Woody Leonhard

TEACHES

Microsoft®

OFFICE 2000

G000055807

201 West 103rd Street,
Indianapolis, Indiana 46290

Woody Leonhard

Woody Leonhard Teaches Microsoft® Office 2000

International Standard Book Number: 0-7897-1871-5

Library of Congress Catalog Card Number: 98-87075

Printed in the United States of America

First Printing: June 1999

01   00   99   4   3   2   1

Trademarks

Warning and Disclaimer

Executive Editor
Jim Minatel

Acquisitions Editor
Jill Byus

Senior Development Editor
Rick Kughen

Managing Editor
Brice Gosnell

Project Editors
Kevin Laseau
Gretchen Uphoff

Copy Editors
Pamela Woolf
JoAnna Kremer

Indexer
Larry Sweazy

Technical Editor
Kyle Bryant

Proofreader
Billy Fields

Interior Design
Dan Armstrong

Cover Design
Michael Freeland

Layout Technician
Cheryl Lynch

Contents at a Glance

Table of Contents

About the Author

Woody Leonhard describes himself as "a Microsoft Office victim." A contributing editor at *PC Computing* magazine, prolific book author, Office add-in software developer, and electronic newsletter publisher, Woody is best known for his offbeat writing style and dead-on accurate technical content. He has earned an unprecedented six Computer Press Association awards and two American Business Press awards. Woody is also a Tibetan human rights advocate and cofounder of the Tibetan Children's Fund.

Dedication

To the Que crew who made this book work, especially Jill—who always knows where I am, even when I'm not too sure myself—and Rick, my literary alter ego.

Acknowledgments

As a guy who tends to look at Office through tech-colored glasses, I never would've thought of writing an introductory book had my agent, Claudette Moore, not insisted that I consider it. Thanks, Claudette. You were right. People starting out with Office need to know where the bodies are buried.

Thanks to Jay Munro for the most excellent icons. I never looked so good!

Most of all, I want to express my admiration and appreciation to the teams at Microsoft who created, designed, wrote, and support Office. We may have our differences at times, but the simple fact remains: Office is the most useful piece of computer software ever invented.

What You See Is What I Got

Don't be too surprised if your screens look different from the pictures you see in this book. To make them match, you'll have to take Office into your own hands and turn off "adaptive" menus—a bit of Microsoft skullduggery that I find particularly irksome.

See the section called "Crucial Changes" in Chapter 6 for details.

Tell Us What You Think!

As the reader of this book, *you* are our most important critic and commentator. We value your opinion and want to know what we're doing right, what we could do better, what areas you'd like to see us publish in, and any other words of wisdom you're willing to pass our way.

As an associate publisher for Que, I welcome your comments. You can fax, email, or write me directly to let me know what you did or didn't like about this book—as well as what we can do to make our books stronger.

Please note that I cannot help you with technical problems related to the topic of this book, and that due to the high volume of mail I receive, I might not be able to reply to every message.

When you write, please be sure to include this book's title and author as well as your name and phone or fax number. I will carefully review your comments and share them with the author and editors who worked on the book.

Fax: 317-581-4666

Email: office_que@mcp.com

Mail: Associate Publisher
Que
201 West 103rd Street
Indianapolis, IN 46290 USA

Do You Need This Book?

This isn't a normal "Intro to Office 2000" book. It doesn't assume you're dumb. It won't show you ten dozen ways to save a document. You won't find tables laden with arcane key combinations that you don't have time to memorize. Most of all, it doesn't follow the Microsoft Party Line—there's no attempt to highlight the features that Microsoft's Marketing Department feels will sell more copies of Office 2000. What you find here works, and works well.

Why is that important? So many of the books on store shelves simply parrot what Microsoft wants you to believe. I remember glancing through one of the most popular Office 97 books a couple of years ago, only to discover that it started with a discussion of Binders—surely among Office 97's least useful and most confusing features, but a Microsoft exclusive and thus a marketer's dream. I just about croaked. Binders were so bad, Microsoft buried them completely in Office 2000: You have to install the feature manually, and you'll find Binder details mentioned only in the most obscure places. Thank heavens.

I'm not going to overload your little gray cells with features that don't work or insult your intelligence by recommending (or even talking about) the parts of Office 2000 that are better forgotten. Instead, I'll show you how to cut through the garbage, bypass the cute stuff, and get down to business.

None of the leading Office books (except the *Special Edition Using Microsoft Office 2000* reference book, which Ed Bott and I constructed meticulously) tell you what you need to know about Word viruses—or about keeping up-to-date on bug fixes. Most books also don't tell you about overriding ludicrous Office settings. Many books explain how pieces of Office fit together, but they don't warn you about the parts that don't match up at all! That's how *Woody Leonhard Teaches Microsoft Office 2000* is different. I'll give you the straight scoop and hold the sugar coating in a way that you can understand and use. Right now.

So why listen to me? Heaven knows the computer industry is full of self-appointed experts who can't tell a font from a formula. The simple fact is that I've been struggling with Microsoft Office and its predecessors for almost a decade now. I've been working with Microsoft's development teams since the days of Word 2.0. (Don't blame me for their mistakes! Sometimes they listen to me, sometimes they don't.) I've written more than a dozen books on Office—especially Word—and Windows. I've taught hundreds of people how to use Office and answered tough technical questions from thousands more. My electronic newsletters, *WOW* (*Woody's Office Watch*) and *WWW* (*Woody's Windows Watch*), reach more than 200,000 people every week, and my articles and Help column in *PC Computing* magazine go out to more than a million.

In short, I see a lot of Office problems—lots of things that work and lots of things that don't. I've distilled that experience, that school-of-hard-knocks know-how, translated it into plain English, and put it into this book. Follow along and I'll get you started on the right track—and, with a bit o' luck, keep you pointed in the right direction as you pursue Office enlightenment.

This book tackles the main Office applications, the ones you're most likely to encounter: Word, Outlook, Excel, and PowerPoint. I don't even try to cover the other applications that appear in some versions of Office because, frankly, they each live in a world of their own. Microsoft Access, arguably the closest to being a "real" Office application, is an excellent database program, but just tackling database concepts would take several chapters. FrontPage builds dynamite Web sites, but most people can do what needs to be done with Word—they don't need to learn a new application. PhotoDraw can help you touch up artwork, but it bears almost no resemblance to the rest of Office. And Publisher...well, don't get me started. Publisher is in the Office package because Microsoft executives ran out of "value added" goodies to toss in the box; it doesn't look or work like an Office application— never has, never will. As far as I'm concerned, Publisher could—no, *should*—be replaced by a handful of well-written Word wizards.

Okay, okay. I'll climb off my soapbox. For a while, anyway.

I'm going to assume that Office 2000 is installed on your computer, and that you know how to start the various Office components: Word, Outlook, Excel, and PowerPoint.

DAZED AND CONFUSED?

Don't have Office 2000 yet? Thinking about upgrading, but not sure whether it's worth the effort? Wondering which version of Office you need to buy? Skip down to Chapter 3, "Executive Summary." In the section called "Other Office Oddities," I discuss all the flavors of Office that are on the market—and the pros and cons (oy! Are there cons!) of each.

I'm also going to assume that you know how to click, drag, select text (by dragging the cursor across characters, turning them black), double-click, and right-click, and that you have a nodding acquaintance with Windows Explorer and the Control Panel. I'm going to assume that you either have access to the World Wide Web or that you can find somebody who does. Finally, I'm going to assume that you want to get the most out of Office even if you have to rearrange things a bit. Don't worry. I'll show you each step, in great detail. It won't hurt a bit.

How This Book Is Organized

I've put this book together in a rather unusual way. Instead of diving straight into intensive drills with each of the Office products, I step back a bit and take a look at what you really need to do to make Office work.

Part I, "In the Beginning—Before You Start," covers two cold, hard facts of Office life: bugs and viruses. As far as I'm concerned, if you don't protect yourself against both bugs and viruses, you're just begging for a heap of trouble. I'll show you the best defenses against Word viruses, and then I'll show you precisely how to get the latest, least buggy version of Office. You'll save yourself a lot of time and frustration if you take a few simple precautions.

In Part II, "Office 101," I take a look at the various Office components and how they fit together, and then segue into strategies for making Office an effective tool. Whether you use Office in your dorm room to tap out an occasional letter home to Mom or you've vowed to become the alpha Office geek attached to a gazillion-dollar corporate computer network, you need to see how Office fits into what you're doing and how you can take advantage of its capabilities to make your life easier.

I don't start hands-on work with Office components until Part III, "Word." By far the largest component of this book, Part III deals with Microsoft Word. I'll have you up and churning out documents—good looking documents—in no time. More than that, though, I'll show you why things work the way they do, and I'll point out where you're bound to have problems. Much of what you learn in Part III about Word carries over to the other Office components, so any additional effort you make here is time well spent.

Part IV, "Outlook," tackles Outlook. I know that it's traditional for introductory books to move from Word to Excel, but it's been my experience that many Office users spend more time with Outlook than any other piece of Office, with the possible exception of Word. And now that Microsoft has given Office a decent, stable email program and personal information manager (Outlook 97 definitely didn't meet these criteria), it's more important than ever that you learn how to take advantage of Outlook's capabilities—and avoid its quirks.

Part V, "Excel," takes Excel all the way up to PivotTables. I know that some people feel that PivotTables are too advanced for a beginning Office user, but I say malarkey. They aren't hard at all. And if you ever hit a problem that's solved best by a PivotTable, you'll be glad you learned how to do the Pivot.

Part VI, "PowerPoint," runs through PowerPoint, far enough to get a presentation going with animation and those fancy interslide transitions.

In Part VII, "Advanced Topics," I look at Office's advanced topics. Although it's true that some of the Office applications work with others, the number of interconnections might underwhelm you—and the capabilities of the few that do work might leave you shaking your head. Don't try to connect two Office apps without reading this part. Office on the Web is also discussed in this part; the Office apps work surprisingly well on the Web. I'll show you how to get them going. I'll also point out the parts that—Microsoft marketing's demos to the contrary—don't work worth a hill of beans.

All in all, I hope you find this book an interesting, absorbing, occasionally funny but always dead-on accurate way to learn about the high points (and the low points!) of Office.

Conventions Used in This Book

I assume, right from the get-go, that you're an intelligent person interested in learning about Office. You needn't be a computer expert. You needn't be a typesetter or graphics designer. But you do need to have a voice inside of you, constantly asking, "Why?"

There's an awful lot of meat in this book and very little fluff. No inscrutable cartoons. A minuscule amount of repetition. There are some funny parts, a few of which were intentional. In short, *Woody Leonhard Teaches Microsoft Office 2000* is designed for people who are serious about learning what Office has to offer, although it doesn't hurt to have a sense of humor.

Gimmicks

I've come up with some gimmicks—Geeks, Scuttlebutts, Tips, Notes, and Cautions—to call your attention to parts of the book and help guide you through all this material.

TIP

TIPS

When I have a tip that deserves your special attention, I'll set it aside this way. *Woody Leonhard Teaches Microsoft Office 2000* comes chock full of tips, so this device is reserved for the really special tips that come along from time to time.

WHAT'S A GEEK?

If you're very interested in a particular topic, it might behoove you to take a gander at the Geek material. Note that these aren't limited to Computer Geek topics—you might qualify as a Font Geek or a Web Geek—so peruse the title to see whether the topic interests you.

NOTES

Notes point out items that you need to be aware of, although you can skip these if you're in a hurry. Generally, I've added notes as a way to give you some extra information on a topic without weighing you down.

CAUTIONS

Pay attention to Cautions! These can save you precious hours in lost work. Don't say I didn't warn you.

Exercises

Most of the hands-on material comes in the guise of an exercise. I've taken great pains to ensure that Exercises include very detailed, step-by-step instructions for exploring a particular Office feature or technique. I think you'll find them fun and, in some cases, absolutely tail-saving.

WHAT'S A SCUTTLEBUTT?
Scuttlebutt material runs the gamut from Office insider gossip to catch-up material for complete novices. In any case, Scuttlebutts aren't required reading—but they can be fun.

An Exercise on Exercises

1. Start the Exercise with Step 1.

2. If you survive, try to tackle Step 2.

3. Continue with Step 3. And so on.

Type

One more tiny convention: When I want you to click something, I've made that something **bold**. So if I say, "Click **File**, and then **Open**," you click File, and then Open. I'll also identify text that you'll see on the screen in **bold**. Anything you'll be required to type or any Web addresses are set off in computer font like this: `computer_font`. Don't worry about it. You'll catch on right away.

Woody Leonhard
Coal Creek Canyon, Colorado

Woody Leonhard

TEACHES

OFFICE 2000

IN THE BEGINNING— BEFORE YOU START

Woody Leonhard

TEACHES

VITAL
UNMENTIONABLES

Bugs and Viruses. I don't know why introductory books fail to tackle bugs and viruses. Maybe the authors don't want to air dirty linen in public. Maybe publishers are afraid that Microsoft will get mad. But the simple fact is that you need to know about bugs and viruses—even before you learn how to use Office 2000. Why? Because you'll waste a lot of time and subject yourself to untold misery if you don't know how to protect yourself from these unmentionables up front.

Such is computing at the turn of the millenium.

Bugs

What's a bug? Good question. There's no simple answer. For the purposes of this book, we'll concentrate on *hard* bugs—errors in Word that will make your documents look strange or give you incorrect answers in Excel worksheets.

Most beginners start out believing that Office has no bugs—that every weird thing they experience is their fault. (One fellow actually wrote to me a couple of years ago and asked how I could be so derogatory. "Mr. Gates certainly knows how to make software that works right. Look at how much money he's made!" Uh, right.) As novices gain more experience and more confidence, they flip-flop and tend to think that every problem they encounter is due to a bug, and couldn't *possibly* be their fault. I still tend to fall in the latter category.

The truth, of course, lies somewhere in between.

Every computer program has bugs—at least, every computer program that does anything interesting. It's a simple, unfortunate, fact of life. Microsoft spends millions and millions of dollars every year wringing bugs out of Office. And they're damn good at it. By any objective measure ("bugs per line of code," "bugs per developer," "bugs per square inch"), Office comes out remarkably well. Still, there are thousands and thousands of bugs left in Office.

Don't believe it? Ah, you trusting soul! Here's an interesting bug that Ed Bott, my co-author for *Special Edition Using Microsoft Office 2000*, discovered. (Okay, okay. This is also a tricky way to get you accustomed to exercises. You caught me. What can I say?)

WHAT'S THIS SPECIAL EDITION THING?

Throughout this book you'll find references to *Special Edition Using Microsoft Office 2000*, which Ed Bott and I wrote (Que, ISBN 0-7897-1842-1). It's a gigantic, hernia-inducing encyclopedia—truly, everything you ever wanted to know about Office, and then some. *Special Edition* doesn't have all the answers, but it sure nails most of 'em. Once you've learned the basics, it's a good reference book to have on your desk (or under your pillow, if you learn by osmosis).

 EXERCISE

Automatic Color Bug

1. Start Word. (In Windows, click **Start, Programs, Microsoft Word**.) Type something interesting such as, oh, You can see me.

2. Select the text you just typed (click in front of the Y, and then drag the mouse pointer to the right of the period, so the sentence is *highlighted*).

3. Click **Format** then **Borders and Shading**. Pick the **Shading** tab. Choose the blackest black you can see. Click **OK**. The text you typed should appear in white on the black background (see Figure 1.1).

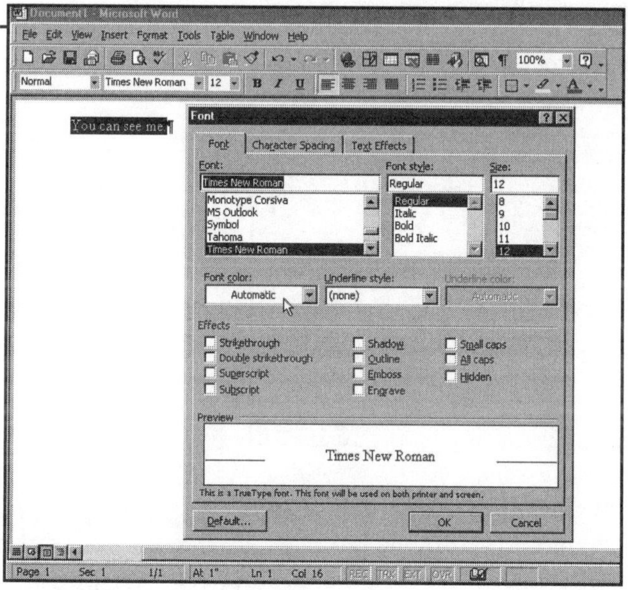

FIGURE 1.1

When a text font's color is set to "Automatic," Word adjusts the text color so it contrasts with the background. In this case, the background was set to black, so the text automatically turns white, and you can "automatically" see it.

4. That's as it should be—to see why, click **Format**, **Font**, and look in the box marked Font Color. The font's color is *Automatic*, which means that Word is supposed to adjust the color of the text so you can see it easily against any background. All is well in Word. Click **File**, **Exit** to leave; **No** you don't want to save changes.

5. Now start Excel. Type something in the upper-left cell, such as But you can't see me! Then press **Enter** to put the text in cell A1.

6. Click on **cell A1**, and then click **Format**, **Cells**, and the tab marked **Patterns**. Under **Color**, pick the blackest black you can see, and click **OK** (see Figure 1.2).

7. Excel should be setting the text to white—click **Format**, **Cells**, and then click the **Font** tab and look in the box marked **Color**. Just like Word, the font here has a color of *Automatic*. But the color isn't automatic at all. It's just... a bug. Click **File**, **Exit** to leave Excel, and **No** you don't want to save changes.

FIGURE 1.2

Under precisely
the same
circumstances
in Excel,
though, the
"Automatic"
font color
doesn't show at
all—the black
background
makes the cell's
text completely
incomprehensible.

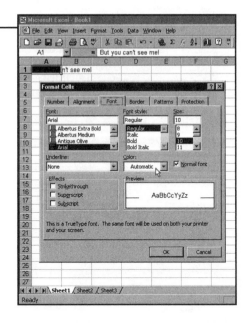

Microsoft internally tracks bugs and
assigns them numbers. This bug has
existed since the release of Office 95.
As of this writing, anyway, Microsoft
hasn't fixed it.

Bugs, unfortunately, rate as a way
of life in Office 2000—and all
other major software packages
for that matter.

Viruses

As of this moment, there are more
than 4,000 identified and catalogued
Word viruses, and several dozen Excel
viruses, along with a handful that
ping-pong back and forth between
various Office applications. Virus writing rates as a major growth industry.

**WHY DO BUGS GET
THROUGH?**

At any given point in time, Microsoft has
many hundreds to many thousands of known,
identified Office bugs on file. Why don't they
rush out to fix every one? Because the cure,
often, is worse than the disease.

Changing a single line of code in Office 2000
can (and probably will) introduce dozens of
ancillary bugs—most of which are impossible
to predict. So the analysts have to review every
reported bug and determine if it's really worth
upsetting the apple cart to cure a particular
problem.

In the end, the really nasty bugs get greased.
Sooner or later. But other known, less intimidating,
bugs can and do live on from version to version.

What are *macro viruses*? They aren't nearly as mysterious as you probably think. A virus (in this context anyway) is a computer program that can reproduce. We tend to think of viruses as being destructive, or at least inconvenient, but those are cultural attributes that really have nothing to do with viruses. If a computer program can reproduce, it's a virus. Simple.

For the other half, a macro (in this context) is just a computer program that's attached to a Word document, Excel spreadsheet, or PowerPoint presentation. It's a bit odd to think of computer programs attached to documents. When you write to Aunt Emma, you probably don't compose a program to go along with the letter. But in many cases it's convenient to be able to let a program hitchhike on the back of a document. Think of form letters that have programs to help you retrieve information about clients, or worksheets that have special rules built-in so you don't flub a complex calculation.

Unfortunately, a few miscreants discovered that they can use Office's programmability—its macro language—to write computer viruses. By subverting a few common programming functions built into Office, they found they could write programs that reproduce.

CAN I GET INFECTED BY READING EMAIL OR LOOKING AT A WEB PAGE?

The short answer is yes; it's possible but extremely unusual. The more complete answer: Computer jocks (both good guys and bad guys, if you'll pardon the gross generalization) bump into Windows security holes all the time. Most of them are really obscure—you have to be a hotshot programmer to take advantage of them, and your average lower-than-spit virus writer is rarely a hotshot programmer.

If the security hole allows a virus (or other type of bad computer program) to wreak havoc on your machine when you read an email message or view a Web page, all hell breaks loose. Microsoft puts a round-the-clock team on the problem and generally solves it within days. It then posts program corrections (called a *fix*) to its Web site. You're encouraged to download and run the fix.

There are three *very* important steps you can take to help prevent the spread of Windows viruses:

● If you receive a program (that is, an .exe file) attached to an email message, or a newsgroup posting (or on a diskette from your Aunt Matilda, for that matter), make sure you know that the program is not infected before you run it (or double-click on it). The safest approach is to save the *.exe file to disk and test it with an antivirus program before you run it. There's a particularly obnoxious program called happy99.exe that's been making the rounds, attaching itself to email messages—do yourself a favor and don't run it.

continues

Some of the viruses, such as the original Concept.A, are relatively harmless. They attach themselves to Word documents and do nothing more than propagate to other Word documents. That makes the documents a little bigger, and it leads to some strange behavior when you try to save them (Word insists on saving them as templates), but by and large Concept.A doesn't do much. When you get right down to it, the worst damage you'll suffer from a Concept.A infection is to your ego, when you have to tell your friends and co-workers that the documents you sent to them might be infected.

Other viruses aren't so nice. They have payloads that can clobber important files on your disk, wipe out most of your documents, or make Word do weird things. The most insidious viruses, called *data diddlers*, make subtle changes to your documents and leave very little evidence of their activity. You can go for months without noticing the effect of a data diddler. Once you catch the bugger, the illicit changes it has made can be impossible to track and correct. Nasty beasts.

CAN I GET INFECTED BY READING EMAIL OR LOOKING AT A WEB PAGE?
continued

- If you receive a document (that is, a Word document, Excel worksheet, or PowerPoint presentation) attached to an email message, a newsgroup posting, or just about anywhere else, make sure you save it and run an antivirus program on it. The infamous Melissa virus never would've spread if Office users had only taken that simple precaution.

- If you ever get the message "An ActiveX object on this page may be unsafe. Do you want to allow it to initialize and be accessed by scripts?" Just click No! That poorly worded, lousy ultra-techie message is trying to tell you that there's a program running that could mess you up. Stop it dead in its tracks by clicking No.

Office 2000 has some very sophisticated hooks for trapping viruses—although, as you'll see, you need to buy a separate antivirus product to make full use of them. For starters, it's important that you ensure Word, Outlook, Excel, and PowerPoint all have their virus protection features turned on.

Virus protection in Office 2000 hinges around the concept of a *signed macro*. People who write *macros*—that is, programs—for Office 2000 usually *sign* their work using a digital signature. Signatures aren't infallible—just as in the real world, they can be faked—but they're reasonably reliable.

If you download a file from the Microsoft Web site and it's signed by Microsoft, there's an extremely high probability that it's a legitimate Microsoft file. Conversely, if you receive a file has an attachment to an email message from DarthVader@HackerzNCrackerz.com and it's signed by Bill Gates, you're entitled to be a bit skeptical. Signatures don't take the place of common sense, but they're a good starting point for protecting your Office 2000 installation.

And that leads us to our second exercise.

OUTLOOK VIRUSES—A HORSE OF A DIFFERENT COLOR

With occasional exceptions, Word viruses travel in documents, Excel viruses attach themselves to worksheets, and PowerPoint viruses lurk in presentations. But Outlook works a bit differently. If there were an Outlook virus—and there aren't any at the moment—it would be stored inside the program's main data file, usually outlook.pst. Since it's very rare for people to pass around Outlook data files, Outlook isn't a likely candidate for widespread contamination. That's why you won't find the same antivirus hooks for Outlook that you'll find in the other Office applications.

EXERCISE

Turn on Virus Protection

1. Start Word 2000. Click **Tools**, **Macro**, **Security**. Unless you're an experienced hand at Word macro viruses, make sure the Security Level tab has **High** checked (see Figure 1.3). Click **OK**, and then **File**, **Exit** to leave Word.

2. Start Outlook 2000. Click **Tools**, **Macro**, **Security**. You'll get the same dialog box shown in Figure 1.3, except for the note at the bottom about a virus scanner being installed. In Outlook, **Medium** security is sufficient. Click **OK**, **File**, **Exit** to leave Outlook.

3. Start Excel 2000. Click **Tools**, **Macro**, **Security**. You know the drill by now. **Medium** is probably good enough for Excel, but you should consider bumping it up to **High** if you receive a lot of worksheets from other sources—including co-workers. Click **OK**, and then **File**, **Exit** to get out of Excel.

4. Start PowerPoint 2000. Click **Cancel** if you need to, to clear out the pesky dialog boxes. Then click **Tools**, **Macro**, **Security**. Again, **Medium** is probably good enough unless you run presentations from other sources, in which case **High** might be a better choice.

FIGURE 1.3

High security in Office 2000 means that signed macros from sources you've already said you trust— say, Microsoft or Que—can run uninterrupted.

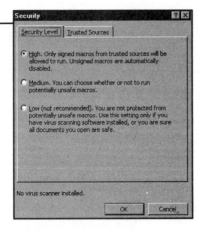

There. Your first-level virus protection is in place and working. And, yes, while you were checking, I tricked you into starting all four of the major Office programs that you'll be using in this book.

Remember this exercise. Before long you'll look back on it with some degree of nostalgia. This is one of the very few features in Word, Outlook, Excel, and PowerPoint that works more-or-less the same way in all four programs!

Don't stop with Office's built-in antivirus protection. After all, it's totally dependent on signatures, and signatures can be faked. It's absolutely imperative that you buy, install, update, and religiously use one of the major antivirus programs, such as Norton Anti-Virus or McAfee VirusScan; we'll talk about the details in the next chapter. After they're properly installed, you'll see the "No virus scanner installed." note at the bottom of the Security dialog box disappear, replaced by an indication that your antivirus program is installed and working.

WHERE DID VIRUSES COME FROM?

Nobody knows where the original Word macro virus, now called Concept.A, originated. We'll probably never know for sure, unless the author steps forward some day. (And if he or she is watching, I'd sure like to meet you!)

What we do know for sure is that there were no identified Word viruses prior to July 1995. Then, in the course of a month, a very large percentage of all the PCs at Microsoft's Redmond campus got infected. By the end of 1995, the Concept.A virus had spread to hundreds—possibly thousands—of PCs all around the world.

The virus protection available in Office 2000 far surpasses that in any previous version of Office. In fact, many knowledgeable Office users, including this one, believe that upgrading Office 97 (or 95) to Office 2000 is imperative, simply for the antivirus protection. Take full advantage of the protection being offered, and get an antivirus add-on. Some day you'll thank me for it.

There are over 4,000 known and catalogued Office macro viruses; the number's probably over 5,000 by the time you read this. You can get more information on macro viruses by visiting the Web pages offered by any of the major antivirus software companies, such as `http://www.symantec.com/avcenter` (Symantec/Norton), and `http://www.nai.com/vinfo` (NAI/McAfee).

VIRUS BIOLOGY 101

How does a macro virus reproduce? Although the details vary from virus to virus, in Word it usually goes something like this: The virus writer creates a macro—a program—that runs when you do something pretty common such as, oh, open a document. He (and it's usually a he) attaches that program to a document. When you open that document, the virus is *triggered* and the virus program takes over.

The virus program usually tries to make a copy of itself—a copy that will hang around, even when the infected document is long gone. If the program succeeds in making a copy of itself that will persist even after you stop and restart Word, you have an *infected system*.

To be truly successful as a virus, the program must in turn infect other documents. There are many ways of writing programs to ensure that an infected system will create more infected documents. Most often, the program takes over a common function inside Word itself and whenever you use that function, the program puts a copy of itself in the document that's currently open.

That's how daddy viruses make baby viruses. The worst viruses also have a payload, which runs occasionally and wreaks havoc on your machine. But the payload is just icing on the viral cake; not all viruses have destructive payloads.

So now you know how a virus can travel inside documents and infect other documents.

2

Woody Leonhard

TEACHES

PRECURSORS TO USING OFFICE

YES, I KNOW YOU WANT TO GET TO THE PROGRAMS. Bear with me a minute or two. There are four more things you have to do before you get started:

- Get the latest versions and patches
- Install virus-protection software
- Register your software
- Make two simple Windows modifications

If you follow the straightforward instructions coming up, you'll pay for this book right off the bat. Then you can sit back and relax, secure in the knowledge that you're attacking Office like a pro, and take the rest of the book at your leisure.

Get the Latest Versions and Patches

If you're using Office 2000, you might not be using the latest version of Office 2000. Why is that important? Because Microsoft is constantly updating Office, fixing bugs, patching security holes, and—even though they frequently won't admit it—adding important new features. If you're using the *old* version of Office 2000, you may well be confronted by all sorts of headaches that simply disappear if you get the *new* version.

 NOTE

TRUTH IN BUG FIXING

Fixes come at unpredictable times. That's why it's important you get the latest update information you can find. Unfortunately, you can't always trust Microsoft to give you the straight scoop (if you were around in the days of Office 97 and its many, varied and conflicting Service Releases, you know what I mean). I strongly suggest that you or a friend log on to the World Wide Web and check the site www.wopr.com. That's my site. I work with a bunch of people who hold Microsoft's feet to the fire—and keep the world at large apprised of our findings. We can be ornery at times, so don't be too surprised if you find us taking Microsoft to task over something. At the same time, though, if we praise a Microsoft product, the praise comes from the heart.

WOODY'S OFFICE WATCH

Office changes all the time. Between the bugs, workarounds, fixes, warnings, viruses, and plain old-fashioned tips and questions, there's something new every week.

An old buddy of mine from Australia, Peter Deegan, and I put our heads together a few years ago and decided that we really needed to send out a regular email message to our friends to keep them abreast of the latest Office news. And since both of us answer dozens of Office questions every week, we also figured we'd copy the questions and answers in the email bulletin, so we didn't end up answering the same questions over and over again.

That's how Woody's Office Watch (WOW) started. Yeah, *that* Woody is *this* Woody.

Now WOW (and its sister publication, Woody's Windows Watch) goes out to about 200,000 people, free, every week. Hard to believe, eh?

WOW prides itself on being fiercely independent: we don't kowtow to Microsoft; Peter and I have nobody to answer to but our readers. We frequently run articles with opinions that vary widely from ours, and we encourage readers to think critically about Office. WOW has been instrumental in fixing Office bugs, getting security holes plugged, improving Microsoft customer service, and generally giving us poor, forgotten Office users a voice in the halls of Redmond.

WOW will keep you abreast of every new development in the world of Microsoft Office. Think of it as a chance to learn the latest, every week, free. (I'll also use WOW to make updates—and corrections!—to this book.) To get WOWd, send a blank email message to wow@wopr.com or drop by our Web site, www.woodyswatch.com. The 'bots will take care of the rest.

Office Service Releases

From time to time, Microsoft releases big bug fixes for Office, dubbed *Service Releases*. In the past, these Service Releases have covered quite a gamut of crucial bug fixes, security patches, new features of the "jeez, you should of done it that way in the first place" variety, and an array of other new features that make Office work faster and better. Instead of dribbling out fixes piecemeal, Microsoft knows it's better for everybody if they hold off and fix a whole bunch of problems at once. That, at its core, is the reason for Service Releases.

While Microsoft is, at least theoretically, under no obligation to keep your copy of Office updated, the 'Softies frequently find that it's in their own best interest to make sure their most savvy customers (that means *you*) get the latest version of Office. After all, if you call or write to Microsoft and ask for technical support, the first thing they're going to ask is, "which version are you running?" It just makes sense to get on top—and stay on top—of your Office destiny.

Several years ago Microsoft tried to charge money for bug fixes. The game, at the time, was that you could get a free fix if you called Microsoft and described a known bug that was solved by the fix. Office insiders, of course, spent a great deal of time figuring out which bugs qualified for free upgrades, and then posted details for reproducing the bugs in all the online forums. Fortunately that ludicrous "don't ask, can't tell" policy went by the wayside, and almost always the fixes are available for free—at least to U.S. and Canadian customers who bought shrink-wrapped copies of Office off of store shelves. (Large corporate customers have always received the patches free. You expected any different?)

What Version of Office Do You Have?

It's unfortunate but true that Office has never had a standardized way of telling its users which version is installed. Just for starters, the shrink-wrapped box Office comes in isn't marked with a version number—and if you bought some old inventory, you might not have the latest version, even if you bought your copy of Office 2000 last week.

In general, you can tell more-or-less which version you're running by starting any of the Office applications and clicking **Help**, **About** *the product* (for example, **About Microsoft Outlook**). You should see a dialog box that looks similar to Figure 2.1.

It's impossible to tell, at the moment I'm writing this, what the Help/About box will look like when you have Office 2000 Service Releases installed. If we're lucky, though, Microsoft will have figured out a way to make the version number obvious—and if we're *very* lucky, they'll put it right here in the Help/About box where it belongs.

FIGURE 2.1

The original version of Office 2000 has a Help dialog that looks something like this.

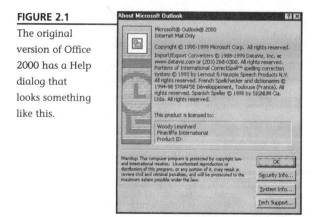

Patches Versus Replacement CDs

Just to make things, uh, challenging, Microsoft has, in the past, released *different* Service Releases with the same name. For example, there were two *different* Office 97 Service Release-1s, and two *different* Service Release-2s. It seems likely that Microsoft will continue this way for future Office Service Releases, so I want to warn you about the sleight-of-hand right up front, and make sure you know what to ask for.

The two versions of an Office Service Release have two different internal code names:

- The *patch* (the one you don't want) is a downloadable file available on the Microsoft Web site. It's a program that you run on a PC that already has Office 2000 installed; the patch goes in and modifies your existing copy of Office 2000, supposedly turning it into the newer, better version. Microsoft likes patches because they don't cost much to distribute—once a patch is on the Web site, that's pretty much the end of it.

- The *replacement CD* (the one you do want), however, is a brand-spanking-new copy of Office 2000, with all the fixes applied. It's the same CD that Microsoft puts in all the new boxes of Office 2000 that it's selling. Microsoft doesn't like to send out replacement CDs because it costs the 'Softies a bundle to take your order, manufacture the CD, and ship it. Hard to blame 'em, really.

So what's wrong with the patch? In my experience, three things:

- Patching is inherently more risky than reinstalling. There's no guarantee that a patched version of Office 2000 will be identical to the version on the replacement CD. And if you ever uninstall a part of Office, use the patch, and then reinstall that component—who knows what kind of bit stew you'll end up with?

- The patch rarely includes all the goodies on the replacement CD. In the past, I've seen patches that didn't include key help files, sample templates, and much more.

- If you have to reinstall Office 2000, wrestling with a patch is a monumental pain in the neck. But if you have the replacement CD, everything you need is in one place.

So a word to the wise: When Microsoft comes out with an Office 2000 Service Release, if you have a choice, don't settle for the patch. Go for the full replacement CD.

Problems Obtaining Service Releases

If you're in the U.S. or Canada (or have an address in the U.S. or Canada), and you bought your copy of Office 2000 from a computer store in the U.S. or Canada, you shouldn't have any problem receiving free Service Releases. At most you may be required to call a specific telephone number and recite your product's ID number (from the Help/About dialog box) to the clerk on hand. We run full details on ordering Service Releases in WOW (see *Woody's Office Watch* at the beginning of this chapter).

Of course that leaves two distinct problems:

- If you aren't in the U.S. or Canada, you'll have to deal with the local Microsoft franchisee. Our experience with local Microsoft offices around the world has ranged from not very good to truly abysmal.

- If you didn't buy a shrink-wrapped box with Office in it, you might have problems. Many people get Office when they buy a new computer. These so-called *OEM versions* (OEM stands for *Original Equipment Manufacturer*— which just means a PC maker) are sold to the manufacturer at a steep discount, and Microsoft is under no obligation to support them. In fact, it's Microsoft's position that the OEM itself should put together and distribute Service Releases. I bet you didn't realize that, did you?

In either case, you should expect some difficulty obtaining Service Releases for Office 2000. The best advice I can offer is to be patient but firm (the person answering the phone rarely has any authority in the matter), and ask to speak to a supervisor if you don't get what you feel you deserve.

Oh. And watch WOW, of course, for specific tips—and occasional commiseration.

Install and Update an Antivirus Program

One question I hear over and over again is "Woody, which antivirus program should I buy?" There's a simple answer: It doesn't matter which one you buy. All the major antivirus software packages work very well. The only real difference among them is in the *user interface*—the part of the package that you see on the screen—and that's largely a matter of personal taste (or lack thereof). The antivirus software companies will cite tests and reviews trying to prove that their product is superior. But where the rubber meets the road—the ability to uncover and eliminate macro viruses—there isn't a hair's difference among them.

By all means, check the latest reviews in the magazines to see which antivirus program seems to best meet your needs. (Personally, I look at *PC Computing*'s A-List. But I'm biased.) More than anything, though, don't let your pursuit of the ultimate antivirus package deter you—not for a minute—in buying and installing one of the major packages.

Depending on the package you buy, you'll either be forced or asked to connect to the Web immediately after installation. That's a vital step in the process. Antivirus packages use something called a signature file to identify and eradicate viruses. The software manufacturers update these signature files weekly; some are even updated hourly. With dozens of new viruses coming to the forefront every week, you can't afford to get too far behind the curve.

TIP

GET YOUR MONEY'S WORTH

Download the latest signature file immediately, and use your antivirus program's automatic download feature to update that signature file at least once a month—preferably once a week.

Register Your Software

If you haven't called Microsoft and registered Office 2000, you should. Even if you have registered, it's a good idea to call and make sure Microsoft has the correct mailing address and your email address. If you don't register your software— maybe you figure Uncle Bill already has enough info about you; maybe you aren't convinced it's worth the hassle—follow the other steps in this section anyway. It shows you how to get your ducks lined up just in case you have to reinstall Office 2000 after some future catastrophe.

How many CDs do you have lying around your desk? Is the Office 2000 CD among them? Good. Now a trick question: Where's the *jewel case*, the little plastic doohickey your Office 2000 CD came in? What, you threw it away? Yeah. Me, too. I hate the things. Just more wasted, rarely recycled plastic.

Guess what? There's a little sticker on the back of your Office 2000 CD's jewel case that could be vitally important if you ever have to reinstall Office. Assuming you always keep all your jewel cases filed away and know precisely where your Office jewel case is located at all times, you won't have any problems when the Office installer program asks you for your Key Number. (That's the number printed on the sticker on the back of the jewel case.) If you're somewhat, uh, lax in that respect, here is the most important exercise you'll find in this book:

EXERCISE

Mark Your Office 2000 CD

1. Right now, *as you're reading this book*, take a minute or two to locate your Office 2000 CD and its jewel case. If you can find the jewel case, and can read the Key Number on the sticker (it's 25 letters and numbers), breathe a sigh of relief.

THE REGISTRATION WIZARD

If you have a copy of the *Academic Version* of Office 2000 (that's a super-discounted version which is supposed to be available only to students and faculty members), or if you got your copy of Office 2000 in Australia, New Zealand, the People's Republic of China, or a handful of additional countries, you're going to be confronted by something called the Registration Wizard. Microsoft is using the Academic Version, plus the versions sold in those countries, to test the concept of forced registration. If it works well with Office 2000, well, who knows? Maybe it will catch on with other Microsoft products.

Personally, I think it stinks.

The Registration Wizard has two main purposes: to limit pirating of Office 2000—where people install copies they aren't entitled to use—and to improve the quantity and quality of information in Microsoft's registration database (the so-called RegBase).

Under the terms of your license for Office 2000, you are entitled to install one copy on your main machine, and a second copy—for your personal use only—on a portable. (Big companies with site licenses play by different rules.)

The Registration Wizard lets you use Office 2000 a grand total of 40 times—reminding you to register each time—before it locks you out. You can register electronically, by phone or fax, or even the mail, but you have to register. Without the registration key, your copy of Office 2000 is toast.

continues

2. Start Word 2000, and then click **Help**, **About Microsoft Word**. At the bottom of the dialog box you'll see the Product ID, something such as 82503-001-0012945-12345.

3. With your Product ID number in hand (remember, that's the one shown in the Help/About dialog box) call Microsoft and make absolutely sure that you're registered, and that Microsoft has your correct address. In the U.S., call 800–360–7561; outside the U.S., call your local Microsoft office.

4. If you couldn't find your Key Number in step 1, ask the 'Softie on the phone if they can provide you with one. You're going to need it if disaster ever strikes; better to get it now than call in a panic a month or two from now.

5. While you're on the phone with the 'Softies, ask them if you have the latest version of the various Office 2000 applications. Don't be too surprised if their advice about patches and Service Releases differs from mine—and if there are any discrepancies, be sure you follow the instructions at the beginning of this chapter!

6. Now that you have your Key Number, don't lose it! Get an indelible pen (I use a Sharpie) and write the Key Number on the top—the printed side—of the first Office 2000 CD. Be careful not to screw up the shiny side of the CD; that's where the program lives.

THE REGISTRATION WIZARD *continued*

If you come up against the Registration Wizard, go ahead and register. But keep in mind two things:

● Even though the form makes you think you have to give Microsoft all sorts of information, you *really* only need to tell them what country you live in and how to contact you with your registration key. If you don't want Bill and Big Bro to have any more information about you, call from a pay phone or rent a mailbox.

● As soon as you get your registration number, write it down on the printed side of the Office CD, using an indelible marker. (See step 6 of the preceding exercise.) You may need it some day.

While I strongly recommend that users register their copies of Office (and always have), and I have little sympathy for people who try to cheat Microsoft by installing pirate copies, I also oppose forced registration such as this on near-religious grounds. Why? It always ends up hurting the legitimate user, and rarely stops anybody who's determined to cheat.

Modifying Windows to Work with Office

One final step before you're ready to use Office 2000 for the first time. (They didn't tell you about all these glitches when you bought Office, did they? *Heh heh heh.*) There are two little things in Windows itself that have to be changed. Even if you've been using Office since the dawn of time, you should make these changes. Don't worry, they're easy.

Explorer Show Extensions

I've been fighting Microsoft on this one for years.

When you create a new Word 2000 document and give it a name such as, oh, *Manifesto*, Word automatically puts some extra stuff on the end of the file's name— Manifesto.doc, in this example. The .doc on the end of the file's name tells Windows (and Word, and the world, for that matter), that this is a Word document. The few characters at the end of the filename are, collectively, called a *filename extension*. Excel worksheets end with .xls. PowerPoint has .ppt and .pps's. Outlook stores data in files with .pst extensions. It's a bit of old-fashioned computer gobbledygook that dates back to the earliest days of PCs and <shudder> DOS.

Somebody inside Microsoft (hi, Bill!) has decided that filename extensions are too complicated for normal people like you and me. They want to pretend that the .doc and .xls and .pst filename extensions don't exist, and hide them from *novices* (whomever they may be). The Windows Explorer itself—whether you use Windows 95, Windows 98, Windows NT 4, or Windows 2000—hides filename extensions from you. That wouldn't be so bad, except Explorer also hides filename extensions from programs like Word and Excel. (Outlook shows you filename extensions in all their glory!) And *that* wouldn't be so bad, except you can get in a whole lot of trouble if you learn that filenames have extensions, and you try to play around with them a bit. Even a little bit.

More than that, the moment you get outside the Office cocoon, you're going to bump into filename extensions—and you might as well get used to them sooner, rather than later. So here's our first Power User exercise.

EXERCISE

Make Explorer Show Filename Extensions

1. In Windows, right-click **My Computer** and choose **Explore**.

2. Click **View, Folder Options** (on some machines it'll just say **Options**). Choose the **View** tab.

3. Check the box marked **Show all files**.

4. If you're using an early version of Windows 95, uncheck the box marked **Hide MS-DOS file extensions for file types that are registered**. If you're using a later version of Windows 95, Windows 98, NT or 2000, uncheck the box marked **Hide file extensions for known file types** (see Figure 2.2). Click **OK** all the way back out.

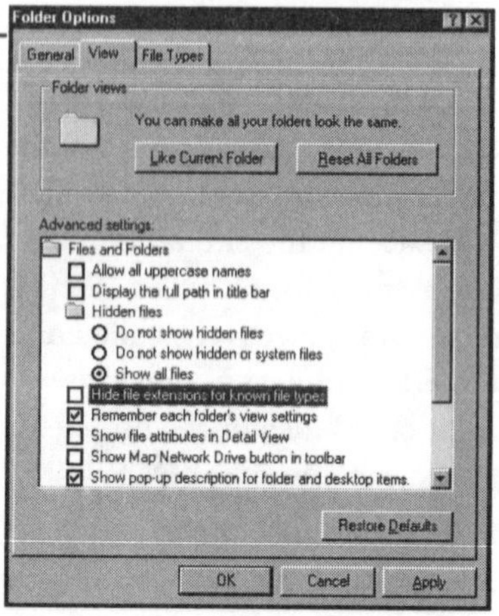

FIGURE 2.2

Removing
the Explorer
blinders.

Now Windows Explorer will show you all the files on your drives; Office will show you filename extensions; and your PC's screen will match the screen shots in the rest of this book. Bet you never thought you'd be a Power User so soon in your Office career, eh?

Turn Off Find Fast

And who says Microsoft doesn't listen? Find Fast debuted in Office 95, and—at least from my point of view—it was an unmitigated disaster. I griped about it in the Office 97 edition of this book. Guess what? Microsoft now includes Find Fast in Office 2000, but it isn't installed unless you specifically ask for it. From where I stand, that's almost as smart as pouring coffee on your keyboard to see if it'll loosen up the keys.

Still, it's possible to have Find Fast activated without you knowing much about it. That most commonly happens when you install Office 2000 over the top of an older version of Office, but there are all sorts of weird circumstances that could let this particular bloodsucker out of its casket. Best that you take a minute or two to check, and make well and truly sure that there's a wooden stake driven through its cold, cold heart.

EXERCISE

Clobbering Find Fast

1. Go out to Windows, click **Start**, **Settings**, **Control Panel**. Then double-click the **Find Fast** icon.

2. If Find Fast hasn't been installed, you might see a message saying that Office is installing it. If so, don't panic. What you really want to know, after the installer comes up for air, is whether Find Fast has been activated, and thus whether any drives or folders are being indexed. Look at the Find Fast dialog box (see Figure 2.3). If Find Fast has been activated, you'll see a line for each drive or folder being tracked. If Find Fast hasn't been activated, there won't be any lines, and you can click the **X** in the upper-right corner to get rid of the dialog box.

3. If there are any lines in the main part of the dialog box, click each one, in turn, so you highlight it. Then click

Index, **Delete Index**. Find Fast comes up for a last gasp (see Figure 2.4). Just click **OK**, and Find Fast will never darken your door—or slow down (or crash!) your machine again. When you're done, click the **X** in the upper-right corner, and you need never fear Find Fast again.

WHAT IS FIND FAST?

Here's how it's supposed to work: Whenever you aren't using your PC for an extended period of time, Find Fast is supposed to kick in, look at all your documents, and create an index of every word in those documents. That way, when you want to find, say, all of your Word documents that contain the word *Fubar*, Find Fast will jump in, use its index, and find the documents lickety-split.

Here's what happens in the real world. You're typing along in Word for a while and rest your hands for a few seconds, to let your fingers cool off. (You *are* a fast typist, aren't you?) Just as you're about to start typing again, Find Fast kicks in. The hard drive starts whirring. Lights flash. You type, type, type—and nothing appears on the screen. It's like the innards of your PC have been cryogenically treated so the little squirrel inside runs at one-hundredth its normal pace. You sit and watch the hard drive light go on and off, and sooner or later the machine unfreezes. If you're lucky.

If you're unlucky, Windows goes south, with one of those **General Protection Faults** staring at you on the screen. I've actually left my machine on overnight, only to return to a precisely arranged series of General Protection Fault messages, cascading 10 deep on my lovely Windows desktop, all caused by Find Fast.

FIGURE 2.3

Find Fast lives.

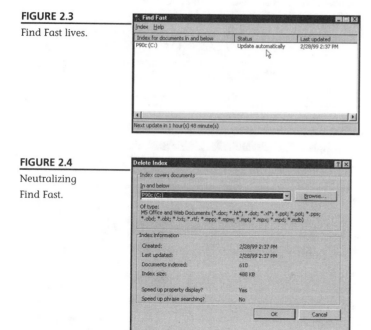

FIGURE 2.4

Neutralizing
Find Fast.

Getting Help

Human tech support for Office leaves a, uh, little bit to be desired. (That's why you buy books like this one, eh?) Once they've exhausted all the Office Assistant (that %$#@! paper clip) has to offer, most people turn to the telephone. While many tech support reps who answer the phone are knowledgeable, competent, and interested in helping you solve your problems, others can be a challenge.

If you bought Office 2000 preinstalled on a PC, you'll have to check with the PC manufacturer to see what kind of support they offer, and how best to contact the tech support people.

On the other hand, if you bought Office 2000 in a shrink-wrapped package—and you registered the way I told you to earlier in this chapter—you're eligible for unlimited free (but not toll-free) support on Office features, menu commands, and installation.

Here are the numbers you should call:

Table 2.1   Microsoft Office 2000 Phone Support Numbers

Product	U.S.A.	Canada
General Office 2000	425-635-7056	905-568-2294
Word	425-462-9673	905-568-2294
Outlook	425-635-7031	905-568-2294
Excel	425-635-7070	905-568-2294
PowerPoint	425-635-7145	905-568-2294
Publisher*	425-635-7140	905-568-3503
FrontPage	425-635-7088	905-568-3503

Note that this number is only valid for people who bought Publisher as part of Office 2000. Commercial printers in the U.S. and Canada can receive help for Publisher, whether they bought it as part of Office 2000 or not, by calling 425-635-3142.

In the U.S., phone support is available from 6:00 a.m. to 6:00 p.m. Pacific time, Monday–Friday excluding holidays. In Canada, it's 8:00 a.m. to 8:00 p.m. Eastern time, also Monday–Friday excluding holidays.

Note that *all this information was provided by Microsoft*. I'm not going to swear that it's all valid at this moment. Don't call me at home, Okay? If the 'Softies change their phone numbers (and that happened a couple of years ago, when the area code in Redmond changed), you might have to do a little hunting. You get the idea.

The Office Assistant is rigged to get you help on the Web, but if all else fails, I'd like to suggest you drop by the WOPR Lounge, at www.wopr.com/lounge.

WHAT TO DO IF YOU FIND A BUG?

First, make sure that the bug is replicable—try to write down a simple series of steps that demo the bug, and then give the instructions to a friend and have him or her try it on a different PC. If the bug replicates, start by calling Microsoft and telling them you have the steps to *repro* a bug. Chances are pretty good Microsoft already knows about the problem and may be able to steer you to a workaround.

Some of the time, though, the Microsoft support reps don't have the slightest idea what is causing the problem, and they're unwilling (or unable) to find somebody who can solve it. That's where WOW comes in. (See *Woody's Office Watch* earlier in this chapter.) Simply write down your steps for replicating the problem, and send them to ask.woody@wopr.com.

continues

We have a dedicated group of volunteers who do a wonderful job of helping people with their problems. Just be nice to them—an occasional offer of pizza and beer goes a long way.

Well, that's about it for the preliminaries. With all that under your belt, you're finally ready to start using Office 2000. Easy, eh?

WHAT TO DO IF YOU FIND A BUG? *continued*

We'll take a look at it and, if it smells like a bug to us, we'll make sure the higher-ups at Microsoft have a look-see. We'll also keep you advised of any fixes Microsoft might post, and keep the world informed through WOW.

It's sad that Microsoft doesn't have a problem escalation procedure that identifies bugs and brings them to the attention of upper management—the folks at Microsoft who can bang a hand on a table, reassign some workers, and get a problem solved. Until Microsoft gets better at it, we at WOW have taken it upon ourselves to short-circuit the system. It works.

Woody Leonhard

TEACHES

OFFICE 2000

OFFICE 101

3

Woody Leonhard

TEACHES

EXECUTIVE SUMMARY

TAKING A PEEK UNDER THE HOOD. Even if you aren't an executive, and you can't stand summaries, you might be interested in knowing something about the parts of this Office 2000 beast that bears (and beats) you.

Office Roots

Microsoft Word has been around since the early days of DOS. It was one of the first computer applications Microsoft ever sold—and it has turned out to be the most lucrative application ever invented. Once Windows 3.0 took off, Microsoft stopped investing in the DOS version and turned almost all its efforts to Word for Windows. The folks at Microsoft believed in Windows—and Bill put his development resources where his mouth was. Word's current hegemony in the word processing realm can be traced directly to Microsoft's betting on Windows—and WordPerfect's failure to back the winning operating system horse.

The creation of Excel led to the development of Windows—not the other way around. Hard to believe nowadays, but Windows 286 was specifically invented to support Excel 1.0, and for years the demands of the Excel development team drove the people designing Windows. Around the time of Windows 3.0 the cart and horse reversed positions, but even now Excel sports innovations that the rest of the Office pack only imitate in later versions.

PowerPoint started out as a Microsoft-internal project: The people in Redmond were making so many presentations they had to come up with a package to make their lives simpler. Little did they know that they'd be creating one of the most ubiquitous time sinks on the face of the planet. PowerPoint has long suffered as Office's poor stepchild. Although many smart people work on the PowerPoint team, they've never received the attention or the resources that other parts of Office have commanded.

Outlook started out on a very weak note. Outlook 97, the first incarnation of Outlook, was a typical Microsoft version 1.0 product: buggy, hard to use, and very frustrating. Still, the brilliance of including all of Office's missing links—from an address book to email to scheduling, and much more—in one package couldn't be denied. Outlook remains one of the most promising products Microsoft has ever conceived, and it is starting to deliver on that promise: Outlook 98 brought the program out of the version 1.0 blues, and Outlook 2000 (finally!) added Visual Basic for Applications support. If it doesn't already control your life, someday it probably will.

Office itself arose as a shotgun marriage between the long-established Word, the upstart Excel, and whatever else Bill could throw into the original package to make it sell. The first few versions of Office made a mockery of the terms "uniformity" and "interoperability"—each application worked its own way, the teams developing the applications rarely spoke to one another, and the whole she-bang was held together with baling wire and chewing gum—lousy chewing gum at that.

Over the years, Microsoft has put a lot of effort into making the four core applications work similarly and together. While I wouldn't say Office has been a screaming success in either category, the fact is that learning about one of the four major Office applications generally gives you a good leg up on learning the others.

Still there are many differences between Word, Outlook, Excel, and PowerPoint—and many of those differences go straight to the core of the products. (For example, if you talk about a "template" in Word, it's very different from a template in Excel or PowerPoint.) So you can't always assume that the terminology stays uniform as you switch between the applications. And don't get me started on FrontPage (which looks and acts a little bit like an Office application), PhotoDraw (I swear it must've been designed by people who had never seen Office), and Publisher (yes, I still insist Publisher should be replaced by a bunch of Word Wizards).

Some folks may disagree, but in my opinion, each of the four main Office applications are best of breed. You won't find a better word processor than Word, a better spreadsheet manipulator than Excel, a presentation package that beats PowerPoint, or an all-in-one email/personal information manager that surpasses Outlook. Without a doubt, Office 2000 is an excellent choice.

Not that Office 2000 isn't without its warts! I've already talked about the bugs. Since Office sits in more offices than any other package (by, oh, an order of magnitude), it's a big target: industry pundits love to take potshots at it; virus writers love to write for it; and the chances of bugs appearing and being identified increase enormously. You can feel smug, though: you're using the best. Even if you do love to hate it. I sure do.

Let's take a 30-second tour of each of the four major applications, and put each one in perspective, particularly as they apply to this book.

Word in a Nutshell

What's a word processor? That's a very good question indeed. Best I figure it, a word processor is a program that helps you take ideas out of your head, organize them in a somewhat linear fashion, and put them in a computer. From that point they can be printed, posted on the Web, or sent to co-workers in a file—whatever.

People get enormously frustrated over Word for all sorts of reasons. If I had to pick the one main reason why people have problems with Word, it has to be this: Word doesn't work like a typewriter. You can't type fill-in-the-blank forms, say, and have all the blanks line up. You can't press the Tab key and watch as the platen goes *ziiiiing* over to the next tab stop. Sometimes Word gets so all-fangled confused that it keeps centering lines when you don't want them centered or makes characters bold for no apparent reason.

Sometimes you'll feel like tossing your PC out the window and yearn for the good old days of the IBM Selectric typewriter. I know I do.

The people who designed Word wanted it to do much more than a typewriter—and they succeeded admirably. But in the process of making Word more than a typewriter, they had to surmount a few conceptual hurdles that are very confusing. In the end, I think it's fair to say that Word is more like a typesetting program than a typewriter—and therein lies many a difficulty.

One of the primary goals I have in writing this book is to acquaint you with the ways in which Word differs from a typewriter, and quite possibly get you to understand why Word *can't* work like a typewriter. There are hidden parts of Word that contain key pieces of information—parts of Word that Microsoft, in its infinite wisdom, has decided are too obscure for normal users. We'll "out" those hidden components, and I bet in the end, you'll see why and how Word works the way it does—an understanding that's completely impossible if you use Word the way it's shipped.

Remember the Wizard in *The Wizard of Oz*? (The movie version anyway.) Think of me as Toto. I'm going to yank that curtain back and show you the machinations going on behind the scenes. I'll bark and growl a bit, too, while I'm at it.

Outlook in a Nutshell

Most introductory Office books go straight from Word to Excel, and mention Outlook parenthetically, back somewhere near the fourteenth appendix. There are (at least) three reasons for this odd ordering:

- So many introductory Office 2000 books around today are minor updates of their Office 97 editions, which in turn are minor updates of their Office 95 editions. Since Outlook didn't even exist in the days of Office 95, the authors threw in information about Outlook as something of a last-minute sop to the Microsoft marketing miracle.

- In the old days of Outlook 97, the product was so buggy it was hard to say anything good about it. That's changed with Outlook 2000.

- Even now, Outlook has failed to capture the mindshare that it deserves. Ask most people which products are in Office, and they'll inevitably start out by mentioning Word and Excel. That's changing, too. Outlook is rapidly becoming the most-used piece of Office, particularly for wired folks who have to contend with a lot of email.

I don't want you to get the idea that Outlook 2000 solves all Office's (manifest) problems; it doesn't. However, for the vast majority of Office users—which is to say, for the vast majority of office workers with PCs—Outlook holds the potential for productivity gains on a grand scale.

Think of Outlook as a combination email program, contact manager (with an address book), calendar and group scheduling program, to-do task nagger, and all-around office organizer, with electronic sticky notes, appointment calendar, a capability to track and retrieve Office documents, and even an alarm clock that warns you when you need to run to an important meeting. In other words, Outlook is the catchall application that handles most business needs not met by Word, Excel, or PowerPoint.

Many Office users would be well advised to keep Outlook running as their main application. Outlook 2000 has a special screen called "Outlook Today" (see Figure 3.1), which is particularly well-suited to the task.

FIGURE 3.1

Outlook 2000's ""Today"" mastermind screen.

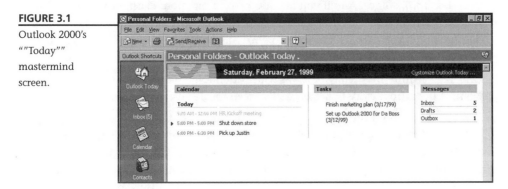

What's not to like about Outlook? My number one gripe is that it doesn't fit into the Office mold very well: It doesn't always behave like other Office applications. That makes it harder to learn in the first place and harder to discover new features by poking around.

Excel in a Nutshell

Excel is a spreadsheet program. Some of you might not be very familiar with spreadsheets, but don't let that put you off. You know how much fun it is to balance your checkbook? Well, think of a spreadsheet as a kind of checkbook that can balance itself, once you figure out how to put in the formulas for calculating balances. If you've ever used a calculator for more than two minutes at a stretch, you're a good candidate for Excel.

At its most basic, Excel has rows and columns—like an old-fashioned columnar pad, if you've ever worked with one of those—with a built-in calculator that can be told to calculate just about anything. The grid sits behind every spreadsheet, physically and metaphorically, and cells on the grid hold the information you want.

But Excel reaches beyond numbers and cells. Its charting capability—where you can turn a table of numbers into any of a gazillion different graphs—is so good it has very nearly destroyed an entire segment of the software industry. Five years ago, you could choose from a half-dozen well-known graphing programs. Nowadays, the vast majority of business graphs come straight from Excel. Later, we'll take a close look at how to create and manipulate graphs.

In a pinch you can also use Excel as a database program. (For that matter you can even use Excel to type business letters. Not that I would recommend it.) For simple databases—"simple" here refers to the structure of the database, not necessarily its size—Excel will suffice. And if you already know a bit about Excel, jury-rigging it to handle databases rates as one whole heck of a lot easier than learning how to use a database program such as Access or FoxPro. At some point, though, you'll get the feeling that using Excel as a database manager is like using a shoe as an ice cream scoop.

One Excel feature that really deserves wider attention: PivotTables (see Figure 3.2). None of the introductory Office books I've seen tackle PivotTables, and that's a shame.

Some information naturally fits into a two-dimensional table. Say your company sells 10 different products, and you want to track sales by quarter. That's easy. List products down the left side and quarters across the top, and you're done. But most information isn't so two-dimensional. If your company has a half-dozen sales people, you might be interested in sales by sales rep by quarter—or sales by rep by product. And flipping between the various spreadsheets can frequently tell you something that isn't obvious by looking at any of the static two-dimensional spreadsheets. As part of the Excel graduate course in this book, I'll show you how to set up a PivotTable and use it. Once you've used PivotTables, PivotCharts—a new and much ballyhooed addition to Excel 2000—are like falling off a log. Even if you've never put together a spreadsheet.

FIGURE 3.2

PivotTables—
an important
but often
overlooked
Excel feature.

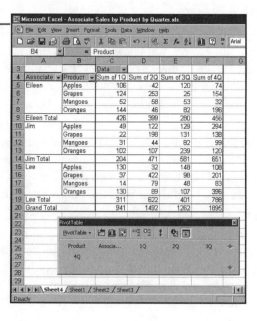

PowerPoint

Few Office users ever take the time to learn how to use PowerPoint. It's almost certainly the most sink-or-swim Office application: The boss asks you to throw together a presentation, you dive into the PowerPoint cesspool… er, lagoon, push a few buttons, type some stuff, and pray that the resulting presentation looks good enough that you don't embarrass yourself. That's what I call the YAPPP approach—Yet Another PowerPoint Presentation. You kinda pray that it turns out okay.

That's a shame, really, because PowerPoint has a lot to offer. Most Office users spend a lot of time with Word. Some also put a bit of effort into learning Excel. After all, a document that looks like a second-grader's scrawl, or a spreadsheet that doesn't add up can make you look like a dunce. Few folks give PowerPoint the time investment it deserves. Once you get over the strange terminology and figure out the tweaks (which, admittedly, don't bear much resemblance to other Office tweaks), PowerPoint can turn a mediocre presentation into a mediocre presentation that won't put people to sleep.

PowerPoint's power lies in its capability to pull together a slide-show style presentation quickly, accurately, and (if you either use the built-in templates or know how to make your own) with a minimum of fuss. Fancy features, such as wipes and fades and picture animation, can be added to presentations in no time. In fact, PowerPoint is so powerful that you have to use its bells and whistles in moderation: by far the largest downside to PowerPoint is that it gives you too much flash, and makes it too easy to create a presentation that outshines the subject matter.

Components You'll Find in Some "Office" Packages

Those are the four Office 2000 components that we'll discuss at length in the remainder of this book. Office, though, contains other flotsam and jetsam that you'll occasionally bump into. For the sake of completeness, I'll dismiss them here.

Microsoft has a huge Office marketing staff; by and large its job is to milk the most profit possible out of Office. Fair enough. That's what a good marketing department should do. In the process of adapting Office to fit various market niches, Microsoft has come up with these flavors of Office 2000:

- **Office 2000 Standard Edition**. Word, Outlook, Excel, PowerPoint. You'll also get Internet Explorer 5. You *do* use IE 5, don't you? Solid choice. If you're still wondering about upgrading from an earlier version of Office—well, in my opinion there's no question, as long as you have a hefty enough PC to run it. I'm running Office 2000 on a Pentium 90 with 64MB of RAM, and it runs much, much faster than Office 97. Run out and buy Office 2000; hock your car if you have to.

- **Office 2000 Small Business Edition**. Word, Outlook, Excel, IE 5, Publisher, Small Business Financial Manager (includes Excel templates for producing charts and reports, for example, the Buy versus Lease Wizard), Direct Mail Manager (automatic direct mail from Outlook's Contacts; help with InfoUSA and other mailing list vendors), Small Business Customer Manager (templates and a contact database manager that will import data from, for example, QuickBooks), and Business Planner (legal forms, business plan skeletons, and so on). No PowerPoint, and that can be a significant shortcoming for many business professionals—even those in small businesses.

- **Office 2000 Professional**. Word, Outlook, Excel, PowerPoint, IE 5, Publisher, Access, plus the four "Small Business Tools" (SB Financial Manager, Direct Mail Manager, SB Customer Manager, Business Planner). Note that this is Standard + Small Business Edition + Access. That's important because you can upgrade from either Standard or Small Business Edition and not lose any features. (With Office 97, you lost out if you upgraded.) A good, uh, suite spot if you don't do much work on the Web, specialized graphics, or need to touch up photos.

- **Office 2000 Premium**. The big kahuna. Word, Outlook, Excel, PowerPoint, IE 5, Publisher, Access, PhotoDraw, and FrontPage. A good choice if you're going to be creating a lot of material for the Web and can take advantage of FrontPage's features. PhotoDraw is a useful all-around photo editing and general "draw" package, although it isn't going to drive Corel or Adobe out of business. Whether it's worth the premium price over the Professional Edition depends on how much you need those features—and how much more you need to spend.

- **Office 2000 Developer Edition**. All the "Premium" stuff, plus printed and online documentation about the Visual Basic for Applications programming language, a Code Librarian, lots of code samples, extra COM controls, Designers, and more. Note that all the macro programming languages are available directly in any version of Office (or even the component applications). If you considered buying the Developer Edition because you wanted to try writing a macro someday, forget about it. You already have everything you need. But if you write, or intend to write, more than a few macros, MOD (as it's known), is well worth the money.

If you bought Office 2000 preinstalled on a PC, chances are good you either received the Standard Edition or the Small Business Edition. The easy way to tell: Do you have PowerPoint? If not, you got the Small Business Edition.

Microsoft also offers a Multilanguage Pack (which is available with the Standard, Professional, and Premium editions) and separate proofing tools for languages other than the one you originally purchased. They're inexpensive and, if you do much work with a second or third language, they'll pay for themselves very quickly. Contact your friendly local software dealer for details.

That's the entire Office 2000 shtick. Let's take a closer look at the lesser-known parts.

Office's More Obscure Parts

Sure Office 2000 contains a handful of stellar applications—Microsoft likes to call them "best of the breed," and they probably are. But there are smaller applications that ship in most Office boxes, and many of these unsung heroes deserve more attention than they usually receive. A couple of them are complete turkeys though, so don't get your hopes up too high.

Office Assistant

No doubt you've bumped into the little paper clip sitting in the corner of any Office program's screen. Probably bumped into it literally. Anyway, I'll have a lot to say about "that damn paper clip" in Chapter 5, "Help from a Paper Clip." Generally it's a pain in the neck, but under some conditions it can save your life. Bet you can't wait, eh?

Binders

I don't care what you've read in other introductory books. Binders are almost completely without redeeming social value, and most users—particularly new users—should avoid them like the plague.

Office 2000's Binder feature is a way to put related documents in one place and keep them all together. There are two very good reasons why you might want to use Binders:

- If you need to print both Word documents and Excel spreadsheets, interleaved, with a single header or footer. This can actually be handy if you have to put together a report where full-page Excel spreadsheets are interleaved with different Word documents, and you need to have the pages numbered continuously across both types of file. (Note that Binders won't help unless each spreadsheet and each document is in a separate file.) There are some similar weird circumstances where Binders can help with printing reports, but that's the main use.

● If you commonly send multiple documents to other people across your company's network, or over the Internet, and you don't know how to use a ZIP program. Binders can help you keep all the pieces together, but that's about it.

Microsoft tried hard to sell Binders in Office 97, but failed miserably. (Who says you can fool all the people some of the time?) In apparent admission of defeat, Binders aren't even installed in the "typical install" of Office 2000, although you have the option to load them during a custom install if you really want to abuse yourself. Unless you've got a really good reason for installing Binders, I say turn the other cheek. Good riddance.

Visual Basic for Applications

Word 2000, Outlook 2000, Excel 2000, and PowerPoint 2000 all contain a macro programming language. I talked about it in Chapter 2, "Precursors to Using Office," when we were looking at viruses. Although the methods used for programming each of the different applications is quite distinct, the languages in all three are very similar. They're called Visual Basic for Applications. As the name implies, VBA rates as a first cousin (well, maybe a second cousin, removed) to Visual Basic, the Windows programming language.

Believe it or not, if you have any of those three programs installed on your machine, you have a verypowerful programming language available to you any time. Click **Tools**, **Macro**, **Visual Basic Editor** to get it going.

I won't be discussing macros in this book. I was tempted to talk about the Macro Recorder—a part of Office that can be made to watch over your shoulder as you do things, and translate your actions into a macro program, which can be replayed to mimic your actions—but it's pretty hard to record a useful macro. If the macro doesn't do exactly what you thought it would, you have to dive pretty deep into the underlying VBA code to figure out why. And, besides, once I start talking about macros, I find it very hard to shut up. They really can do amazing things. I made a living off them for years.

How the Components Work Together

You would think that Office, being the monolith it's marketed to be, would have all sorts of robust interconnections among its various components. Well, you'd be wrong. The fact is that each Office component grew up independently—of the four core components, only Outlook was born after the debut of Office as a whole—and the differences really show up when you try to tie the pieces together.

Here's a thumbnail sketch of which parts of Office work with other parts, along with a little bit of heckling from Woody's infamous Peanut Gallery:

- Excel tables and charts plop into Word documents and PowerPoint presentations with little heartburn.

- Word can bring names and addresses into documents from your Outlook contacts list, but there are several gotchas. (I'll tell you about them toward the end of this book.) Word can also suck in a list of names from Outlook and use them to perform a mail merge (that is, Word can generate form letters and envelopes for people in your Outlook contacts database).

LEARN MORE ABOUT MACROS

If you have a hankering to learn more about macros, I strongly recommend that you pick up a CD from Microsoft called Mastering Office Development. (Hint: If you have kids around the house who want to tackle a real programming language, this is a great way to start.) The CD will set you back $100 or so, but it's worth every penny, even if it does toe the Microsoft party line. To get the CD, which can be surprisingly hard to find, in the U.S., call Microsoft directly at 800-621-7930. Outside the U.S., start at the Web site msdn.microsoft.com/mastering, and pray.

If you really want to learn more about macros, I suggest picking up a copy of (what else?) *Special Edition Using Microsoft Office 2000*, by Ed Bott and (ahem) Woody Leonhard (Que ISBN 0-7897-1842-1).

- It's also relatively easy to send a fax from Word via Outlook out on your modem—providing all the connections work right, anyway.

- Outlook can keep a log—called a *journal*—of all your Word, Excel, and PowerPoint files. The journal shows you when you opened, updated, and stored the files. That can be handy if you get into a situation where you can remember when you did something, but not remember what it was. For example, "Jeez. I updated that Word document last Wednesday or Thursday, but I can't remember the name of the file."

INTEROPERABILITY OUTSIDE THE CORE

The four core Office components I discuss in this book—Word, Outlook, Excel, and PowerPoint—have a hard enough time working together. The other Office apps, from the various flavors of Office (which were forced into Office more than "integrated") rarely even speak to one another, much less cooperate.

- You can move files between Excel and Outlook. That can be handy if you want to pull your Contacts list into a spreadsheet.

- There's a handy, but horribly inflexible, way to turn a Word outline into a PowerPoint presentation.

While the pieces of Office can work together in other ways, these are the biggies. I'll cover them in-depth—and take you through the ins and outs—in Part VII, "Advanced Topics."

Woody Leonhard

TEACHES

MAKING OFFICE WORK YOUR WAY

WRANGLING THE OFFICE BEAST. You'll find my favorite mantra repeated throughout this book: Take Office into your own hands! There's absolutely no reason why you should suffer along with the decisions Microsoft has made for you. Office can be changed every which way, and you'll save yourself an enormous amount of time if you'll just set it up the way that works best for you.

4

Organizing My Documents

I'm going to start this customizing extravaganza, which will recur throughout the book, with some simple apple pie changes. Every single Office user should take these steps to make Office work better. A few minutes spent on these changes will pay off day after day as you use the product. Besides, digging through all this is a simple way for you to get a good feel for how Office fits into Windows at large.

Windows lets you store files—letters, faxes, invoices, memos, stories, spreadsheets, presentations, pictures, and the like—in folders. Office 2000 (and some versions of Windows) sets up a special folder called *My Documents* and encourages you to store your files in that folder. While the name My Documents might strike you as a trifle cute, it's still a decent starting point to help you get organized.

TIP

KEEPING YOUR FILES ORGANIZED

People tend to put all their Word documents in one folder, all their spreadsheets in another, graphics in yet another, and so on. You'll find it much easier to keep track of things if you keep related files together—never mind whether the files are Word documents, Excel spreadsheets, PowerPoint presentations, scanned photos, or artwork. (Outlook files tend to look after themselves; you don't need to be concerned about them at this point.)

ANARCHY IN THE OFFICE

Some companies force you to go along with Microsoft's absurd customizing decisions. There are a few tools that limit the customizing you can perform, both on Office and on Windows itself. Companies that force employees to swallow a specific collection of settings often do so in the name of Total Cost of Ownership—but their TCO calculations are frequently fallacious.

My favorite example: there are ways to keep users from changing the buttons on their Office toolbars. Microsoft created a specific set of toolbars and, dammit, Big Brother (most often in the guise of an inflexible IT department) doesn't want you to change those toolbars so they work better for you. It's all hogwash.

Big Brother will proffer an argument along the lines of, "Hey, if you change the toolbar buttons, our tech support people won't be able to help you. It'll cost us a lot of money to cover for your mistakes!"

What a crock. If you're advanced enough to change your toolbar buttons, you'll know which buttons you have, and what they do. Besides, any tech support person worth their salt should be able to work through toolbar changes. When the IT folks make decisions like this, they're lowering the IT's TCO—not yours. Just don't get fired for tinkering with the settings, Okay?

Occasionally you'll find that some of the customizing recommendations in this book won't work on your machine at work. (They should work on a PC at home, though, unless you've done something weird with the installation.) If you get shut out of an important customization at work, you may well be the victim of Big Brother. I suggest you yell, real loud.

Think about the best way to organize your information. Someone in a small business, for example, might find it easier to work with separate folders for each client. That can get a bit cumbersome if you have more than a few dozen clients, but if that's the case, you might be able to group the clients together and put each client into the appropriate group (see Figure 4.1).

FIGURE 4.1

How a typical small businessperson might want to arrange My Documents.

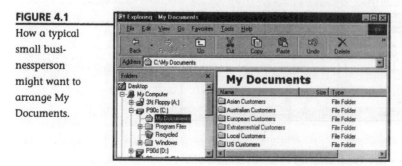

Students can group assignments in a folder and put all the folders for a specific class in yet another folder. Human resources folks might want to use different folders for different functions—hiring, reviews, the HR manual, whatever (see Figure 4.2).

FIGURE 4.2

An HR manager might try this arrangement.

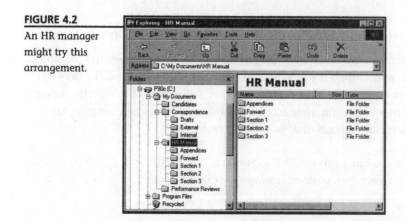

Writers could put each of their projects in a separate folder. For example, I have a folder for articles with subfolders for each feature, review, and Help column; another folder for books, with subfolders for each book, plus separate folders for clients, accounting, and taxes—even one for my son (see Figure 4.3)!

A Place for Everything

You'll save an enormous amount of time in Office 2000 if you set up a place for everything, and keep everything in its place. (I sound like your mother, eh?) Folders can be split, combined, moved, added, and deleted as your needs change.

FIGURE 4.3

My Documents.

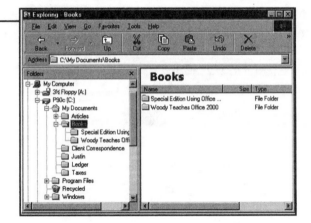

EXERCISE

Think Through My Documents

1. Forget about computers for a minute. Think about the kinds of things you need to organize. Do you work with clients? Courses? Do you put together handouts? Take out a pencil and write down the basic groups of things that drive your daily life.

2. Take a look at each of those things, in turn. Can they be broken down further? If you have clients as a major group, list all your clients. You get the idea.

3. Work out the kinks. Everyone will have some overlap between the categories. A common example: If you send invoices to clients, should all the invoices go into one giant folder, or should each invoice go into the respective client's folder? There's no right answer. Choose whatever works best for you. And remember that you can always change your mind.

Now that you have a blueprint for My Documents, let's go through the steps necessary to set up your very own customized My Documents folder.

EXERCISE

Get Your Bearings with Windows Explorer

1. Right-click **My Computer** and choose **Explore**. If you're working with a virgin Windows installation, you should see a Windows Explorer window (see Figure 4.4).

2. Take a moment to look at the screen. As you can see in Figure 4.4, it's split into two sections. The section on the left, which starts out with the lines **All Folders and Desktop**, is called the *left pane* (as in *window pane*—get it?).

The section on the right, which starts out with **My Computer and My Documents** is called the right pane.

FIGURE 4.4

Windows
Explorer on a
clean Windows
98 system.

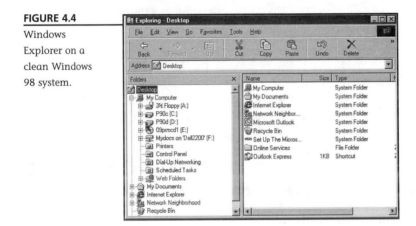

3. Move around a bit. See those plus signs in the left pane? There's one next to P90c (c:) and all the other disk drives. Clicking that plus sign *expands* the folder, showing you all the folders immediately underneath. Click the plus sign + next to your c: drive. You should see a folder called My Documents. That's the folder you need to work with.

4. In the left pane, double-click the folder called **My Documents**. If you haven't been using Office at all, the right pane will be empty (see Figure 4.5)—in geek terminology, you don't have anything stored in the folder c:\My Documents. If you have been using Office 2000, you might be surprised to discover that this is where all those My Documents files are actually stored on your computer.

FIGURE 4.5

A clean My
Documents
folder.

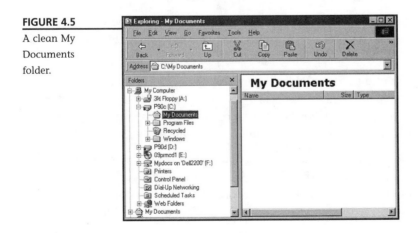

Creating Folders in My Documents

Now that you've discovered where My Documents lives, it's time to build the super-structure that will hold all your files. I'll start by showing you the simple folder-building features you have at your disposal.

 EXERCISE

Create a New Folder in My Documents

1. With your Windows Explorer window looking like Figure 4.5—that is, My Documents selected in the left pane, and nothing in the right pane (with the possible exception of some old files)—right-click a blank area in the right pane. Choose **New, Folder** (see Figure 4.6).

FIGURE 4.6

Creating a new folder in My Documents.

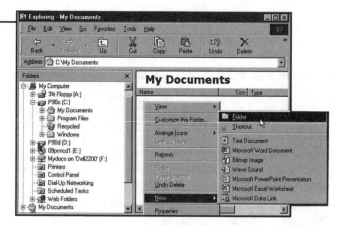

2. Windows creates a new folder and hangs it underneath My Documents. That new folder is called, uh, *New Folder*. Clever, ain't it?

3. Immediately, without pressing Enter or any of the arrow keys on the keyboard, type in a new name for this folder. In a fit of pique, I typed the name *Taxes*. When you're done, press **Enter**.

4. You've just created a new folder underneath the My Documents folder. Since you're bound to be a little skeptical at this point (hey, if I'd spent my life believing in Microsoft's party line, I'd be skeptical too), click the plus sign next to My Documents in the left pane (see Figure 4.7). See where the new folder sits?

5. Fill out the rest of the folders that sit underneath My Documents. In each case, click **My Documents** in the left pane. Then right-click a blank space in the right pane, choose **New, Folder**, and type the new folder's name and press **Enter**. I created the folder structure you see in Figure 4.8.

FIGURE 4.7

Verifying that
the folder
named Taxes
now sits under-
neath My
Documents.

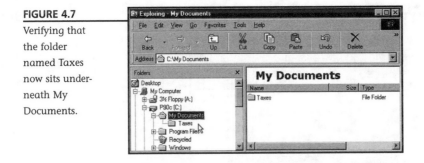

FIGURE 4.8

The first level of
My Documents
on my
machine.

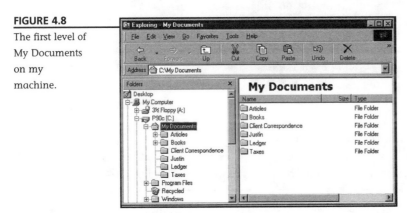

This is a good point to take a break.

Renaming and Deleting Folders

You now know how to create new folders underneath My Documents (or anywhere
else on your disk drives, for that matter). What remains is fine-tuning and
embellishment.

 EXERCISE

Rename, Delete Folders in My Documents

1. It probably won't surprise you to know that you can delete a folder by
   clicking it and pressing the **Delete** key on the keyboard.

2. And if you've used Windows for more than a couple of weeks, you might
   already know that renaming a folder is as simple as right-clicking it,
   choosing **Rename** (see Figure 4.9), and typing the new name.

FIGURE 4.9

Renaming an
existing folder.

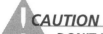CAUTION

DON'T RENAME MY DOCUMENTS!

While it's entirely possible to change the name My Documents to anything you like—the
names *Letters* or *Work* or just plain *Documents* come to mind immediately—in some versions of Windows it's harder than you might imagine to redirect Office's various components
so they can use the new name. Until you've become quite proficient at manipulating Office,
it's a good idea to succumb to Microsoft's naming convention and keep all your Office documents in a folder called My Documents or in subfolders directly beneath My Documents.

Creating Multiple Folders in My Documents

What about multiple levels of folders? For example, what if you need to have several
folders underneath the Articles folder shown in Figure 4.9? Piece o' cake.

EXERCISE

Create Subfolders in My Documents

1. Double-click the folder under which you want to put new folders. For example, if you want to put folders under the Articles folder, double-click the
   Articles folder.

2. Right-click in a blank area on the right pane. Choose **New**, **Folder**. Type in
   the name of the new folder, just as you did in the "Create a New Folder in
   My Documents," exercise in step 3 (see Figure 4.10.)

FIGURE 4.10

Adding new folders underneath the Articles folder.

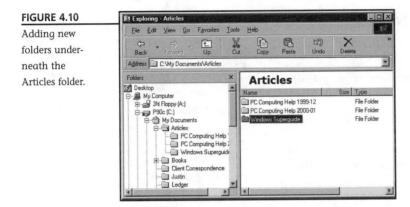

3. Follow these steps to fill in all the folders you think you'll need. Remember that folders can be nested just as deep as you like—although things can get pretty hairy, mentally, if you try to keep on top of more than five or six levels. My final My Documents looks like Figure 4.11.

FIGURE 4.11

Final configuration of My Documents on my machine.

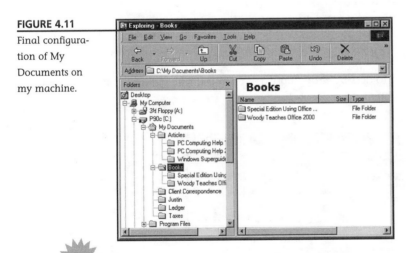

TIP

SORTING FILES

Generally Windows Explorer shows folders and files in alphabetical order, with all the folders appearing above all the files. When you're adding and renaming folders, though, Explorer doesn't bother to re-sort the list until you tell it to. You can re-sort at any time by pressing **F5**, or by closing and restarting Windows Explorer.

Moving Folders in My Documents

Here's one final practice exercise to show you how to move folders (and files) around once they've been created.

EXERCISE

Move Folders in My Documents

1. Click and double-click around Windows Explorer until the folders you want to move appear in the right pane.

2. Select the folders you want to move. To choose one folder, click it. To choose a contiguous block of folders, click the first folder, hold down the **Shift** key and click the last folder. To pick and choose a bunch of folders, click the first one, hold down the **Ctrl** key, and keep clicking all the others.

3. Move the folders by dragging them from the right pane to the left pane (see Figure 4.12).

HEY WOODY, CAN'T YOU DO ALL THIS INSIDE OFFICE 2000?

Yes, it's true. Inside every Office application, when you click **File**, **Open**, you have a chance to make changes to folders—add new ones, rename existing ones, even move them around. But the methods available inside Office's **File Open** box are very cumbersome: Moving files from folder to folder is difficult, and you can never see the whole folder structure at once. Besides, even novice users need to know where the documents in My Documents really reside. That's why I strongly recommend that you do your heavy work outside Office, in the Windows Explorer.

FIGURE 4.12

Explorer lets you move folders by dragging them—usually from the right to the left pane.

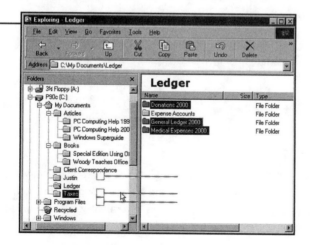

Customizing My Documents

It's time to put all your Windows Explorer talent to work now, and create your very own customized My Documents.

EXERCISE

Build Your Own My Documents

1. Re-create the folder structure you traced out in the first exercise in this chapter. Play with it a bit. Don't be afraid to move folders around until the structure seems right to you.

2. If you already have files in My Documents, use the technique explained in the preceding exercise to move them into the folders where they now belong. If you're bringing files over from an old machine, use Windows Explorer to move them into their correct new locations.

3. Exit Windows Explorer by clicking **File**, **Close**, or by clicking the **X** in the upper-right corner.

Your Office 2000 house is now in order, with My Documents ready to take on your work in your way. Next, let's take a look at what you'll need in case your disk drive ever decides to go bye-bye. Disk drives do die. Oh, my, yes they do.

Backing Up Your Office Files

Someday, somewhere—probably in some parallel universe—Microsoft will come up with one of its famous wizards to handle the chore of backing up your Office files. Until that day arrives you're pretty much on your own.

⚠ CAUTION

THINK DISASTER WON'T STRIKE YOU? THINK AGAIN

I know that backup is boring. I know you're tempted to blow right by this section and go onto something a little more sexy; resist the temptation. I say this from bitter personal experience: Until you have a backup plan in action, you'd be a fool to do any important work in Office 2000.

SURVIVAL ON THE CORPORATE NETWORK

Those of you working at companies with local area networks (you'll hear these called LANs) should feel pretty secure if you keep your Office 2000 data files on the *server*. (A server is just a hefty PC that provides services—printing, file storage, security, and sometimes online access—to other machines on the network. It sounds mysterious, but it isn't.) The IT people usually back up the server religiously, but if you're not sure, ask!

If you keep your data on your own PC's hard drive, though, you should take a good look at what we're doing here and modify things so your backup goes to the server. That might sound complicated, but about any computer geek will no doubt do it for you, for the price of a beer and a pizza. Cheap insurance.

Fortunately, Windows 95 and 98 have good backup routines built into the product. While you can write your own program to perform backups, the built-in Windows Backup programs work well enough for most purposes.

Regardless of what you use, or how you do it, someday a good backup will save your, uh, neck. I won't regale you with my tales of woe. Suffice it to say that having your c: drive die a day before a big assignment comes due is just about as much fun as having a root canal while being audited by the IRS *and* undergoing a digital prostate probe—simultaneously.

Putting together a good backup plan involves three steps. First, you have to figure out which files to back up. Second, you have to figure out how to get those files onto the backup drive or tape. Third, you have to use the backup process every single day.

I can help you with the first two. For the third, you're on your own.

Which Office 2000 Files Need to Be Backed Up?

Office 2000 uses an enormous number of different files. Most of those files can be identified by their filename extensions.

☞ *For details about filename extensions, see Explorer Show Extensions, Chapter 2, **page 21**.*

WHADDYA MEAN, "VARIES"?
Man, Microsoft seems to put its .pst files any old place, depending on which versions of Outlook you use, whether you upgraded over an old version, the phase of the moon…

Moral of the story: use Windows Start/Find/Files and Folders to locate *.pst files.

Table 4.1 shows a list of all the filename extensions that the four major Office 2000 applications use, what they're used for, and where those files are usually located on a single-user PC.

Table 4.1   Office 2000 Filename Extensions

Extension	Type of File	Usual Location on a Single-User PC
.doc	Word Document	c:\My Documents
.dot	Word Template	c:\Program Files\Microsoft Office\Templates
.dic	Custom Dictionary	c:\Program Files\Microsoft Office\Proof
.xls	Excel Worksheet	c:\My Documents
.xla	Excel Add-In	c:\Program Files\Microsoft Office\Templates
.xlt	Excel Template	c:\Program Files\Microsoft Office\Templates
.ppt	PowerPoint Presentation	c:\My Documents
.pot	PowerPoint Template	c:\Program Files\Microsoft Office\Templates
.htm	Web Document in HTML	c:\My Documents Format
.html	Web Document in HTML	c:\My Documents Format

Extension	Type of File	Usual Location on a Single-User PC
.wiz	Office Wizard	c:\Program Files\Microsoft Office\Templates
.obd	Office Binder	c:\My Documents
.obt	Office Binder Template	c:\Program Files\Microsoft Office
.oft	Outlook Template	c:\Program Files\Microsoft Office\Templates
.pst	Outlook Data	varies
.acl	Office AutoCorrect	c:\Windows Entries

Windows NT 4 puts the .acl files in the primary Windows folder, which is frequently called c:\winnt. The .pst file might hang underneath that. If you're using NT or a system with multiple user profiles, you might have to look around for some of these files.

If you've done something weird and installed Office 2000 in an odd folder—or (shudder) changed the name of the My Documents folder—you might have to go searching your hard drive to see where these files got scattered. That's not terribly difficult if you use Windows File Find utility. Click **Start**, **Find**, **Files or Folders**, but I won't go into the gory details. If you get in that deep, find some knowledgeable help.

If you look at Table 4.1 long enough, you'll probably come to the conclusion that what you really want to do is back up the folder called My Documents, plus the folder called Microsoft Office (which sits under the My Programs folder). You'll also want to back up all the folders underneath My Documents and Microsoft Office. You should probably pick up the .acl and .pst files, too, sitting in and under the Windows folder. That's the general strategy.

IDENTIFYING OFFICE DATA FILES

Is all this Greek to you? Don't get freaked out! That table isn't nearly as mysterious as it appears at first glance. Just take a deep breath and I'll walk you through it slowly.

You need to figure out which files on your hard drive are Office data files—those are the ones you want to back up. It ends up that you can identify all of Office's major data files if you look at the *filename extension*—the final few characters after the period on the end of the filename. This table just lists the 17 filename extensions that Office 2000 uses to identify its data files.

Take the table's first row. (Please.) It says that Word documents have the filename extension of .doc. (You knew that already, based on our discussion in Chapter 2, right?) So if you call a Word document, oh, *Letter to Ma*, its filename comes out *Letter to Ma.doc*. If you want to back up all your Word documents, you'd better snag every file that has a name ending with .doc. So far, so good.

The first row also says that Word documents are usually stored in c:\My Documents. That's just geek shorthand for saying they're usually stored in the folder called My Documents that sits on the c: disk drive. In fact, as you discovered in the previous section of this chapter, Word documents are usually in the My Documents folder or in one of the folders that hang off of My Documents.

How to Back Them Up

If you have a commercial backup program, you have all the information you need to get going. (Sorry, I can't step you through the backup program itself; each one is different.) Make sure you get c:\My Documents, c:\Program Files\Microsoft Office, and all the folders underneath them in your backups, plus the .pst files wherever they may be, and you'll be in good shape. The .acl AutoCorrect files would be nice to have, but believe me, if your hard drive goes down you'll be thanking your lucky stars to have anything you can get.

If you don't have a commercial backup system, and you're using Windows 98 or 95, your next best choice is to use Windows' own Backup system. I'll walk you through the Windows 98 Backup; the steps for Windows 95 are quite similar.

EXERCISE

Using Windows 98 Backup

1. Click **Start**, **Programs**, **Accessories**, **System Tools**. Do you see an entry called **Backup**? If so, go on to step 4. If not, you'll have to install Windows Backup from your original Windows installation CD.

2. To install Windows Backup, click **Start**, **Settings**, **Control Panel**, and double-click **Add/Remove Programs**. Click the **Windows Setup** tab. Double-click **System Tools** (see Figure 4.13).

FIGURE 4.13

Changing system tools in Windows Setup.

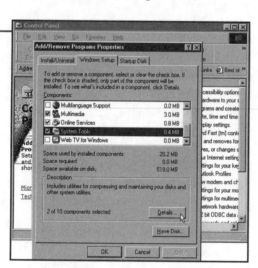

3. Check the box marked **Backup** (see Figure 4.14). Click **OK** twice. When your PC asks you to insert your Windows CD, do so, and click **OK**. Backup will be installed.

FIGURE 4.14

Installing
Backup from
the Windows
CD.

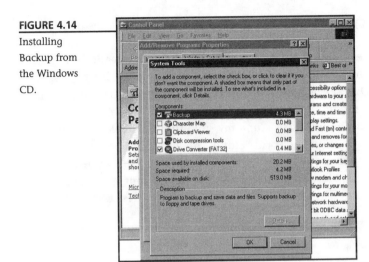

4. Start Windows Backup by clicking **Start**, **Programs**, **Accessories**, **System Tools**, **Backup**. Windows will ask what kind of backup work you want to do (see Figure 4.15). Click **Create a new backup job** and click **OK**.

FIGURE 4.15

Tell Windows you
want to create a
new backup job.

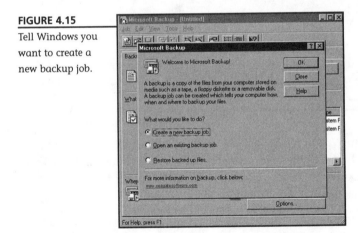

5. The Backup Wizard will ask if you want to back up all of My Computer or if you want to back up selected files, folders, and drives. Assuming you just want to back up your Office files, choose the selected files, folders, and drives option, and click **Next**.

6. Select the files you want to back up. In most cases, the easiest way to do that is to check the box next to My Documents in the left pane. Then double-click **Program Files** in the left pane and check the box next to Microsoft Office in the right pane (that selects the Microsoft Office folder under the Program Files folder). Double-click the **Windows folder** in the left pane and check all .acl files in the right pane. Finally, check the .pst files—in Figure 4.16, the PC is set up with multiple users, and my son Justin's outlook.pst file is in c:\Windows\Profiles\justin\Local Settings\Application Data\Microsoft\Outlook. Use Windows File Find feature (**Start**, **Find**, **Files or Folders**) and type `*.pst` in the **Named** box to locate .pst files on your PC. When you have all your files selected in the Backup Wizard, click **Next**.

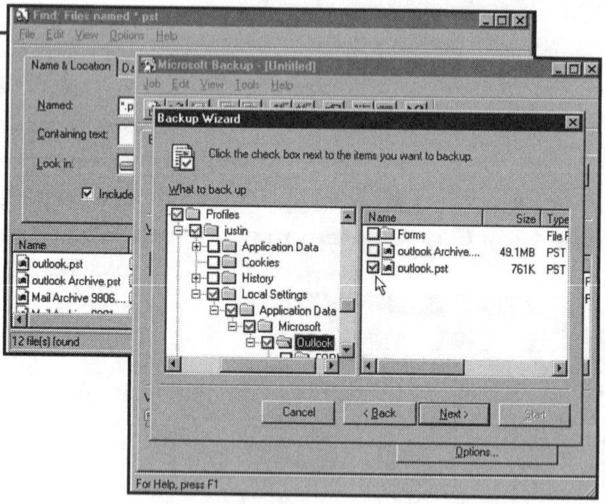

FIGURE 4.16

Select the folders and files you want to back up.

7. Then the Backup Wizard needs to know if you want to back up all the files that are selected, or only the files that are new or have changed. If you keep all your old backups (and you can rely on them!), **New and changed** files is sufficient. Click **Next**.

8. Choose a place to put the backed up files. In Figure 4.17, I've chosen to back up to a file on a different hard drive. Click **Next**.

!CAUTION

DON'T CREATE A BACKUP ON THE SAME DRIVE CONTAINING YOUR DATA

If you're backing up files on drive c:, don't put the backup itself on drive c:! You'd be surprised how many people place backups on the same drive as the original files and don't understand the consequences until the drive flies south for the winter, taking both the original files and the backup along with it.

FIGURE 4.17

Choose a backup location.

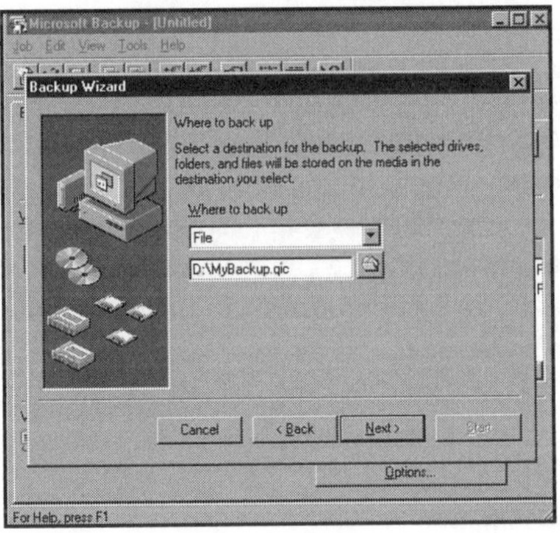

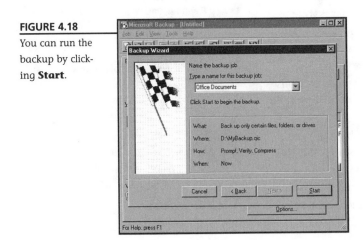

9. The Backup Wizard wants to know if it should compare original and backup files, once the backup is done, to make sure they're the same. In my experience, this is a vital step if you're backing up to tape, but not really necessary if you're backing up to a hard drive or removable drive (such as a Zip or Jaz drive). The wizard also wants to know if you want to compress the backup to save space, and the answer to that is almost always **Yes** (unless your backup drive is unreliable). Click **Next**.

10. Finally, the Backup Wizard asks you to give your backup job a name (in Figure 4.18, I used Office Documents), and invites you to begin the backup process by clicking **Start**. Do it, and you'll be backed up. Congratulations!

FIGURE 4.18

You can run the backup by clicking **Start**.

Now you can breathe easy. If you've followed all the nostrums up to this point, you're fully protected and ready to start using Office 2000 in the real world.

Starting Office

Unless you've gone to great pains to keep Internet Explorer off of your PC, you almost undoubtedly have a Windows taskbar down at the bottom of the screen with a bunch of little icons immediately to the right of the **Start** button (see Figure 4.19). That bunch of icons is called the *Windows Quick Launch toolbar*. It's very handy because single-clicking on any icon in the Quick Launch toolbar automatically starts the associated program. (Your collection of icons in the Quick Launch toolbar might vary a bit from the set in Figure 4.19.)

FIGURE 4.19

The Windows Quick Launch toolbar.

It just so happens that the Quick Launch toolbar is the greatest place in the Windows universe to put little icons that launch the Office applications. Here's how to take the toolbar into your own hands.

Office on the Quick Launch

 EXERCISE

1. Let's employ a little critical thinking—stretch those little gray cells. Take a hard look at the icons in your Quick Launch toolbar. *Hover* your mouse over them to see which programs they launch. If you're like most Office users, you'll see that two of the icons (the first and third in Figure 4.19) are quite useful: they launch Internet Explorer and the Windows Desktop. But the other two (one for Outlook Express, the other for Viewing Channels) are real slackers.

CLEANING UP THE SCREENTIPS—AN ADVANCED COURSE

As you can see in Figure 4.21, the only problem with your new Word Quick Launch icon is the ScreenTip—the yellow text that appears when you hover your mouse over it. **Shortcut to Winword.exe** it says. Blecch. You can change the ScreenTip, but it takes a bit of spelunking in Windows Explorer, unless you installed Internet Explorer 5. In IE 5, just right-click the button, choose **Rename**, and type in the new ScreenTip.

If you aren't running Internet Explorer 5, and you're up to the challenge, first use Windows File Find (**Start**, **Find**, **Files or Folders**) to locate the \Quick Launch folder (type `quick launch` in the box marked **Named**). On my multiple-user Windows 98 machine running Internet Explorer 5, that folder is located at c:\Windows\Profiles\woody\Application Data\Microsoft\Internet Explorer\Quick Launch. (What a mouthful, eh?)

continues

After all, if you have Office 2000, you probably look down your nose at Outlook Express—and you'd rather read spam than view channels. If there are any icons on the Quick Launch toolbar that you don't want, right-click on them and choose **Delete**. They're germs. They deserve to die.

CLEANING UP THE SCREENTIPS—AN ADVANCED COURSE *continued*

Start Windows Explorer (right-click **My Computer**, and choose **Explore**) and navigate to the \Quick Launch folder. There you'll find a file named **Shortcut to Winword.exe**. Right-click on the file and choose **Rename**. Give it whatever name you'd like to appear as a ScreenTip—if you call the file *Word*, for example, the ScreenTip *Word* will appear over the icon.

2. Let's put an icon down there on the taskbar that will launch Word 2000. (I bet you start Word 2000 more frequently than you view channels, eh?) Start Windows Explorer by right-clicking **My Computer** and choosing **Explore**. Navigate down to the c:\Program Files\Microsoft Office\Office folder (see Figure 4.20). See the line marked **Winword.exe**? That's the Word program. Click it once.

3. Click **Winword.exe** and drag it down to the Quick Launch toolbar. When you've positioned the I-beam where you want it, release the mouse button. You'll have a fully functional Word icon available in the Windows Quick Launch toolbar (see Figure 4.21). Try clicking on it to start Word.

FIGURE 4.20

Winword.exe, the Microsoft Word program, in the \Office folder.

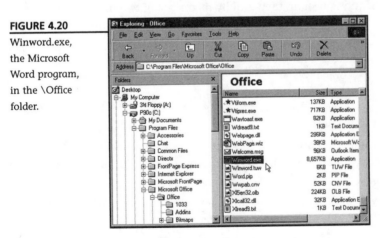

FIGURE 4.21

A Word icon on the Quick Launch toolbar.

4. Similarly, click and drag any other Office applications that you use frequently onto the Windows Quick Launch toolbar. In Figure 4.22, I've included Outlook (outlook.exe), Excel (excel.exe), and PowerPoint (powerpnt.exe). If you have other Office applications, you might want to drag them onto the Quick Launch toolbar, too, while you're at it. Look for Access (msaccess.exe), FrontPage (frontpg.exe), PhotoDraw (Photodrw.exe), and Publisher (mspub.exe), all in the \Office folder. If you make a mistake, right-click the offending icon and choose **Delete**.

5. Test your new icons. You should be able to click once on any of them and have Windows launch the respective application.

FIGURE 4.22

Word, Outlook, Excel, and PowerPoint— where they're easy to find.

Making Office 2000 Run Better

I'd like to finish this chapter with a very short discussion concerning the question I'm asked most frequently: "Woody, how do you make Office 2000 run better?"

When folks ask me that question, they usually mean one of two things: How do you make the bloody thing run faster; or, how do you keep it from crashing so often?

Fortunately, each of those questions has a series of simple answers.

Speed

The very best way to make Office 2000 run faster is to buy a faster PC. (Okay, okay. I'll wait while you finish groaning.)

The next best way to make Office 2000 run faster is to get more memory. The difference between Office running on 16MB and Office running on 64MB will impress you mightily.

The third best way to make Office 2000 run faster is to upgrade to Windows 98. You'll find that Office loads much faster and runs a tiny bit faster.

Anything else you try to do—faster hard drives, fancy video cards, souped up controllers—won't amount to a hill of beans. Spend your money on something you'll use, like a bigger screen, a second hard drive, or a tray to lower your keyboard below normal desk height.

Stability

Which brings me to the problem with crashes. Yes, it's true, if you use Office 2000 hard—I mean, day in and day out—you're going to watch it crash. Sometimes the crashes turn out relatively benign: Word might freeze and swallow a few minutes' worth of typing. Pressing **Ctrl+Alt+Del** and rebooting Windows brings everything back to life. Sometimes, though, you won't be so lucky. That's why you have backups, eh?

The single most important way to improve Office 2000's stability is to get all the fixes (such as Service Release-1) and to apply them religiously. You should do that regardless of what other stability improvement techniques you might attempt.

The next way to improve Office 2000 stability is to run it on Windows 98. Yeah. It's surprising. I have, oh, maybe half the number of crashes under Windows 98 that I did under Windows 95.

The very best way to improve Office 2000 stability? Use Windows NT. This is the first book I've ever written entirely with Word 2000 and NT 4, and it's like the difference between night and day. I haven't had a single crash yet—knock on wood—and I haven't rebooted NT more than once a week—simply stunning.

There. You just paid for this book. Again.

5

Woody Leonhard

TEACHES

HELP FROM A PAPER CLIP

A LITTLE HELP FROM OUR FRIENDS IN REDMOND. No book on Office 2000 can cover the entire product. No, not even those 1,500-page behemoths. Er, especially not those 1,500-page behemoths. This, I know firsthand. Office 2000 has so many nooks and crannies it would take 10,000 pages or more to describe all of its nuances—maybe 20,000.

That's why online help is built into Office itself.

Help Shortcomings

There are three significant disadvantages to the help available inside Office 2000:

- The help is official help, so it parrots the Microsoft party line. Often that means the help you'll find explains how Office is supposed to work, not how it actually does work.

- It can be very difficult to find help on the specific topic that interests you, particularly when you don't know the technical jargon.

- Sometimes the help you find leaves you hanging in mid-air. You'll find instructions for solving part of the problem, but not all of it. Even the built-in help doesn't cover all of Office's capabilities.

Fortunately, there are some tactics you can employ to ameliorate each of those problems. I'll show you how, but first let's start with the basics.

The Office Assistant Character

Every time you start an Office application, you'll be accosted by a paper clip. He/she/it has a name: Clippit. (Cute, eh?) More than anything else, Clippit resembles the ancient oracle at Delphi. Ask it a question, and you'll get an answer. Depending on your luck and the oracle's mood, that answer could be spot-on correct, utterly unrelated to the question, or totally inscrutable (see Figure 5.1). Such is the nature of oracles.

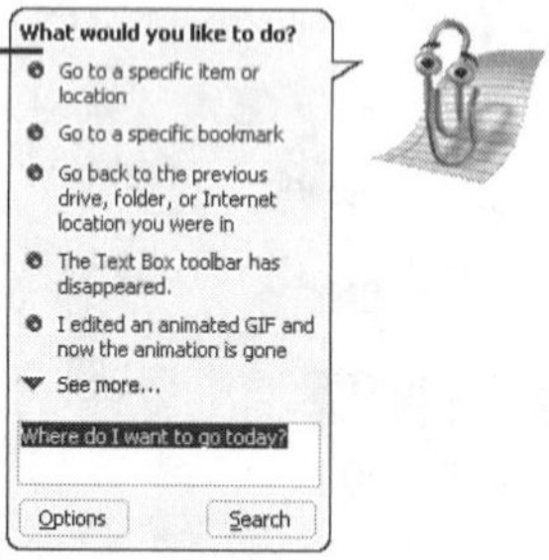

FIGURE 5.1

Clippit answers, "Where do I want to go today?"

> **What would you like to do?**
> - Go to a specific item or location
> - Go to a specific bookmark
> - Go back to the previous drive, folder, or Internet location you were in
> - The Text Box toolbar has disappeared.
> - I edited an animated GIF and now the animation is gone
> ▼ See more...
>
> Where do I want to go today?
>
> Options   Search

EXERCISE

Ask the Oracle a Question

1. Start any of the Office applications.

2. Click **Clippit**.

3. Type a question—any question.

4. Press **Enter** (or click **Search**). Did you get a reasonable answer? I didn't think so.

5. Click any of the offered topics. You'll be transported into the less-visual (and much less friendly!) Office Help system. See how it works? Click the **X** in the upper-right corner of the Help box to get rid of it.

Although it's considered somewhat fashionable among the Office cognoscenti to belittle the Office Assistant, sometimes ol' Clippit really hits the spot.

The Office Assistant watches over your shoulder as you type. Whenever you click it, the character tries to figure out what you're trying to do and gives you a series of tips that may be appropriate—in true oracular tradition, you needn't even ask a question before the oracle will give you an answer. Sometimes the Office Assistant will look at what you're doing and come to the conclusion that you could be accomplishing the same thing with less work. In such circumstances, a light bulb appears in the upper-right corner of the Assistant. Click the little guy to see if he/she/it has any worthwhile tips.

Unfortunately, the Office Assistant character, aside from being cloyingly cute, frequently gets in the way. Yes, it's supposed to scoot around, moving out of the way as you type or enter data in spreadsheet cells. In practice, I find the scooting to be vastly over-rated: Clippit just gets in the way, obscuring things I want to see onscreen. It would be easier if I could make him smaller, or confine him to the Office applications' title bars (nothing worse than seeing a totally bent paper clip in a bar, huh?), but alas there's no such shrinking capability in Office 2000.

BOB INVADES MICROSOFT OFFICE

Microsoft has long pioneered usability improvements in its products, and one of the best—or worst—examples has to be Microsoft's ill-fated Bob. Good ol' Bob (if you're old enough to remember him) beamed a broad yellow smile, incorporated something called a social interface, and did just about nothing else. Buyers shunned Bob in droves. Tons of boxes sporting Bob's smiling face piled up in warehouses. Microsoft couldn't give 'em away.

In the end, though, Bob may steal the last laugh—at your expense. When Bob failed to get off the ground, the team that developed Bob found itself out of work, until the Office Assistant project came to the rescue. The Office Assistant—that, uh, cute little paper clip you might have seen lurking at the corner of your screen—owes its existence to Bob's demise.

Microsoft lore (possibly apocryphal) has it that the first incarnation of the Office Assistant looked like a clown, not a paper clip. Supposedly the Bob team presented an Office Bob prototype to Bill one day. Gates played around with it a bit and pronounced it good—except, "I kept wanting to strangle that damn clown."

The next time you feel like strangling the Office Assistant character, remember this: You're in good company. Bill couldn't stand it either.

Toggling the Office Assistant On and Off

That's why I usually turn the Office Assistant off. It's easy to do—just right-click on the critter, pick **Options**, and uncheck the box marked **Use the Office Assistant** (see Figure 5.2).

FIGURE 5.2

Click here to silence Clippit.

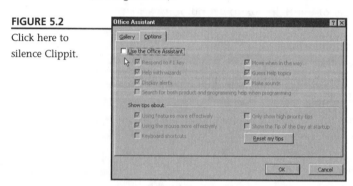

Once the Office Assistant has been zapped, it's easy to resurrect from any Office application: click **Help**, and then choose **Show the Office Assistant**.

Changing Characters

Maybe you don't want to get rid of the little critter. That's not a bad decision, really, at least until you're accustomed to the fact that the Office Assistant is only a click away.

If you do decide to stick with the Office Assistant box, at least you can rotate the characters. When Clippit gets boring, you can switch to an Einstein clone, a cat, or dog. (And who says Microsoft doesn't have a sense of humor?)

EXERCISE

Changing Office Assistant Characters

1. Right-click the **Office Assistant**. (That'll be Clippit, if you haven't already changed it.) Choose **Choose Assistant**. You'll be transported to the Office Assistant Gallery (see Figure 5.3).

2. Click the **Back** and **Next** buttons until you find a character you like. Click **OK** and your new character will appear in the Office Assistant box.

From time to time Microsoft releases new Office Assistants and, if you have access to the Web, you can get new characters free (for the price of a download, anyway).

These new characters will no doubt keep you moderately amused for a little while. Whether they're worth the time to download (at 2+ MB—these aren't tiny files) depends a lot on how easily you're amused.

FIGURE 5.3

Links the Cat, showing that Office really does have claws.

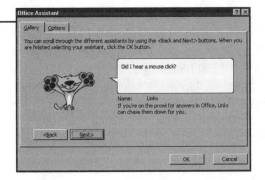

As of this writing, you could get the new Office Assistant characters by surfing to `officeupdate.microsoft.com/search.htm` and typing `Office Assistant` into the Search box. (The location changes from time to time, though, and you might have to start at `www.microsoft.com/office`, and look from there.) Once you've downloaded the file, run it and the character will appear in the Office Assistant Gallery. Select your new character using the instructions in the previous exercise.

Tactics

I know of several tactics for using the Office Assistant.

First and foremost, if you don't find the answer you're looking for, try rephrasing your question using completely different terminology. The natural language recognition routine buried in the Office Assistant isn't very natural at all, and sometimes using one wrong word can throw the whole gizmo out of whack. Remember that there's very little native understanding going on here—mostly, the Office Assistant throws away nonessential phrases such as "How do I?" "Where is?" and tries to identify, and then search on the keywords in your question.

MAKE HIM DANCE!
You can make the Office Assistant of your choice display its full range of tricks by right-clicking on the Assistant and choosing Animate.

Or, you *could* get a life. Heh heh heh.

Second, the light bulb tips shouldn't be taken as gospel. Although Microsoft has made some great strides in help technology, the Office Assistant's attempts to follow along, analyze what you're doing, and offer ideas to improve your work often fall flat on their face. If the light bulb tip you get in any particular situation doesn't seem to make sense, it probably doesn't.

Finally, you can make some crude adjustments to the Office Assistant's sensitivity, using the checkboxes shown in Figure 5.2. Click the **Office Assistant**, choose **Options**, and you'll find several choices that might make the Office Assistant more useful to you. In particular, if you see that light bulb appearing too often—that is, the suggestions offered when the light bulb is on don't matter much to you—consider checking the box that says **Only show high priority tips**. That will keep the light bulb flashes down to a minimum. It also prevents the Office Assistant from appearing unbidden at strange times.

Less Animated Help

Novice Office users tend to identify the Office Assistant character with Office's built-in help. In fact, the characters are simply window dressing: they make the Office Help system a little more palatable by using a friendly face.

The real Help system (including the natural language recognition engine) sits behind the characters' pretty faces.

Native Help

To see the real Help system, start any Office application and turn off the Office Assistant (right-click on the critter, pick **Options**, and then uncheck the **Use the Office Assistant** box). With the Office Assistant well and truly out of the way, click **Help**, and then click the first line in the menu—in Word, it's **Microsoft Word Help**; in Outlook it's **Microsoft Outlook Help**, and so on. (Even better—if you can remember—just push **F1**.) You'll connect directly with the mother lode (see Figure 5.4).

Think of the Help contents page as a table of contents, just like a book's table of contents, organizing and

MOVING THE HELP WINDOW

As you can see in Figure 5.4, Office 2000 Help has a nasty habit of taking over a big part of the screen, shoving the application you're working with out of the way, and monopolizing the right half. This boorish behavior can be most distracting—windows flash around and the screen goes nuts for a bit while Help rearranges things.

Believe it or not, you don't have to put up with the light show. The Help window on the right can be changed just like any other window: click and drag to resize and move it. Once you've moved the Help window to a more suitable location, Office remembers, and it will leave its mitts off your application window.

pointing you to the vast amount of information stored in Office's Help files. If you want to read about a general topic, this is the place to start.

If you click the **Index** tab, you'll see an index into the Help documentation (see Figure 5.5).

FIGURE 5.4

Full native help
appears after
you banish the
"social" Office
Assistant.

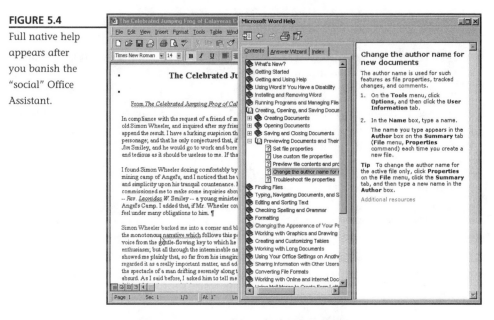

FIGURE 5.5

The native Help
index.

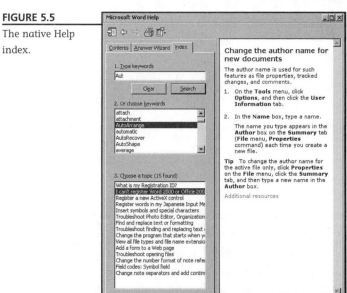

In my experience, the index is the weakest part of Office Help. If you look at
Figure 5.4, you can see that native Help has a section on changing the author name
for new documents. But if you look in the index, shown here in Figure 5.5, there's
no reference to author or author name—none whatsoever. I rarely use the index.

Office's designers have also built the Office Assistant's natural language search capability into native Help. You can see it by clicking the **Answer Wizard** tab. The Answer Wizard here has all the benefits—and drawbacks—of the natural language search engine you've no doubt used with the Office Assistant.

As you can see in Figure 5.6, the Answer Wizard does a decent job of finding the author name change information we looked for earlier—although it helps if you know the precise words that the wizard will be looking for. In general, the Answer Wizard is much more useful than the prebuilt index.

FIGURE 5.6

The Answer Wizard responds correctly to "How do I change the author name for new documents?"

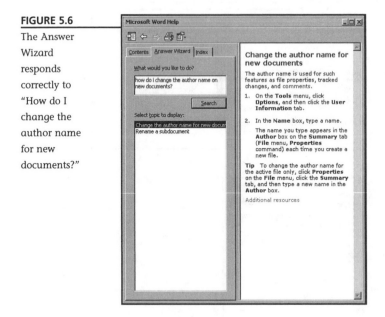

Microsoft on the Web

While native Help has much to offer, it pales in comparison to the quantity (and, yes, quality) of information Microsoft has available, free, on the Web. To get at that information, click **Help**, **Office on the Web** (see Figure 5.7).

After you're acquainted with the basic functions of Office, I strongly recommend that you spend a few hours poking around Microsoft's Web site. While the site itself can be maddeningly slow and occasionally hard to navigate, you just can't beat it for Office information and support. I've found that I can save loads of frustration visiting the site only at odd hours: early in the morning and on workday evenings. If there's any way you can avoid working hours during the week and evenings on the weekends, do it.

FIGURE 5.7

Office on the
Web takes you
to the Office
Update page,
and from there
you have many
options.

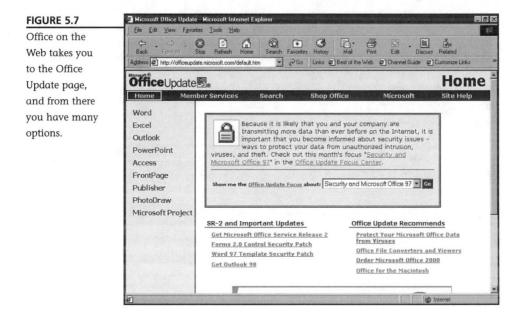

Microsoft's most important source of Office information sits well hidden on the Office
Update page. To get there, first click the **Search** button near the top of the screen (see
Figure 5.8). Then type your question into the box above the **Search** button, there on
the left. *Before* you click **Search**, make sure you check the box marked **Include
Microsoft Technical Support Content**. That's how you get into the MSKB.

FIGURE 5.8

Gateway to the
Microsoft
Knowledge
Base.

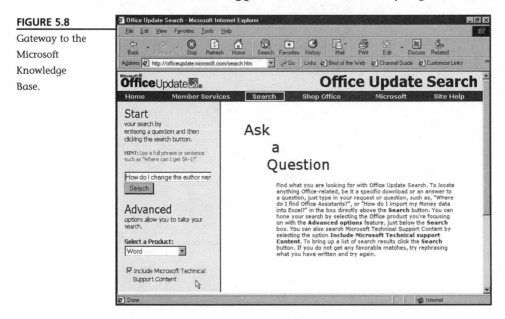

The MSKB consists of tens of thousands of articles, each one addressing a specific problem, solution, or feature of a Microsoft product. While they're written by Microsoft staff, and thus utilize some interesting euphemisms (that is, articles always say a bug is an issue), the MSKB is as close as you'll come to revealed truth in the Microsoft realm.

MSKB: THE ANSWER TO (ALMOST) EVERY QUESTION

Do you have a really tough question about Office 2000? After you've exhausted the online Help—both via the Office Assistant and digging directly into native Help—log on to the Microsoft Knowledge Base (MSKB). Bet you'll find the answer there. That's where I go.

Woody Leonhard

TEACHES

OFFICE 2000
WORD

6

Woody Leonhard

TEACHES

WORD PRELIMINARIES

WHAT A LONG, STRANGE TRIP IT'S BEEN...After a somewhat rocky start, Microsoft's Word for Windows has become the most-often-used computer application ever created. Considering how much it's used, you'd think it would be easy to understand, eh?

Not a chance. Not even close.

Crucial Changes

Word 2000, like all the other Office applications, contains an enormous number of options. Thousands of 'em. The people who designed Word included enough options to make Word usable in every imaginable situation, from jotting short notes to rewriting the U.S. Tax Code (I wish!). Rank novices might only use Word once a week; Microsoft assumes (rightly or wrongly) that beginners don't want to understand *why* things happen—they just want to type a bit and print the result, desultory as their results may be. Microsoft chose Word's standard options for these folks. They dumbed down Word as much as they dared, and then tossed a few whiz-bang features on the toolbar to make it easier to demo and sell the product.

As I introduce each of the Office applications to you, I'm going to step you through a series of crucial settings—options that will help you see what's going on and make your life a little simpler. At first some of these settings won't make much sense, and for that I apologize. By the time you get to the end of the book, I bet you'll be able to go back and see precisely why I had you change each and every one of them.

YOUR MILEAGE MAY VARY
None of these settings I suggest here should be considered gospel: When you get comfortable with the setting and its side-effects, by all means go ahead and change it to suit the way you work. But in the absence of strong evidence to the contrary, I think you'll find these settings most conducive to getting your work done.

I have a secondary motive for showing you each of these groups of settings. If you've been poking around a bit, you might have inadvertently changed something and now you don't know exactly how to get everything back to normal. Forget about uninstalling and reinstalling the application—Microsoft's usual answer to weird Office behavior. Reinstalling usually doesn't change any of your settings: if they were screwed up, they'll stay screwed up. Instead, take a few minutes to go through these steps to restore your application to some semblance of sanity.

Remove Rulers

Unless you can afford a 21-inch computer screen and run Windows at some ungodly high resolution, every square inch of Word's window is precious. The less space Word itself occupies the more peerless prose you'll see onscreen. Let's start by getting rid of something you don't need: Word's rulers.

EXERCISE

Don't Show Rulers

1. Start Word 2000. Make it appear full-screen (what Microsoft calls *maximized*) by clicking the **Maximize** icon— it's in the upper-right corner of the Word window, immediately to the left of the X icon.

2. Click **View** and make sure **Print Layout** is checked. Choosing Word's Print Layout view ensures that you'll see things on the screen pretty much as they will appear on your printer.

3. Type a sentence or two. If you haven't changed anything in Word, your screen will look more or less like Figure 6.1. If it doesn't look like that, don't worry. We'll go through all the settings shortly and get them reset.

4. Click **View,** and then click **Ruler** to clear away the check mark next to the word Ruler. The rulers on the top and left side will disappear from the screen (see Figure 6.2).

5. What? You want to see your rulers? No problem. To see the upper ruler (what Word calls the *horizontal ruler*), move your mouse around until the cursor is just underneath the box that says **Times New Roman**.

WHAT YOU DON'T KNOW WON'T HELP YOU...

Don't laugh. It's true. Microsoft's official position is that they have to hide all the parts of Word that will help you understand the product, because those parts are too intellectually challenging for the novice user. If you become an advanced user, so the Microsoft party line goes, you'll become smart enough to discover and use the hidden tools, *deus ex machina*. Literally.

(Latin lesson for today: *deus ex machina* translates to "god from (out of) a machine." A stage term dating to the times of Euripedes, which describes the resolution of poorly written, hideously complex plots that can only be unraveled by the expedient of having a god drop onto the stage, via a mechanical crane, to sort things out. When Kenny in *South Park* avoids volcanic immolation thanks to a previously unseen Scuzzlebutt monster with a Patrick Duffy leg, you're watching *deus ex machina*, updated a little bit for the '90s. And, yep, they killed Kenny.)

Life isn't like that simple, of course. I don't care if you've only used Word for 10 minutes and consider yourself an unrepentant dummy, you've no doubt poked around in the menus a bit. It's as if Microsoft handed you a loaded shotgun and left you to discover the finer points of its operation by trial and error.

If you're very lucky, you might have found some non-standard settings that make your work easier. (Although you probably don't remember where they were, eh?) If you're very unlucky, you discovered the Tools/Options menu and accidentally changed something really important. Kaboom.

You may have to jiggle it a bit—the position you want is on or just below the dark horizontal line that separates the menus from the document itself (see Figure 6.3). Hold the mouse there for a second and the top ruler appears. The ruler disappears after you move your pointer away.

FIGURE 6.1

Bone-stock
Word 2000,
at 800×600
resolution.

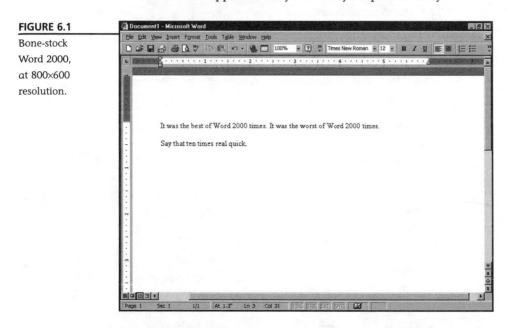

FIGURE 6.2

Uncheck the
View/Rulers
setting.

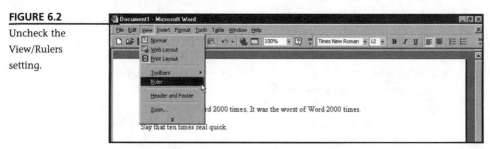

6. Similarly, you can see the left-side ruler (the *vertical ruler*) by hovering your mouse on the left side, near the vertical dark line (see Figure 6.4).

FIGURE 6.3

Hover at the top
of the page for
the horizontal
ruler.

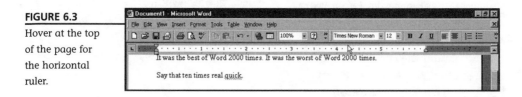

FIGURE 6.4

Hover at the left of the page for the vertical ruler.

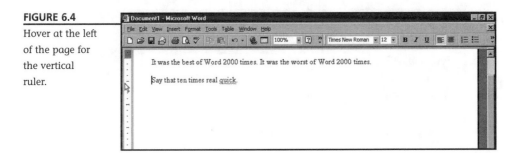

Very good. You've now reclaimed some precious screen space—and lost absolutely nothing in the process. Your eyes will thank you.

See All That You Can See, Adaptively

I hate *adaptive* menu bars and toolbars. Microsoft calls them *personalized* because that sounds so much more politically correct—as if *you* were in control instead of the computer. Ha! To me, they're yet another intrusion, where somebody figures the computer is so damn smart it knows what's best for me. I say "bah humbug," and urge you to nuke them immediately.

Adaptive… er, personalized menus (see Figure 6.5) are the stunted menus that only show you a few of your choices, and then change when you click on them and wait for a second or two, or when you click the downward double-chevron at the bottom of the list. They adapt (can you say *personalize themselves* with a straight face?) as you use them, so the menu items you click on frequently appear on the stunted menu, and the ones you don't use so often fall down to the invisible bottom.

WHAT'S A VIEW?

Word supports several views—ways of looking at the information in a document. I always work in Print Layout view because it most closely mimics the way pages will appear on the printer. If your PC gets sluggish with large documents, you might want to consider switching to Normal view: In Normal view, Word concentrates on showing you the text in the document, but doesn't go to any great lengths to lay out the pages. That lets Word run faster, but it can also lead to surprises when you finally print the page.

YOUR SCREENS DON'T LOOK RIGHT

Until you've made the changes to *adaptive* menu bars and toolbars, as described in this section, your screen will *not* look like the screen shots in this book.

If, for some strange reason, you decide to leave adaptive menus and toolbars in effect, your screen will *never* look like the shots in this book.

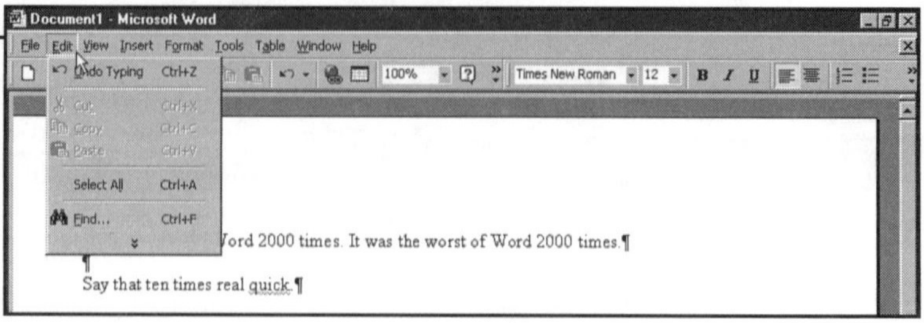

FIGURE 6.5

The stunted, er
adapted, uh,
personalized
Edit menu.

Adaptive toolbars work much the
same way, except buttons appear
and disappear in accordance with
their frequency of use. Use an adaptive menu or toolbar twice, and
you'll never have the same choices
in the same location. Okay, that's an
exaggeration; maybe 10 times. Still,
it's unnerving. And it really slows
you down once you get to know
where things are supposed to be.

SOME PEOPLE LIKE 'EM

Yes, I have to admit that some of my
closest friends like the adaptive menus.
Some will even put up with the adaptive
toolbars. I think they're nuts, but if you've
become accustomed to your menu items and
toolbar icons hopping around like grasshoppers
on a sizzling cast iron griddle, and you really
don't want to make them stay put, skip this
section. I won't mind. Promise.

To make menus *un*adaptive, click
Tools, **Customize**, and Tools menu-
clear the box marked **Menus show
recently used commands first** (see Figure 6.6). To make the main toolbars
*un*adaptive, click **Tools**, **Customize**, and clear the box marked **Standard and
Formatting toolbars share one row**. That doesn't, literally, get rid of toolbars'
adaptive behavior, but it gives the two main toolbars enough room so they don't
have to adapt—so Word keeps its mitts off.

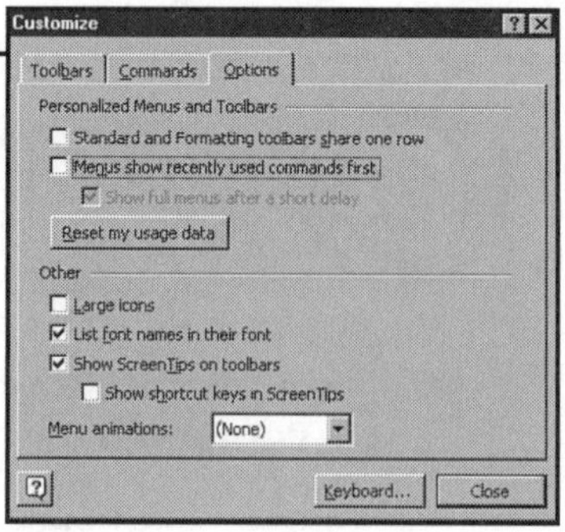

FIGURE 6.6

Turn off the
adaptive menus
and toolbars.

Show Paragraph Marks

I've been ranting about this one for years. If you've used Word more than a day, I bet you've hit a situation where the paragraphs don't line up correctly: suddenly all your paragraphs start centering themselves or appear right-justified, hard up against the right margin. Maybe you typed a couple of bold words, and now everything you type turns to bold or you indented a paragraph, and now all your new paragraphs get indented. Or somehow you

- Started getting bullets (those dots on the left are called *bullets*—probably because you feel like shooting Word when they appear unbidden) like these

- And you don't know why they started,

- Or how to get rid of them.

No, you aren't going crazy. Word is supposed to work like that. But in order to understand what's going on—and I'll show you exactly what's happening, in Chapter 10, "Making Documents Look Good"—you have to be able to see a little marker that Word keeps in your document. The Redmond gods, in their infinite wisdom, have determined that this marker is too confusing for the average reader to see—thereby condemning legions of Word users to untold hours, days, and weeks of frustration.

That little marker is called a *paragraph mark* and, as you might imagine, it marks the end of every paragraph. No, the marker doesn't appear on the printer when you print a document. (That's why Microsoft thinks most people would be confused if it showed up onscreen.) But if you can make that little leap of faith—that something in your document which shows up on the screen won't appear on the printer—you'll stand a fighting chance of understanding what is going on with your documents and why. It's a small price to pay for some regained sanity.

I mean, can you imagine trying to learn how to drive a car when the car manufacturer insists that the steering wheel remain invisible?

EXERCISE

Show Paragraph Marks and Tab Characters

1. If you've just finished the previous exercise, fine. If not, start Word and type in a sentence or two.

2. Click **Tools**, **Options**. Make sure the View tab is showing (click **View** if there's any question), and check the box marked **Paragraph marks** (see Figure 6.7).

3. While you're here, also check the box marked **Tab characters** (refer to Figure 6.7). That will let you see tabs inside your documents—another invisible character that can lead to no end of confusion.

FIGURE 6.7

Show paragraph marks and tab characters. You don't stand a chance if they're invisible.

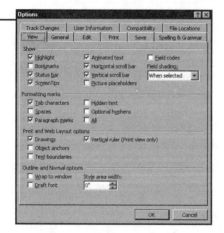

4. Finally, double-check all the settings on the View tab on your machine. Do they match the ones shown in Figure 6.7? If not, seriously consider changing the settings so they do match, particularly if you aren't quite sure what the settings mean. Click **OK** when you're finished.

PARAGRAPH AND TAB MARKS ARE VITAL

A little lesson from Woody's School of Hard Knocks and Broken Hearts. Don't ever work on a Word document unless both paragraph marks and tabs are showing onscreen. So many things depend on both the paragraph mark and the tab character that you're literally shooting in the dark if you try to figure out what's going on without those two showing.

Now take a look at the sentence you typed. See the backward-P character at the end of the sentence, as in Figure 6.8? That's a paragraph mark.

If you type a little more, you'll soon discover that the paragraph mark appears at the end of each paragraph—in other words, every time you press the **Enter** key. It doesn't appear on printouts. Click **File**, **Print** or click the **Print** icon on the toolbar to print a page; you'll see.

FIGURE 6.8

The paragraph mark appears!

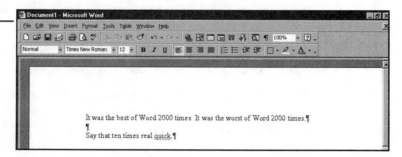

Disable Overstrike Mode

Here's another lousy decision that was made for you by the user-friendly folks at Microsoft. Take a look at your keyboard. Somewhere, typically to the right of the **Enter** key, you'll find a key marked **INS** or **Insert**. That key can cause you no end of grief, whether you've been using Word for a day or a decade.

As it ships right out of the box, Word uses the **Insert** key to go into something called Overstrike mode. The easiest way to describe Overstrike mode is to take you through a little experiment.

EXERCISE

The Dread Overstrike Mode

1. You have Word running and a sentence or two (or more) on the screen, right?

2. Use your mouse and click somewhere in the middle of one of the sentences; doesn't matter where.

3. Start typing. See how the stuff you type goes into the document, pushing all the words that were already there to the right? Good.

4. Now click the **INS** or **Insert** key. Word goes into Overstrike mode—you can tell that it's in Overstrike mode because the letters **OVR** down in the lower-right corner switch from gray to black (see Figure 6.9).

WHAT'S A FAST SAVE?

There's a setting on the **Tools/Options/Save** tab that you may be tempted to engage. It's called **Allow fast saves**. Fortunately, Word 2000 turns it off when you install it. I strongly recommend that you resist the urge to turn it back on. Fast saves don't make Word much faster, and they can certainly give you a headache. Here's why.

Normally when you save a file, Windows overwrites the older version: The whole new file gets written out to disk, replacing the older one. That can take a lot of time. Word's Fast Save updates a document by leaving the old version out on the disk and writing changes to the end of the file. So, for example, a fast-saved document might have instructions at the end that tell Word, "go back and change the second sentence to this and that, and then make the fourth paragraph bold." Word continues to append these instructions to the document until it figures that the changes take up more room than the original document. At that point, it rolls all the changes into the document, gets rid of the old version, and replaces it with the new one.

This can lead to some embarrassing situations. Say you start a letter with, "My boss is a dingbat!" Later, you change your mind and modify the document to say, "My boss is wonderful!" If you Fast Save that document, your original words will be stored in the file; there will be an entry later in the file that says something like, "remove 'a dingbat' and replace it with 'wonderful.'" If somebody looks at the contents of the file, bypassing Word, they'll discover your original sentence. Oops.

A couple of years ago the mainstream computer press picked up on this idiosyncrasy. Some writers touted it as a major bug. It isn't. It's the only way Fast Save could possibly work.

Just leave it turned off, okay?

FIGURE 6.9

Word enters
Overstrike
(Overtype)
mode.

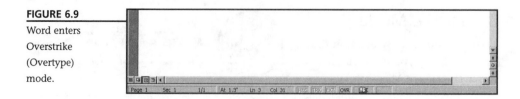

5. Type some more. See that? The characters you type *replace* the characters in the sentence. That's what Overstrike mode does.

Ninety-nine times out of a hundred, Overstrike mode is a mistake: You accidentally click the **INS** or **Insert** key when you really wanted to click **DEL** or **Home** or some other key. And if you're a fast typist, chances are good you don't discover your mistake until you've typed a sentence or two—and clobbered whatever good things might have gone before. Yes, you can use Undo—but why bother?

Fortunately, Word gives you an easy way to disable this madness.

EXERCISE

Use Insert Key to, uh, Insert

1. With Word running, click **Tools**, **Options**; then click the **Edit** tab.

2. Click the box marked **Use the INS key for paste** (see Figure 6.10). Make sure the box is checked.

3. Double-check the other settings to make sure they match Figure 6.10 (or, if they don't, make sure you understand why you want them to be different). Click **OK** and you're done.

FIGURE 6.10

Tools Options
Edit settings.

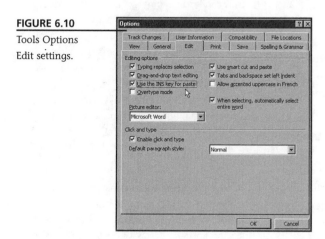

The Case Against Hyperlinks

You have to admire Microsoft for one thing: When they jump on a bandwagon, you can hear the wagon's springs squeal from the weight. When Microsoft embraced the Internet a couple of years ago it went overboard in trying to Webify everything in sight. That's how this final crucial change item came into existence.

In Word 2000, when you type a Web address such as www.que.com, or an email address such as woody@woodyswatch.com, Word takes it upon itself to convert that address into a hyperlink. A *hyperlink* is just a fancy name for a hot button— you can click a hyperlink, and you're supposed to be transported to whatever location is mentioned in the link, or have your email program open up, ready to type a message. In this case, if you click the hyperlink **www.que.com**, Word will take you to the Web site called **www.que.com**; if you click on **woody@woodyswatch.com**, Outlook appears with a message ready to rumble.

Which is all well and good if you're in a hyperlinking mood—that is, if you're looking at a document somebody else wrote, *and* it's on the screen of a machine that's connected to the Web or running a decent email program, *and* you don't mind having your machine go absolutely bonkers for a couple of minutes any time you accidentally click the hyperlink.

Here's the clincher. Not only does Word turn your perfectly reasonable typed Web address and convert it into a rarely useful Web wonderland rabbit hole, it makes the link so ugly you'd be ashamed to print it. When Word identifies a hyperlink, it makes the hyperlink underlined and blue! (The old version of Word 97 also made the hyperlink bold—an assault on the senses rarely matched in annals of modern computing.)

Anyway, it's easy to turn off this nonsense if you know the trick.

EXERCISE

Leave My Web Addresses Alone

1. Get Word going. If you want to see how Word mangles Web addresses, type a simple Web address, say, www.que.com. See how Word makes it blue and underlined? Blecch.

2. Stop the insanity by clicking **Tools, AutoCorrect, AutoFormat as You Type**, and clear the check box marked **Internet and network paths with hyperlinks** (see Figure 6.11).

3. Double-check and make sure your settings match the ones in Figure 6.11. Again, it's all right if they're different, as long as you understand why you've changed them. Click **OK**.

Now you're ready to tackle Word on your own terms. Congratulations.

FIGURE 6.11
Keep Word's
mitts off your
Web addresses.

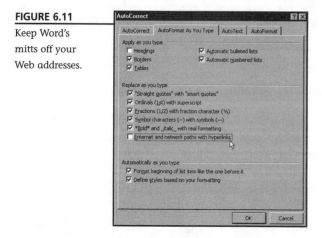

The Screen

Time for a quick guided tour around the Word screen (see Figure 6.12). No need to
memorize anything, but you might want to dog-ear this page so you can refer back
to it if something puzzles you in the future.

FIGURE 6.12
Word 2000 in
all its glory.

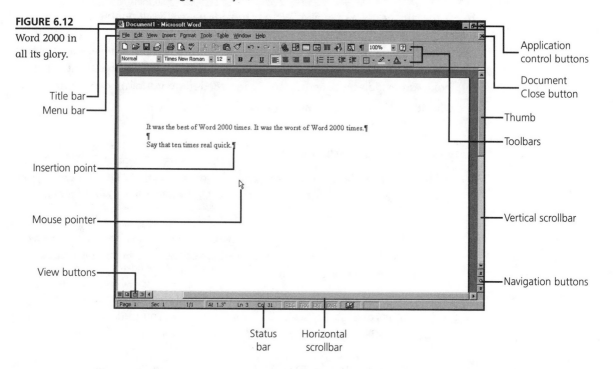

Title Bar

Across the top of the Word window you'll see the title bar. It's just like any other title bar you'll find in any other Windows application. You can click it and drag the Word window around, or resize the window by grabbing any of the Word window's edges.

Over on the extreme right of the title bar, the three Application Control buttons work just like any others in Windows: from left to right, they minimize, maximize/restore (toggle between Word filling up the entire Windows desktop, and floating the Word window on the desktop), and shut down Word.

The flying W icon at the far left duplicates the functions of the Application Control buttons. I never use it, and you probably won't either.

If you aren't familiar with all these Windows housekeeping chores, crank up Word and play with them. Don't worry, you won't hurt anything.

Menu Bar

The next row down contains Word's menu bar. This is Word's working class bar, the place where you can get anything and everything done. You can spend years getting lost in all the options buried in Word's menus.

There might be an X on the far right of the menu bar. It only appears if there's just one Word document open. You can click that **X** to close the document without closing Word. I know it's confusing—no other Office application works like this. The people who designed Word 2000 made Word this way because they were having trouble getting it to work with Outlook. I say phooey. Word should work like all the other Office applications, and I don't care if the programmers can't figure out an easy way to do it. Ignore the X if it exists, and curse the Word gods for this truly crazy "Single Document Interface" insanity.

WHAT'S THE DIFFERENCE BETWEEN A MENU BAR AND A TOOLBAR?

At first blush you'd think that Word's menus and toolbars have little in common: after all, a menu has words on it, while the toolbars have pictures on them. Click something on the menu and you get, well, menus. Click an icon on the toolbar, and you get actions. Surprisingly, the difference isn't nearly so clear-cut.

In fact, in a stroke of true genius, the people who designed Office 97 a few years ago decided to make menus and toolbars quite similar. We won't go into detail about it in this book, but you can put menu items on a toolbar, and you can put icons on menus. There's essentially no limitation on how you can mix and match menus and icons.

So if you've been wondering what the real difference is between the menu bar and the toolbars (a question that surely rates right up there with The Meaning of Life and Everything), you can rest easy. There really isn't any difference.

Toolbars

Below the menu bar sit two toolbars. (Assuming you made the changes I so strongly recommended earlier in this chapter, anyway.) This is where Word starts to get interesting. Toolbars exist solely to let you work faster. They're nothing but shortcuts to actions that you can perform just as well by hunting and pecking through Word's menus. If you've been mystified by the funny buttons and wonder what all of them mean, let me warn you in advance: about half of the toolbar buttons you see in Figure 6.12 will become old friends, rather quickly. A few of the others come in handy from time to time, but lots of the toolbar buttons you see there are very esoteric. You won't use them in a 100 years, so don't get too hung up on Word's toolbar buttons, trying to decipher what those tiny pictures really mean. They don't *mean* much of anything.

Word has lots of toolbars hidden away until you've learned how to use them. We'll work with a couple of them in subsequent chapters.

The Document

Right smack dab in the middle of the screen you'll see a mock-up of your document. When you type, Word stuffs the characters you type into your document and shows them right here on the screen.

As you get more proficient at Word, you'll want to reduce the clutter on the screen and open up as much room as possible for the document. After all, that's why we're here—the document serves as the Alpha and Omega of Word's existence. Everything else you see onscreen is just a means to the document's end.

Inside every document you'll find a blinking vertical line called an *insertion point*. This mark indicates where the next letter you type on the keyboard will appear in the document.

The mouse pointer, which can take on the appearance of an arrow, an I-beam pointer, or any of a dozen additional shapes, indicates where your mouse is located within the document or on the screen.

GIVE US OLD-TIMERS A BREAK...

If you talk to old-timers, they'll refer to either the insertion point or the mouse pointer as the cursor. That's because they spent their formative years B.M.—before the mouse, back when the only controllable moving item onscreen was called a *cursor*. Forgive them.

I'm an old-timer, too, and a bit addled to boot. I try hard to use the terms insertion point and mouse pointer the way I'm supposed to—but sometimes I forget. Cut me a little slack, okay? You should always be able to tell from the context whether cursor means the insertion point or the mouse pointer. Think of it as an exercise for dealing with crusty old PC users, wherever they may be.

If your mouse pointer looks like an I-beam with four horizontal lines to the left, bottom, or right of the beam, Word is in its *click and type* mode.

Click and type—which should be called *double-click and type*—lets you double-click in most blank parts of a document, and start typing with the text aligned to the left, middle, or right. I find double-click and type very confusing, particularly because it's easy to type the first line, but if you then hit **Enter** and try to type any more lines, it's hard to tell where they'll end up or how they'll behave. Double-click and type uses an odd combination of paragraph justification formatting and tab stops to work its magic. I suggest you avoid it.

Status Bar

Way down at the bottom of the screen, Word maintains a status bar. From time to time, some of the information shown on the status bar may interest you. Many of the statistics shown here relate to the insertion point.

Reading from left to right

- **Page.** This tells you the page number of the page you're looking at. This is the number that will print on that page, if you have Word print page numbers. (Sounds complicated, eh? Hang on. It gets worse.)

- **Sec.** This is the section number of the current section. Word lets you break documents (usually large documents) into sections. This tells you which section you're in.

☞ *For details about Sections, see "Interlude: What is a Document Anyway?" in Chapter 8, page 110.*

- **x/y.** This shows you which page you're on (x), and the total number of pages in the document (y). The x here can be different from the page mentioned earlier because Word lets you restart page numbering in each section. This x is the number you would get if you printed the document and then started counting the number of pieces of paper that come out the printer—one, two, three—stopping when you get to the current page. (Still sound complicated? Don't worry about it.)

> **WHAT DO YOU MEAN MORE OR LESS?**
>
> Don't take the information on the Word 2000 status bar too seriously. All sorts of things can throw the numbers off. Probably the worst offender: embedded pictures—if you have pictures in your document, all bets are off for the At, Ln, and Col numbers. I've also seen situations where the page numbers (even the section numbers) don't get updated properly, so *caveat emptor*, er, *writer…*

- **At x.** This tells you, more or less, how far down the page the insertion point sits. It's a quick way of judging vertical distance without having to use that obtrusive ruler.

- **Ln x.** This tells you, more or less, which line on the page contains the insertion point.

- **Col x.** This tells you, more or less, how many characters sit to the left of the insertion point, plus one. In other words, Col 1 means there are zero characters to the left of the insertion point; Col 2 means there's one character to the left; and so on.

The **Spelling and Grammar Status** icon on the right side of the status bar indicates that Word is caught up with formatting and displaying the document onscreen. If Word gets behind a little bit (say, when you're typing fast), the X turns into a pencil. When Word prints, the whole icon turns into a printer, counting off the pages printed. When you save a file, a pulsing disk appears to the right of the icon. In general, if you can't figure out why Word 2000 isn't responding to what you're doing, look around that **Spelling and Grammar Status** icon. It might tell you why Word can't keep up.

Vertical Scrollbar

The scrollbar on the right side of the screen, commonly called the vertical scrollbar, helps you move through your documents. Like most Windows scrollbars, you can click the up or down arrow to move a little bit at a time, or drag the gray rectangle (it's called a *thumb*) to maneuver more quickly.

Unlike other Windows scrollbars, though, clicking the thumb tells you exactly what page you're on (see Figure 6.13). As you drag the thumb up and down, Word 2000 keeps track of where you'll go in the document. Let go of the mouse button, and you're transported to the page indicated next to the thumb. Although the page numbering occasionally gets out of whack by a page or two, I rate this as one of Word's niftiest features for those of you who work with long documents.

Down at the bottom of the vertical scrollbar, below the scrolling down arrow, sit three navigation buttons. They help you move quickly through a document. The **Select Browse Object** button in the middle of the three lets you choose what you want to search for. (Most commonly you'll be looking for specific text inside the document, but Word also lets you search for all sorts of things, for example, pictures, tables, even footnotes.) The up and down buttons let you repeat your previous search, moving toward (respectively) the top or the bottom of the document. We'll cover the Navigation buttons at length in Chapter 9, "Getting Around Word."

FIGURE 6.13

The vertical scrollbar's thumb knows all, tells all.

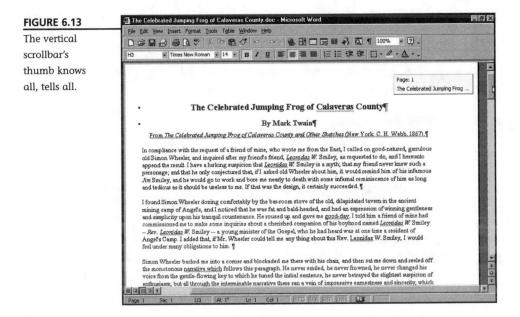

Horizontal Scrollbar

While the vertical scrollbar lets you move through the pages in your document, the horizontal scrollbar only controls the centering of the document onscreen. For most Word users it's nearly useless once you set the zoom factor properly (see the next exercise).

On the far left of the horizontal scrollbar you'll find four icons. These let you switch quickly between Normal, Web, Print Layout, and Outline view, respectively. If you hover the mouse pointer over these icons, a ScreenTip appears to identify each.

☞ *I talked about Normal and Print Layout view on in "Crucial Changes," Chapter 6,* **page 76.**

The other views are less likely to be of interest to you. Web view shows you how the page will look if it's posted on the World Wide Web. Outline view collapses the document down to an outline. All these views can be controlled by clicking the appropriate item in the (surprise!) View menu.

Adjusting Zoom

There's one more setting that varies so much from computer to computer that it's hard to give general advice about it. That setting is the *Zoom factor*. As the name implies, it affects how much of a document appears onscreen at any given moment. I suggest that you first set the zoom following these guidelines, and then refer back here from time to time, particularly if your eyes start driving you crazy.

EXERCISE

Adjust Word 2000's Zoom

1. Start Word 2000. Click **View**, **Zoom**. Your screen should look something like Figure 6.14.

FIGURE 6.14

Where the Zoom factor lives.

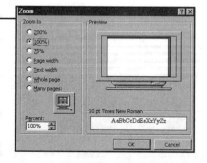

2. For a first approximation, click the button marked **Page Width**. You're trying to juggle two competing goals here: you want to show as much of the page on the screen as possible, but at the same time you want your letters to look good. If you try to show too much of the page onscreen, the letters will be too small; if you enlarge the letters so they're more readily visible, you reduce the fraction of a document that will appear onscreen at any given moment.

3. Click the arrows on the Percent box up and down and try to find a Zoom percentage that shows the entire width of a document, but also makes the letters large enough so you can see them without straining your eyes.

4. When you're happy with the Zoom percent—for now anyway—click **OK**.

If you were lucky enough to get the entire width of the document onscreen without aggravating your myopia, there's one final step you should take: get rid of the horizontal scrollbar. It only takes up precious screen space, and if you don't need to scroll left and right all the time, why put up with it?

EXERCISE

Ditch the Horizontal Scrollbar

1. Get Word running and, using the Zoom factor, make sure you can see the entire width of the document onscreen.

2. Click **Tools**, **Options**; then click the **View** tab. Uncheck the box marked **Horizontal scroll bar**. Click **OK** and the horizontal scrollbar is history. As shown in Figure 6.15, you should be able to see the entire width of the page.

FIGURE 6.15

The full width of the document is visible, so why waste space on the horizontal scrollbar?

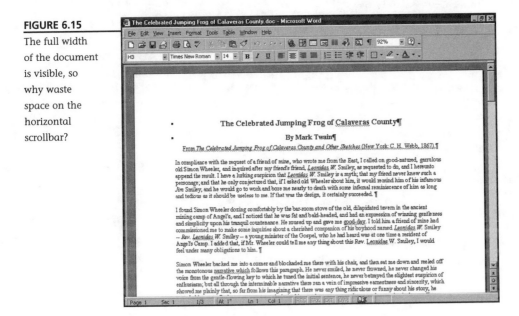

3. Come back to this exercise and turn the horizontal scrollbar on again if you need to—say, work with an odd-sized sheet of paper.

7

Woody Leonhard

TEACHES

WORKING WITH DOCUMENTS

EVERY WORD DOCUMENT HAD TO ORIGINATE SOMEWHERE, RIGHT? Word documents don't exactly grow on trees. Each one starts out with a paragraph mark—and, I swear, a mind of its own. From that point, it's all down hill. This is where I get to show you the options you have for creating new documents.

Easy Plain Documents

Every time you start Word it figures that you probably want to work with a new document, so it creates one for you, and gives that document the name Document1.

The first one's free. After that, you have to make your own. Creating a new, blank document couldn't be simpler.

EXERCISE

Make a New Empty Document

1. Click the **New** icon and a new document appears.

2. Word gives the document a name such as Document2, Document3, and so on. The numbers get assigned sequentially. You can see the new document's (temporary) name on the title bar.

Almost-as-Easy Fancy Documents

Microsoft has spent an enormous amount of time and money coming up with alternatives to the plain, blank document. It pays to spend a little bit of time poking around the different kinds of documents Word offers. While Word doesn't ship from the factory with a copy of your company's next annual report on the CD or even the term paper that's due next week, you might find a document that can save you gobs of time and effort. And, hey, you've already paid for it!

Microsoft distributes its prefab documents in two different forms, *templates* and *wizards*. You've probably bumped into Windows wizards. They guide you by the hand, asking questions, helping you make choices and set options. Word wizards behave quite similarly. If you can find a wizard to help you through the hard spots—say, writing a résumé, or creating your first Web page—you should take the wizard up on the offer to help. When you're done, the worst that you'll do is throw the document away.

THE OTHER 10,000,000 TEMPLATES

Microsoft has zillions and zillions of templates—and a few more wizards—that you can use, free. There's a large collection on the Web, at officeupdate.microsoft.com. You'll find templates to help you create dozens of business documents, legal documents, thesis and term papers, and much more.

Templates are a lot like fonts: At first you'll be tempted to gather all you can find, but sooner or later the sheer volume of them forces you to be more selective. Go for the good ones.

Templates are similar to wizards, but they're dumb. In general, they don't ask questions or guide you through options. More than anything templates resemble cookie-cutter images of documents that you can create. Because of that, templates rate as a good place to store boilerplate text and standard forms. Even though they're dumb cookie-cutter prototypes of real documents, they can still be valuable, particularly if they show you how to lay out a tricky kind of document (for example, a newsletter), or if they contain a skeleton of a document that you can readily adapt to your work.

You get to Word's templates and wizards by clicking **File**, **New**, and choosing the template or wizard that interests you.

EXERCISE

Create a New Résumé with Word's Résumé Template

1. Click **File**, **New**. Click the **Other Documents** tab. Pay particular attention to the thumbnail sketch in the Preview box over on the right. That's where Word shows you a postage-stamp size mock-up of how the new document will look.

2. Double-click **Contemporary Resume.dot** (see Figure 7.1).

FIGURE 7.1

Choosing the Contemporary Resume template in the File Open dialog box.

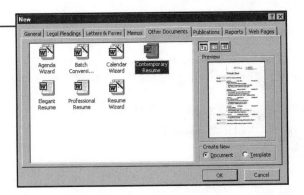

3. Word creates a new document based on the Contemporary Resume.dot template. Basically, it copies everything in the cookie-cutter template (the stuff you saw in the Preview box) into a brand new document (see Figure 7.2).

4. At this point the template has done its work. You can click on the document, type, move, or delete text—do anything you would normally do to a document.

Contrast the *dumb* template approach to the *smart* Word Wizard that also produces a résumé.

FIGURE 7.2

The text from the template is poured into the new document.

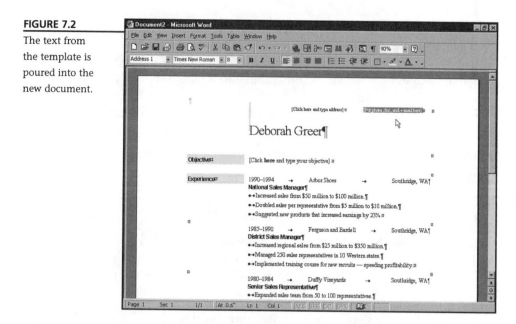

EXERCISE

Create a New Résumé with Word's Wizard

1. Click **File**, **New**. Click the **Other Documents** tab and double-click **Résumé Wizard.wiz**. The Word Résumé Wizard kicks in (see Figure 7.3). Click **Next**.

FIGURE 7.3

Word's Résumé Wizard starts with an overview.

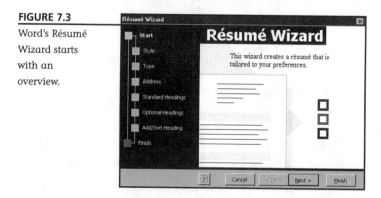

2. The Résumé Wizard asks what kind of Résumé you'd like. I chose **Professional** (see Figure 7.4).

3. Next, the wizard takes you through a series of questions about your name and address, and which headings you want to appear in your résumé. Choose something appropriate.

FIGURE 7.4

The Résumé
Wizard offers
several different
types of
resumes.

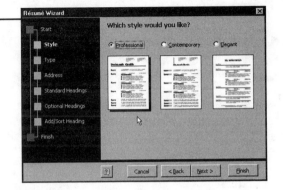

4. When you hit the final screen in the wizard, click **Finish**. You'll be presented
   with a custom résumé, ready for your embellishment and shameless puffery
   (see Figure 7.5).

FIGURE 7.5

The final
résumé created
by the Résumé
Wizard.

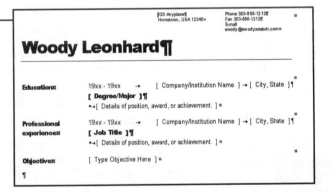

So, which is better—the wizard or the template? Personally, I like the dumb template-
generated résumé a little more than the fancy-schmancy wizard-generated one. Just
as in real life, smarter ain't necessarily better!

TIP

OTHER WAYS TO START ANEW

You aren't limited to using the **New toolbar** icon for creating empty new documents. You
can create a new blank document via the **File**, **New** route, by choosing **Blank Document**
under the **General** tab.

Saving Your Documents

Save often, save well. It's a mantra for our times.

Although the act of saving a document might strike you as terribly simple, the nuances of selecting an appropriate file name and locating the document in a reasonable folder rate right up there with the greatest problems in biological taxonomy. Take some time and do it right!

 EXERCISE

Save Your Résumé

1. Do you still have the résumé showing from the previous exercise? Good. (If not, start Word, and type a few sentences.)

2. Click the **Save** icon 🖫, or click **File, Save**. They both do the same thing. You should get Word's Save As dialog box, as shown in Figure 7.6.

3. Navigate around to the folder you'd like to have hold this document. Navigating, in this case, involves clicking on the big folders in the Place Bar on the left, or double-clicking on folders you want to dig into in the folder list on the right, clicking the **Up One Level** icon 🔼 to move up to a higher level folder. You can also click the down arrow next to the Save in box to hopscotch around all the drives available to Word (see Figure 7.7).

WORD'S AUTOSAVE FEATURE IS A LIFESAVER

Are you really new to computers? Not to worry. We've all been there. If you're just getting your feet wet, you might think that any document you can see on your computer's screen is safely stored away inside your computer. And you'd be wrong.

At the risk of over-simplifying just a little bit, the document you see on Word's screen only exists in your PC's main memory—you know, those memory chips that look like boxy black cockroaches with silvery legs? If the power to your PC goes kaput, main memory craps out, and the document goes with it. From time to time you need to save your documents. Save is a rather strange term, but the idea behind it is quite straightforward: when you save a document, you copy it from main memory onto something else—usually a hard drive. Once it's on a hard drive, your document will stick around through power outages and almost any other calamity you can imagine (short of a crashed hard drive).

I was a little sneaky in Chapter 6, "Word Preliminaries." I glossed right over something called AutoRecover. Unless you do something to change it, Word automatically saves a copy of all the open documents—that is, all the documents in main memory—every 10 minutes. That way, unless you're extraordinarily unlucky, you'll never lose more than 10 minutes' worth of work if the power goes out.

If you frequently make lots and lots of small changes—as, say, an editor might—you might want to think about having Word save your documents every five minutes or even every minute. That way you'll give up control of your PC more often, letting Word come in and do its save thing, but you'll also know that you're never more than a minute or two away from a full restore, should the worst happen.

FIGURE 7.6

Saving a file for the first time.

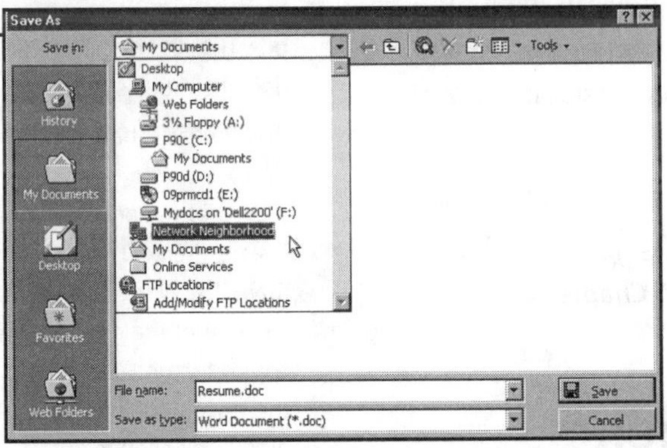

FIGURE 7.7

The drop-down save list for hopping around all available drives.

4. Type a meaningful name in the box marked **File name**. (You can use letters, numbers, spaces, and the underscore character (_), but should avoid weird characters such as * / ? – and almost anything else.) In this case, I would like to call the document resume.doc. Click **OK** and Word saves the document to disk.

Choose that **Save** icon ▦ from time to time as you're working. It'll keep a recent copy of your document on disk, and protect you just in case your two-year-old walks by and punches your PC's off button.

You've probably noticed that Windows in general (and Word in particular) usually shows lists of filenames sorted in alphabetical order.

WHEN WINDOWS DOESN'T SORT

When you put a new file in a folder, Windows automatically sticks the name of the file at the bottom of the list. It won't re-sort the file names until you refresh the window—typically by pressing F5, or closing and re-opening the dialog box.

If you're very clever in the way you assign names to your documents, Word will keep them in order for you. For example, if you commonly write letters to a client named John, you might consider ordering them by date. Thus, a letter written on January 14, 1999 could be called John 19990114.doc, and one written on February 27, 1999, could be John 19990227.doc. Simple tricks like this one can make sorting through documents much simpler in the future.

Finally, remember that the folder structure you have established isn't set in concrete.

 You can change it at any time by following the instructions in "Creating Folders in My Documents," Chapter 4, on **page 46.**

WHAT'S THE DIFFERENCE BETWEEN SAVE AND SAVE AS?

You caught me. I tried to finesse that one right by you. Sheeesh. If you save a document and that document already has a name, Word copies the document from main memory onto your disk drive. But if the document doesn't have a name—and in this case, the Résumé document didn't have a name—Word has to ask you what to call the document and where to put it. So instead of simply copying the document to disk, Word pops up this Save As dialog box, gets the info it needs, and then copies the document to disk.

Any time you have a document open inside Word, you can tell Word that you want to save a copy of the document with a different name. That's where Save As comes in. If you click **File**, **Save As**, Word asks you for the name and location of the new document, and then copies the document from main memory to the disk. The old document—the one still on disk—isn't changed at all.

Closing Documents

Once you're done working on a document, you can close it by clicking **File**, **Close**. That takes it off the screen so you don't have to deal with it any more. Closing consists of two steps:

1. Word figures out if you've made any changes to the document since the last time you saved it. If there have been changes made, Word asks you if you want to save the changes. If you choose **Yes**, Word goes through the normal Save process described in the preceding section. If you choose **No**, Word doesn't save the document, so the copy on disk doesn't change.

2. Word then removes the document from main memory. It gets zapped off the screen.

EXERCISE

Close Resume.doc

1. In the preceding exercise you saved resume.doc. Make sure that it's still the document that's *on top* in the Word window.

2. To close Resume.doc, click **File**, **Close**. There; that wasn't too difficult, was it? Heh heh heh.

Opening Documents

Word offers several methods for opening documents ranging from quite straightforward to incredibly complex. Let's take a look at the two most common—and least difficult—methods.

Say you want to open resume.doc, the document you closed in the preceding exercise. You can click the **Open** icon 📂, which displays the Open dialog box; then click once on **Resume.doc**, and click **Open** (see Figure 7.8).

FIGURE 7.8

Resume.doc in the File Open dialog box.

QUICKLY OPEING RECENTLY USED FILES

Alternatively, you can click on **File**, **Open**, and then double-click **Resume.doc**.

If you know that you've used the document recently, though, there's a much faster way to open it. Word maintains a most recently used (*MRU*) file list under the **File** menu. Opening a document from that list is very fast and easy.

To open Resume.doc from the MRU list, click **File**, slide your mouse pointer down to **1 Resume.doc**, and let go of the mouse button (see Figure 7.9). Boom!

Word includes a very powerful, comprehensive search engine, built into the product itself. That search engine can help you find, say, all the documents on your hard drive that include the phrase, "Free Bill!" or "Peter Piper picked a peck of pickled peppers."

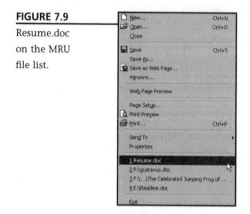

FIGURE 7.9
Resume.doc on the MRU file list.

To use the search engine, click the **Open** icon 📂, or click **File**, **Open**. When you see the Open dialog box (refer to Figure 7.8), click **Tools** in the upper-right corner, and then click **Find**. Now call up Word's built-in Help by pressing the **F1** key, typing find files, clicking **Search**, and clicking the button marked **Search for files** (see Figure 7.10). If you've banished the Office Assistant from your screen, the **F1** key will bring up Word help; just type find files in the Answer Wizard's What would you like to do? box.

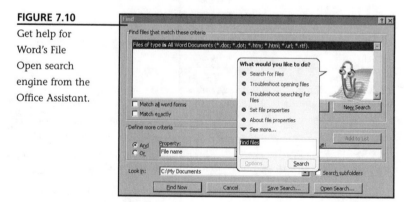

FIGURE 7.10
Get help for Word's File Open search engine from the Office Assistant.

Starting Over

Have you ever screwed up something so badly that you just wanted to throw it away and start over? Word gives you that opportunity. In fact, if you think and plan ahead, there are two different ways to recover from disastrous flubs.

The easy way: Only save a document if you know it's *good*. Once you have a good saved copy, make all the changes to the document that you like. If you get to the point where you want to throw away your current version and retrieve the last saved version, simply close the document (click **File**, **Close**), and when Word asks if you want to save the changes, click **No**. You can then open the old version of the document—the one you saved—as it's still on disk.

The hard way: Word will actually maintain versions of a document for you. While there's a considerable amount of overhead involved (each version is a document unto itself, and takes a fair amount of storage space), this approach gives you great flexibility, as you can retrieve any old version at any time.

To make Word save versions of adocument, click **File**, **Save As**. When you get the Save As dialog box, click **Tools**, **Save Version** (see Figure 7.11).

FIGURE 7.11

Setting up a
document to
save versions.

TIP

VERSIONING HELP

Word has an excellent online help article on versioning. Just press **F1** and either type save versions into the Office Assistant's search box, or type save versions in the Answer Wizard's What would you like to do? box.

Undo/Redo

Word contains one of the most sophisticated Undo/Redo capabilities you'll find in any computer program. If you ever get a hankering to throw away all your work, check first to see if you can undo the part that really gives you heartburn.

Undo and Redo

1. Start a new document by clicking on the **New** icon [image].

2. Type a sentence or two.

3. Click the loopy arrow part of the **Undo** icon to undo your typing. Poof! The sentence disappears.

4. To bring it back—*redo* in Microsoft-speak—click the loopy arrow part of **Redo** .

TIP

UNDOING MULTIPLE ACTIONS

Sometimes you'll want to undo a whole bunch of actions all at once. If that's the case, click the down-wedgie part of the **Undo** icon, and choose however many actions you want to undo. If you overshot your mark, the Redo has a similar feature for redoing any number of changes.

As long as you keep a file open, you can undo or redo a nearly unlimited number of steps. The undo/redo information sticks around even when you save the file, but the minute you close the file, all that history is tossed away. The actions available for *undoing* can be seen by clicking the arrow next to the **Redo** icon.

Printing Documents

Most of the time you'll want to print a single copy of the current document on the printer you normally use (if you have more than one printer). Word has you covered.

To quickly print one copy of your document, make sure the document you want to print is showing in Word's window. Click the **Print** icon . One copy goes straight to your printer.

Occasionally you'll want to do something a bit more complicated than run off one quick copy. Word has you covered there, too.

EXERCISE

Fancy Printing

1. Once again, make sure the document you want to print is the top one in Word's window.

2. Click **File**, **Print** (see Figure 7.12). Your Print dialog might look different from this one, but it should be pretty close.

3. If you have more than one printer attached to your computer (or your network), or if you have fax software on your PC, you should choose the desired printer or fax from the options offered in the Name box.

FIGURE 7.12

A plethora
of printing
options.

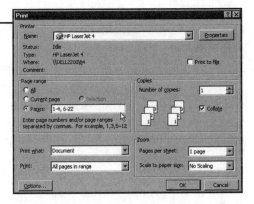

4. To print the current page or any range of pages, choose the appropriate option from the Page range box. In Figure 7.12, I've told Word to print pages 1–4, and 6–22.

5. Choose how many copies you want to print and whether you want the pages collated. If you print more than one copy and check the **Collate** box, Word will print the entire document, and then print it a second time, and so on. If you don't check the **Collate** box, you'll get all the copies of page 1, followed by all the copies of page 2, and so on.

SAVE TIME BY PRINTING UNCOLLATED COPIES

On most printers it's much, much faster to print copies uncollated. Why? Most printers support a command that says something like, "Print 14 copies of the following page." So if you want 14 copies of your document, Word only has to send the pages out once—with each page preceded by the **Print 14 copies of the following page** command. On the other hand, if you want those 14 copies collated, Word has to send the printer all the instructions for printing page 1, and then page 2, and so on. And when the first copy of the document is done, it has to start all over again, sending page 1, page 2, etc., and that sequence is repeated 14 times.

DUPLEX PRINTING ON A SHOESTRING

The box in the lower-left corner, disingenuously marked **Print**, usually allows you to print all the odd pages or all the even pages in a document. (Again, your printer may be different.) Why would you want to do that? If you figure out the correct sequence—and believe me, it can be tricky—you can use this feature to print on the front and back of every sheet of paper, odd pages on the front and even pages on the back. Printing this way is called *duplex printing*, and it's a capability found only on very expensive printers.

You can play around with the other settings on the Print dialog box (refer to Figure 7.12), without fear of breaking anything, as long as you don't change the settings in the box you'll see when you click **Options**.

In particular, the **Pages per sheet** setting in the lower-right corner can let you print more than one page *squished* on a single sheet—two, four, eight, or even 16 pages on a single piece of paper. These printed *thumbnails* can save you time and storage space if you don't mind pulling out a magnifying glass from time to time. Combine thumbnail printing with duplexing, and you can store up to 32 pages on the front and back of a single sheet of paper.

8

Woody Leonhard

TEACHES

BUILDING DOCUMENTS

DOCUMENTS, DOCUMENTS, DOCUMENTS. I've been talking about documents so much, you probably think I'm document eccentric. Could be; I've been accused of worse.

Most people think the term *document* has something to do with paper; after all, the memos you type, the reports you read, and the books you buy are all documents, aren't they?

Interlude: What Is a Document, Anyway?

In the computer milieu, a document has nothing to do with paper. A document is merely a computer file—a collection of ones and zeros, stored away somewhere—nothing more, nothing less.

Word 2000 documents are special kinds of computer files, ones that can be read and understood by, *mirabile dictu*, Word 2000 (and Word 97, too). If you spend a few years working with Word documents, twist and turn and squint real hard, you'll come to the conclusion that Word documents contain very specific parts, built up like Lego® toys in a rather inflexible order. The parts go something like this.

NOTE

LATIN LESSON FOR THE DAY

Mirabile dictu means "wondrous/miraculous to relate." Frequently stated with tongue firmly in cheek. As in: I went to the Microsoft Web site and it recommended, *mirabile dictu!*, that I go buy the latest version.

Word Building Blocks—Characters

Characters form the basic building blocks of Word documents.

Every Word document contains at least one character, and every *empty* new Word document starts out with one character—the paragraph mark. (Since you followed my suggestion in Chapter 6, "Word Preliminaries," you can see the paragraph marks in your documents, right?) Yes, it's pretty weird to think of a paragraph mark as a character—usually *characters* are letters, numbers, punctuation marks, and the like. But Word's different. In fact, when it comes to understanding how Word works, paragraph marks are the *most important* characters.

Put a bunch of characters together and what do you get? Sentences? Well, maybe yes and maybe no. In fact, Word is pretty haphazard in identifying sentences. (Writers can be awfully haphazard about sentences, too!) Word has to accept sentence fragments, disembodied phrases, columns of numbers, and the like without croaking or giving the writer too much guff. It does so by pretty much ignoring sentences and moving on to the next level of aggregated characters—paragraphs.

Word Building Blocks—Paragraphs

You know what a paragraph is, right? Miss Smith in your sixth grade grammar class taught you. In the real world, a paragraph is a collection of sentences with a unified theme, or something along those lines. (Hey, I didn't do any better in sixth grade grammar than you did.)

Microsoft's Bookshelf declares that a paragraph is

"A distinct division of written or printed matter that begins on a new, usually indented line, consists of one or more sentences, and typically deals with a single thought or topic or quotes one speaker's continuous words."

Yeah, sure. That kind of definition may keep English professors fully employed, but it doesn't do squat for a computer.

As far as Word is concerned, a paragraph consists of

1. A paragraph mark

2. All the characters sitting in front of the paragraph mark, up to but not including the preceding paragraph mark (if there is one)

I really prefer that definition, don't you? It would've made my English composition class a whole lot easier. It's also the kind of definition you—and Word—can sink your teeth into. No wishy-washy "thought or topic or quotes" stuff. A paragraph mark and the preceding characters. Period.

Because every *blank* Word document starts out with a single character—a paragraph mark—it's also true that every *blank* Word document starts out with one paragraph. There's nothing in the paragraph but a paragraph mark, but them's the breaks, eh?

Word has paragraphs nailed cold. In the next few chapters, you'll see just how staked out Word paragraphs can be.

So what's the next building block? You put a bunch of paragraphs together and what do you get, a page? Well, no, not necessarily: Pages can have parts of paragraphs, and the paragraphs can flip-flop all over the place as you add more characters to a document, appearing first on one page and then on another.

Word Building Blocks—Sections

I'm going to simplify things a bit and tell you a lie. The next basic building block in constructing Word documents is called a *section*. (No, that isn't the lie.) Sections consist of one or more paragraphs. (There. That's the lie.)

Almost all the documents you'll work with consist of just one section, and that shouldn't bother you a bit.

☞ We'll talk about a few reasons for setting up multiple sections in "Sections," Chapter 8, on **page 112**.

But in almost all cases, working with sections is more hassle than it's worth.

Word Building Blocks— Documents

The ultimate Word construct, the document, consists of one or more sections. Every document contains at least one character (you guessed it, a paragraph mark), and at least one paragraph.

See how these parts fit together? Each one of these components has a slightly different affect on a document, and each can be manipulated in a slightly different way. Word builds them up, piece by piece, characters turning into paragraphs, paragraphs turning into sections, as it constructs your documents. Remember that and you'll be a long way ahead of the game.

THE HORRIBLE TRUTH ABOUT SECTIONS

All right, all right. I can't stand lying. The truth is that Word has relaxed the concept of section a bit, and if you're a geek (like me), you may be curious about the details. Almost all the time, sections are large parts of documents consisting of many paragraphs. People typically use sections to separate out chapters in books or major parts of reports. But in certain extremely unusual situations you can define a section as part of a paragraph. That is, you can break a paragraph into more than one section. Why would you want to do that? Usually it's because you want to vary the number of newspaper-like snaking columns in a large paragraph. Sometimes it's to change the line numbering (as in a legal document, where numbers appear on each line). But it's really, really rare, and I'm going to ignore it from this point on.

Word Building Blocks— Drawing Layer

Word documents have one additional component that's a bit hard to describe. It's called the *Drawing layer*, and it floats like a ghost on top of each document—or even underneath it. You can see right through the drawing layer. In fact, it's frequently difficult figuring out what's in the Drawing layer, and what's in the document itself, and finally what's in the Drawing layer underneath the document.

When you put drawings (such as, oh, clip art) in a document, they usually go in the document itself. They behave more or less like big characters—you can copy them, move them, and push them around like normal characters.

But when you start playing with Word's drawing tools (see Figure 8.1), making free-hand drawings or putting arrows and circles on things, those drawings go in the Drawing layer. They float above the text itself, and sometimes it can be maddening nailing down the floaters so they stay put.

Now you know the complete anatomy of a Word document. Let's see what kind of trouble you can get into by manipulating those parts to best effect.

FIGURE 8.1

Word's drawing
tools—doorway
to the Drawing
layer.

Deleting Text

You know how to get characters intoa document: you type. (And who said Word was tough?) But exactly how do you get rid of them? Ends up that's pretty easy, too.

You have two choices: You can zap out characters from in front, or you can zap them from behind. If you position the mouse pointer directly in front of the characters you want to delete, and then click the mouse, you can press the **Del** or **Delete** key to get rid of subsequent characters.

If you prefer sneaking up from behind, click the mouse after the character(s) you want to delete, and press the **Backspace** key.

Selecting and Moving Text

Word sports a variety of tools for picking up text and moving it around in a document. The easiest is the old select-click-and-drag.

EXERCISE

Move Text by Dragging

1. Start with a new document. Click **New** 🔲 if you need to.

2. Type a sentence or two.

3. Select some text near the end of the sentence (see Figure 8.2). Remember to let go of the mouse button when you're done selecting. The stuff you've selected should appear white on a black background.

SELECTING TEXT: WHAT YOU NEED TO KNOW

If you're new to computers, selecting might be a foreign concept. Not to worry. You've undoubtedly seen it in action before. In Word, when you select something you turn it black—the characters appear white against a black background. Invariably, you select something before you do something to it—move it, delete it, something along those lines.

To select some text, move the mouse pointer to the beginning of the text you want to select, and push the left mouse button down. Hold the button down while you swipe it across the text you want to select. It's a lot like wielding an electronic paintbrush.

If you've never selected much, practice a bit when you get to step 3 in the next exercise. You'll be selecting like an old pro in no time.

FIGURE 8.2

Selecting "if you don't mind." at the end of a sentence.

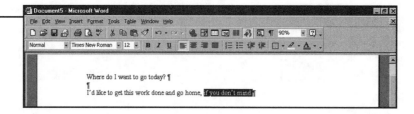

4. Move the selected text to a new location by clicking inside the selected area (that is, the area that has a black background), and dragging it to the desired location (see Figure 8.3).

FIGURE 8.3

Moving the selected text to the beginning of the sentence.

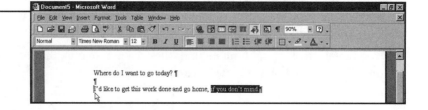

5. Finally, drop the text in its new location by letting go of the mouse button (see Figure 8.4).

FIGURE 8.4

Releasing the text in its new location.

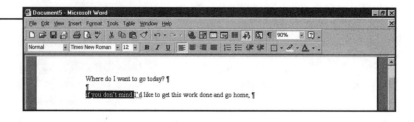

Using that basic select-click-and-drag method you can rearrange documents till the cows come home.

TIP

COPYING INSTEAD OF MOVING

If you want to copy text instead of move it, hold down the **Ctrl** key before you start dragging. A little box with a plus sign shows up underneath the mouse pointer, and a new copy of the text appears wherever the mouse pointer was sitting when you let go of the mouse button.

TIP

CANCELING DRAG AND DROP

If you start to move or copy text using this drag-and-drop method, and you suddenly decide that you don't want to finish the job, drag the text back to where you started, or press the **Esc** or **Escape** key. That cancels out the whole thing, quickly and easily.

If you select a bunch of characters and press the **Del** or **Delete** key, they'll be deleted. Another round of rocket science, eh?

Using the Clipboard

People talk about the Windows Clipboard as if it were an actual place. You move this to the Clipboard, you shove that off the Clipboard—back and forth.

In fact, the Clipboard is just a figment of Windows' imagination. It's a convenient fiction that's been concocted to make it easier for you to visualize how Windows lets you move data back and forth within a document, and between documents and even different programs.

Okay. So let's just pretend there's this thing called the Windows Clipboard.

When you work inside Office (not just Word, but Excel, Outlook and PowerPoint, too), you get to work with a beefed-up version of the Windows Clipboard called—not too surprisingly—the Office Clipboard (see Figure 8.5).

WORD: A SPEED DEVIL?

You can use drag and drop to move text a long way. If you drag the text to the top or the bottom of the screen, Word will scroll forward or backward in your document, only stopping when you move your mouse pointer back into the middle of the screen.

There's only one problem. Sometimes Word moves too fast! (You'll hit this problem, too, if you try to select a lot of text by moving the mouse pointer off the screen.) Yes, it's hard to believe, but sometimes Word turns into a speed devil when you least want it to. I haven't found a solution yet, aside from running on a slower computer.

Yeah. Sure.

SELECT FIRST

Okay, I'm being a little flippant. Sorry. There's actually an important principle sitting around here, one that may not be apparent if you haven't thought about it before. Almost always, Word wants you to act in a two-step fashion. First, you select whatever you want to change. Second, you apply the changes to whatever has been selected.

While that isn't a universal requirement, if you ever have trouble figuring out why Word won't do what you want it to do, keep it in mind. Select first; then act.

You'd be surprised how many experienced Word users forget that simple principle.

Sometimes the Office Clipboard is very handy. Much of the time it pops up when you least expect it—or want it. The only redeeming social value is that the Office 2000 Clipboard (unlike the Windows Clipboard) can hold 12 different chunks of your documents at once: you can pick up a sentence here, a picture there, and a dozen pages (or even a thousand!) from someplace else.

At its very simplest, working with the Clipboard usually goes like this:

- You select whatever part of your Word document that you want to put on the Clipboard

- You tell Windows to copy the selected stuff onto the Clipboard

- You move to a different place in the document

- You tell Windows to take the stuff out of the Clipboard and stick it in your document at the indicated place

CLIPBOARD EXPOSED
Yes, what I'm saying is true. There is no physical location inside your computer where the Clipboard lives. It's just an imaginary thing, set up with typical programming smoke and mirrors. That may explain why you can lose stuff that's *on the Clipboard*. If the application holding the information you put on the Clipboard goes south, it takes the Clipboard contents along with it.

WHAT'S AN OFFICE CLIPBOARD?
Starting with Office 2000, Microsoft has created its own version of a Clipboard with multiple cubbyholes. The old Clipboard—the one still used in Windows—only holds one thing at a time. Unfortunately, this new clipboard is so in-your-face (it pops up at the most frustrating times), many people wish they could turn it off. We haven't found a way to do that. Yet.

FIGURE 8.5
The Office Clipboard.

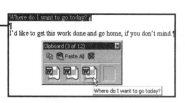

There's one minor variation in working with the Clipboard that's pretty common. Instead of copying the selected stuff onto the Clipboard, you can tell Word to copy it, but then delete it from inside the document. The usual method is called a *copy*. This variation is called a *cut*.

In both cases, when you copy stuff from the Clipboard into your document, it's called a *paste*.

 EXERCISE

Using the Clipboard, Part I

1. Once again, start with a clean document and type a sentence or two.

2. Select some text (see Figure 8.6).

FIGURE 8.6

Selecting
text for the
Clipboard
exercise.

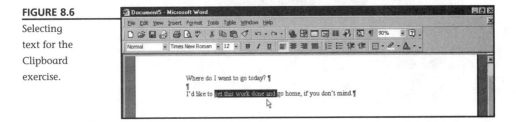

3. Cut the text and put it on the Clipboard. There are three easy ways to cut text: click **Edit**, **Cut** (as shown in Figure 8.7); click the **Cut** icon ✂ on the toolbar; or—the fastest way, once you get used to it—press **Ctrl+X**. If you've never used **Ctrl+X**, now's a good time to try it out.

FIGURE 8.7

Cutting the
text.

4. Move the insertion point to wherever you want the text to go. In this case (see Figure 8.8) I'm putting it after the word "mind".

5. Now paste the text from the Clipboard into the document. There are four easy ways to paste text: click **Edit**, **Paste** (as shown in Figure 8.9); click the **Paste** 📋 icon on the toolbar; press **Ctrl+V**; or, if you followed my advice in Chapter 6 to change Word's default setting, press the **Ins** or **Insert** key.

FIGURE 8.8

Relocating the insertion point to the destination.

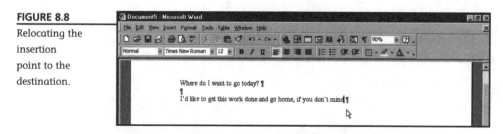

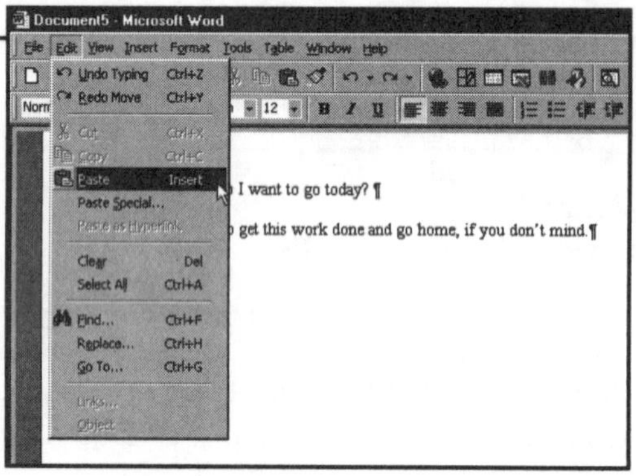

FIGURE 8.9

Pasting the Clipboard contents back into the document.

Most of your work with the Clipboard will go more or less like that: select, copy (or cut), move to the new location, and paste. But if you're ready to look at something a bit fancier, try this exercise.

EXERCISE

Using the Clipboard, Part II

1. The primary problem you'll have with the Office Clipboard is figuring out when, why, and how it's going to appear. (Tell you the truth, I never really know for sure.) You can get rid of much of the suspense by making it appear all by yourself. Just click **Tools**, **Customize**, and then click the **Toolbars** tab and check the box marked **Clipboard**. Click **OK** and the Office Clipboard appears.

OFFICE CLIPBOARD—GOOD BUT OBNOXIOUS

The advanced Word users I know all hate the way the Office Clipboard can appear out of nowhere, for no reason. It's yet another instance of the %$#@! computer thinking it's smarter than I am—and I *hate* that.

So many people have complained that you can expect this will be one of the first things Microsoft will change in its first Office 2000 Service Release. Be sure to read the story on Service Releases in Chapter 2, "Precursors to Using Office." And if your Office Clipboard doesn't act the way I describe here, thank your lucky stars (and the people who griped so loud and hard): You probably have an Office 2000 Service Release installed, whether you know it or not.

2. Select some text in your document. Now copy it to the Office Clipboard by clicking **Edit**, **Copy**; clicking the **Copy** icon on the toolbar; or pressing **Ctrl+C**.

3. Note how the copied text becomes the last item on the Office Clipboard. Hover your mouse over one of the rectangles to see. In Figure 8.10, I copied the first sentence of the document, and then I copied the second sentence. When the mouse hovers over the first rectangle, you can see it contains the text **Where do you want to go today?**

FIGURE 8.10

Hovering the mouse over a rectangle will tell you what appears in a specific cubbyhole in the Office Clipboard.

4. Click somewhere else inside the document. Then click the rectangle that contains the text you want to paste.

5. For a thrill—well, not *that* big of a thrill—try clicking **Paste All**. When you tire of the Office Clipboard, click the **X** in the upper-right corner of the Clipboard and it'll go away. At least, it'll go away until it starts feeling obnoxious, and then it'll suddenly reappear, for no apparent reason. You can always click the **X** to make it stifle.

Building a Test Document

You're now in a position to put together a test document, one you can use for exercises through the remainder of this book. I won't presume to tell you what to put in your test document, but, uh, creativity counts.

EXERCISE

Create a Test Document

1. Start with a blank document. Type an interesting sentence or two. I've used one of my favorite passages from Mark Twain.

2. Select the text you've typed, *but not the paragraph mark* (see Figure 8.11).

3. Copy the selected text to the Clipboard. I use **Ctrl+C**, but you can click **Edit**, **Copy**, or you can click the **Copy** icon on the toolbar.

FIGURE 8.11

Selecting text in
a test docu-
ment, omitting
the paragraph
mark.

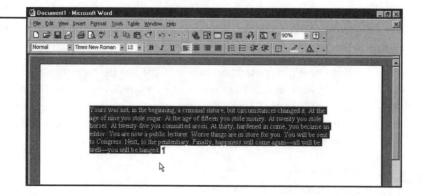

4. Put the insertion point immediately in front of the paragraph mark. Press
   the Spacebar, and then paste the Clipboard contents into the document via
   your favorite method
   (**Ctrl+V**, **Ins**, **Paste**, or **Edit**,
   Paste. See Figure 8.12).

5. Repeat step 4 one more
   time—press the **Spacebar**;
   then copy the Clipboard contents into the paragraph.

6. Now select the whole paragraph, *including the paragraph
   mark* (see Figure 8.13). Copy
   the whole paragraph onto
   the Clipboard.

7. Repeatedly paste from the
   Clipboard back into the document. Do it 10 or 20 times,
   or more—whatever it takes to
   build a document that's three
   or more pages long.

8. Save the document in the My
   Documents folder. Give it a
   name such as test.doc. (Click
   File, **Save**, type test in the
   File name box, and click
   Save. See Figure 8.14.)

THE TWAIN CONNECTION

Did you know that Mark Twain was an
original American gearhead? He pioneered the use of that new-fangled contrap-
tion we now call the typewriter. Some say he
was the first person in the world to submit a
book manuscript that was completely written
by typewriter. This at a time when typing
required no small amount of physical sta-
mina—typewriter keys invariably locked
together and unlinking them invariably left ink
all over your hands. A very accomplished typist
could manage, oh, five words per minute, tops.

Whenever I feel like swearing at Word (oh, a
couple of times a day, at least), I try to think
back on the grizzled Sam Clemens, stooped
over his typing machine, and what he must've
gone through—not only experimenting with
the new technology, but proselytizing it to an
indifferent (if not downright skeptical) public.

Then I figure, hell, he probably swore at his
machine too. Time to get back to work.

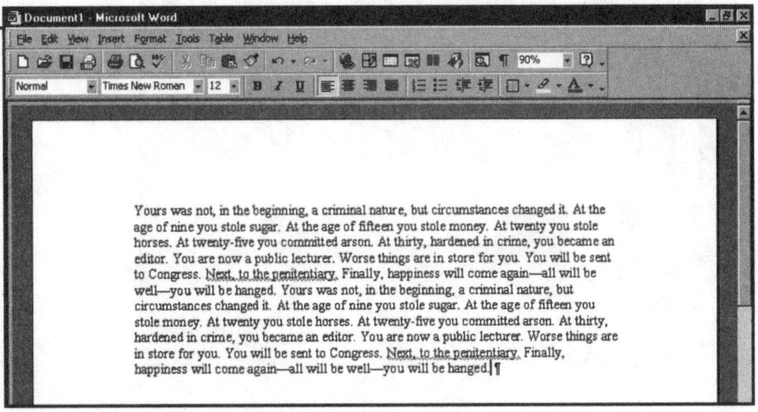

FIGURE 8.12

Making a second copy of the text in the first paragraph of the test document.

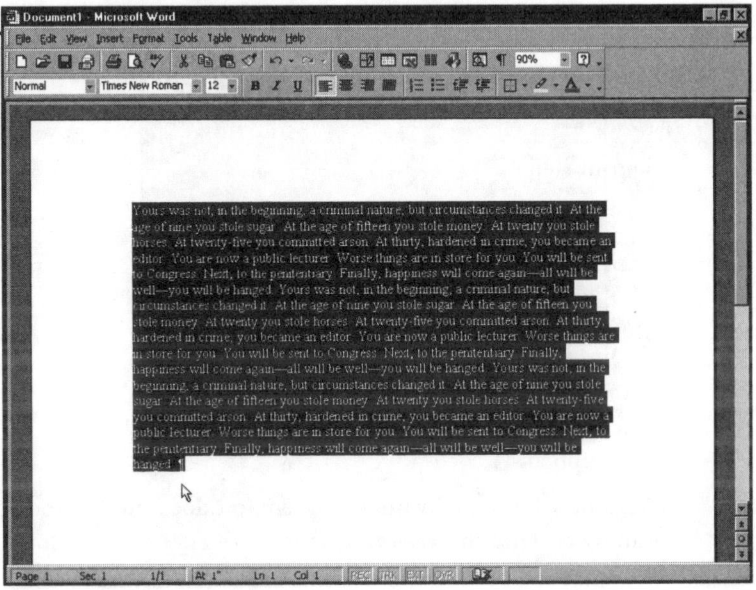

Yours was not, in the beginning, a criminal nature, but circumstances changed it. At the age of nine you stole sugar. At the age of fifteen you stole money. At twenty you stole horses. At twenty-five you committed arson. At thirty, hardened in crime, you became an editor. You are now a public lecturer. Worse things are in store for you. You will be sent to Congress. Next, to the penitentiary. Finally, happiness will come again—all will be well—you will be hanged. Yours was not, in the beginning, a criminal nature, but circumstances changed it. At the age of nine you stole sugar. At the age of fifteen you stole money. At twenty you stole horses. At twenty-five you committed arson. At thirty, hardened in crime, you became an editor. You are now a public lecturer. Worse things are in store for you. You will be sent to Congress. Next, to the penitentiary. Finally, happiness will come again—all will be well—you will be hanged. ¶

FIGURE 8.13

Copy the entire paragraph onto the Clipboard.

We'll use test.doc frequently. In fact, if you have Resume.doc from the preceding chapter (or any other Word 2000 document, for that matter) handy, we'll use it and test.doc in this interesting multiple-document exercise.

EXERCISE

Copying from Document to Document

1. You should have test.doc open and freshly saved from the preceding exercise. In addition, you're going to need a second Word 2000 document, such as Resume.doc, which you saved in Chapter 7, "Working with Documents."

FIGURE 8.14

Saving c:\My
Documents\
test.doc.

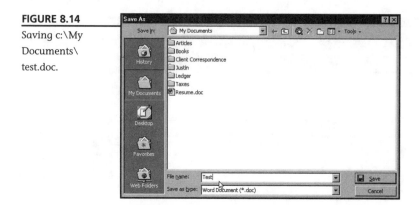

2. Open Resume.doc by clicking **File**, **Open**, choosing **Resume.doc**, and clicking **Open** (see Figure 8.15).

FIGURE 8.15

Opening
Resume.doc for
the copying
exercise.

3. Word now has two documents open: test.doc and Resume.doc. You can verify
   that by clicking the **Window** menu (see Figure 8.16). Both documents
   should be listed.

4. It's easy to flip back and forth between the two documents. Just click
   Window, **2 test.doc** to look at test.doc; and click **Window**, **1 Resume.doc**
   to get back to Resume.doc.

5. Let's copy that big, bold name from Resume.doc to test.doc. Start by putting
   Resume.doc on top (if necessary, click **Window**, **1 Resume.doc**).

FIGURE 8.16

Two documents are currently open.

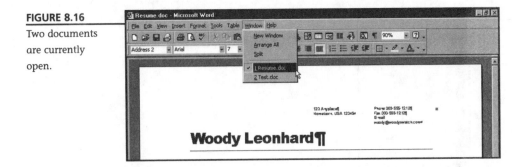

6. Select the text you want to copy. (In my case, it's **Woody Leonhard**. See Figure 8.17.)

FIGURE 8.17

Selecting the name in Resume.doc.

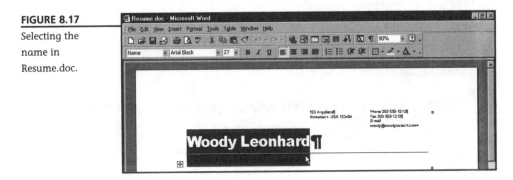

7. Copy the selected text to the Clipboard. I'll use **Ctrl+C**; you can pick whatever method you like.

8. Switch over to test.doc by clicking **Window, 2 test.doc**.

9. Let's put that name at the beginning of test.doc. Position the insertion point by clicking at the beginning of test.doc (see Figure 8.18).

10. Now paste that big, bold name into the beginning of test.doc. I'll use **Ctrl+V**; you can use whichever method you like (see Figure 8.19).

11. What the %$#@!? What happened to that big, bold name? Why is it a puny, scrunchy thing? What's going on here?

FIGURE 8.18

Positioning the insertion point where the pasted text should go.

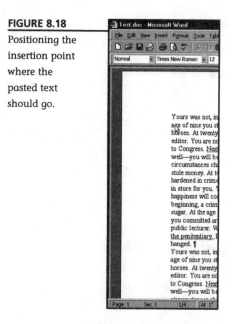

FIGURE 8.19

Pasting the big, bold name into test.doc.

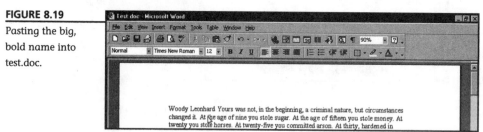

For the answer to that perplexing question, my friend, you're going to have to read Chapter 10, "Making Documents Look Good." Heh heh heh. Gotcha, didn't I?

Oh, Okay. Here's the answer. The big, bold name turned into a puny, scrunchy one because you didn't copy the paragraph mark from Resume.doc to test.doc! Remember: *The paragraph mark is the most important character in Word.*

9

Woody Leonhard

TEACHES

GETTING AROUND WORD

GETTING THERE FROM HERE… Word has dozens—many dozens—of key combinations for moving around inside a document, selecting text, and manipulating items that exist in documents. Truth be told, I don't know more than a handful of people who use more than a very few key combinations.

How the Keys Work

No doubt you've already figured out the common navigation keys and how they work.

TIP

TAKE CTRL

Combining **Ctrl** with those keys turns them into super keys. **Ctrl** + the **down arrow** goes to the beginning of the next paragraph. **Ctrl** + the **up arrow** goes to the beginning of the preceding paragraph. **Ctrl+Home** goes to the start of the document. **Ctrl+End** goes to the end.

EASY SCREEN SHOTS

From time to time you might want to take a snapshot of the Word screen, particularly if you need to show somebody how something is going wrong. Few people realize it, but you have all the tools you need built into Word. To take a shot of the entire screen, press the **PrtScr** or **Print Screen** key. Then click **Edit**, **Paste**, and the whole screen will appear in your document. It's a high-quality shot: People will be able to see all the details from the screen in the document. It prints pretty nicely, too.

If you only want to take a shot of the active window (that is, the window that has its title bar highlighted), press **Alt+Print Screen**. That puts the current active window on the Clipboard. You can then paste it into your document (or any other Windows application, for that matter).

Common Keys

At the risk of restating the obvious:

- **Arrow keys** move up, down, left, or right.

- **Home** goes to the beginning of the current line.

- **End** goes to the end of the current line.

- **Page Up** (or **PgUp**) and **Page Down** (**PgDn**) go up or down a screen—*not* a page.

- **Scroll Lock** and **Pause** don't do anything.

- **Print Screen** (**PrtScr**) takes a snapshot of the current screen and puts it on the Clipboard. Not exactly what you expected, eh?

If you're an extremely fast touch typist who dreads the thought of moving your fingers to the (*eek!*) mouse, you might want to run down and memorize the key combinations. You can find endless lists of shortcut keys by clicking on the Office Assistant (if it isn't showing, click **Help**, **Show the Office Assistant**), typing keyboard shortcuts, and pressing **Enter** (see Figure 9.1).

FIGURE 9.1

All the shortcut
keys fit to print.

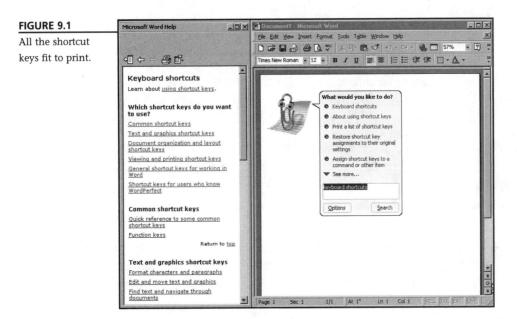

Worthwhile Key Combinations

If you're basically lazy like me and unwilling to spend hours wading through (much less memorizing) that key combination garbage, chances are good all you want to know is the important stuff.

Great. That's what I'm here for.

Table 9.1 contains 10 key combinations most people find useful. Don't bother memorizing them. You'll remember them if you use them enough to make it worthwhile. Write these out on a stick-on note and put them on your monitor, down at the bottom where they're easiest to see. Most of all, remember that they're meant to be shortcuts—if you have to search around for them, don't bother. Almost all of them have equivalents sitting under the **Edit** menu.

Table 9.1   Common Key Combinations

Key	Description
F1	Brings up the Office Assistant, unless it's been turned off (in which case it brings up Help)
Ctrl+A	Selects the whole document
Ctrl+C	Copies whatever is selected to the Clipboard

continues

Table 9.1   Continued

Key	Description
Ctrl+V	Pastes the contents of the Clipboard into the document
Ctrl+X	Cuts whatever is selected to the Clipboard
Shift+F5	Goes to the last place you were editing
Ctrl+Home	Goes to the beginning of the document
Ctrl+End	Goes to the end of the document
Print Screen	Puts a shot of the screen on the Clipboard
Alt+Print Screen	Puts a shot of the current active window on the Clipboard

You might find a few more useful key combinations hidden in Word's darker regions, but by and large they're a pain unless you have a photographic memory. As the saying goes, don't sweat the small stuff. And when it comes to memorizing key combinations, it's all small stuff.

Using the Find Tool

Quite possibly the most powerful and most frequently used, document navigation method is Find, which searches a document for characters that you specify. For example, if you want to search through a document and find every occurrence of the phrase "Party of the First Part," the Find function hops through the document, at your command, stopping each time "Party of the First Part" appears.

It's important that you understand some of Find's nuances, so I'm going to take you through several variations on the standard Find. Let's start with an easy one: bone stock Find.

EXERCISE

Basic Find

1. If you still have test.doc sitting on the screen from the previous exercise, you're in good shape. If not, open it (click **File**, **Open**, **test.doc**, **Open**).

A LÁ MODE

This is one of the few Word dialog boxes that lets you play around with the document while the dialog box stays on the screen. The techie term for this kind of dialog box is a *modeless* box. Don't ask me why Microsoft chose that weird terminology, but it makes a great trivia question. Enjoy this step while you can, because it'll be a long time before you see another modeless Word dialog box.

2. Pick a word from test.doc—doesn't matter which one. For this example, I'm going to choose "editor." (Book editors just love it when I do that.) You're going to search for all occurrences of that word.

3. Click **Edit**, **Find**. You should see the Find and Replace dialog box, as in Figure 9.2. If you can see the screen animation, and you look closely, you'll notice that the Find and Replace dialog box springs from the **Select Browse Object** dot near the bottom of the vertical scrollbar. Word, in its inimitable way, is trying to show you that **Find and Replace** lives in that little dot.

FIGURE 9.2

The Find and Replace dialog box, which ,also covers Go To.

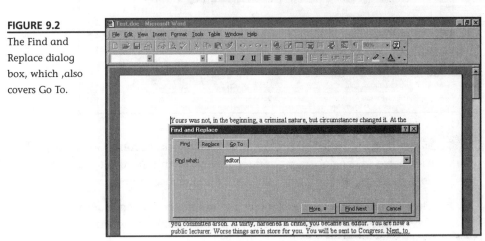

4. Let's visit **Find and Replace** where it lives. (Those of you who disabled the vertical scrollbar will have to bypass this step.) Click **Cancel** in the Find and Replace dialog box. Then click the little **Select Browse Object** dot, and click the **Find** pair of binoculars ![binoculars] (see Figure 9.3). The Find and Replace dialog box (previously shown in Figure 9.2) comes back.

FIGURE 9.3

You now know where Find and Replace lives.

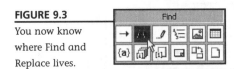

5. Type the word you want to find in the Find what box. In my case, I've typed in "editor".

6. To find a match in the document, click **Find Next**. Word hops down to the first occurrence of the characters you're searching for (see Figure 9.4). Sometimes the Find and Replace dialog box will cover up the characters that Word has found. If you don't see the highlighted characters, move the box around until they become visible.

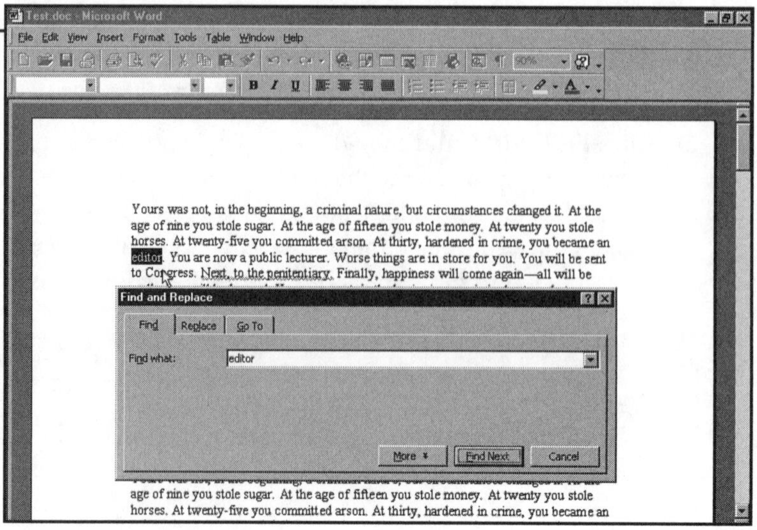

FIGURE 9.4

Word finds
the characters
of the word
"editor".

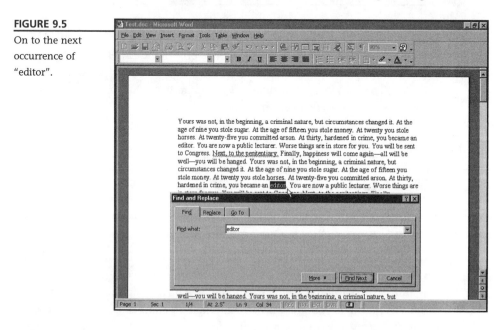

7. Notice how the Find and Replace dialog box sticks around. Go ahead and click down in the document and see how you can type, delete characters, or do just about anything while the Find and Replace dialog box just sits there.

8. Click **Find Next**. Word jumps down to the next occurrence of the characters you've typed (see Figure 9.5). Cool, eh? Hang on. It gets considerably cooler.

FIGURE 9.5

On to the next
occurrence of
"editor".

9. Let's face it. That big Find and Replace dialog box on the screen really takes over things. It's hard to see what you're doing while the box just sits there—and the box doesn't help much once you've set up the search. So click **Cancel** and get rid of the box.

10. See the blue double-wedgie just below the Select Browse Object dot where Find and Replace lives? Move your mouse over there and let it sit (or hover) for a second or two (see Figure 9.6).

FIGURE 9.6

Next Find/GoTo on the vertical scrollbar.

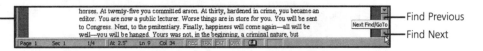

horses. At twenty-five you committed arson. At thirty, hardened in crime, you became an editor. You are now a public lecturer. Worse things are in store for you. You will be sent to Congress. Next, to the penitentiary. Finally, happiness will come again—all will be well—you will be hanged. Yours was not, in the beginning, a criminal nature, but

Next Find/GoTo

Find Previous

Find Next

11. Guess what? To do a Find Next, you don't need that huge dialog box. All you need to know is the trick! Click that blue down double-wedgie and Word moves on to the next occurrence of your Find characters. But wait! There's more!

12. See the blue up double-wedgie, just above the Select Browse Object dot where Find and Replace lives? Can you guess what that one does? Yeah. You're pretty bright. Go ahead and click it, and watch as Word searches backward—toward the beginning of the document—for the text you seek.

Practice that exercise a couple of times. I think you'll find it one of the best time-saving devices Word has to offer.

TIP

SPEEDING UP YOUR SEARCH

When Word does a search, it starts from the current location of the insertion point. So if you want to skip over a bunch of stuff—say, start your search in the middle of a document—go to the place you want to start the search and click the mouse to move the insertion point to that location.

That's the most basic kind of search Word offers. Now let's try a somewhat more complex search.

EXERCISE

A More Interesting Search

1. Click the **Select Browse Object** dot where Find and Replace lives. You'll get the Find and Replace box, of course, as shown in Figure 9.2.

2. Click the **More** button. You'll see a variety of options—ways that Word will modify your search to narrow it down to snag only those characters you want to find (see Figure 9.7).

FIGURE 9.7

The More part
of the Find and
Replace dialog
box.

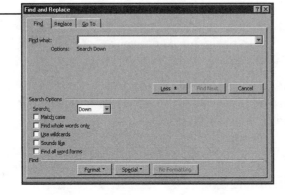

3. Look for a capitalized word in test.doc. In Figure 9.8, I've chosen the word
   Worse. Type that word in the Find what box. Then click the check box
   marked **Match case**. Word will tell you that it's going to search down (that
   is, toward the end of the document), and that it will only stop when it
   matches the upper/lowercase characters in the **Find what** box.

FIGURE 9.8

A Match case
search in Word's
Find.

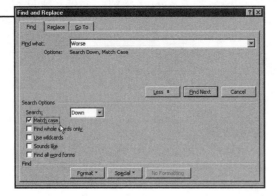

4. Click **Find Next**. Word will scan through test.doc, starting wherever the insertion point happens to be, and look for the characters in the Find what box,
   but only stop if there's an exact match on the upper/lowercase characters (see
   Figure 9.9).

5. Try playing with this extended Find feature for a bit. I bet you'll find lots of
   interesting combinations. If you want to know precisely what each of those
   More options mean (and, believe me, they aren't exactly intuitive!) click the
   ? in the upper-right corner; then click the option that befuddles you.

In general, I haven't had much luck with the **Sounds like** and **Find all word forms**
choices. In my experience, computers don't do very well at listening or verb declensions.

(I'll probably hang up my keyboard when they do.) But the others work quite well. Your mileage may vary, of course.

FIGURE 9.9

An exact match for "Worse", both upper- and lowercase.

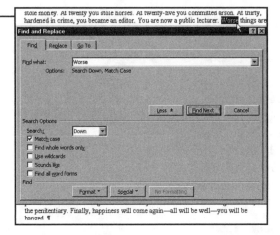

NOTE

TARGETING YOUR SEARCH

You can limit a search to a specific part of your document. Just select the text you want to search before clicking on the **Select Browse Object** dot. Word will look through the selected text and, if it doesn't find a match, ask you if you want to continue searching the rest of the document.

To tell the truth, I've only touched the surface of all the things Find can do. If you want to look up something you've searched for recently, click the down arrow at the end of the **Find what** box. If you want to look for an odd-ball character—a paragraph mark, say, or any number of consecutive spaces (*white space*), click the **Special** button. You can also try playing with the **Format** button, but you'll probably want to go through the next chapter before you tackle that one.

WHAT'S A WILDCARD?

One of the most powerful Find options—and one of the hardest to figure out—is the **Use wildcards** check box, which lets you specify parts of words and have Word fill in the blanks. Single missing letters are represented by **?** and multiple letters are denoted *****. For example, if you ask Word to find **b?ll** it will stop on both **bill** and **bull**. If you specify **b*ll**, Word will stop on both of those, plus **blackball**.

To get a full list of wildcards that Word will recognize (and there are many of them!), bring up the Office Assistant (or use native Help), type the phrase `find wildcards`, and then click the link marked **Fine-tune a search by using wildcard characters**.

For a thorough discussion of wildcards—and, believe me, they can get *wild*—check out *Special Edition Using Office 2000*, by Ed Bott and Woody Leonhard, from Que, ISBN 0-7897-1842-1.

Using the Replace Tool

Word will not only search for characters 10 ways from Tuesday, but it can replace the characters it finds with other characters of your choosing. That's what the Replace function does.

EXERCISE

Replace

1. If it isn't already open from the preceding exercise, open test.doc. Move to the beginning of the document either by scrolling and clicking at the beginning, or by pressing **Ctrl+Home**.

2. Click the **Select Browse Object** dot where Find and Replace lives; then click the **Replace** tab. (If you have disabled your vertical scrollbar, click **Edit**, **Replace**.) If you can see a button marked **Less**, uncheck all the boxes in the lower half of the dialog box—**Match case** may be checked, if you're following along here closely—then click the **Less** button. The dialog box should look like Figure 9.10.

WATCH OUT!

Be careful! **Replace All** is a mighty dangerous option. One of the first Windows books I ever wrote had an address book in it, listing products and addresses from all the major Windows-oriented hardware and software manufacturers. One of the editors at that publishing company (no, it isn't Que!) got tired or lazy or whatever one night, and decided he didn't like my abbreviating the word "Road" as "Rd". So he did a Word **Replace All** of "rd" to "Road". Unfortunately, he didn't limit the replace to match case, or whole words only.

I didn't notice until the book came out. It was embarrassing to see how some hardware manufacturers offered, oh, Video boaRoads.

FIGURE 9.10

The Replace dialog box in abbreviated form.

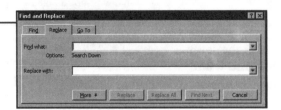

3. Choose a word or phrase you'd like to change in test.doc and what you'd like to change it to. Type the former in the **Find what** box, and the latter in the **Replace with** box. In Figure 9.11, I chose Mark Twain's phrase "in the beginning" and decided to replace it with "originally".

FIGURE 9.11

Replacing "in the beginning" with "origi-nally".

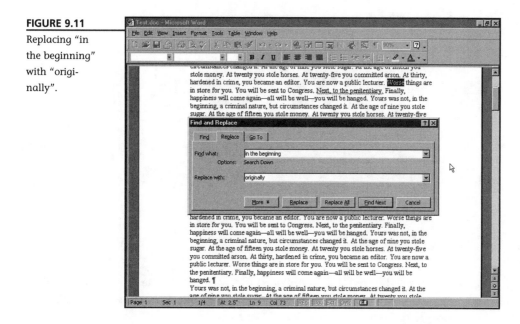

4. Click **Find Next**. Word should find the first occurrence of the characters you want to replace and stop there so you can consider whether you really want to replace them (see Figure 9.12).

FIGURE 9.12

Stopped at "in the beginning".

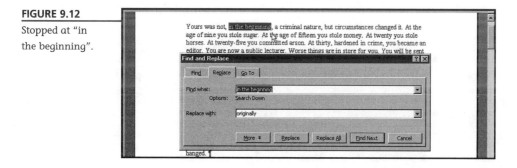

5. If, upon consideration, you really do want to replace the characters—in this case, replace "in the beginning" with "originally", click the **Replace** button. In a lightning-fast move, Word not only replaces the chosen characters, it moves down to the next occurrence of the characters in the **Find what** box (see Figure 9.13). If you're not convinced that it all happened that quickly, scroll back to the first occurrence and confirm that it's been replaced.

FIGURE 9.13

One replace done, another in progress.

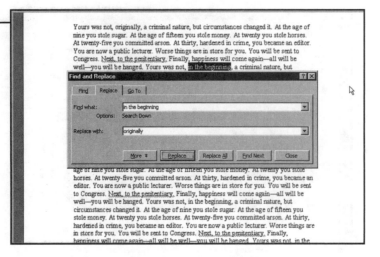

6. Continue through the document this way. If you decide that you don't want to replace a particular occurrence of the Find what characters, don't click the **Replace** button; just click **Find Next**.

7. If, at some point, you decide you want to replace all the occurrences of the Find what characters, click **Replace All**. Word will do your bidding, and then pop up a message that tells you how many times the string was replaced.

8. This is a good point to give test.doc a rest. Click **File**, **Close**. When Word asks if you want to save changes, click **No**.

Replace is quite smart in many respects. For example, it adjusts capitalization: If the word you replace is capitalized in the original document, its replacement will be capitalized as well.

⚠ CAUTION

STICKY SETTINGS

Word's Find and Replace settings are *sticky*. For example, if you try to find a phrase and click the **Match case** box, the next time you do a Find, the **Match case** box will still be checked—even if you search for a different bunch of characters.

Worse, the settings are sticky across both Finds and Replaces. If you find a phrase and click the **Match case** box, the next time you do a Replace it too will have the **Match case** box checked.

Beware! Many a Word buff has gone utterly insane trying to figure out why running a Find suddenly won't find something right in front of Word's nose.

Go To, Good Man, Go To

You may have noticed there's one more tab on the Find and Replace dialog box. It's marked **Go To** and, well, it lets you Go To various places in a document (see Figure 9.14).

FIGURE 9.14

Go directly to a specific page with Go To.

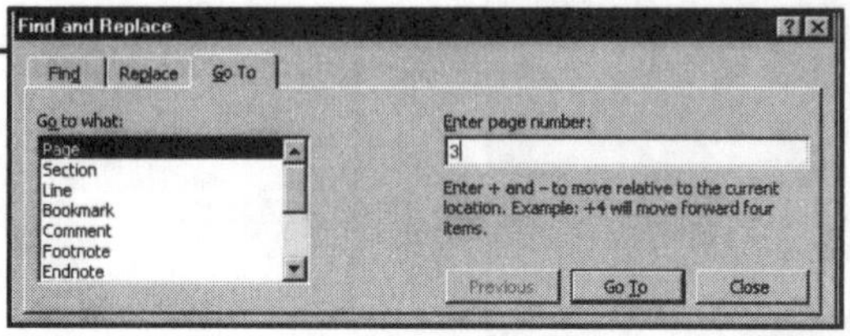

I won't go into too much detail on **Go To**, simply because it's rarely all that useful for the garden-variety Word user. If you want to go to a specific page number, you'll probably find it easier to click the vertical scrollbar's thumb and slide it to the page in question. The other things you can Go To are pretty esoteric, at least for beginners.

Using Mouse Wheels

The vertical scrollbar on the right side of the screen lets you move through your documents. Click the little up or down wedgies to move a few lines at a time. Click inside the scrollbar to move a screenful at a time. Grab the thumb and drag it to whatever page you are interested in and let go.

If you decide that you like the wheel, you can always get rid of the vertical scrollbar. That frees up a little extra space on the screen—although most people want to reclaim more space at the top and bottom of the screen rather than the right edge. Anyway, to get rid of the vertical scrollbar, click **Tools**, **Options**, **View**, and uncheck the box marked **Vertical scroll bar** (see Figure 9.15).

I don't recommend that you get rid of the scrollbar. If you zap it, you'll be losing Word's (nifty) show-the-page-number-when-you-click-the-thumb feature. You'll also lose the repeat Find function, which I'll describe in the next section. But, well, de gustibus non est disputandum, eh?

☞ *I talk about the vertical scrollbar under "Vertical Scrollbar" in Chapter 6, on* **page 90**.

HUH?

Latin lesson for the day: de gustibus non est disputandum translates to "there is no disputing tastes." Or, as R. Crumb so succinctly put it, "Diff'rent strokes for diff'rent folks, I guess."

FIGURE 9.15

IntelliMouse (or other wheeled mouse) users might want to consider removing the vertical scrollbar.

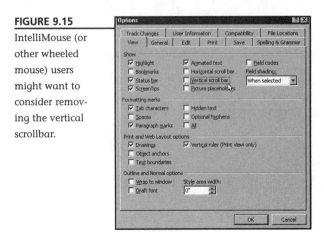

Around the same time Microsoft released Office 97, the folks in Redmond came up with a redesigned mouse that promised to revolutionize navigating through Office documents. The Mickey Marketeers anointed it with the moniker *IntelliMouse*. Some early versions of Office 97 came with the IntelliMouse inside the box—an interesting way to kick-start sales of a commodity with only questionable improvements over the plain, generic mouse attached to every PC sold in the past century or two.

About a year before the introduction of Office 2000, Microsoft got rid of the IntelliMouse entirely and replaced it with a very different, lopsided rodent called the IntelliMouse Pro. Now Microsoft is bundling this new RatPro with copies of Office 2000. If you're struggling with the generic five-dollar mouse that came free with your PC, the IntelliMouse/Office bundle is a worthwhile combination, in my not-so-humble opinion.

Microsoft isn't the only game in town. Several mouse manufacturers have jumped on the roller bandwagon, so you'll see wheeled rodents of various stripes on retailers' shelves. Some are good; some don't roll right, so try before you buy, okay?

Personally, I have a couple of IntelliMouse Pro's (IntelliMeese Pro's?), and I love them. They just fit my hand right. But, with one exception, I don't use the roller very often. It takes a little more brain power than I can muster to keep the roller going in the right direction while trying to accomplish some real work. Maybe I just haven't used it enough to get accustomed to the different feel. Whatever. The one exception: I've finally trained my brain to click the roller, and then slide the mouse down to slowly scroll through a document while I'm reading it. That trick works in all the Office applications and in Internet Explorer.

If you own an IntelliMouse, Pro, or one of its clones, you might want to use the mouse, and you should certainly try it. Here are several wheel moves that really can come in handy, in the right circumstances:

- Roll the wheel to go up and down, just as if you were clicking on the scrollbar.

- Click (push down on) the wheel and move the mouse up or down to scroll up and down in your document. The farther up or down you go, the faster you will scroll. Click the wheel again to stop scrolling.

- You should try zooming with the wheel—just once. (That's probably all it will take for you to give up, because you'll likely develop an advanced case of motion sickness or vertigo.) Hold down the **Ctrl** key and roll the wheel.

10

Woody Leonhard

TEACHES

MAKING DOCUMENTS LOOK GOOD

PUTTING ON YOUR SUNDAY BEST. In this chapter we're going to take a look at *formatting*—changing the appearance of various components of your documents. When most people say they want to learn Office, the very first thing they think about is making their Word documents look professional. So, I'm going to take some extra time in this chapter (the longest chapter in the book) and make sure you get a very thorough look at the formatting options available to you, and how best to use those options.

Select First; Then Apply Formatting

Before we get going, I want you to tattoo this mantra on the inside of your eyelids:

Select first; then apply formatting

- If you want to change the appearance of a few characters in your document, select the characters first; then apply the new formatting.

- If you want to change a few words, select the words; then change them.

- If you want to change a few sentences, select the sentences; then change them.

- If you want to change a few paragraphs, select the paragraphs; then change them.

Word just works like that. If you want to change the appearance of something, Word wants to know *what* you want to change before it applies the changes. Select first, and then apply the formatting.

I'll have one more mantra for you, later in this chapter. Both mantras are *crucial* allies in the battle to get Word to work for you, not against you.

Select first, and then apply formatting. Got it?

ANOTHER ABSOLUTE RULE, EH, WOODY?

Okay, okay. There are a couple of minor exceptions to the select first then apply formatting rule. (For example, you don't have to select an entire document before you change page margins.) But the exceptions are few and far between, and I'll point them out when we discuss them.

Formatting Characters

We'll start with Word's most fundamental component: characters. You probably know all about changing fonts or making words bold, but bear with me. It's not quite as simple as you think.

Font Changes from the Toolbar

Fonts drive the general appearance of your document. Choose your fonts wisely, and use them frugally. No other single formatting choice will have such a great impact on the appearance of your words.

EXERCISE

Changing Fonts

1. Open test.doc.

2. Select a few words. It doesn't really matter what or where. I chose a random sentence from Mark Twain's priceless prose (see Figure 10.1).

3. Change the font. The easiest way to do that is to click the down-arrow to the right of the font list, and choose a different font. In Figure 10.2 I've chosen Arial Black, a thick font frequently used for headings and posters.

FONTS GALORE!

If you've never played with fonts very much, you're in for a treat. Back in the good old days (say, five years ago), fonts were expensive—I once paid $119 for a font I really wanted—and many of the old fonts weren't all that good. Nowadays, fonts practically grow on trees and it's easy to find collections of excellent fonts for less than a buck apiece. Much less.

Font purists insist that there's a difference between a font and a typeface, and quibble over other terminology. They're right. But I'm going to succumb to popular lingo and use terms here the way you'll hear them used on the street.

FIGURE 10.1

First, select the text where you want the font changes to appear.

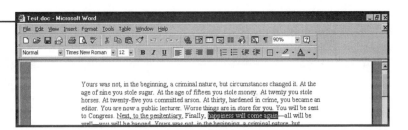

FIGURE 10.2

Change the font to Arial Black. Note how the font names appear formatted in their respective fonts—so Century Gothic, for example, appears on the Font name list formatted as Century Gothic.

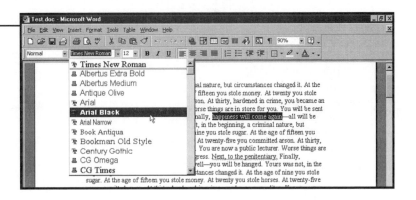

4. Change the font size. With the text still selected, click the right-arrow next to the **Font size** icon and choose a big font size. I chose 28 point in Figure 10.3.

SO WHAT'S A POINT?

A *point* is a rather esoteric measurement equal to one-72nd of an inch (meaning that 72-point type creates letters that are an inch tall). Suffice it to say that 28 point is pretty big (a tad under half an inch), 6 point is pretty small, and most text looks best at 10, 11, or 12 point.

FIGURE 10.3

Boost the font size to 28 points.

5. Make the text italic. With that same text still selected, click the **Italic** icon [*I*]. That makes the text italic.

6. You probably won't be too surprised to discover that the **Bold** icon [**B**] turns text bold, and the **Underline** icon [U] puts an underline under whatever you have selected. Play with those buttons if you like.

7. Word has a feature that lets you highlight text, just as if you'd run over it with a semi-transparent highlighting pen. To put a yellow highlight on the selected text, press the **Highlight** icon (see Figure 10.4). Word isn't limited to yellow highlighting, of course. (*Ach! So pedestrian!*) You can choose from a rainbow of colors by clicking the down arrow next to the **Highlight** icon [✎].

FIGURE 10.4

Adding a high-light to selected text.

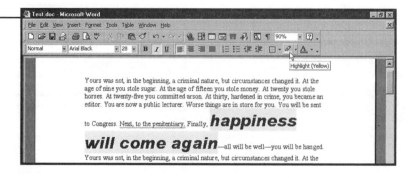

8. Finally, you can play around with Word's capability to change the color of selected text. Just click the **Font Color** icon to get the hang of it.

9. When you're done monkeying around with all these toolbar-based font choices, close test.doc without saving changes. (That is, click **File**, **Close**, and when Word asks if you want to save changes, click **No**.)

That's what you can do to fonts from that lower toolbar. (It probably won't surprise you too much to discover that the lower toolbar is called the **Formatting toolbar**.) It ends up that's just a small part of the Word character formatting shtick.

WEIRD HIGHLIGHTING MOVES

I don't know why, but when you apply highlighting to characters in Word 2000, Word takes it upon itself to scoot your cursor (uh, the insertion point) to the end of the stuff that has just been highlighted. That's very distracting if you're expecting Word to act consistently—no other formatting pops the cursor off the selection. Don't let it take you by surprise.

Ah well. As Emerson said, way back in 1841, "A foolish consistency is the hobgoblin of little minds, adored by little statesmen and philosophers and divines. With consistency a great soul has simply nothing to do."

Font Changes from the Dialog Box

To see the whole panoply of Word character formatting choices, you have to open up the Format Font dialog box. It really should be called the Format Character dialog box, but sometimes you just have to go with the Microsoft flow.

EXERCISE

The Format Font Dialog Box

1. Open test.doc.

2. Select some random text. In Figure 10.5, I've selected a different sentence from Twain's writing.

FIGURE 10.5

Selecting text for major font changes.

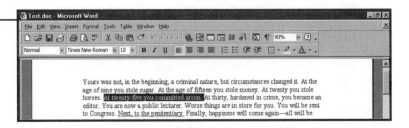

3. Click **Format**, **Font**. You'll see the Font dialog box, shown in Figure 10.6.

FIGURE 10.6

The Font dialog
box—the fount
of all font
changes.

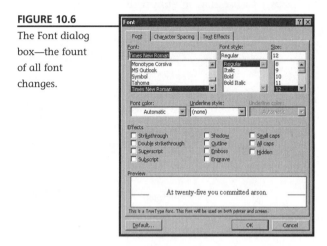

4. Many of the choices in the Font dialog box mirror those available from the Formatting toolbar: font name, size, bold, italic, underline, color, and the like. The major advantage this dialog box has over the toolbar lies in its **Preview** screen: You can actually see the changes being made to your characters before those changes take effect

5. Try one or two of the effects. For example, in Figure 10.7 I've chosen both the **Shadow** and **Outline** options. Yes, the result does look just as horrible as what you see here.

FIGURE 10.7

Shadow and
Outline on
Times New
Roman.

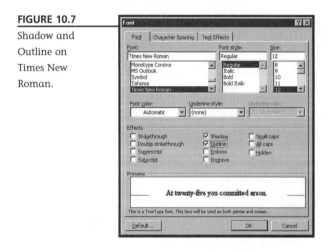

6. The one font formatting option that's worthy of mention here is **Hidden**. When you mark characters as Hidden, they don't appear onscreen or in printouts unless you take specific steps to unhide them. I know teachers who use hidden text to jot down answers to exams. They'll print the exams out normally to hand to students, and then they'll go back and print all the hidden text (the answers) along with the questions to create a key. To learn about hidden text, or any other option in this dialog, click the **?** button in the upper-right corner; then click the option that you want to have clarified.

7. We've only just started working with character formatting. Click the **Character Spacing** tab (see Figure 10.8).

8. Try fiddling with these settings a bit. They can come in handy. The **Scale** setting adjusts your characters horizontally—makes them fatter or skinnier, without making them taller. The **Spacing** option lets you squish characters closer together or give them more breathing room. **Position** makes characters superscript or subscript.

9. Now click the **Text Effects** tab (see Figure 10.10). Here you'll find formatting special effects—cool and colorful ways of highlighting text that will show up on the screen but not on the printer. Sometimes they're useful if you're creating a Web page. Most of the time they're merely distracting.

KERNING

The last setting you'll see in the Character Spacing dialog box reads **Kerning for fonts**. Kerning is a method of squishing specific pairs of letters together. For example, you'll frequently see A and W squished together because they nestle up so nicely (see Figure 10.9). Kerning is something you can only do to specific fonts, ones that have been set up by the font manufacturer with kerning information. Most of the time you don't want to make the computer do all the extra work involved with kerning. For small fonts, it usually isn't worth the effort, as the effect of kerning is very subtle. But for larger fonts, perhaps 14 or 16 or 20 points or above, kerning can be worthwhile; it's mostly a question of what you like, and how much you're willing to slow down Word to achieve your desired effect. In the **Points and above** box you tell Word how big characters have to be before Word should worry about kerning them.

FIGURE 10.8
Adjust character spacing.

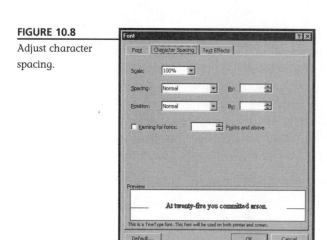

FIGURE 10.9
AWAY, in 72 points, unkerned (above) and kerned (below).

FIGURE 10.10
Word's font animation effects.

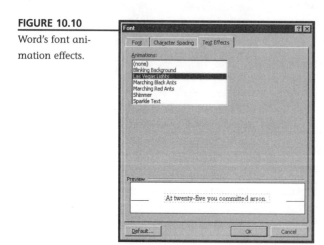

10. One last experiment before we leave this exercise. There's a fast way to get to the Font dialog box. Try it and you may get hooked. If you can see the Font dialog box right now, click **Cancel** to get out of it. Make sure you have some characters selected in test.doc, and then right-click the characters. As shown in Figure 10.11, one of your choices will be Font. Click it, andthe Font dialog box appears quick as a wink.

FIGURE 10.11

The right-click
context menu
that tunnels
straight into the
Font dialog box.

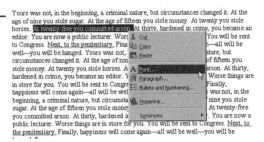

11. Close test.doc without saving your changes.

Changing the Default Font

In the lower-left corner of all three
Font dialog boxes (refer to Figure
10.7, Figure 10.8, and Figure 10.10),
you'll see a button marked **Default**.
That's a very powerful button with a
very lousy description. If you click it,
you'll get a message (see Figure
10.12) that tells you it'll change the
"default font... (for) all new documents based on the NORMAL template." Let me explain what that
technobabble means.

WHERE'S THE HIGHLIGHTING FORMAT IN THE FONT DIALOG BOX?

If you were watching very carefully, you
might've noticed that one of the toolbar
buttons— the **Highlighting** icon—doesn't
have an associated entry in the Font dialog
box. In fact, it's true. There's no way to control
highlighting from any Word dialog box. The
only way you have to work with highlighting is
from the toolbar.

It all has to do with the odd way Microsoft's
programmers decided to handle highlighting.
Don't get me going on that one...

FIGURE 10.12

The quick way
to change fonts
in all your new
blank docu-
ments.

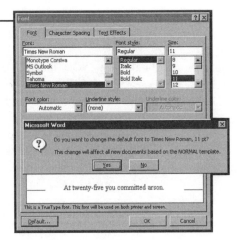

Right now, with Word 2000 running the way it comes straight out of the box, whenever you create a new, blank document, Word turns all the characters you type into Times New Roman font at 12 point. (If you installed Word 2000 over the top of Word 97, chances are good your default font is Times New Roman 10 point.) You can change the font around, of course, by selecting the characters you want to change and applying the changes. Still, everything starts in Times New Roman 12 point, and it takes extra effort if you want to make the primary text in all your documents, say, Garamond 11 point.

You can change the default font—the font Word automatically uses whenever you create a new, blank document—by selecting the font here, clicking the **Default** button, and responding **Yes** to that atrociously worded message about "…all new documents based on the NORMAL template."

Note that this changes the font in the current document and for all new, blank documents created in the future. It does nothing to documents that already exist.

WHICH FONT IS BEST?

There's no single *best* font for your documents. (If there were, the inventor would make a bundle!) Of all the fonts that get installed in a typical Office installation, my top choice for business correspondence is Garamond 11 point. I'm rather partial to Garamond—been using it for years—as it gives a bit of personality to my documents. As for size: 10 point is too small (unless all your correspondents are teenagers), 12 point is too big (unless they're all past middle age), and 11 point is just about right.

But that's just my opinion. What was it Justin Wilson used to say about the old red wine with beef/white wine with fowl conundrum? Something like, "the kind of wine you should drink is the kind of wine you like." Smart guy. That's why I named my son after him.

Sticky Font Formatting

By far the fastest way to write a paper, report, or book is to get the words down, and then go back later and apply formatting. If you don't confuse yourself with italics here and bolds there, the words can be cranked out much more quickly and the appearance can follow much later, almost as an afterthought.

YOU'RE NOT THE ONLY ONE WHO IS CONFUSED

I'm told that this is the most frequently asked question among all Word users. Too bad the folks answering the phone at Microsoft have to wade through all this gobbledygook to answer the question. (Why can't Word have a Format menu item that says "Format/All new blank documents"?)

That's sure a great theory, isn't it? Truth be told, I can't work like that, and I bet you can't either. Just about everybody formats as they type.

There are three tricks for those of us who don't want to take the time to go back through what we've typed, carefully selecting the characters we want to format, and then applying the formatting. Each needs to be used with a bit of understanding and caution.

EXERCISE

Quick Tricks for Character Formatting

1. Open test.doc.

2. Click once inside any word, and then click the **Italic** icon *I* on the tool-bar. The whole word turns italic. In Figure 10.13, I clicked inside the word *Yours*, and then clicked the **Italic** icon. *Yours* turned italic. This is a very handy two-click trick that can save you a lot of time.

FIGURE 10.13

Click once inside a word, and the whole word gets formatted.

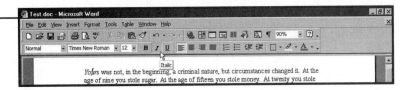

3. Click anywhere inside test.doc and start typing. After you've typed a few letters, click the **Bold** icon **B**, and resume typing. See how all the subsequent characters are bold? Type a few more characters and click the **Bold** icon **B** again. That turns bold off so you can go back to typing normally.

4. Click once inside the group of bold characters you just typed in step 3. See how the new characters come out bold, too? When you're typing in Word, each new character you type inherits the formatting of the immediately preceding character. The inheritance works with the font name, point size, bold, italic, underscore, color—just about everything except highlighting.

TIP

TAMING BERSERK FONTS

How many times have you been typing along when character formatting goes berserk? Suddenly your characters turn bold or italic (typically because you accidentally press the **Ctrl+B** or **Ctrl+I** key combinations, which turn text bold or italic respectively), and then everything you type from that point on comes out bold or italic. To fix the problem, select all the text that has gone haywire, click the **Bold** **B** or **Italic** *I* icon, and your typing should go back to normal.

5. Word has one more way to accomplish quick, on-the-fly formatting. I call it *character stropping*. Some people find it very helpful; others go ballistic when they find out what's happening. To see how character stropping works, click once in a random location inside test.doc. Type a few words, and then type an asterisk (a *****, or a "capital 8"). Type a few more words; then type another asterisk. See what happens? All the characters between the two asterisks turn bold, and the asterisks themselves disappear.

> **WHENCE THE STROP?**
>
> Those of you who have worked much with email will recognize these strop characters as commonly used characters for adding formatting to plain text email messages. That's where Microsoft originally came up with this idea. (The term *strop* is an old programmer's word, which this old programmer used to use back in his college days. It's probably the wrong word for the concept, but I don't know of any better one.)

6. Word has one more recognized strop character. It's the _ underscore, which appears above the hyphen, to the right of the zero on your keyboard. Again, go to a random point in test.doc. Type a few words; then type an underscore. Type a few more words or characters and another underscore. Everything between the underscores turns italic.

7. If you like these quick formatting strop characters, great! They'll save you lots of time. But if you don't like them—and many people don't—there are two things you can do. First, if you catch the problem immediately after it happens—just after you type that final asterisk or underscore—simply press the **Backspace** key and Word will restore what you rightfully typed. If that becomes too much of a bother, you can turn the feature off permanently by clicking **Tools**, **AutoCorrect**, and then the **AutoFormat As You Type** tab. Then uncheck the box marked ***Bold* and _underline_ with real formatting** (see Figure 10.14). In the World According to Microsoft, bold and underline are "real" formatting, whereas the * * and _ _ pairs are not.

8. Good. You survived another exercise. Close test.doc and tell Word not to save the changes.

Now you know the high points about character formatting in Word.

FIGURE 10.14

Disabling the * and _ strop characters.

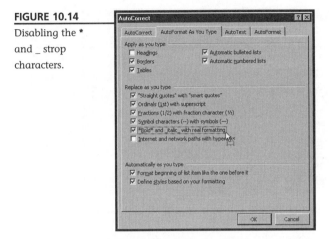

Formatting Paragraphs

Next we'll tackle the second major component of Word documents, the paragraph. Remember that a paragraph consists of a paragraph mark, along with all the characters up to, but not including, the preceding paragraph mark. Also remember that you need to select the paragraphs you want to format before you apply the formatting.

Paragraph Changes from the Toolbar

While it usually isn't the fastest or easiest way to change paragraph formatting, working directly from the Toolbar has the distinct advantage of being hard to screw up.

EXERCISE

Paragraph Formatting on the Toolbar

1. Open test.doc.

2. Select a paragraph or two. Note that, for paragraph formatting, you don't have to select an entire paragraph—as long as you have any part of a paragraph selected it'll be changed when you apply formatting. (In fact, if there's nothing selected, the formatting will be applied to the paragraph that contains the insertion point.) In Figure 10.15, I've selected the first paragraph.

FIGURE 10.15

The first para-
graph of
test.doc is
selected.

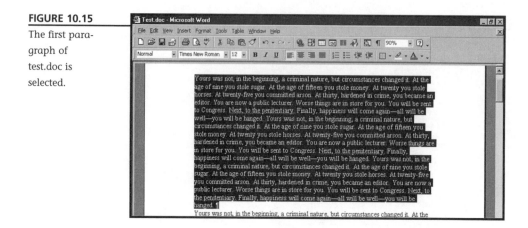

FIGURE 10.15

The first para-
graph of
test.doc is
selected.

3. See up on the toolbar that the **Align Left** icon ▤ has been selected? That's
   because this paragraph is left justified (also called *left-aligned* or *ragged
   right*), which means that the text lines up on the left, but flip-flops all over
   the place on the right.

4. Click the **Center** icon ▤. As you probably guessed, that's the icon for
   centering all the lines in a paragraph (see Figure 10.16).

FIGURE 10.16

Centering each
of the lines in
the paragraph.

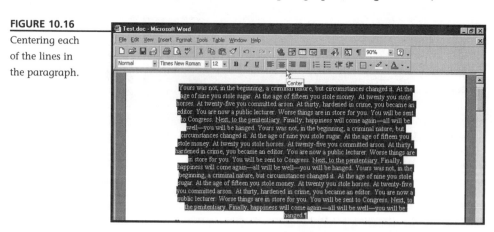

5. Now click the next icon, **Align Right** ▤. Word will right-justify (also
   referred to as *right-align* or *ragged left*) the paragraphs, as shown in
   Figure 10.17.

FIGURE 10.17

Right alignment from the toolbar.

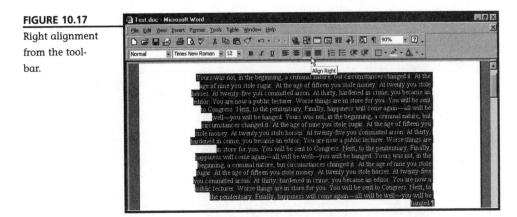

FIGURE 10.17

Right alignment from the toolbar.

6. Finally, as you've probably guessed, the fourth icon, **Justify** 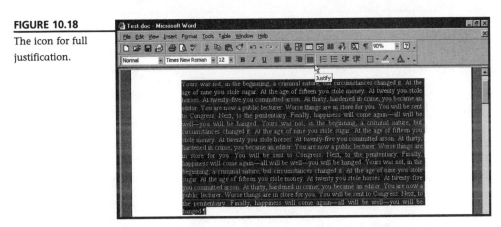, makes all the lines extend fully from the left margin of the page to the right margin (sometimes called *fully justified*, sometimes just *justified*). See Figure 10.18.

FIGURE 10.18

The icon for full justification.

7. Now select two or three paragraphs. Click the **Numbering** button . Your selected paragraphs turn into a numbered list, as shown in Figure 10.19.

8. Click that **Numbering** icon again and the numbering disappears. With the same two or three paragraphs selected, click the next icon, **Bullets** . See how the paragraphs are now bulleted, as shown in Figure 10.20?

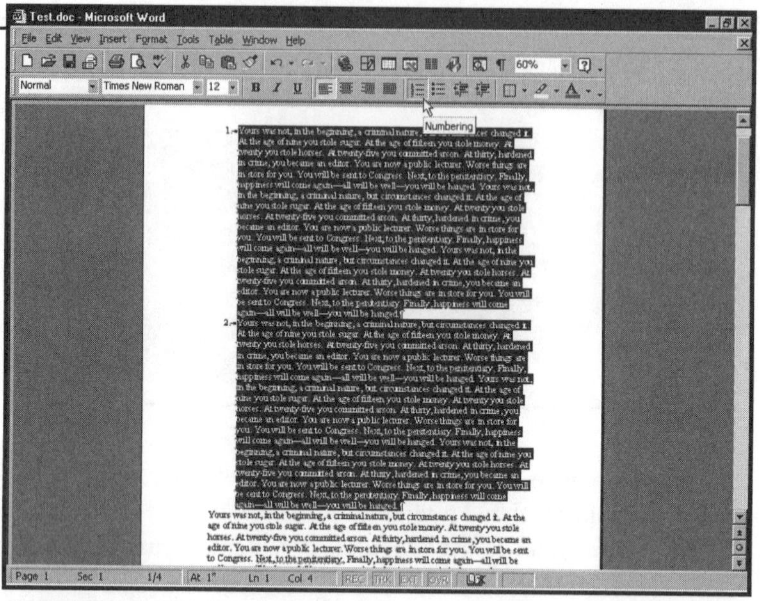

FIGURE 10.19

Creating a numbered list from the toolbar.

FIGURE 10.20

Making a bulleted list using the toolbar.

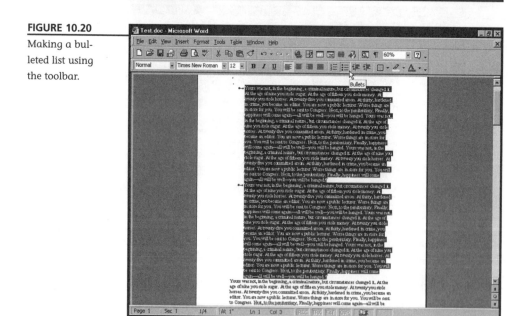

9. This is, far and away, the most accurate way to make bulleted or numbered lists. We'll look at other methods later in this section, but they're all sloppy compared to this toolbar approach.

10. Click the **Bullets** icon ▦ again to remove the bulleting. Then play with the next two icons on the toolbar, **Decrease Indent** ▦ and **Increase Indent** ▦. They move the left edge of the chosen paragraphs in and out by half an inch per click (see Figure 10.21). You can move the left edge just about any-place you like, except this button won't let you move text beyond the left margin of the paper. When you're finished with this step, leave the para-graphs flush with the rest of the document, back where you started.

FIGURE 10.21

Moving the left indent in by an inch (two clicks of the toolbar icon).

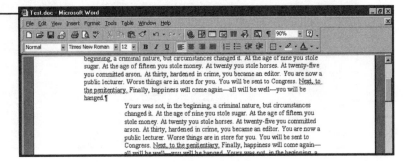

ABOUT THOSE INDENTS...

Microsoft calls the distance from the paper's left margin to the left edge of the paragraph an *indent*. I find that really confusing because I use the term indent to refer only to the initial line of a paragraph. Not so with Word. In the World According to Word, the indent distance controls the entire left edge of a paragraph. Something called a *first line indent* distance affects the first line of the paragraph. We'll see that setting shortly.

11. The next button draws lines around words, sentences, or paragraphs. Word calls such lines borders. This is a very important and powerful toy, er, tool, with a lot of options. Let's try a few of the more basic machinations. Start by selecting two or three paragraphs and clicking the **Outside Border** icon ▦. Word draws a box all the way around the selected paragraphs (see Figure 10.22).

12. Click the **Undo** icon ↺ to get rid of that box. Now, with the same two paragraphs selected, click the down-arrow next to the **Outside Border** icon, and choose the **All Borders** icon, which is the second icon in the list. Word draws independent boxes around the top and the bottom paragraphs, as shown in Figure 10.23.

FIGURE 10.22

A single border
(box) drawn
around two
paragraphs.

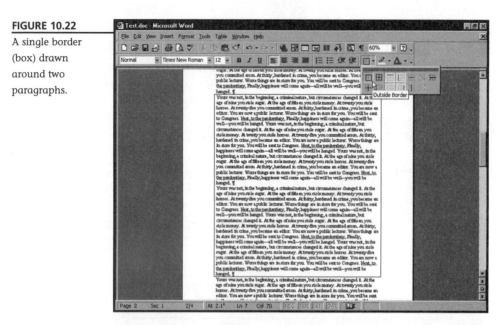

FIGURE 10.23

Use **All
Borders** to
create indepen-
dent boxes
around each
paragraph.

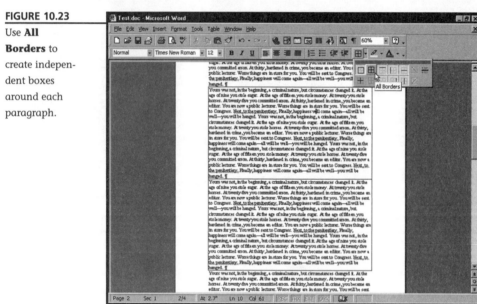

13. Again, click the **Undo** icon 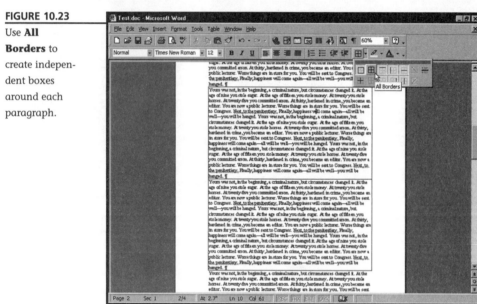 to remove the boxes, uh, borders that you
just inserted. Now select some random text inside test.doc and click the
Outside Border icon. Word draws a rather distinctive box around the
selected text, per Figure 10.24.

FIGURE 10.24

Boxing up random text.

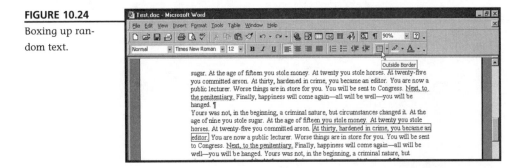

14. I could step you through dozens of similar examples, but you get the idea. Try selecting various combinations of words, sentences, and paragraphs and applying the various border types. I think you'll come away impressed with Word's extensive repertoire.

15. When you're done, close test.doc and don't save changes.

Paragraph Changes from the Dialog Box

As was the case with character formatting, Word only puts a small subset of its available options on the toolbar.

EXERCISE

Paragraph Formatting in the Dialog Box

1. Open test.doc again. Don't get too discouraged: This is going to be fun. Word can do all sorts of amazing things to paragraphs when you dig into the belly of the beast.

2. Your cursor (er, the insertion point) should be at the beginning of test.doc. That's fine for now; we'll only mess around with the first paragraph.

3. Click **Format**, **Paragraph**. (If you're feeling your oats, you can also right-click inside that first paragraph and choose **Paragraph**.) The Paragraph formatting dialog box comes up, as shown in Figure 10.25.

4. Click the **Alignment** drop-down box. The choices you see there—**Left**, **Centered**, **Right**, and **Justified**—are the same choices you had on the toolbar. Ho-hum. Nothing new here.

FIGURE 10.25

The Paragraph formatting dialog box.

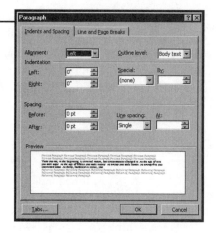

5. The **Outline Level** box sets the heading level for the selected paragraph. That's a rather esoteric setting that only applies to Outline mode, and a wonderful feature called Document Map that finally (*Finally! I've been kvetching about it for years!*) works right in Word 2000 (more on the outline level setting in Chapter 14, "Advanced Features"). You might think that **Outline Level** would change how things appear in Word's automatically generated Table of Contents, but it doesn't.

(Yiddish lesson for today: *kvetch*—in this context— means "complain, gripe." Leo Rosten in *The Joys of Yinglish* illustrates it in this way. The owner of a dress-manufacturing firm received the following telegram from his best on-the-road sales-man: BLIZZARD HAS HIT THIS AREA. COMPLETELY SNOWED IN. ALL FLIGHTS CANCELLED. ADVISE." The owner did not waste a minute before replying: "STOP KVETCHING. START VACATION AT ONCE.")

WHERE DOES MICROSOFT GET THESE NEAT FEATURES?

From Woody's Office POWER Pack, of course. Document Map appeared in WOPR *years* before Microsoft ever put it into Word. Although WOPR's version wasn't quite as slick (because we couldn't hook directly into Word to update the table of contents in the left pane), Microsoft's implementation is practically a pixel-for-pixel duplicate of the feature we created way back in WOPR 6.0.

Nope, of course Microsoft never acknowledged the source of the idea. You expected any different?

If you want to use WOPR 2000—to see the future of Word, *today*, as I like to say—pick up a copy of *Special Edition Using Office 2000*, ISBN 0-7897-1842-1. It includes a fully licensed copy of WOPR 2000, free, on the bonus CD.

6. The **Left Indentation** box controls the distance from the left edge of the paragraph to the left margin of the page. You played with that already when you clicked on the **Decrease Indent** 🔳 and **Increase Indent** buttons 🔳. The **Right Indentation** box controls the distance from the right edge of the paragraph to the right margin of the page. You can crank that up and down for a few seconds of, uh, marginal amusement.

7. Things start getting interesting when you get to the **Special** box. (Why it's called Special I'll never know.) Here's where you adjust paragraph indentation—you know, in the old-fashioned sense of the term. It's just as easy to create indented paragraphs (regular, old-fashioned indented paragraphs) as it is to create hanging indents (where the first line of the paragraph juts out to the left of the body of the paragraph). For the former, choose **First Line** in this box (see Figure 10.26); for the latter, choose **Hanging** (see Figure 10.27). The **Preview** box at the bottom of the dialog box gives you an excellent thumbnail view of what the various options look like.

FIGURE 10.26

First line indentation of half an inch.

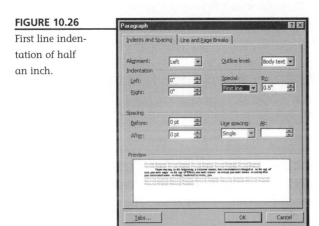

8. The **Before** and **After Spacing** boxes control how much white space appears (respectively) before or after the selected paragraphs. The spacing is additive—if one paragraph has **After Spacing** of 12 points, and the next paragraph has **Before Spacing** of 24 points, there's going to be a 36 point gap (read: lots of white space) between the paragraphs. The easiest way to see this interaction is to select the first two paragraphs in test.doc and try a few different numbers for **Before** and **After**.

FIGURE 10.27

A hanging indent of half an inch.

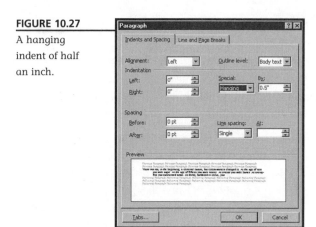

9. The **Line spacing** box on the Paragraph dialog box controls the amount of white space within the paragraphs—between the lines of the paragraph. (So, for example, if there's only one line in the paragraph, this setting doesn't change anything at all!) If you use just one font at one point size, in any given paragraph, the choices offered here—**Single** (plain old single spacing), **1.5 Lines**, **Double** (that's just double-spaced), **At Least** (where you specify a minimum distance between lines), **Exactly** (for a precise, fixed distance between lines), and **Multiple** (so, for example, **3** means triple-spaced)—work pretty well and make sense (see Figure 10.28).

FIGURE 10.28

First paragraph set to Exactly 16 point spacing— note how there's extra white space in that paragraph.

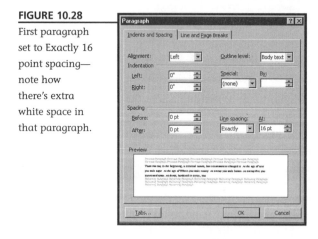

10. If you click the Paragraph dialog box's **Line and Page Breaks** tab (shown in Figure 10.29), you'll find several settings of interest. Checking **Widow/Orphan control** keeps Word from printing just one line from a paragraph on a page. Usually you don't want Word to split up a paragraph, so one line dangles. It looks pretty bad when the first line of a paragraph prints at the end of a page (that's called a *widow*) or when the last line of a paragraph prints at the top of a page (an *orphan*).

TRUTH IN LINE SPACING

The actual rules for line spacing are quite complex and depend on certain font characteristics. Suffice it to say that if you mix two fonts on a line, you might get different spacing on that line than on other lines in a paragraph. If you're concerned about weird line spacing inside a paragraph, try to use the **Exactly** setting. If that doesn't work and you want the full gory details, check the *Hacker's Guide to Word for Windows*, 2nd ed., ISBN 0-201-40763-9, pp 15–17. As far as I know, that's where you'll find the only accurate description of all these settings.

FIGURE 10.29

The Line and Page Breaks tab.

11. The **Keep lines together** setting requires Word to keep all the lines in each of the selected paragraphs together—on the same page. **Keep with next** requires Word to print both the selected paragraph and the following paragraph together on the same page. (If you use **Keep lines together** or **Keep with next** to the extent that there's too much to put on a single page, Word is smart enough to effectively tell you to buzz off, and breaks the pages the way it thinks it should.) No, there's no Keep with previous setting. **Page break before** makes Word start the selected paragraph on a fresh page. The other two options are pretty esoteric, and I won't bore you with them.

12. When you're done experimenting with paragraph formatting, close test.doc and do not save changes.

Borders and Shading

We had a taste of Word's bordering (box drawing) capability when you used the **Outside Border** icon earlier in this chapter. In fact, Word offers a veritable cornucopia of paragraph bordering and background shading when you click **Format**, **Borders and Shading**.

The **Borders** tab (shown in Figure 10.30) lets you choose from prebuilt borders representing several commonly used styles, or it lets you build your own borders by clicking specific areas in the **Preview** box.

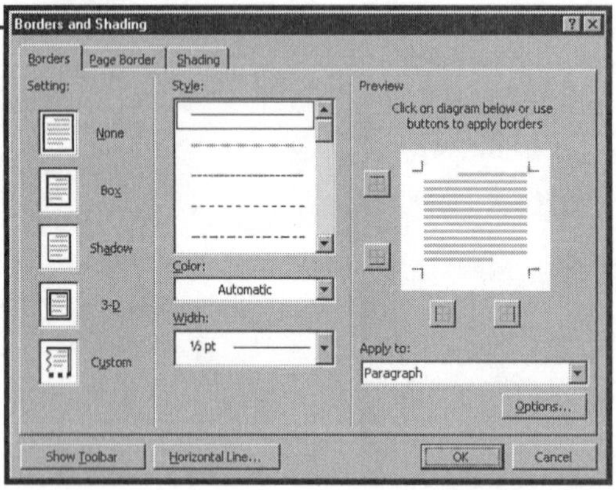

FIGURE 10.30

Word lets you draw almost any kind of box around paragraphs or characters.

If you want to build a custom border, click in the **Preview** box on the edge where you'd like to have a line. For example, if you want a line at the right side of the paragraph, click the right side of the dummied grayed-out text in the **Preview** box.

The **Shading** tab (see Figure 10.31) has Word Word's apply background colors or grayscales to the selected paragraphs or characters. You can even change the intensity of the color (or grayscale) by changing the setting in the **Style** box.

You'll see, if you flip back and forth between the **Borders** and **Shading** tabs, that Word keeps track of all your colorific settings and presents them to you in the Preview pane.

FIGURE 10.32
Both back-
ground color
and grayscale
lurk on the
Shading tab.

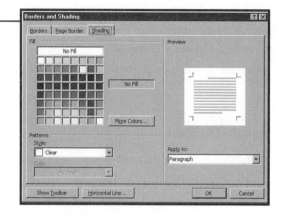

TIP

ADDING BORDERS TO PARAGRAPHS

Word has a quick way of adding borders to paragraphs. If you start a new paragraph, type three or more equal signs, and then press **Enter**, Word formats the previous paragraph with a double line border on the bottom. Similarly, if you start a new paragraph, type three or more dashes or hyphens, and press **Enter**, Word formats the preceding paragraph with a single line border on the bottom. Give it a Word's try!

Sticky Paragraph Formatting

Here's the other mantra you need to tattoo to the inside of your eyelids. (Hey, that's why you have two eyelids, isn't it?)

Paragraph Formatting Is in the Paragraph Mark

More blood, sweat, and tears Word's have been lost to Word over that little observation than all the other hassles combined—well, pretty close.

All paragraph formatting sits in the paragraph mark: centering, indenting, bullets, numbers, borders, line spacing, widow and orphan control, and on and on. It's all stored in the paragraph mark. When you delete a paragraph mark, the paragraph formatting disappears. *Poof!* When you move a paragraph mark, the paragraph formatting moves with it.

TELLING LIES AGAIN, ARE WE WOODY?

Okay. You caught me again. That "the new paragraph mark picks up the formatting of the old paragraph mark" part isn't 100 percent true, but it's almost always true. When you press **Enter**, the new paragraph mark almost always picks up all the formatting of the old paragraph mark. The only exception has to do with Styles and a funny setting called **Style for following paragraph**. For now, we're going to ignore it. When you get to be a hot-shot Word expert, we'll talk about it.

When you copy a paragraph mark, the paragraph formatting is copied too. When you create new paragraph marks (by pressing **Enter**), the new paragraph mark picks up the formatting of the old paragraph mark.

Let me show you what I mean about paragraph formatting sitting in the paragraph mark.

EXERCISE

Paragraph Formatting's on the Mark

1. Open test.doc. Your cursor should be at the beginning of the document.

2. Apply some weird paragraph formatting to the first paragraph. In Figure 10.32 I've formatted the first paragraph with a half-inch hanging indent.

FIGURE 10.32

Use **Format**, **Paragraph**, **Special** to set a hanging indent.

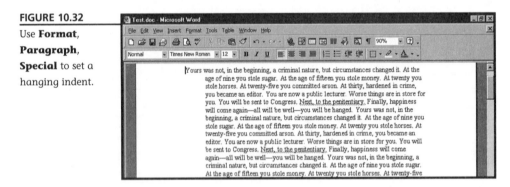

3. Now stick your cursor anywhere inside the paragraph. Press **Enter**. See that? The paragraph formatting settings are sticky—both of the new paragraphs have the same formatting as the old paragraph (see Figure 10.33). When you press **Enter** inside a paragraph, the new paragraphs both take on the formatting of the old paragraph.

FIGURE 10.33

Press **Enter**, and all the old paragraph formatting applies to both the old and new paragraphs.

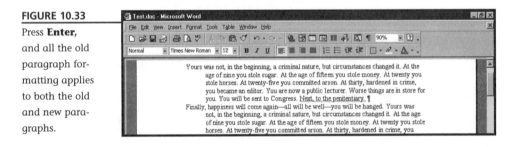

4. Select the paragraph mark at the end of the first paragraph. Copy it (with the **Copy** button 📋 or **Ctrl+C**). Move your cursor into the middle of the first paragraph, and paste the paragraph mark. As you can see in Figure 10.34, both of the newly created paragraphs also have the same hanging indent formatting.

FIGURE 10.34

Copying a paragraph mark also copies the formatting.

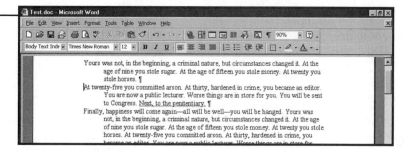

5. See how that works? Play with it a bit. Try copying parts of a paragraph, with and without a paragraph mark, into other locations in test.doc. Put your cursor immediately in front of a paragraph mark, press **Enter**, and verify that all the formatting in the old paragraph gets copied to the new paragraph.

6. Don't fall asleep on me. This may sound pretty trivial at the moment, but when we start talking about tab stops and bulleting/numbering in the next sections, it'll explain all sorts of odd behavior—things that can't be explained any other way. Oh ye of little faith.

7. When you're through watching the bouncing Paragraph marks, close test.doc and do not save changes.

WHAT HAPPENS WHEN PARA-GRAPH MARKS DIE?

Try deleting a paragraph mark. Note how the new, combined paragraph takes on the formatting of the first paragraph. In other words, the formatting in the deleted paragraph mark is transferred to the paragraph mark of the new, combined paragraph. Weird, huh? Hard to believe, but Microsoft intentionally made Word work this way. In spite of, uh, vociferous objections.

Once again, with feeling: Paragraph formatting lives in the paragraph mark. *Ommmmmm...*

Tabs

The world of Word users can be divided into two camps: those who have tried to use tab stops the way you would use them on a typewriter (perhaps to construct a fill-in-the-blanks kind of form), and those who have not. I can always identify people in the former group: their blood pressure has gone up 30 points, their faces are flushed, veins protrude from their necks, and they hurl epithets like sailors in a storm. The latter group just doesn't understand. Why do so many people hate Word? Spend an hour (or day or week) battling tab stops and you'll see.

My mission for this section is to introduce you to tab stops, tell you how (and even why) they behave so oddly, and then step you through an exercise that shows you a relatively easy way to get tab stops to behave themselves. No other introductory Office book covers this ground. Yet, at least in my experience, *every* first-time Word user bumps into these problems soon after they start using the program. Few ever figure out what's going on. You'll be one of the few.

In Word, a *tab stop* consists of a rather complex combination of two electronic concepts. First, there are the stops themselves—invisible locations on each line that you can set up to stop the progress of tab characters. Second are the tab characters—genuine characters that get placed in your document when you press the **Tab** key.

THE SKINNY ON TAB STOPS

In the days of the typewriter, a tab stop consisted of a very simple combination of two mechanical devices. First, there was the stop itself—typically a piece of metal that jutted out of the back of the typewriter, cleverly positioned so it would stop the platen (typewriter roller) at a predetermined location. If you set up tab stops every half inch, you could turn the typewriter around and see pieces of metal sticking out every half inch, ready to stop the platen dead in its tracks.

The second device was a Tab key. That key worked a little bit like the Spacebar, except it released the platen, sent it merrily zipping along, only to be halted when the next tab stop reared its little metallic head. The only major improvement to the tab stop came with the invention of the Selectric. On those machines the ball head, not the platen, moved along. Still, the concept was the same: a tab key that released the internal mechanism and a stop that physically stopped the movement.

Naturally, computers don't have metal pegs sticking out the back. (Or do they? Sometimes I wonder.) There's no way to duplicate the action of typewriter tab stops: Your monitor wouldn't appreciate being sent zinging across your desk. Computer people had to come up with a replacement to the tab stop—lots of folks wanted to use them—but the electronic version is only vaguely related to the original—very vaguely.

When Word builds a page onscreen or on the printer, it handles tab characters in a very straightforward way. Word builds the line the way it always does and, when it hits a tab character, it moves the insertion point to the next tab stop.

EXERCISE

Intro to Tabs

1. Start with a new, blank document. If you don't have one showing, click the **New** icon .

2. Straight out of the box, Word ships with tab stops set up every half inch: there's a stop at 0.5", 1.0", 1.5", 2.0", 2.5", and so on. To see that, type an A then press the Tab key. Type another A and press **Tab**. Do it a couple more times. Your document should look something like Figure 10.35. See how the A's line up every half inch? (You might want to bring down the ruler by hovering your cursor just below the toolbar. Or, if you're really skeptical, print the document and use a real ruler. Go ahead. I won't be offended.)

FIGURE 10.35

Word's default tab stops are at every half inch.

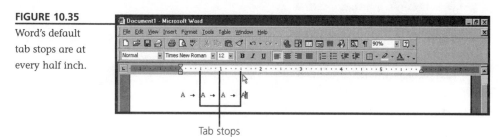

Tab stops

3. To see how tab characters and tab stops interact, type a long word or two, press the Tab key, and type one more A. You can see in Figure 10.36 that tab character lines the final **A** up at another half-inch hitching post.

FIGURE 10.36

Tab characters always move the insertion point forward to the next tab stop.

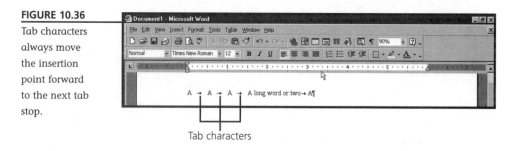

Tab characters

4. It's important that you see how Word puts this line together. It lays down the characters as you typed them. When Word hits a tab character, it zips down the line to the next tab stop. Then it continues laying down the characters you type.

5. Change the first tab stop so it appears at 1.25 inches instead of half an inch. To do so, click **Format**, **Tabs**, type 1.25 in the box marked **Tab stop position**, and click **Set**, **OK** (see Figure 10.37). When you set up a tab stop manually, as we just did, Word wipes out all the preceding default tab stops. So now, instead of having tab stops at 0.5", 1.0", 1.5", 2.0", 2.5", and so on, this line has tab stops at 1.25", 1.5", 2.0", 2.5", and so on.

FIGURE 10.37

Setting a new tab stop at one and a quarter inches.

6. Note in Figure 10.38 how the whole line has moved to the right, because the first tab character doesn't stop Word until it gets to the 1.25 inch mark.

7. Play with this document until you feel comfortable with the way Word handles tab stops and tab characters. Remember that tab characters are just characters—they can be copied, deleted, and moved from one document to another. But the tab stops are buried (invisible) in the line. When you're finished, close the document and don't save changes.

DIFFERENT TYPES OF TABS

You might have noticed in Figure 10.37 that Word supports different tab alignments. A left-aligned tab is the kind of tab you're accustomed to. A right-aligned tab forces characters to sit to the left of the tab stop. Centered tabs center text on the tab stop. Decimal aligned tabs are usually for currency, so all the decimal points line up. The Bar tab listed in Figure 10.37 has nothing whatsoever to do with tabs. It draws a vertical line inside the paragraph at the indicated location. It's like a Borders setting, except it's inside the paragraph. I've been railing against Microsoft about this one for years—it doesn't belong in the Tabs dialog box.

After my diatribe in the previous section, it probably won't surprise you very much to learn that *tab stop information is stored in the paragraph mark.* Think about that for a minute. It's not at all what you would expect. But it goes a long, long way toward explaining why tabs can be so infuriating!

FIGURE 10.38

The first tab stop changed to 1.25 inches.

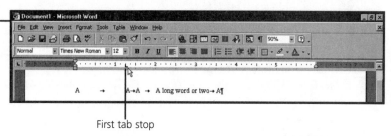

First tab stop

 EXERCISE

Tab Stop Propagation

1. Start with a new, blank document.

2. Press **Enter** five or six times, and then click back at the beginning of the document. Each of the paragraphs in this new document has "default" tab stops at 0.5", 1.0", 1.5", 2.0", and so on.

3. Type an A, press the **Tab** key, type another A, press the **Tab** key again, type a long word or two, press **Tab**, and type one more A. Your document should look like Figure 10.39.

4. Change the first tab stop. Click **Format**, **Tabs**, type 1.25 in the box marked **Tab stop position**, and click **Set**, **OK** (refer to Figure 10.37). Again, the tab stops for this paragraph are now at 1.25", 1.5", 2.0", 2.5", and so on.

SETTING TAB STOPS

In the old days of the typewriter, tab stops were typically set up for an entire document. (Although you could, if you felt sufficiently masochistic, change tab stops at any moment.) Word doesn't work that way. Word has you set up tab stops for each paragraph, and it stores the tab stop information in the paragraph mark.

You can't even change tab stops for the various lines inside a paragraph. If a paragraph is 10 lines long and the first line has tab stops at 1.0", 3.0", and 5.0", then *every* line in that paragraph has tab stops at 1.0", 3.0", and 5.0". Period.

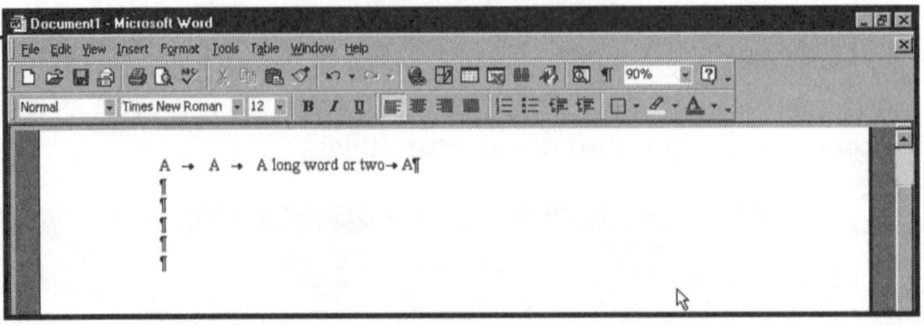

FIGURE 10.39

Tab stops at the default locations.

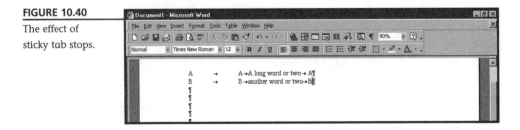

5. Now, with the insertion point sitting immediately in front of the paragraph mark on the first line, press **Enter**. The new paragraph will inherit the tab settings from the original, first paragraph. Verify that by typing a B, pressing the **Tab** key, typing another B, pressing the **Tab** key again, typing a long word or two, pressing **Tab**, and typing one more B (see Figure 10.40).

FIGURE 10.40

The effect of sticky tab stops.

6. Move on to the next line by pushing the right arrow or down arrow. (*Don't* press the **Enter** key.) Try typing a C, and then press **Tab**, type another C, press **Tab**, type a long word, press **Tab**, and type one final C. See in Figure 10.41 how the tab stop information in this paragraph hasn't changed?

FIGURE 10.41

But the original paragraphs still have the old tab stops.

7. When you're done working with the file, close it and don't save changes.

I'd guess that 90 percent of the beginning Word users I know start trying to use tabs within a few weeks of discovering Word. They'll change the tab stops in one paragraph, and then start pressing **Enter** and they can't figure out why in the world the tab stops stick. Then they wonder how to get their old tab stops back. I personally wasted several days (weeks?) trying to figure out how this works. Far as I know, it isn't documented anywhere. But Word has always worked this way, and it behaves very similarly with bulleted and numbered lists. We'll see that in the next section.

TIP

RULES TO LIVE BY

There are three hard and fast school-of-hard-knocks rules I've come up with for dealing with tabs. Ignore them at your own peril!

1. Don't use tabs unless you have to.

2. If you have to use tabs, press **Enter** many times before you start setting tab stops. That way, you can always move down in your document and pick up a *virgin* paragraph mark—one with no tab stop formatting information, other than the default tab stop every half inch—if you need one.

3. The only real way to deal with the multiple-line/single-paragraph dichotomy is to simplify the way you set up lines that will contain tab stops. I *always* set things up so each line that will contain a tab stop is one single paragraph. Sounds complicated? It isn't. Let me illustrate what I mean in this final tab stop exercise.

SO WHEN DON'T YOU NEED TO USE TABS?

Tabs rarely rate as the easiest solution to a Word problem. If you want to indent the first line of a paragraph, don't use a tab, set the **Format**, **Paragraph**, **Special First line indent** value, as discussed earlier in this chapter. If you just need columns of text or pictures, use a table. (We'll discuss tables in the next chapter.) If you want to put an entire paragraph on the right edge of the page, use the **Align Right** icon.

EXERCISE

A Fill-in-the-Blanks Form

1. Start with a new blank document.

2. We're going to create a simple fill-in-the-blanks form, the kind of form you see every day. It will have slots for a name and two lines for address (city,

state, and Zip). Sounds like it should be easy, but it isn't. In fact, if you've tried to do this on your own, guided by those other books and Word's online help, you might think it's impossible!

3. Press **Enter** 8 or 10 times. You can never have too many virgin paragraph marks. Move the cursor back to the beginning of the document.

4. Type Name: and press the **Tab** key twice. Your form should look like Figure 10.42.

FIGURE 10.42

Starting the first line of the form.

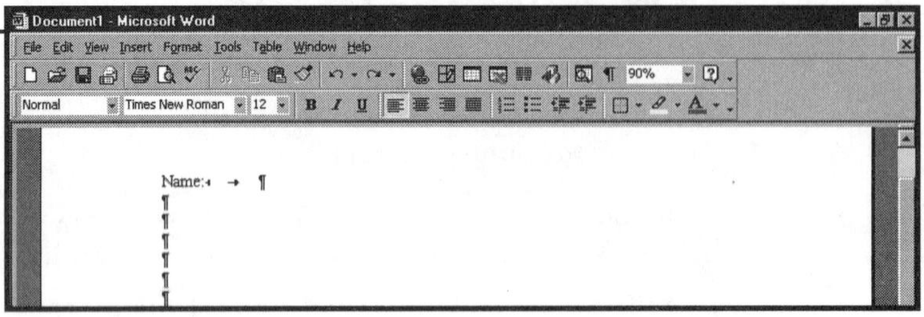

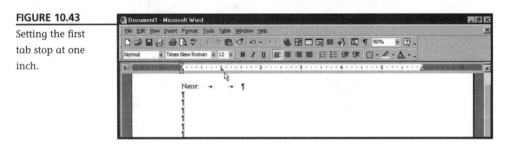

5. We want to set this line up so **Name:** appears on the left margin then there's a space, and then a line where the respondent can type her name. Measuring from the left, we'll make that line begin at 1.0" and extend to the 6.0" point. There are lots of ways to draw that line, but here's the easiest.

6. Click **Format**, **Tabs**. Type 1 in the box marked **Tab stop position**, and click **Set**, **OK**. That puts a tab stop at 1.0", so the tab immediately after **Name:** will advance Word up to the 1.0" mark (see Figure 10.43).

FIGURE 10.43

Setting the first tab stop at one inch.

7. Now you need to draw an underline from the 1.0" point to the 6.0" location. One way to do that is to set up a tab stop at 6.0" and tell Word that you want to use an underline *leader*. A *leader* (rhymes with *feeder*) is just a bunch of repeated characters that lead up to a tab stop. You've no doubt seen the period used as a leader, for example, "John Smith.........800-555-1212". We'll use the underline character as a leader.

8. To do so, click **Format**, **Tabs** again. Type 6 in the box marked **Tab stop position**, click **4** (that's the underline) in the Leader pane, and click **Set**, **OK** (see Figure 10.44).

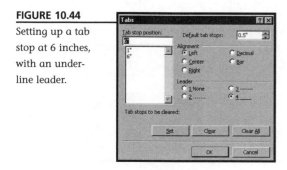

9. You should see a line that looks like the one in Figure 10.45. Congratulations. You've finished the hard part.

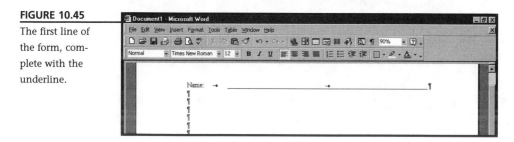

10. Now press **Enter**. Remember, Word copies the tab information from the old paragraph into the new paragraph—so you now have all the tabs set up for the next line of the form. Type `Address:` and press the **Tab** key twice. Your form should be taking shape, as shown in Figure 10.46.

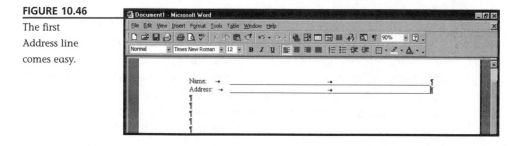

11. For the second address line, we just want a blank on the left with a line on the right, so press **Enter**, and then press the **Tab** key twice (see Figure 10.47). Do you see how the inherited tab stop information can come in handy?

FIGURE 10.47

The second address line with a blank on the left.

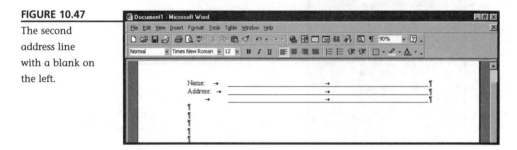

12. The next line has to hold city, state, and Zip, so we can't use the tab stops we've set up for the first three lines. Go down to the next line by pressing the right arrow or down arrow. (*Don't* press **Enter.**) That puts the cursor in front of a *virgin* paragraph mark.

13. Type City:, press **Tab** twice, type State:, press **Tab**, type Zip:, and press **Tab** one more time. Your document should look like Figure 10.48.

FIGURE 10.48

The last line of the form goes on.

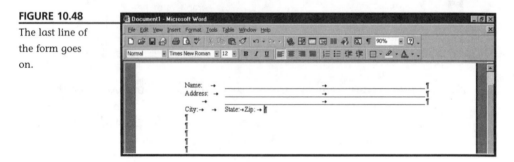

14. All that remains is setting up the tab stops for the last line. Here's how I did it. (No, you never get it right the first time. This one took a few tries, but each time I screwed up I pressed the **Undo** icon and started over again.) Click **Format**, **Tabs**, type 1, click **Set** (that's to start the first underline at 1 inch, so it'll be underneath all the others). Type 4; click **4** in the Leader pane and click **Set** (that's for the underline leading up to **State**). Type 5; click **4** in the Leader pane and click **Set** (that's for the underline leading up to Zip). Finally type 6, click **4** in the Leader pane and click **Set** (that's for the final underline). Click **OK** and your form will appear as shown in Figure 10.49.

FIGURE 10.49

The finished fill-in-the-blanks form.

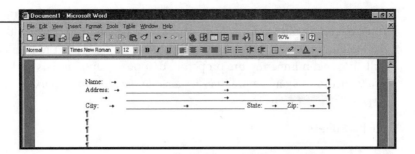

15. You really should be proud of this form. I know people who have used Word for years who haven't the slightest idea how to solve this problem. When you're done, close the document and don't save changes. (Or save it, just for bragging rights if you like.)

There's a definite rhythm to building fill-in-the-blank forms. Figure out what you want on a line, including how many tab characters you'll need. Type those in. Then go back and use **Format**, **Tabs** to draw the lines correctly. That works pretty well.

DID YOU SEE THAT?

There's one last technique from this example I'd like to emphasize. Did you see how I greatly simplified the problem by making each line its own paragraph? That's why I say, when you use tabs, create one line per paragraph, and one paragraph per line.

TIP

AVOID TABBING WITH THE RULER

You've probably noticed that tab stops appear on Word's horizontal ruler. Some people swear the only way to work with tabs is to drop and drag them on the ruler. Personally, I get so confused by the different kinds of tabs and indents and their funny pictures on the ruler, the bizarre rules for using the ruler to create new tabs, and the poor control offered by mousing tabs—how often do you want a tab at 1.01 inches?—that I gave up on tabbing with the ruler long ago. I suggest you avoid it too.

Bulleted and Numbered Lists

Word has an amazingly thorough—although not by any means complete—set of tools for bulleting and numbering lists. The only difference between a numbered and a bulleted list is that Word uses the same character (the *bullet*) to start out each paragraph in a bulleted list, and it uses different characters (typically, but not always, a sequence of numbers) to start out each paragraph in a numbered list.

You might be surprised to learn that the bullets and numbers aren't real characters. You can't select them, move them, copy them, delete them, change their colors using the toolbar, or do anything else you would expect to do with real characters. Nope. Bulleting and numbering are properties of a paragraph, and as such (tell me if you've heard this one before) *they're stored in the paragraph mark.*

EXERCISE

Sticky Bullets

1. Start with a clean new document.

2. Type a few paragraphs and press **Enter** once or twice more so there will be a supply of virgin paragraph marks at the end of the document, if you ever need them. In Figure 10.50 I've typed three paragraphs and pressed **Enter** one extra time.

FIGURE 10.50

Setting up a document for bulleting.

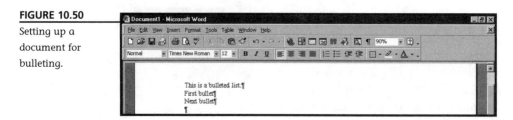

3. Select a couple of paragraphs in the document. Click the **Bullets** icon ▦ on the toolbar. You'll get two bulleted paragraphs, as shown in Figure 10.51.

FIGURE 10.51

Applying bullets to two of the paragraphs.

4. Put your cursor just before the paragraph mark at the end of the second bulleted paragraph. In this example, you'd put the cursor immediately after the text **Next bullet**.

5. Press **Enter**. The new paragraph is bulleted, as shown in Figure 10.52. Remember, bulleting is a formatting property of the paragraph mark, and when you press Enter, Word copies the formatting from the old paragraph mark into the new one. That's how you get a new bulleted paragraph. (If you've used Word more than a few days, I'll bet you've been wondering about that.)

FIGURE 10.52

Bulleting is another one of those sticky settings stored in the paragraph mark.

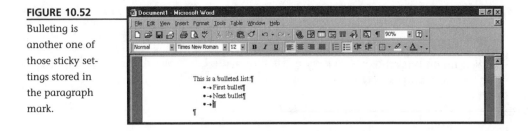

6. Fortunately, Microsoft built a bail-out sequence into this bulleting behavior. Press **Enter** one more time. Word has the smarts to realize that you probably didn't want another bullet point, so it bails out—automatically removes the bullet from the previous (empty) paragraph, and creates a new, non-bulleted paragraph (see Figure 10.53).

FIGURE 10.53

Press **Enter** again, and Word bails out of bulleting.

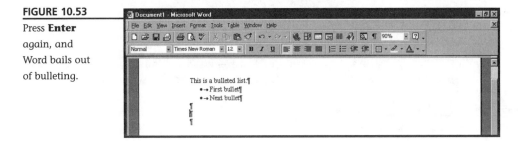

7. When you're finished, close the document and do not save changes.

Word behaves precisely the same way with numbered lists: Numbering is a sticky paragraph formatting option stored in the paragraph mark. If you press **Enter** while your cursor sits in a numbered paragraph, the next paragraph mark picks up the numbered formatting from the previous paragraph and the new paragraph is numbered too.

Just as with bulleted lists, numbered lists will bail out if you press **Enter** while the cursor is in an empty numbered paragraph.

As you've probably guessed, you can apply all sorts of bullets or numbers using the **Format**, **Bullets and Numbering** dialog box. Simply select the paragraph you want to format, click **Format**, **Bullets and Numbering**, and have at it.

USING HAPPY FACES

Yes, I know what you're wondering. If you want to use Happy Faces as bullets, click **Customize**, **Bullet**, scroll down to the Wingdings font, and look in the second row. You're welcome.

Bulleting options, on the **Bulleted** tab (see Figure 10.54), run the gamut from fairly subdued to absolutely wild. If you click the **Customize** button in that dialog box, you'll have a chance to choose any character—any character at all—as your bullet. If you pick **Picture**, you can use any picture available to Word, including clip art and heaven-knows-what-else.

FIGURE 10.54

The standard bullets Word has on offer.

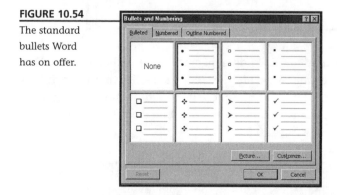

Similarly, the numbering options on the **Numbered** (see Figure 10.55) and **Outline Numbered** (Figure 10.56) tabs can be modified via the **Customize** button.

FIGURE 10.55

The stock Word numbering options.

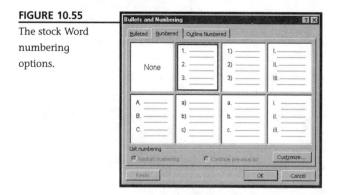

FIGURE 10.56

Word's outline numbering allows you to create different kinds of numbers at different levels.

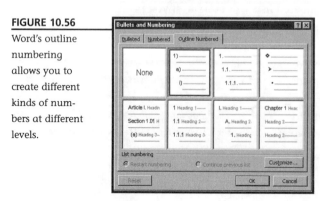

TIP

WORD NUMBERING AND SUB-NUMBERING LIMITATIONS

If you work in a legal office, you're bound to be wondering, just about now, if Word can do the kind of fancy numbering and sub-numbering that so seem to enamor attorneys and judges. The short answer: probably not. (Yes, I know; WordPerfect has been doing it for years. Don't yell at me. Yell at Microsoft.) Poke around the Outline Numbered tab's Customize dialog box and give it a shot—there's an enormous array of choices there—but don't be too surprised if Word just can't handle the peculiar breed of numbering that your office requires.

Ed Bott and I cover odd numbering schemes in detail in *Special Edition Using Office 2000* (Que, ISBN 0-7897-1842-1). To get more advanced numbering, you have to resort to Word's fields, but even then not all numbering methods—not even the common ones, for attorneys and legislators—can be accommodated.

Auto Bullets and Numbers

I hate it when computers think they're smarter than I am. (I particularly hate it when they *are* smarter than I am.) This is one of those situations, but if you're just starting out with Word, these automatic features might amount to more of a help than a hindrance. That's why I didn't tell you to turn them off in Chapter 6 "Word Preliminaries."

If you start a new paragraph, and then type the number 1 followed by a tab, Word assumes that you want to start a numbered list. It swallows up the real character 1 and replaces it with the imitation-numbering-formatted paragraph you came to know in the previous section. In most cases that's what you want, but in some cases, though, it's a pain.

MORE AUTONUMBERING TRIGGERS

In fact, Word will interpret any of a large number of things as the beginning of a numbered list. Typing **1** followed by a period, a space, and some characters will do it. Ditto for an A followed by a tab, or an A followed by a period, space, and characters. A closing parenthesis behaves the same way as the period. If you already have a numbered list somewhere in your document and you type a number that's close to the last number on the list, Word might pick that up too. So if your paragraphs suddenly kick into autonumbering—a very disconcerting experience for many—realize that what you're witnessing is Microsoft trademarked IntelliSense at work (I call it "In-telly-NON-sense"), and seriously consider turning it off.

TIP

HIT THAT BACKSPACE KEY!

If you press the **Backspace** key immediately after Word pulls its numbering-formatted paragraph switcheroo, you'll get your number back as a real character, and be able to continue typing without Word interfering.

Bulleting can kick in similarly if you start a paragraph with an asterisk, a dash (hyphen), a greater-than sign, or any of several combinations including -> and =>.

If you like the way Word does that, more power to ya. If you want to zap the behavior out, now that you understand what's going on, click **Tools**, **AutoCorrect**. Click the **AutoFormat As You Type** tab, and uncheck the boxes marked **Automatic bulleted lists** and **Automatic numbered lists**.

Formatting Sections

In general, I strongly recommend that beginners stay away from sections and using multiple-section documents. To tell the truth, I avoid sections, too, unless I have to change page numbering in the middle of a document. Even then I'm tempted to break the document into multiple pieces, put each piece in a separate document, and manage the page numbers in each separately.

If you feel you absolutely must use multiple sections in a document, flip over to Normal view (click **View**, **Normal**)—that way you can see the section breaks—then bring up the Office Assistant and search on **Section Breaks**. There isn't much information there, but it's more than enough to get you in all sorts of trouble. Just don't say I didn't warn you.

STARTING WITH A PAGE NUMBER GREATER THAN 1

Yes, it can be done, but boy is it difficult. If you want to start page numbering in a document with a number greater than one, you have to click **Insert**, **Page Numbers**, **Format** (see Figure 10.57). What a place to hide a setting, eh?

FIGURE 10.57
The starting page number gets set in this very obscure dialog box.

Formatting the Whole Document

Word gives you complete control over:

● The printable area on a piece of paper (which is to say, the margins);

● Whether pages should be laid out as Portrait (with the short side on top) or Landscape (turned sideways, with the long side on top); and,

● Which tray the printer should use to print the document, if it has more than one paper tray.

These and several other settings are in the Page Setup dialog box. Occasionally people can actually use these settings, but all too frequently they get screwed up, and you find that you need to change the settings back so your documents look normal.

Let me step through each of the four tabs in the Page Setup dialog box and warn you about the things that can, and do, go wrong.

⚠ CAUTION

BE CAREFUL!

One overriding warning: If you ever change anything in the Page Setup dialog box, make sure the **Apply to** box shows **Whole document**. If that box has **This point forward** showing, it means that Word has inserted a surreptitious (and nearly invisible) section break in your document, and your only hope—short of becoming an expert in Word sections—is to make a copy of the file, open it in Normal View, and delete all the section marks.

You needn't select the entire document before applying these formatting options. They're automatically applied to the entire document as long as the **Apply to** box shows **Whole document**.

Margins

The Page Setup dialog box's **Margins** tab (see Figure 10.58) lets you set margins— the boundaries of white space around the top and bottom of a document.

FIGURE 10.58

Beware of margins that are too small for your printer.

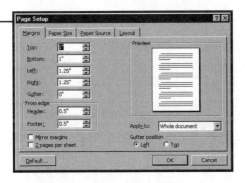

I commonly see three problems under the **Margins** tab.

- First, most printers can't print all the way out to the edge of a piece of paper. Many laser printers, for example, can't print in the last quarter inch. So if the margin on any side is less than the printer allows, you'll get a nasty message every time you try to print that says, **The margins are set outside the printable area of the page. Do you want to continue?**

- The second problem arises when someone mistakenly checks the **Mirror margins** box. That causes Word to print pages with margins that flip-flop, with odd numbered pages having different margins from even numbered pages. This is a very useful setting if you're printing both sides of each piece of paper and the printed pages will be bound into a book or stored in a binder. In most cases, though, it's just a mistake.

- The third problem arises from that funny box marked **2 pages per sheet**. If you suddenly see vast wastelands of empty space in the middle of your pages, look to see if this box has been checked accidentally. The setting can be useful—you can employ it to create brochure-like printouts, with two pages on a single sheet of paper—but you need to be working in Landscape mode (see the next section), and even then it's almost always easier to use the **Pages per sheet** setting in the File Print dialog box, if you don't mind the *squished* fonts.

☞ *For details about the Pages per sheet setting, see "Printing Documents," Chapter 7,* **page 106**.

Paper Size

The **Paper Size** tab (see Figure 10.59) on the Page Setup dialog box controls the size of the page you see on your screen. It doesn't necessarily have anything to do with the size of the paper you'll ultimately print on.

FIGURE 10.59

Where you control the size of paper Word thinks it will print on.

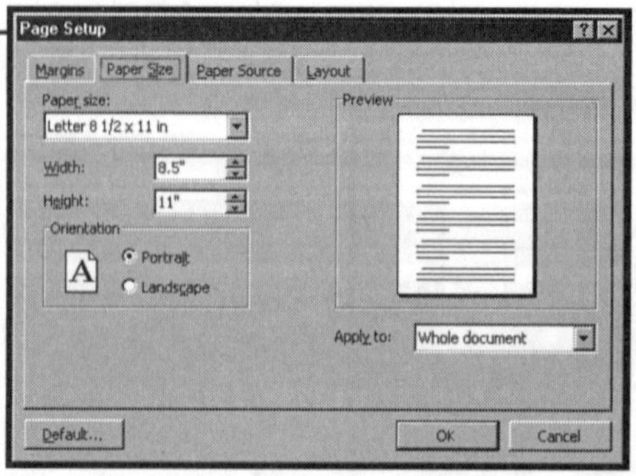

For example, if you want to design wedding invitations, you might find it advantageous to put the size of the invitation in this box, but print on normal-sized paper until you get the pages laid out precisely the way you want them. There's no requirement that these numbers match the dimensions of the physical piece of paper.

Sometimes the **Portrait** and **Landscape** get messed up, particularly if you've been poking around a bit and don't really work them much. If your pages suddenly start printing 90-degrees rotated from the way they should, this is where to look.

Paper Source

The **Paper Source** tab (see Figure 10.60) controls which paper bin your printer uses to print the document, assuming your printer has more than one paper bin.

FIGURE 10.60

Where the paper comes from.

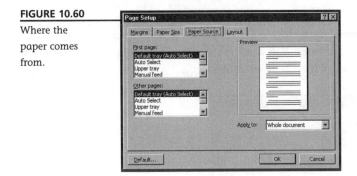

If you suddenly start getting weird error messages on your printer (typically appearing on the light panel on the front of the printer), this is one place to check. Similarly if your documents start printing on envelopes pulled from your printer's envelope feeder, chances are good this setting is causing the mayhem.

Layout

The **Layout** tab (see Figure 10.61) controls all sorts of things that can, and do, go wrong.

FIGURE 10.61

If your documents get spaced out this is the place to look.

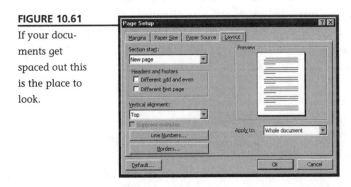

We'll talk about headers and footers in the next chapter, but this is where you tell Word if your document is to have a different header or footer for the first page (common in most kinds of manuscripts and reports), and whether there should be different headers or footers on even and odd pages (common for documents printed on both sides of the paper).

The truly bizarre setting on this dialog box is the one marked **Vertical alignment**. When Word is putting together pages in a document it looks at this setting to see how you want your paragraphs aligned, from top to bottom. If you start to get a lot of white space *between* paragraphs, it's possible that this box has been switched to **Justified**. In a worst-case situation, if you have Word keep the lines of paragraphs together, and the paragraphs are pretty long, each paragraph in a document could appear centered—centered from top to bottom—in the middle of its own page.

Ah, yes, it happens. More often than you think.

Finally, the **Borders** button in the lower-left corner of this dialog box connects you to the Borders and Shading's **Page Border** tab (see Figure 10.62). You can get to the same tab by clicking **Format**, **Borders and Shading**.

FIGURE 10.62

To put a border around an entire page—whether a simple line or fancy graphics—work on the Page Border tab.

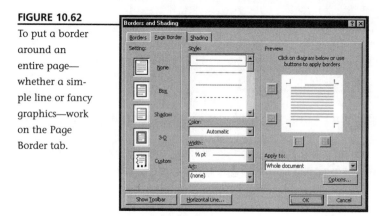

Page borders can be very simple or incredibly ornate. The rules for applying the borders are similar to the ones discussed earlier in this chapter for applying borders to paragraphs—with one important addition. Word also allows you to use any of a huge number of built-in graphics as page borders—from apples to firecrackers, from Christmas trees to palm trees, and many abstract designs to boot. To look through Word's extensive collection, click the down-wedgie in the **Art** box.

11

Woody Leonhard

TEACHES

KEY CAPABILITIES

TROUBLE AHEAD, TROUBLE BEHIND. Formatting only covers part of the Word story, of course. Working wordsmythes need much more. Learn to use Word's features the way they were meant to be used, and you'll save yourself an enormous amount of time every day. Ignore the features, and they'll pop up from time to time and bite you.

Features You'll Use Every Day

In this chapter I'm going to cover a hodgepodge of the most important Word features that most people will use every day:

- Headers and footers, which print at the top and bottom of every page in a document

- Spell checking, one of Word's niftiest features, is only one click away

- Using AutoCorrect to correct common mistakes and, more importantly, to speed up your typing

- Putting symbols of various types in your documents

- Printing envelopes and labels

- Forcing page breaks

By the time you're done with this chapter, you should have enough techniques under your belt to start whipping out documents like a-ringin' a bell.

Headers and Footers

Chances are pretty good you'll want a header or a footer in any document that runs longer than one page. Headers appear at the top of each page, and footers appear at the bottom. Word has a built-in toolbar that helps you with the most common kinds of text you'll want to see in your headers and footers—as you might imagine, the page number falls at the top of that list.

EXERCISE

A Simple Header and Footer

1. Open test.doc. (You probably have one left over from Chapter 10, "Making Documents Look Good"; if not, start with a new, clean document, and type a few paragraphs of text.) If test.doc is less than one page long, copy some text and repeatedly paste it until you have more than one page, and then save the new test.doc (click the **Save** icon on the toolbar).

2. Click **View**, **Header and Footer**. Word propels your cursor up into the top margin, where the header goes, and present you with the Header and Footer toolbar (see Figure 11.1).

FIGURE 11.1

Word prepares
you for creating
a header.

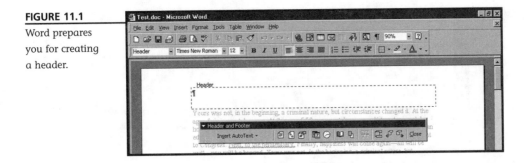

FIGURE 11.1

Word prepares
you for creating
a header.

3. Type a few words, press the **Tab** key, type another word or two, press **Tab**, and type a few final words. Word sets things up so the words you typed are left-aligned, centered, and right-aligned on the page (see Figure 11.2).

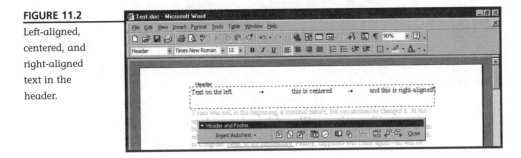

FIGURE 11.2

Left-aligned,
centered, and
right-aligned
text in the
header.

4. Click the **Switch Between Header and Footer** icon on the Header and Footer toolbar. You'll end up in the document's footer (see Figure 11.3).

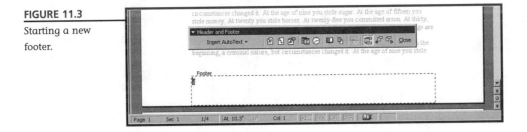

FIGURE 11.3

Starting a new
footer.

5. Press the **Tab** key, type Page and a space, and then click the **Insert Page Number** icon. Next type a space, the word of, and another space, and then click the **Insert Number of Pages** icon (see Figure 11.4). See how Word helps you out with these nifty features? They can be very handy, if you know they're there!

FIGURE 11.4

FIGURE 11.4

Using Word's
page number
and number of
pages values in
the footer.

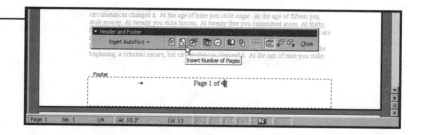

6. Press **Tab** again, type `Printed` and then a space, click the **Insert Time** ⊘ icon, type another space, and then click the **Insert Date** 📅 icon (see Figure 11.5).

FIGURE 11.5

Time and date
in the footer.

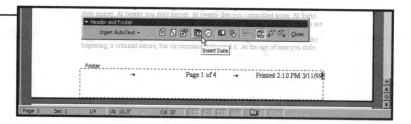

7. Click **Close** on the Header and Footer toolbar. That puts your cursor back inside the document, and your new headers and footers appear grayed out at the top and bottom of each page. Scroll through test.doc and verify that the same headers and footers (with the correct page numbers) appear on every page in the document.

8. If you want to change a header or footer, just double-click it. Word puts your cursor inside the header or footer, brings up the Header and Footer toolbar, and lets

BUT WHICH TIME IS IT?

Although you see the current date and time in test.doc right now, every time you print test.doc the time and date (and page number and total number of pages, for that matter) get updated by Word before the document is printed. All these icons—page number, number of pages, date and time—put fields in your headers or footers. We'll talk about fields in Chapter 14, "Advanced Features," but for now suffice it to say that these fields get updated immediately prior to printing. So if you save this version of test.doc and print it a week from today, the time and date shown on the printed page will be the time and date when the document was printed.

you make whatever changes you like. Note, however, that any changes you make show up on *all* the pages in the document. You can put anything you like—even pictures—in headers and footers.

TIP

GET BACK, JACK

You needn't click **Close** in the Header and Footer toolbar to get back to the document—simply double-clicking inside the document does the trick.

9. Close test.doc without saving changes.

Different First Page

Although there are many tricks you can play with headers and footers, the most important trick you're likely to need concerns headers and footers on the first page of a document.

NOTE

WHY DIFFERENT?

In most documents you're going to want to have a different header (and possibly a different footer) on the first page. For example, if you put together a multiple-page letter, the first page probably won't have any header at all. But the second and subsequent pages might list who the letter is from (or to) and a page number. Frequently, multiple-page memos work the same way.

Similarly, most reports won't have a header on the first page—you'll put the report title at the top of the first page and won't want the header to kick in until page two.

Word has a name for this concept: 'It's called Different First Page, and it frequently confuses the living daylights out of first-time Word users. I'll show you how to cope in the following exercise.

EXERCISE

Different First Page Headers

1. Open test.doc. I'm going to show you the easiest way to put page numbers at the bottom of all the pages in a document, and only put the document's title on the top of the second and subsequent pages.

2. Click **File**, **Page Setup**. Click the **Layout** tab. Then check the box marked **Different first page** (see Figure 11.6). This tells Word that you want to have different headers and footers on the first page of test.doc—different in the sense that headers and footers on the second and all subsequent pages are the same, but the header and footer on page 1 are different. Click **OK**.

FIGURE 11.6

Setting the document to have different headers and footers on the first page.

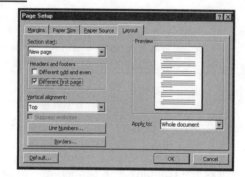

3. We don't want a header on the first page, so let's start with the second page. Scroll down to the second page of test.doc and click anywhere on the second page. Click **View**, **Header and Footer**. Word goes to the header (this is the header for the second and subsequent pages), and shows the Header and Footer toolbar. Type something appropriate (see Figure 11.7).

FIGURE 11.7

The header for the second and subsequent pages.

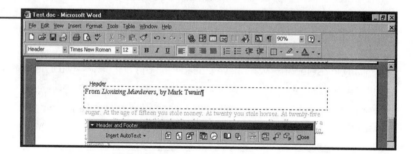

4. Click the **Switch Between Header and Footer** icon on the Header and Footer toolbar. Word goes down to the footer for the second and subsequent pages. Type whatever you like down here. In Figure 11.8, I pressed **Tab** twice, typed **Page** and a space, and clicked the **Insert Page Number** icon.

5. Click **Close** (or double-click inside the document). Now scroll through test.doc. You'll find headers and footers starting on page 2, and going for the length of the document. But you won't find hide nor hair of a header or a footer on page 1.

FIGURE 11.8

Setting up the page number on the second and subsequent pages.

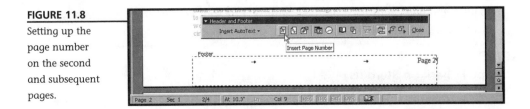

6. To put a footer on the first page, click once on the first page, and then click **View**, **Header and Footer**. Word puts you in the header—note how it's marked First Page Header—so click the **Switch Between Header and Footer** icon on the Header and Footer toolbar.

7. You are now inthe First Page Footer. Type something interesting. In Figure 11.9, I've pressed the **Tab** key twice, typed Page and a space, and clicked the **Insert Page Number** icon—the same way I put together the second (and subsequent) page footer.

FIGURE 11.9

Setting the first page footer.

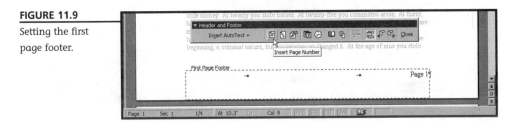

8. Click **Close** or double-click inside the document. On page 1 you should have a footer with the page number, but no header, and the other headers and footers throughout test.doc should remain unchanged.

9. Close test.doc and don't save changes.

That's how you put together professional headers and footers.

Right-click Spell Check

When you type a word that Word doesn't recognize, Word puts a red squiggly line underneath it. You can right-click a word with a squiggly red line under it and, most of the time, Word offers you a correctly spelled version of the word. Move down to whatever spelling you like, let loose of the mouse button, and *boom!*—the chosen word takes the place of the misspelled word.

Right-click spell check is a very cool feature, one that you've probably already discovered and used. But it's only the tip of the iceberg. Let's look a little deeper.

EXERCISE

Spell Check on Steroids

1. Create a new document. Type something that Word's built-in dictionary won't recognize. In my case, that's easy—Word doesn't know how to correctly spell my last name (see Figure 11.10). When you type something Word doesn't recognize, it'll get a squiggly red underline.

FIGURE 11.10

Word's built-in dictionary doesn't *recognize* Leonhard, so it gets the *squigglies.*

2. Right-click a word with the red squiggly underline. Word makes a guess—usually a very good guess—at what you meant. If you misspelled the word and can find the correct spelling on the list, scroll down to the correctly spelled word and let go of the mouse button. In Figure 11.11, Word guesses that I meant either *Leonard, Leon hard,* or *Leonardo.* I didn't, of course.

FIGURE 11.11

Word guesses *Leonard, Leon hard* or *Leonardo.* Bzzzzzzt.

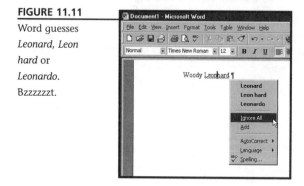

3. Each of the options listed in the right-click context menu, shown in Figure 11.11, holds interesting possibilities. The first option after the suggested correct spellings, **Ignore All**, tells Word to ignore this word throughout the current document. If you've typed a word that you aren't likely to use again in other documents, that's a good choice.

4. On the other hand, if you expect to use the word in other documents, it is a good idea to choose **Add** (as in Figure 11.12). By doing so, you're telling Word to put this particular word in your custom dictionary. The custom dictionary is treated like other Word dictionaries, so the next time you type this particular word, it'll be in the dictionary. That way, Word knows that it shouldn't receive a red squiggle.

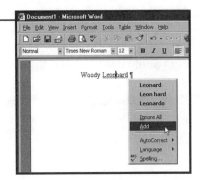

5. Ah, but what if you make a mistake? What if you put a word into your custom dictionary, and you discover that you screwed up? How do you *remove* a word from your custom dictionary?

6. It's amazingly easy, if you know the trick. Click **Tools**, **Options**, and then click the **Spelling & Grammar** tab. Highlight the name of your custom dictionary (which, per Figure 11.13, is usually custom.dic); click the **Dictionaries** button, and then click **Edit**. Word opens the custom dictionary and lets you add, delete, or change any of the entries.

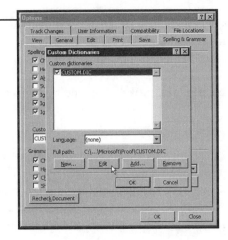

SPELLCHECKUS INTERRUPTUS

Word stops spell checking whenever you edit a custom dictionary. To get automatic spell checking going again, click **Tools**, **Options**, and then the **Spelling & Grammar** tab, and check the box marked **Check spelling as you type**.

7. The next option in the right-click context menu lets you add this word to your AutoCorrect list. I'll talk about AutoCorrect in the next section, but here it's important to note what Word is offering to do. In Figure 11.14, Word offers to automatically correct the word *Leonhard*, turning it into *Leonard*, every time you type *Leonhard*. That might or might not be what you want to do—it certainly isn't anything *I* would do—so make an informed decision.

FIGURE 11.14

A quick tunnel to AutoCorrect, from the right-click spelling context menu.

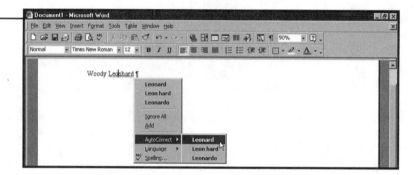

8. In the final entry, Word offers to send you into the full-blown Spelling and Grammar dialog box—the same one you can get to by clicking **Tools**, **Spelling and Grammar**. This batch-mode spell checker, where Word checks spelling for the whole document, almost always amounts to overkill; I never use it.

9. Play with right-click spell check for a bit. When you're comfortable with the options, click **File**, **Close**, and don't save changes.

Remember, you *can* fix any mistakes you make when adding items to your custom dictionary.

AutoCorrect

AutoCorrect is Word's number one productivity enhancer—hands down. If you learn the tricks to using AutoCorrect, you can boost your effective typing rate enormously. Some of those older Word books tell you to use a feature called AutoText. *Balderdash!* For most people, in most situations, AutoCorrect has AutoText beat to smithereens. I'll show you why.

When a Correct Is a Correct

By now you've no doubt seen AutoCorrect in action. If you type *teh*, Word changes it to *the*—and doesn't even bother to tell you. Here's what's happening behind the scenes. Word keeps track of what you're typing. When you press the spacebar or type a punctuation mark, Word looks at the word you've just typed and checks to see if it has an entry for that word in the AutoCorrect list. If there's an AutoCorrect entry, whatever you typed is replaced with whatever sits in the entry.

So, for example, Word has an AutoCorrect entry for *teh*. That entry says that *teh* is to be replaced by *the*. Every time you type *teh*, followed by a space or a punctuation mark, Word looks up *teh* in its AutoCorrect list and changes it to *the*. And the change occurs very, very quickly.

Check Out Word's Built-in AutoCorrect Entries

1. Start with a new document.

2. Type a commodate. Note the misspelling (see Figure 11.15). I misspelled that word in a fourth-grade spelling bee, and never forgot it. Amazing how Word can effectively cope with so many childhood traumas!

FIGURE 11.15

Word "acom-modates" many misspellings.

3. Now type a space or a punctuation mark. Word changes *acommodate* to *accommodate*, as any, uh, accommodating program should.

4. Let's go see why. Click **Tools**, **AutoCorrect**. At the bottom, scroll down to the entry marked **acommodate** (see Figure 11.16). That's where Word picked up on the idea that it was supposed to swap out *acommodate* and swap in *accommodate*.

5. Scroll through the list of words that Word will correct for you. It's an enormous, impressive list—thousands of words.

6. Click **Cancel** to back out of the dialog box.

FIGURE 11.16

Where the
accommodation
occurs.

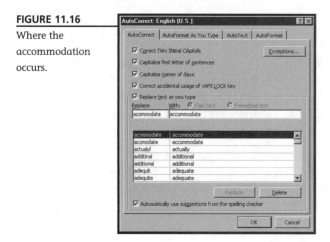

Bending AutoCorrect to Your Own Devices

You can add your own entries to the AutoCorrect table. It's very important that you understand that *these entries need not be spelling corrections!* You can put anything you like in here, and if you organize things well, you can speed up your typing enormously.

EXERCISE

Make Your Own AutoCorrect Entry

1. You can keep working with the document you used in the previous exercise, or you can start a new one. Say you work for a company called Spacely Sprockets, Inc., and you type that company name a gazillion times a day.

2. Press **Enter** a few times, and then type Spacely Sprockets, Inc. in the document.

3. Select **Spacely Sprockets, Inc.** (see Figure 11.17). Be *very* careful not to select the paragraph mark at the end.

FIGURE 11.17

Selecting
**Spacely
Sprockets,
Inc.**

4. Click **Tools**, **AutoCorrect**. Type spac in the **Replace** box (see Figure 11.18), and then click **Add**.

FIGURE 11.18

Adding *spac* to the AutoCorrect list so it comes out *Spacely Sprockets, Inc.*

5. Back out in the document, type spac, and press the spacebar. See how Word now "corrects" the, *ahem!*, misspelled *spac* into *Spacely Sprockets, Inc.*?

6. When you're done, delete any bogus entries you've placed in the AutoCorrect list by clicking once on each entry and clicking **Delete**. Click **OK** and close the document without saving changes.

Note how I didn't use the abbreviations *sp* or *spa*, both of which appear from time to time in various kinds of documents. You might see *sp.* as an abbreviation for spelling or space; and *spa* might appear any time. But *spac* is long enough that it shouldn't cause any confusion, yet short enough to memorize. I also could've used *ssi* or even something really short, such as *s#*, where the punctuation mark at the end would trigger an AutoCorrect replacement before you even pressed the **Spacebar**.

AutoText entries are a lot like AutoCorrect entries, except they require you to press the **Tab** key to expand. That's why they tend to be much more cumbersome than AutoCorrect entries—and why I recommend that you use AutoCorrect.

Symbols

Word supports an enormous variety of characters, as Dr. Seuss used to say, "On beyond zebra." Many weird characters appear in the common fonts that you're likely to have on your computer. If you install even stranger fonts, you're bound to see characters you've never even imagined—at least, not in this dimension.

To put an odd symbol in your document, first position the insertion point wherever you want the character to go. Then click **Insert**, **Symbol**, and click the **Symbols** tab. Leaf through the various fonts listed in the **Font** box (see Figure 11.19). When you spy the character that you want to put in your document, click it once and click **Insert**, or—much simpler—just double-click the character.

FIGURE 11.19

Inserting the Wingdings font's Wheel of Dharma character.

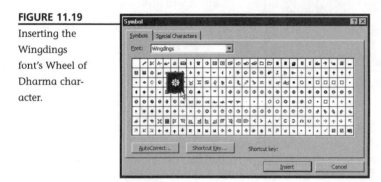

This same dialog box lets you turn a weird character into an AutoCorrect entry (so, for example, you can make the word *greekpi* automatically change into a Greek pi from the Symbol font), or assign a shortcut **Ctrl+Alt** style key combination to the character.

The **Special Characters** tab on this dialog box (see Figure 11.20) lets you insert common and page markup characters without the hunt-and-peck searching that is generally required to find other symbols. It's also a good place to find the shortcut key combinations that let you put those characters in your documents with a minimum of fuss, if you are so inclined.

FIGURE 11.20

Special characters—primarily typesetting and markup characters—sit on the Special Characters tab.

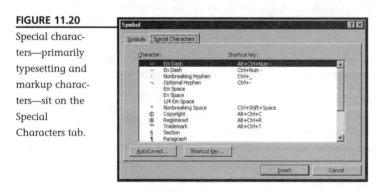

Envelopes and Labels

You'll never need to hand-address an envelope again. After you've printed your first Word envelope, it'll be faster to type an address into Word, select it, and print an envelope than it ever would be to address it by hand. Plus, if you use Word's built-in features, the envelope will get there quicker because it will include the correct POSTNET bar code.

EXERCISE

Print an Envelope

1. Start with a new document. Type a name and address.

2. Click **Tools**, **Envelopes and Labels**, and then the **Envelopes** tab (see Figure 11.21). Make sure that the recipient's address (**Delivery address**) and your return address are correct.

FIGURE 11.21
Verify addresses in the Envelopes dialog box.

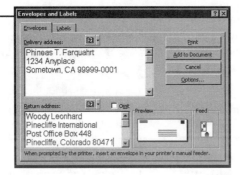

TIP

THE NAME GRAB

Word usually does a good job of snatching the name and address from an underlying document, but if it has trouble with one of yours, select the name and address before clicking **Tools**.

3. If you haven't set up Word to print envelopes the way you like, click the **Options** button.

4. If you want to print a USPS POSTNET bar code on your envelopes (that's the bar

WHAT ARE THOSE FUNNY ICONS?

The Envelopes dialog box has two funny icons, both of which look like an open book with a down-arrow to the right. When you get Outlook set up, these icons transport you to your Outlook Contacts list. The one on top sticks a Contact entry into the recipient box. The one on the bottom does the same for your return address. They can be very handy if you need to double-check an address or swap among several different return addresses.

code that enables automatic sorters to route your mail), click the box marked **Delivery point barcode** (see Figure 11.22). Note that Word prints the POSTNET bar code immediately above the name and address of the recipient.

FIGURE 11.22

Printing enve-
lope bar codes
is just a click
away.

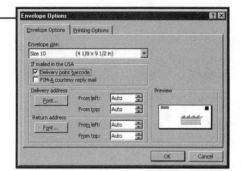

5. Chances are pretty good that Word figured out how you need to feed envelopes into your printer. (Check your printer manual, but you probably need to feed them manually, possibly through a special tray.) Just to make sure that Word got it right, click the **Printing Options** tab, and make any necessary changes (see Figure 11.23). Click **OK** to return to the Envelopes dialog box.

6. When you're convinced that everything is set up properly, click **Print**. Don't be too surprised if the envelope doesn't turn out right the first time—it rarely does. Keep jiggling the **Printing Options** tab settings and refer constantly to your printer manual until it comes out right. It's definitely worth the effort.

WHY DOES THE BAR CODE PRINT ABOVE THE RECIPIENT'S NAME?

I've wondered about that, too. Apparently Microsoft took the U.S. Postal Service's original recommendations—several years old at this point—and decided that bar codes should go on top. In fact, the USPS doesn't require that the bar code go above the name. Their own machines put it in the lower-right corner, where the mail gods intended.

<Shameless self promotion alert> The first macro I ever wrote for Word 1.0 printed envelopes. Word's envelope features have improved greatly since then, but they still leave a lot to be desired. It's nearly impossible to put the bar code at the bottom of the envelope; you'll have a hard time printing a logo on the envelope; heaven help you if you need to center the return address. If you want a professional envelope printer, use WOPR, Woody's Office POWER Pack. If you buy *Special Edition Using Office 2000* by Ed Bott and Woody Leonhard(Que; ISBN 0-7897-1842-1), WOPR is included, free, on the book's companion CD.

FIGURE 11.23

Sometimes Word doesn't get the paper feed options quite right.

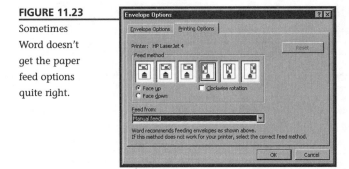

7. When you're done, keep the document open. We'll use it for labels in the next exercise.

Although Word's label printing capabilities might not win any awards for innovative features—it's impossible to print a return address on a large label at the same time you print the delivery address, for example—you will nonetheless discover that it handles the basics pretty well.

 EXERCISE

Make a Label

1. When you're back in that document with a name and address showing, click **Tools**, **Envelopes and Labels**, and then choose the **Labels** tab (see Figure 11.24).

FIGURE 11.24

Printing labels is easy and quick.

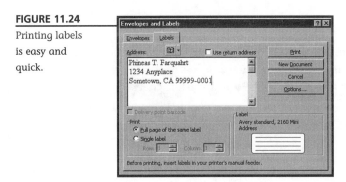

2. You have to tell Word what kind of labels you're using. To do so, click the **Options** button. You'll see the Label Options dialog box (see Figure 11.25).

FIGURE 11.25

Choose the
labels you're
going to use in
the Label
Options dialog
box.

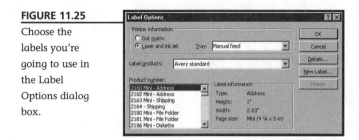

3. Those numbers you see on the left side of the **Product Number** box are
   Avery label product numbers. There's a good reason for that: Avery helped
   Microsoft build this part of Word!

4. If you're feeling very, very lucky, you can set up your own custom label sizes
   by clicking on **New Label**. Yes, it can be done, but it's not something I recommend for the faint of heart or the marginally sane. You'll have more fun
   watching *Teletubby* reruns. Don't say I didn't warn you.

5. Choose the type of label you're using, and then click **OK**.

6. If you want to print an entire sheet of the same label, click **Print**.
   Otherwise, follow the instructions in the dialog box or ask the Office
   Assistant how to print labels.

7. Close the document. Don't save changes.

Force a Page Break

Amazing how something so important can be so hard to find, eh?

If you want to force a page break—that is, force Word to start putting text on a new
page—put your cursor right in front of whatever is to appear on the new page, and
then click **Insert**, **Break**; make sure that **Page break** is checked, and click **OK**.

Speaking of breaks, now's so a good time to take one. When you're ready, come
back and we'll start to tackle some of Word's more esoteric features in Chapter 12,
"Special Purpose Tools."

12

Woody Leonhard

TEACHES

SPECIAL PURPOSE TOOLS

That Notion Just Crossed My Mind. In the preceding chapter we took a look at features you're likely to use all the time, day in and day out. In this chapter, I'm going to try to introduce you to some key features that most people won't use every day—but can be extremely handy if you come up against a specific problem.

Features You Won't Use Every Day

Word contains an enormous litany of features. If I tried to list and (barely) describe them all, you'd fall asleep after the first hundred pages or so. Riveting prose can only do so much.

The trick lies not so much in a recitation of features as in a synopsis of the features that can really come in handy, under the right circumstances. I've chosen to dwell on the following features:

- Word's tables
- Document Map, which is an essential tool for managing documents more than a few pages long
- Putting dates (and times) in documents, and why some of them change and some don't
- Putting pictures into your documents
- Combining existing documents to create new documents

Each of these features, under the right set of circumstances at the right time, can save your tail. So play with them a bit and remember that Word can cover these problems, too.

Tables

Word has several built-in methods for creating and formatting tables. The very first question you want to ask is, "Why would I use Word, instead of Excel, to make tables?" Here is the short answer: Use Word if you don't want to do any arithmetic. The minute you need to add columns of numbers or draw fancy graphs based on calculated numbers inside tables, Word craps out completely (although it can draw reasonably usable graphs if you have the data already crunched).

Someday, Microsoft will integrate Word and Excel a bit better. When that day comes, drawing tables in Word might fade into obscurity. For now, though, Word tables are the best way to solve a wide variety of common business problems.

Fast Pre-Fab Tables

Word has a high-level menu devoted entirely to tables, so it shouldn't surprise you too much to learn that there are lots and lots of table-related commands inside the program. Some of them actually crank out respectable-looking tables very quickly.

EXERCISE

A Quick Table

1. Start with a new, clean document.

2. Click **Table**, and then **Insert Table**. You'll see the Insert Table dialog box shown in Figure 12.1.

FIGURE 12.1

A very quick and dirty way to create a new table.

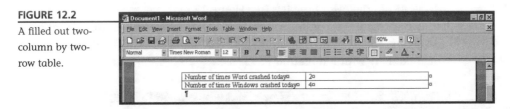

3. Type 2 in the box marked **Number of columns**, and then click **OK** to create a new two-column by two-row table. Type something in the first cell of the table, press **Tab** to move over to column number two, type something else, press **Tab** again, type more, and press **Tab** one last time to move to the final cell and type even more. Your screen will look like Figure 12.2.

FIGURE 12.2

A filled out two-column by two-row table.

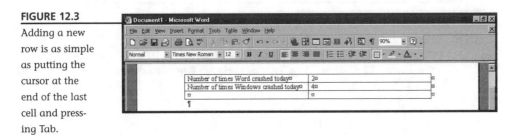

4. Here is the easiest way to create a new row in the table: Put your cursor at the end of the text in the final cell, and then press the **Tab** key. Word adds a new row on the bottom of the table and lets you fill it in (see Figure 12.3).

FIGURE 12.3

Adding a new row is as simple as putting the cursor at the end of the last cell and pressing Tab.

5. The table in Figure 12.3 has several components with which you might not be familiar. The sunburst-like stars at the end of each cell are called *end of cell markers*. They resemble paragraph marks in that they appear on the screen, but they don't print on the printer.

6. You'll also notice starburst markers at the end of each row, after the table cell proper. These are called *end of row markers* (ingenious terminology, eh?) and they, like the end of cell markers, contain formatting information. The last end of row marker, the one at the bottom, is an *end of table marker* (bet you saw that one coming). These markers aren't as mysterious as Word's paragraph marks because you can't easily copy, move, or delete them. Still, they hold important information. Treat them with respect.

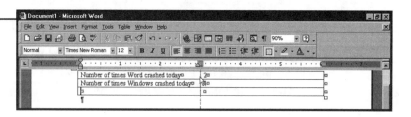

WHY HAVE AN END OF CELL MARKER?

Paragraphs end with a paragraph mark, and as you know (if you survived Chapter 10, "Making Documents Look Good," anyway), Word puts paragraph formatting in the paragraph mark. Well, Word table cells end with an end of cell marker, and Word stuffs both paragraph and cell formatting information into the end of cell marker. It's something of a super paragraph mark.

7. Move the cursor so it's hovering over the vertical line in the middle of the table. You'll see it turn into a double-headed arrow. Click and drag that middle vertical line toward the left (see Figure 12.4). Note how Word automatically pops a ruler up on the screen to help you align things. You can also adjust the height of rows or individual cells using this click-and-drag method. Play with it a bit and you'll see.

FIGURE 12.4

Click and drag any of the lines to adjust table dimensions.

8. Let's get rid of that blank row on the end. To do so, click over in the left margin, to the left of the first blank cell. The entire last row should be selected, as in Figure 12.5. Then click **Table**, **Delete**, **Rows** to delete the row.

FIGURE 12.5

Delete rows in
Word tables by
selecting them
and clicking
**Table, Delete,
Rows**.

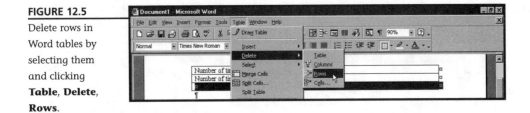

9. Try clicking on any of the **Table** menu items. You'll become immersed in the lore of Word tables.

10. When you're done, close the document and don't save changes. We'll create several more tables shortly.

Fast Free-Form Tables

If you know that your table is going to be rectangular, that is will have neat and orderly cells, and that it needs rows that are all of equal width, the **Table**, **Insert Table** method can't be beat. But if you're a bit more freewheeling, you'll probably get a kick out of this.

EXERCISE

Roll Your Own Table

1. Start with a new, clean document.

2. Click **Table**, **Draw Table**. Word responds by displaying the Tables and Borders toolbar, and turning your cursor into a table-drawing machine. Use the mouse to draw the outer boundary of your new table (see Figure 12.6).

3. Use the cursor to draw a couple of vertical lines in appropriately eclectic places. As soon as you let go of the mouse button, the lines turn into vertical lines in the table and cells appear (see Figure 12.7).

4. Now repeat the drawing motions, this time dragging left-to-right to come up with horizontal lines—the rows. Note that these rows don't have to go all the way across the table; they can begin or end on any vertical line. Cool!

5. When you're done being creative, step back and take a look at the table you've created, freehand. In Figure 12.8 I've come up with a table that contains five cells.

FIGURE 12.6

If you start by drawing the outer edges of your table, marking off the inside cells is quite simple.

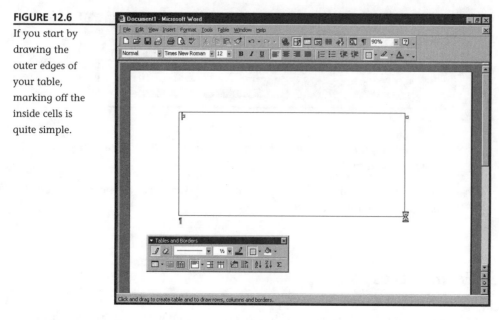

FIGURE 12.7

Simply draw vertical lines to define the columns of the table.

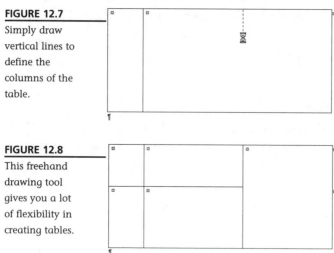

FIGURE 12.8

This freehand drawing tool gives you a lot of flexibility in creating tables.

6. What? You say you don't want one of the lines? Okay, nothing to it. Simply click the **Eraser** icon 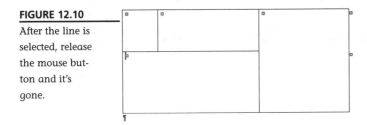, and then click the line you don't want anymore (see Figure 12.9).

FIGURE 12.9

Click on the Eraser and choose a line to erase.

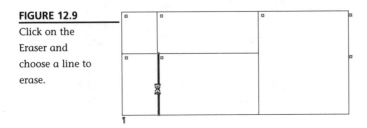

7. Let go of the mouse button and *poof!* The line disappears just like that (see Figure 12.10).

FIGURE 12.10

After the line is selected, release the mouse button and it's gone.

8. Try anything you want with the new table. Type text into the cells. Move the rows and columns around. You're the boss. When you get bored, close the document and don't save changes.

Note that the freehand drawing tool will work on any table—even tables that were originally created with the Table, Insert Table dialog box. In Figure 12.11 I've gone into just such a table, which was created originally as two-column by two-row, and added a mole's nest of odd cells. If you ever need to fabricate a bizarre table, this is the way to do it.

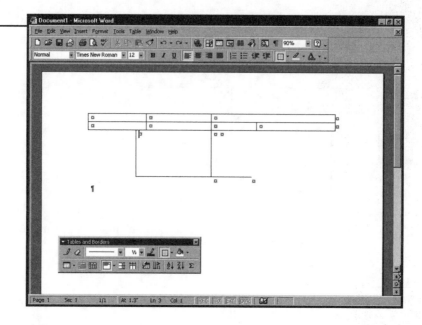

Fancy Tables

Although I can't begin to cover all the tools Word has available for drawing and modifying tables, there's one final table trick I use all the time, and I'd like to show it to you.

EXERCISE

AutoFormat—The Table Wizard

1. Start with a new, clean document.

2. Click **Table, Insert Table**, and then **AutoFormat**.

3. Word will present you with a huge array of table formats (see Figure 12.12). Simply choose one, click **OK**, and start typing in data.

4. The generated tables are real tables: You can modify them any way you want, or poke around to change some of Word's formatting options.

5. When you're done, close the document and don't save changes.

NOTE

AUTOFORMAT AT YOUR LEISURE

You can AutoFormat a table at any time. Simply click once inside the table, and then click **Table, Table AutoFormat**. The built-in tables pretty much assume that the first row in your table includes labels for all the columns. Other than that, it's pretty flexible.

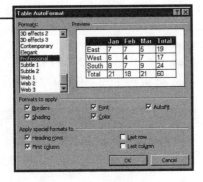

FIGURE 12.12

The Professional AutoFormat table offers quite a bit of built-in formatting.

Odd Ways to Use Tables

Most people think of tables as little boxy things, usually filled with boring statistics or streams of mind-numbing data. While it's certainly true that you can use Word to put anything to sleep—Word stands second only to PowerPoint in that department—it's also true that tables can solve all sorts of formatting problems.

TIP

THINK TABLES, NOT TABS

Here's a simple rule of thumb: If you're thinking of using tabs to organize a page in some way, chances are very good you can solve the problem easier, faster, and better by using tables.

One classic example is the résumé. In a résumé you typically want to keep headings on the left side of the page and line up detailed information indented on the right. If you try to create a résumé with indents or tabs, you'll be pulling your hair out before the first résumé even gets printed.

The trick is to build a big table with two columns. The leftmost column contains the headings, and the rightmost column contains text.

TABLES WITHIN TABLES

Starting with Word 2000, you can draw tables inside individual table cells. That becomes very important in a situation like the one in Figure 12.13, where you might want to use a table to format entries on the right side of the résumés. There's no trick to putting a table within a cell: just click inside the cell and insert the table.

The people who built Word's templates used this trick. Click **File**, **New**, and then go over to the **Other Documents** tab and double-click **Professional Resume.dot** (or any of the other résumés, for that matter).

What you see is a table. It's a bit difficult to visualize because you can't see the table's gridlines—but you *can* see the end of cell markers, which are a dead give-away. The people who created the template hid the gridlines. Click **Table**, **Show Gridlines**, and you'll see the whole table, as in Figure 12.13.

Tables have many uses. Don't get boxed in by table stereotypes. Get creative!

FIGURE 12.13

Word's prebuilt résumés all use tables.

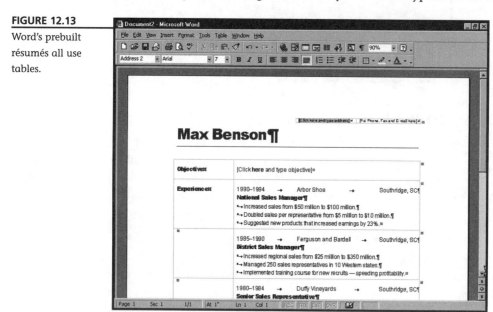

Document Map

If you ever work with documents that are more than a few pages long, you've prob-ably struggled with navigating through the beast: Scroll here, scroll there; move a paragraph from this spot to that; and *oops!* you forgot to add that little bit of text in the fourth chapter—if you could only *find* the fourth chapter.

Word 2000 has a wonderful feature called Document Map (DocMap for short) that gives you a "hot" outline of the document in a pane on the left-hand side. In Figure 12.14 you can see the text of *Alice in Wonderland*, with DocMap visible to its left. If you click on one of the DocMap entries—Chapter II, for example—Word propels you directly to Chapter II.

Note that you don't have to construct the document in any strange way—in particu-lar, sections don't matter (the document in Figure 12.14 is a single-section docu-ment). All that's necessary is an appropriate outline level for each paragraph. Using styles for chapter and sub-chapter headings helps you keep track of which outline levels appear where, but even styles aren't strictly necessary.

FIGURE 12.14

DocMap puts a fully navigable outline of the document in the left-hand pane.

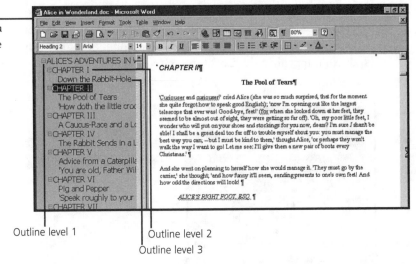

Outline level 1

Outline level 2

Outline level 3

To show the DocMap for an open document, just click the **Document Map** icon on the toolbar.

Entries in the DocMap are very similar to table of contents entries. They're controlled by paragraph outline levels: Level 1 paragraphs are at the "highest" level, so they appear all the way to the left in the DocMap; Level 2 paragraphs are next, so they're indented once from the left; Level 3 are next highest, so they're indented twice from the left; and so on.

There are two easy ways to change a paragraph's outline level:

- **You can apply a built-in Heading style to the paragraph**. To do so, click inside the paragraph, and then select a heading level in the **Style** drop-down box (the one that frequently says "**Normal**"). In Figure 12.14, you can see that the selected paragraph is formatted as "**Heading 2**". As you can probably guess, all "**Heading 2**" paragraphs are given an outline level of 2.

HEY, I THOUGHT THAT WAS NEW IN WORD 97!

While it's true that Microsoft put a Document Map feature into Word 97, the whole thing was so badly botched that only a masochist would live with it. Here's the primary problem: Word 97 takes it upon itself to scan every document as it's opened and assign heading levels to all the paragraphs. By doing so, any heading levels you've assigned are thrown away—and there's nothing you can do about it.

So here's a word of advice. If you use DocMap on a particular Word document, don't let *anybody* with Word 97 (or any earlier version of Word, for that matter) open the document. As soon as your carefully DocMapped Word 2000 document is opened in Word 97, all the level formatting will be irretrievably lost.

● **You can apply the outline level manually**. If you click inside a paragraph, and then click **Format**, **Paragraph**, Word gives you a dialog box (see Figure 12.15) that lets you set the outline level to "**Body Text**" (which doesn't appear in the DocMap), or to any level from 1–9.

FIGURE 12.15

The outline level drop-down list controls the "level" of a particular paragraph in the DocMap hierarchy.

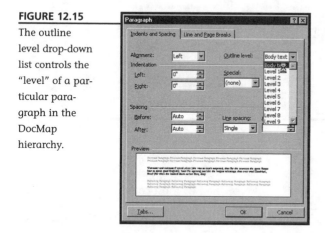

If you work with long documents—anything over, oh, three or four pages that has some sort of structure—try DocMap, and play with assigning outline levels both with the Heading styles and with the Format Paragraph dialog box. It's truly one of the most useful Word features.

Dates

If you want to put the current date or time in a document, the easiest way, by far, is to simply click **Insert**, and then **Date and Time**. You'll get the Date and Time dialog box, as shown in Figure 12.16.

FIGURE 12.16

Word lets you insert dates and times easily—but the Update automatically box can really fool you.

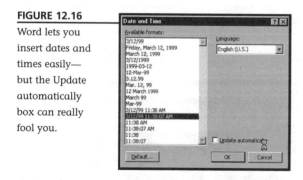

Unfortunately, there's a little box at the bottom of the dialog box that might drive you nuts. It says **Update automatically**, and you're to be excused if you don't understand what Word means by *automatically*. It's a simple concept, hard to explain, made even more difficult because there isn't much room in the dialog box to explain what's going on.

If you don't check that box, Word puts today's current time or date in the document, and that's that. Open the document an hour, a week, or a century from now, and the date or time you'll see there will be identical to the date or time you originally put in the document. Print it next month, and you'll get this month's date. It isn't updated.

On the other hand, if you check the **Update automatically** box, Word puts something called a *field* in the document. Fields can do many things—as we'll see in Chapter 14, "Advanced Features"—but on occasion this particular field retrieves the current date or time and puts it in the document. The process of looking up the current date or time and putting it in the document is called *updating the field*. Word updates fields under several circumstances, but the two most common ones are

- When the document is opened

- Just before the document is printed

There's an easy way to see what's going on.

EXERCISE

Updated Dates

1. Start with a new, blank document.

2. Click **Insert**, and then **Date and Time**. Choose one of the times that includes seconds, such as the one shown earlier in Figure 12.16. Make sure that the **Update automatically** box is unchecked, and click **OK**. You'll see the current time in the document.

3. Press **Enter** a few times. Then click **Insert, Date and Time**. Choose the same time as before—one that shows seconds—and check the **Update automatically** box. Click **OK**, and a later time will appear in your document (see Figure 12.17).

4. Now click the **Print** icon ⊞. Watch the second line in the document, the one with the "**Update automatically**" time. If you look very closely, you'll see it flicker, and then change, immediately prior to printing (see Figure 12.18).

FIGURE 12.17

There are two times in the document; the first is not updated, the second is.

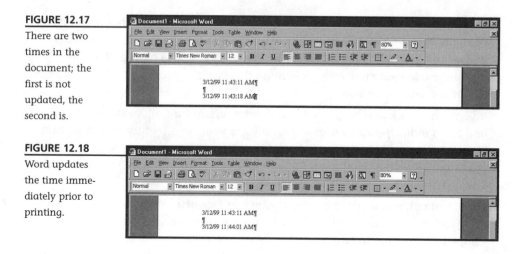

FIGURE 12.18

Word updates the time immediately prior to printing.

5. You can repeat that printing as often as you like. Immediately prior to printing, Word updates the time on the second line—but it leaves the time on the first line intact.

6. Close the document and save changes. Call it, oh, temp.doc. Open it. See how the second line has changed again? Whenever Word opens the document, it updates fields—and thus updates the time on the second line.

Inserting Pictures

And now for something completely different.

Word lets you place almost any kind of computerized drawing inside your documents. These same techniques work pretty much the same way in the other Office components, too, so let's take some time to explore them thoroughly.

Clip Art

The term *clip art* once referred to artwork that could be cut (thus the term, *clipped*) and pasted onto a sheet of paper. As far as Office is concerned, clip art is just a picture, sound, or video loop that you don't intend to change—you can move it around, resize it, chop off (*crop*) one or more of the edges, adjust the contrast or brightness, or draw a box around it, but you aren't going to change what's in the image itself, at least not from inside Office. That's what makes Office clip art, well, clip art. Therefore, if you're creating illustrations with another program (say, using

Collage to take screen shots, as I have with this book, or putting together freehand drawings with Microsoft's PhotoDraw or Corel Draw), those illustrations are just clip art from Office's point of view.

Office's Clip Art Gallery

Office ships with a fairly limited collection of clip art. To see it, click **Insert**, **Picture**, and then **Clip Art**. That brings up the Clip Art Gallery, shown in Figure 12.19.

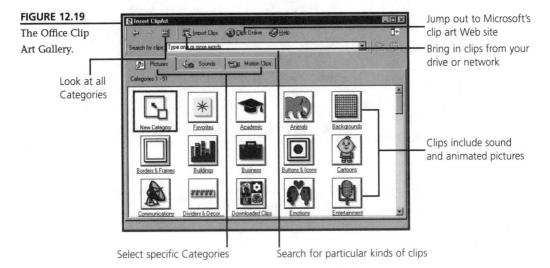

FIGURE 12.19

The Office Clip Art Gallery.

Jump out to Microsoft's clip art Web site

Bring in clips from your drive or network

Look at all Categories

Clips include sound and animated pictures

Select specific Categories

Search for particular kinds of clips

You can spend some time rummaging through the pictures that are offered here; when you find a picture that you want to put in your document, click on it, and then click the **Insert clip** icon; the picture gets transported back into your document.

I want to point out two specific features in the Clip Art Gallery. First, if you have clip art that you use all the time, it's relatively easy to import it into the Clip Gallery. Click the **Import Clips** button 🖳 and follow the instructions from that point.

Second, Office really does ship with a huge selection of clip art—it's just that you have to pop onto the Web to find it! If you have a Web connection established on your PC, click the **Clips Online** button 🌐 . Wait a little while (if you do this in the middle of a business day, wait a *long* while), and you'll ultimately be rewarded with thousands and thousands of high-quality clips, free, from the Microsoft Clip Gallery Live Web site (see Figure 12.20).

FIGURE 12.20

Getting to the mother lode Microsoft Clip Art Web site is as easy as clicking a button.

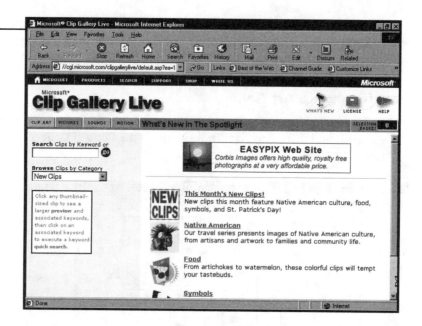

When you download clips from the Microsoft Web site, they're automatically stored on your hard drive and added to the Clip Art Gallery, so if you want the same clip again, there's no need to hook up to the Web.

Click the different tabs—**Pictures**, **Sounds**, and **Motion Clips**. Try going through the **Cartoons Category**, which has the largest collection. In particular, you might want to click on a **Motion Clip** and pick **Play clip**. Some of them are pretty interesting! No, it's not exactly high art, and you aren't going to want motion clips in documents that you print and send to the boss. But it is a neat trick that you can shove away in the back of your mind, just in case you might use it some day.

PUT THAT WALLET AWAY!

If you've ever thought of spending a hundred bucks (or even half that) on a clip art collection, make sure you've explored Microsoft's free site first. You might be surprised how extensive a collection you already own!

All the clips on the Microsoft site are royalty-free, so as long as you don't try to redistribute or sell them, you shouldn't have any problems. Full legal details are on the Web site.

Using Your Own Clip Art

If you ever need to put your own artwork into a Word document—and artwork in this context can mean almost any kind of picture file, sound, or animated video clip—you'll likely use the Insert Picture dialog box (see Figure 12.21). To get to it, click **Insert**, **Picture**, and then choose **From File**.

FIGURE 12.21

Office lets you insert any kind of artwork from this dialog box.

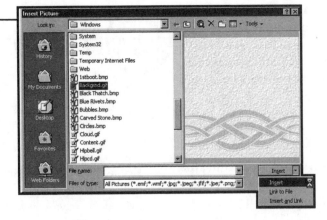

If you use the Insert Picture dialog box to bring artwork into your documents, the three choices in Figure 12.21 deserve your undivided attention:

● **Insert**. Puts the picture in your document.

● **Link to file**. Word doesn't actually put the picture in the document. Instead, it puts a *link*—a pointer to the file—inside the document. On the plus side, that means your document will be much smaller—pictures tend to consume a lot of space, whereas links take hardly any space at all. On the minus side, it means that you can't move the picture, and if you give this document to anybody else, you have to give them the picture file, too. Worse, they have to reconstruct your exact file structure and put the picture file in the same folder that you used in order for the picture to work right.

WHAT HAPPENED TO FLOAT OVER TEXT?

If you used the original version of Word 97 to put a picture in a document, you encountered some truly bizarre behavior: The picture was "floated over" the text (which is to say, Word put it in the Drawing layer). With the picture "floating" you couldn't attach a caption, the picture didn't move or adjust to inserted text the way most people thought it should, and it was awfully hard to understand that the picture you thought was firmly in the document was actually floating off in la-la land.

Microsoft heard so many screams from irate and horribly confused customers that they were forced to back off this dumb design decision. It was the single most frequently asked question about Word 97 that I encountered. I can only imagine how many tens of thousands of phone calls MS Technical Support had to field.

continues

● **Insert and link.** Puts the picture and a link in your document. That way, Word will try to pull the latest version of the picture into your document—but if it can't find the picture, it will use the one that's stored there. On the plus side, you're always assured of getting the latest version of the picture, if it's available; if it isn't available, Word can fall back on the image that is stored in the document. On the minus side, storing the picture in the document takes up lots of room.

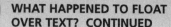

WHAT HAPPENED TO FLOAT OVER TEXT? CONTINUED

The first Service Release for Word 97 fixed this problem, but if you use documents created in the original version of Word 97 you might still encounter it. If you find a picture in an older document that's behaving very strangely, right-click on it, choose **Format Picture**, bring up the **Position** tab, and uncheck the box marked **Float over text**. That will take the picture out of the Drawing layer and put it in the document, where it belongs.

☞ talk about the Drawing layer in the "Drawing Layer" section of Chapter 8, on **page 112.**

Office supports a wide variety of file types. To see what kinds of files you can put into documents, click the down arrow on the **Files of Type** box and scroll through the list.

Of course, you can bring almost any picture into any Office document if you can get it on the Clipboard. Just create the picture by whatever means, click **Edit**, **Copy**, and then flip over to your Office program and click the **Paste** icon. We'll look at one way to do that in the next exercise.

GIMME MORE IMPORT FILTERS

Office uses small programs to bring picture files into documents. These programs are called *import filters*. They're necessary to translate from the format of the picture file into something that Office can understand. When you click the down arrow on the **Files of Type** box in the **Insert Picture** dialog box, what you're really looking at is a list of the import filters that have been made available to Office.

If you need to bring a particular type of file into an Office document and no import filter for that kind of file appears in this **Files of Type** box, try reinstalling Office, choosing a **Custom install**, and choosing from the import filters that are available there.

If that still doesn't get you the import filter you need, check the extensive collection indexed by Microsoft's Knowledge Base at www.microsoft.com/support.

Freehand (AutoShapes and the Drawing Toolbar)

If you're going to do extensive freehand drawing for a picture in an Office document, you'd be crazy to use the tools that are built in to the Office applications. They simply aren't robust enough to support any serious drawing effort.

Microsoft has a far more capable drawing program called PhotoDraw, which is available as a separate product or as part of the Office 2000 Premium Edition. If you need a full-blown drawing program, CorelDraw is still the most capable program on the market.

TIP

CALLOUTS?

What is a *callout*? Good question. In the World According to Word, a callout is a line that points to a picture, usually with some explanatory text attached. You'll see a Word-style callout in the next exercise. Unfortunately, the terminology for these things varies, so don't be too surprised if your favorite graphics artist has a different definition for the term *"callout."*

On the other hand, for the occasional quick drawing or picture callout, Office's AutoShapes and Drawing toolbars may suffice. Let me show you how.

EXERCISE

Picture and a Callout

1. Start with a new, clean document.

2. Let's take a screen shot, using the current screen, and put that in the document. (Cool, huh?) Press the **Print Screen** key on your keyboard (the Print Screen key might be marked as **PrtScr**, or some variation on that theme). That puts a shot of the current screen on the clipboard. To put it into your document, click the **Paste** 📋 icon. Your document should look something like Figure 12.22.

3. At this point you can move or resize the picture almost any way you want. Simply click it once, and then click and drag a corner to resize the picture without distorting it; drag an edge to resize and squish; or use the four-headed arrow to move the picture any place you like. You can even use the Format Picture toolbar that appears when you click the picture to really change things around.

4. Click **Insert**, **Picture**, **AutoShapes**. Word responds by putting the Drawing toolbar at the bottom of the screen and setting up an AutoShapes toolbar. We want the kind of AutoShape that is called a Callout, so click the **Callout** icon, as shown in Figure 12.23.

FIGURE 12.22

Using Word's built-in capabilities to put a screen shot in a document.

FIGURE 12.23

The AutoShapes toolbar organizes Office's extensive collection of prebuilt shapes.

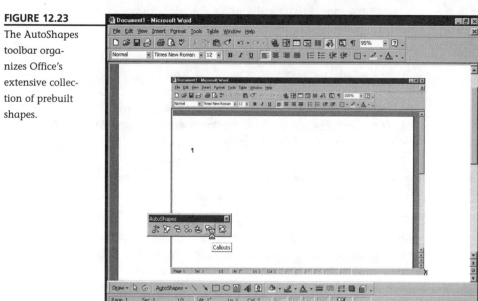

5. The type of callout that I like to use for most pictures is the one Word identifies as **Line Callout 3 (No Border)**. Look for it in the third column, fourth row of the various callouts that Word offers. Click it, and Word sets you up with a callout AutoShape.

6. Move your cursor next to the paragraph mark in the screen shot and press the mouse button. Then, holding the button down, draw to the bottom and right. When you have something that looks like Figure 12.24, let go of the mouse button. It's a little hard to describe but very easy to do.

FIGURE 12.24

Drawing a Line
Callout 3 (No
Border)
AutoShape.

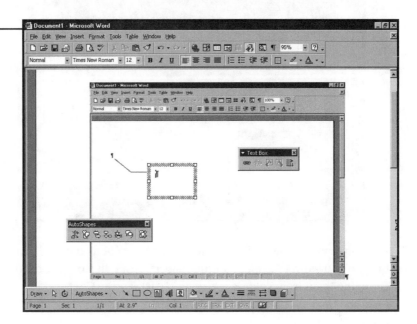

7. Here's the easy part. Type This is a paragraph mark, and then click outside the text box. Your document should look like Figure 12.25.

8. I won't take you through all the various formatting options available at this point, but they are extensive: colors, backgrounds, shapes, lines, all sorts of things.

9. You can spend days playingwith AutoShapes and the Drawing toolbar. When you figure you've had enough, close the document and don't save changes. To get rid of the Drawing tool-bar, right-click on an empty spot in any toolbar and uncheck the box marked **Drawing**.

WHO SHOT THAT ARROW?

Okay, just one formatting option. Click once on the callout, right-click on the callout's line, and choose **Format AutoShape**. Use the **Colors and Lines** tab to, oh, put an arrowhead on the callout. It's amazingly easy to do.

FIGURE 12.25

The finished callout.

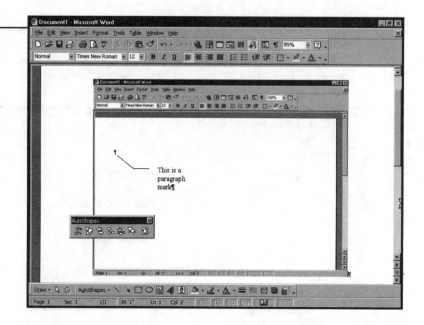

I've only touched the surface of the formatting options that are available with pictures. If you want to explore a little deeper—say, adjusting the contrast of pictures or changing them from color to grayscale—click **Tools**, **Customize**, check the **Picture** box, and then click **OK**. From that point, the Office Assistant can take you on a fantastic journey.

WordArt

Word hosts a program called WordArt, which can be used to create all sorts of fancy font effects; see, for example, Figure 12.26. You can use WordArt in any Office application.

I won't go into any detail here, except to say that you get to WordArt by clicking **Insert**, **Picture**, and then **WordArt**. Microsoft has written an extensive help system for WordArt. To get to it, click **Help**, **Contents and Index**. On the **Index** tab, type WordArt, and follow help from there.

WORDART IS COOL, RIGHT?

Well, yes and no. In certain circumstances, when you want to create a graphic that has a bit of stretching and bending, WordArt can churn out something worthwhile in a very short amount of time.

In most cases, though, the graphics that are generated by WordArt aren't all that impressive. People tend to over-use the fancy parts, just because they're available. 3D extruded text can be mighty hard to read, unless it's done just right...

FIGURE 12.26

WordArt Works!

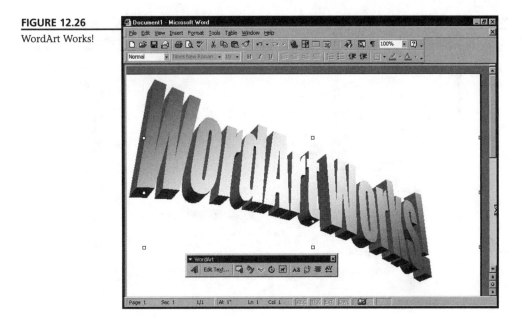

Charts

Word and PowerPoint both support an older Microsoft application called Microsoft Graph. If you have very simple charting requirements and you have all the data already calculated, and if you want to avoid linking to Excel (for, say, performance reasons), you might want to try Microsoft Graph. Maybe.

To set up a chart, click **Insert**, **Picture**, **Chart**. Word responds by bringing in a dummy spreadsheet—Microsoft calls it a *datasheet*, no doubt so you don't think that you have access to all Excel's spreadsheet capabilities. Word also draws a graph on the page, tied to the numbers in the datasheet (see Figure 12.27).

Microsoft Graph has its own toolbars, as you can see in Figure 12.27, and a substantial number of graphing options available through those toolbars.

Once again, I'm not going to bore you with the details because Microsoft has provided a thorough Microsoft Graph tutorial. Bring up the Office Assistant, or the Answer Wizard in native help, and then type chart. Follow the links from there.

FIGURE 12.27

Microsoft Graph
provides lim-
ited, but some-
times useful,
charting capa-
bilities.

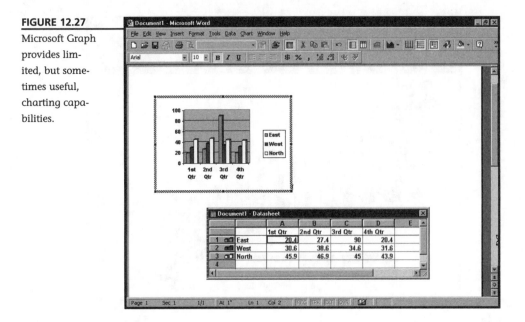

Inserting Files

Some of you might construct Word documents by assembling them from prebuilt
pieces of boilerplate text, mixing and matching as the need arises. That can be a
very efficient way to churn out enormous quantities of Word documents.

To put an entire file into your current document, simply put the insertion point
wherever you want the file to go, click **Insert**, **File**, and then choose your file and
click **Insert** (see Figure 12.28).

FIGURE 12.28

Put an entire
file inside your
document.

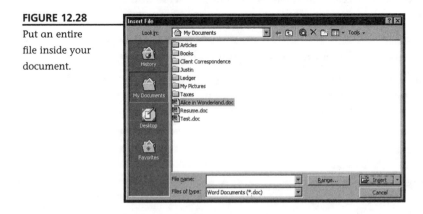

There are a few tricks to inserting files (aren't there always). Here are the ones you need to be aware of:

- There's no real limit to the size of the file you import. You can create files that contain just a single sentence or one picture. On the other end of the spectrum, you can assemble documents from files that are megabytes in size; that is, if you have a high tolerance for pain and infinite patience.

- At the same time, though, you have to realize that when you perform a File Insert, everything in the inserted file goes into your current document. So, in particular, if you're inserting a Word document into a Word document, you will *always* bring the paragraph mark at the end of the inserted file into your current document. (Remember: Every document contains at least one paragraph mark!)

- If you insert a Word document into a Word document, sometimes Word brings across formatting that you don't want. The best way I've found to guard against this problem is to avoid inserting Word documents at the very end of other Word documents. It only takes a moment to put a few "virgin" paragraph marks at the end of a document, and then back up before clicking **Insert**, **Paragraph**.

Follow those little suggestions, and you can build documents from documents from documents.

13

Woody Leonhard

TEACHES

ON THE SHOULDERS OF GIANTS

YOU'LL NEVER WALK ALONE. Tens of millions of people have gone before you, trying to get work done with Word. No matter what problem you've encountered, what word processing crosses you've had to bear, rest assured that somebody, somewhere has confronted the same problem. With any luck at all, they might've found a solution, too.

This chapter concentrates on leveraging the solutions others have found and setting up Word so that you don't have to repeat many of the mundane tasks you encounter every day.

Templates and Wizards that Work

If you need to create and work with a document that you've never encountered before, spend some time looking to see if there's a template in existence that paves the way. So much of Word's useful genetic memory lives inside templates and wizards that were assembled by experts to tackle specific problems.

The Web abounds with templates—some free, some expensive, and admittedly of varying quality—which can be useful in tackling specific Word jobs. A few minutes spent with your favorite Web browser can yield dozens, even hundreds, of Word templates for almost any imaginable project. Check Web sites such as www.wopr.com, www.kmt.com, www.payneconsulting.com, and of course Microsoft's site, officeupdate.microsoft.com.

If you performed a typical install of Office 2000, many of the templates and wizards that are available on the CD won't be on your hard drive. If you have the CD handy, though, it's easy to retrieve them. This exercise shows you how, and at the same time gives you an example of how well one of them—the Calendar Wizard—works. The Calendar Wizard creates catchy, free-form calendars, ready for you to type whatever suits your fancy. Because the resulting calendars are 100% Word documents, you can doctor them up with pictures, fancy fonts, or just about anything you can imagine.

EXERCISE

The Calendar Wizard

1. Start with a clean, new ocument.

2. Click **File**, **New**, and then the **Other Documents** tab. Double-click on the **Calendar Wizard** (see Figure 13.1).

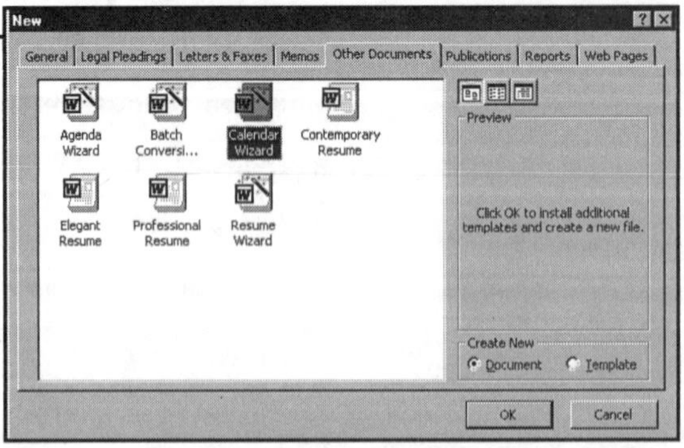

FIGURE 13.1

The Calendar Wizard is "advertised" on the Other Documents tab—it doesn't actually exist on your hard drive, but if you have the installation CD, it can be retrieved quite readily.

3. If you performed a typical installation (as was the case for the system in Figure 13.1), the dialog's Preview pane will say, **Click OK to install additional templates and create a new file**. Click **OK**, and put the Office CD in your CD-ROM drive; Word retrieves and then runs the wizard. (If you installed everything, the wizard is already on your hard drive, and clicking OK will simply run it.)

4. The Calendar Wizard kicks in (see Figure 13.2). Follow the steps in the wizard to place a calendar in your new document.

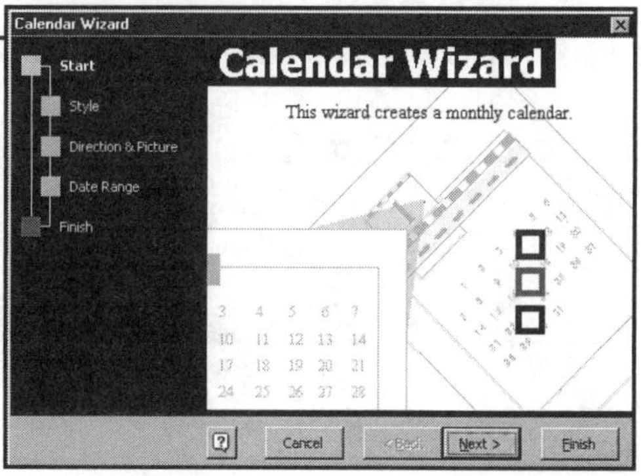

FIGURE 13.2

The Calendar Wizard is one of Word's most powerful wizards—and it's free.

5. It's important to realize that the resulting document is a normal, everyday (sometimes very fancy!) Word document. If you poke around a bit, you'll find that the calendars produced by this wizard (see Figure 13.3) primarily consist of tables.

6. Feel free to change the tables around—resize the boxes by clicking and dragging, change the fonts, whatever you want. When you're done, close the file and don't save changes.

I hope that this exercise has shown you how a well-designed template or wizard can save you hours, even days, of frustrating, nitpicking work. Whenever you tackle a new type of document, seriously consider downloading—even buying!—a template that's customized to solve your specific problems.

FIGURE 13.3

A banner calendar, demonstrating an innovative way to use tables.

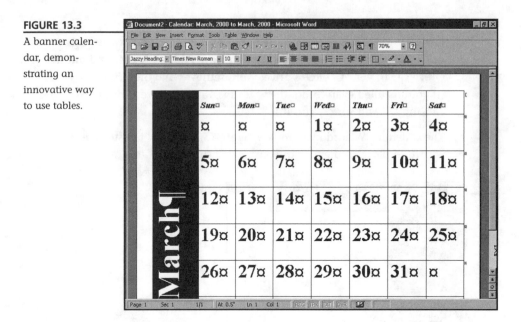

Doing It with Styles

I don't know why people get all sweaty when they hear the term *styles*. It's as if folks are convinced that Word styles are some sort of programmer's mumbo-jumbo, a feature that only advanced Word users or absolute loonies would even consider.

Well, that simply isn't the case. Word styles, which appear in the **Style** box, amount to nothing more (or less) than formatting shortcuts. They let you set up formatting just once, after which you can easily apply that formatting, consistently, throughout your document. There's nothing remotely mysterious or off-putting about them. Styles solve all sorts of problems.

Let me give you an example, a little thought experiment.

You're creating a report for The Boss, and The Boss has determined that the company name is to appear throughout the report as **Tremulous Tribbles, Inc.**, bold, just like that. You spend a lot of time making sure that the name gets typed in correctly, and alert everyone who reads the manuscript to make sure it shows up precisely the way The Boss wants. You hand in the report a couple of days before a Board meeting, and all is well.

Now tell me this hasn't happened to you: The day of the Board meeting, The Boss's Boss's Boss hits the fan, suddenly deciding that the company name must show up as ***Tremulous Tribbles, Inc.***, in bold italic. And you have all of about two minutes to make the change and reprint the reports.

If you had typed in all those **Tremulous Tribbles** and applied the formatting by hand, dutifully clicking the **Bold** icon as you typed, you could run a search and replace and stand a fair chance of picking up most of the **Tribbles**. (That's the trouble with tribbles, eh?) If it's a long report, running through the replace—and double- and triple-checking it—might take quite a while.

On the other hand, if you had set up a *character style* for the company name and applied the style as you typed, it would take just a few seconds to update the style, and thus change the appearance of ***Tremulous Tribbles, Inc.*** throughout the document. Of course, it might still take all morning to get the report out of the printer, but I think you understand where I'm coming from.

Styles are good. Styles let you control your documents with a minimum of fuss.

Character Styles

Word's character styles allow you to apply a bunch of character formatting in one simple step. Let me show you how they work by going through the kind of ohmigosh last-minute changes that you saw in the Tribbles thought experiment.

EXERCISE

Apply Character Styles

1. Open test.doc.

2. Pick a word or phrase in test.doc that you want to emphasize, and select it. In Figure 13.4, I've selected the word **Congress**.

FIGURE 13.4

Start by choosing a word or phrase you want to make different from the surrounding text.

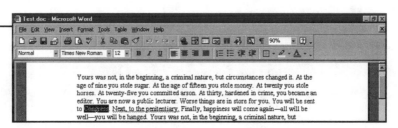

3. Let's create a new character style, one that we can use throughout the document to provide similar treatment to any text. Click **Format**, **Style**. Click **New**. You'll see the New Style dialog box, as shown in Figure 13.5.

4. In the **Style type** box, in the upper-right corner of the New Style dialog box, choose **Character**. Then type a name for your new character style. In Figure 13.5, I've called the new style Emphasize.

FIGURE 13.5

Setting up a
new character
style.

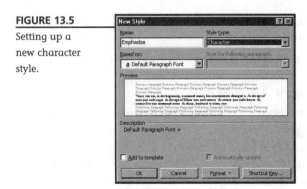

5. Click **Format, Font**. Then set up the font you want for the **Emphasize** style.
In Figure 13.6, I've decided that **Emphasize** is to be Arial, bold, 18-point.

FIGURE 13.6

Specify font for-
matting for the
new style.

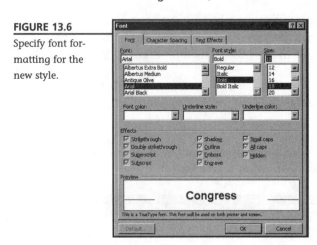

6. Click **OK** twice, and then **Apply**. Word sets up the new character style and
applies it to whatever you've selected. In Figure 13.7, note how the word
Congress has taken on the new formatting—but also note how the Style box
in the upper-left corner now says **Emphasize**. That's how Word tells you
that you're working with a different style.

7. Next, select some other text in the document (it needn't be the same text
that you originally set to the **Emphasize** style). In Figure 13.8 I've selected
public lecturer. Apply the **Emphasize** character style to what you've selected
by clicking the down-arrow next to the Style box and choosing **Emphasize**.

8. The text you've selected turns into the **Emphasize** style, and takes on all
the formatting characteristics embodied in that style.

FIGURE 13.7

The Emphasize style is applied to the selected text.

FIGURE 13.8

Applying the Emphasize character style to other text in the document.

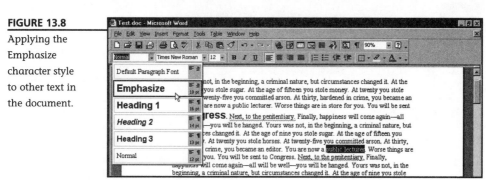

9. To see how changing a character style can ripple modifications throughout a document, let's make a change to the **Emphasize** style. To do so, click **Format**, **Style**. On the left, click **Emphasize**, and at the bottom click **Modify**. Once again, you'll see the Font dialog box. Choose something outrageous. In Figure 13.9 I redefined **Emphasize** so that it becomes Arial, bold italic, 28-point, all caps. That's pretty outrageous.

FIGURE 13.9

Change the font for the Emphasize character style.

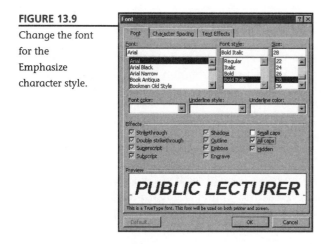

10. Click **OK** a couple of times and you'll see how **Emphasize** has changed. Each of the pieces of text in the document that have the **Emphasize** character style applied change to conform to the new **Emphasize** style (see Figure 13.10).

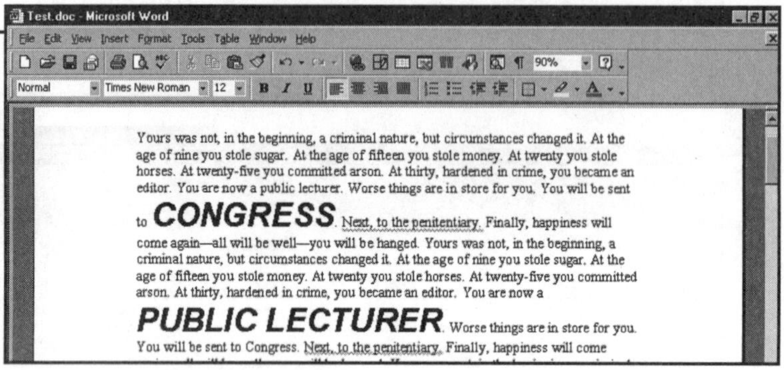

FIGURE 13.10

The new Emphasize character style formatting ripples all the way through the document.

11. As you might imagine, there are lots of options available in these dialog boxes. If you use character styles fairly frequently, take a look behind the **Shortcut Key** button on the New Style dialog box in Figure 13.5, which was shown earlier in this chapter. That lets you set up a simple keystroke—say, Ctrl+Alt+E, for **Emphasize**—to apply character styles quickly and easily.

12. When you're done, close test.doc, and don't save changes.

Character style formatting can come in very handy. Learn to use it, and the neck you save may be your own.

Paragraph Styles

Paragraph styles control both paragraph formatting and character formatting. That's a bit hard to grasp, but once you've used paragraph styles a few times you'll see what's happening.

EXERCISE

Modify Word's Heading Paragraph Styles

1. Start with a clean, new document. Word ships with quite a few built-in paragraph styles. The ones you're most likely to see if you pull down the **Style** box are called **Heading 1**, **Heading 2**, and **Heading 3**. They appear, for example, in Figure 13.8.

2. Type This is a level 1 heading, click the arrow on the Style box and choose **Heading 1**; then press **Enter** a few times. Type This is level 2 and, again using the Style box, format it with the **Heading 2** style; then press **Enter** a couple more times. Finally, type This is level 3 and apply to it the **Heading 3** style; then press **Enter** a few more times. Your document should look like Figure 13.11.

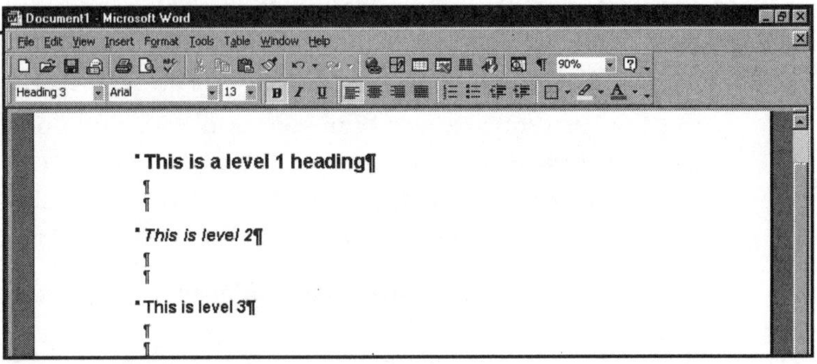

FIGURE 13.11

The standard, built-in Heading 1, 2, and 3 paragraph styles.

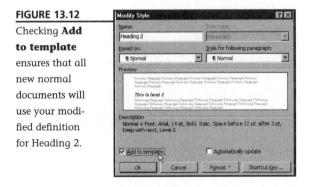

3. These built-in heading styles are a bit garish. Level 1 shows up as Arial 16-point bold, which is all right, but level 2 comes out Arial 14-point bold italic. To most graphic artists, that's a mortal sin. Bold italic is what you expect to see on ransom notes, for Pete's sake!

4. Let's say you want to change level 2 headings so that they're Arial 14-point italic, but not bold. Easily done.

5. Click once anywhere inside the **This is level 2** line. Click **Format**, **Style**, make sure **Heading 2** is showing on the left, and click **Modify**. If you want to permanently change Word's definition of the **Heading 2** style, check the box marked **Add to template** (see Figure 13.12).

FIGURE 13.12

Checking **Add to template** ensures that all new normal documents will use your modified definition for Heading 2.

6. Click **Format**, **Font**, and change the **Bold Italic** setting to just plain **Italic**. Click **OK**, and then **OK** again, and finally **Apply**. From this point on, every time you use the **Heading 2** style, Word makes the heading Arial 14-point italic, but not bold.

7. Feel free to play with other changes to your built-in Word headings, but be aware of the fact that whenever you check that **Add to template** box you're making permanent changes to the way Word works.

8. If you want to change the **Heading 2** style back to Word's built-in setting (there's no overwhelming need to do so, unless you feel more comfortable trusting Microsoft's experts than your own eye), click **Format**, **Style**; then choose **Heading 2** on the left, check **Add to template**, and click **Modify**. Then click **Format**, **Font**, and set the font back to Arial 14-point Bold Italic. Blecch. A couple of **OK**s and you're back to the way Word originally worked.

9. When you're done, keep the document open for the next exercise.

Although we didn't explicitly go through it all, paragraph styles can include any sort of paragraph formatting—from alignment to tabs, bullets to borders. If you want to center all your **Heading 1** styled paragraphs, for example, simply choose **Modify**, **Format**, **Paragraph**, and set **Alignment** to **Center**.

Setting the paragraph style, as you've seen, also changes all the character formatting in the paragraph. You can go back and apply your own character formatting on top of the paragraph style, so to speak. Here's a quick exercise to show you how.

EXERCISE

Character Formatting on a Paragraph Style

1. Start with the document you just created in the previous exercise.

2. Select a few characters from the level 1 heading. In Figure 13.13, I've selected the phrase "is a level".

FIGURE 13.13

Choose some characters in the paragraph that are formatted as Heading 1.

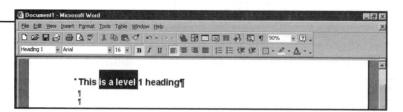

3. Apply some weird character formatting to the selected characters. In Figure 13.14, I've made them 28 points tall by clicking the **Font Size** icon.

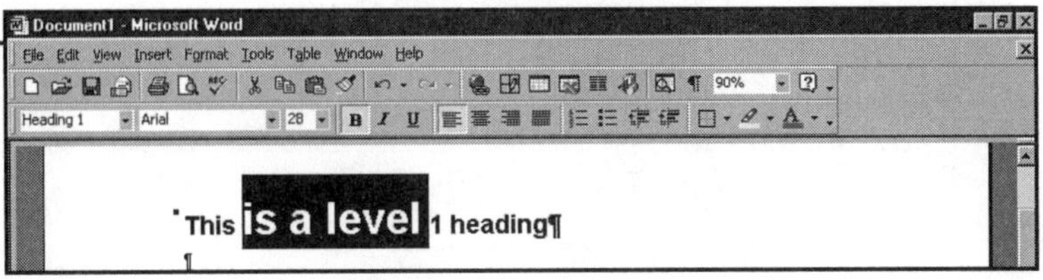

FIGURE 13.14

Change the character formatting of the selected characters.

4. See how you can change character formatting by going in and manually applying the formatting over the top of a paragraph that has already been formatted with a different style?

5. Keep the document up there. We'll use it one last time, in the next exercise.

You probably expect that you can even apply a character style over the top of a paragraph style—and you're right. The character style takes precedence over the underlying paragraph style, just as manually applied character formatting takes precedence over a paragraph's style.

One last little, nagging question. What if you make a mistake? For example, what if you apply manual formatting to some characters in the middle of a paragraph, but later you decide that you really want to make those characters normal?

The easiest way to unformat characters is to undo the formatting with the **Undo** button 🔄 immediately after you screw up the formatting. Unfortunately, sometimes you don't catch your mistake in time to undo; then you really need a reset button, to turn the character formatting back to its original state.

Ah, your wish is Word's command. Well, sometimes anyway.

EXERCISE

Using the Default Paragraph Font

1. Start with the document you created in the preceding exercise.

2. Select the text that's been incorrectly formatted—the text that you want to change back to normal text for the paragraph's style.

3. Click the down arrow to the right of the **Style** box and choose **Default paragraph font** (see Figure 13.15).

FIGURE 13.15

Resetting text to the default paragraph font—the font dictated by the paragraph's style.

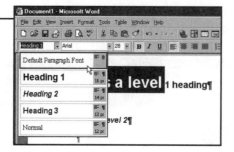

4. You can think of Default paragraph font as being a kind of *reset* character style— one that removes all manually applied formatting. Try applying character formatting to paragraphs with other styles (even the **Normal** style) and see how Default paragraph font resets things.

5. Close the document, and don't save changes.

That's what I wanted to show you about styles. Get accustomed to them and you'll wonder how you ever lived without them.

FASTER WAYS TO RESET FORMATTING

Now that you've seen the slow way to restore a style's default character formatting— via the Default paragraph font setting—you might be interested to know that there's a shortcut. If you select the text you want to return to the default paragraph font and press **Ctrl+Spacebar**, the characters will all go back to the default paragraph font. If you commonly apply manual formatting—and just as commonly change your mind—that's a good key combination to memorize.

Similarly, you can remove all manually applied paragraph formatting by selecting the paragraph and pressing **Ctrl+Q**. That returns the whole paragraph back to whatever settings are established by the paragraph's style.

Customizing Toolbars

Toolbars were originally designed to save you work: Instead of having to wade through a series of menus, you could simply click a toolbar icon and *poof!* Word would respond to your every desire. Obviously, you can't put all Word's commands on toolbar buttons. (Well, I guess you could, but trying to figure out what all those tiny pictures mean might drive you nuts.) So there's a natural give-and-take between having too few toolbar buttons—thus limiting your choices and forcing you to use the menus, slowing things down—and having too many toolbar buttons, far more than you could ever grasp.

Word comes with 22 built-in toolbars that you can turn on and off (there are, in addition, dozens of specialized toolbars that you can't control directly). The two you see on your screen right now—the so-called Standard and Formatting toolbars—merely scratch the surface. To see the other toolbars that are available to you, click **Tools**, **Customize**, and make sure the **Toolbars** tab is showing (see Figure 13.16).

If you want to see a specific toolbar, just check the box next to its name. To hide a toolbar, uncheck the box.

WHY CAN'T I HIDE THE MENU BAR?

I just knew you'd try to do that. Geeks are so predictable. Word's menu—the **File**, **Edit**, **View**, **Insert**, and so on thing up at the top of the window—stands sacrosanct. Even though you see a check mark in a box in front of the menu bar on the **Toolbar** tab, Word won't let you uncheck it; in other words, there's no way you can get rid of Word's menu. (At least, not by using this dialog box.) Don't mess around with it, Okay? You need your menu.

FIGURE 13.16

The 22 toolbars Word has available for you (plus Menu, which is always there).

Word lets you put your own icons on toolbars. (It also lets you put your own commands on the menu, but I won't talk about that here.) I firmly believe that this feature rates as one of Word's most powerful capabilities, yet the feature is so rarely discussed you'd think that it had the plague.

Let me show you how customizing toolbars can save you gobs of time.

Did you ever notice how Word's Standard toolbar has icons for creating new documents, and for opening and saving documents, but no icon for closing them? That's one of the most amazing oversights in all Word-dom. I mean, you're going to close at least as many documents as you open, right?

Here's how to add a **Close** button to your Standard toolbar.

EXERCISE

Close on the Toolbar

1. Click **Tools**, **Customize**, and click the **Commands** tab. Make sure the **Save in** box shows **Normal.dot** (which ensures that this toolbar change appears in all new, clean documents). On the left, under **Categories**, choose **File**. On the right, under **Commands**, click **Close** once (see Figure 13.17).

2. Drag the **Close** command up to the standard toolbar. In Figure 13.18 I've dragged it up to a point immediately to the right of the **Save** ▣ button. As you can see, Word puts a big I-beam pointer on the toolbar to indicate where this **Close** button will be dropped.

A FASTER WAY TO CHANGE BUTTONS

If you look at the far right edge of the Standard and Formatting toolbars, you'll see a little down-wedgie thing. Click on the down-wedgie and you'll see a button that says **Add or Remove Buttons**. Click on *that* button (are you still with me?) and Word offers you a checklist of all the buttons on the toolbar, plus a few common buttons that aren't.

You can use this technique to put a **Close** button on your Standard toolbar. Just one little problem: Word doesn't give you an easy way to specify where you want the button, so it'll always end up at the end of the toolbar.

That stinks—the **Close** button should be right next to the **Save** button—so I recommend that you follow this exercise to add new buttons.

FIGURE 13.17

Choosing the **File**, **Close** toolbar button from the options that Word offers.

3. Release the mouse button. Congratulations! You now have a **File Close** icon on your standard toolbar (see Figure 13.19). Play with it a bit and assure yourself that it behaves precisely the same way as clicking **File**; then click **Close**.

FIGURE 13.18
Click the command and drag it to any desired location on a toolbar.

Drag and drop buttons on a toolbar

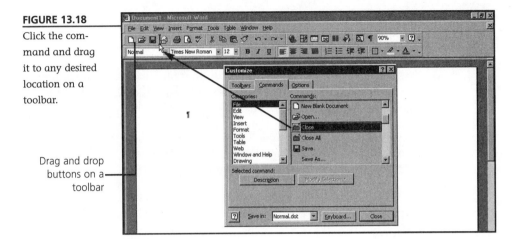

FIGURE 13.19
The brand new **File Close** icon appears on your Standard toolbar.

4. Word lets you make these toolbar changes with impunity. If you ever get to the point where you want to restore the original buttons on all your toolbars, click **Tools**, **Customize**, and then click the **Toolbars** tab. When you see the dialog box shown earlier (in Figure 13.16), click the **Reset** button. Word resets all the toolbar changes you've made.

5. I went back in and Reset the toolbar change we just made, just to make the screen shots in this book look like typical Word. You can make your own decision.

FIGURE 13.20
Right-click an icon to change its name or picture.

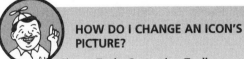

HOW DO I CHANGE AN ICON'S PICTURE?

Choose **Tools**, **Customize**, **Toolbars**. You can then right-click any toolbar icon and change the picture, name, or just about anything else you can imagine on that toolbar icon (see Figure 13.20).

Note that Word lets you do much more than place menu commands on the toolbars. If you scroll down the **Categories** list shown earlier in Figure 13.17, you'll find three very interesting entries.

- The **Fonts** category lets you put a single button on a toolbar that changes the font of the selected text. That icon behaves much like scrolling down the **Font** box and picking the font—but it's very quick and easy.

- The **Autotext** category lets you put entire Autotext entries on a toolbar—just click the icon and the chosen Autotext appears in your documents. (This is one of the very few occasions where Autotext beats AutoCorrect.)

- The **Styles** category lets you apply styles with a single click. Just like icons in the **Fonts** category, this one behaves the same as shuffling through the **Style Box**, but it works very quickly.

Bookmarks

With all the fancy ways I've shown you for getting around documents, you might think that the old-fashioned concept of bookmarks might be passe[as]. Not so. Bookmarks remain one of the easiest and fastest ways to get around a Word document. They also form the cornerstone of hyperlinking, a topic we'll explore in the next section.

Out in the real world, you stick a piece of paper in a book so you can get back to the indicated location. Simple enough. In the Word world, a bookmark consists of a location and a name. The location covers just about anything you can select: a single point, a few words or paragraphs, even many pages of text. The name may only contain letters and numbers (no spaces).

EXERCISE

Create a Bookmark

1. Open test.doc.

2. Select some text. In Figure 13.21, I've selected the first word of the second paragraph.

3. To create a bookmark, click **Insert**, **Bookmark**. Type a meaningful name—in Figure 13.22, I've chosen Kilroy—and click **Add**. That places a bookmark named Kilroy over the first word in the second paragraph.

FIGURE 13.21

Start setting up a bookmark by selecting text (or clicking something interesting).

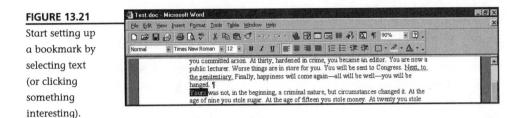

FIGURE 13.22

Creating a new bookmark called Kilroy.

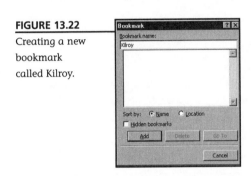

4. Click anywhere else in the document. Now let's see how to get back to Kilroy. There are several ways to navigate around a document's bookmarks. Probably the easiest is to click the **Select Browse Object** icon on the bottom of the vertical scrollbar, the one where **Find and Replace** lives (remember talking about it in, "Getting Around Word"?), and then click the **Go To** arrow in the upper-left corner.

5. In the box marked **Go to what?**, click **Bookmark**. As shown in Figure 13.23, **Kilroy** should be there.

FIGURE 13.23

Jumping straight to a bookmark, compliments of the **Go To** dialog box.

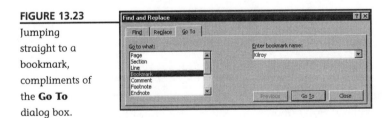

6. Make sure **Kilroy** is highlighted, and then click **Go To**. Your cursor springs to whatever location you chose for the Kilroy bookmark.

7. Add as many more bookmarks as you like. Note in particular how a bookmark can be a simple insertion point or any selected characters.

8. Don't close the document just yet. We'll use it for hyperlinking in the next section.

Bookmarks are quite flexible and very useful. Bookmarks can overlap—you can create bookmarks inside of bookmarks, or you can overlap them partially to the left or right, or just about any way you can imagine. You can put as many bookmarks as you want in a document. You can even bookmark the same selection with as many different names as you might desire.

Hyperlinks

Hyperlinks are just hot buttons inside Word documents. Click a hyperlink, and you're magically transported somewhere else—onto the Web, into another document that's on your PC (or your network, if you have one), or even to another location inside the current document.

☞ *For details about turning off Word's annoying tendency to turn Web references and email addresses into hyperlinks, see "The Case Against Hyperlinks," Chapter 6,* **page 85**.

I recommend that you turn off Word's automatic hyperlinking for all sorts of reasons:

- Word users rarely want a Web address in a document to be hot—usually you're just typing a Web address or email address that you want to print on a piece of paper.

- It's easy to accidentally click a hyperlink in one of your own documents and be hurled onto the Web.

- Sometimes Word misidentifies Web and email addresses.

- Even when Word gets everything right, the formatting of hyperlinks leaves a lot to be desired.

Still, hyperlinks can be quite useful in two very specific situations: when you plan to distribute a document for other people to look at, using Word; and when you use Word to create Web pages. I won't address the latter topic until the very last chapter in this book. But, with Word becoming more and more ubiquitous, you may find the former intriguing.

EXERCISE

Create a Hyperlink Inside a Document

1. Start with the version of test.doc that you used in the preceding exercise. It has a bookmark called Kilroy. We're going to create a hyperlink inside the document that jumps to Kilroy.

2. A hyperlink has two parts: the stuff the reader is supposed to click, and the place to which the link is supposed to jump. We're going to put a picture inside test.doc and hook it up so that when you click the picture, you're whisked away to the Kilroy bookmark. Cool, eh?

3. Let's start by putting a suitable picture in the document. Click inside the document somewhere. Click **Insert**, **Picture**, **Clip Art**. There's a little arrow in the Clip Art Gallery I'd like to grab. Click the button marked **Navigation Controls**. Then click the little red right-facing arrow and pick **Insert Clip** (as in Figure 13.24). Click the **X** in the upper-right corner of the Clip Art Gallery dialog box to get rid of it.

FIGURE 13.24

Inserting a small arrow from the Clip Art Gallery into test.doc.

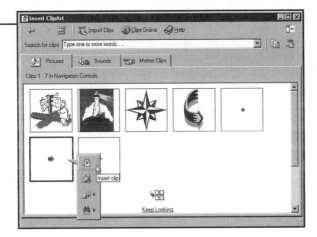

4. We're going to convert that picture into a hyperlink, so click once on the picture to select it, and then click the **Insert Hyperlink** icon 🖼 on the Standard toolbar. You'll get the Insert Hyperlink dialog box that is shown in Figure 13.25.

5. Now tell Word where you want the hyperlink to jump to. In our case, we want it to jump to a bookmark. So click the **Bookmark** button to bring up the **Select Place in Document** dialog box that is shown in Figure 13.26.

FIGURE 13.25

First, select the hot spot, and then click the **Insert Hyperlink** icon to bring up the Insert Hyperlink dialog box.

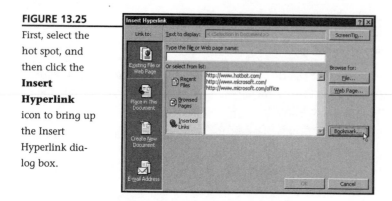

FIGURE 13.26

The **Bookmark** button is used to hyperlink to bookmarks in the current document.

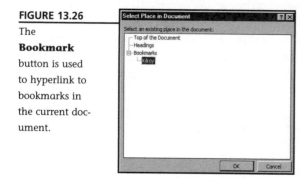

6. Well, b'gosh and b'gorrah. There's **Kilroy**. Click once on **Kilroy** (or any other bookmark you may have set up in the document, for that matter), and then click **OK** twice.

7. That's all there is to it! Word sets up the picture as a hot link. Click it (you see your cursor turn into a pointy finger), and you'll jump all the way to **Kilroy**.

8. Create hot links to your heart's content. When you're tired of it, close test.doc without saving changes.

This is the general method for creating hyperlinks. First, select the *hot spot*—it can be a picture, as you've seen here, or it can be text, or just about anything else in a Word document (outside of the Drawing Layer). Then click the **Insert Hyperlink** icon 🔗 on the Standard toolbar. Choose a destination, whether it's on the Web, inside a document, or even an email address, and click **OK**.

At that point, the hot spot becomes hot—very hot. Click on it, and you'll be whisked away.

14

Woody Leonhard

TEACHES

ADVANCED FEATURES

ON BEYOND ZEBRA. I can't begin to list all Word's advanced features, and I only have one chapter left to talk about Word! So I've crammed into this chapter quick overviews of the features that I'm asked about most frequently. As Dr. Seuss explains in On Beyond Zebra, there's so much more available when you venture beyond the well-known.

The Most Popular Advanced Features

I don't claim to have a scientific study to justify which of Word's many, many advanced features are the most popular, but I seem to get more questions about the following features than any others:

- Page Borders
- Watermarks
- Drop Caps
- Fields
- Mail Merge
- Macros

After lightly touching on each of these topics, I'll give you my best take on the Word 2000 features you want to *avoid*. Yeah, I know that isn't the kind of stuff you usually see in introductory Office books. (Advanced Office books, either, for that matter.) But it's important information—the kind of info you accumulate gradually as you beat your head in the school of hard knocks.

Borders

Want to draw a fancy border around each page in your document? I hear that question more and more frequently, particularly from people who have color printers. Yes, it's very easy to draw a border—even a color border—around Word pages.

EXERCISE

Draw Page Borders

1. Open test.doc. We're going to draw the same border around every page in the document. If you aren't in Print Layout view, click **View**, and then **Print Layout**.

ROLL YOUR OWN BORDERS?

I don't know of any way to add more borders to the list that is offered in the **Art** box. A shame, really, because border frame collections are almost as common now as clip art collections. If you want to get more creative, you'll have to work more or less freehand with the Drawing layer and the Drawing toolbar, or with Microsoft Draw.

STICK WITH ONE BORDER PER DOCUMENT

If you want to draw different kinds of borders around different pages in a single document, you can do it by using Word sections and establishing a different border for each section. But for most people, novice to guru, sections are just too full of lurking headaches and inscrutable behavior. You'll find it much simpler to create separate documents for each border type and stick to one border per document.

2. Click **Format**, **Borders and Shading**, and then click the **Page Border** tab. You'll see the Page Border dialog box, shown in Figure 14.1.

FIGURE 14.1

Word makes it very easy to add a border around entire pages.

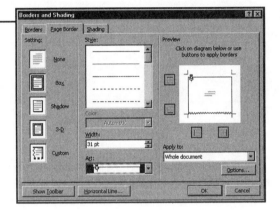

3. Click the arrow to the right of the **Art** box, and choose a suitable border for the pages in your document. In Figure 14.1, I've chosen a border with a push-pin in the upper-right corner.

4. Click **OK** and your new page border will appear, as shown in Figure 14.2.

5. Leave test.doc the way it is. We'll add a watermark in the next exercise.

FIGURE 14.2

The new page border.

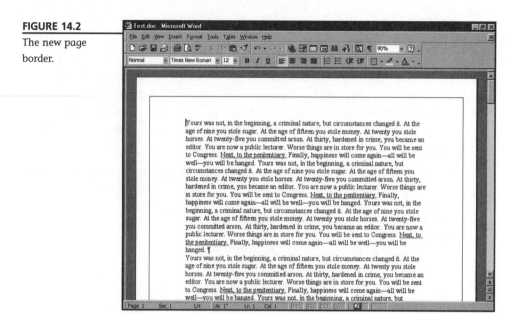

Watermarks

You might not know the official name, but you've definitely seen a watermark: Most frequently a watermark appears as the light gray DRAFT or CONFIDENTIAL printed diagonally on a sheet, with darker text showing above the watermark.

Microsoft recommends that you place Word watermarks in the document header. Yes, that's a strange place. Still, the general strategy works quite well. Here's how.

EXERCISE

Watermark Pages in a Document

1. Start with the document you created in the preceding exercise, or just open test.doc. If you aren't in Print Layout view, click **View**, and then **Print Layout**.

2. Click **View**, **Header and Footer**. To make Word hide the distracting document text for the moment, click the **Show/Hide Document Text** icon in the Header and Footer toolbar (see Figure 14.3).

3. We're going to put a CONFIDENTIAL watermark in the document, so click **Insert**, **Picture**, and then **WordArt** (see Figure 14.4).

4. Pick whatever kind of WordArt you want to use. I chose the simplest version, the one in the upper-left corner, for this watermark. After you've chosen the style of WordArt, type the watermark text. In Figure 14.5 I've typed CONFIDENTIAL.

FIGURE 14.3

When you're in the document's header, click here to hide the document text.

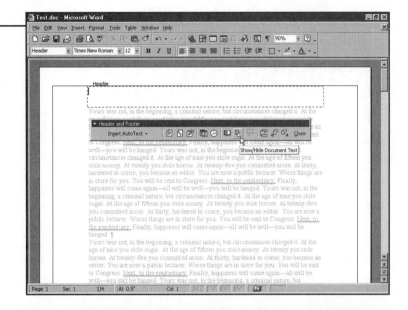

FIGURE 14.4

Put a WordArt object in the document's header.

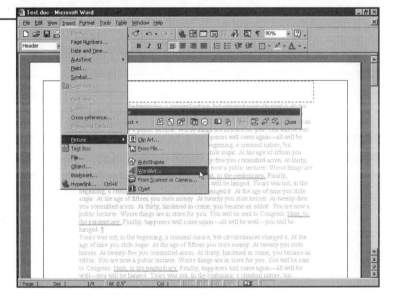

NOTE

CHOOSE ANYTHING YOU LIKE

You can use anything you want for a watermark—clip art, a picture file, even a piece of text in a text box. In this case, WordArt is the easiest because it gives me the handiest tools for manipulating the image.

FIGURE 14.5
Setting up the
watermark text.

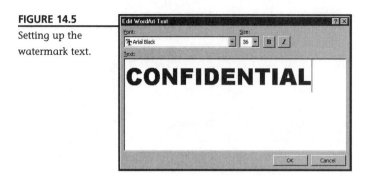

5. Here's where your artistic skills come in. (Or, in my case, where the lack of artistic skills comes to light.) You need to rotate and stretch that WordArt text so it fills the page just the way you want. I start by clicking the **Free Rotate** icon [icon] shown in Figure 14.6, and then I click and drag until it seems to be heading in the right direction.

FIGURE 14.6
To rotate the
watermark text,
click here.

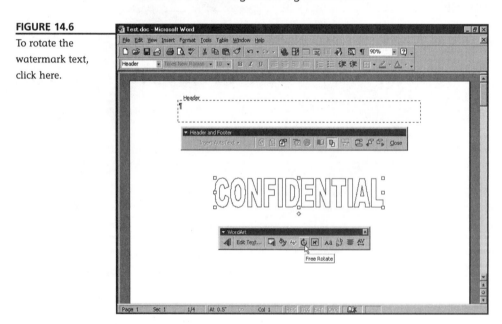

6. You might find it easier to orient yourself if you zoom out to look at the entire page. To do so, click **View**, **Zoom**, and take note of the number in the **Percent** box; then click the button marked **Full Page**, and then **OK**. To increase or decrease the size of the text, click the **Edit Text** button on the WordArt toolbar. In Figure 14.7, I ended up with the text at 36-point, rotated, placed about halfway down the page.

FIGURE 14.7

Enlarged, rotated, and moved down the page.

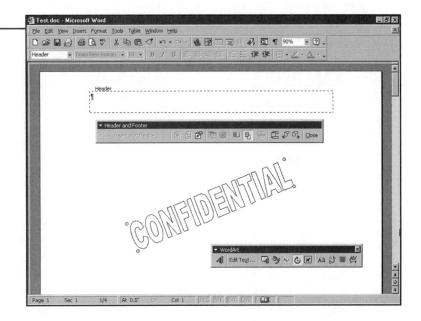

7. Now here's the part they don't tell you in the online help or in any of the books I've seen. The actions you've taken up to this point cause Word to print the outline of the word CONFIDENTIAL, in thick black lines, stomping all over the document. It looks terrible. What you really want is a soft, gray, filled-in CONFIDENTIAL, right? Here's how you do it.

8. Down on the WordArt toolbar, click the **Format WordArt** icon . That brings up the Format WordArt dialog box. Click the **Colors and Lines** tab. You'll notice that the **Line Color** (the color of the line that's drawn around each of the letters of the word CONFIDENTIAL) is black, and that the **Fill Color** (which is the color inside the letters in CONFIDENTIAL) is set to white. That's all wrong. You don't want any line around the letters at all, and you want the fill to be a soft gray. (In fact, if you have a color printer, you might want to use a light blue or red for the fill.)

MY PRINTER CROAKS ON AN OVERRUN

Yeah, it happens to me all the time, too, when I'm printing watermarks. First, it takes forever for anything to print. Then, more often than not, the printer stops right in the middle of printing the first page, usually with a Printer Overrun error. Believe me, this isn't a Word error. It's a problem in how your printer handles the data that's thrown at it.

continues

9. Start by getting rid of the outline around the letters. Click the down arrow next to the **Line Color** box and choose **No Line**. Next, choose your own fill color by clicking the down arrow next to the **Fill Color** box and choosing **More Colors**. At this point you'll see Word's **Colors** dialog box (see Figure 14.8), and you can choose the color you want. When you're ready to try a test printout, click **OK**.

10. Right now, with the Headers and Footers and WordArt toolbars showing and the text invisible, click Word's **Print** icon 🖨️. Check to see if you got the positioning and the colors the way you want them. If not, go back and change the settings until you get them right.

MY PRINTER CROAKS ON AN OVERRUN continued

Although each printer is different, and I can't swear this will work in all situations, you can commonly bypass Printer Overrun errors on HP LaserJets by using something called Page Protection. Lousy name, eh? Here's what you do:

1. Reset the printer. Sometimes you have to flip the power switch off and then back on again.

2. Way out in Windows, click **Start**, **Settings**, **Control Panel**, and then double-click the **Printers** icon. Right-click your printer, and choose **Properties**.

3. With many LaserJets, you'll see a tab marked **Device Settings**. Click it. Then click the button marked **Page Protection** (see Figure 14.9). This enables Page Protection—a scheme used to prevent printer overflows.

4. Click **OK** until you get back out, and try to print again. Chances are pretty good that it'll workthis time.

FIGURE 14.8
I've found that this gray works well as a watermark fill color on most printers.

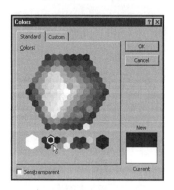

11. Click the **X** in the upper-right corner of the WordArt toolbar to get rid of it, and then click **Close** on the Headers and Footers toolbar. Finally, set your Zoom factor back to wherever you had it by clicking **View**, **Zoom**, and adjusting the **Percent** number to what you saw in step 6. Your watermark now appears, faintly, in the document.

12. Close test.doc and don't save changes.

FIGURE 14.9

If your printer overflows—a very common problem while printing water-marks—see if you can enable **Page Protection**.

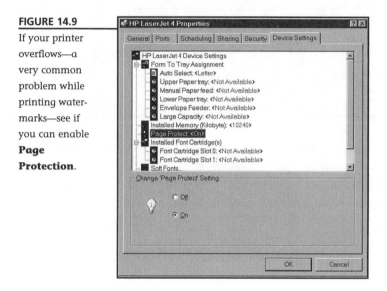

Drop Caps

A *drop cap* is an enlarged initial letter for a paragraph. Word makes drop caps easy.

EXERCISE

Drop a Cap

1. Open test.doc. We'll turn the first letter of the first sentence into a drop cap.

2. Your cursor should be in front of the first letter of the first sentence. Click **Format**, **Drop Cap**. You'll get the Drop Cap dialog box, as in Figure 14.10.

FIGURE 14.10

Easy drop cap choices.

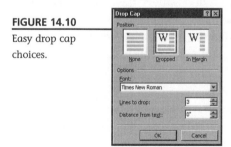

3. In this case, I chose to convert the first letter of the paragraph into a large drop cap, spanning three lines of text. Click **OK** and Word makes the drop cap for you (see Figure 14.11).

FIGURE 14.11

The drop cap is generated for you.

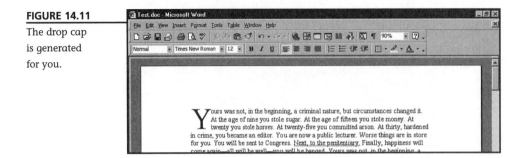

4. It's important to note that the drop cap is a regular character—you can go in and change the letter or delete it. Perhaps most importantly, if you have a font that consists of fancy drop-cap-ready characters, changing the font after the drop cap is created is as easy as selecting the drop cap character and setting the font in the Formatting toolbar's font drop-down list.

5. Close test.doc and don't save changes.

Fields

Word has many, many different fields. Most of them rate as esoteric—Word uses them internally to keep track of things—but many of them support all sorts of powerful capabilities.

☞ *For details about date fields and how they retrieve and update the date and time, see "Dates" in Chapter 12, page 216.*

Think of fields as little computer programs that can go out and retrieve information for you. The various date and time fields that we discussed in Chapter 12, "Special Purpose Tools," for example, check with your PC and retrieve the current date and time. You might be surprised to know that the page number you insert in a header or footer (as we did in Chapter 11, "Key Capabilities") is also a field: In that case, the field goes out and asks Word which page it's on, and returns the page number.

Other fields can retrieve the filename and location of the current document, report on the date the document was created, generate sequential numbers (I used a field to keep the figures in this book numbered sequentially), perform extensive calculations, snatch the characters that are covered by a bookmark (see Chapter 13, "On the Shoulders of Giants"), create entries for an index or table of contents, and much more.

You can look at fields in two different ways: If you look at the field itself, the *field code*, you'll see a mini-program for retrieving data; if you look at the stuff produced by the field, the *field result*, you'll see what will print in your document. Let's take a good look at both.

EXERCISE

Field Codes and Results

1. If you still have temp.doc left over from the date exercise in Chapter 12, open it. If not, start with a new, clean document, and click **Insert**, **Date and Time**. Make sure the **Update automatically** box is checked, click one of the lines that has a date and time, and then click **OK**. Either way, your document will look more or less like the one in Figure 14.12.

FIGURE 14.12

A document with a date field.

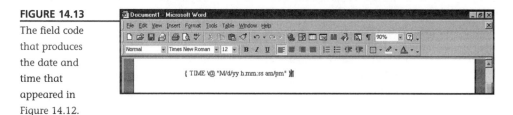

2. What you see in the document is the field result—the date and time, as retrieved by this field. To see the field code, the little program that retrieved and then displayed the data and time, click **Tools**, **Options**. Click the **View** tab and check the box on the right marked **Field codes**. Click **OK**, and you'll see the field code that generates the date and time (see Figure 14.13).

FIGURE 14.13

The field code that produces the date and time that appeared in Figure 14.12.

3. Under normal circumstances, you only want to see field codes when something is really screwed up with one of your fields, and you can't figure out what or why. Switch back to viewing field results by clicking **Tools**, **Options**, **View**, and then unchecking the **Field codes** box.

4. In Chapter 12, I showed you how Word updates field codes just before you print. You can verify that again by watching the Date and Time field, noting how the seconds don't tick (kinda like watching a broken clock, eh?), and then clicking the **Print** icon 🖨 and seeing how the time is updated immediately before Word prints the document.

5. You can force Word to update a field. Here's how: Select the field—Date and Time—and press **F9**. Word goes out to Windows, retrieves the current time, and displays it in the document. Press **F9** a few more times, until you're comfortable with the idea that Word, under your command, can change what's in your documents.

6. Keep this document open. We'll use it again in the next exercise.

I don't have anywhere near enough room in this book to dig in depth on the subject of fields, but I want to show you the fields that I use frequently and give you a few tips for their care and feeding.

EXERCISE

A Few Fields I Have Known

1. Start with the document you used in the previous exercise.

2. If you looked hard when you flipped over to view field codes in the preceding exercise, you know that there's a field in the document that looks like this: **{TIME \@ "M/d/yy h:mm:ss am/pm"}**. That field tells Word to retrieve the current time, and then format it as month/day/year hour:minute:second and append an am or pm. Most fields work like that: They tell Word to fetch something and display it in the document, sometimes with specific formatting instructions.

3. Let's try another field you've already seen. Press **Enter** a few times, and then click **Insert**, **Field**. On the right, scroll down to **Page** and click it (see Figure 14.14). Then click **OK**. Word inserts the current page number—probably 1—into the document.

FIGURE 14.14

Using a page field to insert the current page number.

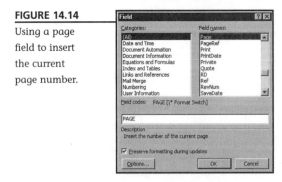

4. That's an honest-to-goodness field in your document. To see the field code, click **Tools**, **Options**, **View**, check the **Field codes** box, and click **OK**. You'll see the field **{PAGE *MERGEFORMAT}**, as shown in Figure 14.15. (The *MERGEFORMAT part just means that Word is to keep the formatting that's been applied to the result, even when the field is updated.)

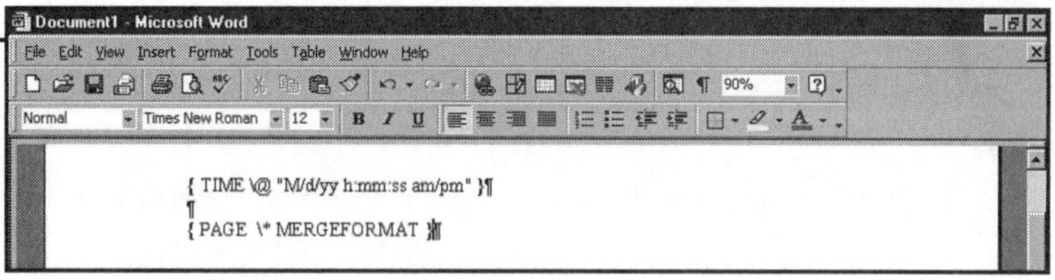

FIGURE 14.15

How Word puts a page number into a document.

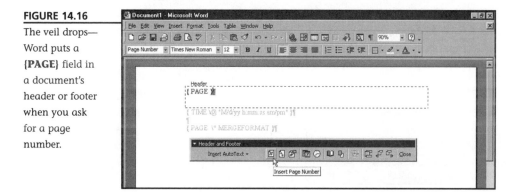

5. This is precisely the same field that's used when you put a page number in a header or footer. It's easy to see: Leave things just how they are—so Word shows field codes, not field results—and click **View**, **Header and Footer**, and then click the **Insert Page Number** icon to put the page number in the header. In Figure 14.16, see how you *really* got a **{PAGE}** field. Click **Close** on the View Header and Footer toolbar to get rid of it.

FIGURE 14.16

The veil drops— Word puts a **{PAGE}** field in a document's header or footer when you ask for a page number.

6. Now, flip back to viewing field results by clicking **Tools**, **Options**, **View**, and clearing the **Field codes** check box. You now have something that looks like Figure 14.17.

7. I hope that "AHA!" light just went off in your head. Word uses field codes to put "update automatically" dates and times in your documents. It uses field codes to put page numbers (and the total number of pages) in headers and footers. In fact, Word uses field codes all over the place to accomplish all sorts of magic, from building tables of contents to managing cross references.

FIGURE 14.17

Results of the
field codes
shown in
Figure 14.16.

8. Here's another field I use frequently. Say you want to put the name of the current file at the end of a document. More than that, say you want to include the full filename—path and all. Go to the end of your current document and Press **Enter** a few more times. Click **Insert**, **Field**. On the right, scroll down to **FileName** and click it once. Click inside the box near the bottom and type the switch \p (see Figure 14.18). Click **OK**, and the full pathname of the current document appears. Change the filename (by clicking **File**, **Save As**), put it in a weird folder, do anything you like—this name will get updated. (Of course, you need to print the document, or select the field and press **F9**, to force Word to do the updating.)

FIGURE 14.18

The **{FILE-
NAME \p}** field
puts the current
path and file-
name in the
document.

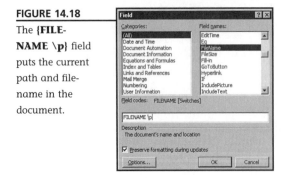

9. Want to maintain a series of numbers in a document? I've done that here in this book, with the figure numbers. You can do it, too, and it's much, much simpler than you think. The trick lies in the **{SEQ}** (sequence) field.

10. We're going to create a sequence of numbers called, oh, DuhFigs. Move your cursor up somewhere near the beginning of the document. Click **Insert**, **Field**. In the Insert Field dialog box, scroll down on the right and click once on **Seq**. Down in the box at the bottom, type DuhFigs, as shown in Figure 14.19. Click **OK** and you'll get a **{SEQ DuhFigs}** field in your document.

FIGURE 14.19

Creating a
{SEQ DuhFigs}
field.

11. Because this is the first **{SEQ DuhFigs}** field in the document, the result is 1. Move down to another random location in the document and repeat the procedure to put another {SEQ DuhFigs} field there. See how it comes up with a value of 2?

12. Now hop all over the document, inserting **{SEQ DuhFigs}** fields in random places. Copy one from the bottom of the document to the top. Move one from the middle to the end. The numbering won't always come out right, but if you select the whole document and press **F9**, you'll find that the various fields are numbered sequentially—the first one comes up 1, the second one 2, the third one 3, and so on. This is by far the simplest way to keep a sequence of numbers going in a document.

13. Word will maintain a nearly infinite number of different sequences—all the **{SEQ DuhFigs}** fields are numbered independently of, oh, the **{SEQ MyTables}** fields. I bet you can think of a few ways to use the **{SEQ}** field right now.

14. You can play with any of the fields listed in the Insert Field dialog box, and you can flip back and forth between field codes and field results. When you're done, close the document and don't save changes.

WORD CAN HELP—SOMETIMES, ANYWAY

Word has a very poor overview of field codes (to see the little bit that's available, ask the Office Assistant "About fields?"), but it has very good help for individual codes—if you can find the entries! When you're in the Insert Field dialog box, click once on the field you think might be interesting, and then click the **?** in the upper-right corner. Bring the **?** down to the field that you clicked, and click the field again. Word responds with downright useful information about that particular field.

For the mother lode of field code descriptions, undocumented tips and more, get a copy of Special Edition Using Office 2000, by Ed Bott and (ahem!) Woody Leonhard, from Que, ISBN 0-7897-1842-1.

Mail Merge

Word includes very powerful tools for performing mail merges—in other words, for spinning out form letters with customized information, matching envelopes, mass fax campaigns, or even sending email to people on a list. (Just don't spam anybody, okay?)

The tools work well, although the technique can be a bit hard to understand at first. In a nutshell, Word needs two different kinds of files: a main document that gets populated with the merged data and a data source that contains names, addresses, and the like.

The main document must be a specific kind of Word document, one peppered with fields (you thought otherwise?) that tell Word how to perform the merge. Fortunately, Word contains tools that make setting up a merge document relatively painless.

The data source can be a simple text file, an Outlook Contacts folder (the mail merge helper calls it the "Outlook Address Book"), a Word table, an Excel spreadsheet, or an Access, FoxPro or dBase database.

There's a comprehensive series of help topics available online. Crank up the Office Assistant and type mail merge. Then pick the topic **Use mail merge** to create form letters, mailing labels, envelopes, or catalogs.

Here's a hint taken from Woody's Graduate School of Mail Merge Hard Knocks. If you plan to do a mail merge, tackle the problem in this order:

- Figure out specifically what data you'll need. If you have to sketch out the final document, go ahead and do so, but don't get hung up on any of the details at first.

- Review Microsoft's rules for the data source (see previous Tip), and then put together a tentative data source file. Write down the steps you take to gather and massage the data because chances are very good that you'll have to reassemble the data source file two or three times.

- Use Word's extensive assistance to build the merge document. To do so, create a new document, click **Tools**, **Merge Documents**, and follow the steps, one at a time.

- If you have to go back and rebuild the data source file, do so without worrying too much about it. I warned you, eh?

- Don't expect perfection the first (or second or third) time you try. In particular, don't waste that fancy letterhead or send out a thousand faxes before you've spun the merged documents out to a file—and studied that file forward and backward for any oddities.

● Mark my words: Minor problems will appear on the first hundred or so merged documents. But the real screw-ups will sit buried way, way down in the pile. Try to get a good night's sleep and look at the merge afresh before you commit to spending a lot of money printing (or faxing or emailing) a merged run.

● Your printer will always jam halfway through a long merge. Shortly after, your envelope feeder will start swallowing #10s, and then the Zip codes won't print right. Anticipate problems, make sure you have a contingency plan (extra toner cartridges, a backup printer you can borrow), and never delete the merged file until all the envelopes have been in the mail for at least a week.

● Keep written notes of the precise steps you followed. The next time you run a similar mail merge, it'll take half as long—but only if you have a good record of what went wrong the first time.

When all else fails, imagine how much fun mail merge would be if you had to do it with a Selectric and a copier.

☞ *For details about mail merge, see Special Edition Using Office 2000, by Ed Bott and Woody Leonhard (Que, ISBN 0-7897-1842-1).*

Macros

A *macro language* is a programming language that hooks into an underlying application such as Word. You can use a macro language to automate repetitive actions that might otherwise take hundreds or thousands of keystrokes. More importantly, programmers can use a macro language to make the application jump through all sorts of awesome hoops. Word, straight out of the box, includes Visual Basic for Applications, which is hands-down the most powerful macro language ever invented.

I used to try to teach Word novices how to use Word's built-in macro recorder. Ultimately, it was a waste of time. The macro recorder is supposed to watch you as you perform a sequence of tasks and then replay those tasks with a click or two. For example, if you always inserted a picture and formatted it a certain way, you could record the steps to perform the formatting, and then replay the recorded macro to avoid having to repeat the steps.

Why is it a waste of time? There are two reasons. First, you can frequently find a much faster and easier (and less obtuse) way to solve most repetitive-typing problems—in the example that was just cited, for instance, it's much easier to put all the formatting in a style and apply the style to the picture. Second, the macro recorder doesn't always record things the way you think it should, and trying to manually change a recorded macro is a bit like trying to change the end of *Titanic*—on videotape.

Nonetheless, you need to be aware of this wondrous, powerful programming language that lies just beneath Word's surface. Yes, it's the tool that's used to create Word macro viruses. But in the right hands—maybe *your* hands!—it can make Word sing, perform precisely the way you want it to, and save enormous amounts of work.

If you have a nodding background in programming (say, an introductory course in Basic at the local community college or a few weeks with

IN PURSUIT OF VBA/WORD

If you want to get started with VBA/Word, I'd strongly recommend that you part with about $100 and buy Microsoft's *Mastering Office Development* CD. Any of Microsoft's online partners, listed at `http://www.microsoft.com/isapi/referral/results_online.asp?q01=3&r01=354&country=223`, will sell it to you.

Visual Basic or any other modern programming language), VBA/Word is well worth a look-see, even if you're just starting out with Office. And if you give it an hour or two, you'll be able to make use of the pre-written VBA code found on Web sites, book CDs, and many other places.

What to Avoid—If You Can

As promised, the very last thing I want to discuss about Word are the features you want to avoid, and why. Some of the biases you'll see here—and I freely admit that they're personal biases, albeit based on years of work and hearing the screams from tens of thousands of Word users—won't apply to you at all. If you use any of these features lightly, you probably won't find anything wrong with them at all. That's as it is supposed to be. But your mileage might vary.

But if you get to the point where you're betting the Office farm on a particular Word 2000 feature, you should feel particularly queasy if any of these appear in your corral.

Gad, that was a terrible metaphor, wasn't it?

The Rogues' Gallery

I've already lambasted quite a number of Word 2000 features, but I wanted to bring them all together here, for your quick reference:

- **Binders**. The devil spawn of the Microsoft Marketing Machine. Although binders have a few very limited uses, mostly they're an over-hyped, needlessly complex artifice where none is needed or wanted.

- **Rulers**. Surely the worst way in the world to set tab stops or indentations, rulers can help from time to time—but mostly they get in the way.

- **Fast Save**. An open invitation for Windows to eat documents. It's the number one source of corrupted documents, and old data that sticks around in the file can prove highly embarrassing. At least Microsoft got rid of it as the default setting—Word 97 (and earlier) users weren't so lucky.

- **Find Fast**. Microsoft's most effective tool for bringing down Windows. Why take a performance hit when you're in the middle of editing a document? Until Find Fast gets to be much more reliable, and a lot less obtrusive, I say pass on it.

- **Normal View**. Who needs ya, baby? Back when computers relied on floppies, working in Print Layout view took up too much processing power. Nowadays, you need to think about how much time *you* lose by not seeing what you're going to get. There is one exception: when you need to see every paragraph's style name, quickly and easily.

- **Recorded Macros**. Except in very simple situations, you just can't rely on them to faithfully reproduce the keystrokes that you want to repeat.

The Other Half

The other Word features I'll mention in this section haven't been discussed before in this book, simply because I didn't want you to get the impression that I endorse them!

- **Print Preview**. A throwback to when people had to use Normal view to keep their PCs from crawling on their knees, Print Preview has almost no redeeming social values.

- **Grammar Checker**. HA! Ha ha ha ha! Hahahahahaha! Okay, yes, I do keep the Word Grammar Checker running (and I didn't recommend that you turn it off, back in Chapter 6, "Word Preliminaries") because once in a very blue moon it'll pick up something and bring it to your attention with that squiggly green line. Most of the time, though, my eleven-year-old does a much better job.

- **Format Painting**. Some people swear by the **Format Painter** ; I swear at it. You never know precisely what formatting has been chosen, or what will be applied. Learn to use character and paragraph styles.

- **Style Gallery**. If you think a computer can do a better job of laying out a document than you can, heaven help us all. Don't believe it's that bad? Take a raw, unformatted document (say, a piece of text from the Web) and click **Format**, **Theme**, and then **Style Gallery**. Then shield your eyes. It's so bad Microsoft buried it on a backwater button.

- **AutoSummarize.** Yet another reason why dictionaries should define four kinds of intelligence: human, animal, military, and computer—in that order.

- **Letter Wizard**. If you want to take the time to tailor your templates so that they work with the Letter Wizard, more power to you. (Ed Bott and I provide extensive details in *Special Edition Using Office 2000.*) But if you aren't adept at changing templates, this wizard is much more hassle than it's worth. The worst possible way to use it is by starting with a blank document and clicking **Tools**, **Letter Wizard**—which is the way most novices (and many grizzled old veterans) approach the Wiz.

- **Snaking Columns**. My choice for Word's worst toolbar button. You might be forced to use snaking columns if you're writing a newsletter. But by the time you're done, I bet you'll wish you had a better tool, like Microsoft Publisher (and I don't say that lightly 'cuz I have *very* little respect for Publisher).

- **Gigantic Files**. Word chokes and gags on large files. There are lots of strategies for tackling large documents, but none of them work very well. Link to File on pictures might make the files smaller, but it makes handling them much more of a hassle.

- **Master Documents**. Speaking of large documents, Microsoft still hasn't gotten all the bugs out of the Master Documents feature. (It's a method for breaking a document up into small pieces, and then dealing with the pieces, only reassembling them for tables of contents, indexes and the like.) If you have no other choice, Master Documents works, but it doesn't work well. Make sure you read and understand all the nuances that are explained in Microsoft's Web page on the topic, `support.microsoft.com/support/kb/articles/q180/1/42.asp`, and back up often.

Snake Oil

From time to time I hear rumors about other features that might make their way into Word someday. As far as I'm concerned, if you ever hear these bandied about, you should scoff and be wary of the speaker: They're trying to sell you a bill of goods:

- **Voice Recognition**. Not yet ready for prime time, and it won't be for quite a few more years. It's wonderful for those with special needs, but for the typical business user, don't waste your money!

- **Thin Client**. In other words, running Word on a PC without a hard drive, or with a tiny hard drive, with all the data stored in some benevolent location in the sky. What a crock. It didn't work 20 years ago with mainframes and guys in white lab coats, and it won't work now. Here's the primary reason:

Thin client proponents are sliding down the wrong side of the price/
performance curve.

- **Java**. HA! Ha ha ha ha! Hahahahahaha! (Is there an echo in here?) I think
  Bill would rather fill Lake Washington with Sun-logo'd baseball caps than
  even think about rewriting Office in the Java programming language.
  Imagine the overhead! Imagine the bugs! Imagine the other ways Bill can
  throw away a few billion dollars and accomplish absolutely nothing!

That's my best take on Word things to avoid, past, present, and future.

Where to Go Next

There are so many good Word features I've had to skip over because they just didn't
fit. (Or, more accurately, if you got me going on them, I never would've been able to
finish this book!) I really feel guilty about that, but you can rest assured that if
you've made it this far, you know more than enough to make Word dance on its
ear—far more than those dummies
guys will learn in ten lifetimes.

At this point, in my not-so-humble-
opinion, you're ready for the ultimate Office reference book, *Special
Edition Using Office 2000*. (Yeah, I
know I've mentioned it a few times
in this chapter. I can't help it.) You
can't read *SEU Office 2K* from cover
to cover—unless you like to read
encyclopedias from cover to cover—
but if you get hung up on a problem, it's the best single source of
information you'll find. As I'm fond
of saying, "The truth is out there…it
just ain't in online help."

FREE SUPPORT ON THE WEB?
Yes, it's true. I won't vouch for the
speed or accuracy of answers (in my experience, Microsoft Product Support Services
answers vary from pretty poor to surprisingly
good), but if you bought your copy of Office at
a store, you probably qualify for free Web-based
support. Drop by support.microsoft.com/
support/webresponse.asp, click the line
marked **Submit a question using standard
no-charge support**, and give it a shot.

In addition to my free weekly newsletter, *Woody's Office Watch*—which I plugged mer-
cilessly in Chapter 2, "Precursors to Using Office," and which I won't inflict upon
you again, except to point you to www.woodyswatch.com—there are several other
online sources you need to keep an eye on:

- The Microsoft Support Online site, support.microsoft.com. This is where
  you'll find Microsoft's Knowledge Base, the distilled collection of all (well,
  most) of Microsoft's know-how.

- The Word site, www.microsoft.com/word, where you can download all sorts of freebies, from the Legal Resource Kit (for law offices), to file viewers and converters.

- Finally, you're most welcome to post questions at my own Office site, er, portal, which supports this book and all my other far-flung endeavors. Kick off your shoes and drop by the WOPR Lounge, www.wopr.com/lounge. I can't guarantee that I'll be able to answer every question that's posted, but a large group of very helpful people congregate there.

Woody Leonhard

TEACHES

OFFICE 2000

OUTLOOK

15

Woody Leonhard

TEACHES

Outlook Preliminaries

Is it DIM? Microsoft calls Outlook a Desktop Information Manager. Aside from the wonderful acronym (hey, it takes cojones to call your product DIM), there's much to like about Outlook. Although it takes some getting used to, Outlook combines a top-notch email handler with a good-to-very-good PIM (Personal Information Manager), consisting of an address and phone book, a calendar, a group scheduler, a to-do list organizer, and a yellow sticky note manager.

Components

Unfortunately, Outlook doesn't work the same way as the other major Office applications. It doesn't look like other big Office applications, either. Adding injury to insult, some parts of Outlook don't work the same as other parts of Outlook. So you have to resign yourself, right up front, to a considerable learning curve.

What will all that learnin' get you? A magnificent entre[as]e to Office's "all other" application—Outlook's a powerful, if quirky, place to work with and store everything that doesn't fit into the other Office components.

It's well worth the effort. Trust me.

From the 20,000-foot level, here are the major parts of Outlook:

- **Outlook Today**. An easy-to-locate summary of all the email that's piled up (how many messages are waiting for your action), along with calendar appointments and your current to-do list.

- **Email**. Outlook handles the traditional email inbox and outbox, along with excellent message preview and filing capabilities. It also gives you a lot of flexibility in sending and receiving messages. Outlook can keep copies of all your incoming and outgoing messages, archiving them automatically. Outlook's email address book is part and parcel of the overall address book, so you can finally keep email addresses in the same place as physical addresses and phone numbers. Outlook's spam/bozo filter rates as one of the best: It can automatically dismiss many "Betty's Bouncing Bimbos" and "Make $10 Million in Heating Oil Futures" messages. I'll show you how.

- **Calendar**. Start with a personal calendar, much like those gazillion-dollar At-A-Glance calendars you're probably still buying: appointment scheduling; day, week, month views; so many printing options you couldn't describe them all. Add a group scheduling component, where you can automatically set up a meeting date, time, and location via email, even checking to see if others are free without bothering them. Top it off with an alarm system that pops up messages on the screen at selectable intervals prior to a meeting. In short, Outlook has all the calendaring components you might expect from a modern PIM.

- **Contacts**. Names, addresses of every imaginable type, phone numbers up the wazoo, email addresses, notes, define your own fields, and much more. Outlook is not an ordinary address book—if you know the secrets, anyway.

- **Tasks**. Although Outlook won't ever be mistaken for a project tracking system, the Tasks feature has more than a few tricks up its sleeve: tracking progress and due dates, helping you assign tasks to others—and having them report their progress back to you via email—and much more.

- **Notes**. Yep, those yellow sticky notes get a thorough treatment in Outlook. What's more, you can search all your notes for specific text. So you can think of Outlook Notes as something of a free-form database with a few organizing capabilities. Very cool.

- **Journal**. Someday Outlook's Journal will be a dynamite application. As it stands right now, though, Journal's a major disappointment. It will help you keep track of the amount of time you spend on the phone with an individual, but the other journaling activities—email messages, meeting requests, Word, Excel, Access, PowerPoint, and Binder files—all fall short of the mark.

Outlook is not a real contact manager, not by any stretch of the imagination. As far as logging phone calls goes, you get to record the time you spend on the phone with a client and write notes. That's it. The records end up in Outlook's Journal. While the Journal entry identifies the record as a phone call, you can't even mark an entry as covering an incoming or outgoing phone call.

There's no facility for rescheduling calls if you get a busy signal. There's no easy way to gather information about all contacts with an individual client, and there's no way to organize or analyze it. There's no support for totaling times, or for billing. All in all, phone contact support in Outlook can be described only as minimal—but it does exist.

If you need full contact management capabilities, you'd best look elsewhere. And if you fear Internet Explorer, you can pass on Outlook: This version requires IE 4, at least, and installing Outlook automatically means you'll install IE.

Outlook Express Versus Outlook

Outlook Express, an email-and-newsgroup-only product that looks amazingly like (and actually donated a significant portion of its genetic code to) Outlook, first appeared as the email and newsgroup reader for Internet Explorer 3.0, where it was called Microsoft Internet Mail and News. It was upgraded significantly for Internet Explorer 4.0, and it was changed a bit for Internet Explorer 5.

With one exception, anything you can do in Outlook Express, you can do better in Outlook. That exception is newsgroups. For reasons known only to Microsoft, Outlook itself doesn't have a newsgroup reader. When you ask to read newsgroup messages (either in Outlook or in Internet Explorer), you're automatically shuffled off to Outlook Express. Since that transition comes *gratis*, compliments of the software, you never need to click on the Windows Desktop's Outlook Express icon again.

Outlook Installation

If you haven't installed Outlook yet, be sure you read through this section before attempting it. If you have installed Outlook, read this section to figure out what you should have done. Then, at the end of this section, I'll tell you how to fix the mess you might already be in.

Internet Only Versus Corporate/Workgroup

It's absolutely crucial that you install Outlook properly. There's one tricky dialog box during the installation (see Figure 15.1) that makes a huge difference in how Outlook behaves on your system. In fact, I think it's fair to say that if you screw up the choice on this one dialog box, you'll doom yourself to days and weeks of pain, and probably end up throwing away Outlook in disgust.

FIGURE 15.1

The Outlook installation dialog box that completely controls your Outlook destiny.

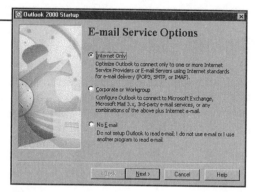

Something else they don't tell you in the advertisements, eh?

So bear with me, and walk through this slowly. I'm going to explain what that installation dialog box is supposed to say, and the details it really is supposed to give you—and probably would, if Outlook's developers had a few thousand extra words to talk it out. This might sound like geek-speak, but at heart the choices are quite simple, really, and they'll control your Outlook destiny forevermore.

MAPI—THE BOTTOM LINE

Okay, okay. I've made MAPI sound like the worst thing since Lotus Notes, and for that I apologize. In all fairness, Exchange Server is an excellent program, and it's built on MAPI. There are plenty of good reasons why companies might require you to use a MAPI-savvy email program. But if there's any way you can run Internet Only on your PC, I strongly suggest that you do so. Outlook will run faster and much more reliably if you select the Internet Only option; furthermore, there are a whole passel of Outlook features that don't work with the Corporate/Workgroup option.

If you look at Figure 15.1 you'll no doubt think that Outlook can be installed with one of three different options for email. Although that's literally true, there are, in fact, *three different versions of Outlook*. Which one gets installed on your machine is dictated by the choice you make in this installation dialog box:

WHICH VERSION DO I HAVE?

So you've already installed Outlook, eh? If so, it's easy to figure out which version of Outlook you're running. Start Outlook, and then click **Help**, **About Microsoft Outlook**. The second line of the dialog box (see Figure 15.2) will tell you.

Sometimes Outlook doesn't give you a choice. If the Outlook installer detects a program that requires MAPI (for example, cc:Mail or the old Microsoft Mail), it might install the Corporate/ Workgroup version without asking. In such cases, the installer is usually right: You probably do have to use the Corporate/Workgroup version.

- **Internet Only**. If you plan to use Outlook to handle email, check this box, unless there's a huge, overriding reason not to. This option— the Internet Only version of Outlook—includes all sorts of new, fast, relatively stable programs that connect you directly to the Internet.

- **Corporate or Workgroup**. There's only one situation in which you have to check this box: if you're connected to a corporate network, and that network requires your PC's email program to support something called MAPI (pronounced *garbage*... er, *mappy*). If you're connected to a corporate network and couldn't care less what MAPI means, it is a good idea to call somebody who understands your corporate network and ask them if you absolutely must have mappy support in your email program. Networks that run Microsoft's Exchange Server, cc:Mail, or ancient programs such as Microsoft Mail demand MAPI support; in that case you don't have any choice.

- **No E-mail**. If you aren't using email (do such people exist nowadays?), or if you're using a different email program (for example, Eudora) and you're installing Outlook only to take advantage of the calendar, address book, and other PIM-like components, choose this box.

For the remainder of this book, I'll try to briefly point out the differences between the Internet Only and Corporate/Workgroup versions. In general, though, when I talk about Outlook, I'll be referring specifically to the Internet Only version. Why?

If you have to use Corporate/Workgroup, that means somebody in your company has decided for you that MAPI is the way to go, and life is too short—er, this book is too short to tackle all the obstacles that MAPI will throw your way. Besides, your company probably has a help desk that's well acquainted with MAPI's idiosyncrasies. They're your first line of defense.

Heaven help us all.

FIGURE 15.2

Help/About will tell you which version of Outlook is installed.

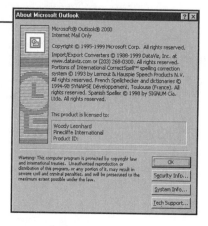

Installing Outlook Fresh

Most of the Outlook installation process is pretty straightforward—you double-click on the Outlook icon and, if you choose the correct option in Figure 15.1, you're pretty much home free. With one exception.

If you choose the Internet Only flavor, Outlook has to figure out how to get at your email. You'd think that would be pretty straightforward in this day of Whiz-Bang Wizards and billion-dollar fiber-optic networks, but it isn't. In fact, it's so difficult

YOU HEARD IT HERE FIRST

In spite of what some Senators might have you believe, shipping Internet Explorer 5 with Outlook 2000 doesn't amount to a Microsoft conspiracy to take over the Web browser marketplace. It's a very legitimate reuse of a huge amount of programming code.

While Internet Explorer 4.01 is supposed to work with Outlook 2000, I wouldn't trust it. Stick to Internet Explorer 5.0 or later.

that you need to prepare for the problems before you install, and you need to brace yourself for entry into one of the most jargon-infested areas still left in the PC arena: networking.

In particular, as part of the Internet Only setup process, Outlook might need three pieces of information that you might not have at hand—and might not even understand, for that matter.

It's possible that Outlook might be able to find the email connection information already inside your PC. If that's the case, breathe a sigh of relief. You'll be spared. But if the information is nowhere to be found, the Internet Connection Wizard pops up, asks a few simple questions (for instance, your name and email address). Then, as in Figure 15.3, it asks for the names of your incoming and outgoing mail servers.

Don't worry: This isn't an intelligence test. There's no way you're going to know the names of your incoming and outgoing servers off the top of your head. You'll need to call your email service provider and ask them. (And don't hang up the phone before you read the rest of this section!)

The second question you'll be asked (see Figure 15.4) is a more reasonable one—and something you might know. The Internet Connection Wizard needs your email logon ID and password. Sometimes that's the same as the logon ID and password you use when you log on to your email service provider; sometimes it isn't.

IS IT REALLY THAT HARD?

The first time I installed a test version of Outlook 98, years ago, I tried setting it up with my Microsoft Network (MSN) account. A Microsoft product with a Microsoft email server, I figured, what could be simpler?

I hit the dialog box in Figure 15.3 and I was stumped. Tried to call MSN tech support, but after ages on hold, I got disconnected. Furious, I logged on to the MSN Web site. For the life of me I couldn't find the names of MSN's incoming and outgoing mail servers there. I switched over to the Microsoft Knowledge Base and looked and looked. After more than an hour of looking for those blasted names, I finally found them.

And I'm supposed to know what I'm doing. Blech.

(By the way, if you use MSN, I'll save you the bother: incoming mail is on `pop3.email.msn.com`; outgoing is on `smtp.email.msn.com`.)

FIGURE 15.3

The Internet Connection Wizard needs to know the names of your email servers.

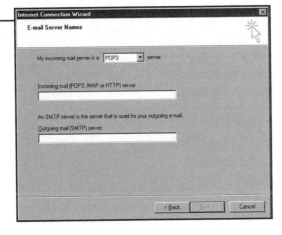

FIGURE 15.4

The Internet Connection Wizard needs to know your email logon ID and password.

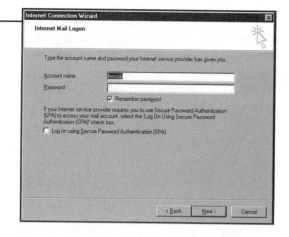

Ah, but there's a trick here, too! Some email service providers require you to log on via something called *Secure Password Authentication*, or *SPA*, which is another one of those MTLAs (Meaningless Three-Letter Acronyms) that so bedevil the computer industry. There's no way a normal person would know whether their email service providers require SPA, so once again you'll have to call and ask. The Microsoft Network, for one, requires you to use SPA.

Outlook uses Internet Explorer (version 4.01 or later) to read certain kinds of email messages—so-called HTML messages—so when you install Outlook, you get a copy of Internet Explorer whether you want it or not. If you already have a different Web browser, such as Netscape Navigator, it remains and should survive the Outlook installation unscathed; IE contents itself with lurking in the background.

BUT THAT AIN'T ALL

Locations of all these files can vary, too, if you upgraded Outlook from version 97 or 98 to 2000. To get all the facts about file locations, see *Special Edition Using Office 2000*, by Ed Bott and Woody Leonhard, from Que, ISBN 0-7897-1842-1.

HELP IS ON THE WAY FROM MICROSOFT

If you have trouble setting up your email account in Outlook, Internet Only version, Microsoft has a thorough review of the steps and the foibles at `support.microsoft.com/support/kb/articles/q179/9/50.asp`. If you've already installed Outlook and you can't get email to work at all, this is a good starting point.

If you install the Internet Only version of Outlook, all—and I do mean all—of your Outlook data gets stored in one file. It's usually in a file called outlook.pst in the c:\WINDOWS or the c:\WINDOWS\Profiles\yourname\Application Data\Microsoft\ Outlook folder, where yourname is the name you use to log on to Windows. On some machines you might find it in c:\WINDOWS\Profiles\yourname\Application Data\Microsoft\Office\9.0\Outlook. That file holds all your family jewels. Treat it well.

(With a Corporate/Workgroup installation, Outlook files can be scattered all over the place, with names ending in .pst and .pab.)

Switching from Corporate/Workgroup to Internet Only

The Corporate or Workgroup flavor of Outlook includes support for most of the features found in the Internet Only version—you'll still be able to connect to your own Internet Service Provider to send and receive email, for example, and all of the address book, calendar, journal, and other capabilities also appear in Corporate or Workgroup. The primary downside to using Corporate or Workgroup lies in the enormous overhead and relative instability of MAPI.

If a glance at Outlook's Help/About dialog box (shown previously in Figure 15.2) shows that you're running the Corporate or Workgroup version, and you want Internet Only, it's relatively easy to switch. Click **Tools**, **Options**, and then the **Mail Service** tab, and click the box marked **Reconfigure Mail Support**. If you want to go the other way—change Internet Mail Only to Corporate/Workgroup—click **Tools**, **Options**, and, on the **Mail Delivery** tab, click **Reconfigure Mail Support**.

Crucial Changes

By and large, Outlook's default settings are pretty reasonable. I have problems with only a few of them, and minor suggestions for a few more.

Adaptive Menus

If you haven't already turned off adaptive, er, "personalized" menus, you can do so by clicking **Tools**, **Customize**, and then bringing up the **Options** tab and clearing the check box that says **Menus show recently used commands first**.

☞ For details about adaptive menus, refer to "See All That You Can See, Adaptively," Chapter 6, **page 79**.

Email Options

Start Outlook, and then click **Tools**, **Options**; click the **Preferences** tab (if it isn't already visible), and then click the **Email Options** button. I make two changes to this dialog box (see Figure 15.5), and recommend that you do the same:

FIGURE 15.5

Improving the way Outlook handles your email.

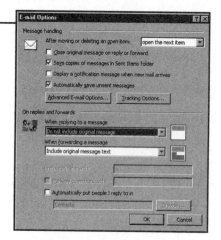

- I find it's much easier to work through lots of email by starting with the first message in my inbox and working my way down. You probably will, too. Make it easier to navigate by changing **After moving or deleting an open item** to **Open the next item**.

- In the not-so-good-old-days, courteous emailers included a copy of the original when replying to a message. Nowadays, some people think the copy is rather redundant because most people have massive email programs (such as Outlook!) that make it easy to look up the original message. Personally, I drop the copy, thus reducing the amount of data going over the wires. If you agree, change the **When replying to a message** box to read **Do not include original message**.

Click **OK** and your new email options take effect.

Mail Delivery

In the Options dialog box, click the **Mail Delivery** tab (see Figure 15.6).

Most of you will want to make two changes on this tab:

- Yes, some people remain connected to the Internet all day, every day. I turn green with envy every time I hear about people with monster Web connections: Watching friends use their T1 connections, even ADSL, can bring tears to my eyes.

But most of us live in the real world where frequently connecting to the Net to retrieve email messages gets really expensive, really quickly. Those with limited Net connections (and real world budgets) need to consider unchecking the box that says **Check for new messages every x minutes**. When you do that, Outlook checks for messages only when you specifically instruct it to do so. Of course, if you have bandwidth to burn, and don't mind the (minimal) overhead on your PC, you can always spin the number down to check for new mail every minute.

WHAT'S THE TECHNOBABBLE?
T1, ADSL, Cable modem—they're all different ways to provide more bits into your home or office, and to remove more money from your pocket. Basically, anything you hear about is faster than using a regular modem. But don't be fooled into believing the marketing claims: a T1 line may or may not be 10 times faster than you 56K modem, for example. Each telephone line is different. So keep your hand on your pocketbook, and insist that any fancy-schmancy new connection live up to its reputation—or your money back.

FIGURE 15.6

Changing Mail Delivery options to reflect a more typical user.

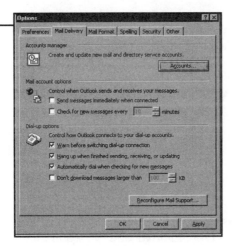

● Those who uncheck the box that says **Check for new messages every x minutes** need to also check the box marked **Automatically dial when checking for new messages**. That allows Outlook to dial the phone every time you tell it to retrieve or send messages.

In most cases, Outlook is smart enough to see whether your PC is already connected to the Web and, if so, to use that Web connection for sending and receiving mail instead of trying to connect independently (say, through a network or a modem).

Spelling

Outlook lets you use Word to compose messages. For reasons that I'll explain in Chapter 16, "Email," I strongly recommend that you don't avail yourself of this capability. If you don't use Word for composing email, you'll probably want Outlook itself to run a spell check for you.

To do so, click the Spelling tab and check the three boxes marked **Always check spelling before sending**, **Ignore words in UPPERCASE**, and **Ignore words with numbers** (see Figure 15.7).

FIGURE 15.7

Have Outlook check spelling on email messages.

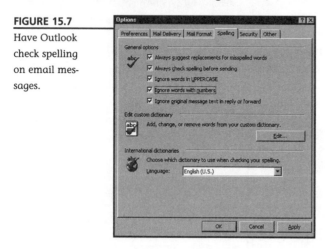

Click **OK** to put all of your options into effect.

Backup

No other Office program comes close to Outlook's, uh, delicacy. With all Outlook data stuffed into one file (the Corporate/Workgroup version uses a few files), you'll frequently feel that all of your Outlook eggs sit in one basket—and they do.

Although Microsoft has gone to great lengths to help you take care of your outlook.pst file, ultimately you have to shoulder the responsibility for keeping it nurtured and coddled. Quite simply, if outlook.pst gets hosed, you lose all your email, all your contacts, all your appointments…well, you get the picture.

Daily Backups

Every Outlook user needs to back up their .pst files daily. Corporate/Workgroup version users also need to back up their .pab files.

 *I covered backup way back in the "Backup" section of Chapter 4, on page 51.*

If you didn't make full preparations for backing up your .pst (and possibly .pab) files back then, flip back to Chapter 4, "Making Office Work Your Way," and get things straightened out.

! CAUTION

NO ONE IS SAFE

I'm warning you: Sooner or later, your outlook.pst file or archive.pst file will get screwed up, and the only recourse you'll have is that old copy you remembered to make the day before.

AutoArchive

Fortunately, Outlook's designers understand—perhaps better than we do—how important it is to keep outlook.pst trim and happy. They also understand that some of us like to keep copies of our correspondence, practically in perpetuity. (Yes, I do think I have a copy of every email message I've received or sent since 1985. Don't you?)

Outlook's solution to these rather diametrically opposed goals is called AutoArchive (see Figure 15.8). With AutoArchive, Outlook makes copies of old email messages (and appointments, notes, and so on), stores them in a different .pst file, and then deletes them from outlook.pst.

WHY CRAM IT ALL IN A .PST FILE?

Why did Microsoft put all the Outlook information in a single file? It certainly wasn't for stability's sake: .pst file corruption problems probably rate as the most common, and potentially the most devastating, Outlook exposure.

There's a reason for it, though. Back in the old days (before Windows 98 and NT 4), DOS and Windows used exceedingly wasteful methods for storing small files on hard drives. You could easily consume an entire hard drive with a few months' worth of email messages if each message got stored in its own file.

Microsoft learned long ago that they had to squish messages together and handle them efficiently, or people wouldn't put up with the overhead.

So now we have just one gargantuan file, and everything in Outlook hinges on that file's ability to keep itself in good shape. As files get larger, the chance of mishaps increases dramatically. If my son knocked my PC's power cord out of the socket, for example, he could easily take out a file of that magnitude, if Outlook were running—and it usually is.

I just checked, and the outlook.pst file on my main production machine weighs in at 62MB! Scary…

FIGURE 15.8

Although it normally happens once every other week, you can trigger an early AutoArchive by clicking **File**, **Archive**.

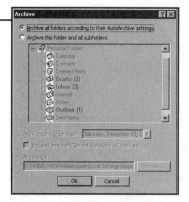

Note how this approach differs from making a backup: When you make a backup copy of outlook.pst, all of your current Outlook data is copied into the new file—and none of it gets removed from outlook.pst. On the other hand, when you AutoArchive outlook.pst, only older information gets copied over, and then that older data is actually removed from outlook.pst, trimming down the file and making it more manageable.

In general, AutoArchive works quite well. It kicks in every two weeks, gives you a chance to abort the archive and, if you give the okay, goes about its business without interfering with your use of Outlook. I strongly recommend that you let AutoArchive do its thing whenever it wants.

There's one crucial AutoArchive setting that many of you will want to change, though, and I guess this is as good a place as any to talk about it. Outlook automatically AutoArchives copies of every email

ROTATING ARCHIVES

I bet you've been sitting back, thinking to yourself, "Well, Woody, if you keep shoveling all this old Outlook data into the same archive file, what happens when the archive file gets so big it goes POP?"

You got me there.

The fact is, Outlook doesn't have an elegant way to cycle archives: It sticks all the old data into the same file and, just as sure as Kenny meets his doom in *South Park*, some day the file's going to get overwhelming. By that I mean incredibly huge.

Here's how I handle the problem. Every few months, right after Outlook goes through its AutoArchive cycle, I close Outlook and rename the archive.pst file to something more informative: for example, Outlook Archive 2000Q1.pst, for first quarter, 2000 data. Outlook will create a new archive.pst file when it requires one. If I ever need to look back at that data, I open the archive by choosing **File**, **Open**, **Personal folders file**.

message you send out, and that's as it should be. Unfortunately, the default setting for archiving the email messages that you receive isn't as thoughtful.

In the normal course of events, you receive an incoming email message; more often than not you reply to it; and when you're through dealing with the incoming message, you'll delete it. Of course, Outlook doesn't really delete the message when you delete it. Instead, Outlook moves the message to a different location—in Outlook parlance, the message gets shoved into the Deleted Items folder.

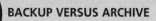

BACKUP VERSUS ARCHIVE

Backup and AutoArchive are different, complementary methods for keeping your Outlook data safe. Outlook sets up AutoArchive automatically when you install the program. For backups, though, you're on your own. You need both.

That way, you can go back and look up a deleted message, if the need arises.

⚠ CAUTION

OFF TO SEE THE BIG BIT BUCKET IN THE SKY

Unless you go in and change things manually, Outlook doesn't archive any messages you receive and then delete. Instead, it holds the deleted incoming messages for two months, and then throws them away. I mean, it really *deletes* them. Permanently. There's no Recycle Bin, no reprieve for good behavior. The **Deleted Items** incoming messages go to that Big Bit Bucket in the Sky, where they sit next to Elvis, and nothing in heaven or on earth can bring them back.

Sound a bit drastic? It is.

If you want to archive deleted incoming messages, here's how.

EXERCISE

Make Outlook Archive Copies of Incoming Messages

1. Start Outlook. You'll probably see the **Inbox** screen, which looks something like Figure 15.9.

2. Over on the left, you'll see a series of icons. Near the bottom, there's a down-pointing arrow, floating disembodied near the icons. Press that down button until you can see the **Deleted Items** icon .

3. Right-click the **Deleted Items** icon and choose **Properties** (see Figure 15.10).

4. In the Deleted Items Properties dialog box, click the **AutoArchive** tab. If you want to force Outlook to automatically archive email messages that you receive, click the button marked **Move old items to** (see Figure 15.11).

FIGURE 15.9

Outlook's

Inbox.

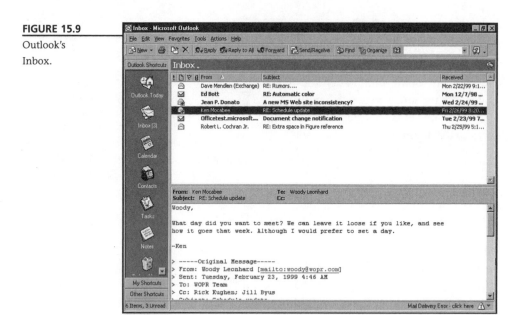

FIGURE 15.10

The right-click

context menu

for Deleted

Items.

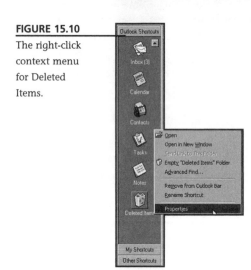

CAUTION

READ THIS! YOU'LL BE GLAD YOU DID

If you want to keep copies of old messages that other people have sent to you, it's very important that you not choose the **Permanently delete old items button** shown in Figure 15.11. As the name implies, this choice tells Outlook to completely delete the old messages—and there's no way to recover them once they're gone.

FIGURE 15.11

Setting up
Outlook to
AutoArchive
Deleted Items
(primarily
incoming email
messages
you've deleted).

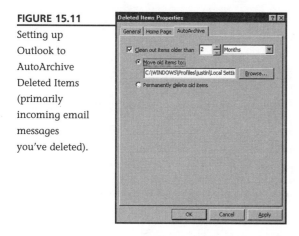

5. Click **OK** and Outlook starts AutoArchiving deleted email messages during
   the next AutoArchive round. That can be as much as two weeks away, so
   don't hold your breath.

Manual Archive

I'm not sure why, but Outlook doesn't have the capability to AutoArchive your
Contacts, that is, the people in your address book. From time to time, you want to
archive your Contacts by clicking **File**, **Archive**, and then choosing **Contacts** and
clicking **OK**, as shown in Figure 15.12.

FIGURE 15.12

From time to
time, be sure to
manually
archive the
Contacts folder.

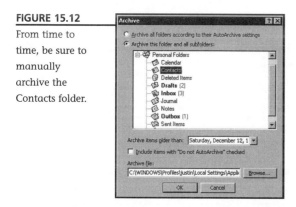

Compacting

As your .pst file grows older and you delete items from the file—really delete them, as
opposed to moving them to the Deleted Items folder—the .pst file gets flabby.
Although Outlook is supposed to compact the .pst file from time to time, you might
want to compact it manually, especially if you've just gone through a lengthy archive.

If you're running the Internet Only version of Outlook, here's how to compact your main .pst file.

EXERCISE

Compact outlook.pst

1. Start Outlook. If you're just starting out, the screen should look more or less like Figure 15.9.

2. Right-click the big **Outlook Today** icon  in the upper-left corner. Then choose **Properties**.

3. On the Personal Folders Properties dialog box, click the **Advanced** button.

4. The Personal Folders dialog box appears (see Figure 15.13). Click **Compact Now** and Outlook will start compacting your primary .pst file.

FIGURE 15.13

This is where the compacting program hides.

For those of you running the Corporate/Workgroup flavor of Outlook, you'll find a similar dialog box by clicking **Tools**, **Services**; then click **Personal Folders** on the **Services** tab, and, finally, click **Properties**.

The Screens and Views

Outlook uses more screens than all the other Office applications put together, and each of those screens can be modified by myriad so-called Views. The bad news is that each of the screens looks so different that you can expect to spend some time getting used to them. The good news is that you can change parts of many of them to reflect the way you work. In fact, Outlook has so many customizing options that you can easily get lost in the mire.

The Outlook Shell

Outlook itself takes over the top and left side of the screen. It leaves most of the screen for the Outlook application that happens to be in charge at the moment— Email Inbox, Calendar, Contact list, and so on—but the prime screen real estate at the top and left side remain firmly in control of Outlook itself. I call that reserved area at the top and left the *Outlook Shell*.

FIGURE 15.14

The anatomy of Outlook's Inbox screen.

Menu bar
Toolbar
Folder List

Email message List
Outlook bar

Preview Pane

Separator bar

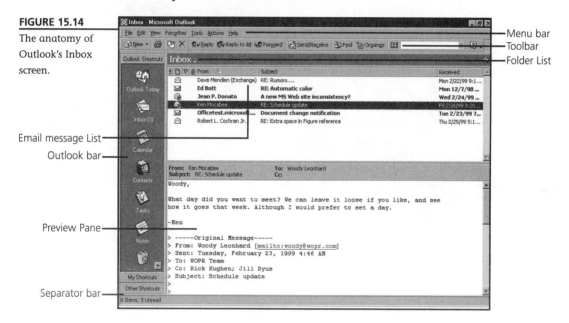

Working from top to bottom, and left to right, here's what the Outlook Shell offers:

- Just below the window title sits Outlook's menu bar. This menu bar resembles other Office menu bars in that it can be modified, if you feel so daring. But it's different in one important aspect: When you change the Outlook application—in other words, move from the Email Inbox to the Calendar, to the Contacts list, and so on—the contents of the menu bar change. The top-level menu items (File, Edit, View, Favorites, Tools, Actions, and Help) remain the same, but almost everything underneath changes. Most confusing.

- Under the menu bar sits the toolbar. It, too, changes when you change applications, but you'll see the toolbar change immediately, and that's less confusing.

● Over on the left sits the Outlook bar, Microsoft's sop to pretty pictures—er, a more friendly user interface. I won't dwell on its obvious deficiencies, but I want to point out that you can get to the Outlook Today screen, the Inbox, the Calendar, the Contacts list, the Tasks list, the Notes and the Deleted Items by pushing the up and down arrows and single-clicking on the related icon.

● At the bottom of the Outlook bar squat two separator bars: one marked My Shortcuts, the other marked Other Shortcuts.

● Click the **My Shortcuts** separator bar (see Figure 15.15). Here you'll find an odd collection of icons with different purposes. Drafts contains drafts of messages you haven't yet sent. Outbox includes messages that are ready to be sent. Sent Items contains copies of all the messages you've sent out. The Journal—Microsoft hid it away here—has little that is worthwhile for most Outlook users. And Outlook Update connects you to the Web, specifically to the Office Update's Outlook site.

FIGURE 15.15

My Shortcuts contains an eclectic collection of icons.

● If you click the **Other Shortcuts** separator bar, Outlook displays three icons that you probably won't use: My Computer, My Documents, and Favorites. Someday, it might make sense to get at your files or onto the Web from inside Outlook. For now, I think it's more effort than it's worth.

● If you click **Inbox**, Outlook shows you its Folder List (see Figure 15.16)—a very compact, easily accessible list of all the locations that correspond to those pretty icons over in the Outlook bar.

TIP

RECLAIMING SCREEN SPACE

Personally, I reclaim a lot of screen space, get rid of the Outlook bar (by clicking **View**, and then unchecking **Outlook bar**), and use this Folder List when I need to navigate around Outlook's folders. I realize that many of you won't be comfortable with that approach while you're growing accustomed to Outlook, so I left the pretty icons showing when taking screen shots for this book.

FIGURE 15.16

The Outlook Folder list drops down from the upper left.

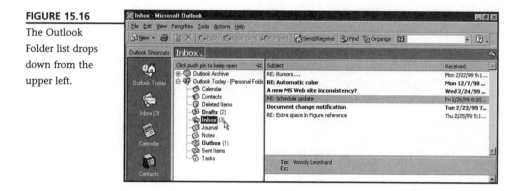

Inbox

If email controls your life, as it does mine, you will find yourself spending much of your working day sitting inside Outlook's Inbox screen. Click the **Inbox** icon 📬, if the Inbox isn't already visible, and you see a screen much like Figure 15.14.

The vast majority of the screen, the part outside the Outlook Shell (Microsoft calls this application-specific area the *Information Viewer*), contains information about your email:

- Just below the Inbox folder list, you'll see yet another bar that starts with an exclamation point (!). That bar (which doesn't seem to have an official Microsoft name) tells you what information Outlook is currently displaying about your email messages. You can change what information appears by changing the Inbox view—a topic we'll explore in the next exercise. Below the bar sits a list of all the messages in your Inbox—that is, all the messages you've received, but haven't yet deleted.

- Reading from left to right, the ! column contains a picture only if the person who sent the message took the extra effort to mark the message as high or low priority. The envelope icon tells you whether you've looked at the message—redundant, usually, because the messages you haven't looked at are listed in bold—and whether you've replied to or forwarded the message. The next column shows a flag if you've, uh, flagged the message. There's a paper clip showing next if the message has an attached file. Most of those fields don't mean much, unless you really go hog wild with Outlook email.

- Now comes the important stuff. The **From** field lists the person who sent you the message. Then there's the **Subject** field the sender typed into the message and the date and time your Internet email service provider received the message.

- Although you might not know it to look at them, those column headings are hot. Click the **Subject** box, for example, and Outlook re-sorts your messages alphabetically by subject. Click **From**, and they're sorted based on the text in the **From** field (which occasionally bears some semblance to the sender's name). Click once again and they're sorted in reverse order.

YOUR GUESS IS AS GOOD AS MINE

Heaven only knows why it's called a Preview—scroll up and down and you'll see the whole message. Occasionally, you have to open a message (for example, if you want to use Outlook's Edit/Find feature to search for text inside the message), but most of the time the Preview Pane is the only, uh, pane you need.

- You can even adjust the width of the columns by clicking and dragging the vertical bars that appear between the field names. Or right-click a field and choose **Best Fit** to have the column width vary dynamically, making itself just wide enough to cover the widest item in the list.

- Below the list of email messages you'll find one of Outlook's nicest features—the Preview Pane. Whenever you choose a message from the list above, a preview of the message appears below.

We'll go through the ins and outs of email in the next chapter, but for now I want to show you how to change an Outlook view. This general approach works no matter which Outlook application you're using. When you change a view, you tell Outlook that you want to look at the data in a different way: Say, for example, that you want to see the time messages were sent instead of when they were received. That's done by creating a view that includes time sent. As the name implies, changing a view doesn't change any of the underlying data—in the Inbox, for example, your messages aren't modified in any way. Outlook just changes the way you look at them.

Microsoft has created some extraordinarily fancy views. Let's take a look at what's available in the Inbox.

EXERCISE

Check Out Inbox Views

1. Start Outlook and click the **Inbox** icon 📧.

2. Up on the toolbar, click **Organize**, and then click **Using Views**.

3. In the **Change your view** box, click once on **Messages with Auto Preview** (see Figure 15.17). Note how Outlook has changed the way you look at your messages—with this view, it shows the first three lines of each message directly below the message itself, and it ditches the Preview Pane.

FIGURE 15.17

Outlook's AutoPreview shows three lines from each message.

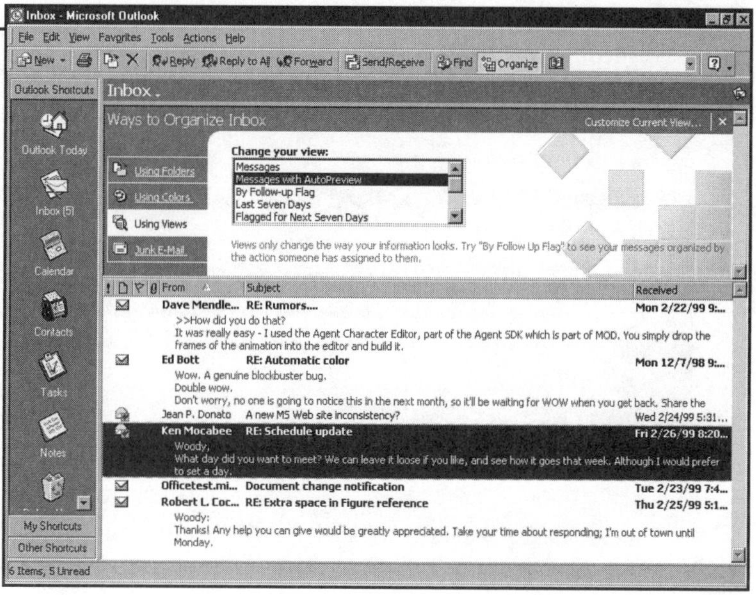

4. I, for one, don't like the AutoPreview mode; I greatly prefer the Preview Pane. But you can make up your own mind. Scroll up and down the **Change your view** box, clicking as you go, and you can see all the different views the Inbox has to offer.

5. If you're really feeling adventurous, click the **Customize Current View** box in the upper-right. Outlook lets you add new columns, delete and move existing ones around, and generally transmogrify any existing view to your heart's content. If you create a new view, make sure you give it a new name so that you can get back to the default setting if and when you get tired of it.

6. As soon as you've found a view you like, click the **Organize** button again and Outlook shows the view you've chosen.

7. You might want to close Outlook (**File, Exit**), to make sure that your changes take.

With one exception—the Contact list—I won't go through the Views that are available in the other applications. Suffice it to say that the defaults Microsoft has chosen for you are pretty good, but you might be able to find something that better suits your needs by plunking around a little bit.

Outlook Today

If you click the **Outlook Today** icon 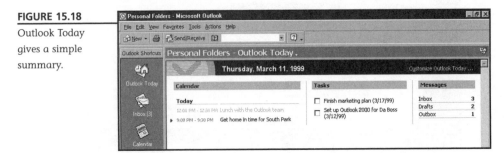 at the top of the Outlook bar, Outlook presents you with a summary of the items in your most important folders (see Figure 15.18).

FIGURE 15.18

Outlook Today gives a simple summary.

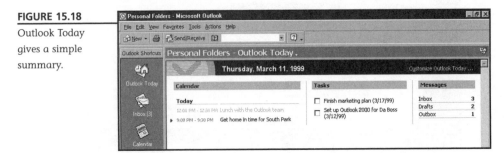

The day's appointments appear on the left, your unfinished tasks appear on the right, and a quick summary of email (with the number of unread messages appearing in parentheses) goes in the upper-right.

You can click just about anything here and be transported to the appropriate part of Outlook: Click **Inbox**, for example, and you end up in the Inbox. (Click **Messages**, and you end up in the Inbox, too.) Ho-hum.

Microsoft built a lot of power into the Outlook Today screen, but they didn't use it very well. Someday, independent developers will come up with much better screens, but for now it's pretty yawn-inspiring.

Calendar

Click the **Calendar** icon in the Outlook bar. Outlook's application appears, as shown in Figure 15.19.

The calendar's toolbar actually focuses on views, with 1-day, 5-day, week, and month options available with just a click.

You can probably figure out what most of the screen elements in Figure 15.19 do, but here are a few pointers:

- The up and down (vertical) scrollbar on the day calendar lets you switch to times early in the morning or late in the evening.

- Click the left or right arrows on the calendar thumbnail to show the previous or next month.

- Click a day in the calendar thumbnail to show that day's activities.

- The TaskPad in the lower-right corner contains task information—the same info you'll see if you click the **Tasks** icon on the Outlook bar.

FIGURE 15.19

The calendar, with a couple of important appointments.

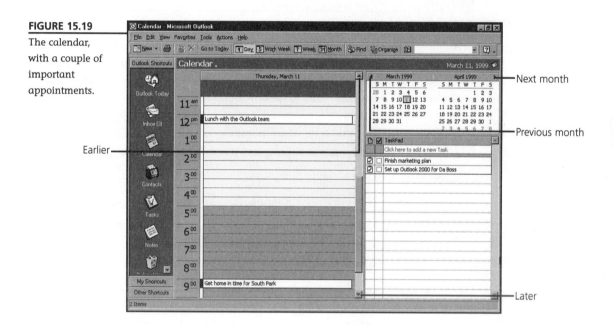

Next month

Previous month

Earlier

Later

Details for each of the major views differ—for example, the TaskPad appears only if you're looking at a single day—but by and large these are the main components of the Calendar application.

Contacts

As far as I'm concerned, this is the only Outlook application that misses the boat in its default view. Click the **Contacts** icon in the Outlook bar. You see the Address Cards view of your Contacts, as shown in Figure 15.20.

REAL ADDRESSES, WOODY?

Yes, I know it's a no-no publishing real addresses in books. Oh well. That really is Bill Gates's business address. Good luck getting through to him. Bill employs living Bozo filters (see the next chapter). And, yep, that really is my business address. Feel free to write! One guess which one of us will answer you first...

FIGURE 15.20

The Address
Cards view in
Contacts.

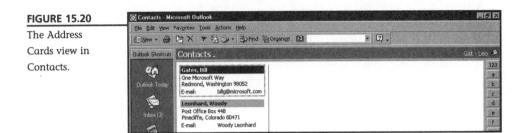

FIGURE 15.20

The Address
Cards view in
Contacts.

Bah, Humbug. The Address Cards view takes up a lot of room, so you can't see very many contacts at a time. Yes, it's pretty. But it won't let you sort your Contacts by, oh, company name. (At least not very easily.) It won't let you visually scan lots of contacts at a time—your eyes have to go down one column, and then up and over to the next, and then the next. And to top it off, the Address Cards View is so... wasteful. Look at all that wasted space! Shameful.

EXERCISE

Get Contacts in Shape

1. Start Outlook and click the **Contacts** icon 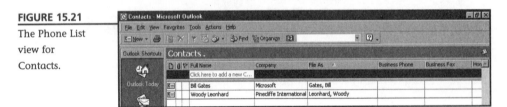 in the Outlook bar.

2. Click **Organize** on the toolbar, and then **Using Views**. In the Change your view box, click **Phone List**. Then click the **Organize** button once again. You see something like Figure 15.21.

FIGURE 15.21

The Phone List
view for
Contacts.

3. As it stands, Phone List view won't let you type a letter and zoom you to the appropriate place in the list. If you want that capability—so that you can type an L, for example, and go straight to the beginning of the Ls, just click **View**, **Current View**, and then **Customize Current View**. Click **Other Settings** and clear the box marked **Allow in-cell editing**. Click **OK** all the way back out, and Contacts will jump to whatever letter you type.

TIP

KEEP THOSE FINGERS MOVING

If you type two letters quickly—say, Le—Contacts hops down to the beginning of the **Le**s. Step lively, though; if you dawdle, Outlook assumes that you want to start a new search on the second keypress, with the **E**s.

4. I don't know about you, but I like to have my Contacts list available all the time, even when I'm working on email. Fortunately, Outlook can keep a copy of the Contacts folder open all the time—if you know the trick. Right-click the **Contacts** icon in the Outlook bar, and choose **Open in new window**. Outlook creates a new window with your Contacts list, and you can place that window anyplace you like. As long as you're careful to use **File**, **Exit** to leave Outlook every time you restart it, the Contacts list appears as a running application on the Windows taskbar.

Tasks, Journal, Notes

The default Tasks screen looks just like the TaskPad that appears on the Calendar. Some of the Tasks views that are available by clicking **Organize** might come in handy, particularly if you use Tasks to manage small projects.

The Journal screen won't do much for you, either, until you start keeping track of telephone conversations via the Journal. Skip it for now.

Finally, the default Notes screen is just a single sticky note—very uninspiring. To take advantage of Notes' flat-file database and organizing capabilities, you'll have to switch to a different view.

The Oops Switch

If you start monkeying around with different Outlook views, sooner or later you'll make a mistake—things will be so totally messed up you'll wish all the customizing would go away.

Have I got a switch for you!

If you ever want to completely wipe out all of your custom views, set them back to the Outlook defaults, click **Start**, **Run**, and then type `Outlook /CleanViews`.

Note that there's a space after Outlook, but no space after the /.

Outlook starts with absolutely pristine views, and you can take it from there.

16

Woody Leonhard

TEACHES

EMAIL

THE NEW KID IN TOWN. For many people, Outlook email rates as the second-most-frequently used Office application, second only to Word. It won't be long before millions of people will rely on Outlook email every day. Astounding.

Setting Up Email Accounts

As the saying goes, "Know thy ass well, for it bears thee." This is one of those big-payoff topics you've heard about. Learning to use Outlook email—and use it well—will pay untold dividends every day. I'm going to assume that you have Outlook running, and that you've clicked the **Inbox** icon on the Outlook Bar so that Outlook is using its email application. Follow along here and I'll have you up and using email like a pro in no time flat.

NOTE

READY FOR A TEST SPIN?

If you already have an email account and you followed the directions I gave in Chapter 15, "Installing Outlook Fresh," there's a better-than-middlin' chance that Outlook is ready to send and receive your email.

There is an easy way to check whether Outlook is ready to handle your email: Click the **Send and Receive** button on the toolbar. If your PC dials in to your email service provider (or connects to your company network) and completes its mission without giving you any sort of weird error messages, you're home free. Breathe a sigh of relief and move down to the next section, "New, Reply, Reply to All, Forward."

Not so lucky, eh? Don't worry. Email problems might be the most common PC problems of all.

If you're using the Internet Only version of Outlook and you can't get Outlook to connect to the outside world, you need to first go back and double-check your account information.

EXERCISE

Set Up an Internet Only Mail Account

1. Start Outlook, click the **Inbox** icon on your Outlook Bar, and make sure you're running the Internet Only version of Outlook by clicking **Help**, **About Microsoft Outlook**.

DON'T TWEAK YOUR EMAIL SETTINGS

After you've got your email set up and working, don't mess around with it! Email is fraught with all sorts of problems—your PC might not be able to establish a phone connection with your service provider, the provider's computers (*servers*) might crash and burn, key programs might get flaky—and the worst thing you can do is monkey around with Outlook's settings in an effort to compensate.

If your email has been working fine and suddenly it stops working, get on the phone and complain to your email service provider! Whatever you do, resist the temptation to blame Outlook and go hunting for a setting gone awry. If email suddenly goes belly up, there's at least a 99 percent chance that your email service provider is to blame.

The second line of that dialog box should say Internet Mail Only. (If it doesn't, see the following discussion for some alternatives.)

2. Click **Tools**, **Accounts**; in the Internet Accounts dialog box, click the **Mail** tab. You see something like Figure 16.1.

FIGURE 16.1

Add or modify email service information here.

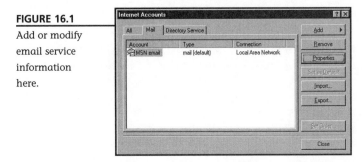

3. If you want to review the settings for an existing email service connection, click the Account, and then click **Properties**. In the Properties dialog box (see Figure 16.2), try clicking the **Servers** tab.

FIGURE 16.2

Server informa-tion for the selected email service.

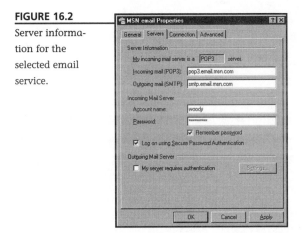

4. Verify that the server names you typed in here are correct: It will take a call to your email service provider to confirm that they're right. (The server name might be a weird Internet name, as you see in Figure 16.2, or it might be a set of four numbers, such as 123.0.123.234.)

GET THOSE SERVER NAMES RIGHT

Here's a weird one: If your connection isn't working right, check to make sure all the letters in the server name are lowercase. Yes, it can make a difference. If the server name is a bunch of numbers, each of the four numbers, separated by periods, should be between 0 and 255.

5. If Outlook can't even get a phone line (frequently you can tell just by listening for a dial tone coming from your PC's modem), click the **Connection** tab (see Figure 16.3) and try to get the Modem box set up correctly. You might have to click the **Add** button and tell Windows how to connect to the outside world.

FIGURE 16.3

Wrestle with phone line access problems on the Connection tab.

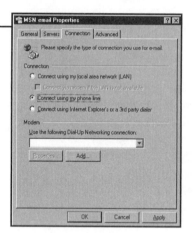

6. Click **OK** all the way back out and see whether Outlook will connect by clicking the **Send and Receive** icon on the toolbar.

MORE WAYS TO GET HELP

There's more information about this approach available on the Web at support.microsoft.com/support/kb/articles/q179/9/50.asp. It doesn't work all the time, but it's a decent place to start.

(If you're using the Corporate/Workgroup version of Outlook, the procedure is quite drastically different. Refer to support.microsoft.com/support/outlook/serviceware/out98/3c4h93uq.asp.)

If you need help installing specific mail services—at this moment, there are very detailed instructions for Microsoft Network (MSN 2.5), AT&T WorldNet, Sprynet, CompuServe, and others—log on to the Microsoft Knowledge Base site at support.microsoft.com/support/c.asp, specify that you want to **Search About Outlook**, and type the name of your service, for example, compuserve.

If that doesn't solve the problem for you, hop onto the Web, go to the Knowledge Base site at support.microsoft.com/support/c.asp, **Search About Outlook 2000**, and try searching on mail setup.

And if that doesn't yield results, get on the horn to your email service provider (don't bother calling Microsoft; they won't have the information you need) and tell them you need help setting up your email account to work with the Internet Only version of Outlook.

For those of you who are stuck with the Corporate/Workgroup version of Outlook, if you can't get email going with all of this heavy artillery at hand, you have no choice but to call your company's help desk. Good luck.

Get your Outlook settings right once, write 'em down so you can go back to a bunch of settings that work in case something goes awry, and then leave 'em alone. If you suddenly have email problems, even if Outlook itself makes you think they're Outlook problems, blame your email provider and you'll be right 99 percent of the time.

New, Reply, Reply to All, Forward

So how do you create a new email message? You'll be happy to know (particularly if you've gone through a lot of hassles to get Outlook connected) that it's like falling off a log.

REAL WORLD VERSUS WOODY

Lemme tell you a story. A couple of years ago I was working with an early beta test version of Outlook 98. Email worked fine for a day or two. All of a sudden, I started getting these weird error messages from Outlook, saying **Unable to establish Dial-Up Network connection. Please go to Dial-Up Networking and make sure your connections are configured properly.** I clicked OK, and Outlook even provided a dialog box for me to do precisely that. I scratched my head and wasted hours trying to pacify Outlook, changing this setting and that, dialing and redialing.

Know what the problem was? Dear old MSN wasn't putting through any calls that day! Outlook 98 was working fine. It dialed MSN, and MSN's computers picked up the phone. But for reasons known only in Redmond, on that particular day MSN in Denver wasn't establishing a connection between its phone-answering computers and its network-connecting computers.

I called MSN, of course, but the tech support people assured me that everything was just fine. I hunted and sweated and swore and pecked, and finally decided that the problem *had* to be on MSN's side. I hopped over to a friend's house (he didn't have Outlook), used his PC to dial in to MSN, and sure enough—I couldn't get onto MSN from his machine, either.

Moral of the story: It doesn't pay to futz with Outlook settings.

EXERCISE

Talk to Yourself

1. Your very first Outlook email message can be a message to yourself, eh? If Outlook is working, and you know your own email address, you have all you need to talk to yourself. Start Outlook, and then click the **Inbox** icon.

2. Click the **New Mail Message** icon 🖾 on the toolbar. Outlook responds by creating a new mail message and placing your cursor in the **To** box (see Figure 16.4).

FIGURE 16.4

Message to myself.

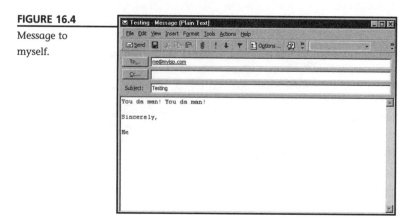

3. Type your email address in the **To** box. Then press **Tab**, down to the Subject box. Type an appropriate subject line, and then press **Tab** again. Type the message that you want to send to yourself. Click the **Send** icon at the top of the message.

4. You might think that clicking **Send** sends your message. If you're permanently connected to the Internet (and some of you might be, through your corporate network), that's probably what happens. For most people, though, clicking **Send** merely puts the message in Outlook's Outbox.

5. To see what's in your Outbox, you have a few choices. The simplest method is to click the **My Shortcuts** separator bar, at the bottom of the Outlook Bar, and then click the **Outbox** icon (see Figure 16.5). Much faster: Click the **Inbox** drop-down to reveal the Folder list, and then choose **Outbox** from that list.

FIGURE 16.5

Switch over to
the Outbox.

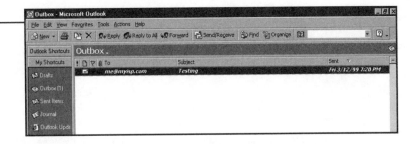

6. Note that you have one message in your Outbox, the one you just
wrote. You can open that message and modify it, if you want to, by
double-clicking it.

NOTE

DON'T LEAVE ORPHANED MESSAGES

If you open the message in the Outbox, make sure that you click **Send** at the end of your
editing. Otherwise, the message will be stuck in your Outbox, and it will sit there forever—
or at least until you go back in and click **Send** again. Weird, eh?

7. To truly send the message, click the **Send and Receive** icon on the
toolbar. Outlook dials the phone (or connects to the local network) and
sends the message.

8. Depending on the speed of your email service provider, the state of the
Internet, and the phase of the moon, it can take anywhere from a few
seconds to a few hours for that message to make its way through the
Internet and back to your email service provider, where it's available for
you to download. Check every so often to see whether the message has
come back by clicking the **Send and Receive** icon.

9. When the message comes back, it'll be deposited in your Inbox (see
Figure 16.6). At this point, you would normally read the message, and
then delete it by clicking the message in the upper pane and pressing the
Del key or by clicking the **Delete** icon ☒ on the toolbar. Don't delete the
message just yet, though. In the next exercise, I'll show you how to reply to
yourself.

FIGURE 16.6

The message
goes all the way
through the
Internet and
comes back to
you.

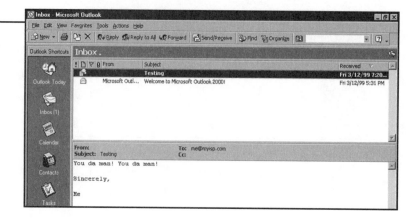

NOTE

WHEN DELETE REALLY MEANS DELETE

Remember, deleted messages aren't really deleted—they're just moved to the Deleted
Items folder. You can see any messages you've deleted by clicking the **Deleted Items** icon
in the Outlook Bar. (At least, you can find them there until you archive your Deleted Items;
see Chapter 15, "Outlook Preliminaries," for details.)

Outlook really does make the standard email functions easy, quick, and—
relatively—easy to understand. In this exercise, we'll reply to the message you just
received and then forward it, just for fun.

EXERCISE

Reply and Forward to Yourself

1. You now have the message you sent to yourself showing in the Inbox's
Preview Pane, as shown in Figure 16.6.

2. To reply to this (or any other) message, simply click the **Reply** button on
the toolbar. Outlook fills out the **To** field with the ID of the person who sent
you the message. It fills out the **Subject** field with **RE:** (presumably meaning "Regarding:"), followed by the subject of the incoming message. Finally,
it puts your cursor down in the body of the message, where you can type
your reply. Go ahead and type something erudite (see Figure 16.7).

FIGURE 16.7

Outlook sets up Reply messages with the important fields filled in.

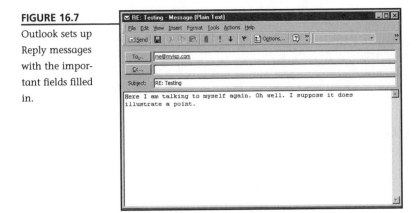

3. When you're through typing your message, click **Send**, and the outbound message is deposited in your Outbox.

4. Now let's forward the message to a friend of yours. Do you have their email ID? Good. With the original talk-to-yourself message showing in the Preview Pane, as shown in Figure 16.6, click the **Forward** button on the toolbar.

5. Outlook fills in the **Subject** field with **FW:** (as in "Forward"), and the subject of the incoming message. It then creates a copy of the original message, puts it in the body of this new message, and sticks the delivery information at the top of that copy, as shown in Figure 16.8.

FIGURE 16.8

Outlook takes care of all the dirty work in a Forward.

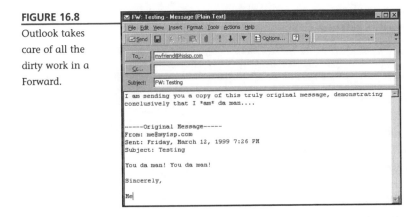

6. All you have to do is type the email address for your friend, add whatever text you like on top of the forwarded message, and click the **Send** button.

7. Both of those messages should've been placed in your Outbox (unless you're directly connected to the Internet). To send the messages, click the **Send and Receive** button.

Congratulations. You now know enough to do serious damage as an email maven.

Using Email Addresses

In this section, we're going to look at Outlook's ways of managing and using email addresses: that is, adding them to the Contacts list, and then using them in email messages.

Can't remember your correspondents' email addresses? Not to worry. Neither can I. Outlook offers myriad ways to get at all your Contacts via shortcuts to the Contacts application.

EXERCISE

Retrieve an Email Address from Contacts

1. If you haven't already, add a few names to your Contacts list. Click the **Contacts** icon in the Outlook Bar, and then click the **New Contact** icon on the toolbar. When you're done with a specific entry, click **Save and Close** to have Outlook save your new Contact. Make sure you have at least one Contact with an email address. In Figure 16.9, I've constructed a Contact for a fellow you've no doubt heard of, complete with his (real) email address, `billg@microsoft.com`. I'll use this Contact entry for various exercises throughout this book.

RULES FOR THE EMAIL NEWCOMER

If you're new to email, you need to be cognizant of the fact that it's a totally different medium—unlike any you've used before. Start out slowly and study the messages that come in. There are a few simple cardinal rules:

- Don't type all capitals. IT MAKES YOU LOOK LIKE YOU'RE SHOUTING.

- Don't compose an emotional message hastily and send it out before thinking about it. So-calledflames always come back to haunt you. In 15-plus years of using email, I've sent out four flames—maybe five—and I've deeply regretted every one of them.

- Remember that email messages can end up in the strangest places. If you use your company's email account, your company owns your messages. If you forward a copy of a message to someone else, make sure the originator of the message won't be offended.

- Don't get too cute (for instance, using emoticons such as :-) and <G>) before you get the hang of it. Patience, patience.

People tend to think out loud when they type email messages, so give them the benefit of the doubt. Even good friends misread messages from time to time.

FIGURE 16.9

Creating a
Contact entry
for BillG.

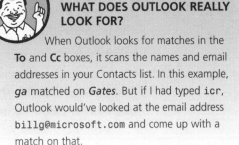

2. I'm going to show you how
Outlook can pluck out email
IDs with almost no effort on
your part. Go back to the
Inbox and click the **New
Mail Message** icon [icon] on
the toolbar. Type just part of
your intended recipient's
name in the **To** box. In
Figure 16.10, I've typed only
ga. Then press **Tab** twice and
start typing the **Subject**.

WHAT DOES OUTLOOK REALLY LOOK FOR?

When Outlook looks for matches in the
To and **Cc** boxes, it scans the names and email
addresses in your Contacts list. In this example,
ga matched on *Gates*. But if I had typed `icr`,
Outlook would've looked at the email address
`billg@microsoft.com` and come up with a
match on that.

FIGURE 16.10

A new message
with only **ga** in
the To box.

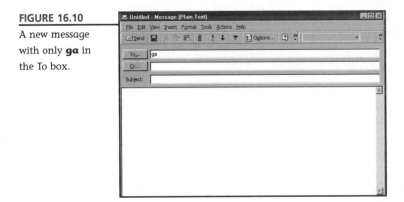

3. *Boom!* As soon as you press the **Tab** key to get out of the **To** box, Outlook runs out
to your Contacts list and tries to match what you've typed with any entry in the list.

If only one entry matches—in this case, the letters *ga* only appear in the entry for William Gates—and that entry has an email address, it's automatically entered into the **To** box. You don't need to lift a finger.

4. Go ahead and type a message to Bill, as in Figure 16.11, but don't click the **Send** key just yet. We'll use this message in the next exercise.

FIGURE 16.11

Message to Bill, ready to send.

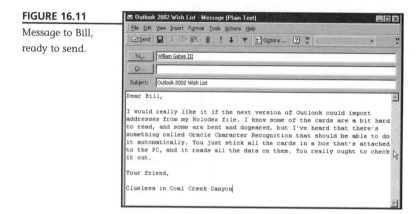

You're probably asking yourself two questions right now:

- **What if I don't know who I'm going to send the message to?** For example, "I think the guy's name is Jim or Harry or something, but I need to look in my Contacts list to jog my memory."

- **What if two (or more) Contacts entries match the bit of text I typed in the box?** Say, for example, that I typed `micr`, but I have six entries that match, ranging from Micron Corporation to `wishlist@microsoft.com`.

Answers coming right up...

 EXERCISE

Contacts in To, Cc, and Bcc Boxes

1. You should still have a message similar to the one shown in Figure 16.11 on your screen.

2. Click the **To** button immediately to the left of Bill's name. You see the **Select Names** dialog box, as shown in Figure 16.12.

FIGURE 16.12

Outlook runs out to the Contacts list for you and presents names for your plucking.

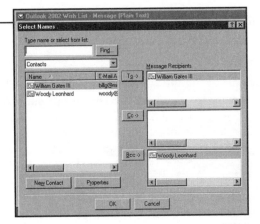

3. You can add as many recipients to the message's **To** or **Cc** list as you like. Just click once on a name, and then click the **To** or **Cc** button in this Select Names dialog box. The name gets added to either the **To** or the **Cc** list, depending on which button you click.

4. Outlook allows you to send blind copies (that's the *B* in *Bcc*). A blind copy recipient receives a copy of the message, but their name and ID don't appear anywhere on the **To** or **Cc** lists. Therefore, other people who are receiving copies of the message have no idea that the Bcc person also received a copy. In Figure 16.12, I've clicked once on Woody Leonhard, and then clicked **Bcc**. That puts, ahem, Woody Leonhard on the blind copy list.

THE SELECT NAMES DIALOG BOX

As you probably noticed in Figure 16.12, the Select Names dialog box has all sorts of buttons. If you're curious, try adding a new Contact directly from this dialog box by clicking **New Contact**. Narrow down the list of Contacts by typing selection criteria up at the top and clicking the **Find** button. Look up all the information you have about a particular Contact by clicking on that Contact, and then clicking **Properties**.

WHAT'S THE DIFFERENCE BETWEEN TO AND CC?

There isn't any. The message gets sent to everybody on the **To** list and to everybody on the **Cc** list, precisely the same way. Some people like to differentiate between **To** and **Cc** simply to show who they expect to follow up on the message. But from Outlook's point of view, there's really no difference at all.

TIP

UNDERSTANDING BLIND COPIES

The blind copy recipient can see all the names on the **To** and **Cc** list, but they can't see the names of any other blind copy recipients.

> **5.** When you've finished using the Select Names dialog box, click **OK**. You now have a message similar to the one that is shown in Figure 16.13. Note how the Bcc recipient appears in a new box marked (of all things!) Bcc.

FIGURE 16.13

A new message, complete with blind copy recipient, ready to go.

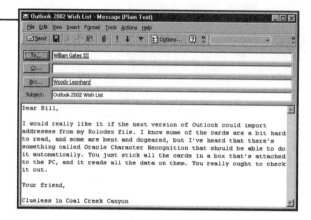

> **6.** If you want to send this message to Bill, by all means, click **Send**. Otherwise, you can delete the message by clicking the **X** in the message's upper-right corner and replying **No** when you are asked if you want to save changes.

Resolving multiple matches in the Contacts list is a piece o' cake, if you know the trick. This rates as a very important trick—Outlook behaves very strangely if you don't do it right—so pay attention!

EXERCISE

Choosing the Right Contact

> **1.** In Outlook's Inbox, start a new message by clicking the **New Mail Message** icon 📷 on the toolbar.

> **2.** I want you to type something in the **To** box that will trigger matches on two or more items in your Contacts list. Here is one possibility: If you have two or more entries in the Contacts list that have email IDs that end with *.com*, you can type com in the **To** box, as I have in Figure 16.14.

FIGURE 16.14

Type something in the **To** box that will trigger multiple matches in your Contacts list.

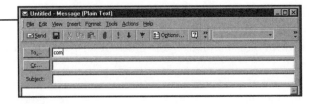

3. Press **Tab** a couple of times to move down to the **Subject** box. Outlook scurries out to the Contacts list, trying to match what you've typed with what exists in the list. If Outlook finds more than one match, it puts a red squiggly line under the entry in the **To** box. In this case, Outlook found two or more matches for *com*, so it stuck a red squiggly line under *com* in the **To** box.

4. If you remember your Word experiences, you might be tempted to right-click the text with the red squiggly under it and choose the correct email ID. (After all, that's what you do when Word identifies a misspelled word and puts a red squiggly line underneath it: You right-click the word and choose one that's spelled correctly.) DON'T DO IT! I'll explain why at the end of this exercise.

5. Instead, finish typing your message. When you're ready to send it, click the **Send** button. Outlook pops up a Check Names dialog box, as shown in Figure 16.15. From the list that is offered here, you can choose the person for whom the message is intended, and then click **OK**. The message goes out properly.

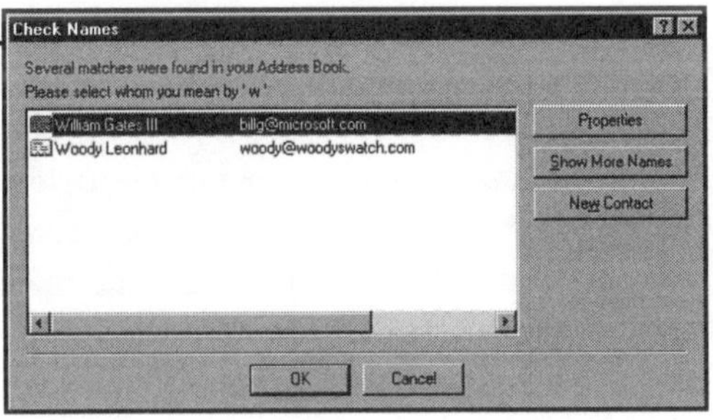

FIGURE 16.15

If you click **Send** for a message with multiple Contacts matches, Outlook presents you with a list.

6. Why shouldn't you right-click the text with the red squiggly line? In point of fact, you can do it—and Outlook presents you with a list quite similar to the one that Word offers. But after you choose a recipient this way—say, if you tell Outlook that *com* really means Woody Leonhard—it remembers the association. After you do it once, every time you type com in the To box, Outlook automatically substitutes Woody Leonhard and flags the substitution with a dotted green underline. If you can always remember to double-check dotted green underlined names, more power to you. But for most Outlook users, it's yet another rabbit hole waiting to swallow you.

Resolving multiple matches in the Check Names dialog box works fine every time. But after you resolve a match using the right-click method, Outlook "knows" that you always want to make that same association—whether you want to or not.

I just hate it when programs think they're smarter than I am.

Adding Contacts

It's probably become crystalclear to you, at this point, that you're going to want to put all your email correspondents' names in your Contacts list. Outlook imports that information from just about every email package imaginable, and from most address books, to boot. If all else fails, you can always type all of them into the Contacts list. Blecch.

There *is* one trick for adding Contacts quickly, and directly from email, however, and you can take advantage of it to add new email addresses whenever new people send you email messages.

EXERCISE

Add Email Address to Contacts—Correctly

1. In the Outlook Inbox, in the Sent Items folder or the Deleted Items folder, choose an email message that was sent to you by someone who you want to include in your Contacts list. Open the message by double-clicking the message in the upper pane, so you can see the full message, as shown in Figure 16.16.

FIGURE 16.16

Right-click to
create a Contact
from an email
message.

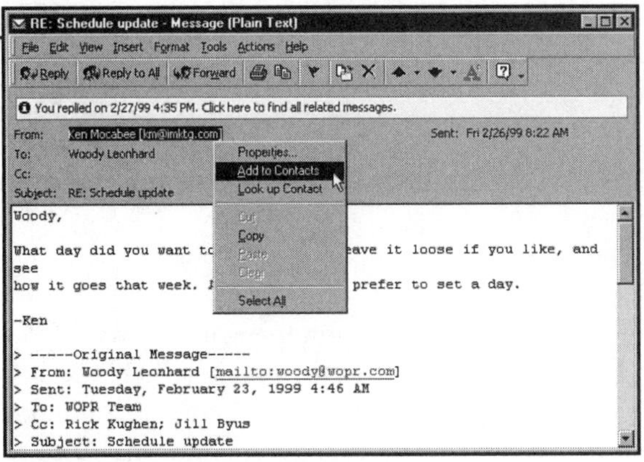

2. Immediately after the word **From** in the message itself, you'll see the
   sender's name, although it's grayed out. Everywhere—I do mean everywhere—in Windows, a grayed-out field is dead, in the sense that you can't
   do anything with it. Outlook decided to do things differently. (Aren't we the
   lucky ones?) Not only is this grayed-out name "live," it's the only easy way
   to get a sender's email ID added to your Contacts list!

3. Right-click the sender's name. In Figure 16.16, I right-clicked **Ken Mocabee**.
   Pick **Add to Contacts**.

4. Outlook presents you with a Contact form, on which you can type the
   Contact's name, address, telephone number, and so on. When you're done,
   click **Save and Close**.

5. If the Contact already exists, you'll get the warning message shown in

   Figure 16.17. You can choose whether you want to update or replace the
   Contact.

FIGURE 16.17

Outlook offers a
number of
options if
there's an exist-
ing Contact
with the same
email address.

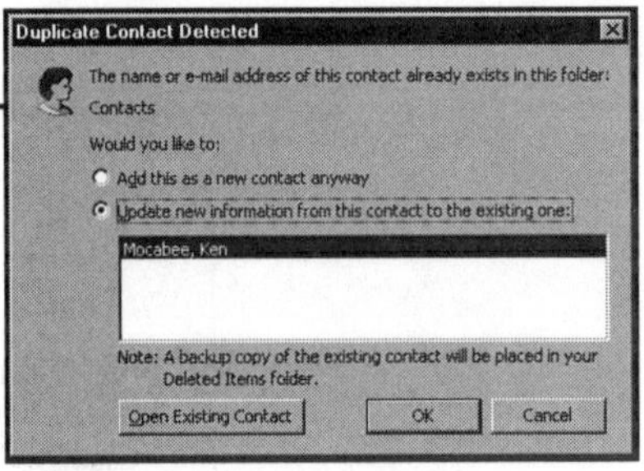

TIP

ADDING CONTACTS WORKS THE SAME WAY EVERYWHERE

You can use this same technique to add Contacts that appear in any From or Cc field, in any message. Just open the message, right-click on the person's name or email address, and then click **Add to Contacts**.

Attaching Files

Once upon a time, attaching files to email messages—the procedure you use to send a file to somebody else over the Internet—owed more to black art and luck than rational thought and science. Things are much better today than they were just a few years ago, but you'll still encounter some sporadic problems sending and receiving files—particularly large files, which can be rejected by Internet Service Providers without any notification. Such is the state of the art at the turn of the century.

Outlook makes it easy to attach a file to a message.

Sending and Receiving Files

1. Start in Outlook's Inbox. Click the **New Mail Message** icon on the toolbar to start a new message. You'll be sending a message, with an attached file, to yourself.

2. Type your email ID in the **To** box, add any subject you like, and when you're ready to attach a file to the message, click **Insert**, and then **File**. Pick the file you want to attach, and click **Insert**. The file will appear as an icon at the bottom of the message (see Figure 16.18).

FIGURE 16.18

Attached files appear as icons at the bottom of the message.

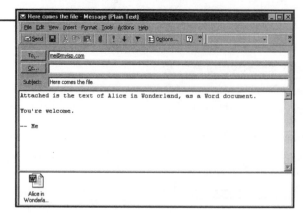

NOTE

A NOTE ABOUT ATTACHED FILES

Files are always attached to the end of the message, so it doesn't matter where your cursor sits when you insert the file.

3. When the message and attached file are to your liking, click the **Send** icon on the message's toolbar. Then click **Send and Receive** on the Inbox toolbar to send the message (with attached file) to yourself.

4. After a few minutes—or a few hours if you're exceedingly unlucky—your message should be ready for you to retrieve. Clicking the **Send and Receive** icon on the Inbox toolbar brings it in to the Inbox.

5. You'll be able to tell that this message has an attached file because of the **Paper Clip** icon that appears to the left of the message.

6. Similarly, a **Paper Clip** icon appears at the top of the Preview Pane. Click it and you'll see a list of the files that are attached to the message. Click one of the files and you'll get the dialog box shown in Figure 16.19.

FIGURE 16.19

Outlook asks what you want to do with the file that is attached to a message.

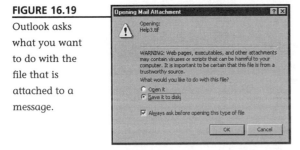

7. When you're done with this message, click it once in the upper pane, and then press the **Delete** icon ⊠ on the toolbar. Your message, along with its attached file, will be sent to the Deleted Items folder.

Note that you can attach as many files as you like to a particular message, but as the message size goes up, the chances of it surviving the trip through the Internet go down. That isn't the fault of the files, necessarily: Long messages always have a harder time getting through the Net than smaller messages. Some email service providers even refuse to send (or receive) messages larger than a predetermined size!

⚠ *CAUTION*

LIMIT THE FILE SIZE FOR YOUR EMAIL ATTACHMENTS

Some files are just huge, and there isn't much you can do about it. Even after you zip a file, it might still be so huge (say, over 1MB, or approximately 1,000,000 bytes) that you'll have trouble getting it sent, or your correspondent might not be able to download it.

If that's the case, consider breaking the file into smaller pieces, if that's possible. (On some files it isn't.) Word documents, for example, can be broken into pieces, with each segment stored in a separate file.

Finally, note that you don't have to use the **Insert**, **File** menu to get a file into an Outlook message. Outlook supports drag and drop just like most other Windows programs. Try dragging files and dropping them onto messages. Most of the time, it works like a charm.

ZIP IT UP

While files up to, oh, 50KB (about 50,000 characters) in size work just fine over the Net, after you get much above that point, it pays to compress the file. Compression removes redundant data from the file. You compress the file on your end, and the person receiving the file has to uncompress it on the other end.

While there are many programs that compress and uncompress files, I've long used a utility called WinZip, and it's served me well. Check out www.winzip.com for details.

AutoSignature

Have you ever noticed how many advanced email users tack a signature onto the end of their messages? Some of them are pretty simple—their name, maybe their email address or Web site, perhaps some personal information or a witty saying. Some of them include cute drawings, or even designs straight from a Grateful Dead poster—kinda makes you wonder what the sender's been smoking. If you set up a signature properly, it can be a real time saver for the people who read your messages.

🔍 *EXERCISE*

Create an AutoSignature

1. Once again we'll start in Outlook's Inbox.

2. Click **Tools**, **Options**, and click the **Mail Format** tab. Click **Signature Picker**, and then **New**. You see the Create New Signature Wizard, as shown in Figure 16.20.

FIGURE 16.20

Give your new
AutoSignature a
name.

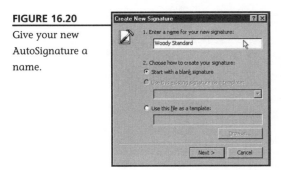

3. Outlook lets you create all sorts of different AutoSignatures, so type a name for this one (in Figure 16.20 I've called it *Woody Standard*), and then click **Next**.

4. Now type whatever you want to appear in your AutoSignature, being careful to add paragraph marks (in other words, press the **Enter** key) only where you want Outlook to force an end of paragraph. In Figure 16.21 I've typed in an AutoSignature that lists my email ID, Web site, and a shameless plug for WOW.

FIGURE 16.21

Enter your
AutoSignature
here.

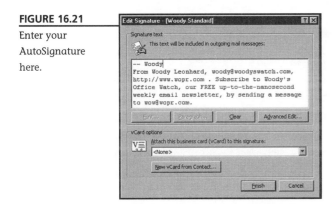

5. Resist the temptation to format the AutoSignature for now. (If you ever decide to use HTML Mail—I talk about it at the end of this chapter—you might want to add some formatting; for now, don't get yourself confused with it.) Click **Finish**, and then **OK**.

6. Back in the Options dialog box, make sure your new signature appears in the **Use this Signature by default box**, and uncheck the box that says **Don't use when replying or forwarding** (see Figure 16.22). Click **OK**.

FIGURE 16.22

Setting up the AutoSignature to work on new messages, replies, and for-wards.

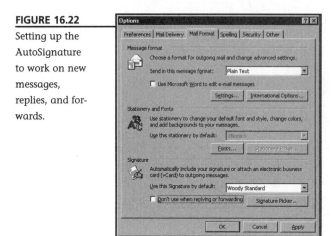

7. Test your AutoSignature. If you create a new message, as shown in Figure 16.23, the AutoSignature appears at the bottom of the message. If you reply to a message, the AutoSignature appears similarly. If you forward a message, the AutoSignature shows up before the forwarded copy.

FIGURE 16.23

A new message with the *Woody Standard* AutoSignature.

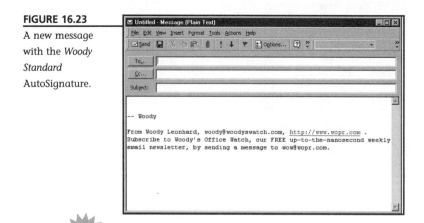

TIP

ADDING A SIGNATURE ANYWHERE YOU WANT

If you ever want to stick your AutoSignature into the middle of a message, click **Insert**, **Signature**, and then choose the AutoSignature you want.

That's all there is to the AutoSignature shtick. If you want to dig into the formatting question a bit more, check out `support.microsoft.com/support/kb/articles/q179/4/36.asp` on the Web.

vCard

The electronic version of business cards, *vCards* (short for *Virtual Cards*), provide a convenient, fast way to send a correspondent your name, address, phone number, email ID, and just about anything else you might normally think of putting on a business card.

Outlook supports vCards; more importantly, however, other email packages do as well. In particular, if you send a vCard to somebody using Netscape, they can add the information to their Netscape address book. Look for all the major email packages to support vCards soon. It's just too good an idea to ignore.

EXERCISE

Create and Send a vCard

1. To create a vCard, you have to flip over to the Contacts application, so click the **Contacts** icon in the Outlook Bar.

2. If you haven't yet created an entry for yourself, do so now. Include all the information you want people to have. At the same time, exclude any information (say, home phone number) you don't want people to have. I've completed an entry for myself in Figure 16.24.

FIGURE 16.24

To create a vCard, start by filling out a Contact entry for yourself.

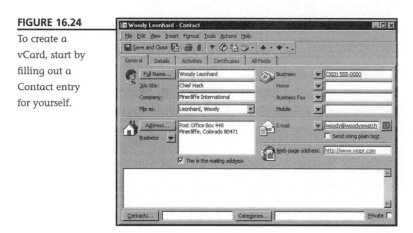

3. Next you need to save this information as a .vcf file. Click **File, Save As**. When Outlook presents you with its Save As dialog box, choose **VCARD Files (*.vcf)** in the **Save as type** box. Outlook chooses an appropriate filename for you—in this case, it suggested Woody Leonhard.vcf. Save the vCard in a convenient location.

4. This .vcf file can be treated the same as any other file. In particular, you can attach it to an email message. Try it by flipping over to the Inbox, creating a new email message, clicking **Insert**, **File**, and inserting the .vcf file you just saved.

5. If you hand out business cards like confetti on Fifth Avenue, you might want to send out your vCard with every email message. I *don't* recommend it, but if you want to, click **Tools**, **Options**, click the **Mail Format** tab, and then click the **Signature Picker**. Either select an existing AutoSignature and click **Edit** or click **New** to create a new AutoSignature. On the Edit Signature dialog box (see Figure 16.25), click **New vCard from Contact**. Choose the Contact you want to include, click **Add**, and then click **OK**. Back in the Edit Signature dialog box, in the **Attach this business card (vCard) to this Signature** box, select the vCard you want to add, and then click **OK**. Click **OK** again, and the selected vCard will go out every time you use this AutoSignature.

FIGURE 16.25

This is where you specify that a vCard is to be included in a particular AutoSignature.

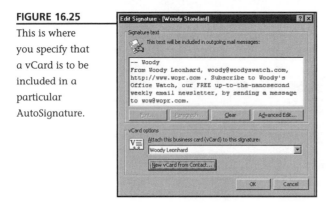

6. When you receive a message with an attached .vcf file, simply click the paper clip icon at the top of the Preview Pane and select the file. Outlook responds by presenting you with a Contact entry, precisely as you saw in Figure 16.24. If you then click **Save and Close**, Outlook adds this new entry to your Contacts list.

Find

Outlook's Inbox, Outbox, Sent Items, and Deleted Items folders all support a very powerful Find function. As the name implies, Find lets you search through messages (either the subject lines or all the text in all the messages) for specific words.

EXERCISE

Find a Deleted Item

1. Say you want to find a message you deleted from your Inbox last week. No problem. Bring up the Deleted Items folder by clicking the **Deleted Items** icon in the Outlook Bar.

2. Click the **Find** button on the toolbar. Outlook responds by tacking a Find panel at the top of the message list (see Figure 16.26).

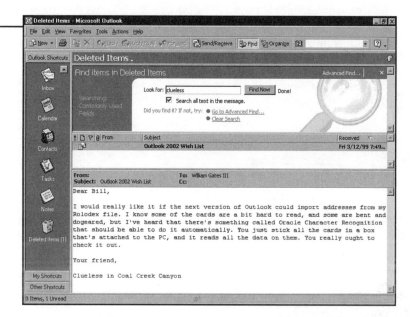

3. Type whatever text you want to search for in the **Look for** box. In Figure 16.26, I typed **clueless**. If you want Outlook to look inside the body of all the messages, check the box marked **Search all text in the message**. (If you don't check that box, Outlook only searches the To, Cc, Bcc, and Subject contents.) Click the **Find Now** button.

4. Outlook will present you with a list of all the messages that match your search criteria. Rummage through those messages and see if you found what you were looking for.

5. Outlook also puts a few lines up on the Find panel, saying "Did you find it? If not, try: Go to Advanced Find.../Clear Search." Although that text is grayed out (sheesh!), it is nonetheless hot. Click **Advanced Find** to see all the extensive search options available to you. Click **Clear Search** to start out fresh.

6. When you're done searching through the messages, you can click the **Find** icon on the toolbar again to clear away the Find panel. The Find panel also clears out if you switch to any other Outlook folder or application.

Organize

Outlook also includes very powerful capabilities for organizing your email. Although organizing is certainly in the eye of the beholder, the ability to highlight mail from important colleagues, to customize the views, and—perhaps most importantly—to shuffle junk email to a special holding area puts Outlook's email handling among the very best.

All of these Organize features apply equally well to Outlook's Inbox, Sent Items, and Deleted Items folders. You'll probably use them most within the Inbox, and that's what I'll focus on in these exercises.

Folders

Organize with Folders

1. Move to Outlook's Inbox and click the **Organize** button on the toolbar. Outlook presents you with the **Using Folders** dialog box, as shown in Figure 16.27.

FIGURE 16.27

Organizing your email with folders.

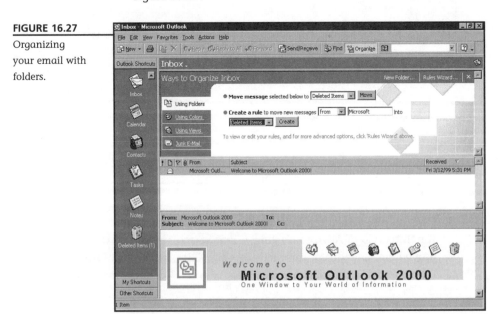

2. The first option in the Using Folders pane lets you move a selected message from one folder to another. That's a real yawner: You can move messages much more readily by clicking and dragging them.

3. The second option is much more powerful. You can create rules that Outlook will automatically apply to all incoming mail. In this particular case you can create a rule that will move any email message coming in from a specific person (actually, from a specific email ID) to any folder you choose. You can even create a new folder to receive all those messages—click the **New Folder** text at the top of the Using Folders pane, or choose **Other folder** in the **into** box.

4. There's more. You can create rules that will move messages sent to a specific ID into a particular folder. If you commonly get messages from more than one email service provider, or if you receive email addressed to all sorts of different IDs, this option lets you organize the mail according to the intended receiver.

5. If you really want to see an amazingly powerful (and quite complex!) message filtering system, click the **Rules Wizard** text at the top of the Using Folders dialog box. I won't try to step you through all the nuances here. Suffice it to say that the Office Assistant (**F1**) does a pretty good job of it.

Colors

If you don't want to shuffle messages to different folders, you should certainly take advantage of Outlook's capability to highlight messages coming from the people who are most important to you. Believe me, when a red message shows up in your Inbox, you'll take notice!

 EXERCISE

Highlighting Important Messages with Color

1. Go into Outlook's Inbox.

2. If you have a message sitting there from someone who's important to you (a boss, a spouse, a significant other, even your stock broker!), click once on the message so it appears in the Preview Pane.

3. Click the **Organize** button on the toolbar, and then click **Using Colors**. You see the Using Colors dialog box, as shown in Figure 16.28.

FIGURE 16.28

Use color to flag messages from important people.

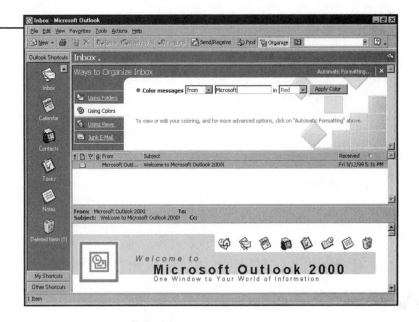

4. Choose a color for all the messages from this particular person by choosing one from the Inbox. When you're happy with the choice, click **Apply Color**.

5. If you really want to feel like you've fallen down the rabbit hole, click **Automatic Formatting** at the top of the Using Colors dialog box. You'll discover that Outlook can color code messages based on the content of the message or the size of attachments—or just about anything you can imagine. The Office Assistant doesn't provide much help with these choices, but there's limited help available if you click the **?** in the upper-right corner of the appropriate dialog boxes.

Views

☞ *I covered views in the section on "Inbox," Chapter 15, on* **page 295**.

We took a look at the various views in the earlier exercise. Check it out if you want to modify your Inbox, Outbox, Sent Items, or Deleted Items views.

Junk Mail

This is quite possibly Outlook's most compelling feature—every email user should set up Outlook to filter out junk mail.

I tend to lump junk mail into three categories:

- **Mail from Bozos**. Some Bozos are people you know; they just can't quit sending you mail that you don't want to read. These Bozos are easily handled—you know their IDs, and you can deal with their mail via the Using Folders dialog box shown in Figure 16.27.

- **Spam, which is email sent indiscriminately to everyone on a mailing list**. Typically the mailing lists are huge, and the ID of the sender changes with every message. Outlook's Junk filter will help you bypass much spam.

- **XXX messages**. Microsoft calls these Adult messages, although I fail to see anything adult about them. Prurient, maybe. Usually XXX messages are a form of spam, but sometimes they're more targeted. Outlook's Adult Content filter will take care of most of them.

EXERCISE

Enable Junk Email Filters

1. Go into Outlook's Inbox.

2. Click the **Organize** button on the toolbar, and then **Junk E-Mail**. You see the Junk E-Mail dialog box shown in Figure 16.29.

FIGURE 16.29

Outlook's built-in junk email filters.

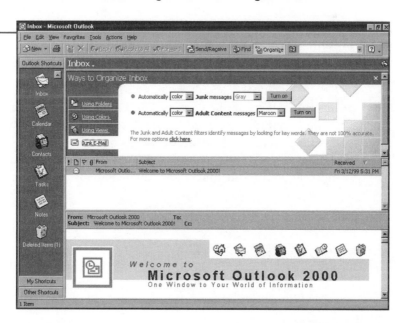

3. Outlook scans the content of each message to see if there are any matches on a specific set of words. These keywords—and Outlook's method for searching for the keywords—are described in a file called filters.txt, which is in your c:\Program Files\Microsoft Office\Office folder. You might want to use Word or Notepad (**Start**, **Programs**, **Accessories**, **Notepad**) to open that file and study it. The one that shipped with my system is shown in Figure 16.30.

FIGURE 16.30

Outlook's junk mail filter rules, in filters.txt.

4. Although Outlook's default settings for Junk and Adult messages (shown in Figure 16.29) assign them colors, I find it much more effective to move the messages out to a folder created specifically for junk mail. If you want to do the same, change the **Automatically** boxes to say **move** (see Figure 16.31). Outlook creates a new folder called Junk E-Mail for you and shuffles messages that match the Junk and Adult definitions in filters.txt into that folder.

FIGURE 16.31

How to make
Outlook move
junk mail into
its own folder.

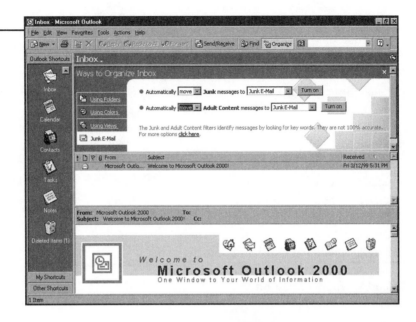

5. Mail filtering isn't a perfect science. For example, if I send you a message that says, oh, "WOPR has always carried a 100 percent money back guarantee," Outlook will see the phrase *money back* inside the message and assume it's junk mail! That's why I strongly recommend that you not direct junk mail to your Deleted Items folder, and why you need to take a look at your Junk E-Mail folder from time to time. You never know—you might have a message from me hiding in there!

DIDN'T MICROSOFT LOSE IN COURT OVER JUNK MAIL?

Yep, they sure did. A company called Blue Mountain Arts sued Microsoft because the junk mail filter in a beta test release of Internet Explorer's Outlook Express—which works much the same way as Outlook 2000—would toss Blue Mountain Arts-generated greeting cards into the Junk Mail folder.

That's a lousy thing to do, of course, but taking Microsoft to court over it? I dunno. I guess I could take Microsoft to court because it tosses my "WOPR has always carried a 100 percent money back guarantee" messages into the Junk Mail folder. Yeah. That would make a lot of sense.

continues

If you constantly get junk mail sent from the same ID, it's easy to tell Outlook that you want all messages from that ID to go in your Junk Mail folder. Just right-click the message (in the upper pane, where all the messages are listed), and choose Junk E-mail.

Microsoft is constantly refining and updating its junk mail filters. If you click the underlined phrase **click here** in the Junk E-Mail pane, Outlook offers several alternatives for handling junk mail, including an automatic tie-in to the Web to download Microsoft's latest filters.

DIDN'T MICROSOFT LOSE IN COURT OVER JUNK MAIL? continued

Let's get this straight: In order to have the Junk mail filter kick in, you have to activate it manually, using the procedure described in the exercise. Once it's activated, it'll send some messages to the Junk mail folder that shouldn't really go there. It'll send any message that says *money back* into the Junk Mail folder. It'll send any card from Blue Mountain Arts into the Junk Mail folder. Get this—it'll even send *Microsoft-generated* greeting cards (from `insider.msn.com/greetings`) into the Junk Mail folder.

That really sounds like a conspiracy against Blue Mountain Arts, doesn't it?

Oh well. Everything's been changed now so you can get your Blue Mountain Arts greeting cards. However, putting the phrase *money back* in a message will still get it kicked to Junk Mail.

Some days I really wonder about American justice.

What to Avoid—If You Can

So much for the high points of email in Office. I hope you agree with me that Outlook contains one humdinger of an email program, and that you have a chance to use it to help tame the onslaught of email that seems destined to engulf us all.

That said, there are two Outlook email options that I think you ought to avoid.

WordMail

Outlook allows you to use Word as your email editor. That feature is known as WordMail, and it stinks.

Yes, I know how nice it is to have all of Word's power available when composing email messages. (Hey, remember, you're talking to Mr. Word here.) Yes, I do hate to give up the red squiggly underline on misspelled words and the simple right-click correction routine that Word offers. Yes, I realize that Document Map can make traversing long email messages a snap.

There's just one problem. For the vast majority of people, WordMail doesn't work.

The reply formatting goes all weird; WordMail-generated replies to messages are hardly legible. WordMail causes all sorts of strange, indescribable problems with Word itself and it frequently makes Windows so unstable you'll see *GPFs* (*general protection faults*) on top of GPFs. If Outlook crashes, you'll have a hidden instance of Word running in the background. If Word crashes, it'll probably take Outlook along with it. Sorry, but as much as I love Word, it still doesn't work well inside Outlook.

If you're using WordMail right now, turn it off. Click **Tools**, **Options**, and the **Mail Format** tab, and then uncheck the box that says **Use Microsoft Word to edit e-mail messages**. While you're at it, switch your messages over to Plain Text in the top drop-down box.

I know, I know. Some of you won't give up on WordMail until Microsoft pries it from your cold, dead fingers. If you fall into that camp, I wish you luck. Back up often, back up well!

HTML Mail

Notice how I just recommended that you send messages in Plain Text, and not HTML (one of the other options in the Mail Format tab's **Send in this message format** box). There's a reason for that.

Using HTML mail doesn't carry with it the huge overhead and instability inherent in WordMail. For that we can all be thankful. But, in my experience, it isn't a good choice for beginning Outlook users, for two reasons:

IDENTIFYING HTML MESSAGES IN THE WILD

If you've never heard of *HTML*, don't worry about it. It's just another computer buzzword. Er, acronym, standing for *Hypertext Markup Language*. HTML is the language of the Web—World Wide Web pages are all constructed in HTML.

Outlook and the Netscape mail reader both allow you to create messages in HTML format and to read them if you get one in your Inbox. If you've ever seen a message that includes more than plain, drab, old everyday text, it's probably an HTML message.

1. HTML just isn't appropriate for some kinds of messages, for example, any message that might receive wide distribution. At this point there's very, very little standardization on HTML mail and its interpretation. Your carefully constructed, pretty message might end up looking like day-old pig slop.

2. New Outlook users are more likely than most to be conversing with people who don't have HTML-speaking email programs. Starting out with email is hard enough without having to answer tough questions from novice email correspondents. "Why did your message come through all garbled, with a weird attached file?" The minute you stray from Plain Text, you invite those problems. By the droves.

That said, if you want to tackle the wacky but glorious world of HTML mail, go ahead and set the **Send in this message format** box to HTML.

After you get your bearings, try adding a background (Microsoft calls it *stationery*) to your email messages. Check the Microsoft Knowledge Base article at `support.microsoft.com/support/kb/articles/q182/4/01.asp` for all sorts of helpful tips.

BUT YOU USE HTML MAIL, DON'T YOU, WOODY?

It's true: I have a newsletter—*Woody's Windows Watch*—that goes out in HTML. We use the additional formatting capabilities of HTML to make the newsletter easier to read and follow. But I still stick to plain text for my email messages.

Brian Livingston has a great article on HTML mail that ran in the March 1, 1999 issue of InfoWorld magazine. Check out "E-mail with rich text: Some Readers Like It, Others Really Don't" at `www.infoworld.com/cgi-bin/displayNew.pl?/livingst/990301bl.htm`.

Someday everybody will use HTML to send formatted email, and all the HTML email readers will produce more-or-less the same results. But for now, plain text is far and above the safest way to go.

17

Woody Leonhard

TEACHES

OTHER OUTLOOKS

LOOKIN' OUT MY BACK DOOR. Although the majority of Office users spend the bulk of their days with Word and Outlook's email component, there's lots more to like about Office in general, and about Outlook in particular. In this chapter, I'll hit the high points of the other, non-email parts of Outlook.

Contacts

No doubt you've struggled with Windows-based telephone and address books before. If you're lucky, you used one of the easy ones (such as Sidekick or Metz Phones) that sit back and get out of the way while you go about your business. If you aren't so lucky, you probably struggled with one of the heavy-duty contact management packages, where it helps to have a Ph.D. in computer science before you make your first entry.

Outlook's Contacts application takes a little more effort than the bone-simple address books: There are some tricks you can employ to make retrieving names, addresses, and phone numbers faster down the road. Still, most people find it remarkably easy to use straight out of the box, and it is amazingly flexible.

Contacts is far from perfect, of course, and we'll delve into some of its idiocies here. (More idiocy will become apparent in Chapter 29, "Tying the Parts Together," where we look at how the Contacts application interacts with Word.) For now, though, it will behoove you to take a moment and think through the way you're going to use Contacts. A little time spent now will greatly speed up things as you become more adept.

Creating a Contact

You'll be amazed at how well Outlook analyzes the information you type. Let's start by putting an entry in your Contact list for little ol' me. (Okay, okay. Big ol' me. Nevermind.)

 EXERCISE

Make Me a Contact

1. Start Outlook. If you followed the instructions in Chapter 15, "Outlook Preliminaries," you now have a separate Contacts program running down on the taskbar. Click it to bring up the Phone List

USE CONTACTS!

If you're new to computerized address/phone books—or if you've tried to use them in the past but have come away with a very bad taste in your mouth—give Outlook Contacts a chance. It's a lot easier to use than you might think, and there are great benefits to having all your contacts' names, addresses, phone numbers, and email addresses in the same location.

Whenever you think about bypassing Contacts, even for a moment—say, for example, that you have a new address you're going to type into a letter, or you're sending out an email message to somebody new—take a moment and create a contact, particularly if you think there's a chance you'll ever write to that person again. Yes, there's a certain amount of overhead involved in switching over to Outlook and typing the name and address, and if you use the address only once it's overkill. But the second time you need that address you'll come out ahead because it's already in Outlook. By the third time you use the address, it's all gravy.

view of your Contacts. (If you didn't follow the instructions in Chapter 15, you'll have to click the **Contacts** 📇 icon on the Outlook Bar, **Organize** on the toolbar, and then **Using Views**. In the **Change your view** box, click **Phone List** and click the **Organize** button again.) In either case, you should be in Phone List view, as shown in Figure 15.21 (Chapter 15).

2. Create a new contact by clicking the **New Contact** 📇 icon on the toolbar. You see the standard Contact entry form, shown in Figure 17.1.

FIGURE 17.1

Name and company information is extracted and presented so you can choose how Contacts sorts names.

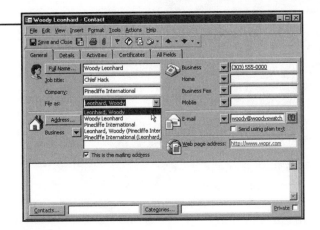

3. Type my name and company information, and watch carefully to see how Outlook's Contacts program handles much of the work for you. When you finish typing the name, Outlook takes a first guess at the File as entry (that's what Outlook uses to alphabetize the list). Type a job title and company, and then click the drop-down list next to File as. See how Outlook has created five entries for you to choose from? In the case of my contact information in Figure 17.1, you can file me away as Woody Leonhard; Leonhard, Woody; Pinecliffe International; Leonhard, Woody (Pinecliffe International); or Pinecliffe International (Leonhard, Woody). It's an amazing bit of wizardry that can save you all sorts of time—the hallmark of a very well designed computer program.

4. In most cases, you'll want to file away names of individuals in *Last name, First name* order. That makes it easy to see your contacts alphabetized by last name. In some cases, though (for example, if you have only a contact name at a company, but all the other information is for the company itself), you might want to use the *Company Name* or *Company Name (Last name, First name)* for sorting. For now, let's file me under Leonhard, Woody.

5. Now type my business address. (You also can type my home address by clicking the down-arrow next to the word Business and choosing **Home**.) When
you're done typing the address, click the **Address** button, and see how the
Contacts application has interpreted the address (see Figure 17.2). It's
uncanny how well Outlook interprets most addresses, picking up many
tough European addresses where the postal code precedes the city name.

FIGURE 17.2

Type my
address, and
Outlook inter-
prets it cor-
rectly—as can
be verified by
clicking the
Address
button.

Check Address
Address details
Street: Post Office Box 448
City: Pinecliffe
State/Province: Colorado
ZIP/Postal code: 80471
Country/Region: United States of America
☑ Show this again when address is incomplete or unclear

6. You can easily enter up to
four different phone numbers
for this contact. (Simply click
the down arrow next to
Business, Home, Business
Fax, or Mobile if you have
other kinds of phone num-
bers to enter.)

TIP

HOW TO ENTER PHONE NUMBERS

It's important to enter phone numbers
correctly. Otherwise, Outlook won't be
able to dial the phone for you properly.
Even if you never use Outlook to dial
voice calls, you probably will use it for
faxes, so listen up!

SOURCE OF THE COUNTRY

There's an important detail to note in
Figure 17.2. If you don't type a country
name (or at least, if Outlook doesn't recognize
a country name in the **Address** box), Outlook
assumes you want to use the country name
that was stored away when you first installed
Windows. If you live in the U.S. and said so
when you installed Windows, *every single*
entry in your Contacts list will be marked
United States of America—even though you
can't see it—unless you explicitly type a country name. When we get to Chapter 29, you'll
see how incredibly frustrating that little detail
can be.

For each entry, the primary question is
whether you have to dial a country code prior to dialing the phone number. If you don't
need to dial a country code, type the area code, followed by the local number; in other
words, 3035550000, *even if it's a local call*. (Force your fingers to ignore spaces, hyphens,
parentheses, and the like; it's much faster.) Outlook will interpret the number correctly.

If you do need to dial a country code, type the number like this: +country code (area code) local number; for example, +61(02)12345678. Again, Outlook will interpret the number correctly.

If you follow these simple instructions, you'll be ready to dial even if your phone company goes to ten-digit dialing or if your area code changes. I'll talk about the details at the end of this exercise.

NOTE

EXTENSIONS AND NOTES

Outlook ignores any letters you type in a phone number box, so typing an entry such as 800-OK-WINWORD gives the Contacts program heartburn. You'll be asked to retype the number.

But you can put any free-form notes you like at the end of the phone number itself. For example, 3035550000X1234 will be interpreted as (303) 555-0000, the number that Outlook is to use when it's dialing the contact, followed by the characters X1234, which appear on the Contact form and on the Phone List but aren't actually used by Outlook.

7. Outlook lets you store up to three email addresses for each contact. Type the one you want to use most frequently in the E-mail box, or click the **Address Book** icon to retrieve an email address that already exists in your Contacts list. For the second and third email addresses, click the down arrow next to the E-mail box.

NOTE

THE FLEETING THREE EMAIL ADDRESSES

It's nice that the Contacts application lets you save three email addresses. Really, it is. But Outlook's Email program—the one we tore to pieces in Chapter 16, "Email"—doesn't yet handle multiple email addresses very well.

Say you have three email addresses stored in the contacts entry for, oh, **Woody Leonhard**. If you start a new email message—look back at Figure 16.4—and type Woody, you might expect Outlook to ask you which email address for **Woody** you'd like to use.

Unfortunately, it doesn't work that way. You have to wait for the email program to find the name; then, after it's in the **To** box, you have to right-click the name to be able to pick the correct email address.

You can't even get at the multiple addresses by clicking the **To** button, where you normally choose recipients' names. The email program doesn't even list the alternative addresses. Amazing how a really neat feature in one part of Outlook can be negated by lousy design in another part, eh?

8. Type the contact's Web page address, if they're so endowed, and any comments you want in the big box at the bottom. You're just about ready to click **Save and Close** to add the contact to your Contacts list—but first there's a very important decision you have to make. It's called a *Category*, and it's so important that I'll cover the topic, all by itself, in the next section.

> **WHAT IS 10-DIGIT DIALING?**
>
> In some locations in the U.S., the telephone company requires you to punch in an area code, even for a local call. For example, I live in the 303 area code. If I want to call my neighbors down the street, I have to dial 303-555-1212; the old 555-1212 doesn't work any more. Another neighbor might have the number 277-555-1212, and to call them I cannot precede the number with a 1. It gets confusing quickly. Outlook handles these kinds of telephone company oddities with aplomb.

Dialing Conventions

How does Outlook know when to dial a 1 before an area code—or whether to dial an area code at all? When the phone company changes your area code, how do you tell Outlook? What happens when the phone company changes to 10-digit dialing (where you have to dial the area code, but not a 1, before dialing any number)? When you're on the road and try to send a fax from your portable to the home office, how do you tell Outlook to start dialing the 1 and area code?

The answers to all these questions are buried so deep inside Outlook you could spend ages hunting them down. In brief, here's where they all sit...

Back out in the Contacts application, click **Actions**, **Call Contact**, **New Call**, and then click the **Dialing Properties** button. You should get the dialog box shown in Figure 17.3.

FIGURE 17.3

Dialing Properties, where you tell Outlook which area code you're dialing from and how to get an outside line.

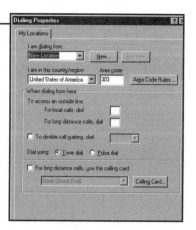

You can set up collections of settings and assign them a name in the **I am dialing from** box. For specific help on each setting, click the **?** button in the upper-right corner and click the appropriate box.

To set the rules for dialing a 1 before the number, or for dialing the area code at all, click the **Area Code Rules** button on the Dialing Properties dialog box to get the dialog box shown in Figure 17.4. These entries are pretty self-explanatory, after you find them!

FIGURE 17.4

Tell Outlook when to dial a 1 and when to dial the area code by using these settings.

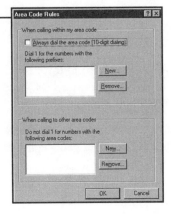

Categories

Plan from the get-go for your Contacts list to become very large. Trust me. Before long you'll be putting the Cub Scout roster in here, along with your holiday card mailing list, the addresses of all your elected representatives, and the name of the local dog catcher.

Outlook's Contacts application includes a marvelous way to help you sort out the various groups of people, without forcing you to create (and manage) ten different Contact lists. It's called Categories. You have to take the initiative to get the categories set up and maintained, but when your Contacts list grows to 100 entries (or 1,000 or 10,000!), you'll thank the day you started out on the right foot.

 EXERCISE

Set Categories for Contacts

1. You should have the Contacts entry form we were working on in the previous exercise open and ready for action.

2. Click the **Categories** button. Outlook presents you with a list of categories that it has predefined for your use (see Figure 17.5).

FIGURE 17.5

Outlook's prede-
fined categories.

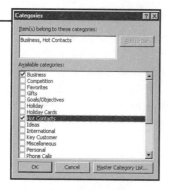

3. In this case, I want to assign Woody Leonhard to three different categories: **Business** and **Hot Contacts**, as shown in Figure 17.5, but I also want to assign him to a category called **TCF** (for Tibetan Children's Fund, of course).

4. The **TCF** category doesn't exist. To create it you need to click **Master Category List**. Outlook responds by showing you the list of all available categories, as shown in Figure 17.6.

FIGURE 17.6

Outlook's list of
all available
categories.

5. Type the name of the new category—in this case TCF—into the **New Category** box, and click **Add**.

![Caution icon] **CAUTION**

WHEN AN ADD DOESN'T

You might assume that clicking **Add** at this point adds the contact called **Woody Leonhard** to the **TCF** category. It doesn't. The **Add** here signifies only that you want to add a new category to Outlook's overall list. Careful!

6. After you've added the new category called **TCF** you have to go back into the Categories dialog box, check the box marked **TCF**, and then click **OK** (see Figure 17.7).

FIGURE 17.7

FIGURE 17.7

The contact is
added to the
new category
only after you
check it in this
dialog box.

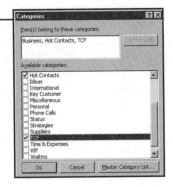

7. Click **Save and Close**, and Woody Leonhard is added to your Contacts list.

Although it's possible to type categories in the Contact form's Categories box, I strongly advise against it. You'll find it much simpler—and more accurate—to click the **Categories** button and check off the appropriate categories as you add new contacts.

So now that you have your contacts assigned to categories, what can you do with them? Good question...

Invariably, whenever I want to look up a contact quickly, one of two situations applies: Either I know the person's (or business's) name; or I can't remember the name, but I certainly know the category. You're probably the same way. Outlook's Contact application gives you some powerful tools to make your lookup job easier.

EXERCISE

Two Views of Contacts

1. You have your Contacts list open, and it's in Phone List view, as shown in Figure 15.21. Good. This is an excellent general-purpose view, the one you should use when you look up a name.

2. You can make this view even better, though, by changing the font of select Contacts, based on their categories. Say I want to make all my Business category contacts bold so that they'll stand out on in the Phone List view. (It's more dramatic, but harder to see in this book, if you actually color code them—say, make them all blue and bold.) Start by clicking **Organizer**, and then **Using Views**. You see **Phone List** in the **Change your view** box. Click **Customize current view**, as shown in Figure 17.8.

FIGURE 17.8

Color code the
various cate-
gories by click-
ing **Customize
Current View**.

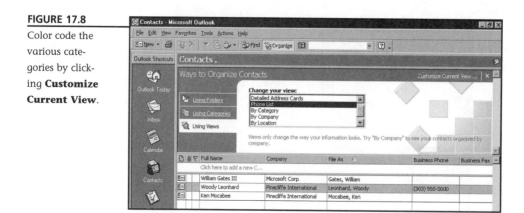

3. When Outlook asks you which View component you want to change, click
   the **Automatic Formatting** button. You'll see the **Automatic
   Formatting** dialog box, as shown in Figure 17.9.

FIGURE 17.9

Outlook has
names for its
various auto-
matic format-
ting rules.

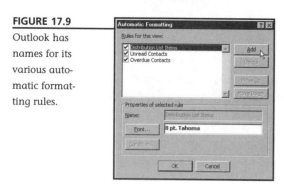

4. We need to add a new automatic formatting rule, so
   click **Add**. Type a name for
   the new formatting rule; I
   chose Business. Then click
   the **Font** button, and apply
   whatever formatting you
   like. In this case, I chose 8-
   point bold Tahoma. You
   may well want to assign a
   color to these particular contacts. Click **OK**, and your
   new automatic formatting rule will appear, checked, in the **Automatic
   Formatting** dialog box (see Figure 17.10).

**WHAT IF THERE'S MORE THAN
ONE CATEGORY?**

If a particular contact belongs to more
than one category and each category has a different font treatment, Outlook makes a game
attempt to combine the fonts. For example, if
you have Business contacts set up for bold and
Hot Contacts set up as red, a contact that's
both Business and Hot shows up in bold red.

FIGURE 17.10

The new automatic formatting rule called Business has been added.

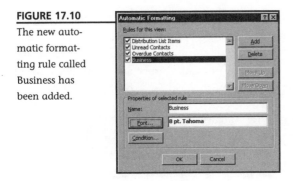

5. Now you have to tell Outlook that you want to apply this formatting to any contact in the Business category. To do so, click **Condition**, and then in the Filter dialog box, click the **More Choices** tab. Click **Categories** and, in the Available Categories dialog box, check the box marked **Business**. Click **OK** and you'll have your new filtering rule set, as shown in Figure 17.11.

FIGURE 17.11

Set the filter to catch any contacts in the Business category.

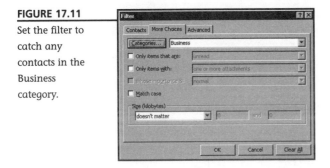

6. Click **OK** three times, and then click the **Organize** icon to get rid of the Organize box. Your custom Phone List view now shows all Business contacts in bold, as shown in Figure 17.12. Neat!

FIGURE 17.12

The new Phone List view puts Business contacts in bold.

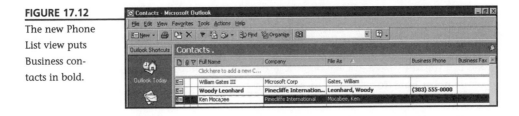

7. But what if you know the category—or want to restrict your attention to a single category—and you don't want to deal with all the other contacts, whether they're blue and bold or green and italic? That's pretty easy, too.

8. Back in Phone List view, click the **Organize** button, and then click **Using Views** (no, not **Using Categories**!). In the Change your view box, choose **By Category**. Suddenly, all of your contacts appear grouped by category, as shown in Figure 17.13. Click the + sign in front of the category that interests you, and only those contacts show up on the grid.

FIGURE 17.13

Outlook will also gladly group contacts by category.

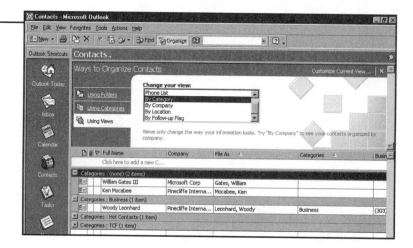

MULTIPLE CATEGORY PROBLEM SOLVED

When you're in By Category view, Outlook will put separate copies of each contact in every appropriate category. Because I put Woody Leonhard in the **Business, Hot Contacts,** and **TCF** categories, the contact will actually show up in three different places in the By Category view, as you can probably surmise from Figure 17.13.

9. You can either flip back to Phone List view by clicking **Phone List** in the Change your view box, or you can stay in By Category view by clicking the **Organize** icon again.

BY CATEGORY VIEW SHOWS ALL

Note that you have all the usual tools at your disposal while in By Category view: Click **Company**, for example, and the displayed contacts are sorted by company.

Copying

For such a clearly brilliant program, Outlook can be awfully dumb at times.

Two important capabilities are nowhere to be seen in the Contacts application:

- It's impossible to put a contact's name and address on the Clipboard so you can use it in some other program.

- There's no easy way to type a company's address once and have it readily available for new contacts (or change it once and have the change ripple throughout my contacts list).

I wish I had a nickel for every time I've typed "One Microsoft Way/Redmond, WA 98052."

That said, Outlook does have one rather anemic method for minimizing the amount of typing involved in setting up a new contact. If you select a contact, and then click **Actions**, **New Contact from Same Company**, Outlook fills in the company name, address, and business phone numbers from the selected contact, and then presents the new Contact form for you to complete.

You can also right-click a Contact and choose **New Contact from Same Company**.

From my point of view, anyway, that's the bare minimum of what you need to understand about Contacts. Keep your categories straight, and Outlook's Contacts application will serve you well. Ignore them and you'll end up with a jumbled mess.

HOW WOULD YOU KNOW THAT?

I have no idea why Microsoft put this under **Actions**. It isn't under **File**, **New**, where most Office users might expect it; nor is it an option under the **New Contact** icon. It isn't accessible when you're filling out a new contact form, either via a tunnel button or the Insert menu. In short, you just have to learn about this feature by osmosis.

Calendar

Outlook's Calendar application rates right up there with the best calendar/scheduling packages available on the market. In fact, for most people, much of Calendar rates as wishful thinking and overkill. I'll show you what I mean.

The Outlook Calendar tracks three kinds of activities: Events, Appointments, and Meetings. There's a very easy way to tell which is which:

- An *Event* is an all-day or multiple-day activity, such as a birthday, holiday, or convention. There's no beginning or ending time.

- An *Appointment*, on the other hand, has a starting and (at least projected) ending time. Appointments are, well, appointments.

- *Meetings are Appointments* where you contact the participants electronically to ascertain whether they can attend.

Let's deal with Meetings first.

Meetings

As you can probably guess, it takes a lot of discipline to get good-sized Meetings—in the Outlook sense of the term—off the ground. Just for starters, everybody attending the meeting has to be running software that is compatible with Outlook. Those needed for a Meeting must maintain accurate calendars online so the Meeting planner software can check to see whether the participant has the time slot free. All the attendees have to be in your Contacts list, and they all must have email IDs. Then everybody has to answer the query email messages in a timely manner to say whether they'll be going to the meeting. If one key person finks out, another round of email is necessary to change times (or locations). And on and on.

Personally, I don't know of anybody who's ever kept their electronic appointment calendar updated, accurately, more than a few minutes in advance. (Present company included.) I figure Meetings are more hassle than they're worth. As anyone who's put together a Meeting—in the Outlook sense of the term—will tell you, it almost never works the way it's supposed to; and if there are more than three or four participants, you can kiss the whole electronic effort good-bye from the start.

Anyway, I'm not going to talk about Meetings in this book. If you work with people who are disciplined enough to maintain their electronic calendars, conscientious enough to respond to email rapidly, and organized to the point that they can make Meetings work, I salute you. I also direct you to your corporate Help Desk for assistance in setting up Meetings with Outlook.

Events

The easiest way to learn about Events is to see how one looks inside the Calendar. Let's set up a week-long Event and take a gander.

EXERCISE

A Convention

1. Click the **Calendar** ![icon] icon in the Outlook Bar to bring up Outlook's Calendar application.

2. This particular Event, Fall Comdex (a big annual tech conference that's supposed to be the largest conference of any kind in the U.S.), runs five days from November 15 to November 19. So start by selecting all five days in the calendar in the upper-right corner, as shown in Figure 17.14.

FIGURE 17.14

To set an Event, start by selecting the days it encompasses.

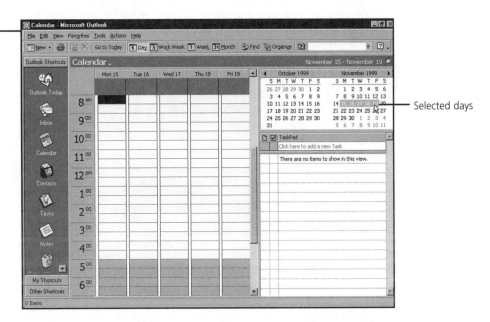

Selected days

3. As you select the days, you'll notice that your calendar automatically changes from a one-day view to a five-day view to give you a visual reminder that you've selected five days.

4. Click the **New Appointment** icon on the toolbar. You'll get the Calendar's **New Appointment** form (see Figure 17.15). Type the Subject and Location, check the box marked **All day event**, and set the **Start time** (which is just a date) and the **End time**. Uncheck the **Reminder** box (you don't want a reminder to pop up on the screen 15 minutes before midnight on Sunday night!). Add a note in the big box at the bottom and click **Save and Close**.

FIGURE 17.15

The Calendar's New Appointment form, set to an all-day (actually, all-week) Event.

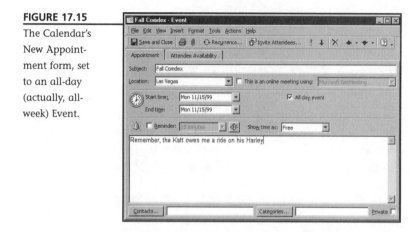

5. When you get back to the Calendar (see Figure 17.16), note how Outlook puts the name and location of the Event up at the top of the five-day calendar. That keeps it out of the way so you still have room add Appointments, even during the Event.

FIGURE 17.16

The Event appears at the top of the calendar.

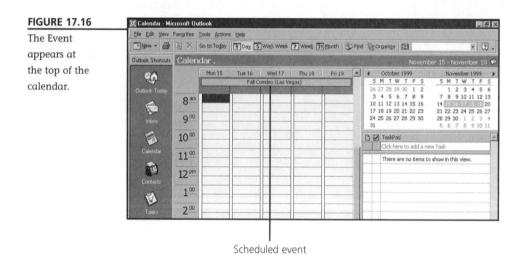

Scheduled event

Appointments

Outlook's Calendar makes it very easy to add appointments during the day. Let's add an appointment at 10:00 Monday morning, during Comdex.

EXERCISE

Making—and Breaking—an Appointment

1. Start with the five-day view of Comdex that you created in the preceding exercise.

2. Put your cursor in the 10:00 box on Monday morning and double-click. Outlook responds with the New Appointment form, much as you would expect (see Figure 17.17). Outlook initially assumes that you want to set up a 30-minute appointment, starting at 10:00.

FIGURE 17.17

Set up a new appointment.

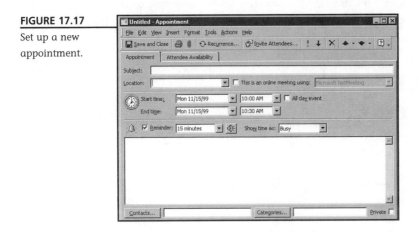

3. Fill in the **Subject** and **Location** (see Figure 17.18), and adjust the **End Time** if it isn't reasonable. Keep the **Reminder** box checked—this time you want a warning to pop up on the screen and a little sound to go off 15 minutes before the meeting. Finally, type any notes you need in the big box at the bottom and click **Save and Close**.

FIGURE 17.18

Filling out the details of a one-hour appointment.

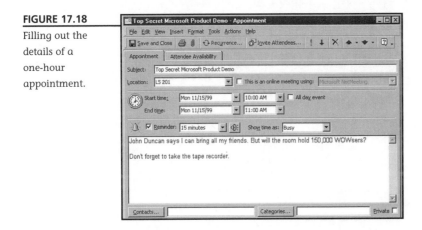

4. Back you go to the five-day calendar. Outlook shows a one-hour appointment starting at 10:00 for New Secret Product. The bell in front of the appointment title indicates that a reminder alarm will go off before the meeting.

5. Sure enough. It's 9:45 on Monday morning, and you overslept. Your portable (which you left on, plugged into the wall) is wailing like Bo-Peep's sheep, and there's no way you can make the 10:00 appointment. You get on the horn and reschedule for 11:00. (Try doing that with an Outlook-style Meeting!) How to change the appointment in Outlook? No sweat. Hover your cursor over the 10:00 appointment. It'll turn into a four-headed arrow. Click and drag the appointment down to 11:00, as shown in Figure 17.19.

FIGURE 17.19

Rescheduling an appointment is as simple as a click and drag.

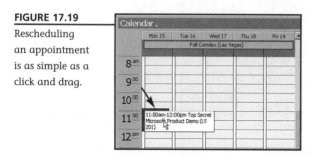

6. Outlook reschedules everything—including the 15-minute warning reminder beep. Go back to sleep. You've got plenty of time.

Recurring Activities

Some events happen on the same day every year: birthdays, anniversaries, and the like. Many appointments also recur: the traditional weekly staff meeting or monthly sales meeting. As long as the activities recur daily, weekly, monthly, or annually, chances are pretty good that Outlook can set up your calendar automatically.

To set up a recurring appointment or event, just bring up the Appointment form (as previously shown in Figure 17.18), and click the **Recurrence** icon. Outlook presents you with the Appointment Recurrence dialog box, shown in Figure 17.20.

FIGURE 17.20

Set recurring appointments and events here. Outlook can even schedule recurrences such as "the third Wednesday of every month."

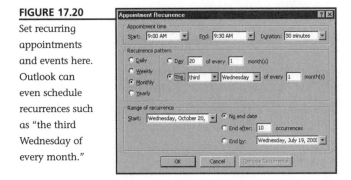

The choices here are pretty self-explanatory. Note that if you want to get rid of a recurring appointment, you merely click it, click the **Recurrence** icon, and then click the **Remove Recurrence** button at the bottom of this dialog box.

Printing Calendars

I won't say that Outlook's capability to print calendars will win any awards, but I'm frequently surprised by how few Outlook users realize that the option exists. In fact, the Calendar application contains a host of options for printing daily, weekly, and monthly calendars, either on a single page or tri-folded.

The printed calendars are generally quite good, and they can be customized very easily.

To see the options that are available, click **File**, **Print**. Outlook's calendar Print dialog box (see Figure 17.21) is considerably more complex than those in other Office applications, but it's ideally suited to the job.

FIGURE 17.21

Outlook prints calendars ten ways from Tuesday.

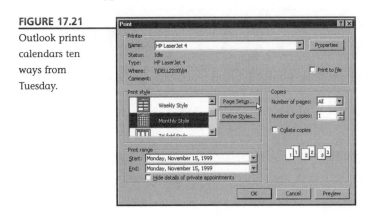

SQUISHED PRINTING

Outlook fills up all the space available in a printed square, but if you have long meeting descriptions, that might not be enough. You can tell Outlook to print with a smaller font. To do so, click **File**, **Print**, **Define Styles**, and then choose **Calendar Details Style** and click **Edit**. From that point, you can make the font as small as you please.

The customizing options that you'll most likely want to use sit under the **Page Setup** button. Click it and have fun!

Tasks: It's What to Do

Outlook's To-Do List (Microsoft calls them Tasks) feature offers much more than first meets the eye. If you get in the habit of keeping your Tasks inside Outlook (instead of, oh, jotting them down on the back of envelopes, as I usually do), Outlook can help you with a number of memory-joggers.

Set a Task

1. Go into Outlook's Tasks application by clicking the Tasks  icon on the Outlook Bar.

2. Underneath the **Subject** heading, click once on the grayed-out text that says **Click here to add a new Task**. Type a description of the Task, press the **Tab** key, and type a due date (see Figure 17.22).

FIGURE 17.22

Creating a new Task from the Tasks application.

WHAT'S IN A DATE?

Note how, in Figure 17.22, I typed next tuesday for a due date. In general, any time you're asked to type a date, you have a great deal of flexibility in what Outlook will recognize as legitimate. Try playing with it a bit and you'll come away impressed.

3. That sequence of actions creates a simple Task; if you do nothing more, Outlook shows you a reminder (and plays a little song) at 8:00 on the morning the Task becomes due. If the Task falls past due, it will start appearing in red on all the Task screens.

4. It probably won't surprise you to know that Outlook has quite a few additional options for Tasks. To see the first level of embellishment, double-click the Task you just created. The Task application shows you a Task form, as shown in Figure 17.23. (Note how **next tuesday** has been translated into a more conventional date.)

FIGURE 17.23

The Task form, where you can gussy up Tasks.

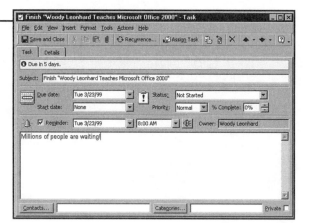

5. Most of the entries on the Task form are self-explanatory, but you need to take note of a few options. The Status box is limited to five choices (Not started, In progress, Completed, Waiting on someone else, and Deferred). Priority can be set only to High, Normal, or Low.

6. The Details tab in Figure 17.23 might be helpful. It contains built-in fields where you can list how many hours

INFORMATION AT SOME FINGERTIPS

Surprisingly, different Task information shows up in different locations. As you've seen, the due date appears in the Task list and in Outlook Today, but not on the TaskPad. (This is not surprising because the TaskPad doesn't have a whole lot of spare room.)

What *is* rather amazing is that changing a Task's Priority doesn't change the Task's icon. Thus, you won't be able to distinguish high-priority Tasks when looking at them in the Tasks list or the Calendar's TaskPad. High-priority Tasks do get an exclamation point, though, when they show up on the Outlook Today page.

Go figure.

you worked on the Task, Contacts and Companies involved, mileage, and billing notes. Don't get too excited, though: There's no easy way to group and total this information or export it to, say, Excel for billing or other analysis.

7. The **Assign Task** icon on the toolbar in Figure 17.23 is another option worth exploring, particularly if you commonly assign tasks to other people via email. It automatically generates email to inform the stuckee, er, assignee, and there are additional hooks to work with status reports, completion tracking, and the like. Hardly a full-blown project management package, but if your needs aren't particularly demanding, it can be handy—and it works much better than the Outlook Meetings feature.

8. Your new task appears not only in the Tasks list, but also in the Calendar's TaskPad. Click the **Calendar** icon in the Outlook Bar, and you'll see the Task in the lower-right corner (see Figure 17.24).

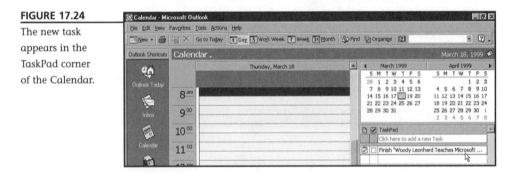

9. Finally, the new task also appears on the Outlook Today page (see Figure 17.25), along with the due date, which doesn't show up in the Calendar's TaskPad. From Outlook Today, you can click the Task, and the full Task form appears to show all the Task's details.

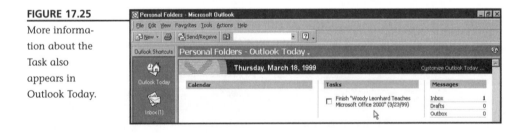

Notes

The great unsung hero of Outlook's back pages, you might think of Notes as the electronic equivalent of little yellow sticky-notes. But if you do, you'll be selling this amazing flat-file database program short. All you have to do is kind of stand on your head and squint real hard, and you'll see how the lowly Notes application can really help you organize all the flotsam and jetsam that crosses your desk every day.

Trust me. Learn Notes and start using it, even if you don't use any other part of Outlook. Let me show you how.

EXERCISE

Organizing Notes

1. Start the Notes application by clicking the **Notes** 📝 icon on the Outlook Bar.

2. Click the **New Note** 📝 icon to create your own new Note. In Figure 17.26 I've created a couple of new Notes, both of which contain quotes from famous (or at least infamous) sources. I collect quotes to use in my writing. So I started both of these Notes with the word *Quote* to show that they're both quotes.

FIGURE 17.26

Creating a couple of new Notes, both Quotes.

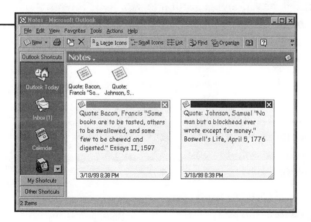

3. You can click on a Note and drag it onto the Windows desktop. That's cool, I guess, but it doesn't show you what Notes are *really* good for.

4. When you click the **List** button (see Figure 17.27), the Notes application sorts all the Notes alphabetically. Because I had the foresight to begin each quote-related Note with the word *Quote*, followed by the author's last name, they all sort together—making them easy to identify and track.

FIGURE 17.27

The List view sorts Notes in alphabetical order.

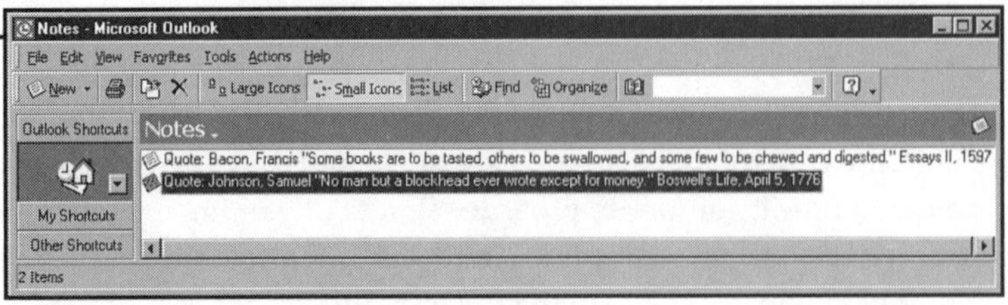

5. If you want to get a little fancier and don't mind spending the time, you can even color code the Notes (five different colors are available by right-clicking the Note and choosing Color) or assign them to Categories, just as we did with Contacts. If you use these more advanced organizing techniques, click the Organize button to get customized views of your Notes sorted every which way.

6. Also available is Outlook's full Find capability, up on the toolbar. That means you can search for any text, in any Note, with just a click. Very powerful.

Journaling Phone Calls

Although Outlook has many screaming lapses, none scream more energetically than its astounding lack of phone call logging support. Many people depend on phone calls for their livelihood, and for those people the poor support of this one feature alone might force them to use a package other than Outlook.

When it comes to phone calls, Outlook has two feeble capabilities:

- If a Contact has a phone number, Outlook will dial the number for you and log that call, with elapsed time and your typed notes.

- If you receive a call from someone on your Contacts list, you can bring up a form that lets you time the conversation and keep notes about it.

CAN THE COMPUTER DIAL MY PHONE?

To use a PC to dial outbound calls, you need to have a suitably capable modem, plus a microphone or telephone handset that works with the modem to enable you to talk on the phone after the number has been dialed by the computer.

EXERCISE

Log an Outbound Call

1. Start in the Contacts application; click the **Contacts** ![icon] icon in the Outlook Bar.

2. Choose the Contact you want to call. Right-click the name, and click **Call Contact**. Outlook responds with the New Call dialog box, as shown in Figure 17.28.

FIGURE 17.28

Have the computer dial the phone with this dialog box.

3. Make sure the **Create new Journal Entry when starting new call** box is checked, and then click **Start Call**.

TIP

MODEM SETUP PROBLEMS

If you haven't set up your modem properly, Outlook will complain. This is pretty common, so don't be too worried about it—but you're pretty much at the mercy of your PC (or modem) manufacturer. Contact them and tell them you're trying to use Outlook to dial an outbound voice call.

4. If all works as it is supposed to, Outlook shows a Call Status dialog box that lets you switch over to the microphone or handset when somebody answers.

5. When you're done with the call, click the **Save and Close** button. The call will appear in the Journal—and we'll talk about that in the next exercise.

To reliably log inbound calls, you need to be right next to your PC, and should probably have your Contacts list (in Phone List view!) already showing when the call comes in. Even then it takes some fancy footwork to get the logging mechanism working.

EXERCISE

Log an Inbound Call

1. Start in Outlook's Contacts application. The telephone rings. You pick up the phone (or use Caller ID) and figure out who's calling.

2. Double-click the Contact who's calling you. You'll get the standard Contact form, as shown in Figure 17.1, way back at the beginning of this chapter.

3. Click **Actions** on the menu, and then **New Journal Entry for Contact**. (Equivalently, you can drag the Contact from the phone list onto the **Journal** icon in the Outlook Bar—if you're a contortionist, anyway.) You'll get the Journal Entry form, as shown in Figure 17.29.

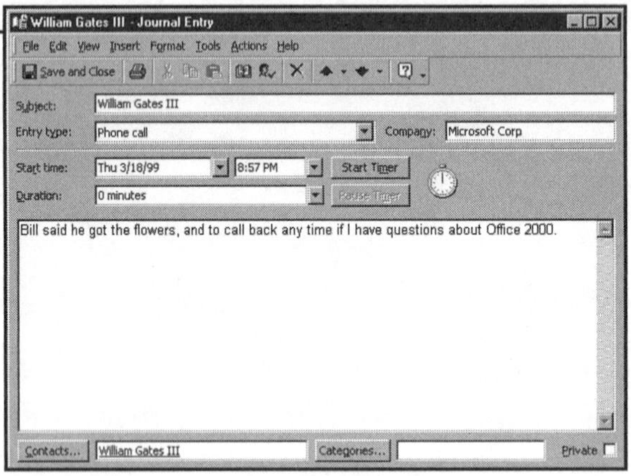

FIGURE 17.29

Creating a
Journal entry
for an incoming
phone call.

William Gates III - Journal Entry	_ □ ×
File Edit View Insert Format Tools Actions Help	
Save and Close	
Subject:	William Gates III
Entry type:	Phone call	Company:	Microsoft Corp
Start time:	Thu 3/18/99	8:57 PM	Start Timer
Duration:	0 minutes	Pause Timer
Bill said he got the flowers, and to call back any time if I have questions about Office 2000.	
Contacts...	William Gates III	Categories...	Private

4. Quickly, before you do anything else, click the **Start Timer** button. Then, at your leisure, as the conversation unfolds, fill in the **Subject** box and type whatever notes you might desire in the big box on the bottom.

5. When your conversation ends, click **Save and Close**. That stops the timer and saves the new Journal entry. You'll be propelled back to the Contact form for this particular Contact, but now you can also see the Journal entry for this phone call (see Figure 17.30).

FIGURE 17.30

The Contact form, showing this most recent phone call.

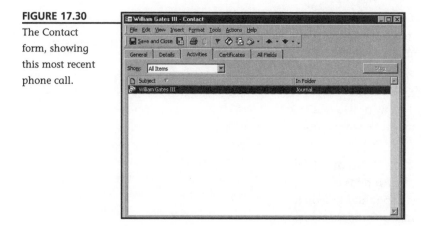

6. In general, you can find all the Journal entries for all your phone calls in Outlook's Journal application (see Figure 17.31). Simply click the **Journal** icon on the Outlook Bar, and you can view your phone log in many different ways by using the **Organize** button.

FIGURE 17.31

Inbound and outbound phone logs can be found in the Journal.

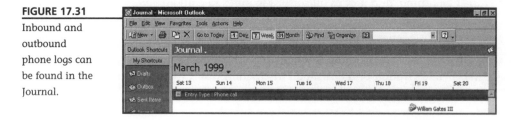

That's the only use I've found for the Journal.

Add-ins

I wanted to conclude this discussion of Outlook with some indication of how it can be made better. Just as the ascendancy of Word generated a host of Word add-ons to make the operation of Word faster, easier, and more reliable, so, too, will the inevitable success of Outlook bring more and better add-ons, spelling relief to all of us long-suffering users.

After all, there's a reason why Personal Information Managers are called Personal. Everybody does things a little differently. That's what makes life interesting, eh?

At this point, I know of two Outlook add-ons that might be worth your perusal.

The first one, called Integrated File Management, which adds an Advanced Find capability to search for files from inside Outlook, comes from Microsoft. While its highfalutin' name might overstate the capabilities a bit, the price is right—it's free. You can read about it and download it from `support.microsoft.com/support/kb/articles/q181/8/21.asp`.

The second package is a commercial add-on that holds great promise, I think. It's called Lightning, and it adds all sorts of features to Outlook: quick Contact look-up, easier entry for Tasks ("Call Jim next Thursday at 8:00"), and far simpler access to Contacts, Categories, and much more.

If you find yourself spending a lot of time in Outlook, it's definitely worth a look. There's a description and download instructions for a free trial version at `www.catalystinnovations.com`.

MORE OUTLOOK TOYS ON THE WAY?

As we went to press, I had a chance to take a peek at several Outlook add-ons that had been developed in-house, inside Microsoft itself. It's still too early to tell if these snazzy packages will ever see light of day, but it's not impossible: after all, the wildly popular Windows PowerToys started the same way. Hey, you folks in Redmond! How 'bout letting some of those goodies out of the bag?

Woody Leonhard

TEACHES

OFFICE 2000

EXCEL

V

18

Woody Leonhard

TEACHES

EXCEL PRELIMINARIES

AIN'T COMPUTERS WUNNERFUL? We've come a long way from the days of green eyeshades, columnar pads, pencil sharpeners, and mechanical pull-down-the-handle calculators. With Excel you can make more calculation errors in a second than an experienced accountant used to be able to make in weeks.

Excel Boot Camp

That's why I'm going to approach Excel differently here than in the other introductory books, videos, online help systems, and the like. They want you to think of Excel as a wonderfully capable upgrade of the old columnar pad with a fast and savvy built-in calculator. I want you to think of Excel as a loaded shotgun aimed directly at your foot with the safety off.

If you're accustomed to looking at computer-generated spreadsheets and believing the numbers are correct just because "they were done on the computer; they have to be right," think of the following chapters as a much-needed dose of reality. Mathematical errors in Excel spreadsheets are almost as common as spelling errors in Word documents. It isn't enough that Excel (and Word for that matter) gives you the tools to avoid most of the problems. You have to learn how to use the tools and then apply what you've learned religiously. Otherwise, one twitch and the Excel shotgun goes kaboom!

Welcome to Excel Boot Camp, recruit.

Heh heh heh.

Terminology

What is the difference between a worksheet and a workbook? Is a spreadsheet the data I see on the screen, the stuff that prints on a page, or the computer program responsible for both? Is a printed spreadsheet the same as a worksheet?

Just accept it right from the get-go: Excel terminology sucks. In fact, terminology throughout the spreadsheet industry (there's that S word again!) runs all over the map. In Excel if you click **File**, **New**, you'll see Excel's default offer to create a new workbook, but at the same time there's a tab marked **Spreadsheet Solutions**. If you then click **File,Print**, you'll be given the option to print the Active sheet. And on and on.

The beast that I call a *spreadsheet* has an official name in Microsoft-speak. It's called a *worksheet*, but Microsoft uses the name so cavalierly, and you'll hear *worksheet* used so infrequently, that I'm going to use the common, vulgar term.

GOSPEL ACCORDING TO WOODY

Throughout this book I'll use the term *spreadsheet* (or occasionally *sheet*) to refer to a single grid with rows and columns and cells.

One or more spreadsheets make a *workbook*. In fact, a workbook is just an .xls file, and I will use that term occasionally as well.

Crucial Changes

Excel's settings, straight out of the box, are certainly more than adequate if you don't intend to use it very much. On the other hand, if you really want to take advantage of what the product has to offer, I strongly recommend you make these simple changes.

No Adaptive Menus

If you haven't yet shut off Office's adaptive menus, consider doing so now. Your eyes aren't pinballs: they shouldn't be forced to go *ping! ping! ping!* when looking for entries on the menu. To make the menus stay put (so they don't adapt on their own moving menu items willy-nilly), click **Tools**, **Customize**, and on the **Options** tab, uncheck the box marked **Menus show recently used commands first**.

While you're there, you might also want to uncheck the box marked **Standard and Formatting toolbars share one row**. Although it takes a little extra screen real estate, getting rid of adaptive toolbar buttons is almost as relieving as zapping out the adaptive menus.

☞ For details about adaptive, uh, personalized menus, see my discussion in *"See All That You Can See, Adaptively"* in the first Word chapter, Chapter 6, "Word Preliminaries," **page 79.**

AutoSave

For the life of me, I have no idea why Excel doesn't install AutoSave automatically.

The very first thing you should do before you start relying on Excel is to install and activate the AutoSave feature. Just as with Word, AutoSave automatically saves a copy of your open workbooks at intervals you can set. Unlike Word, though, AutoSave is considered an add-in and you have to go hunting for it. Bah!

Although Microsoft's implementation of AutoSave in Excel leaves much to be desired—for example, you have to specify a filename for any previously unsaved workbook, which is ludicrous—running with AutoSave still beats the devil out of working without a net. Get AutoSave going now.

OH REALLY?

Okay. Yeah, I *do* know why Microsoft doesn't activate AutoSave automatically. Advanced Excel users tend to play around with their spreadsheets quite a bit and use Save as a safety net. Instead of relying on Undo to back out of a series of mistakes, Excel users frequently save when they've reached a steady point in a spreadsheet's development, and then go back and open the saved file if something major goes awry. (It's important to note that Excel doesn't have anywhere near the Undo capabilities that are embodied in Word, and that all Undo information disappears whenever a workbook is saved; I'll talk about that more in the next chapter.)

continues

EXERCISE

Enable AutoSave

1. Start Excel. (Click **Start**, **Programs**, **Microsoft Excel**.)

2. Click **Tools**, **Add-Ins**. You should see the Add-Ins dialog box, as shown in Figure 18.1.

NOTE

WHAT IF IT ISN'T THERE?

If you performed a standard Office installation, AutoSave might not yet be installed. If that's the case, you'll get a message like the one in Figure 18.2. Click **OK**, and be prepared to insert the Office 2000 CD.

Don't you just love install-on-demand?

OH REALLY?   continued

I don't like that approach for two reasons. First, running without AutoSave leaves you incredibly vulnerable to a power outage or other system screw-up: if you've been playing with a spreadsheet for a couple of hours without saving and the power goes bye-bye, your only option may be cyanide.

Second, Excel should be set up to help novices, right out of the box. That includes AutoSave. More advanced users should be able to figure out how to cycle through several backups using Save As. Novices' spreadsheets shouldn't be sacrificed for the convenience of advanced users who can generally fend for themselves.

FIGURE 18.1

The Add-Ins dialog box, where you can find AutoSave.

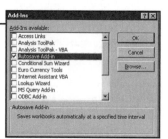

FIGURE 18.2

If you get this message, you did nothing wrong. It's just Office playing with itself, trying to reduce the size of its "footprint."

3. Check the box marked **AutoSave**, and then click **OK**. That activates the AutoSave Add-In.

4. To set AutoSave options, click **Tools**, **AutoSave**. You'll see the AutoSave dialog box, as shown in Figure 18.3.

FIGURE 18.3

AutoSave settings become available under the Tools menu.

5. Personally, I feel comfortable having the active workbook saved every 10 minutes, but your impressions might differ. (Just don't set it too low if you're going to be using large workbooks—the delay from too many AutoSaves will drive you nuts.) I also don't want to be asked if I want to save every time AutoSave kicks in, so I unchecked that box.

If you haven't yet given a new Excel workbook a filename when AutoSave kicks in, you'll have to type a name and put up with AutoSave's nonsense. And I can hardly believe that Excel deletes all Undo information whenever a workbook is saved. Those are two of the worst design glitches in Office today, in my opinion, and the people who are responsible for them should be banished to the seventh level of Excel Hell.

Even given AutoSave's myriad problems, using it is still better than losing all your data if Excel crashes or locks up. And it does. Oh, yes, it does.

Stay Put After Enter

When you type in Word, the program puts whatever you type up on the screen. Simple. But when you move to Excel, you have to be able to tell Excel when you're done typing things into a cell. Although there are lots of ways to do that, most people press the **Enter** key.

Unfortunately, Excel does strange things when you press **Enter**. Generally it moves the cursor down to the next cell, the one directly below the one you've been typing in. (There are circumstances where pressing **Enter** can trigger even more bizarre behavior.) Personally, I rarely want to go down to the next cell when I press **Enter**. Mostly I just want Excel to acknowledge the fact that I've typed a number or a formula and show the result in the spreadsheet. Sometimes I want to move on to the next cell—right, left, up, or down, but when that happens I'm perfectly content to use the arrow keys on my keyboard to specify precisely where I want to go.

If you want Excel to stay put after you type something into a cell and press **Enter**, it's easy to change.

Click **Tools**, **Options**, and click the **Edit** tab. Remove the check mark in front of the **Move selection after Enter** box, as shown in Figure 18.4.

FIGURE 18.4

Make Excel
behave nor-
mally when you
enter data into
a cell and press
Enter.

FIGURE 18.4

Make Excel
behave nor-
mally when you
enter data into
a cell and press
Enter.

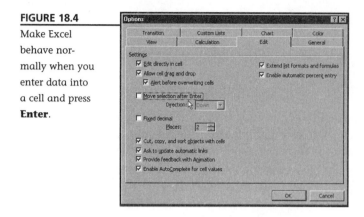

Click **OK** and Excel drops one of its most irritating predispositions.

Max Out the Most Recently Used List

Excel, like Word, keeps a list of most recently used (MRU) files at the bottom of the
File menu. If you have a very tiny screen and run Excel at 640 × 480 resolution, you
might want to succumb to Excel's anemic default setting, showing only the four
most MRU files on the list. Most of us, though, would like to see all that Excel can
offer. In this case, the maximum number Excel will show is nine files.

Click **Tools**, **Options**, and click the **General** tab; then run the Recently used file list
spinner up to **9** (see Figure 18.5).

FIGURE 18.5

Check the
Macro virus
protection set-
ting and run
the MRU list up
to 9 entries.

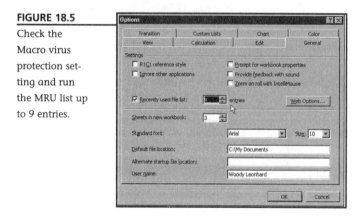

Click **OK** and Excel will start showing nine files on the File menu.

Double-check Virus Protection

Your macro virus protection levels should've been set when you first started reading this book, but it never hurts to double- and even triple-check.

Click **Tools**, **Macro**, **Security**. Make sure the security level is set to **Medium** or **High**—Medium being the default, and an adequate setting for typical Excel users.

FIGURE 18.6

Make sure your security setting is on Medium or High.

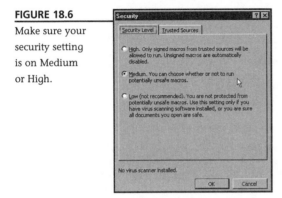

Add Auditing Toolbar

Get ready for the most controversial recommendation you'll find in this book.

Excel ships with one of the most sophisticated set of error-tracking tools available in any computer program, anywhere. For some reason, though, most people don't know they exist, and only a tiny fraction of all Excel-ulites ever use them.

I say "for some reason" as if I didn't know why the tools are never used. Fact is, I do know why. First, they're buried in a weird Excel backwater and if you didn't already know they existed, you'd never find them. (Although I'm delighted to report that Office Bob now tells you about them when you type audit or check formulas.) Second, none of the introductory books even mention them, much less show you how to use them. Third, even if you did know they existed, there's only one way (far as I know, anyway) to get to them—through an obscure toolbar that isn't referenced any-place in the menus, and only rarely in Help.

Here's how you get at Excel's auditing tools, the gizmos that will catch a very large percentage of all your mistakes—before your boss does.

Click **Tools**, **Customize**, and click the **Toolbars** tab. Check the box marked **Auditing**. Personally, I click the area at the top of the Auditing toolbar and drag it down to the bottom of the screen, as shown in Figure 18.7.

FIGURE 18.7

Bring the Auditing toolbar onto the screen and position it someplace handy.

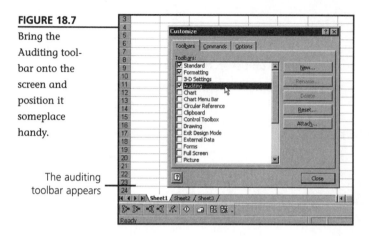

The auditing toolbar appears

I'll show you how to use the Auditing toolbar in the beginning of Chapter 20, "Building Spreadsheets." Think of it as an integral part of your Excel arsenal. Some day it'll save your tail.

The Screen

Let's take a look around the Excel screen. You don't need to get too hung up on any of this terminology, but you might want to mark this page and refer back to Figure 18.8 if you get bogged down at some future point.

FIGURE 18.8

The Excel 2000 screen.

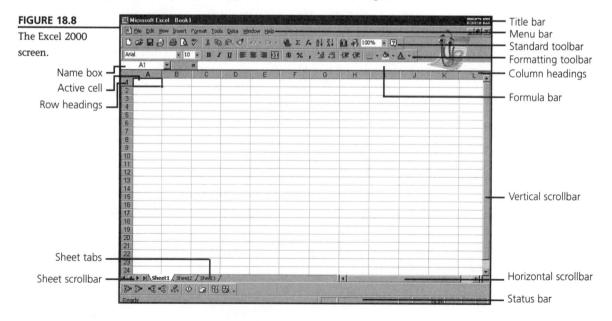

- Name box
- Active cell
- Row headings
- Sheet tabs
- Sheet scrollbar

- Title bar
- Menu bar
- Standard toolbar
- Formatting toolbar
- Column headings
- Formula bar
- Vertical scrollbar
- Horizontal scrollbar
- Status bar

Title Bar

☞ *The Excel title bar is virtually identical to Word's. I talked about the Word title bar in the section "Title Bar," Chapter 6, on* **page 85.**

Menu Bar

Right below the title bar, Excel has a menu bar. The top-level menu items look remarkably similar to those in Word. We'll have a chance to use them all in the next few chapters.

Toolbars

Excel ships with two toolbars showing: the top one is called the *Standard* toolbar and the second one is known as the *Formatting* toolbar. Again, similarities with Word pop up all over the place.

I also had you add the *Auditing* toolbar, in the preceding exercise. It's probably sitting at the bottom of your screen.

Formula Bar

The Excel Formula bar, however, is unique to Excel. On the left side you'll see the Name box, which lets you navigate to different places in your spreadsheets. On the right side Excel has room for you to type things into cells and edit the stuff that already exists in cells.

The Spreadsheet

The major part of the Excel screen is devoted to the spreadsheet, of course.

As you've probably guessed already, each of those little rectangles you see is a *cell*. The cell is the atomic particle of Excel spreadsheets, the basic building block that will ultimately hold all the numbers and formulas.

CELL NAMES

If you're new to spreadsheets, you need to get used to the naming convention. It's a lot like the naming system you'll find in chess or on most maps—or if you've ever played Battleship.

Each cell in a spreadsheet has a name, called an *address*. The cell in the upper-left corner is called A1. (You can tell because it's in the A column, and in the row marked 1.) The cell below it is called A2. The cell to the right of A1 is called B1. Then, working left to right, you'll see C1, D1, E1, and so on. Get the picture?

When Excel runs out of letters, it doubles-up. So, for example, the cell to the right of Z1 gets the moniker AA1, AB1, AC1, and so on. To the right of AZ1 sits BA1, BB1, and then BC1.

If you're ever in doubt, look at the Column headings and Row headings to get your bearings.

Every Excel spreadsheet is limited to 16,777,216 cells, arranged in 256 columns (which run from A to IV), and 65,536 rows (numbered 1 to 65536). That's a lot of cells.

The active cell—the one that has contents currently displayed in the Formula bar—gets outlined with a heavy black line. In Figure 18.8, cell A1 is the active cell.

The horizontal and vertical scrollbars let you navigate through the spreadsheet, much as you would expect. Click the up or down arrows, and the spreadsheet moves up or down. Grab the thumb to slide around long distances. Click in the blank area on the scrollbar to move up, down, left, or right a page or so at a time.

Sheet Tabs and Scrollbar

Unless you tell Excel to do something differently, every time you create a new workbook you get three spreadsheets in that workbook. When you start Excel, it creates a new workbook called Book1. And, lo and behold, Book1 contains three spreadsheets.

Near the bottom of Figure 18.8, you can see three tabs, marked Sheet1, Sheet2, and Sheet3. If you click each of those tabs in turn, you'll jump from the first spreadsheet (called Sheet1) to the second and then the third.

The Sheet scrollbars to the left of the Sheet tabs give you a way to cycle through the tabs. Imagine a workbook with 20 sheets. Only a few Sheet tabs can show at once, so the Sheet scrollbars let you move left to right among the 20 Sheet tabs.

Status Bar

Down at the very bottom of Figure 18.8 you'll find a status bar not unlike the one in Word. It's here that you'll see visual cues about what Excel is up to. There's also a neat feature called AutoCalculate that uses the status bar.

☞ We'll play with AutoCalculate in the section "AutoCalculate," Chapter 20, on **page 405**.

Zoom

More than any other Office application, working effectively with Excel entails a lot of moving back and forth. As your spreadsheets get larger and larger, navigation gets tougher. Many times life would be much easier if you could see your entire spreadsheet—or at least a big chunk of it—at one time.

That's why Excel has a **Zoom** icon on the Standard toolbar. Click the icon and see what your screen looks like at, oh, 50%, as I have in Figure 18.9.

FIGURE 18.9

The Excel screen at 50% Zoom factor.

Zoom from the Standard toolbar is okay. If you can't live with the built-in percentages shown in Figure 18.9, you can click once on the icon and type whatever zoom percentage you like. But Zoom really comes into its own with the Microsoft IntelliMouse or competing roller mice—the ones that have a roller in between the two buttons. (Implementations vary. I've seen roller mice with the roller under the thumb position and several other locations as well.)

Zoom is so important in getting around a spreadsheet that you might want to splurge and get an IntelliMouse (or finally figure out how to use the one you already have).

IntelliMouse

☞ *I talked about using the IntelliMouse with Word in the "Using Mouse Wheels" section, Chapter 9, on* **page 137**.

The roller mouse received a lukewarm endorsement in Chapter 9, "Getting Around." At least in my opinion, it's of limited value if your major Office preoccupation extends no further than word processing. If you do a bit of spreadsheet work—particularly with fairly large spreadsheets—the nature of the problem changes, and the IntelliMouse becomes a reasonably cost-effective addition to your bag of tricks.

Unless there's a roller mouse installed on your PC, you'll have to go out and buy one, and then install it with the software using the manufacturer's recommendations.

WHICH ROLLER MOUSE IS BEST?

Every hand is different, and for that reason I strongly recommend that you try a mouse before paying for it. If you can, use the mouse in some sort of real world environment where you're sitting down in front of a PC and working with applications you use every day.

My experience with Microsoft's IntelliMouse Pro has been uniformly excellent: it's a high-quality beast that keeps rolling and rolling and… well, you get the idea. Even my eleven-year-old son, who has a habit of destroying mice while playing intense simulation games, has a hard time going through an IntelliMouse Pro. He did wear out an old IntelliMouse once, though. I figure it had about 1,000,000 miles on it, and had wasted, oh, 10 times that many aliens.

For you historians, the IntelliMouse was a dovebar shaped mouse that preceded the IntelliMouse Pro. Some diehards still say it was the best mouse ever made. Personally, I prefer the IntelliMouse Pro, which has an arched side. The extra room for my clumsy thumb helps a lot.

Inside Excel, a roller mouse gives you three significant capabilities:

- Roll the wheel up or down and the spreadsheet moves up or down, much as it would if you clicked the vertical scrollbar.

- Click the roller, and then move the mouse. Excel moves the spreadsheet in sync with the mouse—up, down, right, or left. Move the mouse farther, and the spreadsheet moves more quickly.

- This is the feature I use most. Hold the **Ctrl** key down and roll the wheel. Excel responds by zooming in and out, from 10% to 100% zoom factor, in 15% increments.

MORE MOUSING

Microsoft has quite a few IntelliMouse capabilities buried, of all places, inside its (unsupported) TweakUI Windows application. TweakUI lets you modify all sorts of strange Windows settings; the mouse support is just a tiny piece.

You can get Windows 95 and NT versions of TweakUI from www.microsoft.com/windows95/info/powertoys.htm. The Windows 98 version is on the Win98 CD, in the folder \tools\reskit\powertoys; you can install it by right-clicking **tweakui.inf** and choosing **Install**.

Microsoft won't support TweakUI—it would put quite a strain on their phone support system, as parts of it don't work on every PC—but I've found it to be quite stable and, in some cases, indispensable.

There are lots of little features that Microsoft threw in with the IntelliMouse, but by and large I find them bothersome. You can play with them by clicking **Start**, **Settings**, **Control Panel**, then double-clicking the Mouse applet.

I'm not going to assume that you're going to run out and buy yet another Microsoft product, so I won't explicitly talk about the IntelliMouse in the rest of this book. Suffice it to say that any time you need to zoom, roller mice offer substantial benefits.

19

Woody Leonhard

TEACHES

WORKING WITH WORKBOOKS

WORK YOUR WORKBOOKS TO THE BONE. The basics of file manipulation in Excel closely resemble those in Word. If you survived the Word file-manipulation examples earlier in this book, these should come as second nature.

The only conceptual tripping point seems to be terminology. Once again, for emphasis: an Excel workbook is just an .xls file. Workbooks can have many spreadsheets. If you don't do anything to change how Excel works, a new workbook contains three spreadsheets.

Got that?

New, Close, Open

Let's start out easy.

EXERCISE

Start a Test Workbook

1. Start Excel. (Click **Start**, **Programs**, and choose **Microsoft Excel**.) Your screen should look like the one shown in Figure 19.1. Excel starts out with a new workbook called Book1. This workbook has three spreadsheets, called Sheet1, Sheet2, and Sheet3.

FIGURE 19.1

When you start Excel, you get a Book1.

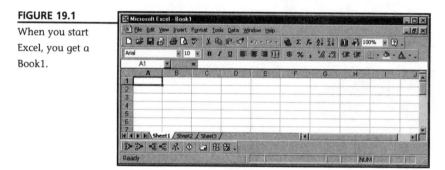

2. Create a new workbook by clicking the **New** 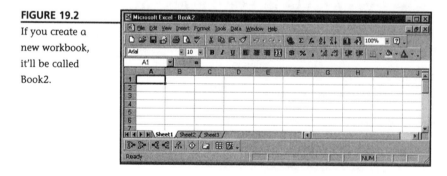 icon on the Standard (top) toolbar. Excel responds by creating a workbook called Book2 (do you detect a pattern here?), as shown in Figure 19.2. It too has three spreadsheets.

FIGURE 19.2

If you create a new workbook, it'll be called Book2.

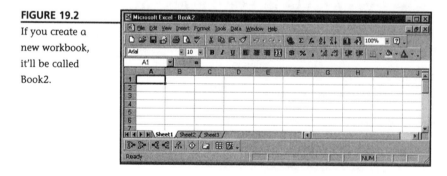

3. We're going to build a very simple test workbook. Click **cell A2**, and then type Apples. Press the down arrow on your keyboard and type Oranges. Then, press the down arrow, type Grapes, press the down arrow again and type Mangoes. (Rocket science, eh?) Click **cell B1** and type Q1 (that's my shorthand for "first quarter"). Press down, type a number in **B2**, and similarly fill in dummy numbers for the cells **B3**, **B4**, and **B5**. If you press down one last time, your Book2 will look much like mine, in Figure 19.3.

FIGURE 19.3

Beginnings of the test workbook.

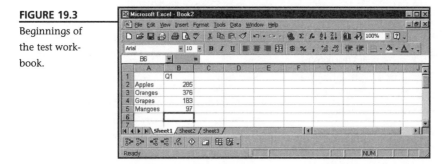

4. To close this workbook, click **File**, **Close**. When asked if you want to save changes to Book2, click **Yes**. You'll see the **Save As** dialog box, as shown in Figure 19.4.

FIGURE 19.4

Excel asks you to give the test workbook a name.

5. Type a name like test in the File Name box, and click **Save**. The workbook with all the fruits and numbers that you just created has been saved as the file test.xls, in the folder called c:\My Documents.

The other Excel file manipulation methods work much like Word, too.

EXERCISE

Open an Existing Workbook

1. With Excel running, click the **Open** 📂 icon on the toolbar. You should see Excel's **Open** dialog box, as shown in Figure 19.5.

2. Choose the workbook you want to open—in this case **test.xls**—and click **Open**. Excel opens the workbook and presents it to you precisely as it was when you last saved it (see Figure 19.6).

WHAT ABOUT PREBUILT FANCY SPREADSHEETS?

Word ships with lots and lots of templates, so you can take advantage of all sorts of prebuilt documents, modifying them to your specific situation. By contrast, Excel only ships with four usable templates (.xlt files), and nine rather boring workbooks (.xls files). You can play with the templates by clicking **File**, **New**, and choosing the **Spreadsheet Solutions** tab (the Village Software template is an ad for the company that made these few samples). For the rest of them, use Windows Find (**Start**, **Find**, **Files or Folders**) to look for *.xlt and *.xls files on the Office CD.

FIGURE 19.5

Opening a workbook.

FIGURE 19.6

The opened test.xls, identical to how it was when you saved it—note how the active cell hasn't even changed.

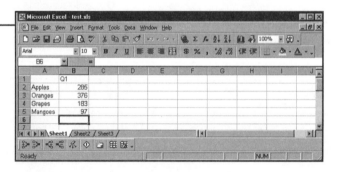

3. Of course, there are many ways to skin the Open cat: you could've opened test.xls by choosing it from the bottom of the **File** menu, or by clicking **File**, **Open**. All the tricks in Word work with Excel too.

If this whole series of exercises has you yawning, there's a good reason why. The **Save**, **Save As**, and **Open** dialog boxes in Word and Excel are identical. Don't believe it? Double-check Figure 7.8. The only difference is in the **Files of type** box, and that only changes because you're looking for .xls files (that is, Excel workbooks), not .doc files (Word documents).

YOU DON'T MEAN ABSOLUTELY IDENTICAL, RIGHT?

Nope. Er, yes. The Word and Excel file handling routines are identical. I mean absolutely, totally, 100 percent identical.

This really is one of the great advances in Office over the years, one that you'll only start to appreciate as you gain experience in Office's more advanced features. It's called *common code*. Office uses the very same program to open and save files, no matter which Office application you're in. So if you mastered the Search or the Advanced features in Word's Open dialog box, you can use *precisely* the same features in Excel.

Sheets

There's nothing worse than an unnamed sheet, eh? Just ask the sheet.

Anyway, one of the first things you're likely to do with a new workbook is to give the first sheet, at least, a name. Here's how.

Renaming Sheets

1. In your test.xls workbook, right-click the tab marked **Sheet1**. You should see several options, as shown in Figure 19.7.

FIGURE 19.7

The right-click context menu for a Spreadsheet tab.

2. Choose **Rename**. Excel selects the name Sheet1, inviting you to type something over the top of it. In Figure 19.8, I typed **Fruit Sales by Quarter**, then pressed **Enter**.

FIGURE 19.8

Renaming
Sheet1.

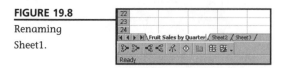

3. Now let's insert a new sheet into this workbook. Right-click **Sheet2** and choose **Insert**. When Excel shows you the Insert dialog box, click the **General** tab, and double-click **Worksheet**. You should get a new spreadsheet, automatically called Sheet4, between Fruit Sales by Quarter and Sheet2 (see Figure 19.9).

FIGURE 19.9

Inserting a new
sheet into
test.xls.

4. Click the **Fruit Sales by Quarter** tab. Then save this latest version of test.xls by clicking the **Save** 🖫 icon on the toolbar.

Undo/Redo

The Undo capability in Excel works much like the same feature in Word, except it's limited to a measly 16 undo's. In other words, you can undo your last 16 actions, but that's it, that's all she wrote.

To undo your most recent action, click the **Undo** 🔙 icon on the toolbar. And then to redo whatever you've undone, click the **Redo** 🔜 icon.

As always, the undo information remains as long as the workbook is open—even when you save it. But the information disappears as soon as the workbook is closed.

Print

Printing in Excel rates as a full sub-discipline. You can spend half your workday setting up a spreadsheet to print legibly. The fundamental reason seems pretty clear: whereas Word documents exist (pretty much) simply to be printed, and printing in PowerPoint comes as a natural byproduct of producing a presentation, printing in Excel is almost an afterthought, something you worry about after the spreadsheet is cranking out good numbers.

It shows.

I'll go into specific tricks for making your printed spreadsheets look good in Chapter 22, "Making Spreadsheets Look Good." We'll cover headers and footers, setting page breaks, and the like. What I'd like to tackle here are general, overall strategies for printing spreadsheets so you can kind of stick them in the back of your mind while you're working through the coming exercises.

The job ain't over till the paperwork's done—and in Excel, that usually involves printing a spreadsheet.

Print Area

Excel spreadsheets tend to get real big, real fast. Quite commonly all you want to do is print a bottom-line summary of all the calculations performed in a spreadsheet: The boss doesn't want to drown in the detailed lists of component numbers when a simple set of totals will do. That's where Print Area comes in.

 EXERCISE

Set and Clear the Print Area

1. Open test.xls, if it isn't already staring at you.

2. Print test.xls by clicking the **Print** icon. So far it's pretty easy, eh?

3. Now say the boss only wants her printouts to cover apples and oranges; she couldn't care less about grapes and mangoes. That's easy to do in Excel with something called the Print Area.

4. Start by selecting the range that you want to print—in this case, click the **cell A1**, hold down the mouse button, and drag it down to **B3**. (You can also click **A1**, hold down the **Shift** key, and then click **B3**.) As you see in Figure 19.10, you'll end up with six highlighted cells, the ones between A1 and B3 (Excel calls that the range A1:B3).

FIGURE 19.10

Selecting the range A1:B3.

5. Because this is the area you want to print, click **File**, **Print Area**, **Set Print Area** (see Figure 19.11). Excel turns the range A1:B3 into the print area.

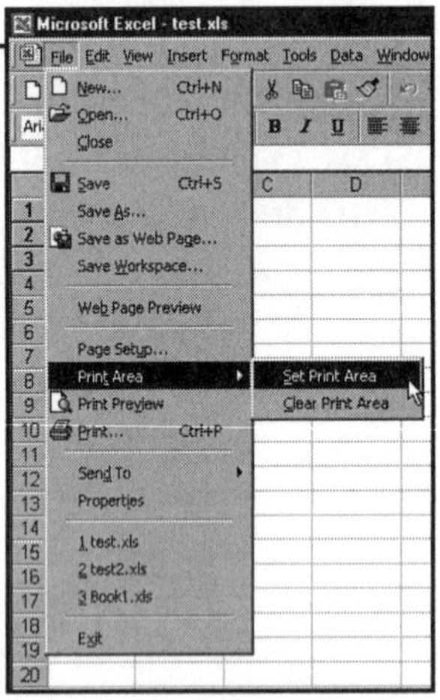

FIGURE 19.11

After the print area range has been selected, you tell Excel about it with this menu item.

6. Now click the **Print** [icon] icon again. See how Excel only prints the cells in the Print Area?

7. Remove the Print Area by clicking **File**, **Print Area**, **Clear Print Area**.

If Excel has no defined Print Area, it prints everything between cell A1 and the very last (bottom-right-most) cell in your spreadsheet. That can cover quite a bit of territory, as you'll see in the next section.

Page Sequence

When Excel can't print all of your spreadsheet on one page, it follows a very simple series of rules for determining where to print what:

- If you've set up a Print Area, these rules are applied to the Print Area. If there's no defined Print Area, Excel takes the entire area between cell A1 and the last cell in your spreadsheet and considers that to be the Print Area.

- Excel prints the upper-left page in the Print Area. It then moves down and prints the next page-full. It continues downward until it's printed all the left-most pages in the Print Area. Then it starts at the top of the next column of pages. It continues that way, working top to bottom, and then left to right, until all the pages are printed.

● If there isn't enough room on a page to fit an entire row, that row is pushed down to the next page. Similarly if there isn't enough room on a page to fit an entire column, that column gets shifted to the next page to the right.

Let's take our little test.xls and make it big enough to demonstrate how Excel prints a four-page spreadsheet.

Print a Big Spreadsheet

1. Start with test.xls.

2. We don't want to screw up the main test file, so let's make a copy of it. Click **File**, **Save As**, and type `test2` in the File name box. Click **Save** (see Figure 19.12). That saves a copy of test.xls; the new copy is called test2.xls.

FIGURE 19.12

Saving a copy of test.xls as test2.xls.

3. You should be working on test2.xls. Verify that by looking up at the title bar. It should say **Microsoft Excel - test2.xls**.

4. Use the vertical scrollbar (or down arrow) and scroll down to cell A40. Type `Hello from the Bottom!` and press **Enter**. Your screen should look like Figure 19.13.

FIGURE 19.13

Putting the text `Hello from the bottom!` in cell A40.

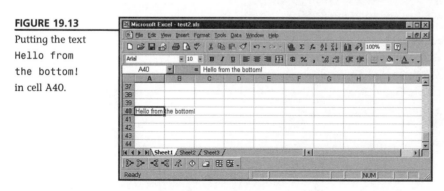

5. Now click the **Print** icon one more time. You should get two pages printed, covering the range from A1 to A40. Excel first prints the upper-left page, which is the one with our Fruit Sales by Quarter figures. Then it prints the page below that one, the one that says Hello from down below!

TIP

IS THAT ENGRAVED IN STONE?

Nope. If you ever need to change Excel around so it prints pages from left to right, and then from top to bottom, you can do so by clicking the **File**, **Page Setup**, **Sheet** tab, and changing the **Page order**.

Portrait and Landscape

Frequently, Excel pages print better if they're turned on edge so the short side of the paper is at the top. (In fact, that's how Excel used to print, before version 2000.) Printing with the short side on top is called Portrait printing.

What happens when we print test2.xls in Portrait? I bet you can guess...

WHY PORTRAIT?

Printers have been using these terms for centuries. A Portrait page is the normal way for printing word processing documents—with the short edge of the paper at the top. Think of a drawing of a person's portrait: typically it's taller than it is wide.

Similarly, Landscape refers to pages printed on their side, with the long side of the sheet on top. Think of a drawing of a landscape.

Print Portrait

1. Start with test2.xls, the test page you just created.

2. Click **File**, **Print**. Make sure the **Page** tab is showing, and click the button marked **Portrait**, as shown in Figure 19.14.

FIGURE 19.14

Setting test2.xls to print Portrait.

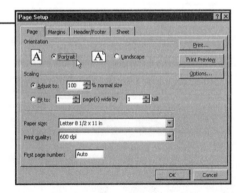

3. Click the **Print** button. Now you'll see the same information coming out the printer, this time printed on just one page.

Wait. There's another option.

Fit to Page

The people who created Excel know that sometimes you just want to print the blasted spreadsheet and you couldn't care less if it's pretty. For those times, they've invented a magical shrinking machine.

 EXERCISE

Just Print the Blasted Thing

1. With test2.xls up on the screen, the Page Setup dialog box showing, and the **Landscape** button pressed, click the **Fit to** button, as shown in Figure 19.15.

FIGURE 19.15

Forcing Excel to print it all on one page.

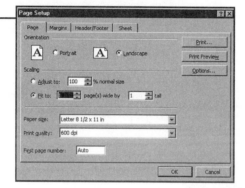

FIGURE 19.15

Forcing Excel to print it all on one page.

2. You can spin the buttons to tell Excel how many pages to squish down to. In our case, just leave it at 1. Click **Print**.

3. You'll get one page coming out of the printer. This one should be pretty easy to see. If you have a larger spreadsheet and try to print it on a single page, you may not be so lucky. Can you read the information?

TRULY ADVANCED PRINTING

If you ever get stuck printing really, really hairy reports from Excel—particularly ones that include certain parts of the spreadsheet and exclude others, perhaps for multiple "what if" scenarios—make sure you look at the Report Manager. You can get a rudimentary introduction to Report Manager by bringing up the Office Assistant and typing report manager.

On some printers the text from a mondo-squished page will be quite legible; on others it'll be totally inscrutable. Only you can decide for sure.

5. Keep this trick in your hip pocket if you ever need to get the data printed; damn the torpedoes, full speed ahead.

Gridlines

Excel will print spreadsheet gridlines—light horizontal and vertical lines that make it easier to pick out individual cells. You almost always want gridlines to appear onscreen; entering data without them can be monstrous. But whether or not they appear on printouts depends very much on your predilections.

WHEN GRIDLINES HELP

I've found that printing gridlines helps when you're shrinking a spreadsheet down, so text appears at less than 10 point. It's also useful for sparse spreadsheets—ones that have few entries.

EXERCISE

Print Gridlines

1. Using test2.xls as it appears now, with the Page Setup dialog box on the screen, click the **Sheet** tab. Down in the Print section, click the box marked **Gridlines** (see Figure 19.16).

FIGURE 19.16

Tell Excel to print horizontal and vertical gridlines with this option.

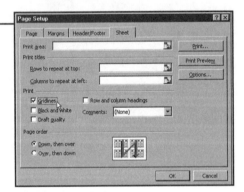

2. Click the **Print** button, and then **OK**. The cells on the printout will be clearly identified with gridlines. Do they help or hinder? It's very much up to you.

That will do for a quick introduction to the major print options. I'll go into much greater detail when we talk about making your spreadsheets look good.

20

Woody Leonhard

TEACHES

BUILDING SPREADSHEETS

DON'T SWEAT THE SMALL STUFF. Okay, okay. I have a little confession to make. I tricked you. Most introductory books make a big deal about Excel values and labels and ranges and whatnot, going into excruciating detail about how you have to click in a cell before typing a value or a label, how values differ from labels, and all sorts of folderol.

Bah! Humbug!

In the previous two chapters I introduced you to all those things and more, and I bet you didn't even blink an eye. The simple fact is that you can do an awful lot in Excel if you don't get bogged down in the details, and go ahead and do what comes naturally.

Let me show you what I mean.

Entering Data

Excel understands data. You'd be amazed at how frequently Excel guesses exactly what you mean, just because of the way you type.

EXERCISE

Excel's Automatically Recognized Data Types

1. Start with a new, clean workbook by clicking the **New** ▢ icon.

2. In cell A1, type $12.34 and press **Enter** (see Figure 20.1). Excel interprets the number as 12.34, and understands that you want to display the number as a dollar amount.

FIGURE 20.1

Excel correctly interprets $12.34 as a dollar amount; also, notice that when you type August 20 also is interpreted correctly as 20-Aug.

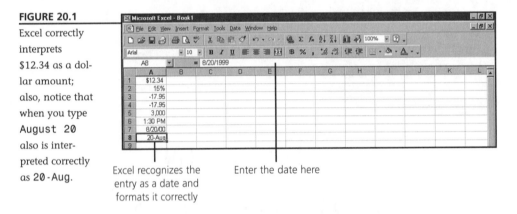

Excel recognizes the entry as a date and formats it correctly

Enter the date here

3. In cell A2, type 15%. Excel interprets that as, uh, 15%.

4. In cell A3, type -17.95. Excel interprets that as a negative 17.95. Stop yawning. It gets better.

5. In cell A4, type (17.95). Excel is smart enough to know that a number in parenthesis is negative. Hey, that's better than some accountants I've known.

6. In cell A5, type 3,000. See how commas don't give Excel fits?

7. Here's a fun one. In cell A6, type 1:30 p. As soon as you press **Enter**, Excel turns that into 1:30:00 PM up in the Formula bar, and puts **1:30 PM** in the active cell. Pretty smart, eh?

8. In cell A7, type 8/20/00. When you press **Enter**, Excel realizes that's a date and converts it into 8/20/2000, which you can see in the Formula bar. In the active cell, you'll see **8/20/2000**, just as you typed.

9. Now for the grand finale: in cell A8, type Aug 20 and press **Enter**. Excel recognizes that as a date, attaches the current year to it (as I write this, that's 1999), converts it to **8/20/1999** in the Formula bar, and then shows **20-Aug** in the active cell. Don't applaud. Throw money.

10. Close the workbook (click **File**, **Close**). No, you don't want to save changes.

All those are pretty cool, but if you think about it a bit, there's no great leap of faith involved. When Excel sees you type Aug 20, for example, it doesn't take a whole lot of imagination to figure that you wanted to type a date.

In fact, in 1999, you can type any of these on the keyboard and get the same date, **8/20/1999**, put in a cell:

- 8/20/99 (no surprise with that one)
- Aug 20
- 8/20
- 8-20

...and I bet you can see the problem right there. What if you want Excel to calculate 8 divided by 20, or 8 minus 20? This automatic recognition of data types is all good and well, but how do you tell Excel when to stop interpreting what you type, and just do the calculation? That's where formulas come in to play.

Using Formulas

What's a formula? Good question.

There's a lot of mumbo jumbo associated with formulas—the Office Assistant spouts a lot of it—but it all boils down to one thing. In Excel, a *formula* is an entry in a cell that starts with an = equal sign. It's that simple.

You write a formula—that is, you start by typing an = sign in a cell—when you want Excel to calculate something for you. Type = and Excel does the calculation. No = sign, no calculation. Nothing to it.

EXERCISE

A Simple Formula

1. Open the test workbook, file test.xls.

2. Click **cell B6** and type this formula: =B2+B3+B4+B5 (see Figure 20.2). That tells Excel to add the values in B2, B3, B4, and B5, and to put them in the current cell, which is B6.

FIGURE 20.2

A simple formula for adding the contents of four cells.

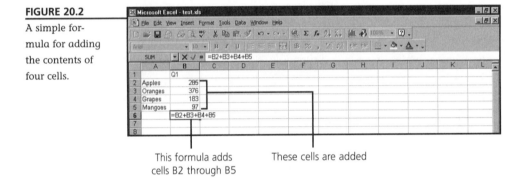

This formula adds cells B2 through B5

These cells are added

3. Press **Enter**. Excel takes the formula, which is displayed in the Formula bar; calculates the result, which is 941 (if you don't believe it, grab a calculator!); and puts the result in cell B6 (see Figure 20.3).

FIGURE 20.3

The result of =B2+B3+B4+B5 gets placed in cell B6.

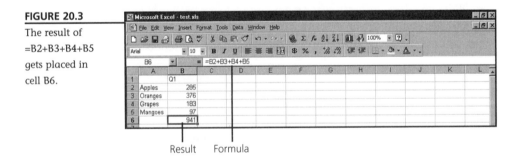

Result   Formula

4. In Figure 20.4, I've filled in three more columns of data to start fleshing out test.xls. Please do the same. You can use my numbers or choose some of your own; it doesn't matter.

FIGURE 20.4

Completing the
sales figures
for Q2, Q3,
and Q4.

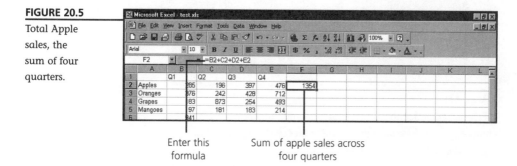

5. Now that you're an old pro at entering formulas, click **cell F2** and type
=B2+C2+D2+E2, as shown in Figure 20.4. Press **Enter** and the total Apple
sales for the four quarters appears in cell F2 (see Figure 20.5). You expected
something different?

FIGURE 20.5

Total Apple
sales, the
sum of four
quarters.

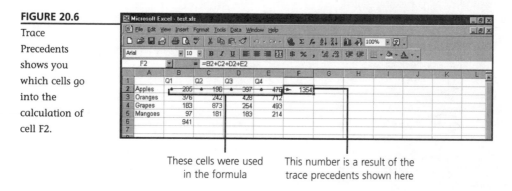

Enter this
formula

Sum of apple sales across
four quarters

6. Here's the most important step, the one most people miss, the one where
you double-check and make sure you got things right. With F2 still the
active cell, click the **Trace Precedents** icon on the Auditing toolbar.
Excel shows you, quite visually, precisely which cells have been used to calculate the number in F2. Take a close look at Figure 20.6 and verify that
there are dots in the cells you expected to be used in the calculation of F2.

FIGURE 20.6

Trace
Precedents
shows you
which cells go
into the
calculation of
cell F2.

These cells were used
in the formula

This number is a result of the
trace precedents shown here

☞ *For details about the Auditing toolbar, see "Add Auditing Toolbar," in Chapter 18, page 373*.

7. In fact, wherever you have a formula the Trace Precedents icon shows you which cells go into the calculations for a given cell. In Figure 20.7 I've clicked **cell B6** and then the **Trace Precedents** 📊 icon, to verify that B6 refers to the correct cells.

FIGURE 20.7

Tracing precedents for the other formula in the spreadsheet.

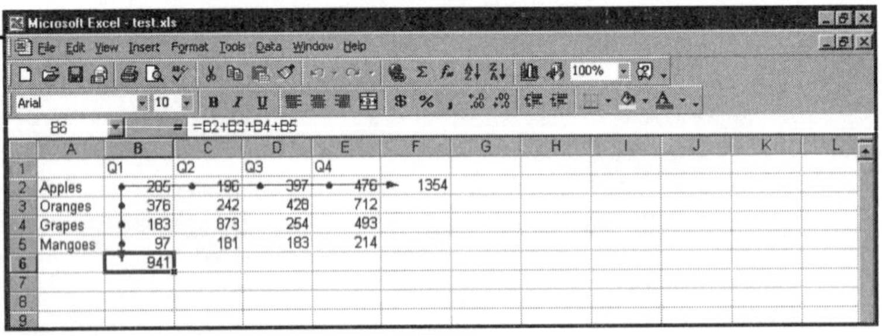

TIP

USE IT!

I can't emphasize this often enough: Whenever you have formulas in a spreadsheet, you should verify them with Excel's Trace Precedents feature. Yes, I know that Trace Precedents is considered to be an advanced feature, something you only need when auditing a spreadsheet. But if you use it, and use it well, from the very beginning, you'll greatly reduce the chances of messing up a formula and nip calculation problems in the bud.

8. Remove the Trace Precedents line for **B6** by clicking the cell once, and then clicking the **Remove Precedent Arrows** 📊 icon. Click **cell F2** and do the same. Then, just to make test.xls a little more legible, click **A6** and type Total; then click **cell F1** and do the same. Your test.xls should look something like Figure 20.8.

FIGURE 20.8

Cleaning up test.xls.

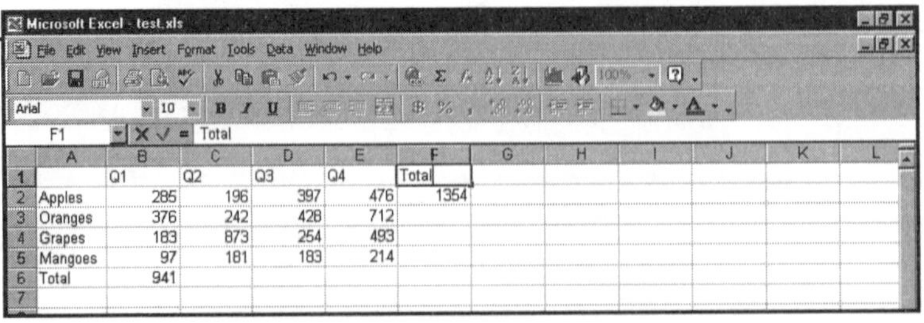

9. Click the **Save** 🔲 icon to save the changes you've made to test.xls.

There are lots and lots of ways to enter formulas. Each of the methods has its own advantages and drawbacks. The method you just used, where you type a mathematical formula and the cell names, rates as the slowest and most error prone method—but the easiest to see and understand.

I'm going to take you through six more methods for adding columns or rows of numbers, just to expose you to the major tricks and concepts. This list is far from exhaustive, but I think you'll find it instructive.

To learn more about Excel's functions, bring up the Office Assistant, type formulas, and follow the link that says **How formulas calculate values (Constructing a formula)**. For more detailed information, see *Special Edition Using Excel 2000*, from Que.

Pointing and Clicking

You don't need to type the names of the cells in your formulas. Excel is smart enough to pick them up, if you click the cell. Here's how.

EXERCISE

Building a Formula by Pointing

1. Click **cell F3**. We want to put the sum of B3, C3, D3, and E3 in there, adding up the numbers in row 3.

WHAT'S A FUNCTION?

Gulp. I thought I'd be able to finesse that question. You're pretty sharp, you know?

When you get down to it, a *function* is just a formula that's built into Excel itself. For example, once you get good at Excel formulas, you could write a formula to figure out the largest number in a list of numbers. (Yeah, it might take a while before you're at that stage, but it can be done.)

Microsoft realizes that there are lots and lots of calculations people need to use all the time, so instead of forcing you to write and rewrite a formula to calculate the maximum number in a list, they've created a function called *Max()* that does all the work for you.

Excel has hundreds of built-in functions. I'll talk about some of them later in this chapter.

NOT JUST FOR ADDING

Although I'll use addition for my examples here, you aren't limited to sums—not by any stretch of the imagination. Most of the techniques adapt to almost any mathematical combination you can imagine, and there are functions far, far more sophisticated than the Sum() function I'll be using. In fact, built-in Excel functions can calculate everything from the number of days between two dates, to the net present value of a series of financial transactions, to sophisticated statistical analyses you've never heard of and wouldn't dare touch without a textbook in hand.

2. Type =, and then click **cell B3**. Magically, as you can see in Figure 20.9, B3 appears in the Formula bar, starting out the formula **=B3**. It also appears in cell F3. And, just for emphasis, Excel sets off cell B3 with *marching ants* that scroll around the cell.

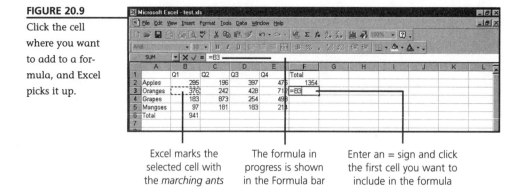

Excel marks the selected cell with the *marching ants*

The formula in progress is shown in the Formula bar

Enter an = sign and click the first cell you want to include in the formula

3. Type + and click **cell C3**. The Formula bar now reads **=B3+C3**, and the ants now march around cell C3.

4. Type another + and click **cell D3**. Now the formula sits at **=B3+C3+D3**, and the ants are running around D3.

5. Finally, type one last + and click **cell E3**; then press **Enter**. As you can see in Figure 20.10, the correct formula appears in the Formula bar, and the total sits in cell F3.

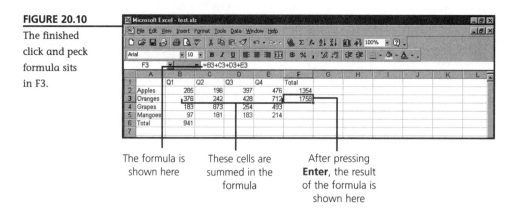

The formula is shown here

These cells are summed in the formula

After pressing **Enter**, the result of the formula is shown here

6. That's how you can construct a formula by clicking and typing.

The Sum() Function

One of the simplest Excel functions, Sum(), takes in a bunch of cells and spits out the total of all the values in those cells. It's simple once you see how to do it.

EXERCISE

Sum() the Total

1. Click **cell F4** once. This is where you want to put the sum of cells B4, C4, D4, and E4, right?

2. Type =sum(b4,c4,d4,e4). That just tells Excel to add up the numbers in cells B4, C4, D4, and E4. Note that you can type lowercase; Excel understands.

3. Press **Enter**, and you'll see the sum in cell F4, along with the formula up in the Formula bar, as shown in Figure 20.11.

FIGURE 20.11

Using the Sum() function to calculate a sum.

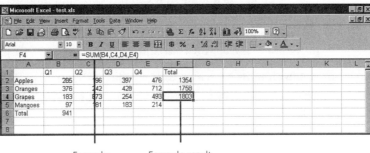

Formula   Formula result

AutoSum

This method rates, far and away, as the best way to calculate the sum of a row or column of numbers.

EXERCISE

Sigma: The Fastest Way to Add

1. Click **cell F5**. This is where you want to put the sum of B5, C5, D5, and E5.

2. Click the **AutoSum** Σ icon on the toolbar. The result should look like Figure 20.12. Whoa!

FIGURE 20.12

Excel's AutoSum
tool, run from
the cell F5.

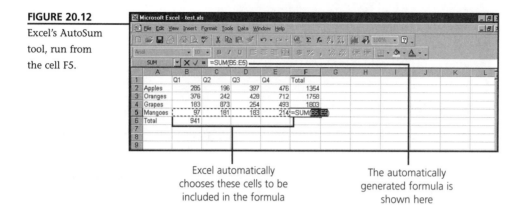

Excel automatically
chooses these cells to be
included in the formula

The automatically
generated formula is
shown here

3. A whole bunch of things kicked in all at once. First, Excel's AutoSum tool realized that you wanted to calculate a sum. It guessed that you want to sum the cells between B5 and E5. (Pretty good guess, eh? AutoSum usually guesses right; when it doesn't, you just click and drag across the cells that you want to sum.) Second, it put the formula **=SUM(B5:E5)** in the Formula bar, indicating which cells should be summed. Third, it drew those marching ants around the cells B5 through E5.

4. Play with those marching ants a little bit. Tease them, er, click one of the edges and drag the rectangle around. See how the AutoSum tool lets you adjust which cells are included in the sum by simply moving around the marching ants? Pretty cool.

5. When you're done playing with the tool, make sure the marching ants cover cells B5 through E5 and press **Enter**. You should get the sum in cell F5, along with the formula you see in Figure 20.13.

FIGURE 20.13

Press **Enter** to
freeze the
marching ants
and put the
sum in cell F5.

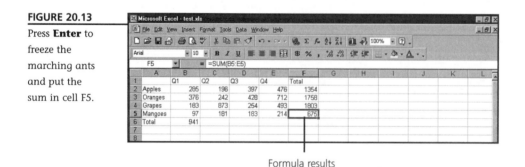

Formula results

Sum() on the Range

Aha! You were watching closely in that last exercise, weren't you? If so, you probably noticed that Excel understands the abbreviation B5:E5 to mean all the cells
between B5 and E5.

In fact, that's an example of Excel's shorthand for any range of cells. The colon does
the trick. If you type A1:D4, you're referring to all the cells between A1 and D4.
C2:R23 means all the cells between C2 and R23, and so on.

That leads us to yet another way to enter sums.

 EXERCISE

Sum() Using Ranges

1. Click the **cell C6**. This is where we'd like to have the sum of all the numbers
   in the range C2:C5, correct?

2. Type =sum(c2:c5) and press **Enter**. Sure enough, the correct sum appears
   in cell C6, and the formula shows up in the Formula bar, as shown in
   Figure 20.14.

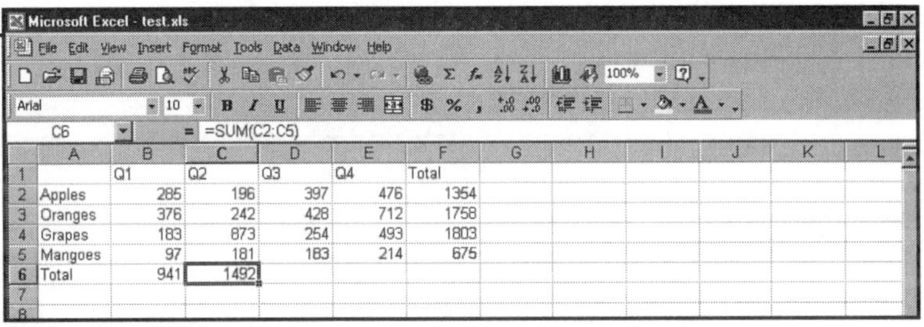

FIGURE 20.14

Using
=Sum(Range)
to calculate
a sum.

 TIP

RANGES RULE

Many operations in Excel work on ranges. As you've just seen, a (contiguous) range is specified by its upper-left and lower-right cells, with a colon in between. It's quite simple, really.

We'll be working a lot with ranges. In fact, we already have. Believe it or not, when you
set the Print Area for printing a spreadsheet in the previous chapter you were actually
defining a range that's used by Excel's print routines.

Discontiguous Sums

The Sum() function has all sorts of tricks up its sleeve. (Thus begging the question, "Do functions have sleeves?") We've already seen how it can add up the contents of a list of cells, separated by commas. We've also seen how it can calculate the total of an entire range. You can also mix 'n' match individual cell locations and ranges.

 EXERCISE

=Sum() on Discontiguous Ranges

1. Click **cell D6**.

2. Type =Sum(D2,D3:D5) and press **Enter**. That tells Excel to add the value of D2 to the sum of the values in the range D3:D5. Once again, as you can verify in Figure 20.15, you'll get the total for the column of numbers.

FIGURE 20.15

The Sum() function can combine any number of single cell entries and ranges.

	A	B	C	D	E	F
1		Q1	Q2	Q3	Q4	Total
2	Apples	285	196	397	476	1354
3	Oranges	376	242	428	712	1758
4	Grapes	183	873	254	493	1803
5	Mangoes	97	181	183	214	675
6	Total	941	1492	1262		

Formula bar: =SUM(D2,D3:D5)

Using Parentheses

I don't want to dredge up bad memories of high school algebra, so I'll make this section very short. Although some might take issue with my assertion, the laws of mathematics apply, even in Excel. And at some point or another, in spite of your successes or failures in algebra class, that might actually work in your favor.

I'm talking about parentheses. When you group a bunch of numbers together and place them in parentheses, Excel evaluates them before it evaluates the stuff outside the parentheses. And then the stuff outside the parenthesis is evaluated from left to right. So, for example

- =2*(3+4) evaluates to 14, whereas

- =(2*3)+4 comes out 10, and

- =2*(3+4)+5 is 19, but

- =(2*3)+4+5 is 15.

Note how Excel uses the asterisk for multiplication.

If you have problems with formulas like that, I'll just refer you to your local math teacher. Heh heh heh. It all has to do with something called the "Order of Operations" or "Operator Hierarchy" and it encompasses more than just the parenthetical portions of formulas.

Our final excursion into writing sums shows how you can put parentheses in Excel formulas.

EXERCISE

In Loco Paren-tis

1. Click **cell E6**.

2. Type =(e2+e3)+(e4+e5) and press **Enter**. Note how this, mathematically, is the same as e2+e3+e4+e5. You'll get the result shown in Figure 20.16.

> ### WHERE HAVE ALL THE LABELS GONE?
>
> In earlier versions of Excel, you could use row and column labels in formulas. For example, you could type =Apples+Oranges+Grapes+Mangoes in cell D6, and Excel would dutifully cobble together a formula that did what you expected—some of the time, anyway.
>
> Microsoft has disabled that capability, by default, in Excel 2000. Good move, in my opinion: All too frequently, people would end up with a formula that didn't change when the underlying data changed, or didn't calculate precisely what was expected in the first place. Experienced Excel users would never rely on such a flaky *feature*, and novice Excel users occasionally fell victim to formulas that didn't get updated properly.

FIGURE 20.16

A total using (totally red undant) parentheses.

	A	B	C	D	E	F
1		Q1	Q2	Q3	Q4	Total
2	Apples	285	196	397	476	1354
3	Oranges	376	242	428	712	1758
4	Grapes	183	873	254	493	1803
5	Mangoes	97	181	183	214	675
6	Total	941	1492	1262	1895	

E6 = =(E2+E3)+(E4+E5)

3. Click **File**, **Save**. We're going to use this version of test.xls for a while.

Verifying Your Calculations

And now, after that heavy dose of typing and clicking, it's time to verify all your calculations. (In fact, I repeated these verification steps while I was performing the original calculations, just because I knew that about 10 million of you would write to me if I added up a column of numbers wrong!)

EXERCISE

Trace Dependencies

1. Start with the test.xls you just saved in the previous exercise.

2. Double-check the precedents for cell B6. Click **cell B6**, and then click the **Trace Precedents** [icon] icon on the Auditing toolbar. You should have a precedent list like the one shown in Figure 20.6.

3. Now click **cell C6**; then click the **Trace Precedents** [icon] icon. This trace looks a little different because the cell C6 relies on the entire range C2:C5. In Figure 20.17, Excel is showing you two things: first, it draws a box around the range C2:C5 to show you that the whole range is involved; then, second, it draws that arrow from the top of the range down to cell C6. Between the two visual clues you should get the impression that the range C2:C5 is used in cell C6.

FIGURE 20.17

Showing that the entire range C2:C5 is used in cell C6.

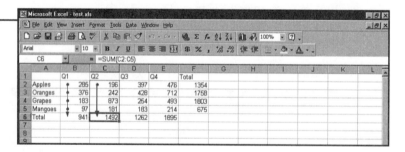

4. Continue tracing precedents for cells D6, E6, and then F2, F3, F4, and F5. Note how F5 is another one of those range precedent cells (see Figure 20.18).

FIGURE 20.18

Double-checking the formulas at the end of each row.

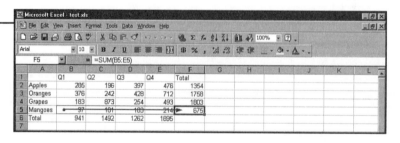

5. Got 'em all checked out? Good. Click those cells, and remove the arrows by clicking the **Remove Precedent Arrows** ⬚ icon on the Auditing toolbar.

There's one other popular way of verifying formula interconnections like these. If you double-click, oh, **cell F2**, you'll see how it works. Excel presents you with color-coded references to each of the cells in the formula (see Figure 20.19). You can then click, drag, move, or otherwise manipulate the individual cells and make changes in the formula. Press **Enter** to go back to normal.

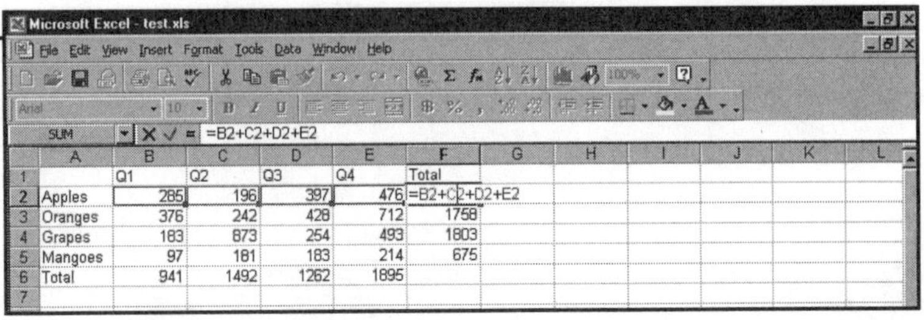

FIGURE 20.19

Excel's color-coded formula verifier.

Although this approach certainly works—and it beats the living daylights out of not verifying at all—I find it harder to use than the trace precedents capability. If you accidentally click inside the spreadsheet before you click **Enter**, or otherwise disturb the color-coded cells, you can really mess up your formula.

Using AutoCalculate

While we're on the subject of building and verifying formulas, there's one more trick you should know about. It's called AutoCalculate, and neither the Office Assistant nor the Help Index will tell you a thing about it.

Every time you select a range of cells, Excel quickly calculates the sum of the values in those cells and puts the number down on the status bar. If you right-click the **AutoCalculate panel**, as you see in Figure 20.20, you can even tell Excel that you'd rather see the average, maximum, minimum, and so on.

This little number can come in very handy to quickly cross-check the answers you're getting in your spreadsheet.

FIGURE 20.20

AutoCalculate sits unobtrusively on the status bar.

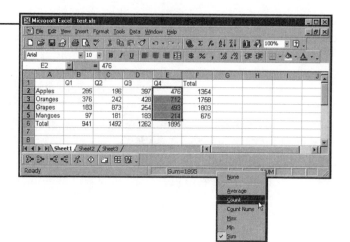

Entry Tricks

Let's take a few minutes right now to look at the ways Excel helps you enter data in a spreadsheet. Learn these tricks well, and you'll save enormous amounts of time—and improve your chances of getting the spreadsheet right the first time.

Enter and Cancel

Have you noticed how you need to press **Enter** every time you type a formula so Excel knows that you're through typing? In fact, there are several alternatives to pressing **Enter** when typing formulas:

WHAT'S A COUNT?

Ah, you noticed that, did you? In Figure 20.20, two of the values you can elect to show in AutoCalculate are called **Count** and **Count Nums**. The Count number is the number of cells with something in them that is selected (blank cells don't, uh, count). Count Nums tells you how many of the selected cells contain valid numbers. So, for example, if you selected cells A2 through B6 in test.xls, you would get a Count of 10, and a Count Nums of five.

- If you press any of the four directional keys (**up**, **down**, **left**, **right arrows**) on the keyboard, Excel understands that you're done typing the formula, and that you want to move on to the next (up, down, left, or right) cell.

- Ditto for the **Tab** and **Back Tab** keys: the formula is finished, and you move left or right one cell.

- If you press **Escape** (the **Esc** key on most keyboards), Excel understands that you want to throw away whatever you've typed and revert to whatever was in the cell before you started typing. **Esc** is the Oops! key.

If you're severely addicted to using the mouse, you can mimic the behavior of the **Enter** key by clicking the **Enter** icon on the Format bar: Clicking that icon makes Excel behave precisely the same way it would if you pressed **Enter**. Similarly, the **Cancel** icon on the Format bar produces precisely the same result as pressing the **Esc** key.

CAUTION

DON'T LEAVE 'EM DANGLING

It's important that you realize new entries in cells don't *take* until you press **Enter** (or, equivalently, click the **Enter** icon). Until you press **Enter**, Excel thinks you're still editing the entry and it will refuse to do all sorts of things—most of the menu items are grayed out—until the editing is done.

If Excel ever seems to be stuck or frozen, first check to make sure you aren't in the middle of editing a cell. The easy way to do that, in most cases, is to press **Enter**.

Correcting Misteaks

What if you've entered something in a cell and it's wrong? You have three choices:

- Click once on the cell and press **Del** or the **Backspace** key. That wipes out the entry and lets you type a new value or formula.

- Click once on the cell; then click in the Formula bar at whatever point you want to start editing. I don't use this approach very much, because the next approach is much faster.

- Double-click the cell. When you do that, Excel makes a pretty good guess where you put the mouse cursor and lets you edit the entry starting at that point. You'll end up editing right there in the cell. This method isn't perfect—it's a little hard to see where the cursor will go before you do the double-click, because the mouse pointer is usually a thick plus-sign, and formatted entries flip-flop like a dying fish when you edit in the cell—but it tends to be the fastest, easiest way to make changes to the contents of a cell.

Entering Functions

Functions intimidate a lot of people because there are so many of them, and some of the functions sound like they're from a different planet. (Tell me the truth: Even if you know how to use a hyperbolic arctangent, how frequently do you need one?)

That's too bad, really, because Excel includes a remarkable support system for functions. Any time you think Excel might be capable of helping you calculate something—whether it's the monthly payment on a mortgage or the day of the week (Monday, Tuesday, and so on)—click the **Paste Function** [fx] icon on the toolbar. Excel responds with its Paste Function dialog box (see Figure 20.21), which lists all the available functions, along with brief descriptions of what the function will calculate and what kind of information you need to feed it.

FIGURE 20.21

Excel's amazingly detailed Function support system.

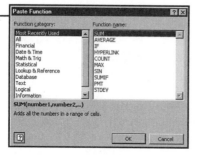

If you click the **?** icon in the lower-left corner, Office Bob, er, the Office Assistant pops up, ready to search for the specific function you want.

Using AutoComplete

Whenever you start typing characters in a cell, Excel takes a quick look at all the text entries in the current column. If it finds a match on the characters you've typed, it offers to fill in the rest of the cell for you.

PARAMETERS, THE BANE OF MY EXISTENCE

Most functions require you to give them information to get an answer back. For example, Excel's WEEKDAY() function tells you the day of the week for a particular date. You feed it a date, and WEEKDAY() returns a number between 1 and 7 that represents the day of the week. (That isn't precisely correct—there are a few additional things the function can do—but it's close enough for our purposes.)

Because different people have different ideas about which day of the week is the first day of the week, you also need to tell WEEKDAY() which day of the week should come back as the number 1.

EXERCISE

AutoComplete

1. Start with a clean, new spreadsheet.

2. In cell B3 type Microsoft Corporation.

3. In cell B4 just type M. See how Excel offers to fill in the rest of the entry? Press **Enter** to accept it.

Excel can't read your mind, of course, so if you have entries for Microsoft Corporation and for Micron Electronics in the same column, you'll have to type all the way out past Micro for Excel to guess which one you want.

This AutoComplete feature (which will be familiar to anyone who's used Quicken) not only saves time, it reduces the chances of typing mistakes. Use it well.

PARAMETERS, THE BANE OF MY EXISTENCE continued

These two things you need to feed WEEKDAY() are called *parameters* and remembering precisely how to feed those parameters to WEEKDAY()—or any other Excel function—can be a monumental pain in the brain.

Excel's Paste Function capability will help you keep your parameters straight, whether you're entering a new formula or modifying an old one. Simply click the cell that's going to receive the formula and click the **Paste Function** _fx_ icon. After you pick the function, or if you're editing an existing function, Excel provides a handy form that sorts out, defines, and manages the function's parameters (see Figure 20.22). It's a godsend. If you ever need to use functions, don't forget the **Paste Function** _fx_ icon.

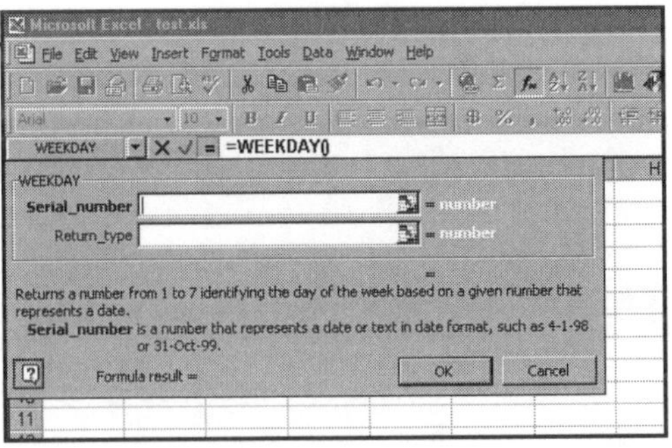

FIGURE 20.22

Excel's parameter support for the WEEKDAY() function.

AutoCorrect

Excel shares Word's AutoCorrect feature: if you type teh, Excel, too, will correct it to the.

☞ *For details about AutoCorrect, see the section called "AutoCorrect," in Chapter 11,* ***page 196***

The care and feeding of Excel's AutoCorrect mirrors Word's precisely, down to its location on the menu (click **Tools**, **AutoCorrect**). Excel and Word even use the same list of corrections, with one minor exception: formatted AutoCorrect entries in Word do not show up in Excel. That's the only difference.

If you aren't yet familiar with AutoCorrect, it would behoove you to go back to Chapter 11, "Key Capabilities," and take a close look. In particular, you should remember that AutoCorrect isn't just for spelling errors! You can use it to store and expand abbreviations of your own choosing. For example, if you commonly type, oh, Sub-Total for this Division of Woody's Widgets Inc., you can set up AutoCorrect so you only need to type a very short string, such as st#, to get the full text put in your spreadsheets.

Using AutoFill

There's one last data entry trick you need to know about. It's called AutoFill and, when the situation's right, it can save you all sorts of time.

EXERCISE

AutoFill as Copy

1. Start with a new, clean spreadsheet.

2. Type 10 in cell B2. Note how there's a little thickening in the lower-right corner of the box around cell B2 (see Figure 20.23). That tiny thick part is called a *fill handle*.

FIGURE 20.23

The fill handle in the lower-right corner of the active cell.

3. Click the fill handle and drag the resulting dotted line (see Figure 20.24) down to cell B10. Watch the little ToolTip, in yellow, as you drag the fill handle. See how it says **10**? That's a little visual clue to tell you that all these cells will be set to 10 as soon as you release the mouse button. Let go of the fill handle, and you'll see it happen.

FIGURE 20.24

Dragging the fill handle down to B10.

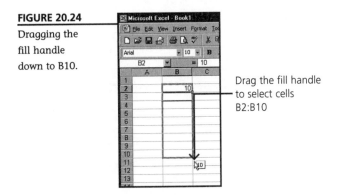

Drag the fill handle to select cells B2:B10

4. At this point, cells B2 to B10 are highlighted, and there's a fill handle at the lower-right corner of B10. Click that fill handle, and drag it over to the D column (see Figure 20.25). All the while you drag, the yellow ToolTip says **10** and, when you release the mouse button, you'll see that the entire range B2:D10 has been filled with 10s.

FIGURE 20.25

The fill handle works in all four directions, for individual cells and for ranges.

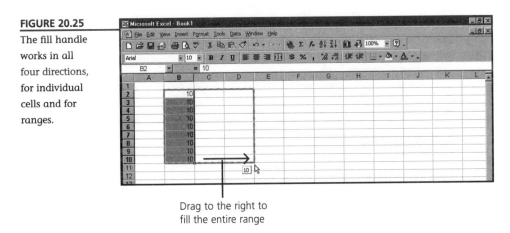

Drag to the right to fill the entire range

5. Push and pull the fill handle until you get the feel for how Excel will copy data from a cell or a region into adjacent cells or regions.

That's pretty cool if you need to copy the same data through a spreadsheet, but it gets much better. AutoFill has some native intelligence you can exploit to generate sequences of numbers and labels. Let me show you what I mean.

EXERCISE

AutoFill a Sequence of Numbers

1. Start with a clean, blank spreadsheet.

2. Type 1 in cell B2.

3. Right-click the fill handle and drag it down to cell B9. Let go of the mouse button, and you'll see the shortcut menu shown in Figure 20.26.

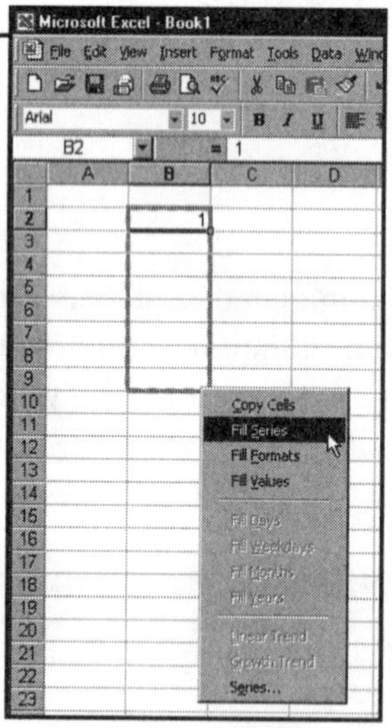

FIGURE 20.26

Various options available when you right-click the fill handle.

4. Click **Fill Series**. That instructs Excel to construct a series of numbers in the filled area. When you click **Fill Series**, you'll get the sequence shown in Figure 20.27.

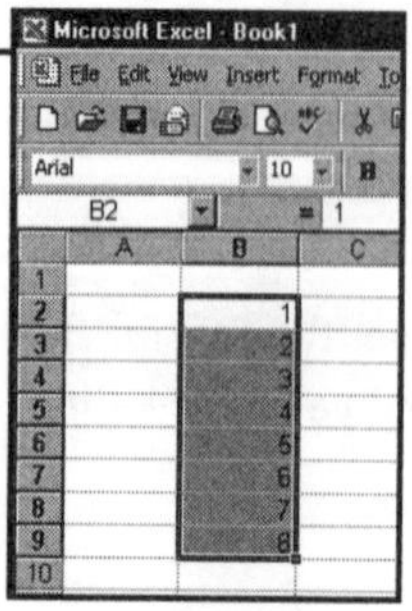

FIGURE 20.27

The sequence formed by choosing **Fill Series**.

AutoFill's smarts aren't limited to simple sequences of numbers. Take a look at this.

EXERCISE

AutoFill Sequences of Labels

1. Start with a new, clean spreadsheet.

2. Type Jan in cell B2.

3. Click B2's fill handle, and drag it out to column I, as shown in Figure 20.28. See how the yellow ScreenTip changes from **Feb** to **Mar** to **Apr**, and so on, until it turns into **Aug** in column I?

WHAT HAPPENS IF I CLICK SERIES?

If you're curious, go ahead and choose **Series** from the list of options offered in Figure 20.26. You'll discover that Excel can create a wide variety of series, based on your choices, including trend lines under various regression models. The mathematics gets a bit hairy, so if you're interested in such things, bring up the Office Assistant and type growth trend.

FIGURE 20.28

Creating a sequence of months with the fill handle.

4. If you release the mouse button over column I, Excel fills in the first row with **Feb**, **Mar**, **Apr**, **May**, **Jun**, **Jul**, and **Aug**.

5. That isn't the only label sequence Excel will AutoFill for you. In Figure 20.29, I've put together quite a few AutoFills, and they're all available in bone-stock Excel.

FIGURE 20.29

A wide variety of AutoFill labels, created by dragging the fill handle.

	A	B	C	D	E	F	G	H	I	J	K	L
1												
2		Jan	Feb	Mar	Apr	May	Jun	Jul	Aug			
3		January	February	March	April	May	June	July	August			
4		Mon	Tue	Wed	Thu	Fri	Sat	Sun	Mon			
5		Monday	Tuesday	Wednesda	Thursday	Friday	Saturday	Sunday	Monday			
6		Jan-00	Feb-00	Mar-00	Apr-00	May-00	Jun-00	Jul-00	Aug-00			
7		10:00	11:00	12:00	13:00	14:00	15:00	16:00	17:00			
8		Q1	Q2	Q3	Q4	Q1	Q2	Q3	Q4			
9		Quarter 1	Quarter 2	Quarter 3	Quarter 4	Quarter 1	Quarter 2	Quarter 3	Quarter 4			
10		15-Jan	16-Jan	17-Jan	18-Jan	19-Jan	20-Jan	21-Jan	22-Jan			
11		12/15/99	12/16/99	12/17/99	12/18/99	12/19/99	12/20/99	12/21/99	12/22/99			
12												
13												

Excel follows some strange rules when deciding if it should just copy, or fill in a full series, when you use the fill handle on a range. (For example, if you AutoFill starting with a row of numbers, the numbers are simply copied. But if you put just one formula in that row, the numbers will be incremented. Weird, but true.) So be careful when you AutoFill starting with more than one original cell.

Copy/Move Data

You would think that Cut, Copy, and Paste—the mainstays of all Windows applications, not just the Office crew—would be incredibly simple in Excel. And you would be wrong—way wrong.

Copying and moving data in Excel gets down right confusing for two simple reasons:

- Excel doesn't behave the way any normal Windows application (or Office application, for that matter) behaves when you paste data from the Clipboard.

- Excel tries to help you by altering formulas behind the scenes when they're copied or moved.

ROLL YOUR OWN AUTOFILL LIST

If there's a series of entries you commonly type into your spreadsheets—say, a bunch of account numbers, or a list of expense categories—you can have Excel do all the dirty work for you.

To see how it works, bring up test.xls and select **cells A2 through A5**. Click **Tools, Options**, and click the **Custom Lists** tab. If you then click the **Import** button (see Figure 20.30), and **OK**, Excel adds the list "Apples, Oranges, Grapes, Mangoes" to the AutoFill feature. From that point on, you can type `Apples`, grab the fill handle, and get the whole list inserted into your spreadsheets.

FIGURE 20.30

Make your own AutoFill lists.

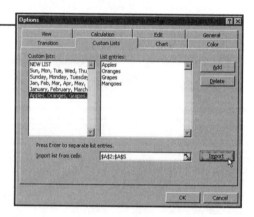

Let's start with the easiest case, and then tackle each of those two tough points in turn.

Simple Copy, Move

By far the fastest and simplest way to move data around in an Excel spreadsheet is to just click and drag.

Move and Copy

1. Open test.xls. Drag your cursor over **cells A1:F6** to select them (or click **A1**, hold down **Shift**, and click **cell F6**).

2. Move your mouse so the pointer hovers just below the range you just selected, as shown in Figure 20.31. The pointer turns into an arrow, indicating that Excel is ready to move or copy the range.

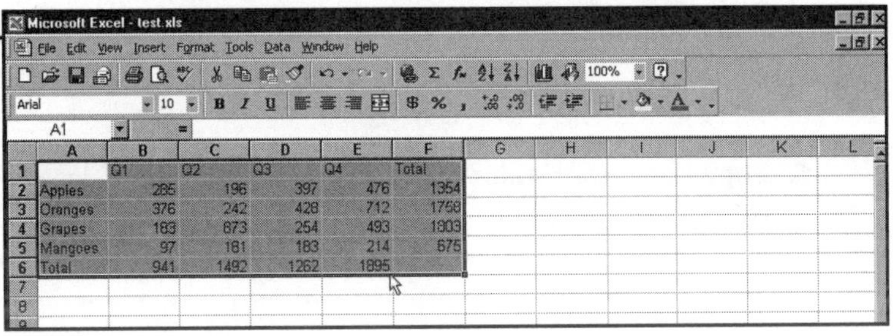

FIGURE 20.31

Select a range and move the mouse pointer to the bottom of the range, to prepare for a move.

CLICK A SIDE, ANY SIDE

While I tend to click the bottom line of a range when I want to move or copy it, in fact you can click any of the outside lines, except the fill handle. It takes a little manual dexterity, but the other edges can come in handy, particularly when you're moving or copying a big range.

3. Click and drag the whole range to some other location on the spreadsheet. In Figure 20.32, I've moved it to C10:H15.

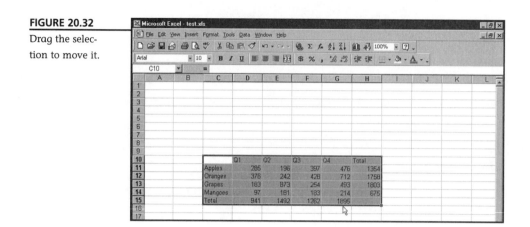

4. That's all it takes to move a range using the mouse. Practice for a bit, and note in particular that you don't have to move the range to a completely virgin location on the spreadsheet; Excel has no trouble at all moving the range just a few cells. When you're done practicing, click the **Undo** 🔄 icon enough times to put the range back in the upper-left corner of the spread-sheet, where it started, at A1:F6.

5. Copying is very similar to moving, except you hold down the **Ctrl** key while clicking and dragging. In Figure 20.33, I started by selecting **A1:F6**. Then I held down the **Ctrl** key and clicked the bottom of the range. (A visual cue that you're copying: the arrow gets a small + sign next to it.) When I had moved the range to **C10:H15**, I released the mouse button, and then the **Ctrl** key, in that order. The result: Excel copied the range to the new location.

FIGURE 20.33

Copying by
holding down
the **Ctrl** key.

6. Again you can practice copying until you're comfortable
with it. When you're fin-
ished, click **Undo** to restore
test.xls to its original
condition.

Excel lets you click and drag ranges
anywhere in a spreadsheet. If you
want to drop a range of cells down
below the bottom of the current
screen, just hold your cursor at the
bottom and Excel will scroll the
spreadsheet for you. All in all, click
and drag is the best way to go. You'll
see why in the next section.

MORE MOVE AND COPY OPTIONS

Sometimes you want to move a row, but
when you're through dragging it, you don't
want to over-write an existing row, you want
to stick it between two other rows.

Excel supports this option and many more. You
can memorize a lot of weird key combinations
to insert, copy, bump, and grind, but the simplest way to take advantage of Excel's multiple
options is to simply right-click, drag, and then
pick what action you want to perform. In
Figure 20.34, I've selected **A5:F5** in test.xls,
right-clicked, dragged, and then released the
mouse button to select my preferred action.

FIGURE 20.34

Right-click and
drag to uncover
a host of
options for
shifting, copy-
ing, and
moving.

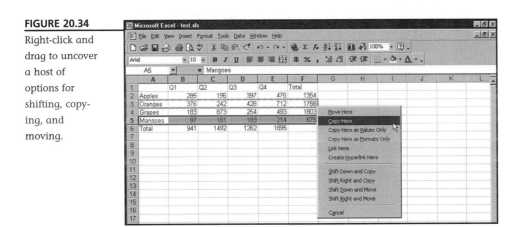

How Excel Pastes

If you can't use the mouse to move or copy ranges in your spreadsheet—perhaps
you need to move the range a long distance, or you're afraid you might miss the
destination area by a cell or two—you need to be aware of the strange way Excel
handles Cut, Copy, and Paste.

EXERCISE

Copy and Paste

1. Open test.xls, if it isn't already open.

2. Click a cell, say **C4**, and then click **Edit**, **Copy**. (Equivalently, if you're accustomed to Windows' shortcut keys, you can press **Ctrl+C**.) Excel responds by placing the contents of C4 on the Office Clipboard, the common Office procedure, and it adds a bit of lagniappe by showing the marching ants around cell C4, as shown in Figure 20.35.

FIGURE 20.35

Cell C4 is copied to the Clipboard.

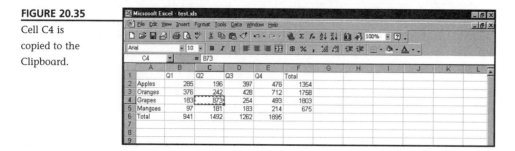

3. Excel is capable of performing a fairly normal paste. Click in, oh, **cell E10**, and then click **Edit**, **Paste** (or press **Ctrl+V**, the Windows shortcut key combination). As you can see in Figure 20.36, that puts a copy of cell C4 in cell E10.

FIGURE 20.36

A standard paste with **Edit/Paste** or **Ctrl+V**.

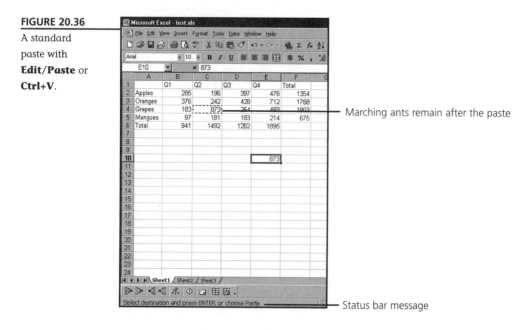

Marching ants remain after the paste

Status bar message

4. Notice two things that are very odd about Figure 20.36: Even after the paste, Excel keeps the ants marching around cell C4, and it continues to show the message **Select destination and press Enter or choose Paste** in the status bar. That's where the problem arises.

5. Say you've performed a copy in this manner, but you get to scrolling to some obscure part of your spreadsheet, and you've forgotten that the ants are still marching around cell C4. You end up somewhere in your spreadsheet—in Figure 20.37, I just happened to get to cell B12—and you press **Enter**.

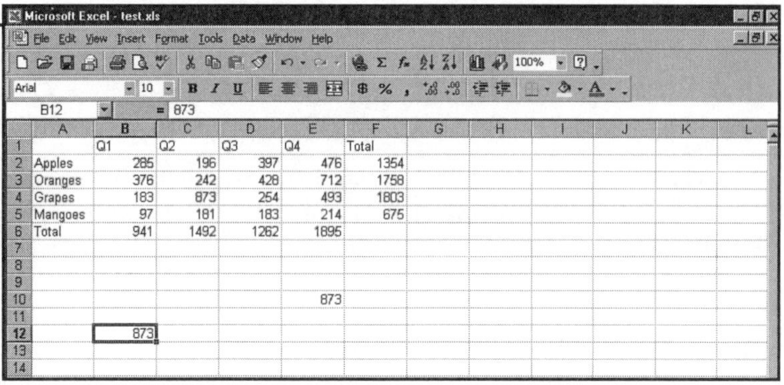

FIGURE 20.37

While the ants are marching around a cell, the **Enter** key is still hot and will copy the contents.

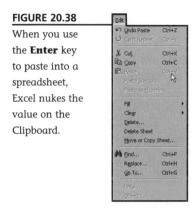

6. *Boom!* For no apparent reason, Excel copies the contents of cell C4 into cell B12. That's a real bummer. But wait, it gets stranger.

7. After you've completed a copy using this weird **Enter** key method, Excel removes the value from the Clipboard! If you then click **Edit**, as you can see in Figure 20.38, the Paste action is grayed out. Excel has literally thrown away the contents of the Clipboard. (It's tossed off the Office Clipboard, too.)

FIGURE 20.38

When you use the **Enter** key to paste into a spreadsheet, Excel nukes the value on the Clipboard.

Some people shrug off this odd (and decidedly un-Windows–like, not to mention un-Office–like!) behavior as another Excel anomaly. Personally, when I was learning to use Excel for the first time, I found it to be one of the most frustrating inanities in Excel.

Anyway, whether you think of this odd paste behavior as another ho-hum stupidity or a major stumbling block to understanding what's going on, the conclusion comes out the same: Use the mouse to copy and move cells, unless you absolutely have to resort to the Edit menu or keyboard shortcuts.

Absolute and Relative Addresses

I was astounded to discover that some introductory Office books don't even mention the difference between absolute and relative cell addresses. When you see how important they are, you'll be astounded as well.

The whole problem stems from a simple fact: Sometimes when you copy (or move) formulas, you want them to change, and sometimes you don't. Let me show you what I mean.

EXERCISE

When You Want Formulas to Change

1. Start with a new, clean spreadsheet. We're going to calculate some salespeople's commissions.

2. Put some numbers in cells B4:C5. In Figure 20.39, I've built a small spreadsheet to hang the numbers in, and give them some context.

FIGURE 20.39

The beginning of a small commission calculator.

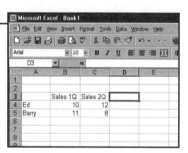

3. In cell D4, type the formula =B4+C4. In the example in Figure 20.39, that calculates Ed's total sales for the first two quarters.

4. Copy the formula in D4 toD5 by clicking and dragging on the copy handle. You would expect this new formula in D5 to calculate Barry's total sales for the first two quarters—and it does (see Figure 20.40).

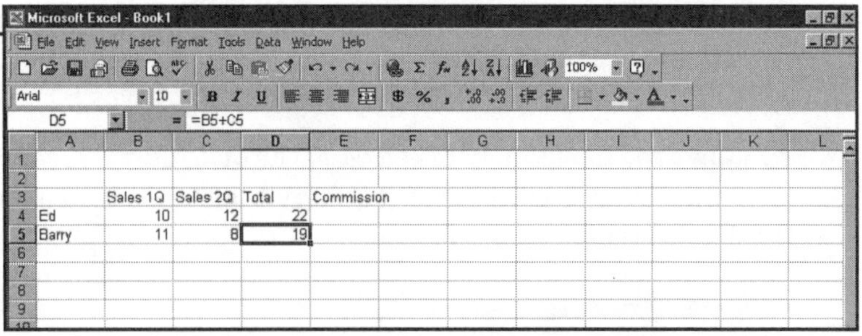

FIGURE 20.40

Copy Ed's total sales formula to Barry's line, and you would expect the total to reflect Barry's sales.

	A	B	C	D	E	F
1						
2						
3		Sales 1Q	Sales 2Q	Total	Commission	
4	Ed	10	12	22		
5	Barry	11	8	19		

(Cell D5 = =B5+C5)

5. Something strange happened when Excel copied the formula from D4 to D5, though, and you can see what happened in the Formula bar of Figure 20.40. Excel changed the cell references around, so the total now refers to Barry's numbers on row 5, and not Ed's numbers on row 4. Cell D5 now reads **=B5+C5**, which is as it should be.

6. If you subsequently move or copy the A3:D5 range to some other place on the spreadsheet, you would expect the total for Ed's line to stay 22, and the total for Barry's line to stay 19. They do—but Excel changes the underlying formulas as the range moves around, so these two formulas refer to the correct cells, no matter where the A3:D5 range might sit.

That's an example of *relative* addressing: When you move or copy formulas around, you let Excel take care of the details and switch the formulas to fit the situation.

Sometimes, though, you don't want Excel to change the formulas—or part of the formulas.

EXERCISE

When You Don't Want Formulas to Change

1. Continue with the spreadsheet you were just using.

2. Let's figure out how much commission I owe Ed and Barry for the first two quarters' sales. I'll put the commission rate in cell A1, as you can see in Figure 20.41.

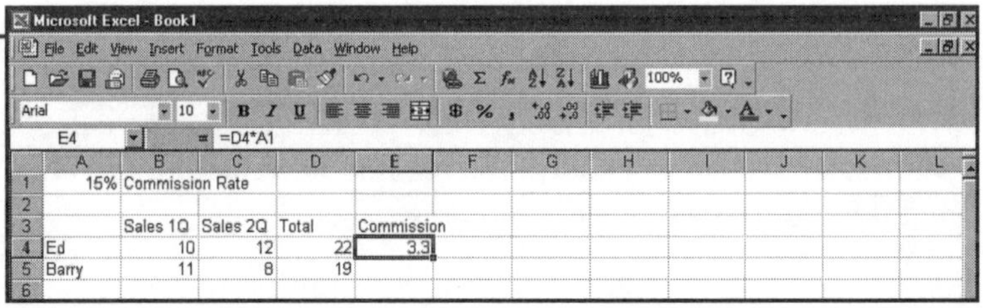

FIGURE 20.41

Commission rate goes into cell A1.

	A	B	C	D	E	F
1	15%	Commission Rate				
2						
3		Sales 1Q	Sales 2Q	Total	Commission	
4	Ed	10	12	22	3.3	
5	Barry	11	8	19		

(Cell E4 = =D4*A1)

3. To calculate Ed's commission, I need to multiply his total sales (cell D4) by the commission rate (cell A1). That's why I put the formula =D4*A1 in cell E4. Sure enough, his commission comes up 3.3, which is 15 percent of 22.

4. Now copy the formula in cell E4 to calculate Barry's commission in cell E5. As you can see in Figure 20.42, Barry would be a bit, uh, perturbed to learn that his commission is 0!

FIGURE 20.42

Copy the commission calculation formula down one cell, and all hell breaks loose.

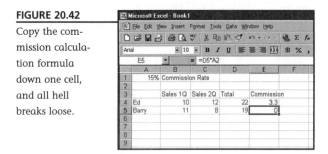

5. What happened? Let's trace the precedents to see. Click **cell E4**, and click the **Trace Precedents** icon on the Auditing toolbar. You'll see in Figure 20.43 that the precedents for E4 look fine.

FIGURE 20.43

Precedents for cell E4 look fine.

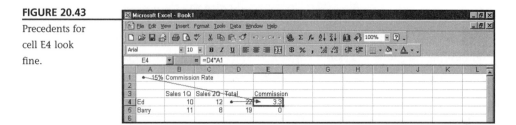

6. But when you run a **Trace Precedents** on **cell E5**, as shown in Figure 20.44, you'll see immediately that the formula in E5 refers to cell A2—and that isn't where the commission rate is located!

This is one of those occasions when you want Excel to keep its mitts off your formula. More accurately, you want these commission calculations to continue to refer to cell A1, no matter where the formula might be moved or copied.

When you want Excel to change a cell address as a formula gets copied or moved, you use the regular cell addressing method we've been using all along: A1, C3, D5, and the like. Those are relative addresses.

FIGURE 20.44

Trace Precedents on cell E5 reveals the culprit—Excel has incorrectly changed the formula.

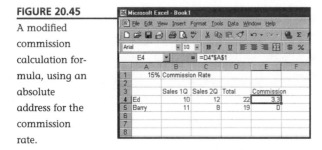

When you want Excel to refrain from modifying a cell address, you have to use something called an *absolute* address. You specify absolute addresses by putting $ dollar signs in front of the row and column: A1, C3, D5, for example. The dollar signs don't have any celestial significance; they're just Keep Off signs warning Excel not to change the addresses.

EXERCISE

Using Absolute Addresses

1. Go back into the commission spreadsheet we've been using, and click **cell E4**.

2. This time, instead of using the (relative) address A1 in the formula, try using the (absolute) address A1. I've modified the formula in E4, as you can see in Figure 20.45.

FIGURE 20.45

A modified commission calculation formula, using an absolute address for the commission rate.

3. Now copy the formula in cell E4 down to E5. Sure enough, the new formula, **=D5*A1**, refers to the correct location for the commission rate, and the commission gets calculated properly (see Figure 20.46). Barry should be a happy guy.

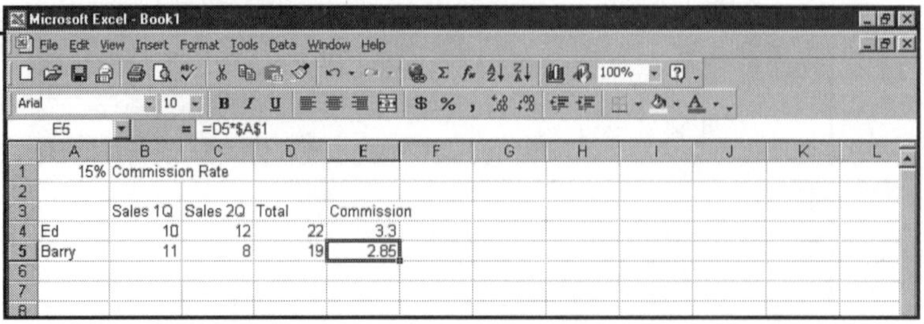

FIGURE 20.46

The formula copies across correctly because you used an absolute address.

[Screenshot: Microsoft Excel - Book1. Cell E5 contains =D5*A1. Spreadsheet shows: Row 1: 15% Commission Rate. Row 3: Sales 1Q, Sales 2Q, Total, Commission. Row 4: Ed 10 12 22 3.3. Row 5: Barry 11 8 19 2.85]

If you start copying formulas and they go haywire, run a quick **Trace Precedents**. If the Trace shows that the formulas aren't referring to the correct cells, chances are very good that you need to use an absolute address.

Add/Delete Rows and Columns

If you knew exactly what your spreadsheet was going to look like at the time you started, you'd never have to add or delete rows or columns.

'Course if you knew exactly what your spreadsheet was going to look like, you wouldn't need me to help, would you?

VARIATIONS ON A THEME

Things aren't quite as neat as I made them out to be. In addition to relative and absolute addresses, Excel also recognizes hybrid addresses, such as A$1 and $A1. As you might imagine, the part of the address preceded by a $ dollar sign is the absolute part, while the other half of the address can be modified by Excel when you copy or move formulas. I'll leave it as a, uh, exercise for you to work out the nuances of those puppies.

EXERCISE

Insert a Column

1. Start with test.xls.

2. Let's say you want to add a new column between the existing columns A and B. As shown in Figure 20.47, you would start by clicking the **B column** heading, thereby selecting all of column B.

3. Up on the menu, click **Insert**, **Column**, and violà, a new column B appears, as shown in Figure 20.48. Remarkably, all the other columns in test.xls are shifted to the right, and all the formulas still work. (Such is the wonder of relative addresses, eh?)

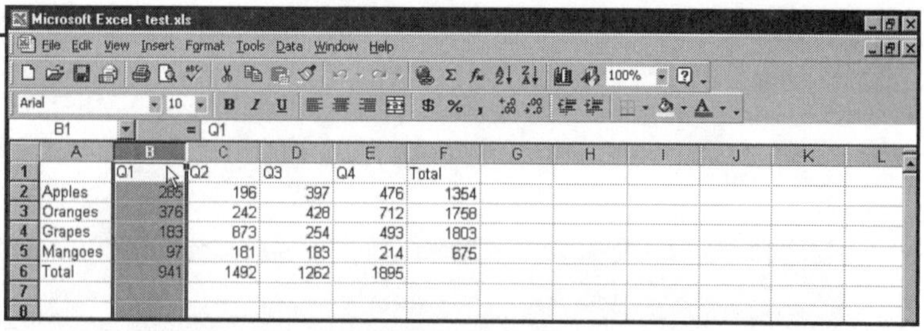

FIGURE 20.47

To insert a column to the left of column B, first select **column B**.

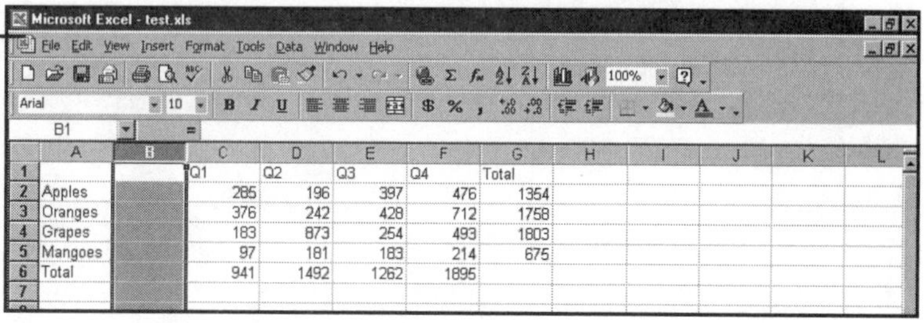

FIGURE 20.48

Click **Insert**, **Column**, and a new column appears to the left of the selected column.

That was easy. Now, what if you want to insert more than one column or row?

EXERCISE

Insert Multiple Rows

1. Continue with test.xls, as in the previous exercise.

2. Say you want to insert three rows directly above the row marked Oranges. Here's the trick: select the **Oranges row**, plus two additional rows, for a total of three rows, by clicking and dragging on the row **headings 3**, **4**, and **5**. See Figure 20.49, where I've selected rows 3, 4, and 5.

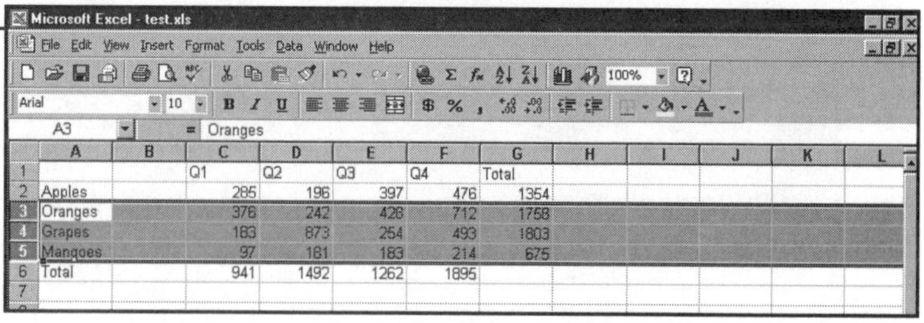

FIGURE 20.49

Select a number of rows equal to the number of rows you want to insert.

3. Now click **Insert**, **Rows**. Excel responds by adding three rows—a number equal to the number of rows you selected—and placing them above the top selected row. In Figure 20.50 you can see how the other rows have been moved down, and once again all the formulas remain intact.

FIGURE 20.50

Click **Insert**,
Rows and
Excel inserts an
equal number
of rows above
the one at the
top of the
selected range.

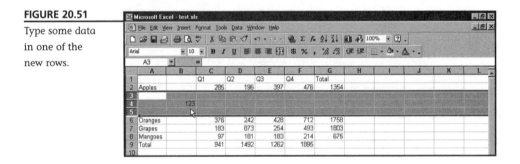

If adding rows and columns is so easy, deleting rows and columns must be easy, too, right?

Well, it is... if you know the trick. (Have you heard that one before?)

 EXERCISE

Delete Rows

1. Start with the modified version of test.xls you just created in the previous exercise. Type a number—say 123—in cell B4. Your spreadsheet should look like Figure 20.51.

FIGURE 20.51

Type some data
in one of the
new rows.

2. Let's say you want to get rid of rows 3, 4, and 5. Select the rows by clicking and dragging on the row headings 3, 4, and 5.

3. You want to delete the rows? Okay. Press the **Del** or **Delete** key on your keyboard.

4. Guess what? The rows don't disappear. Only the data goes away, and you end up with a spreadsheet that looks just like Figure 20.50!

5. To delete the rows, you have to click **Edit**, **Delete**. Similarly, to delete a column, you must first select the entire column, and then click **Edit**, **Delete**.

6. Return test.xls to its original condition by deleting the three rows and one column you added in this section. (You can probably just click **Undo** a few times.)

#Bad Data

When Excel looks at a number and has a problem, it invariably uses some variation of the # sign to alert you to the problem.

The simplest situation is when a number is too big to fit in a cell. In that case, Excel shows ####### in the cell, just to warn you that you need to make the cell wider to display the number. I'll talk about adjusting column widths in Chapter 21, "Getting Around"—and if you haven't already adjusted a

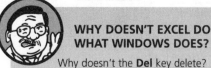

WHY DOESN'T EXCEL DO WHAT WINDOWS DOES?

Why doesn't the **Del** key delete? Probably the same reason why Excel uses the **Enter** key for Paste: Excel has always worked that way, and Microsoft is afraid to change it. Funny, though, that the Redmondians don't let you change this very un-Windows–like behavior in the **Tools** menu. Funnier still when you recall that Windows was essentially invented to support Excel.

column width, Excel should be smart enough to automatically adjust the width to hold your widest entry—but if you hit the problem before you read the next chapter, just double-click the vertical bar to the right of the column heading and the column will expand, growing wide enough to accommodate the widest entry in the column.

Other # warning values aren't so benevolent. These are the ones you're most likely to encounter, in "normal" business spreadsheets:

- **#VALUE!** appears when you try to use a text string in an arithmetic formula. For example, if cell B1 contains the text **Apples**, and you type the formula =B1*3, you'll get the #VALUE! error.

- **#NAME!** will pop up if you forget to put the colon in a range name. For example, the formula =SUM(B2F6) will trigger a #NAME! error.

- **#REF!** usually happens when you delete a cell that's needed for a formula. Say cell D4 contains the formula =B3+7, and you delete the B3 cell. B4 will come up with #REF! error.

To get more details on these and the other error values, #DIV/0!, #N/A!, #NUM!, and #NULL!, bring up the Office Assistant and type formula error values (for some reason, error values isn't good enough!).

Show Formulas

Most of the time you want to look at the results of all the formulas in your spreadsheet. But sometimes it makes more sense to look at the formulas themselves. In Figure 20.52, I've switched test.xls over to show formulas.

FIGURE 20.52

Showing formulas in test.xls.

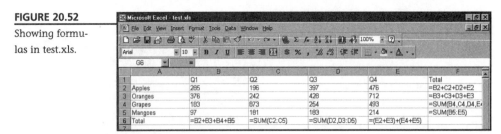

Fortunately, it's easy to switch back and forth between seeing formulas and seeing results. Unfortunately, the key combination is so weird you'll probably have to write instructions down on your monitor to remember it: hold down the **Ctrl** key and press the single open quote key (`), which is usually underneath the tilde, to the left of the number 1 on most keyboards. (On some it's way down near the spacebar.) To bring back the results, press **Ctrl+`** once again.

Comments

A couple of good friends of mine, Lee Hudspeth and T.J. Lee, like to call Excel spreadsheets the largest undocumented computer programs in existence. They have a good point. Spreadsheets that start out as little 8×10 cell quick calculators frequently end up a hundred times that size, and more often than not many such spreadsheets can be found running important parts of major corporations. True fact.

Just as programmers know how important it is to put comments in their programs (present company, ahem, excluded), it's vitally important that you put comments in your spreadsheets to show anything even remotely out of the ordinary, and to document when and why changes were made.

To put a comment in a cell, just click the cell, and then click **Insert**, **Comment**. Excel responds with a little box where you can type whatever you feel is appropriate (see Figure 20.53).

FIGURE 20.53

Comments are easy to insert and can save your neck.

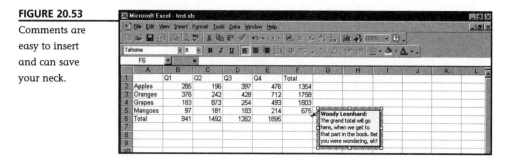

Excel gives you a visual cue that there's a comment attached to a cell by placing a small red triangle in the upper-right corner of the cell. Hover your mouse pointer near the cell for just a second, and the comment appears for your edification.

21

Woody Leonhard

TEACHES

GETTING AROUND EXCEL

ON THE ROAD TO SHAMBALA. You've already seen how to get around a spreadsheet by using the mouse and the directional keys on the keyboard (up, down, left, right). Those all come naturally; they're pretty much the same in every Windows application. Now I'd like to explore navigation a little further and introduce you to one of Excel's most important concepts along the way: named ranges.

Worthwhile Shortcut Keys

Gad, I hate shortcut keys in all the Windows applications. They're hard to memorize, and they almost never do what I expect them to do.

Excel, though, is a little different. At least there's some logic to the key combinations: Just remember to use the **Ctrl** and **End** keys, both individually and together, and you can save quite a bit of time, particularly when you're trying to navigate large spreadsheets.

Here are the two key combinations I find useful. Your results may vary, of course:

- **Ctrl+Home** takes you to cell A1.

- **Ctrl+End** takes you to the last cell in your spreadsheet. Actually, it's a little more complicated than that. Say the last row in your spreadsheet that has any data in it is, oh, line 2345. And say the last column that has any data in it is CD. Pressing **Ctrl+End** would take you to cell CD2345, even if there's nothing in that cell.

- If you have a very dense spreadsheet with values in most of the cells, the **End** key can be helpful. Press **End** and one of the arrow keys, and you'll be transported to the end of the current column (or row) of data.

And the way we have things set up, if you ever want to get back to the active cell (say you've scrolled into the lower forty and aren't quite sure where the active cell went), just press **Enter**.

There are other keys, of course, but most of them are too esoteric for my blood. You can get a list of them by calling up the Office Assistant and typing shortcut keys.

Using Named Ranges

Word has bookmarks. Excel has named ranges. The concepts are very similar, and the uses for both are far beyond what you might imagine. When you start to hyperlink workbooks, connect the various Office applications together with features such as Paste Special, or move your spreadsheets onto the Web, named ranges are the anchor points within workbooks that you can access, retrieve data from, or go to.

WHY SUCH A WEIRD NAME?

Range names can take on only a very specific form. They can contain only letters, numbers, periods, and the underscore (_) character. Capital letters get treated the same as lowercase. No spaces are allowed. Worse, the name can't start with a number or a period, and the name can't look like a cell name. So _KilroyWasHere is a valid range name, while 52Skidoo and L8 are not.

What is a named range? Well, it's a range that has a name. (Rocket science again, eh?) You can assign almost any name you want to any range you like.

EXERCISE

Assign a Name to a Range

1. Start with your trusty test workbook, test.xls.

2. Select the guts of the spreadsheet, range **B2:E5**, by clicking **B2** and dragging down to **E5**, or clicking **B2**, holding down the **Shift** key, and clicking **E5** (see Figure 21.1).

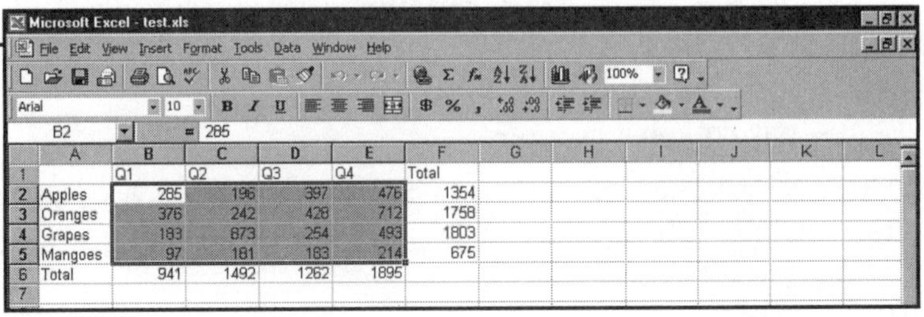

FIGURE 21.1

To define a named range, start by selecting the range.

3. Now click in the **Name** box on the Formula bar. Excel responds by highlighting the current name in the box, inviting you to change it. In Figure 21.2, I typed the name FruitSales, thus giving the selected range a name.

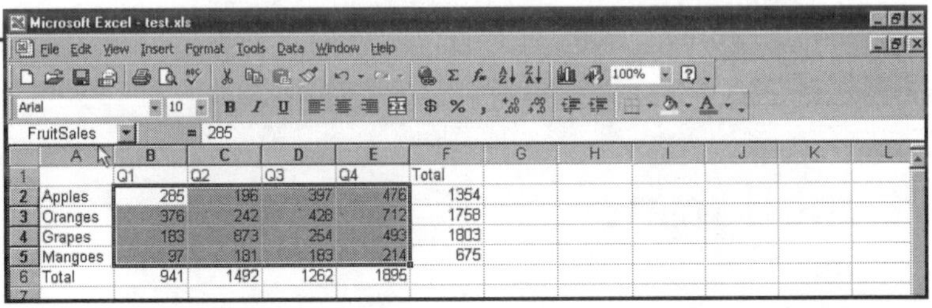

FIGURE 21.2

Type a new name for the range in the Name box.

After a range has been given a name, navigating to it couldn't be simpler.

EXERCISE

Go to a Named Range

1. In test.xls, click a random cell.

2. To go to the range called **FruitSales**, click the down arrow to the right of the Name box, and choose **FruitSales**, as shown in Figure 21.3.

FIGURE 21.3

Using the Name box to go to FruitSales.

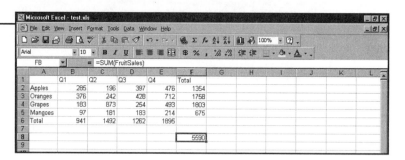

3. Excel selects the entire range called FruitSales, and the result looks precisely like Figure 21.2. Delete the formula when you're done.

 TIP

GO TO UNNAMED RANGES

Have a hankering to jump to, oh, cell F49? Use the Name box. Just click the **Name** box, type F49, press **Enter**, and you're off.

NOTE

OTHER USES FOR NAMED RANGES

You can use a named range just about anyplace you would use the more traditional kind of range (that is, a range indicated by two cell addresses separated by a colon, such as A1:D5).

Take the Sum() function, for example. If you click **cell F8** in test.xls and type =sum (fruitsales), Excel recognizes that as a valid range name and gives you the sum of all the cells located in the FruitSales range (see Figure 21.4).

FIGURE 21.4

Using the named range FruitSales to calculate a sum.

Although creating and using named ranges is quite easy, getting rid of a range name involves a few extra steps.

EXERCISE

Delete a Range Name

1. Start with test.xls.

2. This is a little weird (like clicking **Start** to turn off your PC, eh?), but click **Insert**, **Name**, **Define**. You'll see Excel's Define Name dialog box, as shown in Figure 21.5.

FIGURE 21.5

The only way to delete a range name is via the Define Name dialog box.

3. Click **FruitSales**, and then click **Delete**. That gets rid of the FruitSales name (note that it doesn't touch the range itself!). Click either **OK** or **Close** and you can verify through the Name box that FruitSales is gone.

Using Excel's Find Tool

Excel, like Word, has a Find feature that enables you to scan spreadsheets for words and characters. Surprisingly, though, Excel Find isn't anywhere near as capable as the Word find.

EXERCISE

Find Apple

1. Start with test.xls.

2. Click **Edit**, **Find**. Excel puts the Find dialog box on the screen. In the Find what box, type apple, as shown in Figure 21.6.

FIGURE 21.6

Looking for "apple".

3. Click **Find Next**. As you can see in Figure 21.7, Excel finds Apples in cell A2. (Note that if you had checked either Match case or Find entire cells only in the Find dialog box, Excel wouldn't have stopped in cell A2. Match case is for upper- and lowercase; Find entire cells only forces Excel to look for whole cells that precisely match the text in the Find what box.)

FIGURE 21.7

A match on "Apples" in cell A2.

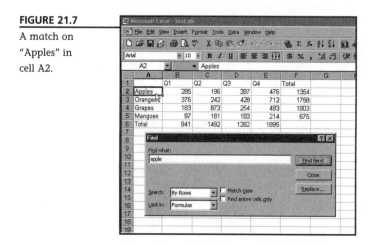

You can limit Excel's searching to Formulas, Values, or Comments, as you can see in Figure 21.8.

FIGURE 21.8

Limiting Excel's searching to Formulas, Values, or Comments.

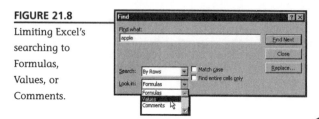

These terms in the Find dialog box are awfully misleading. Excel has a very specific definition for the term *Value*, and it's blown completely away in this dialog box. (In fact, in this book I don't use the term *Value* in the same strict way that Excel does, precisely because of this dialog box!) Here's what the terms mean:

WHAT ABOUT WILDCARDS?

Ah, you remember those from Word, don't you?

Excel supports two wildcards: the **?**, which stands for any single character, and the *****, which stands for any string of characters. Thus, searching for "a*le" will match apple, argyle, and ale, while searching for "gr?pe" will match grape, gripe, or grope.

● *Comments*, as you might imagine, are the Comments put inside cells, as we have in cell F6. That's fine.

● But in this context, *Formulas* means anything that you typed into the cell, whether what you typed is a real formula, or any other kind of data, including text and numbers. Here, a formula is anything that appears in the Formula bar, whether it's an Excel formula or not.

● *Values* in this context means whatever you normally see on the screen, whether that's text you've typed or a number that's been typed or calculated via a formula.

SOAPBOX ON

While I'm taking Microsoft to task over its inconsistent Value terminology and the strange way it scans for Replace strings, I want to throw one more barb in the direction of Redmond. Why oh why are Excel's Find and Replace capabilities so wimpy? Word can Find and Replace 'til the cows come home, with all sorts of patterns, style matches, formatting changes, and the like. Excel can't even perform a simple Replace without some sort of convoluted definition of what it's replacing.

There's no reason in the world—at least, no good reason—why Word and Excel should have different Find and Replace functions. Just as Word would benefit from a "look inside field codes" option, Excel would benefit from a "look inside formulas" option. The entire area of search and replace is just begging for some uniformity. Common dialog boxes would be nice. Common code would be most welcome.

Excel's designers desperately need to differentiate between formulas and formula results, just as Word's designers differentiate between field codes and field code results.

Excel can also perform a Find and Replace just like Word. If you click **Edit**, **Replace** (or click the **Replace** button on the Find dialog box, as in Figure 21.8), you'll get Excel's Replace dialog box, shown in Figure 21.9.

FIGURE 21.9

The options available to perform a replace in Excel.

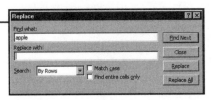

Replace proceeds much as you would expect, as it closely mimics the Find/Replace cycle in Word, but it won't touch formulas. Nothing on heaven or earth will convince Excel to replace one string inside a formula with another.

All this adds up to an enormously confusing situation (to me, anyway). Make sure you go slowly when you use Excel's Replace feature.

Excel's Go To Feature

Excel's Go To dialog box (click **Edit**, **Go To**) works much like the Name box: Type a cell address or the name of a region in the box, press **Enter**, and you move to that location.

The Go To dialog box, though, has two additional capabilities that you won't find in the Name box. They can come in handy for getting around a spreadsheet.

First, it keeps a list of the locations you've jumped to most recently. (Whether or not you used Go To or the Name box.) As you can see in Figure 21.10, returning to a spot you recently visited is as easy as clicking the location, and then clicking **OK**.

FIGURE 21.10

The Go To dia-
log box lists the
most recently
"jumped to"
locations.

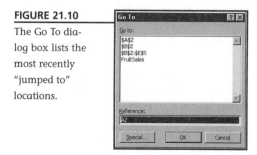

Second, Go To lets you cruise through an entire spreadsheet looking for certain types of entries. If you click the **Special** button in Figure 21.10, you'll get the Go To Special dialog box shown in Figure 21.11. From this dialog box you can look for formulas, precedents, and much more.

FIGURE 21.11

Go To Special
hops through a
spreadsheet
looking for spe-
cific kinds of
entries.

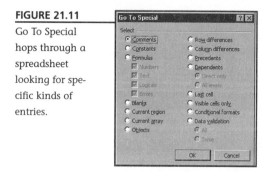

Working with Multiple Sheets

Although all the Excel work in this book concentrates on a single spreadsheet, you can pull data from other spreadsheets in a workbook or even other workbooks.

Welcome to the bang.

EXERCISE

Multiple-Sheet Formulas

1. Start with a clean, new workbook by clicking the **New** 🗋 icon on the tool-bar. This new workbook should have three spreadsheets, identified as Sheet1, Sheet2, and Sheet3.

2. Type some numbers in Sheet1's A1:B2 range. In Figure 21.12, I've typed 2, 3, 4, and 5.

FIGURE 21.12

Type numbers on Sheet1.

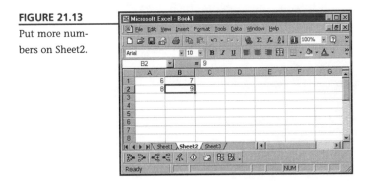

3. Click the tab for **Sheet2**, down near the bottom of the screen, and type some more random numbers, this time in Sheet2's A1:B2 range. In Figure 21.13, I've typed 6, 7, 8, and 9.

FIGURE 21.13

Put more num-bers on Sheet2.

4. Click the **Sheet3** tab. I'm going to make this a total sheet. For example, in Sheet3's cell A1, I want the total of Sheet1's A1 and Sheet2's A1.

5. Nothing to it. Click Sheet3's **cell A1**. Then type an = sign as if you were going to write a formula. In fact, that's precisely what you're going to do, using the old point-and-click method.

6. Click the **Sheet1** tab, and then click **cell A1** on Sheet1. The Formula bar should read **=Sheet1!A1**. Now type a + sign.

7. Click the **Sheet2** tab, and then click **cell A1** on Sheet2. The Formula bar should now say **=Sheet1!A1+Sheet2!A2**. That's the formula you want, so press **Enter**.

8. You're propelled back to Sheet3, where you started, and the number appearing in cell A1 is, indeed, the sum of A1 on Sheet1 and A1 on Sheet2 (see Figure 21.14). Nifty, eh?

FIGURE 21.14

Cell A1 on Sheet3 is the sum of the A1s on Sheet1 and Sheet2.

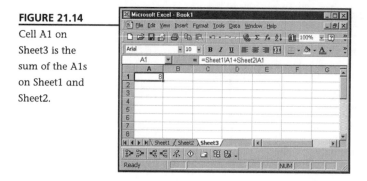

9. You could repeat this laborious procedure for Sheet3's B1, A2 and B2, but why bother? Hold the **Ctrl** key and click and drag to copy the formula in Sheet3's A1 into Sheet3's B1. Do the same for A2 and B2. Excel understands perfectly what you want to do, and modifies the (relative) addresses accordingly. As you can see in Figure 21.15, the formula it puts into Sheet3's B2 is **=Sheet1!B2+Sheet2!B2**.

FIGURE 21.15

Copied formulas mutate properly.

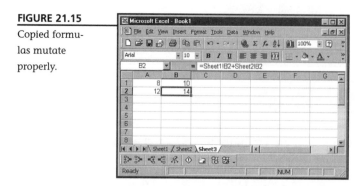

See how the *Sheet name!Cell name* address is such a straightforward extension of the cell addresses you've already used? **Sheet1!A6:D8**, for example, refers to the range A6:D8 on Sheet1. Nothin' to it.

Care to take a guess what Sheet1:Sheet3!A1:B2 refers to in this example? Right. It's the 12-cell range, four cells on each of three sheets, which contains numbers. In fact, it's a three-dimensional range.

Three-dimensional ranges can be named, used in functions (try =sum(Sheet1:Sheet3!A1:B2) in your spreadsheet), cut, copied, moved, sliced, and diced just like any other range. All you need is a little gumption and a big bottle of Excedrin— good-sized 3D worksheets will drive you crazy in no time.

> **SO WHAT'S A BANG?**
>
> I'm not sure where it comes from, but for many, many years UNIX programmers have called the ! exclamation point a *bang*. Somehow the pronunciation has carried over to the PC world in general, and Excel in particular. So, for example, =Sheet1!B2 is pronounced "equals sheet one bang bee two."
>
> New Excel users tend to emphasize the "bang" when reciting a name like that, but experienced users generally pronounce all the syllables with the same, flat tone.
>
> I'll have you talking like an old Excel salt in no time, eh wot?

I won't try to incorporate 3D calculations (or ranges) into the rest of this book. You'll have your hands full formatting and charting single spreadsheets without the added distraction. But remember that anything you can do with a single spreadsheet can probably also be done with a 3D range, although the details may prove, uh, challenging.

22

Woody Leonhard

TEACHES

MAKING SPREADSHEETS LOOK GOOD

YOU LOOK MAHVELOUS. The triumph of appearance over substance. Such is the fate of the formatted spreadsheet. But let's face it. If you need to use your numbers to get a point across, you'll end up spending an amazing amount of time formatting and reformatting those cells, borders, headings, and whatnot.

Format on, I say.

Resizing Columns and Rows

All in all, Excel does a pretty good job of adapting automatically to most column width challenges. In most cases, you don't need to do a thing.

 EXERCISE

The Limits of Column Width

1. Start with a new, clean spreadsheet.

2. In cell A1, type eleven 5s, or 55555555555. Press **Enter**. On most spreadsheets, Excel automatically adjusts the width of column A to accommodate the entire number.

3. Now try typing twelve 5s in cell B2. Excel is smart enough to realize that the number is too wide for column B. Further, it decides that you really don't want to expand the column width all that much, so it converts your number into scientific notation, widens the column, and displays as many decimal places as it can in the allotted space (see Figure 22.1).

FIGURE 22.1

Excel adapts column widths to accommodate reasonably large numbers.

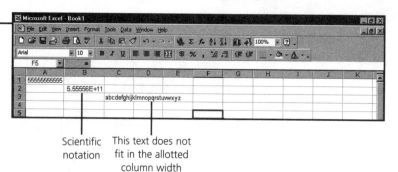

Scientific notation — This text does not fit in the allotted column width

4. Excel doesn't try to change column widths when confronted by text that's too large for a cell. Instead, it flops the excess text into the next cell. You can see that in Figure 22.1, where I've typed abcdefghijklmnopqrstuvwxyz in cell C3. The part that doesn't fit into cell C3 shows up where D3 and E3 would appear.

5. As soon as something else occupies one of those "flop over" cells, though, the excess text disappears. Look at Figure 22.2, where I've typed abc in cell D3. See how the extra text in C3 no longer flops over?

FIGURE 22.2

Putting any-thing in a cell stops the long text "flop over."

Text no longer "flops" into the neighboring cell
once text is placed in the second tail

6. Hold onto this spreadsheet. You'll use it in the next exercise.

Excel starts out with each column about as wide as 8.5 numbers, in the standard font (in this case, Arial 10 point). It then automatically expands up to a little over eleven numbers wide, should you type a large number, but it doesn't get nar-rower if you type smaller (in other words, shorter) numbers. Different auto width-adjustment rules apply for formulas, but let's ignore that for the moment.

In many cases you'll want to make column widths narrower so your spreadsheet will fit on a single printed page or on a screen, and that brings me to an important point.

WHAT'S SCIENTIFIC NOTATION?

It's shorthand for big numbers. Excel uses the letter E to represent *times ten to the following power.* So, for example, 4E+3 is four times ten to the third power—or 4,000. (Remedial lesson: 1 times 10 to the xth power is 1 followed by x zeroes.)

In this case, 5.55556E+11 is 5.55556 times ten to the eleventh power, or 5.55556 * 100000000000, or (roughly) 555556000000. Excel actually knows the number is 555555555555, but it saves your eyes by showing the number onscreen as 5.55556E+11.

TIP

NARROW TO PRINT

If you're only going to adjust column widths to fit a spreadsheet on a single printed page, consider modifying the print settings instead of changing the column widths.

As you saw in Chapter 19, "Working with Workbooks," you can turn the page horizontal (**Landscape**). You can also have Excel automatically shrink the page so it will fit, no matter what. Using print settings is far, far easier than laboriously slogging through spreadsheet columns. The built-in printer options usually create a better-looking spreadsheet, too.

With that bit of warning, here's how you can adjust the width of the columns in your spreadsheet.

 EXERCISE

Widening a Column

1. Let's adjust the width of Column C in the spreadsheet we just created.

2. Hover your mouse pointer over the vertical line that separates the C and D column headings. The pointer turns into a weird Janus-like thing that points both forward and backward at the same time.

3. Click the vertical line, and drag it to the right (see Figure 22.3).

FIGURE 22.3

Adjusting the column width by dragging.

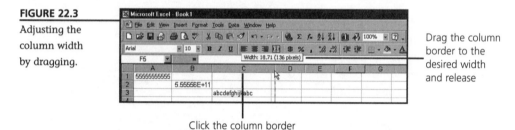

Drag the column border to the desired width and release

Click the column border

4. The Width number you see in the yellow ScreenTip is something of a fantasy. It's approximately how many numbers will fit in the column without overflowing. (Note that all numbers, in most fonts, are the same width.) It has very little use when you're trying to scope out the size of a cell containing proportionally spaced characters.

5. When you figure you're out beyond the z in cell C3, let go of the mouse button. Play with it a bit until you're happy with the width.

Sometimes you want a bunch of columns to all have the same width. Excel makes that easy, too.

 EXERCISE

Adjusting Multiple Column Widths

1. Continue with the spreadsheet we've been using.

2. Let's say you want to make columns D, E, and F wider—and you want them all to have the same width when you're done. It's actually quite simple.

3. Select the **D**, **E**, and **F** column headings by clicking and dragging across all three or by clicking **D**, holding down the **Shift** key, and clicking **F**.

4. Hover your mouse pointer over any of the vertical bars to the right of D, E, or F. When you get the two-headed arrow, click and drag the column to your desired width (see Figure 22.4). Note that the two-headed arrow does not appear in the figure, though you'll see it on screen.

FIGURE 22.4

Setting the width of three columns simultaneously.

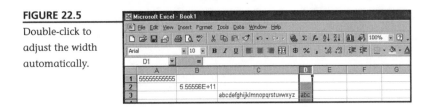

5. Even if columns D, E, and F all started out with different widths, they'll finish this operation all the same size.

There's one more column width trick you need to know—how to adjust a column's width, automatically, so it's just wide enough for the widest entry.

EXERCISE

AutoWidth

1. Continue with the spreadsheet we've been using.

2. Let's say we want to make column D just wide enough to cover the widest entry in the column. Hover your mouse pointer on the vertical bar to the right of the D column heading.

3. When you get the double-headed arrow, double-click. Excel makes column D very narrow, just wide enough to accommodate the one, short entry in cell D3 (see Figure 22.5).

FIGURE 22.5

Double-click to adjust the width automatically.

4. There's no need to save this spreadsheet. You won't be using it again.

If there's no data in a column, and you try to auto-adjust the width, Excel does nothing.

Row height works much the same way as column width: Click and drag the horizontal line beneath a row heading to adjust the row's height; select multiple rows to adjust all the heights at once; and double-click to auto-adjust. (One small difference for the row height auto-adjust: If there's no data in a row, Excel returns the row to standard height instead of leaving it untouched.)

CAN I MAKE A COLUMN AUTOWIDTH ALL THE TIME?

Nope. After you adjust a column's width—even if you use this double-click trick to make it just as wide as the widest entry—the column stays the same size until you change it again. There's no way to say, "Excel, just take care of the width for me" and have it adjust the column's width dynamically, as you enter new data.

AutoFormat

Although I love to deride Word's AutoFormatting capabilities, Excel does a very commendable job of putting a large number of formatting options together—particularly options appropriate to smaller tables—and making them available to you with just a few clicks.

EXERCISE

Format a Table

1. Open test.xls. We're going to put a pretty new face on the old Fruit Sales by Quarter spreadsheet.

2. Click once inside the main part of the spreadsheet. Excel is very good about snagging the whole spreadsheet, as long as you start inside of it.

3. Click **Format, AutoFormat**. You'll see the AutoFormat dialog box, as shown in Figure 22.6.

FIGURE 22.6

Excel's handy-dandy AutoFormat dialog box.

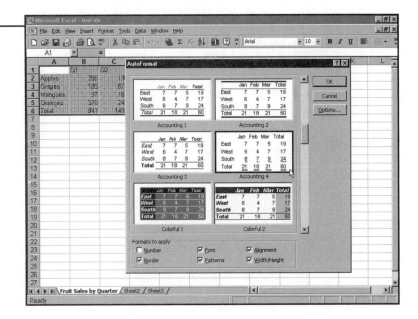

4. Scroll through the various samples. Note that you can modify Excel's built-in formats by the simple expedient of clearing the check box next to the type of formatting that you don't want. For example, the Accounting 4 format, which you can see in Figure 22.6, usually puts dollar signs in front of all the numbers. I didn't want the dollar signs, so I unchecked the Number box—and Excel refrained from formatting the numbers.

5. When you find a format you like, click **OK**. Figure 22.7 shows you how test.xls looks with the Accounting 4 format, but no Number formatting.

6. Go ahead and save test.xls. This one looks cooler than the previous version, doncha think?

TIP

WHAT YOU SEE VERSUS WHAT YOU GET

Some of the AutoFormat formats listed in the dialog box look great onscreen but don't print worth beans. In particular, I've found the background colors on the colorful versions wash out black-and-white printed text.

If you're going to print the spreadsheet some day, take a moment at this point and test print your AutoFormatted spreadsheet to make sure you'll be able to read the results.

FIGURE 22.7

Fruit Sales for-
matted with the
Accounting 2
AutoFormat.

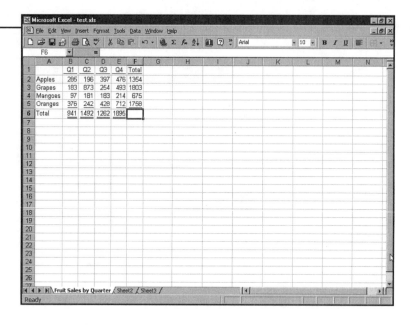

After you've AutoFormatted a table, chances are pretty good you'll go back in and change some of the data. When that happens, column widths may change, you might have additional rows or columns that come up—all sorts of things can (and will) change. Fortunately, it's easy to reapply AutoFormatting. Just click once inside the new table of data, click **Format**, **AutoFormat**, and apply the same formatting style you chose previously.

Formatting Cells

Where AutoFormatting does a good job with small tables, sometimes you just can't avoid formatting a spreadsheet manually. Excel includes a wide variety of tools designed exclusively to make the cells in your spreadsheets look better.

The general rule in Excel is the same as in Word: select first, and then apply the formatting. If you want to format a few characters

WHERE'S THE FORMATTING STORED?

Except for formatting applied to individual characters, all the formatting in Excel is stored in the cell. If you select a column and apply formatting to it, *every* cell in the column gets that particular formatting.

If you subsequently select a few cells in that column and apply different formatting, that new formatting supersedes the old.

If you want to clear formatting out of a cell—whether the cell has any data in it or not—click the cell, and then click **Edit**, **Clear**, **Formats**.

inside a cell, select the characters first. (Do this by double-clicking the cell to go into Edit mode.) If you want to format an entire cell, select the cell by clicking it, and then apply the formatting. If you want to format a whole column, click the column heading. To format a row, click the row. For multiple columns or rows, select all of them before formatting (use the **Ctrl** key to select rows or columns that aren't next to each other). To format an entire spreadsheet, click the rectangle to the left of the A column heading and above the 1 row heading.

Always, always select before applying the formatting.

Number

Excel lives and dies by numbers, and the wide variety of formatting options available for numbers only emphasize their central nature.

EXERCISE

Format Numbers

1. Start with a new, clean spreadsheet.

2. Type a column of numbers that could be dollar amounts. In Figure 22.8, I've typed 6, 7.5, and 8.25 in column B.

FIGURE 22.8

Column B is meant to be a series of dollar amounts.

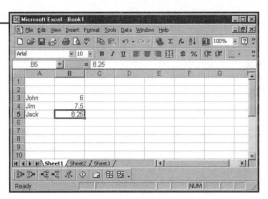

3. Let's have the numbers in column B appear as dollar amounts. Start by selecting the entire B column by clicking the **B column header**.

4. The easiest way to format numbers as dollar amounts is to select the appropriate cells, and then click the **Currency Style** ⑤ icon on the Formatting toolbar. When you do, the result is as in Figure 22.9.

FIGURE 22.9

Currency Style
formatting
applied to col-
umn B.

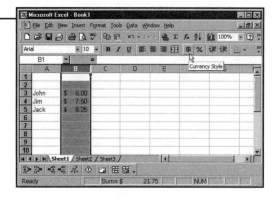

5. Keep this spreadsheet. We'll use it in the next exercise.

Similarly, you can click the **Percent Style** %️ icon to show numbers as percentages, with no decimal places.

TIP

WHY DON'T MY PERCENTAGEES COME OUT RIGHT?

Remember that percentages are fractions: If you type 1 in a cell and apply the **Percent
Style**, you'll get **100%**; type 0.5 and you get **50%**. If you have a hard time remembering
that percentages are fractions, get in the habit of typing a % percent sign after the number
you're entering. Typing 1%, for example, will always result in a value of **1%**, or **0.01**.

The **Comma Style** 📝 icon on the Formatting toolbar formats selected numbers so
commas appear to separate thousands, millions, and so on. The **Increase Decimal**
📝 and **Decrease Decimal** 📝 icons increase and decrease (respectively) the
number of decimal places shown.

Although the Formatting toolbar buttons come in handy, they can't hold a
candle to Excel's mother lode of umber formatting. To see that, choose the cells
you want to format; then click **Format**, **Cells**, and click the **Number** tab (see
Figure 22.10).

I think it's fair to say that if you can't find the right number formatting here, it just
doesn't exist. Well, almost.

FIGURE 22.10

Hundreds of number-formatting options are built in to Excel.

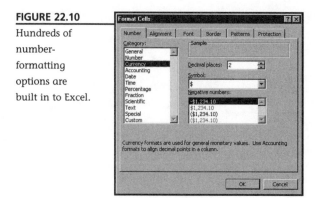

Aligning Data Within Cells

Excel includes some very fancy options for aligning data within cells.

EXERCISE

Center Text in a Column

1. Use the spreadsheet you had in the previous exercise.

2. Let's center the peoples' names in their cells. Click the **A column heading** to select the whole column.

3. Click the **Center** 🔲 icon on the Formatting toolbar. All the names in the A column will appear centered in their cells, as shown in Figure 22.11.

FIGURE 22.11

Center all the selected cells by clicking the **Center** icon.

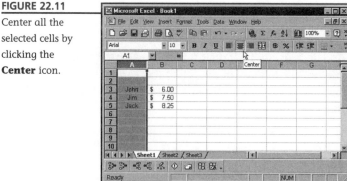

4. Play with the left, center, and right align buttons on the toolbar, and when you're done, click the **Align Left** icon to return the spreadsheet to its original state.

Excel has an alignment tool that works quite well. It's known as Increase/Decrease Indent. Back in the "dark ages" prior to Excel 97, indenting text was a real pain in the neck. Now it's one-click simple.

EXERCISE

Indent Cells

1. Use the spreadsheet from the preceding exercise.

2. Select **cells A4 and A5**. These are the cells we want to indent, so Jim and Jack appear slightly indented below John. Click the **Increase Indent** icon on the Formatting toolbar, as shown in Figure 22.12. Excel responds by indenting the text in the selected cells.

FIGURE 22.12

Click the **Increase Indent** button, and Excel indents the chosen cells.

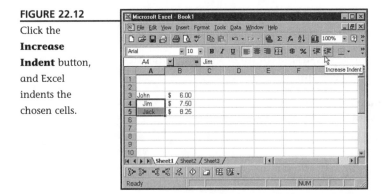

3. Try increasing and decreasing the indent a few times. You'll find that the text will never run out the left end of the cell, but it can be indented by almost any amount. When you're finished, click **Decrease Indent** until the cells are back to where they started.

Although the centering options you've seen so far are just fine for most cells in the body of a spreadsheet, Excel users frequently want more control over headings. These last two alignment options apply more to headings than to normal cells.

EXERCISE

Center a Heading over Multiple Rows

1. Continue working with the spreadsheet you've been using.

2. Say you want to center the heading **Hourly Wages** over the names and dollar amounts in your little table. None of the alignment options we've hit so far will do that—many people resort to typing spaces and jury-rigging things so they look right—sorta. If they only knew how simple this centering trick can be!

3. Start by typing `Hourly Wages` in cell A1. You want to center that heading in **cells A1** and **B1**, so select both A1 and B1, as shown in Figure 22.15, and then click the **Merge and Center** 🔳 icon on the Formatting toolbar.

FIGURE 22.13

Type the heading in the leftmost cell, and then select all the cells you would like to include in the centering.

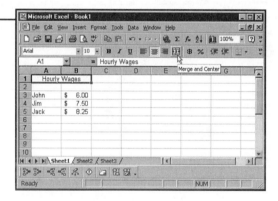

4. Excel obliges by merging together all the cells you've selected—in this case, **A1** and **B1**—and then centering the title text (from the first selected cell) in the newly merged cell.

5. Hold onto the spreadsheet.

There's one last ultra-cool alignment feature in Excel's bag o' tricks. It's very easy to rotate text within a cell.

EXERCISE

Rotate Text

1. Continue with the spreadsheet you've been using.

2. Say you want to put in a couple of column headings, one each over the names and the amounts. And let's say those column headings are either a bit too long to fit nicely into the allotted space, or perhaps that you want to call attention to them by making them different. Easily done.

3. Type Name in cell A2, and Hourly Amount in cell B2. Then select those two cells, as shown in Figure 22.14.

FIGURE 22.14

Lengthy column headings are in place, and the cells that need rotating are selected.

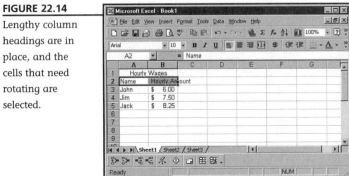

4. Click **Format**, **Cells**, and then the **Alignment** tab. We want to rotate the text in the selected cells by 45 degrees. So grab the **Text** line in the **Orientation** box and twist it until it lines up at the 45 degree mark, as shown in Figure 22.15.

FIGURE 22.15

Rotate all the text in the selected cells by 45 degrees.

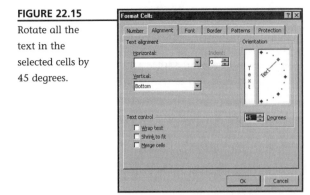

5. Click **OK** and Excel dutifully rotates the titles in row 2 by 45 degrees, as shown in Figure 22.16.

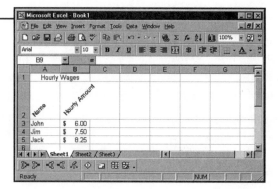

6. The text you see rotated onscreen might not look very good; typically the jaggies take over, and sometimes you can barely read the result. But if you're printing on a laser printer or a good ink jet, I bet you'll be impressed by the quality of the printing. Go ahead and print a test page, just to see how it comes out.

7. When you're done, keep the spreadsheet around.

The actions of all the Formatting toolbar shortcuts we've been using can be duplicated by choosing the appropriate combination of settings on the Alignment tab, as shown in Figure 22.15. If you're curious about the capabilities of a particular setting, click the **?** in the dialog box's upper-right corner, and then click the setting that puzzles you.

Changing Font Formatting

The font choices available to you are similar to those in Word, so I won't belabor the point here. Simply select the text you want to format; then choose the font name, point size, bold, italic, or underline from buttons on the Formatting toolbar. Or you can click **Format**, **Cells**, and then click the **Font** tab to get the choices shown in Figure 22.17.

FIGURE 22.17

FIGURE 22.17

Rather hum-drum font for-matting choices.

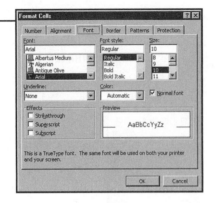

WHAT, NO MARQUEE?

Surprisingly, Excel doesn't have anywhere near the number of font formatting options available in Word. Aside from Word's Animation effects, which exude coolness with no redeeming social value, it's surprising that Excel gives you no fine control over subscripting or superscripting.

To change the default font, the one used in all spreadsheets, click **Tools**, **Options**, and click the **General** tab. On the Standard Font line, choose the font name and size. Click **OK**.

Your choice will take effect in all spreadsheets you create from that moment on.

Adding a Border

Every new Excel user wants to know the best way to draw lines under columns of numbers. Somehow, a total isn't a total unless there's a line above it, right?

The answer: Borders.

Draw a Total Line

1. Continue using the spreadsheet you've been working on.

2. Let's say you want to draw a double-line (all together now: "Oooooh! Aaaaaah!") under cell B5. Presumably you would then put the total of all the hourly wages in cell B6.

3. Start by clicking **cell B5**; then click the down arrow next to the **Borders** icon on the Formatting toolbar.

4. Choose the **double-underline** icon, which is the first icon in the second row of the Borders list. As you can see in Figure 22.18, Excel places a double-underline at the bottom of cell B5.

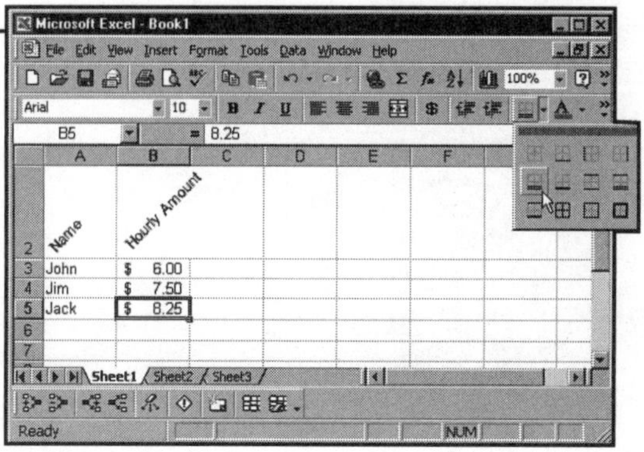

FIGURE 22.18

To draw a line under a cell, select the cell, and then go for the Borders icon. Choose the **double-underline** icon, and a double-underline appears on the selected cell.

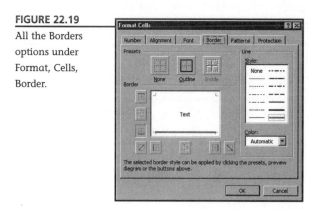

5. When you're done drawing lines, nuke the spreadsheet. You don't need it any more.

Excel has a large number of Border formatting options located on the Border tab of the Format Cells dialog box (see Figure 22.19). Although the choices are similar to those in Word, it's surprising that Excel doesn't support full-page borders or easy methods for constructing watermarks.

FIGURE 22.19

All the Borders options under Format, Cells, Border.

Adding Patterns

Excel lets you apply background colors and designs to cells. To see the variety of options Excel offers, select the cells you want to change, click **Format**, **Cells**, and choose the **Pattern** tab, as shown in Figure 22.20.

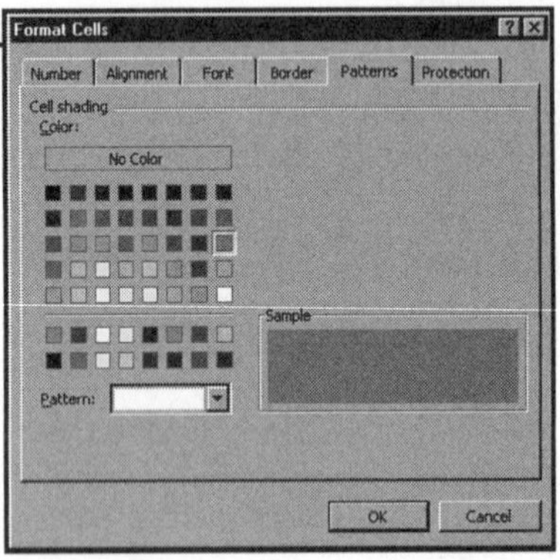

FIGURE 22.20

Patterns you can apply to the background of cells.

Insert Picture

One of the easiest ways to add some visual diversity to your ever-boring long rows of numbers is to add a picture.

Excel's capabilities are similar to Word's for all those kinds of pictures: The picture gets placed in a Drawing layer that floats over the top of the spreadsheet, and a full range of drawing tools are available.

☞ For details about the Drawing layer and Word's picture insertion capabilities, see **page 205** in Chapter 12, "Special Purpose Tools."

Excel also includes a great, if limited, organization chart drawing tool. To get at it, click **Insert**, **Picture**, **Organization Chart**. You'll see an entire Org Chart application in Figure 22.21.

"Microsoft Organization Chart," as it's called, was developed by Banner Blue Software, the makers of Org Plus for Windows—a much larger, but extra-cost, organization charting program. The Office Assistant isn't available inside the Org Chart application, but if you click **Help**, **Index**, you'll find a complete description of the program and its capabilities.

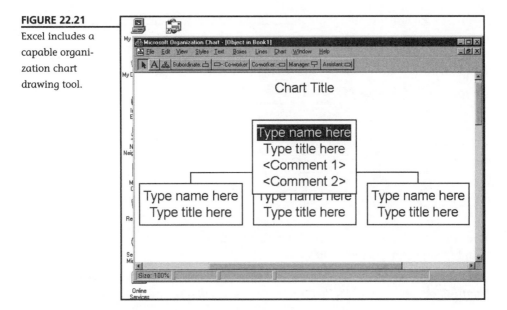

Hide Rows and Columns

Sometimes the best thing you can do to an ugly column is to hide it. That may sound a bit flippant, but frequently spreadsheets look better with less data in them, not more. Other times, you just don't want prying eyes to see where all the data came from.

Hiding a row or column couldn't be simpler. Just right-click the heading of the row or column you want to hide, and then choose **Hide**.

Unhiding rows and columns takes a trick. If you've hidden a row, select both the row above and the row below the hidden row; then click **Format**, **Row**, **Unhide**. If you've hidden a column, choose the column to the left and the column to the right, and click **Format**, **Column**, **Unhide**.

Spell Check

Before you print an important spreadsheet, or send it out for review, you'll always want to check the spelling. In Excel, that's easy: click **Tools**, **Spelling**.

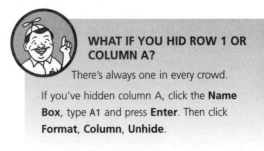

WHAT IF YOU HID ROW 1 OR COLUMN A?

There's always one in every crowd.

If you've hidden column A, click the **Name Box**, type A1 and press **Enter**. Then click **Format**, **Column**, **Unhide**.

Excel uses the batch spelling tool that's also available in Word. It consists of a single dialog box, which looks like Figure 22.22.

FIGURE 22.22

The Excel spell checking dialog box.

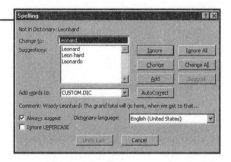

You can change, ignore, or retype a word. You can also add words that weren't found to your own personal dictionary.

 *You can edit your custom dictionary using the tools Word provides. Check out "Right-Click Spell Check" in Chapter 11, "Key Capabilities," **page 187** for details.*

Keep Titles Onscreen

Sometimes you want to keep column or row titles on the screen so that you can see what the columns or rows mean as you scroll through reams and reams of data. The means for doing so is quite simple, if you realize that Microsoft calls this capability Freeze Panes.

EXERCISE

Keep Column and Row Titles Onscreen

1. Let's go back to our old standby. Open test.xls.

2. Imagine that test.xls contains thousands of cells of breathtakingly interesting information. (That's a stretch, eh?) Further, imagine that both the first column and the first row of test.xls contain titles that you'd like to remain onscreen while you flip through that vast quantity of information. (This part's true!)

3. Click **cell B2**. Then click **Window**, **Freeze Panes**, as shown in Figure 22.23.

FIGURE 22.23

Freezing the
first row and
the first column
so they remain
onscreen.

4. Now try scrolling up, down, left, and right. See how column A and row 1 stay on the screen no matter what other rows or columns might appear? That's what Freeze Screen does. It lets you specify which rows and columns should stay put while the rest of your data scrolls on by.

5. To undo the Freeze, click **Window**, **Unfreeze Panes**.

There are many variations on this technique, as you might imagine. For help, bring up the Office Assistant and type `freeze panes`.

Print Titles

These last three "Look Good" topics only apply if you're printing your spreadsheet. The goodies you add here never (well, hardly ever) show up on the screen.

Print Titles is just like Freeze Screen, except it applies to printouts. The intent is precisely the same: show the contents of rows or columns on every page of the printout. That way you can set up your column titles in row 1, say, and have them print on every page.

EXERCISE

Print Column Titles on Every Page

1. Let's set up row 1 in test.xls to print on every page. Open test.xls, if it isn't already.

2. Click **File**, **Page Setup**, and click the **Sheet** tab (see Figure 22.24).

3. Back in the spreadsheet, select **row 1** by clicking the 1 row heading, as shown in Figure 22.25. Excel fills the correct value in the Rows to repeat at top box.

FIGURE 22.24

Tell Excel which rows or columns repeat on every printed page on the Sheet tab.

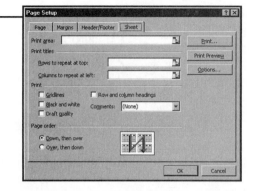

FIGURE 22.25

Go back to the spreadsheet and choose the row that's to be repeated.

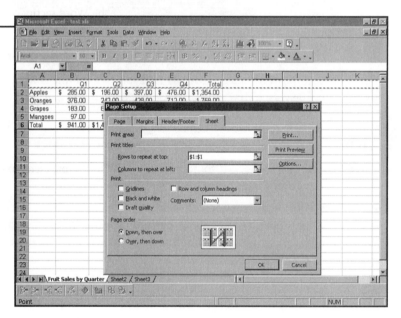

4. Click **OK** and the row (or column) you've selected will print on every page.

5. When you've had a chance to experiment with this, go back to the **File**, **Page Setup**, **Sheet tab** and delete this entry in the Rows to repeat at top box. Leave test.xls in good shape; you'll use it again in the next exercise.

Headers, Footers

Most of the time you'll want to print a header or footer on your spreadsheet pages. (Remember, a *header* is the text that appears at the top of each printed page; a *footer* appears at the bottom.)

This is yet another one of those situations where Word and Excel tackle precisely the same problem in completely different ways. So don't bother looking at the Word section on headers and footers; it won't help you a bit.

PRINT AREA

The row and column you choose to print on every page will print on the first page, too! So adjust the spreadsheet's Print Area, per Chapter 19, "Working with Workbooks," to exclude whatever row or column you have printing on every page.

EXERCISE

Headers and Footers

1. Start with test.xls. We're going to gussy it up so it will print with a header and footer.

2. Click **File**, **Page Setup**, and click the **Header/Footer** tab.

3. Click the down arrow to the right of the Header box (see Figure 22.26). One of the choices there is a good choice for the header—it says **Fruit Sales by Quarter**—so choose it.

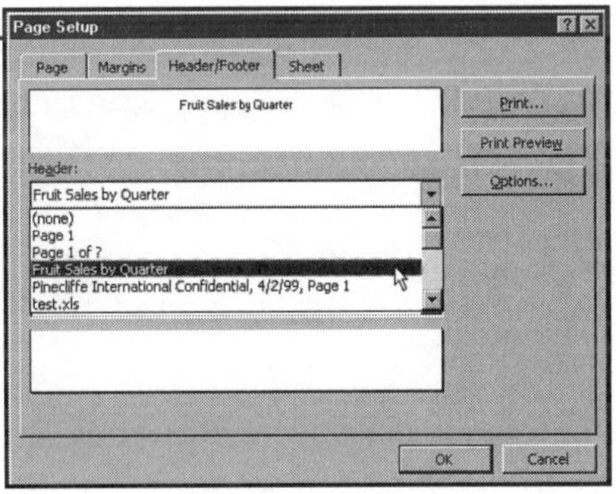

FIGURE 22.26

Choose a header from the drop-down list, if you find one you like.

4. To make a custom footer (the built-in choices are abysmal), click the button marked **Custom Footer**. The Footer dialog box you see in Figure 22.27 appears.

FIGURE 22.27

Excel's poor excuse for a custom footer helper.

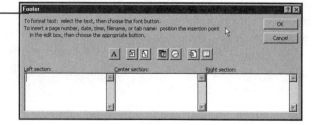

5. In this case, in the Left section I typed Printed at, clicked the fifth icon (which looks like a clock), typed on, and then clicked the fourth icon (the calendar). In the Right section I typed Page, clicked the second icon, typed of, and clicked the third icon (##). You can see the results in Figure 22.28.

6. You can see the results of the typing in Figure 22.29, which shows test.xls in Page Preview (click **File**, **Page Preview**).

7. Save test.xls. It keeps getting better and better, eh?

A HEAD LIKE A FOOT

Don't expect to get much out of this Footer dialog box. The buttons don't even have ScreenTips! Whatever you type in the **Left section** box is left justified at the bottom of each page. The stuff in **Center section** gets centered, and the text in **Right section** gets right justified.

To change the font, select the text you want to change, and then click the **A** icon. From left to right, the remainder of the icons insert the following into the footer: page number, total number of pages, date (short form, as in, 8/19/00), time (AM/PM format, as in, 4:35 PM), the name of the current workbook (for example, book1.xls), and the name of the current sheet (for instance, Sheet1).

FIGURE 22.28

A custom footer for test.xls.

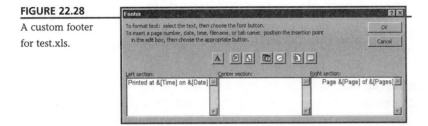

FIGURE 22.29

How the final page looks.

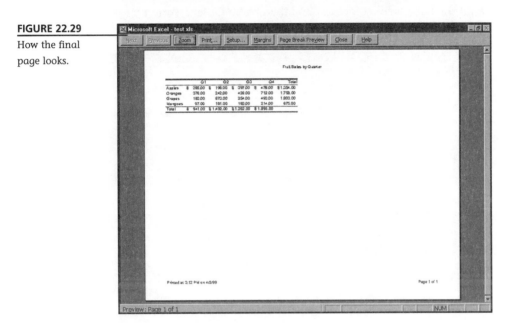

Page Break Preview

There's one last spreadsheet formatting trick that you need to know about, if you ever get to the point where you're printing big spreadsheets. It's called Page Break Preview, and it's the best thing since sliced bread. Unfortunately, the online documentation for Page Break Preview consists of two paragraphs, with no real instructions.

To go into Page Break Preview, click **View**, **Page Break Preview** (see Figure 22.30). That part's easy.

Page Break Preview lets you set page breaks manually by clicking and dragging a dark blue line that marks off where pages begin and end. You can always set a page break by clicking **Insert**, **Page Break**, but that method can be mighty tedious when you have to precisely paginate a 100-page report.

As you can see in Figure 22.30, Excel offers you a preview of how the pages will break, with a heavy dotted horizontal line signifying where the page will end. Changing the page breaks is as easy as dragging that horizontal line to where you want the page break to occur. Excel then reshuffles everything for you, quickly, and you can continue scanning for the next page break.

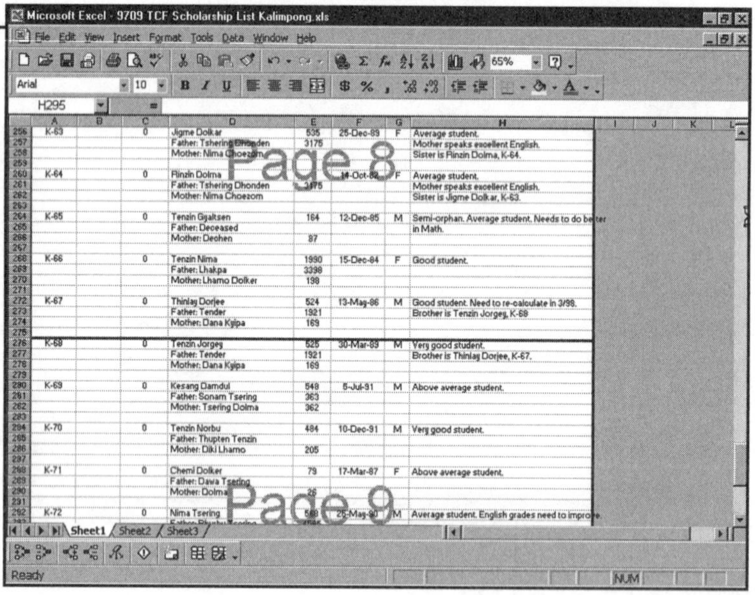

FIGURE 22.30

Page Break
Preview.

Sometimes when you set page breaks manually, the whole document seems to get screwed up, and you really want to start all over again. If you ever want to have Excel remove all your manual page breaks, right-click anywhere inside the spreadsheet, and choose **Reset All Page Breaks**, as shown in Figure 22.31.

HOW TO WORK PAGE BREAK PREVIEW

There's a trick. When working in Page Break Preview, you should always, always move the dotted line *up*! If you move a dotted line down, Excel gets all confused because you're telling it to print more data on a page than the page can hold.

Keep moving the dotted lines up and you'll have your report properly paginated in no time.

FIGURE 22.31

To reset all the manually inserted page breaks, right-click inside the spreadsheet.

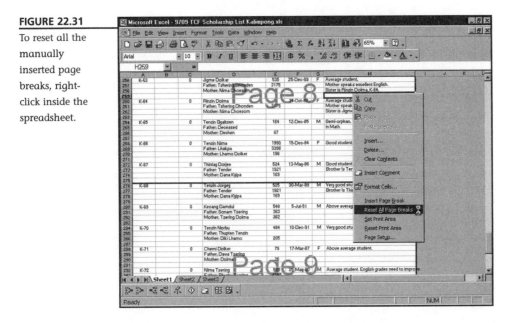

As far as I know, Reset All Page Breaks isn't mentioned anywhere in the documentation.

23

Woody Leonhard

TEACHES

EXCEL-LENT CHARTS

GET FANCY-SCHMANCY WITH EXCEL. Quite possibly the coolest part of Office, Excel's charting feature lets you convert all those boring numbers into whiz-bang pictures. And the most remarkable part? You need to understand only a few simple concepts, and click the right button. Excel does all the heavy lifting. It's amazing.

Making a New Chart

Before you start to create a new chart, you have to ask yourself one simple question: Do you want the chart to appear on the spreadsheet along with the data, or would you rather have it on a special kind of sheet, called a chart sheet, all by itself? If the chart goes on the sheet with the data, you can readily see the data at the same time that you see the graph. If the chart sits on a chart sheet, you won't have to look at that (yech!) dirty data or the gridlines that usually accompany the numbers.

The choice is up to you.

EXERCISE

The Chart Wizard

1. We're going to make a chart out of test.xls, so open it up.

2. First, you must select the data you want to chart. In almost all situations, that means you want to select the raw data, including row and column titles, but without totals. In Figure 23.1, I've selected the range **A1:E5**, which meets those criteria.

FIGURE 23.1

Select the basic data, plus row and column titles, but without totals.

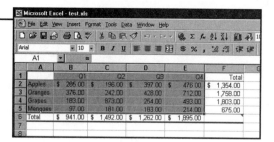

TIP

HOW MUCH IS TOO MUCH?

Although there are no hard and fast rules, you need to be careful that the data you select in the initial step is pretty well consolidated. In most kinds of charts, if you get too much data, the chart starts looking like an abstract painting of a pig pen.

3. When you have the data selected, click the **Chart Wizard** [icon] icon on the Standard toolbar. That awakens the Chart Wizard, one of the most sophisticated pieces of software in Office.

4. First, the Chart Wizard wants to know what kind of chart you want to create. Take your time, because there are hundreds of choices—and you can make up your own chart types on the Custom Types tab. In Figure 23.2, I wanted to check out the 3D Stacked Column chart, which is the Column chart shown in the second row and second column of the Chart sub-type box.

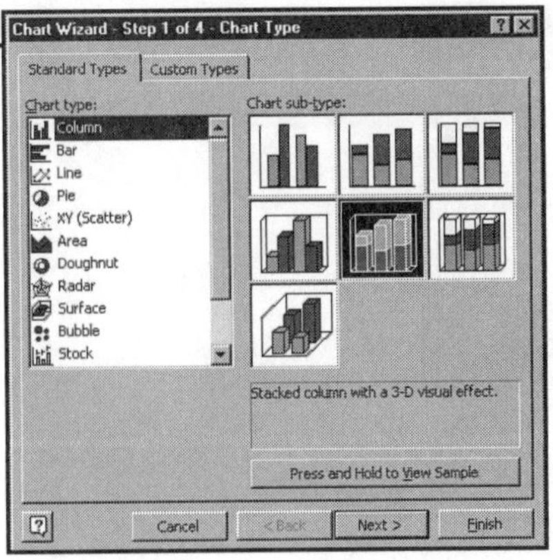

FIGURE 23.2

Choose a Chart sub-type of 3D stacked columns.

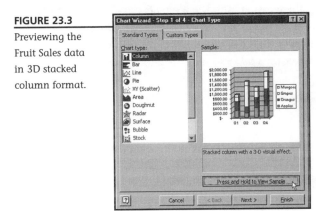

5. Any time you want to see how your data will look when poured into a particular type of chart, click the **Press and Hold to View Sample** button, as I have in Figure 23.3.

FIGURE 23.3

Previewing the Fruit Sales data in 3D stacked column format.

6. When you're satisfied that you have the right kind of chart, click the **Next** button. The Chart Wizard advances to the next step, where it verifies that you've selected the data you really want to show in the chart. In my case (see Figure 23.4), I was careful to select the data properly. But if you flubbed your choice, click the **Collapse Dialog Box** icon next to the Data Range box, and then go back to your spreadsheet and make the right selection.

7. When you have the correct data selected, click the **Next** button. The Chart Wizard now presents you with a fascinating array of options. I won't go through all the details (you'd be sitting here till next Tuesday), but I would like to show you some of the high points.

FIGURE 23.4

Verify that you
selected the cor-
rect data when
you started the
Chart Wizard.

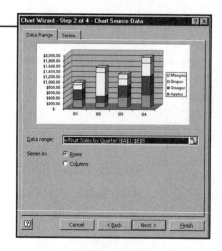

8. Under the **Titles** tab, the Chart Wizard lets you type titles for your x-, y-, and z-axes. (Remedial lesson: The x-axis runs horizontally across the bottom; the y-axis runs vertically up the left side, and the z-axis is a weird thing that's hard to visualize, but for most 3D graphs the z title goes in the same general place as the y title.) In Figure 23.5, I've given my chart a title of Fruit Sales by Quarter; I've identified the x-axis as 1998 and the z-axis as Metric Tons.

FIGURE 23.5

Assign titles to
the chart and
the axes on the
Titles tab.

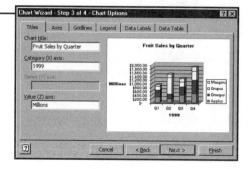

9. Skipping lightly over to the **Data Labels** tab, I wanted to point out that you can put labels—that is, actual values—at various points on the chart. I didn't want to put data labels on this chart because it looks cluttered. But if you want to show actual values to support the numbers on the gridlines, this is the place you set them up.

10. Behind the **Data Table** tab, you can actually have the Chart Wizard show a small table on the chart that lists all the data. To do so, check the **Show data table** box (see Figure 23.6). Again, to avoid clutter, I didn't end up putting Data labels on the Fruit Sales by Quarter chart, but this preview should give you a good idea of what could have been.

FIGURE 23.6

The Chart Wizard will put all the data on the chart, if you ask it.

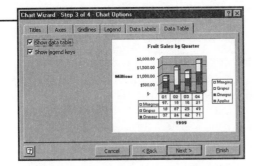

11. When you're done playing with the option tabs, click **Next**. The Chart Wizard asks you its last question: Where do you want to put the chart? In Figure 23.7, I've chosen to put the chart on a new sheet called, imaginatively, Chart1.

FIGURE 23.7

The final Chart Wizard question: Where to put it?

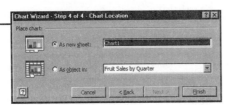

12. Click **Finish** and the Chart Wizard sets up the chart precisely the way you've described it.

The Chart Wizard dumps you out in your spreadsheet, or in your new chart sheet if you chose to put the chart on a new sheet. In Figure 23.8, my chart is almost done.

Note the Chart toolbar, which I've placed in the lower-right corner of Figure 23.8. You can change any part of a chart—including any or all the choices made in the Chart Wizard—by twiddling with settings on this toolbar.

FIGURE 23.8

First stab at the
Fruit Sales by
Quarter chart.

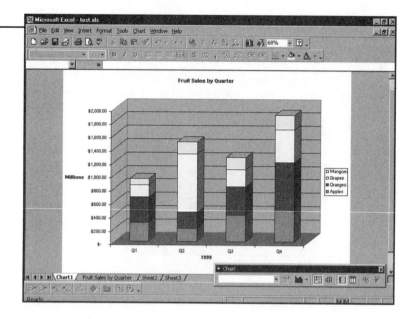

Editing an Existing Chart

Now that the basic chart's in place, it's time to tweak things a bit. I'll start by changing one of the titles on the chart.

EXERCISE

Change a Chart's Appearance

1. We'll continue working with the chart on sheet Chart1 in test.xls.

2. See the axis title over on the left, the one that says **Millions**? (It's actually a z-axis title, but that's only because I decided to use a 3D stacked bar chart; in any 2D chart it would be the y-axis title.) Let's rotate that title by 90 degrees.

3. Click the title you want to change. Then click the **Format Selected Object** icon on the Chart toolbar. Excel presents you with the Format Axis Title dialog box, as shown in Figure 23.9.

4. In this case, you want to change the alignment of the title, so click the **Alignment** tab (see Figure 23.10). Excel shows its alignment dialog box.

5. To rotate the text by 90 degrees, click the Text-graphic handle and rotate it upward. Click **OK** and note how the Millions title has been rotated.

6. Save test.xls. It only gets better and better, eh?

FIGURE 23.9

Select the part of the chart you want to change, and then use the Chart toolbar to change it.

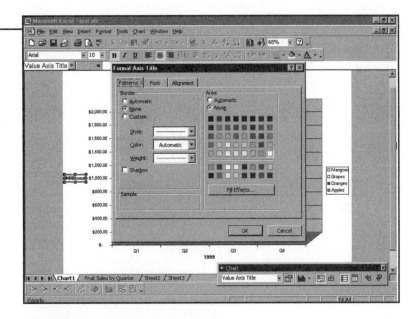

FIGURE 23.10

To align the title, click the **Alignment** tab.

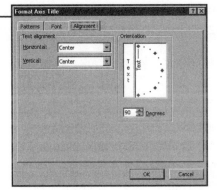

NOTE

CHART CENTRAL

The Chart toolbar holds the key to all your charting options. In general, it's easiest to modify part of a chart by first picking the object on the chart that you want to change. The name of that object will appear in the drop-down list at the left of the Chart toolbar. At that point, you can click the **Format Selected Object** [icon] icon and make changes.

By now you're no doubt asking yourself what happens when the underlying data changes. What do you need to do to redraw the chart?

There's a surprise answer: You don't need to do a thing. Excel goes in and updates the chart without your lifting a finger.

EXERCISE

Change Chart Data

1. Keep working with test.xls.

2. Let's see what happens when the underlying data—the data feeding a chart—changes. Click the **Fruit Sales by Category** tab, and change one of the data points. In Figure 23.11, I've changed cell C4—the value of grapes sold in the second quarter—to 0.

FIGURE 23.11

Change the chart's underlying data.

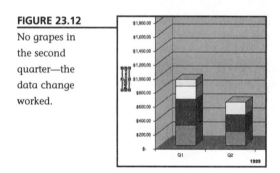

3. Now flip back to the chart by clicking the **Chart1** tab. Guess what? The bar for the second quarter (see Figure 23.12) shows that no grapes were sold!

FIGURE 23.12

No grapes in the second quarter—the data change worked.

4. Just to prove that this trick wasn't done with smoke and mirrors—fingers never leave the hands—click the **Fruit Sales by Quarter** tab again and change **cell C4** back to 873. Flip back to **Chart1** and let your mouse pointer hover over the Grapes portion of the bar for the second quarter. As you can see in Figure 23.13, the value of 873 has been restored.

5. Save test.xls. We'll use it again.

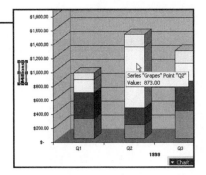

FIGURE 23.13

Restore the value of 2nd quarter grapes sales, and it appears back in the chart.

Deleting Charts

Charts can be moved, resized, or deleted, just like other pictures in the Excel drawing layer. Simply click once on the chart's border:

- To move the chart, click in the middle and drag it.

- To resize the chart, grab one of the resizing handles (the little squares) and push it around. To keep from squishing the chart, use the resizing handles in the corners.

- To delete the chart, press the **Del** or **Delete** key.

NURTURING NEW CHARTS

Many advanced Excel users place charts on their own sheets until the chart looks right, and then copy or cut the sheet onto the main spreadsheet. That's a particularly useful technique because, if you have the foresight to put your chart on a new chart sheet, you can delete the whole sheet by right-clicking the sheet's tab and clicking **Delete**. That's a clean way to get rid of your old, failed experiments.

You can move, resize, or delete elements of a chart similarly. Just click once on the element you want to mangle, and follow the usual procedure.

Entire charts can also be copied, cut, and pasted: Select the chart and use the **Cut**, **Copy**, and **Paste** items on the Edit menu, or the appropriate shortcut keys.

24

Woody Leonhard

TEACHES

ADVANCED FEATURES

IT SLICES. IT DICES. IT'S THE EXCEL-O-MATIC! Excel has more ways to slice and dice data than a county fair huckster. If you know, or can guess, the name of a particular data analytical tool, try typing it into the Office Assistant and see what comes up. Failing that, log on to Microsoft's support site, www.microsoft.com/support, and see whether you get any hits there.

In this final Excel chapter, I wanted to take a look at some of the more widely used, general-purpose advanced features, just to make sure you know they exist.

Working with Excel Scenarios

What if?

That's the question you always hear when working with spreadsheets. What if Jimmy sells 20 percent more widgets next month? What if the weather gets bad in Kenya and the price of coffee goes up 35 percent? What if long-term T-Bill yields drop by two basis points? What if my adjustable rate mortgage goes up half a point next year?

Excel does "What if" like Carter does liver pills. You can create all sorts of scenarios, and compare and contrast them—if you know the tricks.

EXERCISE

Create a Scenario

1. Start with our old standby, test.xls.

2. When you create different scenarios—different "what if?" situations—you have to figure out which numbers in which cells will change from scenario to scenario. Before you start the Scenario Manager, select those cells.

TIP

SELECTING DISCONTIGUOUS CELLS

The cells you select need not be contiguous—that is, they don't have to be next to each other. To select cells anywhere in a sheet, click the first cell, hold down the **Ctrl** key, click the next cell, keep the **Ctrl** key down, click the third, and so on.

3. In Figure 24.1, I've decided to create scenarios based on fourth quarter sales of all four fruits. Accordingly, I've selected **E2:E5**. Then I brought up the Scenario Manager dialog box by clicking **Tools**, **Scenarios**.

TIP

BACK TO THE STARTING POINT

I've found it much, much simpler to use the Scenario Manager if I first create a scenario that reflects the current state of the spreadsheet—in other words, a Baseline scenario. I strongly recommend that you do the same because switching to alternative scenarios and then going back to the Baseline is so easy.

4. To create a Baseline scenario, click the **Add** button. Excel presents you with the Add Scenario dialog box. In Figure 24.2, I've created a scenario called Baseline. With the name chosen and the changing cells specified, click **OK**.

FIGURE 24.1

Scenario
Manager starts
with fourth
quarter fruit
sales selected.

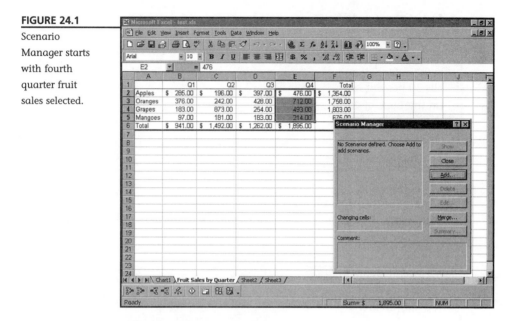

FIGURE 24.2

Adding the
Baseline
scenario.

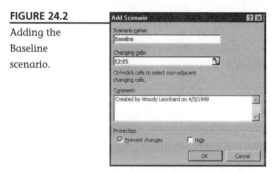

5. Next, you have to tell Excel what values this scenario will use for the chosen
cells. In the case of a Baseline scenario, as in Figure 24.3, you don't want to
change the values, so click **OK**.

FIGURE 24.3

Set values for
the changing
cells in the
Baseline
scenario.

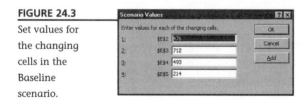

6. Excel hops back to the Scenario Manager (see Figure 24.4). This time, you
have the Baseline scenario firmly established, so you can switch to it
(by clicking the **Show** button) at any time.

FIGURE 24.4

Scenario
Manager now
contains a
Baseline
scenario.

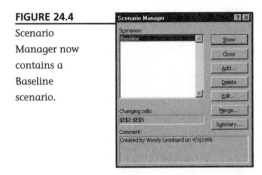

7. Click the **Add** button in the Scenario Manager to add your first scenario. In Figure 24.5, I've called this scenario Fourth Quarter Goes to the Dogs. With the scenario name and changing cells specified, click **OK**.

FIGURE 24.5

Creating a new
scenario, Fourth
Quarter Goes to
the Dogs.

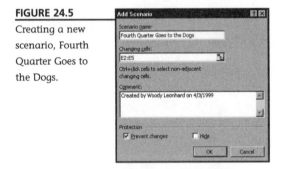

8. Tell Excel which values to use for this scenario. In Figure 24.6, I've typed numbers that are half of the Baseline numbers. When you're done, click **OK**.

FIGURE 24.6

The Fourth
Quarter Goes to
the Dogs sce-
nario posits
sales in the
fourth quarter
that run half
the baseline.

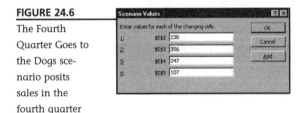

9. The Scenario Manager now contains two scenarios: Baseline, and Fourth Quarter Goes to the Dogs (see Figure 24.7). To see how the two scenarios stack up against each other, click the **Summary** button.

FIGURE 24.7

Two scenarios
are now
available.

10. In the Scenario Summary dialog box, you have to tell Excel what kind of report you want and which cells interest you—that is, which ones you're looking at in the various scenarios. In Figure 24.8, I've chosen a summary report (we'll get to PivotTables by the end of this chapter), and I've specified that I want to look at total sales for the fourth quarter, which is cell E6.

FIGURE 24.8

Choose the kind
of report you
like, and point
Excel to the cells
that interest you
in the various
scenarios.

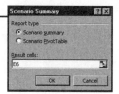

11. Click **OK** and Excel presents you with a Scenario Summary, created on a new spreadsheet with a tab of that name. In the simple example we've been using, see Figure 24.9, the Scenario Summary says that the Fourth Quarter Goes to the Dogs scenario drops total fourth quarter sales by about half. (Not surprising, eh?)

12. Scenarios can do much more than summarize. You can trace through all the details of each scenario by clicking **Tools**, **Scenarios**, choosing the scenario you like, and clicking **Show**. In Figure 24.10, I've chosen the **Fourth Quarter Goes to the Dogs** scenario, and then popped over to the **Chart1** tab to see the sales chart.

FIGURE 24.9

Excel's Scenario
Summary lists
the scenarios,
their dependent
cells, and the
results.

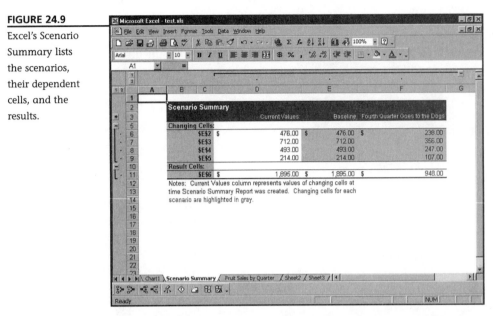

FIGURE 24.10

The Fruit Sales
by Quarter
chart, using the
Fourth Quarter
Goes to the
Dogs scenario.

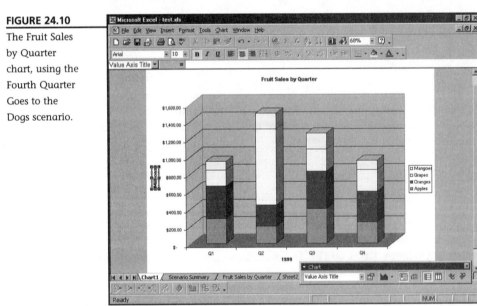

13. Explore a bit and create as many scenarios as you like. When you're finished, return to the Baseline scenario by clicking **Tools**, **Scenarios**, choosing **Baseline**, and clicking **Show**. Save test.xls.

Audit Techniques

After a spreadsheet gets to a certain size—certainly, by the time it's more than a page long—the chances for errors grow enormously. I like to think of errors as falling into three categories:

- Errors where somebody put a bad number into the spreadsheet. For example, if the unit price for an item is negative, you can pretty much bet somebody made a mistake.

- Errors where the spreadsheet doesn't calculate correctly because it wasn't made right. The most common example I've seen of this kind of error is where a Sum() function doesn't cover the first or last cells in a series.

- Errors generated by flaws in Excel. These are quite rare, compared to the other two, but some bugs did crop up in Excel 97, and you can bet your sweet recalculating bippy more will raise their ugly heads in Excel 2000. The best way to stay ahead of these bugs is by following Woody's Office Watch, as I discussed in Chapter 2, "Precursors to Using Office."

Although no sizable spreadsheet is certain to be error-free, you can greatly increase your chances of creating a good spreadsheet by using some of the tools Excel provides.

You already have the number one bug-killing weapon available—that's the Auditing toolbar, which you've used numerous times in this book to trace precedents and nail down formulas. In this section, I'd like to talk about two more features that can save your tail: data validation and conditional formatting.

Data Validation

Sometimes it's easy to tell when data is good and when it's bad. For example, if you type a person's name in a cell that's supposed to contain a date, you probably screwed up. Excel has a very easy-to-use feature called *data validation* that can help you keep data entry errors to a minimum.

> **FOR MORE INFO...**
>
> I don't have anywhere near enough room in this book to introduce you to all of Excel's auditing tools. If you get to the point where you are creating and maintaining sizable, important spreadsheets (say, where your money is involved!), I'd strongly recommend that you pick up a copy of *Special Edition Using Microsoft Office 2000*, by Ed Bott and Woody Leonhard (Que, ISBN 0-7897-1842-1) and devour the Auditing discussion.

EXERCISE

Validate a Date

1. Start with a new, clean spreadsheet.

2. I've created a simple expense report spreadsheet that uses column A for the date, B for the amount, and C for a description (see Figure 24.11). Let's set up the spreadsheet so it checks the date entries to make sure they're valid. Start by selecting **column A** (by clicking the A heading), and then click **Data**, **Validation**. Excel responds with the Data Validation dialog box.

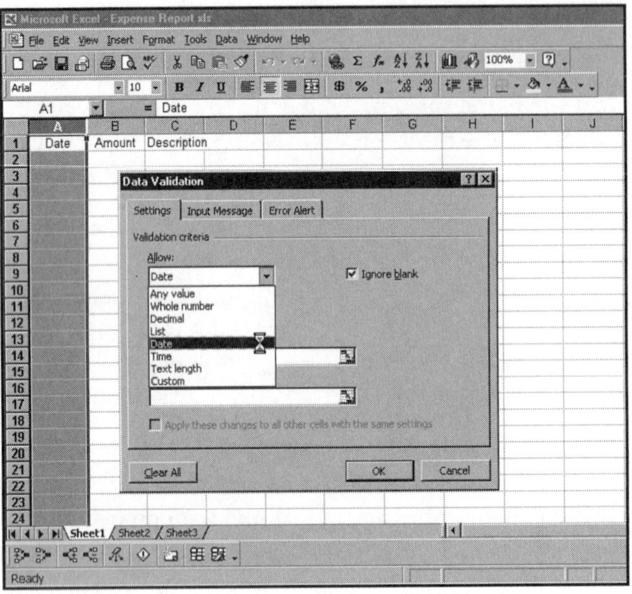

FIGURE 24.11

Setting up data
validation for
column A.

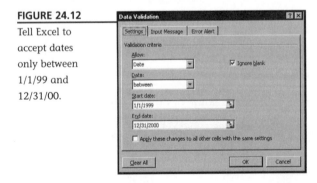

3. In the Allow box, you can choose from several different kinds of valid data. In our case, we want to check for dates, so the **Allow** box gets set to **Date**. More than that, as you can see in Figure 24.12, we want to ensure the dates fall between January 1, 1999 and December 31, 2000. When the criteria look good, click the **Input Message** tab.

FIGURE 24.12

Tell Excel to
accept dates
only between
1/1/99 and
12/31/00.

4. Excel lets you write a custom ScreenTip, which will appear whenever the user clicks a cell in column A, even before they type the data. In this case (see Figure 24.13), I've constructed a friendly message with details about the kind of data I want to see in column A.

FIGURE 24.13

Create a message for the column A ScreenTip.

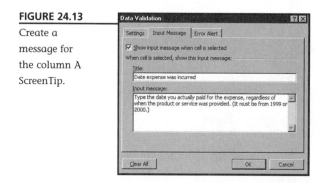

5. What happens if the user types invalid data? That's what you get to decide on the **Error Alert** tab. In Figure 24.14, I've set up a rather terse message to prompt the user (even if the user is me!) to enter only valid dates. Click **OK** and the data validation restrictions go into effect for column A.

FIGURE 24.14

Use the **Error Alert** tab to compose a message for those who dare to enter invalid data.

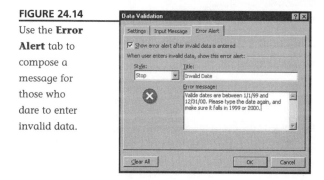

6. To see how the data validation routines work, click a cell in column A. In Figure 24.15, I've clicked **A3**. The ScreenTip I wrote in Figure 24.13 shows up with a yellow background.

7. If I try to type an invalid date, number, name or otherwise—anything other than a date between 1/1/99 and 12/31/00—Excel pops up the dialog box I created in Figure 24.14. In Figure 24.16, I tried to get away with 12/31/98. It didn't work.

FIGURE 24.15

The ScreenTip appears whenever the user clicks a cell in column A.

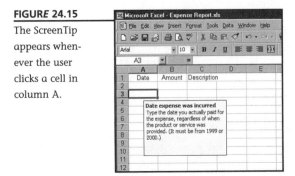

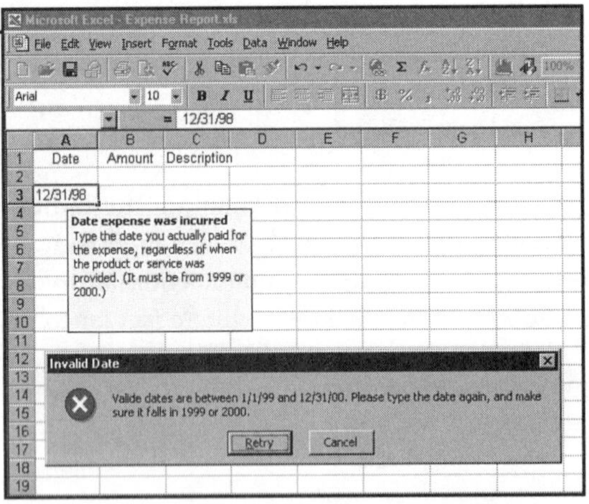

FIGURE 24.16

Type an invalid entry and Excel won't let you put it in the spreadsheet.

8. The two buttons in the Invalid Date dialog box don't give you much choice: Click **Retry** and Excel puts you in the cell, with the original entry highlighted so you can edit it; click **Cancel** and Excel wipes out the cell entirely. Either way, you can't get past the data validation routine until the number satisfies the validation criteria.

9. Hold onto this spreadsheet. You'll use it in the next exercise.

That's how you can use Excel to keep bad data from getting posted in the first place. Now let's take a look at how Excel can help you highlight iffy entries.

Conditional Formatting

We spent a lot of time in Chapter 22, "Making Spreadsheets Look Good," discussing formatting: You can make text in cells big, bold, italic, red, even draw boxes around the cells, or change their background colors.

Now imagine being able to do much of that based strictly on the value of what's in a particular cell. That's the concept behind conditional formatting—and the reason why conditional formatting can be such a powerful auditing tool. It can draw your attention to values that just don't look right and make it much simpler to catch data errors with a glance.

EXERCISE

Highlight Big Expenses

1. Use the spreadsheet you just finished in the previous exercise.

2. Management has declared that no single expense line item may exceed $250. (Do you have management like that? I sure did, back in the days when I worked in the real world. Dilbert's got nothin' on this ol' boy.) By Management Dictate, we're going to set up this expenses spreadsheet so any amount—that is, any value in column B—over $250 appears in red, bold.

3. Start by selecting **column B**. (Real quick, go over and click the **Currency Style** $ icon, so numbers in this column appear in dollars-and-cents form.) Then click **Format**, **Conditional Formatting**. Excel responds as shown in Figure 24.17, with the Conditional Formatting dialog box.

FIGURE 24.17

Select the cells that you want to have conditional formatting, and then click **Format**, **Conditional Formatting**.

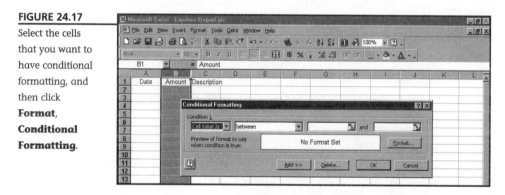

4. We want to make entries over $250 stand out, so click the down arrow next to the middle box and choose **greater than**.

5. In the third box, type 250 (see Figure 24.18).

FIGURE 24.18

Set your selection criteria.

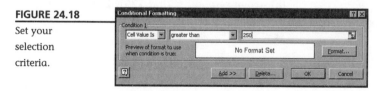

6. Now choose the way you want to format all entries greater than 250 by clicking the **Format** button. Excel gives you the Format Cells dialog box, as shown in Figure 24.19.

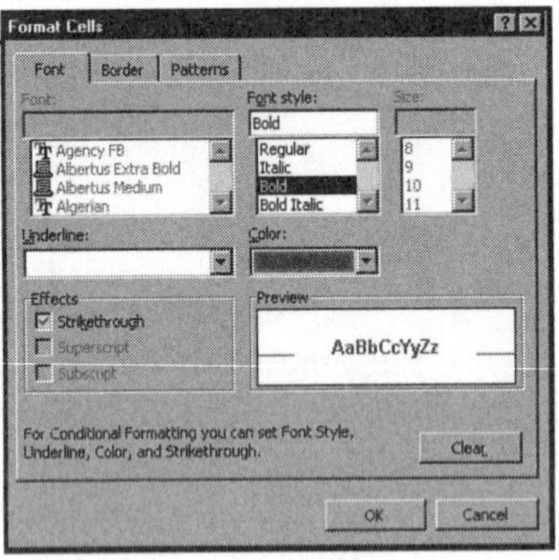

FIGURE 24.19

Choose formatting for cells that match the selection criteria.

7. Note that you cannot change the font, size, or super/subscript for a conditional flag. (This is a limitation imposed by Excel, probably to simplify row height formatting; if Excel let you change fonts or sizes, it would have to dynamically change row heights, and that would pose a significant programming problem.)

8. In Figure 24.19, I told Excel to format numbers greater than 250 as bold and red. You can also specify borders (to draw a box around the cell) or patterns (that is, a background shading or color) for values that match the criteria. With the formatting set, click **OK**. Excel gives you a preview of the formatting chosen in the Conditional Formatting dialog box (see Figure 24.20).

FIGURE 24.20

Formatting for cells that meet the criteria now appears in the lower box.

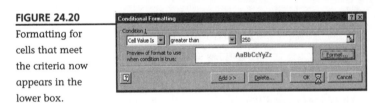

9. Click **OK** one more time and the conditional formatting criteria are set. Test it out by typing a number greater than 250 in column B. In Figure 24.21, I've had the audacity to file an expense report with a $251 dinner at Chez Chez. Excel has responded by turning cell B3 red and bold.

FIGURE 24.21

Any amount greater than $250 in column B now gets the treatment.

10. Try other criteria, in other cells. You needn't select an entire column or row, for example—you can choose just one or a few cells for special treatment. You can also specify different treatment for different values (for example, red if the number's too big, blue if it's too small) by clicking the **Add** button in Figure 24.20.

11. When you're finished, nuke this spreadsheet. We won't need it anymore.

I hope this excursion into creative auditing has given you a few ideas you can use in your spreadsheets, even if you're the only user.

IF in a Crossfoot

Bet you've been wondering when we were going to put that grand total in test.xls.

It's time.

One of the most common problems in spreadsheet land—no, make that *the* most common problem in spreadsheet land—is validating crossfoot totals.

It happens all the time. You have a rectangle of numbers, with totals to the right and totals at the bottom, just as you have in test.xls. The grand total better be equal to the sum of the totals on the right. It also better be equal to the sum of totals at the bottom. If it isn't, something is out of whack.

There's an easy way to make crossfoot totals self-validating. And you now have all the tools at your disposal to do the job properly.

WHY IS "AMOUNT" RED AND BOLD, TOO?

If you follow along with this exercise—or squint real hard at the screen shot in Figure 24.21—you'll see that the word "Amount" in cell B1 is red and bold, too. Why? Excel considers text to be greater than 250. Thus, it gets conditionally formatted. That's what they call artificial intelligence.

To get rid of the eyesore, just click on **cell B1**, uncheck the **Bold** button on the Formatting toolbar, and change the color back to normal.

I just hate it when computers think they're smarter than I am. Don't you?

EXERCISE

A Robust Grand Total

1. Open up test.xls.

2. Click **cell F6**, the place where the grand total should go.

3. You want to compare SUM(F2:F5) with SUM(B6:E6)—the totals on the right and the totals on the bottom—to make sure they're equal. The way to do that is with Excel's IF function. So bring up the IF function by clicking the **Paste Function** f_x icon on the Standard toolbar. You'll see the Paste Function dialog box, as shown in Figure 24.22.

FIGURE 24.22

Start validating crossfoot totals by bringing up the Paste Function.

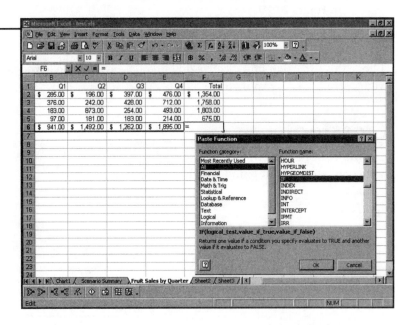

4. On the left, under Function category, choose **All**. Then on the right, choose IF. Click **OK** and Excel presents the **IF** formula construction kit shown in Figure 24.23.

NOTE

"TUNNELING" OUT OF THE DIALOG BOX

Figure 24.23 has three **Hide Dialog Box** buttons, at the right end of each input box. If you need to refer back to the spreadsheet itself to retrieve data, click one of those buttons. The big dialog box shrinks down to a single line. Choose the data you need (perhaps by pointing at cells) and when you're done, click the **Show Dialog Box** button to get the dialog box back.

FIGURE 24.23

Excel's built-in
support for the
IF function.

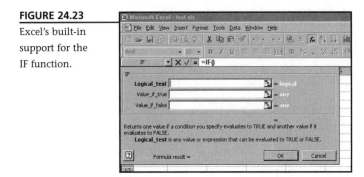

5. We need to retrieve some cell locations from the spreadsheet itself, so click
the **Hide Dialog Box** button to the right of the box marked **Logical_test**.
The entire IF formula construction kit turns into a single line, shown in
Figure 24.24, which floats above the column headings.

FIGURE 24.24

Click the **Hide
Dialog Box**
button and the
IF construction
kit backs off to
let you retrieve
data from the
spreadsheet.

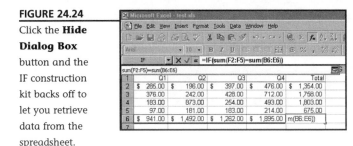

6. We want to see whether the sum of the right side totals equals the sum of the
bottom totals, so start by typing SUM and a left parenthesis, then click the
range **F2:F5**. Type)=SUM(and click the range **B6:E6**. Finally type a right
parenthesis. You're building the formula shown in the Formula bar—
IF(sum(F2:F5)=sum(B6:E6)—so you can use that for guidance.

7. When the IF formula is complete, click the **Show Dialog Box** button,
which appears in Figure 24.24 immediately to the left of the G column heading. The IF construction kit reappears, this time with the Logical_test box
filled out.

8. We want a formula that says something like, "If SUM(F2:F5) is equal to
SUM(B6:E6), the crossfoots match, so put SUM(F2:F5) in the grand total cell;
If they aren't equal, though, something is wrong, so put **ERROR! Totals
don't match.** in the cell." I've filled out the entries necessary to do precisely
that (see Figure 24.25).

FIGURE 24.25

The key test
for matching
crossfoot totals.

9. Before you click **OK** to get out of the IF construction kit, select the text **ERROR! Totals don't match.** and press **Ctrl+C** to copy it to the Clipboard. We'll use it in the next exercise.

10. When you click **OK**, the Fruit Sales by Quarter spreadsheet finally, finally has a grand total, sitting in cell F6, as you can see in Figure 24.26. Congratulations! You've come a long way, baby.

FIGURE 24.26

The Fruit Sales
spreadsheet gets
a grand total.

	Q1	Q2	Q3	Q4	Total		
Apples	$ 285.00	$ 196.00	$ 397.00	$ 476.00	$ 1,354.00		
Oranges	376.00	242.00	428.00	712.00	1,758.00		
Grapes	183.00	873.00	254.00	493.00	1,803.00		
Mangoes	97.00	181.00	183.00	214.00	675.00		
Total	$ 941.00	$ 1,492.00	$ 1,262.00	$ 1,895.00	$ 5,590.00		

11. Don't close test.xls just yet. There's one final embellishment you might want to add, and we'll talk about it in the next Exercise.

Whenever I use an IF() formula to verify crossfooting in a spreadsheet, I like to toss in one little enhancement—I want to make that **ERROR! Totals don't match.** warning stand out. With conditional formatting, it's easy.

WHAT IF SOMETHING GOES WRONG?

If you get that **ERROR! Totals don't match.** message, there's no reason to panic. One of your crossfoot totals isn't right—either the formula for calculating the total got screwed up, or somebody (not *you*, of course) typed a number over the top of one of the subtotal formulas.

The simplest way to find where the error occurred is to break out the **Trace Precedents** function on the Auditing toolbar. You'll have the spreadsheet back together in no time.

EXERCISE

Emphasize Botched Crossfoot Totals

1. You should still be working on test.xls, from the previous exercise.

2. Click **cell F6**, the grand total cell.

3. Click **Format**, **Conditional Formatting**. In the Conditional Formatting dialog box (see Figure 24.27), set things up so the criterion matches when the cell is equal to **ERROR! Totals don't match.**, the text you used in the IF construction kit in the previous exercise.

FIGURE 24.27

Setting up the criteria for conditional formatting of the grand total.

 TIP

HOW TO GET A MATCH

If you paste the text in that third input box precisely as it appeared in the IF construction kit, you'll be sure you get a match when you want it. That's why I had you copy the text at the end of the previous exercise. Sneaky, eh?

4. Click the **Format** button and choose whatever formatting you feel is appropriate. In Figure 24.27, I chose bold red, which stands out pretty well. Click **OK** and your conditional formatting rules take effect.

5. To test the conditional formatting, go back into the spreadsheet and change one of the crossfoot totals. In Figure 24.28, I've changed B6 to 1. Press **Enter** and the message should appear—in bold red or whatever other formatting you might have chosen.

FIGURE 24.28

Trigger an error by overwriting one of the cross-foot totals.

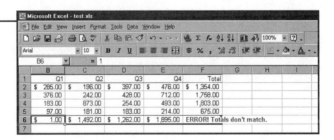

6. Click the **Undo** icon to fix the messed up cell B6. Then save test.xls. It's one robust spreadsheet now. Perhaps fittingly, we won't use it again. Such is the price of perfection...

That's the technique I use for putting grand totals in spreadsheets. It's relatively easy and fast, once you get the hang of it. And it double-checks and triple-checks all the subtotals, automatically, with very little fuss on your part.

I hope that's given you a good feel for the steps you can take to make sure your spreadsheets are solid, and that they'll continue to work for years and years. A little bit of precaution in the Excel world can save you lots and lots of frustration. In fact, it might save you lots and lots of money. Don't skimp on the audits.

Working with Conditional Sums

As we finish with Excel, I want to take you through two key features that can help you analyze data in ways you might not imagine possible. Both of these features, Conditional Summing and PivotTables, work on a specific kind of spreadsheet, one where some of the same data gets repeated. Rather than flapping my gums and beating my arms trying to describe what that kind of spreadsheet looks like, let me show you an example.

EXERCISE

Total Sales by Salesperson

1. Start with a new, clean spreadsheet.

TIP

A LIST

The kind of spreadsheet that best lends itself to conditional summing is called a *list*. There's no formal definition of a list (at least, not as far as I'm concerned), but it has several characteristics. Typically, a list contains a lot of raw data, usually without totals or subtotals. The text entries generally repeat a lot: You see the same text over and over again. The numbers, though, can be just about anything.

WHERE'S THE CONDITIONAL SUM WIZARD?

If you performed a standard install of Office 2000, you didn't get the Conditional Sum Wizard. There's an easy way to tell if it's available on your machine: click **Tools**, **Wizard**. If there's no wizard entry on your **Tools** menu, or if there's no Conditional Sum entry under **Wizard**, you don't have the Conditional Sum Wizard installed.

To retrieve it, you'll need your original installation CD. Click **Tools**, **Add-Ins**, and then check the box marked **Conditional Sum Wizard**. Excel will ask you to insert the CD and complete the installation.

2. I've concocted a rather typical (if short) list in Figure 24.29. It's supposed to show sales by product by salesperson, for four quarters. You can make up a list of your own liking, or just copy the one here.

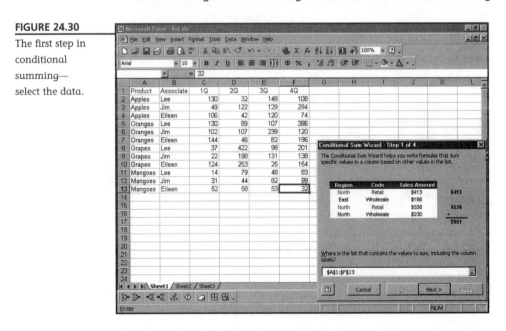

3. Excel implements conditional sums via something called the Conditional Sum Wizard. The Conditional Sum Wizard lets you specify what kinds of data you want to add, and then calculates sums based on those specifications. Click one of the cells in the list, and then click **Tools**, **Wizards**, **Conditional Sum**. You'll get the first dialog box in the wizard, as shown in Figure 24.30.

FIGURE 24.30

The first step in
conditional
summing—
select the data.

4. Excel does a very good job of guessing which data you want to use in the conditional sum. In Figure 24.30, it chose A1:F13, which happens to be the entire list. When you have the data chosen, click **Next**.

5. In the wizard's step 2, you have to set the criteria for summing, and choose the column you want to sum. In Figure 24.31, I've told the wizard that I want to sum all the first quarter sales numbers for the salesperson named Lee.

FIGURE 24.31

Choose the column you want summed and establish the selection criteria.

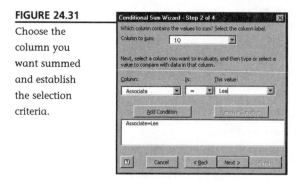

6. The wizard does much more than add all the first quarter sales numbers for Lee. In fact, it creates a formula (a very convoluted formula!) that calculates the total first quarter sales for Lee. That's a very important distinction because it means you can paste the formula into your spreadsheet and, even if the data changes, the formula will continue to give the correct answers. In Figure 24.32, I've specified that I want the formula to be placed in the spreadsheet.

FIGURE 24.32

Tell Excel you want only the formula.

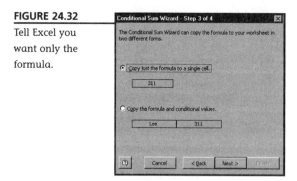

7. Finally, you have to tell the wizard where you want it to put the formula—in this case, the formula that calculates total first quarter sales for Lee. In Figure 24.33, I've told it to put the formula in cell C15.

8. I went back and used the Conditional Sum Wizard to calculate second, third, and fourth quarter totals for Lee and similar totals for Jim and Eileen. It took a few minutes, but not much more than that. Then, just to double-check all the totals, I added the crossfooting and grand total fields that I spoke about in the previous section, making good use of the **AutoSum** Σ icon to generate totals, and Excel's Fill Handles to copy formulas. You can see the result in Figure 24.34.

9. Go ahead and save this spreadsheet. Call it, oh, list.xls. We'll use it in the next exercise.

Using PivotTables and PivotCharts

Here's the one Excel feature everyone talks about and, for the life of me, I don't understand why people think it's complicated. I think it's fair to say that PivotTables rate as the premiere data analysis tool, certainly in Excel and possibly for most business situations, period. If you have a bunch of data and you're trying to understand it, PivotTables let you look at the numbers in many different ways. You provide the insight; Excel provides the spectacles.

What's a PivotTable? Sounds mysterious, but it isn't. Usually when you think of spreadsheets, you think in two dimensions: quarterly sales by product, as we've just seen, or inventory levels by location. There's a series of "things" going across the top of the spreadsheet, and a different series of "things" going down the side. That's fine and dandy; most people think in two dimensions—when they're dealing with data anyway—and spreadsheets are ideally suited to that kind of analysis.

HOW HARD ARE PIVOTTABLES, REALLY?

If you know enough to construct a very basic spreadsheet—say, one on a par with the version of list.xls shown in Figure 24.29—you know enough to use PivotTables. Yes, it may take an hour or two to get the hang of it. But if you follow along here—even if you skipped all the rest of this book—you should be able to construct, analyze, and understand PivotTables in an afternoon—maybe less.

Unfortunately, real data is rarely two-dimensional. Reality strays from the spreadsheet ideal in two very different ways.

First, you might want to change the things going across the top or down the side—looking at different things might give you some insight into what the numbers are saying. For example, while you're looking at quarterly sales by product, it may suddenly strike you that what you really should be looking at is quarterly sales by salesperson. So instead of wondering why, oh, oranges sold so well in the third quarter, you might flip the data around and suddenly realize that the important point is that Lee's total sales in the third quarter went through the roof.

Second, you might want to flip into three dimensions. So instead of looking at quarterly sales by product, you may decide that the nugget of information you seek will best show up if you concentrate on, oh, how well each salesperson sold a specific product in a given quarter, and then step through the information quarter by quarter. Thus, you might discover that most of your salespeople sold a lot of oranges in the third quarter, but that Jim just didn't keep pace. That's how things go with real data. You can take a static two-dimensional view with predefined buckets and hope that the meaty information jumps up and punches you in the face. Or you can go digging for information and insight by varying the things you examine and jumping from two to three dimensions and back again.

PivotTables, uh, excel at allowing you to quickly and easily change things in a two-dimensional view. PivotTables also make it easy to arrange data three-dimensionally, with the third-dimensional slices appearing on separate spreadsheets.

That's why PivotTables are so powerful. They put you in the driver's seat so you don't have to sit back and passively take the data in predefined two-dimensional ways. Instead, you can dig into the data with both hands and, with a bit of luck, come up with an elusive bit of insight.

PivotTables work best with lists. As explained in the previous section, lists are just spreadsheets with lots of raw data, repeating text entries, and numbers by the gazillion.

EXERCISE

From List to Pivot

1. Start with an usable list containing data similar to that shown in Figure 24.29. The first row should include titles for all the columns, and there shouldn't be any blank rows. If you saved list.xls in the previous exercise, open it and delete all the totals. When you feel comfortable with the list, click a cell inside of it, and then click **Data**, **PivotTable and PivotChart Report**. The first step of the PivotTable Wizard kicks in (see Figure 24.35).

FIGURE 24.35

The PivotTable Wizard can work off almost any kind of data, if need be, but it eats spreadsheets for breakfast.

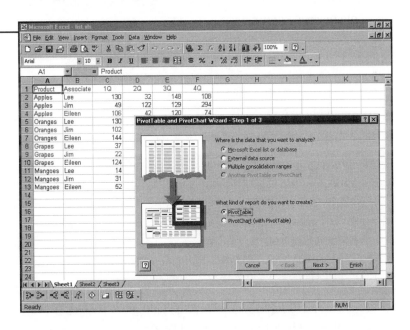

2. We're going to use the list that you can see in Figure 24.35, so make sure **Microsoft Excel list or database** and **PivotTable** are checked, and then choose **Next**.

3. In step 2, the wizard wants to verify that it has your data selected properly (see Figure 24.36). If you have a good list—particularly one without any completely blank rows—it will. Make any changes necessary, and then click **Next** again.

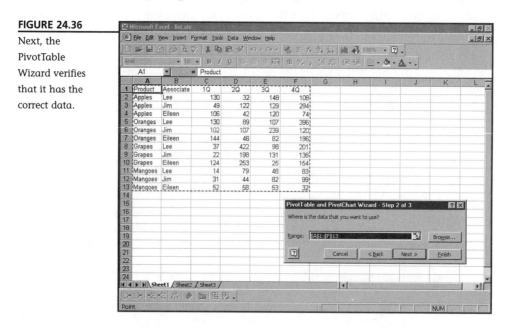

4. The final step in the PivotTable Wizard, Figure 24.37, asks whether you want to put the PivotTable in a new worksheet. I always do because it's easy to delete an entire sheet if I really screw up. Click **Finish**, and Excel constructs your PivotTable.

FIGURE 24.37

Have Excel put the PivotTable in a new work-sheet, and click **Finish**.

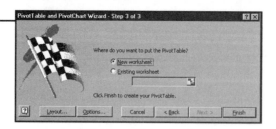

5. Now set up your first PivotTable by dragging the field buttons (which contain the names that the PivotTable Wizard scarfed up from the first row of your list) into one of four locations: Page, Row, Column, or Data. This screen (see Figure 24.38) looks intimidating, but it isn't as bad as you think—and no matter how you start, you'll end up changing things when you pivot your PivotTable.

FIGURE 24.38

Set up the initial pivot of the PivotTable by dragging and dropping field buttons.

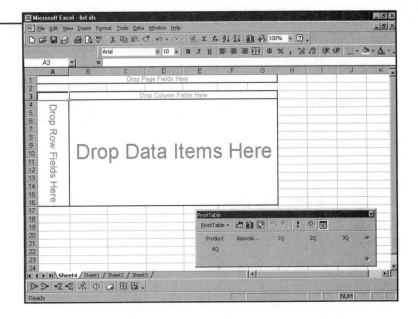

6. In Figure 24.39, I've dragged the **Products** onto **Row**, the **Associates** onto **Column**, and all four data categories—**1Q, 2Q, 3Q**, and **4Q**—onto **Data**.

7. Your first glance at a PivotTable is bound to be a little overwhelming, so let's take the one in Figure 24.39 slowly and see what kind of conclusions you can draw.

8. Looking at the information in Figure 24.39, you can tell at a glance that apple sales in the fourth quarter beat the second quarter by a wide margin (which won't surprise any apple growers out there), and that a lot of that swing is due to Jim's salesmanship in the fourth quarter. Grapes go way up in the second quarter, thanks largely to Lee's efforts. Mangoes go way down in the first quarter, but Eileen somehow manages to keep her numbers up even then. And Eileen does a good job of selling oranges in the fourth quarter, but Lee does better. Pretty neat, huh?

WHICH FIELD GOES WHERE?

In general, the columns in your spreadsheet come in two different flavors: the text columns, where you have many repeating entries, and the data columns, which usually (but not always) contain numbers.

As a first approximation, I like to drag one of the text columns to **Row** and all the rest to **Column**. Then I'll drag all the data columns to **Data**. That doesn't always work real well—and it ignores **Page** entirely—but it's usually a good starting point.

FIGURE 24.39

A first attempt
at arranging
the components
of the
PivotTable.

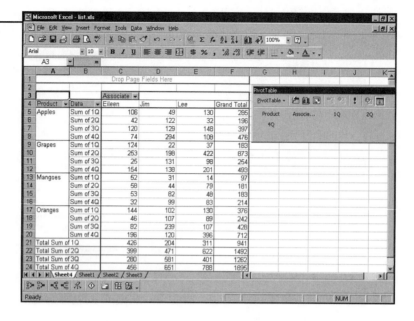

9. Now let me explain what a pivot does by flipping this table over. The numbers you see on the screen won't change, but you should start to get an idea of what we're dealing with in a PivotTable.

10. Click **cell A4**, where it says **Product**, and drag that cell over to the right of cell C3, the one that says **Associate**. Then drag the C3 cell, which says **Associate**, and drop it to the left of cell A5. You should have a PivotTable that looks a lot like Figure 24.40.

> *TIP*
>
> **SCRUNCHING**
>
> Sometimes it's hard to drop these category headings precisely where they belong. In those cases, try clicking the **PivotTable Wizard** 🔢 icon on the **PivotTable** toolbar.

11. What you've just done is a pivot. Admittedly, it isn't terribly interesting because the data is the same in both Figure 24.39 and Figure 24.40, as you can readily verify by looking at the numbers while cocking your head at a 90-degree angle. But now you're in a position to understand what happens next.

12. Pivot the table back to where it stood in Figure 24.39. You might be able to do that by clicking and dragging. If that gets to be too much of a, uh, drag, use the **PivotTable Wizard** 🔢 icon on the PivotTable toolbar and drag **Products** to **Row**, and **Associates** to **Column**.

FIGURE 24.40

Swapping the Associate and Product categories.

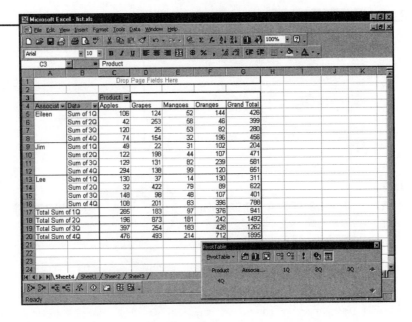

13. Now let's collapse all the **Product** entries. The easiest way to do that is to click **Product**, in cell A4 (Figure 24.39), and drag it to the box that says **Drop Page Fields Here**. Alternatively, you can click the **PivotTable Wizard** icon and drag **Product** to the box marked **Page**. The result, collapsing all the salesperson information, should look like Figure 24.41.

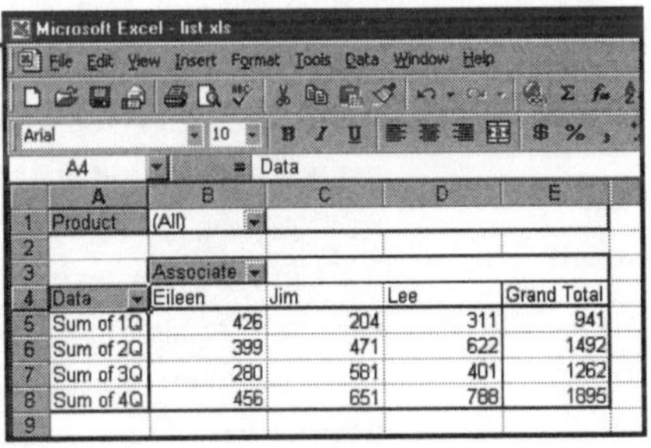

FIGURE 24.41

Collapsing the PivotTable on Product by moving Product to the "Page" block.

14. Play with this a bit. No. Play with this a lot. Try collapsing by Associate, moving **Product** in cell A1 to the right of **Associate** (cell B3), and then dragging **Associate** to cell A1. The result should look like Figure 24.42.

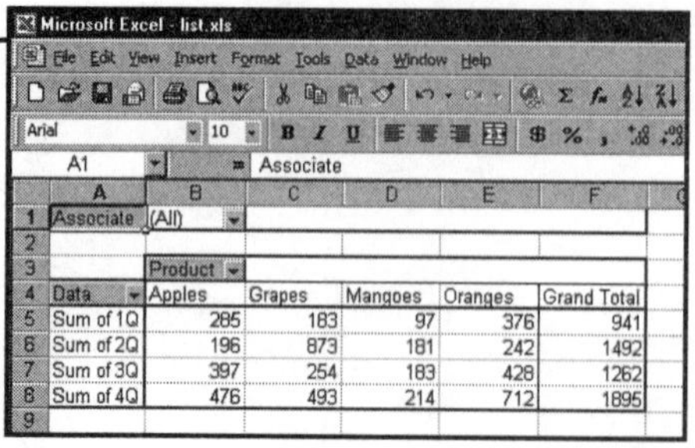

FIGURE 24.42

Collapsing the
PivotTable by
Associate.

	A	B	C	D	E	F	G
1	Associate	(All)					
2							
3		Product					
4	Data	Apples	Grapes	Mangoes	Oranges	Grand Total	
5	Sum of 1Q	285	183	97	376	941	
6	Sum of 2Q	196	873	181	242	1492	
7	Sum of 3Q	397	254	183	428	1262	
8	Sum of 4Q	476	493	214	712	1895	
9							

NOTE

YES, VIRGINIA, IT IS A SPREADSHEET

These PivotTables look really cool, but you
need to keep in mind that they are *real*
spreadsheets, too! If you want to run a
quick total, click a cell, and then click the
AutoSum icon. Insert a picture. Create a
chart. Do anything you can do with any
other spreadsheet. Knock yourself out!

15. I guarantee this gets posi-
    tively addictive, especially if
    you have a stack of real-
    world data that's been bug-
    ging you with unseen and
    unanalyzed relationships.
    You can look at the data in
    so many different ways, so
    easily, that you'll wonder
    how you ever lived without
    PivotTables.

Wait a minute! Wait a minute!

Take another glance at those
PivotTables. Don't the numbers look
familiar?

Compare Figure 24.41 with, oh,
Figure 24.26. Compare Figure 24.42
with Figure 24.31. Is that little light
going off in your noggin'?

WHAT ABOUT PIVOTCHARTS?

Excel 2000 introduced a new, sophisticated, and remarkably easy to use charting capability called the PivotChart. A
PivotChart is nothing more (or less) than a
chart based on a PivotTable. Once you've created a PivotTable, making a chart to go along
with it is as easy as clicking inside the
PivotTable, then the **Chart Wizard** icon.

The Wizard steps you through myriad choices,
paralleling those we discussed in Chapter 23.
Once you're done, the chart you generate will
be a full-fledged PivotChart, and you'll be able
to drag and drop fields along the axes and
three-dimensional "page" slices with ease.

The concepts behind pivoting a chart are nearly
identical to those behind pivoting the underlying PivotTable itself, except you drop the data
fields into the main part of the chart. So if you
want to learn how to use PivotCharts, I urge
you to play with PivotTables for a while, and
get accustomed to the way dragging and dropping data fields works. When you're comfortable with the basics, go ahead and click the
Chart Wizard icon, choose the default
stacked column format, and work from there.

If Excel can come up with PivotTables that generate all these reports from the raw data, why would you want to digest the data in the first place? Why not feed everything into PivotTables, and let Excel do all the hard work?

Why, indeed.

VI

Woody Leonhard

TEACHES

OFFICE 2000

POWERPOINT

25

Woody Leonhard

TEACHES

POWERPOINT PRELIMINARIES

THERE'S A METHOD TO MY MADNESS. There's a reason why PowerPoint takes up less room in this book than the other Office applications. To put it bluntly, there isn't as much to PowerPoint as the other applications. Most PowerPoint users never venture beyond the AutoContent Wizard, and the ones who do frequently expect PowerPoint's concepts and terminology to be similar to Word and Excel's.

Guess what? They aren't.

Experienced Office Users Take Note

In fact, experienced Word, Outlook, and Excel users are going to find the hardest part of PowerPoint lies in just finding things. PowerPoint presents an unfamiliar terrain to Office adepts, and you'll be battling that problem from the minute you start the program and find that you have to make a choice (see Figure 25.1), up front, before PowerPoint will even run!

FIGURE 25.1

PowerPoint's in-
your-face open-
ing screen.

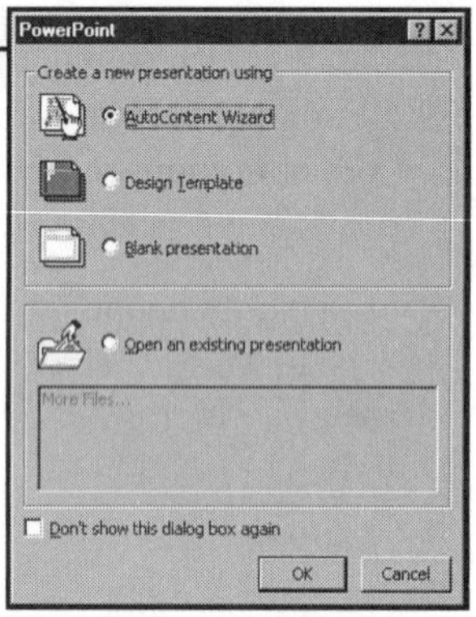

So I'm going to approach the next few chapters as if you knew a bit about the other Office apps—fonts, centering, inserting pictures, and the like—but need to come up to speed on PowerPoint quickly.

Don't worry. You'll survive.

A Note on Terminology

PowerPoint creates presentations. You knew that.

Presentations consist of slides, but these have nothing to do with the slides you put in a slide projector. Each PowerPoint slide is really a computer screen. When I talk about a PowerPoint slideshow, I'm really talking about a series of computer screens, one after another, that together make up your presentation.

Although it's possible to have PowerPoint slides reproduced on 35mm slide film or overhead projection transparencies—indeed, there are companies that specialize in doing precisely that—you'll only be able to take advantage of the vast majority of PowerPoint's powerful capabilities if you deliver your presentation straight from a computer.

So when I say slide, I really mean one screen in the presentation. Got that?

Crucial Changes

PowerPoint's initial settings are an odd mixture of overly protective handholding with one resource-conserving but dangerous default. Very schizophrenic. Let me show you what I mean.

EXERCISE

Set PowerPoint Options

1. Start PowerPoint. You'll get the in-your-face screen shown in Figure 25.1. Click **Cancel**. You can get rid of that obnoxious screen, but if you do, PowerPoint replaces it with an even more obnoxious screen, demanding that you choose an AutoLayout. So I guess we'll have to learn to live with it.

2. Like Word and Excel, PowerPoint has those flighty adaptive—er, "personalized" —menus and toolbars, and they should be given the heave-ho. To do so, click **Tools**, **Customize**, and click on the **Options** tab. Uncheck the boxes marked **Standard and Formatting toolbars share one row**, and **Menus show recently used commands first**. Click **Close**.

3. Click **Tools**, **Options**, and click the **General** tab. Run the **Recently used file list** up to nine entries, the maximum (see Figure 25.2). You might also consider checking the **Provide feedback with sound to screen elements** box, if you appreciate squeaks and squawks to confirm that your work is actually being recognized by PowerPoint.

4. Here's one of those resource-conserving, penny-wise but pound-foolish settings I mentioned. Click the **Edit** tab, and roll the **Maximum number of undos** box up to 100, as shown in Figure 25.3. I have no idea why Microsoft sets this initially at 20; the performance hit seems minimal on any reasonably powerful PC.

> ### YET ANOTHER FILE LOCATION BOX
>
> This is our fourth Office 2000 application—and, if you were watching closely, Figure 25.4 shows yet a fourth, *different* method for specifying the default file location. Word, Outlook, Excel, and PowerPoint all have very different methods for choosing the default file location. It's enough to make you tear your hair out.
>
> Ya know what Microsoft really needs to do for Office 2002 or 2003 or whatever they call it? They need to go back and standardize all the features that are common to the Office applications. Yes, some people will fuss because they've been doing things in their own set way since before Office existed. But why do you and I have to figure out four different ways to set the default file location, change the default font, run a find or replace, or pick a keyboard shortcut for inserting em dashes? It's crazy.

FIGURE 25.2

Roll the
Recently used
file list up to
nine, as you did
with all the
other Office
programs.

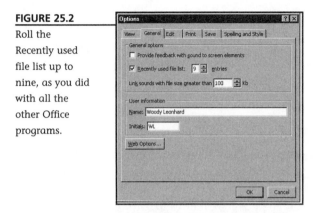

FIGURE 25.3

Give yourself
lots of Undo
breathing
space—cheap
insurance.

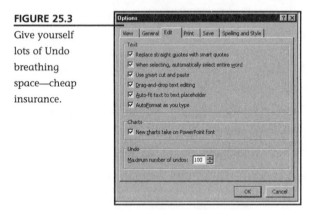

5. Finally, click the **Save** tab. Fast saves are always a bad idea; they don't add that much to performance, they make file sizes swell and, worst of all, they can corrupt files. Drive a stake through Fast save's heart by unchecking the **Allow fast saves** box (see Figure 25.4). While you're here, consider changing the AutoRecover (known as AutoSave in Excel) interval. If you don't often save your files manually, you might want to run this setting down to 5 minutes or less.

6. That sets your Options straight. Click **OK** and that splash screen will never darken your door again.

With those changes in effect, you're ready to start building a presentation with PowerPoint.

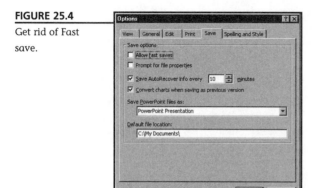

FIGURE 25.4

Get rid of Fast save.

The Screen

PowerPoint 2000 represents a huge improvement over its predecessors, primarily because of its new default screen—the so-called Normal view. (Microsoft also decided to replace the old Common Tasks toolbar with a **Common Tasks** button on the Formatting toolbar. That's a huge help, too.)

Most of your work in PowerPoint will take place in Normal view. In fact, PowerPoint has six different views, each of which provides a different insight into a given presentation.

Let me show you the different views and what they contain. Let's start by creating a very simple presentation.

Create a Generic Presentation

1. If PowerPoint is running, click **File**, **New**. We're looking for the AutoContent Wizard, which should be the second item on the **General** tab (see Figure 25.5). Click the **AutoContent Wizard** and click **OK**.

2. If PowerPoint is not running, start it, make sure the **AutoContent Wizard** button is pressed, and click **OK**.

3. The AutoContent Wizard kicks in. Just click **Finish**. You'll end up with a presentation that PowerPoint simply calls Generic. That's a good description.

4. Let's save this presentation; we'll work with it. Click **File**, **Save**, type Generic Presentation, and click **Save** (see Figure 25.6).

FIGURE 25.5
The
AutoContent
Wizard, first
among
equals.

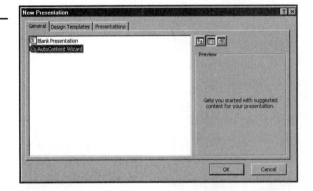

FIGURE 25.6
Saving the
Generic
Presentation.

The AutoContent Wizard leaves you in Normal view. That's as good a place to start as any.

Normal View

Normal view (see Figure 25.7) combines a panel on the left that contains the presentation outline, a big panel on the right that previews the current slide, and a tiny panel on the lower right that holds the notes. For most detailed work with a presentation, this is the easiest view to work in.

THE MORE THINGS CHANGE

Dyed-in-the-wool Word users will probably note immediately the similarity between PowerPoint's Normal view and Word's Page Layout view with the Document Map enabled. Although it was probably entirely unintentional (since when do the design teams for two different Office applications talk to each other? *Heh heh heh*), the parallel is hard to miss. Word users accustomed to navigating through documents with DocMap will pick up on PowerPoint's Normal view in no time, and vice versa.

I wonder how long Excel users will have to suffer before they, too, get a Document Map in the left pane?

Working from the top in Figure 25.7, we have the title bar, menu bar, and then the Standard and Formatting toolbars. Except for the Slide Show menu item and a few icons on the ends of the Standard toolbar and Formatting toolbar, you've seen all this before in the other Office applications.

Similarly, the horizontal and vertical scrollbars and status bar behave much like their counterparts in Word and Excel. The **Previous** and **Next** slide buttons move forward and backward one slide at a time.

The left pane of the screen shows an outline of your presentation. Each line at the highest level of the outline marks the beginning of a new slide. If you think about it a bit, you'll understand why the Slide Number changes with each highest-level entry, and why the text at each highest level is called the Slide Title. The Slide Text—which is to say, all the text under a given Slide Title—appears as a bullet in the outline.

FIGURE 25.7

The first slide of the Generic Presentation, in Normal view.

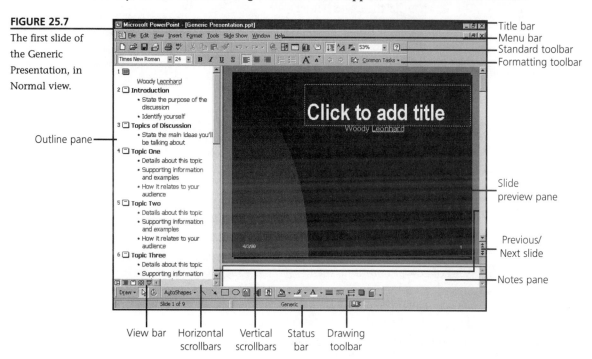

☞ I talk about the Drawing layer extensively in the section called (mirabile dictu) "Drawing Layer," Chapter 8, on **page 112**. You might want to look there if the term Drawing layer doesn't immediately trigger moans and make you break out in a cold sweat.

On the right is the slide itself, try clicking the text. Although the slide might appear to be a solid piece of work, in fact it contains two areas—called *placeholders*—where you can easily click and type your own data. One placeholder has the text **Click to add title**; the other has my name. Clicking and typing into a slide directly is a great way to make sure that what you see is what you get in the presentation.

The View bar in the lower left lets you select among the different views we're discussing here. Clicking the **Normal View** button puts you into Normal view (subject of the current discussion); the **Outline View** button hops into Outline view; similarly, **Slide View**, **Slide Sorter View**, and the **Slide Show** itself get you to those views. There is no button on the View bar for Notes Page view: to get there, you have to click on **View**, **Notes Page**.

A lot of PowerPoint users spend most of their time developing content in Normal view. Almost everything you need to do to a presentation is easy to access here.

TEXT IN THE OUTLINE PANE

All the text you type into the Outline pane (or in Outline view, for that matter) appears on the appropriate slide. However, it's possible to put text on a slide and *not* have the text appear in Outline view.

Yeah, it's confusing, but the problem stems from the infamous Drawing layer—the same Drawing layer we had to deal with in Word and Excel.

If you put text in a slide's Drawing layer— typically by using Text Box from the Drawing toolbar, or the **Insert**, **Text Box** menu item—that text floats above the slide itself and, even though it appears when the slide is shown, the text isn't really stuck inside the slide. Because it isn't really inside the slide, text in the Drawing layer won't appear in Outline view.

If you think that's confusing, you should read the official (and unofficial) documentation on the subject. I swear, if you didn't know what the Drawing layer was, you'd *never* understand what the references were talking about.

Anyway, the only text that appears in the Outline pane (or in Outline view), as far as I can tell, is text that sits inside the predefined areas for the slide's title and body text. Everything else floats above, in the Drawing layer never-never world.

Outline View

Switch over to Outline view by clicking on the **Outline View** button in the View bar. As soon as you do, right-click in the blank area of any toolbar and check the box marked **Outlining**. That brings up the Outlining toolbar, shown on the left in Figure 25.8.

FIGURE 25.8

Outline view with the Outlining toolbar on the left.

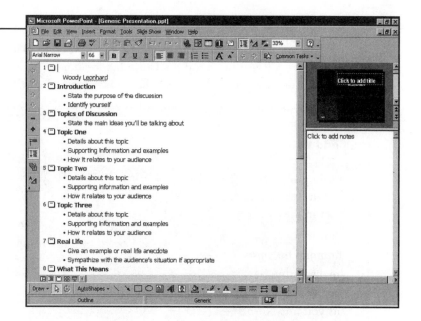

The left and right ⬛ arrows at the top of the Outlining toolbar Promote and Demote selected lines—promoting a line moves it to a higher level in the outline hierarchy, and demoting moves the line lower in the hierarchy.

WHY USE OUTLINE VIEW?
The only real advantage Outline view offers over Normal view is the extra screen real estate devoted to presentation text—and the fact that Outline view gives you enough room to include the Outlining toolbar.

⚠ *CAUTION*

DON'T OVER-PROMOTE

It's very easy to accidentally promote a line to the highest level in the outline, and thus create a new slide. Keep a close eye on the Slide Numbers to make sure you don't fall into that trap.

The remaining icons on the Outlining toolbar are rather ho-hum. The up ⬛ and down ⬛ arrows move selected text toward the beginning or end of the presentation—an action just as easily accomplished by clicking and dragging. The next four icons expand and collapse outline levels, so you can hide the Slide Text underneath a particular Slide Title. And I never use the last two.

Slide View

Flip over to Slide view by clicking the **Slide View** ▣ icon on the View bar (see Figure 25.9). While you're at it, dump the Outlining toolbar by right-clicking on an empty part of any toolbar and unchecking the box marked **Outlining**.

FIGURE 25.9

The first slide of the Generic Presentation in Slide view.

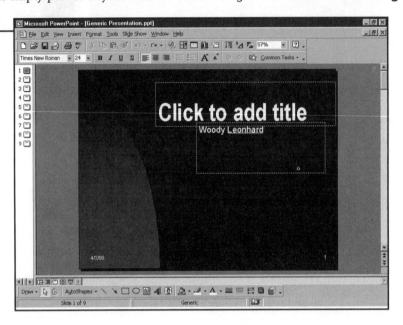

Slide view can be useful for fine-tuning slide details. In most other cases, you'll probably find it easier to work in Normal view.

Slide Sorter View

Click the **Slide Sorter View** ▦ icon on the View bar. PowerPoint shifts to Slide Sorter view (see Figure 25.10), where you have a chance to see thumbnails of all your slides, in order.

WHAT'S WITH THE TIMES NEW ROMAN?

PowerPoint shows Times New Roman 24-point at the top of Figure 25.9. But there's no Times New Roman text anywhere in sight! Surprisingly, what PowerPoint is showing you is the default font for new text added to the slide in the Drawing layer. Go figure.

While working in Slide Sorter view, you can click a slide and move it to a different place in the presentation. That's probably how you'll use Slide Sorter view most often.

FIGURE 25.10

The Generic
Presentation in
Slide Sorter
view.

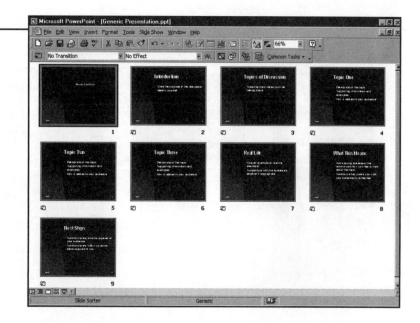

This is also the most logical place to work on transition effects—the way one slide transforms into the next, sounds that should be played when moving from one slide to another, even whether the slide should be changed automatically, not under the presenter's control. We'll look at Transitions in Chapter 28, "Making Presentations Look Better."

Notes Page View

And you thought PowerPoint only did slides.

Attached to each PowerPoint slide is a freehand text page that PowerPoint refers to as Notes or Presentation Notes. If you click **View**, **Notes Page**, you'll get a series of pages like those shown in Figure 25.11.

At the top of each Notes Page is a copy of the associated slide. You can enter any text you like in the lower Notes area. This can be handy if you need to develop notes along with your presentation, or if you want to hand out written notes to accompany your presentation.

I don't use it very much.

FIGURE 25.11

Presentation
Notes Pages are
visible in Notes
Page view.

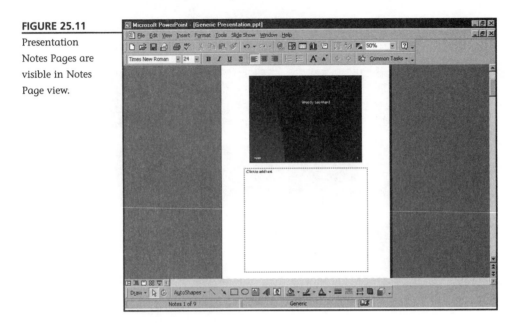

Slide Show

The final view is the slideshow. Click the **Slide Show** 🖳 icon in the View bar,
and PowerPoint launches into the presentation you're currently working on (see
Figure 25.12). Slides in the slideshow appear one at a time, starting with the slide
you've been working on.

FIGURE 25.12

The presenta-
tion, the so-
called Slide
Show view.

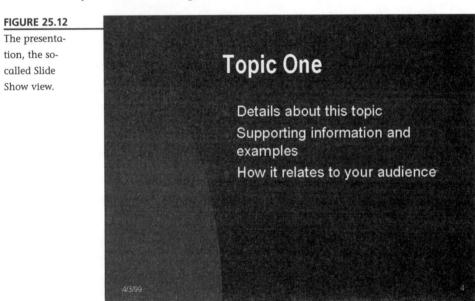

THE WHOLE ENCHILADA

If you want to see the entire slideshow, from start to finish, click **View**, **Slide Show**.

In most cases, you advance to the next slide by clicking onscreen with the mouse. There are several exceptions to that general rule, though. You can program the slides to appear at predefined intervals, whether you click the slide or not. There are dozens of keyboard shortcuts for moving forward, backward, fading to black or white, or quitting the presentation. In addition, if you click the small graphic in a slide's lower-left corner (or if you right-click anywhere on the screen), a host of navigational aids pops up, as shown in Figure 25.13.

FIGURE 25.13

Navigate by clicking the graphic in the lower-left corner.

GET BACK

To quit the slideshow at any point, press the **Esc** key. You'll go back into whatever view you had been using before sliding into Slide Show view.

Now let's take a look at how you can handle PowerPoint presentations.

Woody Leonhard

TEACHES

WORKING WITH PRESENTATIONS

JUST PUT THE MOUSE DOWN AND BACK AWAY... When you start out creating PowerPoint presentations you'll feel mighty proud just being able to put together a presentation that gets your point across. That's as it should be.

Then, if you're like most people, you'll gain enough confidence to start doing fun things with your presentations—add video clips, hot links, multiple customized presentation sequences, fancy wipes, and other effects. And you'll soon discover that, instead of making your presentations better, they'll get worse.

Content Is King

With all due apologies to Marshall McLuhan, when it comes to PowerPoint presentations, the medium is *not* the message.

When people start paying more attention to your whiz-bang effects than they do to the message you're trying to convey, it's time to take stock. In PowerPoint, more than in any other Office application, it's best to keep things relatively simple.

The View from 10,000 Feet

So how does PowerPoint hang together? Excellent question, and one that's relatively easy to answer. I'll spend the next few chapters going into details, but here's what you really need to understand about what's going on behind the PowerPoint scenes.

AutoContent

PowerPoint sports one of the best wizards Microsoft has ever built. It's called the AutoContent Wizard, and in the vast majority of cases it's more than adequate for just about any kind of presentation you can imagine. Answer a few questions, make a few choices, and out pops a presentation skeleton, complete with title slide, decent selections for colors and fonts, and even a few suggestions for what you might want to say. You add the content, and the presentation is ready to go very quickly.

There's much more to PowerPoint than one wizard, though, and sooner

THE POWERPOINT FAMILY JEWELS

This is critical information, and as far as I know nobody has ever put it all together in one place at one time. If you have to use PowerPoint but you don't want to spend time learning about the nuances, you need to read the rest of this section. At least it'll get you started and point you in the right direction when you inevitably get frustrated.

THE JADED AUDIENCE

It'll happen to you some day. You'll give a presentation—a *good* presentation—and as you're walking out the door, you'll overhear a couple of people in the audience saying something like, "Ugh! That's the fourth Bold Stripes presentation this week!"

If you're going to make a presentation to an audience that sees lots of presentations—more than likely, PowerPoint presentations—you'll have to go beyond Microsoft's predefined templates, just to keep them from snoring. It's sad but true: Many of today's presentation-savvy audiences have seen everything PowerPoint has to offer.

There's no easy solution. Designing a killer presentation with custom graphics is every bit as difficult as designing any other kind of multimedia art.

or later you're going to bump into a situation that the wizard can't handle directly. When that happens, you need to know about PowerPoint's, uh, eccentricities.

Types of Slides

The very first slide of a presentation is usually a *title slide*. You're going to hear the term *title* in many different contexts, so don't get confused. Designated title slides are treated differently from the other slides in a presentation. I'll explain all about title slides later in this section. Don't worry about them—yet.

The other slides in the presentation are just called slides. (Whew!) Typically, each slide has a background of some sort, plus room for a title (there's that word again), a body (bullet points, pictures, and the like), a date, a number (for automatic slide numbering), and a footer. In addition, you can use the Drawing layer above each slide to add whatever you like.

Slide Masters

Behind each of the slides sits something called a Slide Master. There's only one Slide Master for each presentation. Anything that appears on the Slide Master appears in all the slides (except title slides). So if you want to change the background on all your slides, move the title, change fonts in the body, add text that will appear in the Drawing layer in all the slides, or even change the whole appearance of your presentation, you need to work on the Slide Master.

WHAT'S A MASTER SLIDE?

Confusingly, the Slide Master is frequently referred to as the Master Slide. In common parlance they're one and the same, but PowerPoint lingo is so confusing that your head is probably swimming by now anyway, so I'll try hard to stick with the official term, Slide Master.

I just told you that anything appearing on the Slide Master appears on all the slides. I lied. It's a little more complicated than that. Take a look at the typical Slide Master in Figure 26.1.

FIGURE 26.1

The Slide
Master for the
Generic
Presentation.

If you change any of these things in the Slide Master, the changes are reflected in every slide in your presentation:

- **Background.** Whatever background you choose for this slide appears on all the slides in your presentation (except on the title slides).

- **Floating Text and Pictures.** If you put text on the Slide Master—typically by clicking **Insert**, **Text Box**, or by clicking the **Text Box**  icon on the Drawing toolbar—that text shows up on all the slides. Similarly, if you put a picture on the Slide Master (with **Insert**, **Picture**), the picture goes on all the slides.

- **Title formatting.** Click once on the box marked **Title Area for AutoLayouts**. Then apply whatever formatting you like—fonts, size, color, centering—and that formatting gets applied to the titles on all the normal slides. If you want to move the title on all your slides to a different location, click and drag this box to whatever location you like. To make the title area bigger on all your slides, click and drag the sizing handles on this box.

- **Body formatting.** Click once on the box marked **Object Area for AutoLayouts** (I just love the way this terminology ping-pongs all over the place, don't you?), and apply the formatting you want for body text. Typically that includes fonts, color, and the like. Frequently, people like to change the bullet character used on their slides, and that's easy, once you know the trick. To change the third-level bullet, for example, click inside the line that says **Third Level**, click **Format**, **Bullet** and choose your favorite bullet. That bullet will be used for third-level text throughout the presentation.

- **Footer formatting.** Click the box marked **Footer Area**, and format away. Again, you can relocate the box, make it larger or smaller, or click once and apply any formatting you like.

WHY CAN'T I PUT TEXT IN THESE BOXES?

I dunno. You'd think that PowerPoint would let you type text in the title, body, or footer boxes, and have that text appear on all the slides. It doesn't work that way. Nothing you type in the **Title** or **Body** boxes appears anywhere else in the presentation. And PowerPoint won't even let you type in the Footer box!

I'll go into some detail on the **Footer Area**, **Number Area**, and **Date Area**, in Chapter 28, "Making Presentations Look Better." They're weird. Don't worry about them for now.

These examples for modifying the Slide Master point out an important difference between PowerPoint and the other Office applications: All the text in PowerPoint appears inside boxes. The easiest way to change formatting for all the text in a box is to select the box by clicking it once, and then applying the formatting. So, in PowerPoint, you don't have to select text before formatting it—merely selecting the box that surrounds the text is sufficient.

Changes made to the Slide Master are reflected in all the slides in your presentation (except title slides). In addition to those changes, you can make changes to individual slides—change formatting for a title, or the bullets in the body, or move the footer. In those cases, the formatting you've applied manually to an individual slide takes precedence over the Slide Master. Thus, if the Slide Master says the title should be in 20-point Arial bold, and you go into an individual slide and make the title 14-point Gotham Condensed, the slide will show the title in Gotham. Subsequent changes to the Slide Master will still be overridden by the changes you've applied manually. The only way to force an individual slide to go back to the Slide Master settings is by selecting the slide, clicking **Format**, **Slide Layout**, and clicking the **Reapply** button, as shown in Figure 26.2.

FIGURE 26.2

To remove manual changes applied to an individual slide, click **Reapply** here.

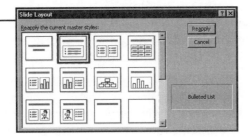

This bears repeating: If you want to change all the slides in your presentation, except for title slides, change the Slide Master. Don't play around with individual slides. I'll show you how to change the Slide Master in Chapter 27, "PowerPoint's Auto Support."

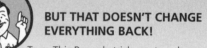

BUT THAT DOESN'T CHANGE EVERYTHING BACK!

True. This Reapply trick resets only manually applied formatting—it doesn't change any text you've typed into the slide.

Title Slides

First of all, there's no such thing as *the* title slide. Your presentation can have one, many, or no title slides. The AutoContent Wizard puts a title slide at the beginning of all the presentations it generates. But you don't have to limit yourself to just one.

In fact, you don't have to have any title slides at all. You can get rid of a title slide just like any other slide—go into Slide Sorter view, click the slide, and press the **Delete** key.

Whenever you create a new slide, PowerPoint presents you with the New Slide dialog box. As you can see in Figure 26.3, if you choose the first layout that's offered, PowerPoint tells you (in the box in the lower-right corner) that you're creating a title slide.

FIGURE 26.3

How to create a new title slide.

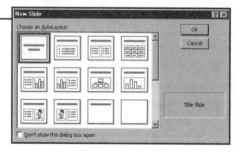

If you click **OK** at this point, the slide that's added to your presentation is a title slide. It's really that simple: You create a title slide at any point in your presentation by creating a new slide and choosing the first layout. I don't know of any way to change a normal slide into a title slide or vice versa.

In many respects, title slides are just like normal slides—you can move them, delete them, copy them—but there's one big exception. Whereas the Slide Master sits behind normal slides, the Title Master controls the appearance of all title slides. If you change the Slide Master, all normal slides change, but none of the title slides do. If you change the Title Master, all the title slides change, but the normal slides stay the same.

More Confusion for the Office Punter

The fact is that PowerPoint behaves strangely in many respects. For example, Outline view doesn't really show an outline. It doesn't even show all the text on the slides—it just slaps an outline-like format onto the text in the Text and Body boxes. Another example: You can specify only footer text in a dialog box, and you can specify only the formatting of that text on the Slide Master! That's okay. The dialog box you type the footer into is called the Header and Footer dialog box—and there are no headers in PowerPoint. *Meshugge*.

(Yiddish/Hebrew lesson for the day: meshugge means "crazy, nuts, absurd." Leon Rosten, in Joys of Yinglish, says, "Perhaps the soundest insight into human behavior is this folk saying: 'Every man has his own *mishegoss.*'")

WHAT'S AN OBJECT?

I thought I knew the answer to that question before I started digging deep into the PowerPoint documentation. The term *object* has a very specific meaning to grizzled old programmers like me. The term has been, uh, adopted by Microsoft in several interesting ways, but I'll have to admit that PowerPoint takes the cake.

As best I can tell, in PowerPoint, an *object* is a *thing*. And that's about as specific as the documentation gets. I'm not going to use the word *object* when referring to PowerPoint.

The minute you start getting confused by a discussion (in the official documents, or in other books) about *text boxes* as opposed to *text box objects* as opposed to *text objects* and on, and on... don't feel bad, just bail out. I can't follow them either. I get the distinct impression that a lot of people who write about PowerPoint get confused, too, and start swinging around a lot of meaningless drivel to throw you off the track.

Even with the inconsistent terminology, the woefully inadequate Help (I dare you to come up with a coherent description of the Slide Master, based on the online Help), and the tendency to flaunt other Office applications' long-standing traditions, PowerPoint still has a lot of capability. It's remarkably easy to use once you know the secrets. And it has some features that are nothing short of amazing.

That's about it for the way PowerPoint hangs together. It's considerably simpler than Word, Excel, or Outlook (in fact, I'm not certain even now that I understand how those applications hang together!). The rest of the PowerPoint story is all embellishment and technique.

General Strategy

Which PowerPoint tools should you use to build presentations? Here's my school-of-hard-knocks series of recommendations:

- Use the AutoContent Wizard. If everybody at your company is using the AutoContent Wizard and management is getting tired of slide shows that all look the same, use the AutoContent Wizard, and then change one simple item (a color, say, or a piece of art) on the Slide Master.

- If you (or your boss) get so sick of presentations generated by the AutoContent Wizard that you're considering throwing all your ThinkPads out the tenth-floor window, use one of the pre-fab presentations provided with PowerPoint. You'll find those pre-fab presentations on the Presentations tab of the File New dialog box.

- When you (or your boss) get so sick of those presentations that you're considering throwing the next presenter out the tenth-floor window, use **Format**, **Apply Design Template** to steal the formats from other presentations. You can do that regardless of whether you start with the AutoContent Wizard or the pre-fab presentations in the Presentations folder, or if you build your presentation slide by slide.

- And when those get stale, get a new job. Nobody except a full-fledged, card-carrying graphics designer should attempt to build a new PowerPoint design scheme from scratch.

You think I'm joking? Hey, if you'd suffered through the kind of presentations I've seen, you wouldn't be laughing. PowerPoint makes it easy to create good presentations—if you stick to the designs provided with the product and add top-notch content. PowerPoint also makes it easy to make execrable presentations, in spite of the quality of the content. The difference between the two boils down to something called artistic talent—and that's a rare commodity.

Content, content, content. Stick to the substance and leave the design to PowerPoint—or hire a pro.

Making a New Presentation

PowerPoint gives you three choices for creating a new presentation: AutoContent Wizard, the pre-fab presentations on the Presentations tab, and building a presentation one slide at a time.

Starting AutoContent

To use the AutoContent Wizard when you first start PowerPoint, click the **AutoContent Wizard** button and click **OK** (see Figure 26.4).

FIGURE 26.4

The initial PowerPoint screen.

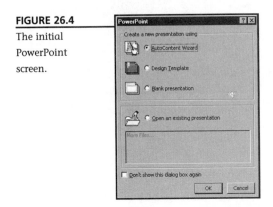

To use the AutoContent Wizard when PowerPoint is running, click **File**, **New**, on the General tab pick **AutoContent Wizard**, and **OK**. I'll talk about the AutoContent Wizard extensively in Chapter 27, "PowerPoint's Auto Support."

Using Pre-Fab Presentations

PowerPoint offers many pre-fab presentations on the Presentations tab, covering topics as diverse as Company Meetings, Financial Reports, Strategy Recommendations, and much more. To use one of the pre-fab presentations, use the initial PowerPoint screen shown in Figure 26.4, check the **Design Template** button, click **OK**, and then choose the **Presentations** tab. If you're already running PowerPoint, click **File**, **New**, click the **Presentations** tab, and select from the proffered presentations.

Going It Alone

If you want to build your presentation screen by screen, you can check **Blank Presentation** in the initial PowerPoint screen. Equivalently, if PowerPoint is running, click **File**, **New**, and choose **Blank Presentation** from the General tab.

For those not quite ready to start completely from scratch, you can start with a design template: simply choose **Design Template** from the initial PowerPoint screen, or via **File**, **New**, and the **Design Template** tab. In PowerPoint a design template is a collection of Slide Master, Title Master, Notes Master (which controls how presentation notes are printed), and Handout Master (which controls how handouts appear). With the design template in place, you're then responsible for creating your own slides one at a time.

TERMINOLOGY ALERT!

It's important that you realize a PowerPoint design template isn't anything at all like a Word template or an Excel template. Not even close.

In PowerPoint, a design template, or a .pot file, is a collection of Slide Master, Title Master, Notes Master, and Handouts Master, which can be applied to a presentation. That's it.

Whereas Word templates and Excel templates are somewhat different, the differences with PowerPoint are like night and day. So don't be confused! The closest PowerPoint gets to a Word or Excel template is in those pre-fab presentations in the Presentations folder.

I will try to avoid using the term *template* when discussing PowerPoint, simply because the term is so completely different here than in other parts of Office.

Man, PowerPoint's odd terminology gets confusing!

WHAT'S A .PPS FILE?

PowerPoint stores files in two forms. The first form, the one you're accustomed to because it's just like all the other Office forms, contains the presentation. Open one of these .ppt files and you can edit, save, and otherwise work with the presentation. Double-click a .ppt file (in Windows Explorer, say, or on the desktop) and PowerPoint comes up with the file loaded and ready to go—typical for an Office file.

The other form, called a .pps form, is the slideshow: If you double-click a .pps file and PowerPoint is available on the PC, the presentation begins. On the other hand, if you open a .pps file from inside PowerPoint, you can edit, save, and work with that version, too.

To avoid the all-too-common problem of having different versions of a file with essentially the same name ("Gee, which one has the more recent version, foo.ppt, or foo.pps?"), I strongly recommend you *not* open .pps files from the Open dialog box. If you absolutely must open a .pps file—perhaps because you lost the original .ppt file, or because somebody gave you the .pps but not the .ppt—you should immediately save the file as a .ppt (click **File**, **Save As** and in the **Save as type** box choose **Presentation (*.ppt)**), and work on the .ppt version.

Page Setup

If you use the AutoContent Wizard, PowerPoint asks what kind of output you're going to use for your presentation. If you use pre-fab presentations or build your presentation one screen at a time, you need to tell PowerPoint whether the presentation is destined to be output to 35mm film, overhead transparencies, and the like. (If you're just going to use the computer's screen, there's no need to change anything: PowerPoint assumes you're going to do the presentation onscreen unless you tell it otherwise.)

It's important that you tell PowerPoint about these alternative output devices, because they'll affect the size (actually, the aspect ratio) of your slides. If you build the perfect onscreen presentation, the 35mm version of that same presentation can flop all over the place.

To tell PowerPoint that you're going to use an output device other than the computer screen, click **File**, **Page Setup**, and set the **Slides sized for** box.

Opening a Presentation

PowerPoint starts out differently from all the other Office applications. PowerPoint's handholding may be a little cloying to most of you, but it could be worse. At least it works.

 On **page 517**, you created a presentation called the Generic Presentation. If you somehow skipped that exercise, pop back there now and get a presentation saved on your disk.

EXERCISE

Opening a Presentation

1. If PowerPoint isn't running, get it going. When the PowerPoint dialog box opens, as shown in Figure 26.4, click the **Open an existing presentation** button and click **OK**.

2. If PowerPoint *is* running, just click **File**, **Open**.

3. In either case, you'll get the Open dialog box, as shown in Figure 26.5. It looks like all the other Office Open dialog boxes, with one exception—in the Files of type box, PowerPoint lists both .ppt and .pps files.

FIGURE 26.5

PowerPoint's Open dialog box—just like all the others, but with one important twist.

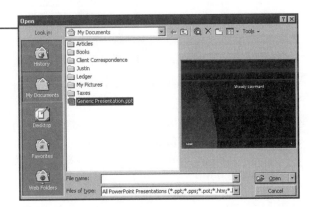

4. Simply click **Generic Presentation.ppt**, click **Open**, and you're in the fast lane. Leave the Generic Presentation up on the screen; we'll use it in the next exercise.

Save, Save As, Close, Exit

PowerPoint's Save, Close and Exit routines are identical to those in the rest of Office.

Save As, however, holds one important wrinkle: This is where you create .pps or slide show files.

EXERCISE

The Generic Slide Show

1. Let's save the Generic Presentation, which should be on your screen, as a slide show or .pps file.

2. Click **File**, **Save As**. You'll get the Save As dialog box, shown in Figure 26.6. In the **Save as type** box, click the down arrow and choose **PowerPoint Show** (*.pps). Click **Save** to save a copy of the Generic Presentation as a PowerPoint slide show.

FIGURE 26.6

Saving the Generic Presentation as a PowerPoint slide show.

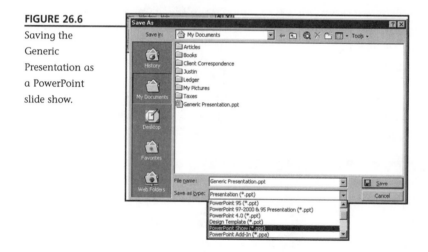

3. Right now you're in a very delicate position, so *follow these instructions very carefully!* If you look in the Window title, you'll see that you're currently editing the file Generic Presentation.pps (see Figure 26.7). You do *not* want to edit the .pps file—the minute you do, the .ppt presentation file will be different from the .pps slide show file, and there's no way you'll ever get them synched up again.

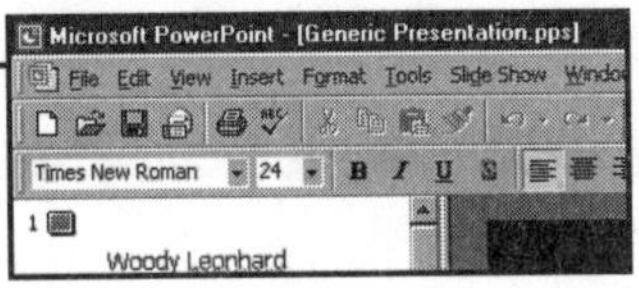

FIGURE 26.7

CAREFUL!
You're editing
the .pps file.
Close it before
you make
changes.

4. Immediately after   saving a file as a .pps slide show file, you should close
   the .pps file and open the original .ppt file. To do that in this case, click **File**,
   Close. Then click the **File** menu item and choose **Generic
   Presentation.ppt** from the list of files at the bottom of the menu. Make
   sure you're working with the .ppt file, shown in Figure 26.8, before you
   continue.

FIGURE 26.8

Make sure
you're using the
.ppt file before
you continue.

> **⚠ CAUTION**
>
> **THIS IS CONFUSING...**
>
> As my son says, "No DUH!" Whoever designed PowerPoint to work this way should be
> forced to spend the rest of his life reconciling users' incompatible changes to .ppt and .pps
> files. I have a few they can start working on right now!
>
> The general rule: .pps files are nice as self-contained slide shows, but never, ever, ever edit
> a .pps file. As soon as you create one (using **File**, **Save As**), close the .pps file and open
> the associated .ppt file.

5. If you want to view the slide show, find the file (using Windows Explorer, or
   Start, **Find**), and double-click the **Generic Presentation.pps** file. The
   slide show is displayed on your screen; click each slide, in turn, to advance to
   the next slide.

6. Make absolutely, totally, 100 percent sure that you have the Generic
   Presentation.ppt file showing onscreen before you continue.

Organizing Slides

After you have a presentation going, adding, copying, moving, and deleting slides couldn't be easier.

EXERCISE

Adding a New Slide

1. Make absolutely, totally, 100 percent sure that you have the Generic Presentation.ppt file showing on the screen before you continue. Yeah, I know I said that already. I mean it.

2. When you need to organize slides, there's only one place to be: Slide Sorter view. So click the **Slide Sorter View** 🔳 icon on the View bar, and your presentation should look like Figure 26.9.

FIGURE 26.9

Slide Sorter view of the Generic Presentation, with nine slides.

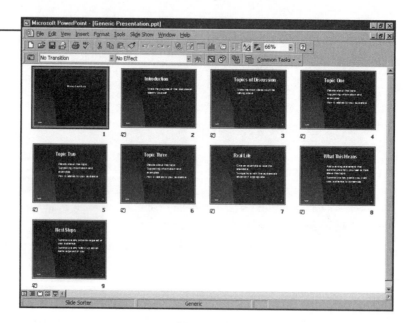

3. Let's say you want to put a new slide in your presentation, immediately after the title slide. Click in the blank area between slide 1 and slide 2. You should see a solid black vertical line appear between the two slides, as shown in Figure 26.10.

4. To add a new slide to the presentation, click **Common Tasks** on the Formatting toolbar, and then click **New Slide**. PowerPoint responds with the New Slide dialog box, as shown in Figure 26.11. I'll talk about the meaning of each of those 12 thumbnails in Chapter 27.

FIGURE 26.10

Click where you want your new slide to go.

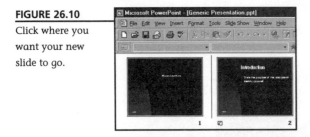

FIGURE 26.11

PowerPoint needs to know what kind of layout you want for your new slide.

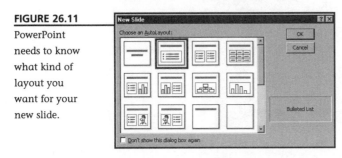

5. Choose a simple bulleted slide, the second thumbnail in the New Slide dialog box, and click **OK**. When PowerPoint comes back to my presentation, Slide Sorter view shows a new slide, number 2, has been inserted, and the subsequent slides have all been bumped down by one slot (see Figure 26.12).

FIGURE 26.12

The new slide takes position 2, displacing the others by one position each.

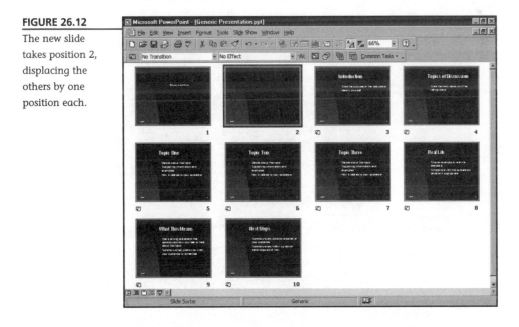

6. Double-click **slide 2**, to go into Normal view. (You also could click the **Normal View** icon on the View bar to get the same effect.) Up pops slide 2, per Figure 26.13, ready for your captivating prose.

FIGURE 26.13

The new slide 2 needs text.

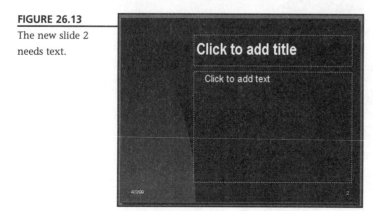

7. Following the displayed instructions, click in the upper box (the **Title** box) and type a new title. Then click the lower box (the **Body** box) and start adding bullet points. The first point you type is at the top level. When you start the second line, press the **Tab** key to indent the line and move in to the second level. On the third line, press **Shift+Tab** (or the backward Tab) to return to the top level. From there, use the **Tab** and **Shift+Tab** keys to move back and forth from first, to second, to third levels (see Figure 26.14).

FIGURE 26.14

Use the **Tab** and **Shift+Tab** keys to move between the various levels of bulleting.

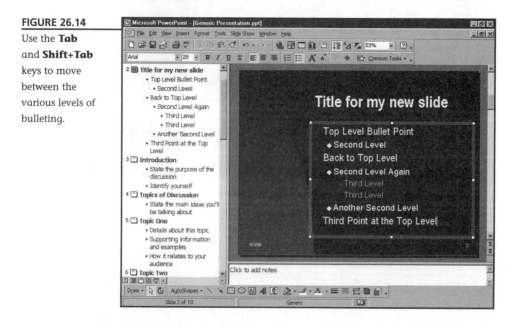

8. All the stuff you type will appear in the Outline pane.

9. At this point, you should try to select individual lines in this new slide and click the **Promote** or **Demote** icons on the Formatting toolbar to move them in or out in the outline levels. You'll not only see the result of your actions in the outline, but they'll also appear in the thumbnail of the slide in the upper-right corner.

10. When you're finished mangling the new slide, leave Generic Presentation.ppt showing on the screen.

If you thought adding a slide was easy, you'll be amazed at moving, copying, and deleting; they couldn't be simpler.

EXERCISE

Move, Copy, and Delete Slides

1. You should have Generic Presentation.ppt open and visible.

2. Managing slides is always easiest from the Slide Sorter view, so click the **Slide Sorter View** 🔲 icon on the View bar.

3. Say you decide that the new slide, number 2, really belongs between slides 7 and 8. To move it, click slide 2 and drag it to the space between slides 7 and 8, as shown in Figure 26.15.

FIGURE 26.15

Click and drag to move a slide.

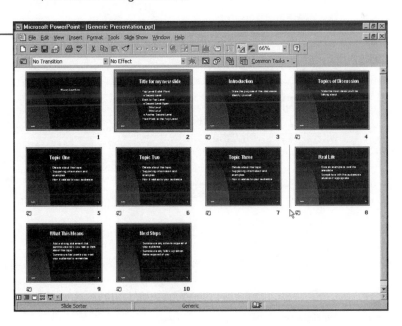

4. When you let go of the mouse button, the old slide 2 turns into slide 7, rearranging the numbering on all the intermediate slides (see Figure 26.16).

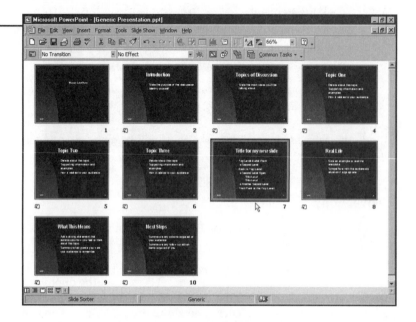

5. Copying slides is just as simple. Say you need to make a copy of this new slide. (Hey, the content's so good you gotta say it twice!) Click the slide, and then click the **Copy** icon on the Standard toolbar. Then click wherever you want the slide to go—in Figure 26.17, I clicked between slides 5 and 6—and click the **Paste** icon.

MOVE LONG DISTANCES

If you need to move a slide a long way, and you can't see both the slide and the destination at the same time, you have three choices. First, you can click the slide, **Cut** it, move to the destination, and **Paste** the slide. Alternatively, you can click the slide and drag it to the top or bottom of the screen; PowerPoint scrolls along with you. Finally, you can zoom (click **View**, **Zoom**) so both source and destination are visible.

FIGURE 26.17

To copy, select the slide you want copied, click the **Copy** icon, click where you want it to go, and click **Paste**.

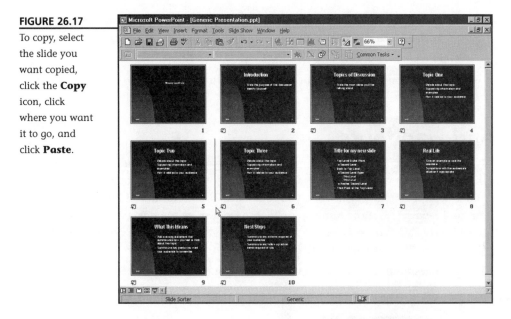

6. When the copy of the slide gets inserted, all the appropriate slides are renumbered and rearranged on the screen (see Figure 26.18).

FIGURE 26.18

When you paste, all the other slides move around.

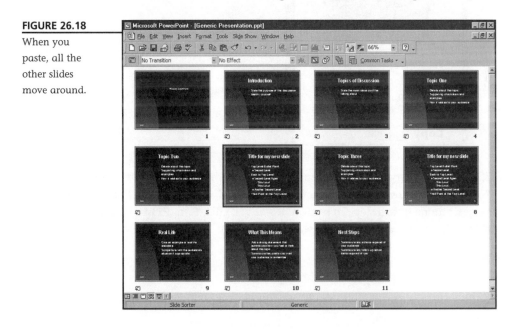

7. Finally, to delete a slide, you select it and press the **Del** key. (Difficult, eh?) To delete the two new slides in Generic Presentation.ppt, click **slide 8** and press **Del**, and then click **slide 6** and press **Del**.

8. We've come full circle. The Generic Presentation is back to how it started.

Notes and Handouts

PowerPoint lets you type notes for each slide. They're freeform and, as the name implies, they're primarily intended as speaker's notes. Unfortunately, the only way you'll be able to read them when you're making a presentation is by printing them out and reading from the hardcopy, flipping from page to page as you go from slide to slide. That's not a very elegant solution. You get one slide on a page, plus whatever text you've typed, and that's it.

To type notes for a slide, click **View**, **Notes Page** (see Figure 26.19).

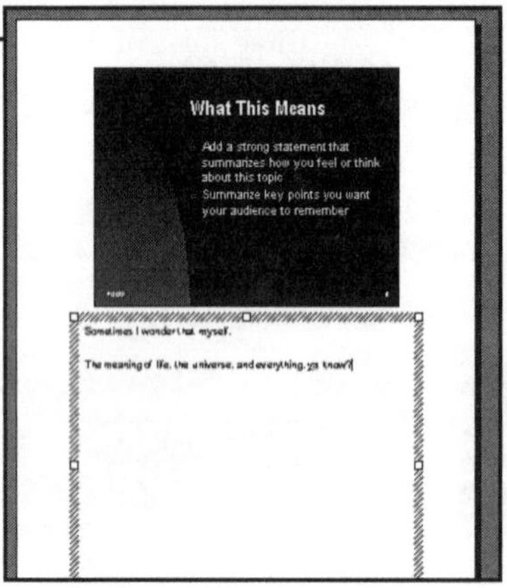

FIGURE 26.19

Notes can be entered in the usual PowerPoint fashion, in Notes Page view.

If you have a very morbid curiosity, you can see the layout of notes pages on the Notes Master (**View**, **Master**, **Notes Master**). Modify the Notes Master, and notes pages change in lockstep. To print notes pages, click **File**, **Print**, and choose **Notes Pages** in the **Print what** box (see Figure 26.20).

FIGURE 26.20

Printing notes.

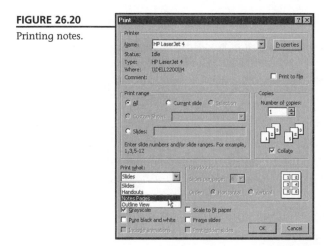

In PowerPoint parlance, *handouts* are just thumbnails of the slides, with no ancillary text. You can have two slides to a page, three-up (along the left side of the page), six-up (two columns of three each), or nine-up (three rows of three). Layout of the pages is controlled by (what else?) the Handout Master, which sits under **View**, **Master**, **Handout Master** (see Figure 26.21).

FIGURE 26.21

The Handout Master for six-up thumbnails of your slides.

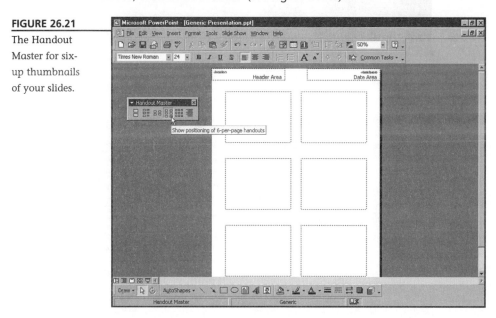

OUTLINE MASTER

Yes, you can print the Outline view—but (wonder of wonders!) you *don't* specify the form of the printing in an Outline Master. Instead, you have to go into the Handout Master and click the last button on the Handout Master toolbar, which is marked **Show positioning of outline**.

Now there's a trivia question for you.

Finally, once you select Handouts, you choose which set of thumbnails you want (two-up, three-up, six-up, or nine-up) in the File Print dialog box, as you can see at the bottom of Figure 26.22.

FIGURE 26.22

The place to go for thumbnails.

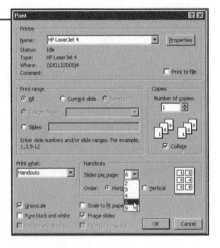

Printing Your Presentation

To print your presentation, click **File**, **Print**, just as you would with any other Office application.

The latest generation of color inkjet printers do an exceptionally good job printing color handouts and overhead transparencies. The usual precautions apply: If you need good color definition, use the expensive paper; don't expect color pages to print anywhere near as fast as black and white; and remember that the ink is water soluble, so don't spill coffee on your overheads!

35mm Slides

If you're going to print your presentation on 35mm slides, you have three basic choices:

● **Genigraphics.** Long a specialist in turning PowerPoint presentations into 35mm slides, Genigraphics knows what they're doing, although they're rarely the least expensive alternative. To send your presentation to Genigraphics, have them turn it into 35mm slides, and deliver the slides back to you via FedEx, get your presentation together, and then click **File**, **Send To**, **Genigraphics**. Have your credit card handy.

WHEN ARE NOTES HAND-OUTS?

Just because Microsoft calls the notes printout *speaker's notes*, there's no reason why you should feel constrained. If you want to hand out copies of your slides with supporting text and a bit of room for viewers to jot down their ideas, you should definitely consider printing the notes and distributing them.

● **Service Bureau.** Many communities around the country have service bureau companies that know PowerPoint inside and out. If you can find a service bureau that will work with you, they can save you money and get the slides back to you fast. To find a local company, check the Yellow Pages under Graphics or Computer Graphics.

● **Film Recorder.** The ultimate do-it-yourself output device, a film recorder acts just like a printer, except it prints on 35mm film. Pop the film canister out of the recorder, take it to your local 1-hour photo shop, and you're in business. If you can't find any locally, check out Publishing Perfection at **www.publishingperfection.com**.

As for other kinds of presentation hardware, you're on your own. The market for projection boxes changes daily (see *PC Week* for lots of ads). LCD panels that sit on top of overhead projectors delight some people, but leave others swearing. Portable panel and screen technology can take your breath away—and relieve you of a substantial amount of capital at the same time. All in all, anything I write today about presentation hardware will be obsolete by the time you read it. So watch the magazine reviews, and put off buying hardware as long as you can, secure in the knowledge that the prices will always go down.

So much for dealing with presentations. Now let's take a look at what kinds of auto goodies PowerPoint provides for your edification and entertainment.

27

Woody Leonhard

POWERPOINT'S AUTO SUPPORT

EVERYTHING BUT AN AUTO PILOT. More than any other Office application PowerPoint abounds with auto tools that help you put together whiz-bang presentations—and you hardly need to get your fingers dirty. In this chapter I'm going to introduce you to the auto features, one at a time, and show you how to use them to create an effective presentation.

AutoContent Wizard

The granddaddy of all PowerPoint wizards, the AutoContent Wizard (what a weird name!), churns out presentations. The presentations that come out of this wizard look good, hang together well, and they even include hints for creating and organizing content. Unless you're going up against a very jaded audience—one that has seen hundreds of PowerPoint presentations—chances are pretty good that the AutoContent Wizard has all you need to get your point across.

Wizard Options

Let's step through the wizard, one point at a time. I'd like to give you an idea of the kind of choices available and what you can expect when you run the AutoContent Wizard. We'll create a new version of the Generic Presentation that served us so well in the preceding chapters.

EXERCISE

A (New) Generic Presentation

1. If PowerPoint isn't running, start it and choose **AutoContent Wizard** on the initial screen. If PowerPoint is running, click **File**, **New**, and double-click **AutoContent Wizard** on the General tab.

2. The AutoContent Wizard presents its splash screen (see Figure 27.1). If you want help from the Office Assistant, click the **?** icon at the bottom. Otherwise, click **Next**.

FIGURE 27.1

The AutoContent Wizard starts.

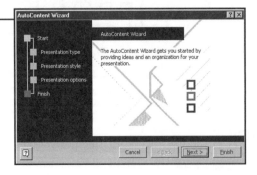

3. In the next wizard panel, you have to make a key decision: What kind of presentation do you want to create? Click the buttons on the left side to see the presentations grouped by category, or scroll through the left box to see what comes closest to your ideal. In Figure 27.2, I've chosen Generic to create a presentation we can play with. When you're done, click **Next**.

FIGURE 27.2

The key AutoContent question—what kind of presentation do you want to build

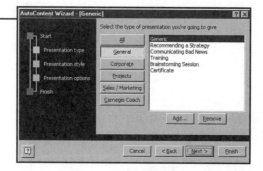

4. You need to tell the wizard how you're going to use the presentation (see Figure 27.3). If it's destined for the Web, PowerPoint inserts forward and backward viewing buttons, and other support details helpful for navigating the presentation. These settings are also used to adjust the size (aspect ratio) of the slides, and set certain printing options.

FIGURE 27.3

Will the presentation go on the Web, or in a kiosk?

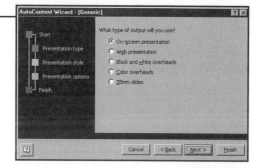

TIP

POWERPOINT IN KIOSKS

Typically a kiosk presentation runs itself, or at least restricts what the observer can do while the presentation is running. Kiosk presentations also frequently start over again once they're done. PowerPoint has extensive kiosk support. To get more information, crank up the Office Assistant, type `kiosk`, click **Search**, and choose **About self-running presentations**.

POWERPOINT ON THE WEB

Finally, with the release of PowerPoint 2000, Microsoft has given us a way to create usable, reliable Web-based presentations. While it's true that PowerPoint-generated Web sites don't "feel" like normal Web sites (they're very much tied to the slide show concepts of forward and backward navigation), it's relatively simple to put your presentation, wholesale, on the Web.

5. In the last informational panel, the wizard wants data for the Title Slide and footers (see Figure 27.4). The AutoContent Wizard invariably creates a single title slide and puts it at the beginning of the presentation. Don't be too worried about getting this right; you can always go back and change what you typed on the slide itself.

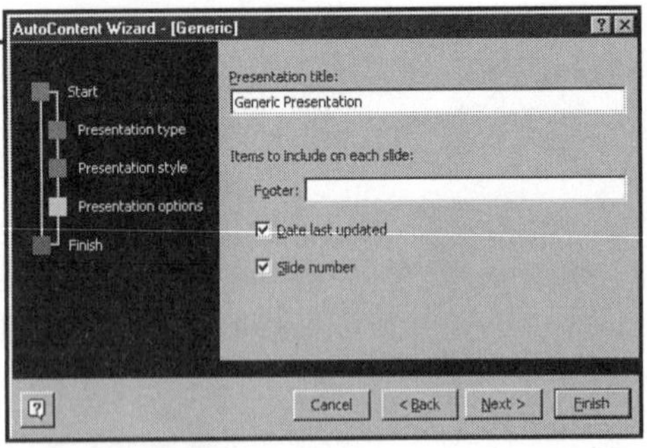

FIGURE 27.4

The wizard generates the presentation's title slide from this information.

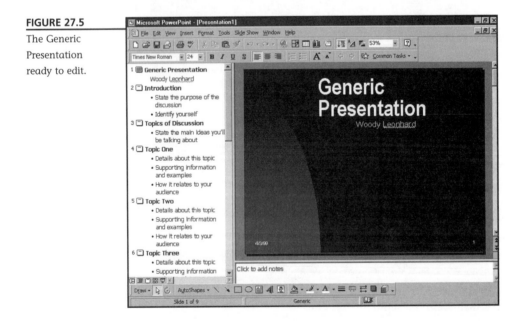

6. Click **Next**, **Finish**, and the AutoContent Wizard creates your new presentation, and then dumps you out in Outline view. Note in Figure 27.5 how the wizard has created a fairly good skeleton onto which you can hang your own content.

FIGURE 27.5

The Generic Presentation ready to edit.

7. We're going to use this presentation, so click **File**, **Save**, type Generic Presentation, and click **Save**. If you already have a presentation with that name (created in the preceding chapters), go ahead and replace it with this one.

Summary Slide

Let's take that Generic Presentation and make it a little better.

 EXERCISE

Summary Slide

1. Start with the Generic Presentation from the previous exercise. Click the **Slide Sorter View** button on the View bar to flip into Slide Sorter view.

2. Slide 3 in that presentation, titled Topics of Discussion, doesn't say much—and, I would argue, duplicates what should go in the Introduction slide, number 2. Let's get rid of that slide by clicking it (see Figure 27.6), and pressing the **Del** key.

FIGURE 27.6

Give slide 3 the deep six.

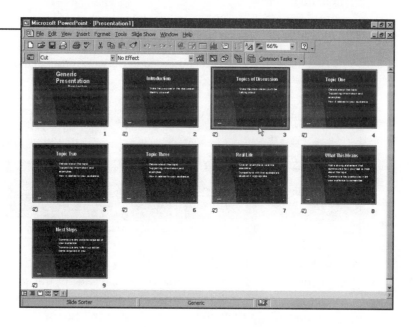

3. There's a nifty PowerPoint feature called Summary Slide, which creates a new slide based on the titles of all selected slides. Here's how to use it. Hold down the **Ctrl** key and click **slides 3**, **4**, **5**, **6**, **7**, and **8**. When they're all selected, click the **Summary Slide** [icon] icon on the Outlining toolbar, as shown in Figure 27.7.

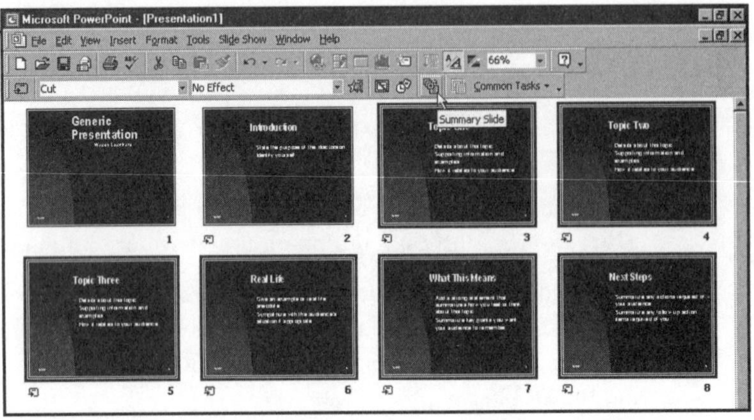

FIGURE 27.7

The **Summary Slide** icon creates a new slide based on titles from all the selected slides.

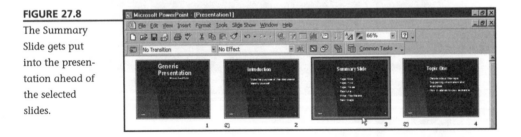

4. PowerPoint creates a new slide, with the title Summary Slide, and inserts it at the beginning of the selected slides—in this case, as slide 3. Note how the body of Summary Slide is composed of bullet points, each of which comes from the titles of the chosen slides (see Figure 27.8).

FIGURE 27.8

The Summary Slide gets put into the presentation ahead of the selected slides.

5. I've found that the Summary Slide often works best as a review slide—sometimes called a snooze slide—that is, a slide at the end of your presentation that reviews all the most excellent points you made during the presentation. So click and drag **slide 3** to the end of the presentation, as shown in Figure 27.9.

FIGURE 27.9

Move the
Summary
Slide to the
end to help
wrap up your
presentation.

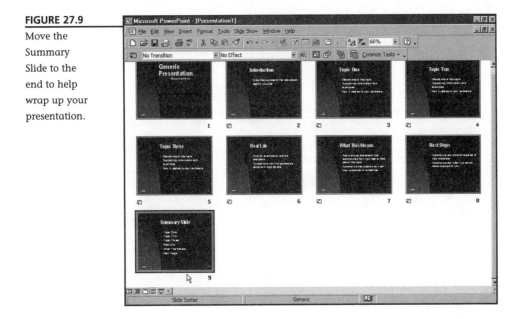

6. Save the presentation as Generic Presentation.ppt. We'll keep using it.

Now let's see what other goodies await our Generic Presentation.

AutoLayout/New Slide

PowerPoint uses the term AutoLayout to refer to its capability to insert new slides—correctly formatted with placeholders for title, body text, and pictures—into presentations. The new slides are hooked up so you can type text into them and have the text appear in Outline view. They're also capable of more-or-less automatically retrieving tables of text from Word, creating Microsoft Chart charts (which don't hold a candle to Excel charts), or inserting clips—pictures, sound, or movies—from the outside world.

If you have PowerPoint running, click **Common Tasks** on the Formatting toolbar, and then **New Slide**. PowerPoint presents you with the New Slide dialog box, which has 24 options; the first 12 are shown in Figure 27.10, the last 12 are shown in Figure 27.11.

FIGURE 27.10

The first 12 pro-
totypical slides
in the New Slide
dialog box.

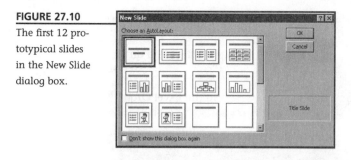

FIGURE 27.11

The last 12 pro-
totypes in the
New Slide dia-
log box.

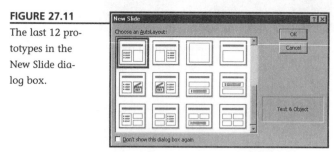

Although that seems like a lot of options, in fact there are just a handful of unique
types of slide placeholders. (Placeholders are those boxes on slides that you fill with
your own content.)

You can see names of the placeholders listed in the bottom right of the New Slide
dialog box. For example, the first slide in Figure 27.11 says **Text & Object**, while
the second slide in the same figure says **Object & Text**. The Text and Object placeholders, in that case, are just reversed.

The following list shows the different kinds of slide placeholders, with their names as
they appear in the box at the bottom right, and what they really mean:

● **Title Slide.** Has room for a title and subtitle. Click this icon to create a genuine designated title slide.

● **Bulleted List.** By far the most common type of slide, the bulleted list has
room for a title and body text. The 2 column text slide is identical, except
that it has two separate placeholders for body text laid out side by side.

● **Table.** This kind of slide contains one large Word table. Only use it when a
Word table would be appropriate, for example, for text.

- **Chart.** The chart placeholders are hard-wired into Microsoft's Chart application, which I discussed way back in Chapter 12, "Special Purpose Tools." Unless you specifically need a very simple, quick and dirty chart, avoid Chart and use Excel.

- **Organization Chart.** This is identical to the Excel Organization Chart application, which I discussed in Chapter 22, "Making Spreadsheets Look Good." Only use it if you want to spend a while drawing an org chart in your presentation.

- **Clip Art.** This is a real misnomer. Clip Art placeholders are hardwired into Microsoft's Clip Gallery, which I discussed in Chapter 12. The Clip Gallery includes sounds and video clips, but it's pretty limited in scope, unless you've added a lot of clips to it, or you're willing to go scouting around on Microsoft's Web site.

- **Object.** By far the most powerful placeholder, Object lets you put anything inside the slide that you can retrieve using Insert/Object—parts of Excel spreadsheets (including charts), Word documents, almost any kind of image, sound, or clip, including those from the Clip Gallery. If you want to put a picture or sound into your presentation, this is the kind of placeholder to use.

- **Media Clip.** If you know that you specifically want a movie clip on a slide, use this kind of placeholder. Otherwise, use Object, because it will enable you to choose movies as one of the options.

Make your choice in New Slide based on the number and type of placeholders on the icon. Don't get hung up about size or location of the placeholders—those are easy to change, once the slide is under construction.

Global Changes

In this section I want to go over the auto features PowerPoint includes to change all the slides in a presentation. I've talked about masters, those phantom slides that sit in the background, affecting all the slides in your presentation, and we'll work with those. There's also a way to apply a set of PowerPoint masters to an existing presentation, and that's done through a command called Apply Design.

Apply Design

PowerPoint templates, as you may recall, aren't really templates in the usual Office sense of the term. Instead, they're collections of four masters in a single .pot file. When you tell PowerPoint to apply a design, what you're really doing is telling PowerPoint to throw away its current set of masters and to bring in a different set from a .pot file.

☞ *I talked about PowerPoint templates in the "Going It Alone" section of Chapter 26, "Working with Presentations," on* **page 535.**

EXERCISE

Apply a Design to the Generic Presentation

1. Open Generic Presentation.ppt, and click the **Slide Sorter View** 🏁 icon to flip into Slide Order view.

2. Click **Format**, **Apply Design Template**. Look through the list of designs in the box on the left. Pick an interesting design template—in Figure 27.12 I've chosen **Dads Tie.pot**. Click **Apply**.

FIGURE 27.12

Apply the Dads Tie design to your Generic Presentation.

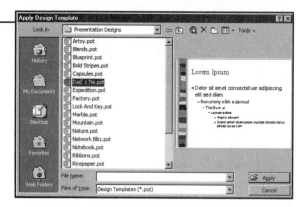

3. PowerPoint gets rid of all the masters it was using and replaces them with the masters stored in the .pot file you've just chosen. In Figure 27.13 you can see how the Dads Tie masters look when applied to the Generic Presentation.

4. Go ahead and save this new version of Generic Presentation.ppt. We'll keep plugging away on it.

FIGURE 27.13

PowerPoint
applies the
design by
swapping out
masters.

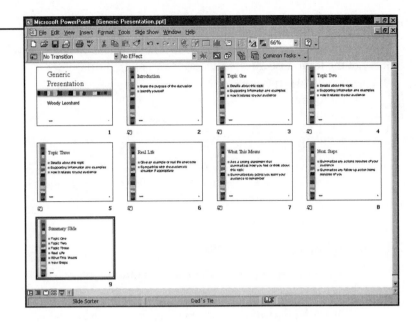

STEAL A SET OF MASTERS

Do you know somebody who's created a really, really cool presentation? If you have a .ppt or .pps file of that presentation, you can steal their masters—and along with them, the backgrounds, font settings, bullets, and everything else that can be set in the masters—and use them in your presentation.

Simply click **Format**, **Apply Design Template**, and in the Apply Design dialog box's **Files of type** box, choose **Presentations and Shows (*.ppt, *.pps)**. Navigate to the presentation in question, click **Apply**, and you've got it.

One note of warning: there may be copyright considerations, particularly if you pilfer a professionally produced set of masters. It's always best to check with the creator of a set of masters before adopting it as your own. (Don't worry about using the masters that ship with PowerPoint; you can use them just about any way you like, as long as you don't try to sell them.)

Slide Master

The Slide Master controls the appearance of all normal slides in your presentation—that is, all the slides except genuine title slides. (Title slides are discussed in the next section.)

USE THE SLIDE MASTER!

If you want to change every slide in your presentation (except title slides), use the Slide Master. Not only does it save tons of time—applying changes manually to every slide in a presentation can take forever—it also ensures that the changes appear uniformly on every single slide.

EXERCISE

Personalizing Your Presentation

1. Start with the version of Generic Presentation.ppt you saved in the previous exercise.

2. Click **View**, **Master**, **Slide Master**. You should see the Slide Master for Generic Presentation, as shown in Figure 27.14.

FIGURE 27.14

Click **View**, **Master**, **Slide Master** to see the Slide Master for this presentation.

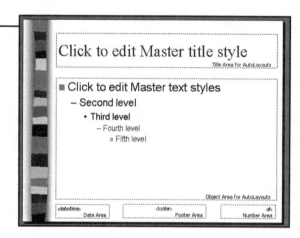

3. This slide master has titles set up in the Times New Roman font. Pardon me, but gag me with a RAMDAC; Times New Roman is *soooo* boring. I want to change that font. So I clicked once on the **Title** box—that is, the box surrounding the title—and used the Formatting toolbar to change the title to Arial Narrow, bold. You can see the result in Figure 27.15.

4. Next, let's change the bullet for second-level lines down in the body boxes on all the normal slides. Start by selecting a second-level line in the Body box, as shown in Figure 27.16.

5. Click **Format**, **Bullets and Numbering**, and choose a bullet you like. In Figure 27.17 I've clicked the **Character** button, and then chosen a **Wingdings wheel of life** symbol as my second level bullet. Click **OK**.

6. The Slide Master is updated to show you the new bullet (see Figure 27.18). Simultaneously, all the second-level text in your presentation is updated to have this new bullet appear in front of it.

YATA—YET ANOTHER TERMI-NOLOGY ALERT!

The first time I saw the Title box at the top of Figure 27.14 I just about croaked. What is a "Master title style?" If you ask Office Bob, he doesn't have any answers. Nor does the Help Index.

PowerPoint is just trying to tell you that, if you change the formatting of the Title box up there—as we just did—your new formatting will ripple through all your normal slides.

I've already complained about the nonsense labels Title Area for AutoLayouts and Object Area for AutoLayouts. Just ignore them. The box on top is the Title box; the box on the bottom is the Body box. Anything else is pretentious garbage.

FIGURE 27.15
Change the title font to something a little less, uh, boring than Times New Roman.

FIGURE 27.16
To change a bullet for a specific level in the body, start by selecting text at that level.

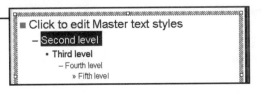

FIGURE 27.17

Choose your new bullet from the Bullet dialog box.

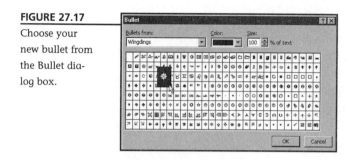

FIGURE 27.18

The new bullet appears on the Slide Master— and thus in the presentation.

7. One last embellishment: I'm constantly running out of room at the bottom of the body boxes in my slides, so I'd like to enlarge the area. I could reduce the size of the fonts in the Body box, but that would make a lot of people squint. Besides, I only need an extra line or two, so it makes sense to make the Body box bigger.

8. Start by moving the **Date**, **Footer**, and **Number** boxes out of the way. This isn't strictly necessary, but it makes it easier to see how far you can enlarge the Body box without falling off the slide. Simply click once on the **Date** box, and drag it to the top of the slide. Then repeat the action with the **Footer and Number** boxes, ending up with the result shown in Figure 27.19.

FIGURE 27.19

Move the **Date**, **Footer**, and **Number** boxes out of the way.

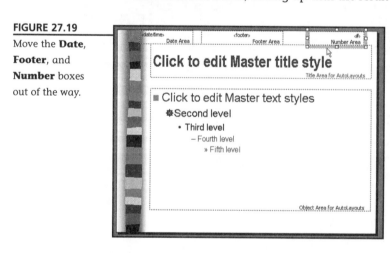

9. Finally, click once on the **Body** box and drag the lower sizing handle to the bottom of the slide (see Figure 27.20).

FIGURE 27.20

FIGURE 27.20

Click and drag the edge of the **Body** box to expand it.

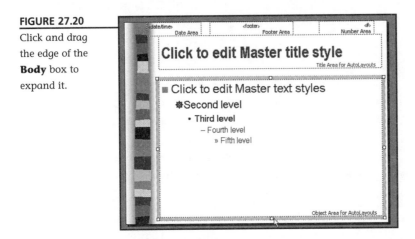

10. To see how the presentation has changed, click the **Normal View** icon on the View bar, and PowerPoint stores away the changes to the Slide Master, reflecting them in all the normal slides in the presentation (see Figure 27.21).

FIGURE 27.21

The new, (slightly) improved Generic Presentation.

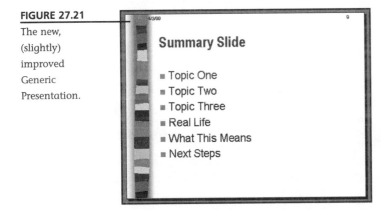

11. We'll continue to use this presentation, so save Generic Presentation.ppt.

That exercise only covers a small part of what you can do with the Slide Master.

For example, although we only moved the Date, Footer, and Number boxes, we could have resized or moved any box on the Slide Master. We also could have specified a background color or chosen to have a line drawn around any of the boxes simply by double-clicking the box.

In addition, we could've applied formatting to the Date, Footer, and Number boxes. If we told PowerPoint to show the date, footer, or slide number—I'll show you how in the next section—that formatting would be applied to all the Date, Footer, and Number boxes in the normal slides.

TIP

COMPANY LOGO

Many companies want to put their logos on all their presentations. It's very easy. Bring up the Slide Master (**View**, **Master**, **Slide Master**), click **Insert**, **Picture**, **From File**, and bring in a picture file that contains your company's logo. Then click and drag the logo to resize and position it wherever you like.

From that point on, all the normal slides in your presentation will include the logo. PowerPoint sticks it in the Drawing layer, floating above the text in your slides.

One final note on the Slide Master: The changes you make to the Title box and the Body box—including formatting, bullets, and the like—are reflected in the title boxes and body boxes of your normal slides (in other words, slides that are not designated as title slides). If you have other boxes on your normal slides, they aren't affected at all. And if you put text on one of your slides using the **Insert**, **Text Box** menu or the **Text Box** ▣ icon on the Drawing toolbar, none of that text will be changed by modifications to the Slide Master.

Title Master

Now let's turn our attention to changing title slides. Real, honest-to-goodness title slides come from three places:

- They can be placed in your presentation by the AutoContent Wizard.

- They can be copied in when you create a new presentation based on one of the pre-fab presentations on the **File**, **New**, **Presentations** tab.

- You can put them in your presentation manually, using the New Slide dialog box (refer to Figure 27.10) and choosing the first prototypical slide.

Most presentations only have one title slide. When you only have one title slide, it doesn't matter if you change that slide directly, or if you change the Title Master and let PowerPoint roll those changes onto the title slide.

However, if you have more than one title slide—or if it's possible that you might want more than one sometime in the future—changing the Title Master makes sense. That way, you'll know that all the title slides will look the same.

EXERCISE

Change Generic's Title Master

1. We're going for overkill. Some day we might want to add a second title slide to Generic Presentation.ppt, so instead of manually changing the title slide in the presentation, we're going to change the Title Master.

2. Start by taking a good look at the title slide in Generic Presentation.ppt. If you're in Slide Sorter view, click the first slide in the presentation, then click the **Slide View** icon on the View bar (see Figure 27.22).

FIGURE 27.22

The original title slide for Generic Presentation.

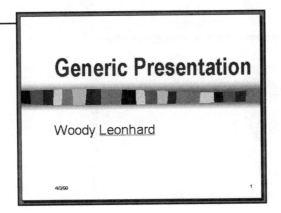

3. Let's say you want to move that picture (it's supposed to be "Dad's Tie") from the middle of the slide to the top, and shuffle the Generic Presentation heading lower. More than that, let's say you want to make those changes to all the title slides in the presentation—even new ones, which you might create at a later date.

4. That's a job for Title Master. Click **View**, **Master**, **Title Master**. You should see a Title Master that looks like Figure 27.23. Because you want to move the tie, click it once to reveal the sizing handles.

5. Move your cursor until it turns into a four-headed arrow. Then click and drag the tie toward the top of the slide. When you have it in position, let it go. Then, because you want to move the **Title** box downward, click once on it, as shown in Figure 27.24.

FIGURE 27.23

Click the graphic on the Title Master.

FIGURE 27.24

Drag the graphic up, and then select the **Title** box.

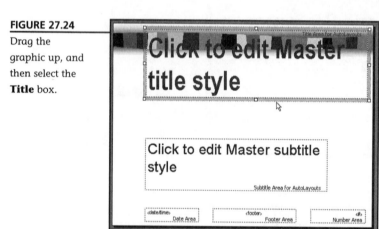

6. Again, jockey around until the mouse pointer turns into a four-headed arrow; then click and drag the **Title** Box down. When you're happy with its new location, let go of the mouse (see Figure 27.25).

7. That's all the changes you wanted to make, so click the **Normal View** icon on the View bar. You'll see how your Title Slide has been changed (see Figure 27.26).

8. Save Generic Presentation.ppt. We'll use it again in Chapter 28, "Making Presentations Look Better."

FIGURE 27.25

Click and drag
the **Title** box
down.

FIGURE 27.25

Click and drag
the **Title** box
down.

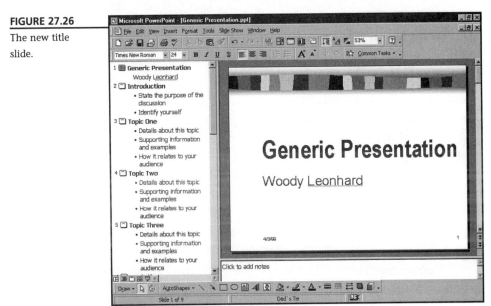

FIGURE 27.26

The new title
slide.

That's how PowerPoint supports global changes. All the strings are being pulled by the masters, and you can find four masters in a .pot file.

Easy, huh?

Footer, Date, Slide Number

Every Slide Master has boxes set up for a footer, date, and slide number. You can format those boxes, add text to them (for example, put the text "Slide" in front of the <#> marker in the Slide Number box), move them, resize them, and so on.

Oddly, though, you don't use the Slide Master to tell PowerPoint that you want to see the footer, date, or slide number on slides. In fact, you can't even use the Slide Master to type a footer that will appear on all the slides—PowerPoint lets you edit the Footer box, but anything you type there doesn't show up on the slides.

To get footers, dates, or slide numbers going on your slides, click **View**, **Header and Footer**. There you can pick and choose which you want to see. If you click **Apply to All** on the way out, the changes are made to the Slide Master. If you click **Apply**, the change is only made to the current slide.

Using the Pack and Go Wizard

I wish all the Office applications had this feature.

PowerPoint's designers realize that it's a PC jungle out there. When you take your presentation to an unfamiliar site, you have no idea if the computers there will have the latest version of PowerPoint available. You don't even know if they'll have the right fonts installed. About all you can depend on is the availability of a 3.5-inch floppy disk drive. Beyond that, you're taking chances.

That's why PowerPoint includes something called *Pack and Go*. This feature packs up everything—and I do mean everything—you need to take your presentation on the road. It'll scarf up the fonts you've used. It can even pack up a PowerPoint viewer that will run on Windows 3.1!

Pack and Go lets you put your presentation on any media you choose, including 3.5-inch floppy disks. (Fair warning: Presentations with graphics of almost any sort will fill several floppies.) When you get to the other site, you insert the first disk into the presentation PC, run a program called pngsetup.exe, watch it all unpack, and then run the PowerPoint viewer, ppview32.exe, and choose your presentation.

To use Pack and Go, get your presentation ready and, with the presentation open, click **File**, **Pack and Go**. Follow along with the wizard (see Figure 27.27) and you'll be done in no time.

FIGURE 27.27

The Pack and Go Wizard makes transporting a presentation easy.

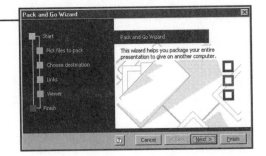

28

Woody Leonhard

TEACHES

MAKING PRESENTATIONS LOOK BETTER

Content, Content, Content. I assume you're only reading this chapter because you have stellar content in your presentation, and you want to jazz things up a bit visually. Okay. I can understand that. But don't lose focus on your content. A zippy presentation with lousy content may keep your audience awake, but it won't do much more.

In this chapter I'm going to assume you have a presentation pretty much put together, but you want to add a few bells and whistles to some of the slides, maybe stick a chart some-place, or add a few transition effects.

Charts

Let's say that we're pretty happy with Generic Presentation.ppt (Generic Presentation.ppt was created in Chapter 27, "PowerPoint's Auto Support"), except we want to add a chart on the slide marked Topic One. You have an amazing array of tools available to you. In particular, if you know the trick, you can take advantage of Excel's powerful charting tools to draw the perfect chart.

THE ADVANCED COURSE

Most books step you through using Microsoft Chart in PowerPoint slides, but I refuse to do it. You don't want to use Chart if you have Excel handy. Yes, I know, this is a topic that should go in the next chapter, where I discuss tying parts of Office together. But you're almost ready for more advanced topics, and you might as well learn how to do this right.

Excel is superior to MS Chart in every respect and should be your first weapon of choice for graphing data on a PowerPoint slide.

 EXERCISE

Put a Chart in a Slide

1. Open Generic Presentation. ppt. Working in normal view, bring up the third slide (by, for example, clicking on the number **3** in the outline pane).

2. Although there are lots of ways to add a chart to this simple bullet slide, by far the best way is to change the Slide Layout. That ensures that all the text on the slide remains intact, and that the precious link between this normal slide and the Slide Master isn't broken. To change the Slide Layout, click **Format**, **Slide Layout**. You'll see the Slide Layout dialog box (see Figure 28.1), which is identical to the New Slide dialog box we saw in Figure 27.11 and Figure 27.12.

3. Although it's true that you can change the layout to Text & Object (reading in the lower-right box in Figure 28.1), a quick check of the New Slide discussion in the previous chapter will remind you that "Chart" refers to that stunted Microsoft Chart application. You don't want that. You want to connect with the mother lode, Excel.

4. So scroll down in Figure 28.1 until you get to the Text & Object layout. Click once on the layout, and click **Apply**. PowerPoint responds by rearranging the text on your slide and putting a placeholder for an Object on the right side, as shown in Figure 28.2.

FIGURE 28.1

PowerPoint
offers to change
the layout of
the slide, in a
dialog box
that's identical
to the New Slide
dialog box.

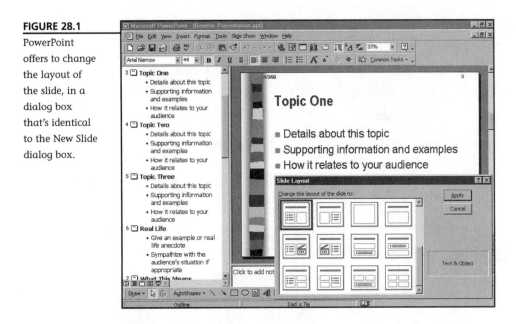

FIGURE 28.2

The Body box
stays on the
left, but a new
Object box
appears on the
right.

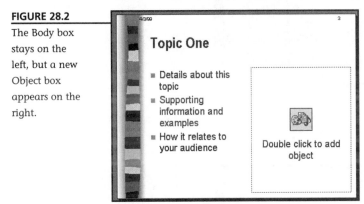

5. Double-click the **Object** box, as indicated, and PowerPoint goes to the Insert Object dialog box (see Figure 28.3). This Insert Object dialog box is identical to the one you'll see in all the Office applications. We want to insert an Excel Chart, so choose it from the Object type box, and click **OK**.

FIGURE 28.3

PowerPoint lets
you choose
what kind of
object you want
to put in the
Object box.

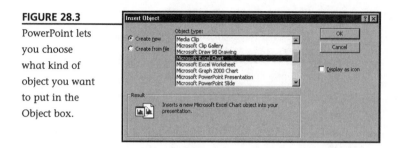

6. Excel responds with a dummy chart attached to a spreadsheet called Sheet1 (see Figure 28.4).

FIGURE 28.4

Excel's initial
chart, with an
attached
spreadsheet.

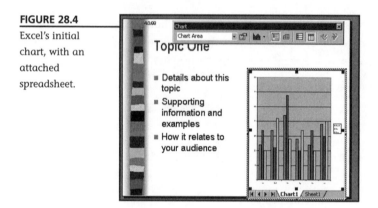

7. Click the **Sheet1** tab and Excel shows you what data it's using to draw that dummy chart (see Figure 28.5).

FIGURE 28.5

The data that
corresponds to
the initial chart.

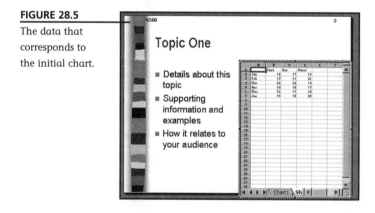

8. Replace the data with some of your own devising. In Figure 28.6 I've used the numbers from test.xls, our test spreadsheet from the Excel chapters.

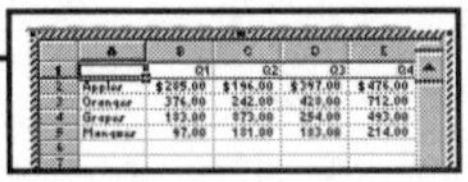

FIGURE 28.6

Type or copy
your own data
into the spread-
sheet.

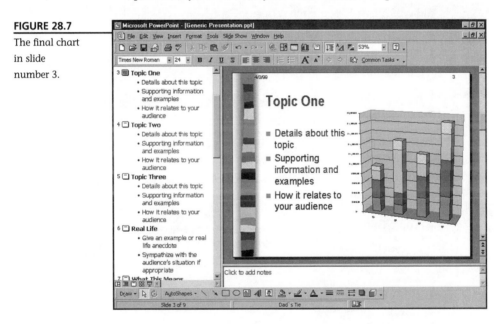

9. Click the **Chart1** tab again and get to work on the chart. Right-click the chart and choose **Source Data** to reset the cells used to draw the chart. Then right-click the chart again and choose **Chart Type**, to choose the kind of chart you'd like to see.

10. After a few more right-clicks and work with the Chart toolbar to reset the axis labels and a little futzing here and there, I came up with the chart shown in Figure 28.7. You should try it, too. It's easy, and if you run into problems you can always check the Excel chapters in this book.

FIGURE 28.7

The final chart
in slide
number 3.

11. Save Generic Presentation.ppt.

Text Boxes

The next common modification most people want to make with their slides involves adding more text to a slide—but not in the main bullet-ridden Body box. (There's something eerie about that phrase, but never mind.)

If you want to add a second column of bullets on one slide, that's easy: click **Format**, **Slide Layout**, and choose the layout with two columns of bullets. (It's the third layout in Figure 27.11.) Your existing bulleted text ends up scrunched in the left side Body box, and a new Body box appears on the right.

But if you want to add free-form text to a slide you have to use a text box.

EXERCISE

Text Floating Above a Slide

1. Let's say you know that your audience will be tired and grouchy by the time you finish the Generic Presentations slide called Topic Two. You want to put some text at the bottom of the slide that says, "Let's take a break!" so they know that there's some relief in sight.

2. Open up Generic Presentation.ppt. The slide called Topic Two is the fourth slide in the presentation, so move to slide number 4 in Normal view, as in Figure 28.8.

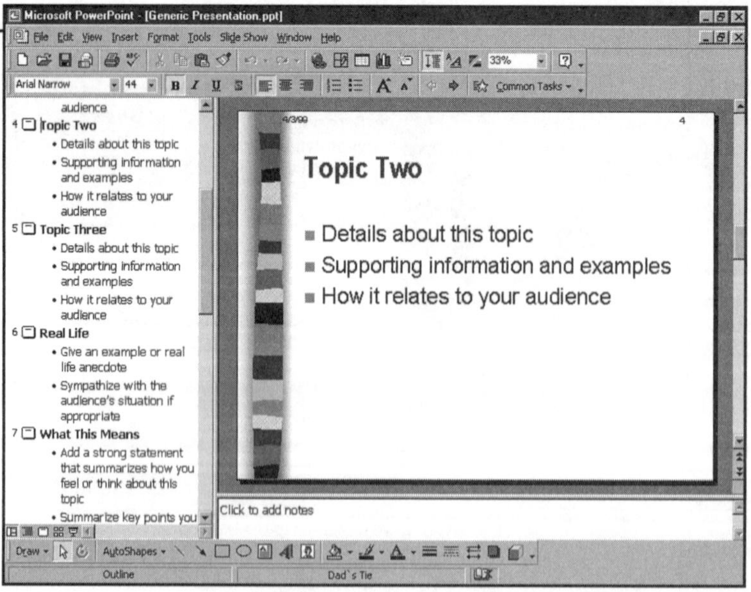

FIGURE 28.8

Slide 4, where we want to put the text "Let's take a break!"

3. There are several ways to put a text box on a slide, but the easiest is to click the **Text Box** 🔲 icon on the Drawing toolbar. Your mouse pointer turns into a weird vertical-line–thingy with a crosshatch. Figure out where you want to put your text, and then click and drag to create a box to hold it (see Figure 28.9).

FIGURE 28.9
Click and drag
to insert a text
box on top of
your slide.

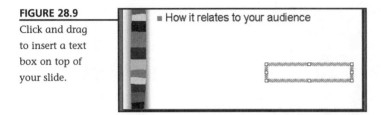

4. You can immediately start typing text. In Figure 28.10, I've typed `Let's take a break!`

FIGURE 28.10
Type the text
that goes into
the box.

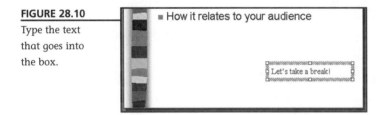

5. You can format the text directly by using the usual formatting tools (font, size, color, centering, and so on), either the ones on the Formatting toolbar or the ones buried in the menus. You can also format the box. If you right-click that new text box and choose **Format Text Box**, PowerPoint responds with the Format Text Box dialog box shown in Figure 28.11.

FIGURE 28.11
You can even
apply format-
ting to the text
box by right-
clicking.

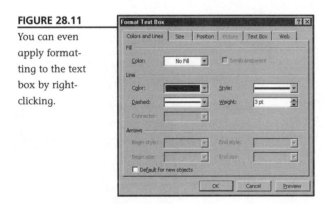

6. Per Figure 28.11, I've chosen to have the text box appear with a dark line around it. After setting the formatting, click **OK** and the properly formatted box will appear on the slide (see Figure 28.12).

FIGURE 28.12

The text box appears with a thick line.

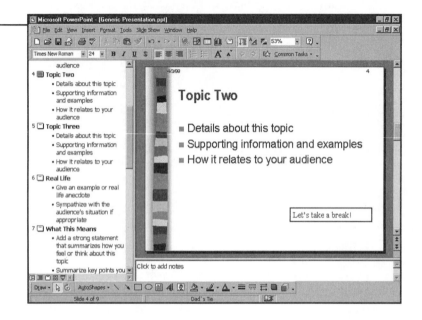

7. Save Generic Presentation.ppt.

It's important to realize that text is "floating" above the slide, in PowerPoint's Drawing layer. As such, the text won't appear in Normal view's outline pane (as you can verify by looking at Figure 28.12), nor will it be changed should you change the Body box in the Slide Master. In fact, nothing you do in the outline pane, or in the Slide Master, will influence this floating text.

Pictures

Pictures, pictures, everybody wants pictures in their presentations. If they help prove your point, there's much to be said about pictures—worth a thousand words and all that. But if they merely adorn, you're running dangerously close to producing an airhead presentation.

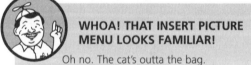

WHOA! THAT INSERT PICTURE MENU LOOKS FAMILIAR!

Oh no. The cat's outta the bag.

Yes, as you can see in Figure 28.13, PowerPoint has the same **Insert Picture** menu that you've seen in Word and Excel. Yes, you can use it in precisely this way to put AutoShapes in your presentations—or Org Charts, WordArt, scanned images (if you have a scanner), even text tables from Word.

continues

By far the simplest way to put a picture on a particular slide is to change the layout. Click **Format**, **Slide Layout**, and choose the layout marked **Text & Clip Art**, or the one marked **Clip Art & Text**, the two layouts in the lower-left corner of Figure 27.11. The current bulleted text shows up either to the left or right of the picture placeholder. Double-click the picture placeholder and you end up in Office's Clip Gallery. From there you can bring any picture you like into the Clip Gallery and, from there, into the picture placeholder.

WHOA! THAT INSERT PICTURE MENU LOOKS FAMILIAR! continued

If you need a refresher on those options, see the section on inserting pictures in Chapter 12. But chances are pretty good you're adept enough at Office's picture handling by now to just dive in.

Don't go overboard, though, okay? Chances are awfully good that any WordArt you put on a slide will be just that… awful.

Most of the time, though, you want to put a picture on a slide without moving around the text that's already there.

EXERCISE

Paste a Picture on a Slide

1. Let's put a picture on the slide titled Topic Three. In Generic Presentation.ppt, the slide called Topic Three is the fifth slide in the presentation, so move to slide 5 in Normal view.

2. Click **Insert**, **Picture**, **From File**, as in Figure 28.13.

FIGURE 28.13

PowerPoint's Insert Picture menu looks familiar, eh?

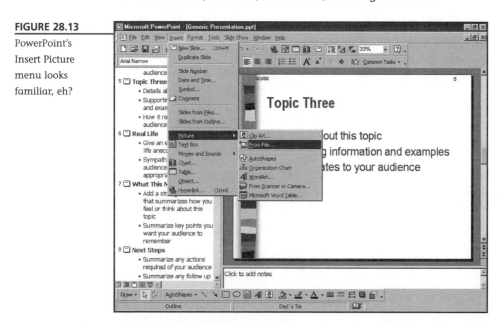

3. When you click **Insert**, **Picture**, **From File**, PowerPoint responds with the now-familiar Insert Picture dialog box, as shown in Figure 28.14. I found a picture of a globe worth snagging in Windows 98's c:\Windows folder. You can hunt around for your own favorite picture. When you've got it, click it and click **Insert**.

FIGURE 28.14

Look for a decent picture.

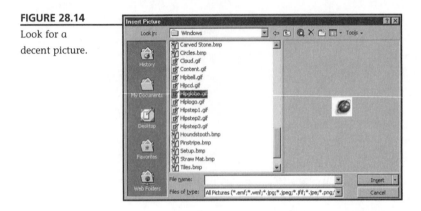

4. The picture—no doubt way too big or way too small, as in Figure 28.15— appears in your slide along with the Picture toolbar.

FIGURE 28.15

The picture appears at a random location inside your slide.

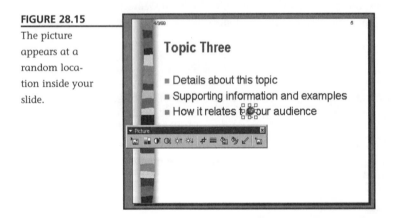

5. Click and drag the picture to whatever location you like. Click the square box sizing handles to make it bigger or smaller (see Figure 28.16), and apply whatever picture-mangling options suit your fancy from the Picture toolbar.

FIGURE 28.16

Click and drag the picture, and resize it to fit the location.

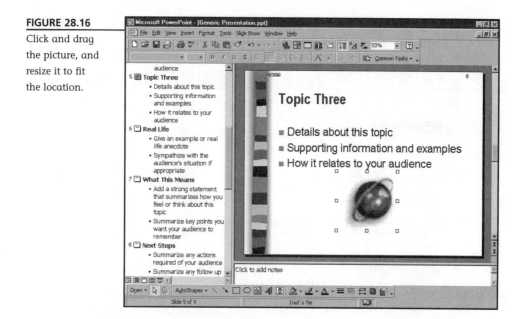

6. Save Generic Presentation.ppt.

Once again, it's important to realize that pictures you put on a slide using Insert Picture (or the Drawing toolbar, for that matter) float above the slide itself. Nothing you do to the Slide Master will change them.

Movies and Sounds

PowerPoint lets you put movie files and sounds in your slides. Many major video file formats are supported, including .avi, .mpg, .flc, and .fli. And sounds can be played directly from a CD in the PC's CD drive. Office comes with a few video clips and sounds in the Clip Gallery. You can pick up many, many more on the Web. (Just make sure you get permission from the owner to use them!)

EXERCISE

Self-Starting Video

1. This time we'll put a self-starting video of a person using a calculator on the slide called Real Life. In Generic Presentation.ppt, that's the sixth slide in the presentation, so bring up slide 6 in Normal view.

2. Click **Insert**, **Movies and Sounds**, **Movie from Gallery**. You'll get the Clip Gallery, open to the Motion Clip tab. Click on Office (appropriate, eh), and you'll see the choices shown in Figure 28.17. Choose the clip with the calculator, click **Insert Clip**, and then close the Clip Gallery.

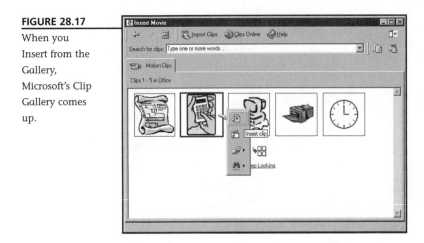

3. PowerPoint puts the video clip in slide 6. Resize it, and then click and drag it to a convenient corner, as shown in Figure 28.18.

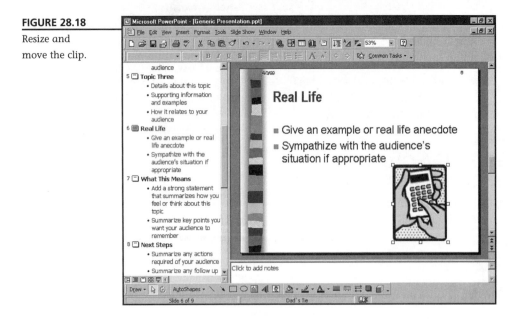

4. Here's the trick. When you nsert a video clip into a PowerPoint presentation, it's set up so you have to click on the video before it will start running. So, when you have a presentation running you must have the presence of mind to click the video—otherwise it just sits there, looking like a simple unanimated picture. But we want to set things up so the video clip runs automatically, as soon as the slide appears onscreen.

5. Right-click the video clip (in this case, right-click the picture of the calculator in the lower-right corner of slide 6), and choose **Custom Animation**. Click the **Order & Timing** tab, and then check the box marked **Picture frame 3**, (that's the picture holding the calculator). See Figure 28.19.

FIGURE 28.19

The self-starting setting sits buried in this dialog box.

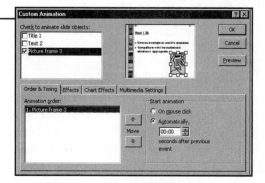

6. In the **Start animation** box, click **Automatically**. You can run the spin number up if you like, to make PowerPoint delay just a bit after it shows the slide on the screen, before it starts running the video. Click **OK**.

7. To see the calculator in action, click **Slide Show**, **View Show**. Go through the presentation normally by clicking each slide in turn. When slide 6 appears, the calculator video runs by itself, and the fingers start zooming. Cool!

8. Save Generic Presentation.ppt.

Sounds work the same way as this video clip: Unless you change the Custom Animation setting, you'll have to click the sound's picture to get it to work.

For more information about playing a selection from a CD in a slide, bring up the Office Assistant (in other words, press **F1**) and type play cd.

Transitions and Builds

When used in moderation, transitions and builds can add a lot to your presentations without becoming overly distracting.

What's a *transition*? It's the way that PowerPoint moves from one slide to the next. You can have PowerPoint simply cut—move from one slide to the next, with no animation in between—or you can make the new slide arrive in a blaze of checkerboard patches, wiping across the screen, zooming in from the top, bottom, lower right, or any of dozens of additional animation techniques.

A *build*, on the other hand, controls how elements of the slide are placed on the slide. For example, you can have the title appear, and then make each bullet point appear, one at a time, when you click the screen or at predefined, timed intervals.

In short, the options would befuddle a movie director, and the potential for visual over-stimulation looms greatest right here.

EXERCISE

Generic Transitions and Builds

1. Open Generic Presentations.ppt and go into Slide Sorter View.

2. Usually you'll want to set the same transition for all the slides in a presentation. It can be distracting having some explode out from the middle, others fly in from the bottom, and still others checkerboard! To set one transition for all the slides in a presentation, click **Edit**, **Select All** to select all the slides. You can then set the transition effect by selecting them from the **Slide Transition Effects** drop-down box on the left of the Slide Sorter toolbar (see Figure 28.20).

FIGURE 28.20

Select a transition effect by choosing it from this drop-down list.

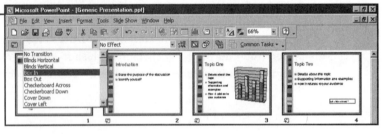

NOTE

TRANSITION FOR ONE

If you want to set the transition for just one slide, select the slide, and then choose the transition from the **Slide Transition Effects** drop-down box. This is the transition that takes effect when the slide appears onscreen—it has nothing to do with the way the slide goes away.

3. If you watch closely, the first selected slide will show a miniature animation of whichever transition effect you choose, so you can get quick visual confirmation of the effect.

4. In Figure 28.21, I've chosen the **Cover Left** transition, which shuffles new slides in from the right to the left. It's a reasonable animation that isn't too distracting.

FIGURE 28.21

Applying the
Cover Left
transition to all
the slides in the
presentation.

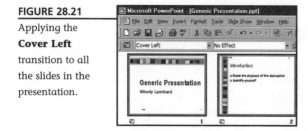

5. Let's also put together a build for the last slide, the one marked Summary
Slide. I'm particularly impressed by the Spiral build, which adds each bullet
item by spiraling it in from the top, gradually making the item bigger, until
it ends up at the correct size in the right location.

6. To apply the Spiral build technique to the final slide, just click the slide (in
Figure 28.22, that's **slide 9**). Then choose **Spiral** in the **Text Preset
Animation** drop-down list on the Slide Sorter toolbar.

FIGURE 28.22

Have
PowerPoint
build the
Summary Slide
by spiraling in
each bullet item
when you click
the mouse.

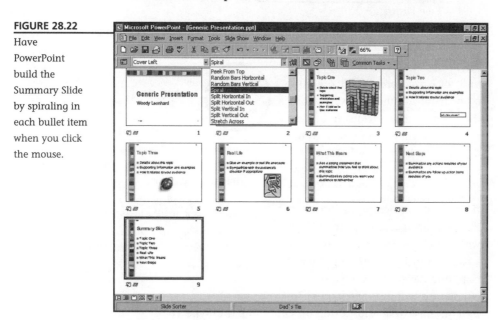

7. Start the presentation by clicking **Slide Show**, **View Show**. Each slide
arrives on the screen from left to right. And the final slide, shown in
Figure 28.23 in mid-spiral, builds the bullet points one at a time.

The Summary
Slide build,
caught in mid-
spiral with one
of the bullet
items.

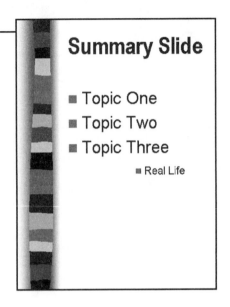

8. Keep Generic Presentation.ppt around just to wow your friends.

That's about all I have to say on the topic of PowerPoint. There are quite a few features I didn't cover, but they're all pretty obvious from the menus and they don't really go to the heart of how PowerPoint works, or what you need to know to get a good presentation up on the screen.

If you have a microphone on your PC, you can record narratives to go with the slides. In fact, it's quite possible to record your entire presentation, and never speak a word. (Audiences will just love it, eh?) To find out how to do that, bring up Office Bob and type voice.

MORE CONTROL

If you want to see the transition effect in greater detail, or if you want to control how quickly the transition takes place, click **Slide Show**, **Slide Transition**. In the Slide Transition dialog box you can also tell PowerPoint that you want the slides to advance automatically—without a mouse click—and if you want a sound triggered as the slides change. *Whoosh! HOOORAY! Gimme a break...*

You can also use PowerPoint to time your presentation and warn you if you're running too fast or too slow, using something called the Slide Meter. To see details on that feature, type rehearse in the Office Assistant.

VII

Woody Leonhard

TEACHES

OFFICE 2000

ADVANCED TOPICS

29

Woody Leonhard

TEACHES

TYING THE PARTS TOGETHER

CAN'T WE ALL JUST GET ALONG? One of Office's still-nascent capabilities, the possibility of making all the Office applications work together in harmony, rates as the Holy Grail of Office suite programmers. Sadly, we're still a long, long way from the time when all the parts of Office work similarly, and all work together. Until that time comes, we're going to hear a lot of marketing hype about how the parts of Office interconnect—the logo on the box shows the pieces coming together as in a jigsaw puzzle, for heaven's sake—whereas the real-world interconnections consist of little more than broad tips and a handful of very obscure tricks.

It Really Doesn't Hang Together

Much as the Microsoft marketeers would disagree, Office hangs together very poorly: it's still much, much too difficult to get information from one part of Office into another. You'll have to struggle to accomplish things that should be very simple.

That's why I put this chapter in the advanced topics category. If you're still a little green behind the ears (as were we all at one time!), tread lightly. You can't expect all the interconnections to work precisely as advertised all the time—your system will lock up unexpectedly every now and then, you'll face weird errors with even weirder error messages, and sooner or later things will go wrong and you'll never figure out why.

That said, Office 2000 has much stronger, more capable, and more reliable interconnections than any previous version of Office—or any other collection of computer applications that I know about. Working with the glue that holds them together can be exciting, challenging, and ultimately make your working day go much more smoothly.

Once you figure out the tricks, of course.

Copying, Embedding, Linking

There are three ways to put data from one Office application into another Office application:

- **Copying.** Office supports copying through the Clipboard, just like every other Windows application. (Office's own Clipboard tends to get in the way, but some day it will be useful, too.) When you copy data into one of the Office applications, there's no memory of where the data came from: The application just scarfs up the data and goes on its merry way.

- **Embedding.** Depending on the applications involved, you might be able to embed data from one Office application into another. When you embed, the data is actually moved from one application to the other, but the receiving application remembers where it came from.

- **Linking.** Similar to embedding, but the data doesn't get shuffled around. Instead, Office sets up a link to the data so it can retrieve the data when it's needed.

Yeah, those definitions seem kind of loosey-goosey at the moment. Cut me a little slack, though, and I'll show you how each of the interconnection methods works.

In the remainder of this chapter, I'm going to look at specific pairs of Office applications and show you how to get data from one into the other. I'll clearly identify whether the data is going from one application to another by copying, embedding, or linking, and thereby help tighten up the loose definitions.

I hope.

Sharing Data Between Word and Outlook

When you think of moving data from one Office application to another, what's the first thing that comes to your mind?

Of course: You want to be able to retrieve names and addresses from your Outlook Contacts list and use them in Word. At least to a first approximation, everybody needs to do that. You'd think it would be the major focus of Microsoft's Office interconnection efforts.

And, of course, you'd be wrong.

A SOLUTION DOES EXIST

This is such a huge, glaring gap in Office's capabilities that somebody had to come along, sooner or later, and plug it up.

Well, that somebody is, uh, us. WOPR, Woody's Office POWER Pack, has a nifty feature that sucks Contact information into Word. Right-click in your document wherever you want the name to appear, wait a few seconds while WOPR builds a list of all your Contacts' names, and then pick the person's name from the list. *Boom*. There it is, in black and white.

Although it normally costs $49.95, WOPR is free when you buy *Special Edition Using Office 2000*, by Ed Bott and the well-known Office under-achiever Woody Leonhard (Que, ISBN 0-7897-1842-1). It's highly recommended.

Retrieving Names and Addresses

You can try to do it manually—get Outlook's Contacts list running, find the person in question, copy their address to the Clipboard, flip back to Word, and paste the address information, but oh! wait!

Guess what? You can't even copy the name and the address from Contacts to Word in one round-trip. You can pick up one or the other, but not both. You can't snag the business name either, or the job title, or the phone number. In short, whoever designed Outlook didn't design it to work with Word, and vice versa.

Fortunately, there are a couple of stopgap measures you can take to make it much easier to copy Outlook Contacts into Word.

EXERCISE

Retrieve a Name and Address in Word

1. Start Word.

2. We're going to put a new icon on the Standard toolbar (that's the toolbar on top), which will insert a name and address from Outlook into the current document. Click **Tools**, **Customize**, and click the **Commands** tab (see Figure 29.1).

FIGURE 29.1

Put a new icon on a toolbar by clicking **Tools**, **Customize**, and bringing up the **Commands** tab.

3. Make sure the box marked **Save in** says **Normal.dot**. On the left side, in the **Categories** box, scroll down to **Insert**. Then, in the **Commands** box, scroll down to **Address Book**.

4. Next, you're going to create a new icon on the Standard toolbar. Click **Address Book** and drag it up to a convenient location on the toolbar. In Figure 29.2, I've chosen to put the new icon to the right of the **Spelling** icon, but you can put it wherever you like.

> **COPY, EMDBED, OR LINK?**
>
> This is copying, pure and simple. After Word snags the name and address from Outlook's Contact list, that data gets pasted into the document at the current insertion point (in other words, where the cursor is sitting). There's no link back into Outlook, or even any memory that the data originally came from Outlook.

FIGURE 29.2

Click and drag **Address Book** onto a handy toolbar.

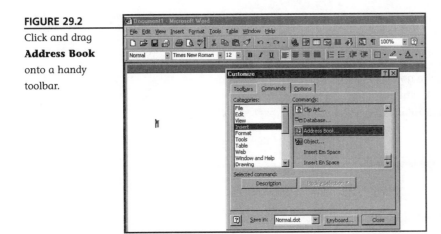

5. Let go of the mouse button, and you'll have a new icon on the toolbar, as shown in Figure 29.3. Close the dialog box. If you hover your mouse over the icon, you'll note how the ScreenTip says **Insert Address**. And that's precisely what this icon does—sorta.

FIGURE 29.3

Drop the new icon on the toolbar.

6. Let's take the new icon out for a spin. Click **Insert Address**. Word chunks and whirrs for a little bit—it has to wake up Outlook to get the names—and when it's done, Word presents a list of names in the Select Name dialog box, shown in Figure 29.4.

FIGURE 29.4

Word lets you select a name from Outlook's Contacts list.

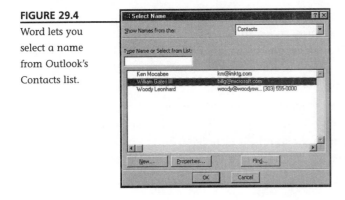

7. Click one of the names in the Select Name dialog box, say **William Gates III**. Click **OK**. The name appears in your document, as shown in Figure 29.5.

When Word retrieves a name from Contacts, it never includes the company name, but always includes the country name.

William Gates III¶
One Microsoft Way¶
Redmond, Washington 98052¶
United States of America¶
¶

8. Yes, what you see is what you get. Word never brings in the company name, and it always brings in the full country name—even if the country name is United States of America.

Fortunately there's a way to get around the problem, although you won't find any documentation for this solution anywhere in the Office package.

WHAT'S WRONG WITH THE SELECT NAME DIALOG?

Just about everything.

The names only appear in alphabetical order—sorted by first name. (It doesn't matter how you sort them in Outlook.) Only the names of people appear, no business names. You can't see addresses, so if you have two separate entries for a person or company, you have to guess which one includes the correct address. You can't sort. And on and on. In short, the only thing worse than this dialog box that I can imagine would be no dialog box at all.

But wait. It gets worse.

On Useful Information

Word uses a hidden AutoText entry called AddressLayout to determine what name and address fields it should retrieve, and how to put them in your documents. Don't bother trying to find it. You won't see AddressLayout anywhere in the AutoText list, or anyplace else in Word, for that matter.

This is a difficult exercise—quite likely the most difficult one in the whole book—so follow along carefully. There's no inherent danger; you won't mess up your machine if you flub some of the typing, for example. But to get a decent name and address imported into your documents from the **Insert Address** icon, you have to follow these instructions exactly.

EXERCISE

Make the Name and Address Useful

1. Word is running. Click the **New** [icon] icon to create a new, blank document.

2. Carefully type this information into the document (see Figure 29.6):

   <PR_DISPLAY_NAME>

   <PR_COMPANY_NAME>

   <PR_STREET_ADDRESS>

   <PR_LOCALITY>, <PR_STATE_OR_PROVINCE> <PR_POSTAL_CODE>

FIGURE 29.6

Type these weird formatting commands in a new document, and be careful to spell everything correctly.

```
<PR_DISPLAY_NAME>¶
<PR_COMPANY_NAME>¶
<PR_STREET_ADDRESS>¶
<PR_LOCALITY>, <PR_STATE_OR_PROVINCE> <PR_POSTAL_CODE>¶
```

3. Select all the information that you typed, and then click **Insert**, **AutoText**, **New**, as shown in Figure 29.7.

4. When asked for the name of the AutoText entry, type AddressLayout (all one word), as shown in Figure 29.8. Word replaces the existing AddressLayout AutoText entry— the one you can't see—with this new one.

ARE THOSE FIELD CODES?

Nope. These formatting directives are complete gibberish, unlike anything I've ever seen in Word (and, believe me, I've seen a lot of strange stuff in Word!). As far as I know, you'll never come across anything quite like this anywhere else in Office.

FIGURE 29.7

Select the entire document and set it up as an AutoText entry.

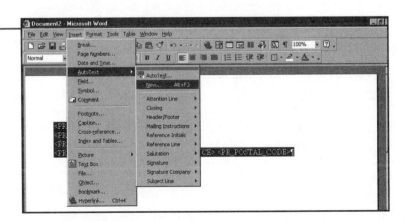

FIGURE 29.8

Call this
AutoText entry
AddressLayout.

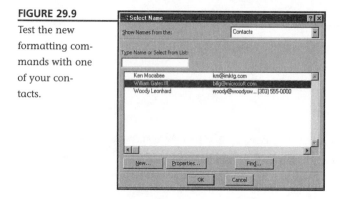

5. Before you delete the document with all those weird formatting commands, test out your new setup. Click the **New** ⬚ icon to crank out a new, blank document. Then click the **Insert Address** icon. Choose one of your contacts, per Figure 29.9, and click **OK**.

FIGURE 29.9

Test the new
formatting com-
mands with one
of your con-
tacts.

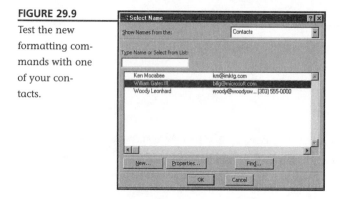

6. The name and address should be inserted in your document, along with the company name, but no country name, as shown in Figure 29.10.

FIGURE 29.10

The new com-
mands have
Word insert the
name, company
name, and
address (but no
country name).

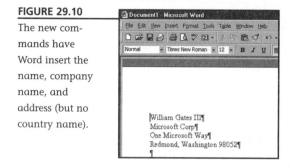

7. Now that you've seen how these new commands work, you might want to change them. For example, you might want to delete the line that says **<PR_COMPANY_ NAME>**. Or you might want to go back to always print-ing the country name, in which case you need to add an extra line at the

end that says <PR_COUNTRY>. If you make either of those changes, make sure you select all the lines and go back through steps 3 and 4 to update the AddressLayout AutoText entry.

There are several other formatting commands that you might want to use:

- **<PR_TITLE>**—Job title

- **<PR_DEPARTMENT_NAME>**—Department name

- **<PR_OFFICE_ TELEPHONE_NUMBER>**— Business phone number

- **<PR_BUSINESS_FAX_ NUMBER>**—Business fax number

- **<PR_HOME_ TELEPHONE_NUMBER>**— Home phone number

- **<PR_EMAIL_ADDRESS>**— Email address

Go ahead and experiment. If you get to the point where you'd just as soon go back to Word's original weirding ways, click **Insert**, **AutoText**, **AutoText**, select **AddressLayout**, and click **Delete**. Word automatically restores its hidden version of the AddressLayout AutoText entry.

WHAT IF I DON'T HAVE A COMPANY NAME?

The way I set up the formatting codes, if there's no company name associated with a particular contact, you get a big, ugly empty line where the company name should go.

Unfortunately I haven't found any way to make those commands conditional, so they can give different results based on the contents of the fields. For example, I don't know how to tell Word "Insert the company name if there is one, but if there isn't, just forget it." I also don't know of any way to say "Insert the country name if it isn't United States of America," or even "Use U.S.A. instead of United States of America." My guess is that the people who invented these bizarre formatting codes never thought anybody would be interested in doing anything with them!

Sharing Data Between Word and Excel

More time, effort, and money have been allocated by Microsoft to tying together Word and Excel than any other two programs in the Office pantheon. That's surprising to me because I'll put an Excel spreadsheet or chart in a Word document once or twice a week, but I need to use the brain-dead Word to Outlook Contacts connection many times a day. And I doubt that I'm unique.

Anyway, the Word-to-Excel connection gives us a good chance to look at all three of the methods for interconnecting Office applications: copying, embedding, and linking.

Copy Excel Data to Word

Office offers not one but three genuinely useful ways to copy spreadsheet data from Excel into Word. Let's try each one.

Excel Spreadsheet to Word Table

1. Start Excel. Open a handy workbook. If you have test.xls available from one of the Excel chapters, it will do nicely.

2. Select some spreadsheet data. In Figure 29.11, I've chosen the range **A1:F6** in test.xls. Click **Edit**, **Copy** (or press **Ctrl+C**) to copy the data to the Clipboard.

FIGURE 29.11

Select a range in the spreadsheet.

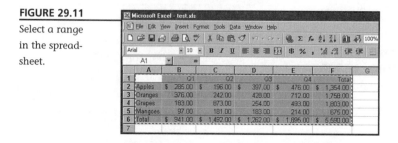

3. Start Word. You should have a new, clean document visible.

4. Paste the Excel spreadsheet into Word by clicking **Edit**, **Paste** (or **Ctrl+V**). The result should look something like Figure 29.12.

FIGURE 29.12

A spreadsheet range copied from Excel and pasted into Word.

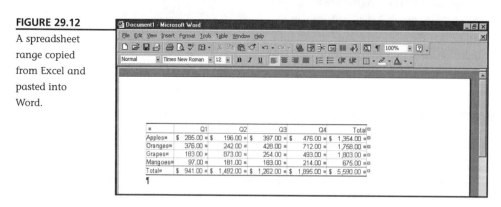

NOTE

IS THAT A SPREADSHEET IN WORD?

Nope. What you have in Figure 29.12 may have originated as a spreadsheet. It may look like a spreadsheet. It even has all the formatting you applied to it in Excel. *But it is not a spreadsheet!* What you see in Figure 29.12 is a Word table. You can resize the rows and columns. You can format it with the Table AutoFormat feature. You can change the text and numbers any way you like. But you have to be very cognizant of the fact that totaling no longer works.

Word does have a few formula functions that will total columns and rows, and do a little bit of arithmetic, but I hesitate to bring it to your attention because the capabilities (built into obscure fields) are so pathetic they'll only lead to madness. If you're going to need the ability to update numbers and get totals to reflect the new numbers, embed or link the spreadsheet (detailed later in this chapter), don't paste it in.

5. Just to prove to yourself that this isn't a spreadsheet, click the **Oranges/Q1** cell, and change the number to zero. Then tab out of the cell. As you'll notice in Figure 29.13, none of the totals change—horizontally, vertically, or even the Grand Total.

FIGURE 29.13

It's a Word table, and as such there are no calculation smarts.

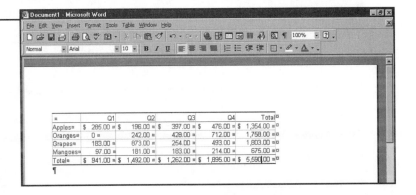

That's the most common way to copy data from an Excel spreadsheet into Word. The next most common way brings the data across without any formatting, so the resulting text doesn't look at all like a table—much less a spreadsheet.

WHY DO I GET FORMATTING WITH A SIMPLE PASTE?

By default, all the Office applications use HTML when copying between the apps. HTML—the type of data used on Web pages—includes rudimentary formatting capabilities. The formatting that you see moving from Excel to Word, in this case, is precisely the formatting that's preserved in HTML.

EXERCISE

Excel Spreadsheet to Raw Data

1. If you're continuing from the previous exercise, you have some spreadsheet data in the Windows Clipboard. (If not, start Excel and copy some data.)

2. In Word, click **Edit**, **Paste Special**. Word shows you the Paste Special dialog box, where most fancy application interconnection takes place. In Figure 29.14, I've chosen to paste the data from Excel into Word as unformatted text.

FIGURE 29.14

Paste as unformatted text.

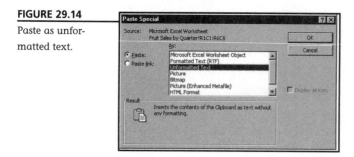

3. When Word pastes a spreadsheet as unformatted text, each row comes across as its own paragraph. Then, within each paragraph, the columns are separated by tabs. You can see the effect in Figure 29.15.

FIGURE 29.15

Unformatted spreadsheet data is separated by tabs and paragraph marks.

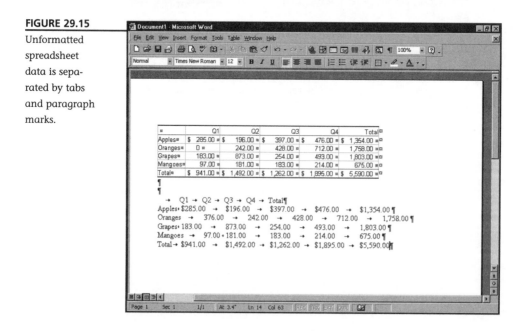

This method of bringing across data as unformatted text is a good choice if you want to apply formatting to the data inside Word, and don't want to carry across any formatting that was applied back in Excel.

EXERCISE

Excel Spreadsheet to Word Picture

1. If you're continuing from the previous exercise, you have some spreadsheet data in the Windows Clipboard. If not, start Excel and get some.

2. Inside Word, click **Edit**, **Paste Special**. Again, the Paste Special dialog box comes up. In Figure 29.16 I've chosen to treat the spreadsheet data as a picture.

FIGURE 29.16

Paste a spreadsheet as a picture in Word.

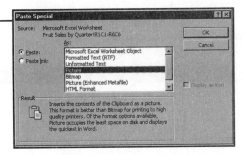

3. A picture, as you might imagine, is precisely that (see Figure 29.17). You can't go in and change the data (which may be a very good thing if you'd be tempted to think that this was a live spreadsheet). You can format the picture: make it larger or smaller, move it around, crop it, and so on.

So there you have three powerful methods for copying data from Excel into Word. In each case, there's no memory of where the data came from. Word hasn't the slightest idea that the table, raw data, or picture originated with its sibling application.

FIGURE 29.17
Spreadsheet
data inserted as
a picture.

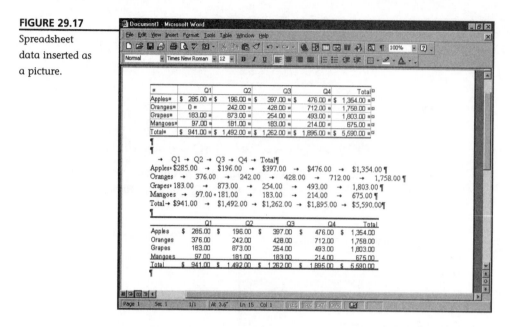

Embed a Spreadsheet in a Word Document

Now we get to go beyond the amnesia stage. When you embed a spreadsheet in a
Word document, Word is fully cognizant of the fact that the data came from Excel
and can be manipulated in Excel. The data stays inside the Word document, but it's
treated in a special way, as you'll see.

EXERCISE

Embed a Spreadsheet

1. Start Word.

2. To create a new, blank spreadsheet at any point in a Word document, click
   Insert, **Object**. You'll see the Object dialog box, as shown in Figure 29.18.

FIGURE 29.18
Word wants to
know what kind
of object you
want to insert.

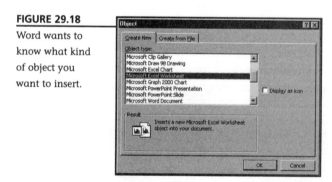

3. If you scroll through the list, you'll discover that Word can insert a couple dozen kinds of objects into documents. In our case, we're interested in an Excel Worksheet, so click **Microsoft Excel Worksheet** and click **OK**.

4. Word undergoes a significant transformation. It may take a while, so be patient. By the time Word comes up for air you'll discover that a spread-

WHY JUST ONE SPREADSHEET?

Actually, Word lied to you. It didn't exactly insert a spreadsheet into your document. It really inserted an entire workbook. You only see one sheet in Figure 29.19 because Word only sets up one sheet initially. But if you poke around a bit, you'll discover that you have an entire workbook on your hands—you can add more sheets, run scenarios, create charts, the whole nine and a half yards.

sheet has been inserted in your document (see Figure 29.19). More than that, though, the Standard and Formatting toolbars suddenly revert to the *Excel* toolbars of the same name, the menus have turned into *Excel* menus, and even your Auditing toolbar appears at the bottom of the screen.

FIGURE 29.19

Word as were-wolf, taking on all the aspects of an Excel window.

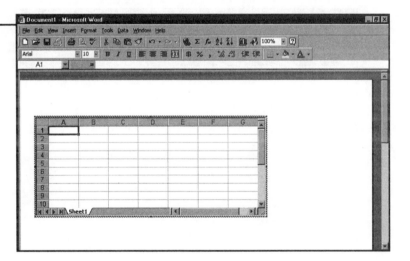

5. Go ahead and create your own little spreadsheet. In Figure 29.20 I've charted sales of widgets and wombats, in two designer colors.

FIGURE 29.20

Anything you can do in an Excel .xls file, you can do right here, inside Word.

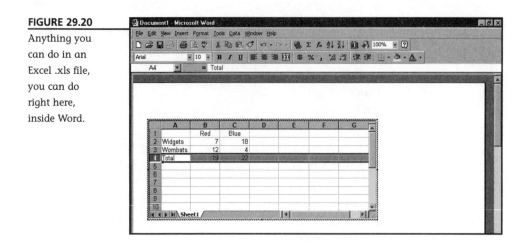

6. When you tire of spreadsheeting, click anywhere in the document outside the spreadsheet area, and Word returns. You can type sentences (as shown in Figure 29.21), bring in pictures, and do everything you normally do in a .doc file.

FIGURE 29.21

Click in the document, outside the spreadsheet, and the Word persona returns.

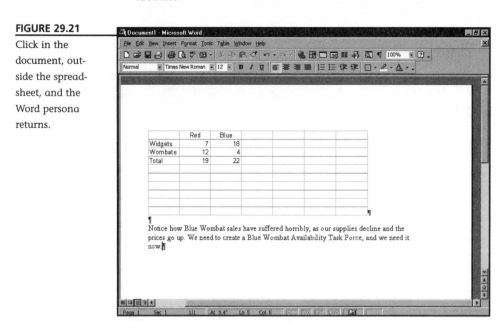

7. Any time you want to return to the spreadsheet, just double-click it. The Word wrapper fades away and Excel takes over once again, as shown in Figure 29.22.

FIGURE 29.22

Double-click to bring back Excel.

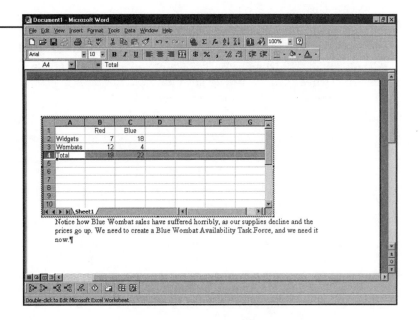

That's how embedding works. Word keeps the data in the document, but it knows that you want to use Excel to manipulate the numbers. This werewolf-like capability of Word to give way to Excel when you're editing the embedded data is, in fact, an enormously complex one that took Microsoft years to make usable.

You can embed a spreadsheet in a Word document going the other way—by selecting the data inside a spreadsheet, doing a copy, moving to Word, running a **Paste Special**, and choosing **Microsoft Excel Worksheet Object** (refer to Figure 29.16).

Now let's look at the fanciest way to put Excel data in a Word document.

DOES PASTE SPECIAL WORK THE SAME AS INSERT OBJECT?

No, it doesn't. When you use **Paste Special** to paste a Microsoft Excel Worksheet Object into a Word document you don't get a worksheet object pasted in your document, in spite of what the dialog box says. You actually get a copy of the whole workbook—the equivalent of the entire .xls file! (Yet another example of Microsoft's inconsistent use of the terms worksheet, workbook, and spreadsheet.)

So if you select a small part of a spreadsheet in a big .xls file and try to use **Paste Special** to get that data embedded into a Word document, you're going to be in for an unpleasant surprise. The Word .doc will grow huge, simply because it has to hold all the data.

Link to a Chart from a Word Document

I don't recommend that try linking unless you have at least 32MB of memory on your machine. Windows has to keep copies of both Word and Excel running at the same time when the links are updated, and that's a bit like feeding Shamu and Willy, simultaneously, from the same bucket.

Linking is a little bit like embedding, except the data doesn't sit in the document. Instead it stays where it came from—in this case, in an Excel spreadsheet—and Word only retrieves the information when it's needed.

EXERCISE

Link a Chart

1. Start Excel, and open a workbook that contains a chart. If you have test.xls handy, it will work. Make the chart visible on the screen (in test.xls, click the **Chart1** tab).

2. Click out near the outer boundary of the chart when the ScreenTip on your mouse pointer says **Chart Area** (see Figure 29.23). Click **Edit**, **Copy** (or press **Ctrl+C**).

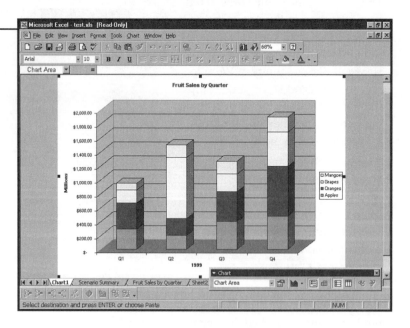

3. Start Word. Put your cursor wherever you want the Excel chart to appear. Then click **Edit**, **Paste Special**. As in Figure 29.24, click **Microsoft Excel Chart Object**, and make sure **Paste link** is chosen on the left. Click **OK**.

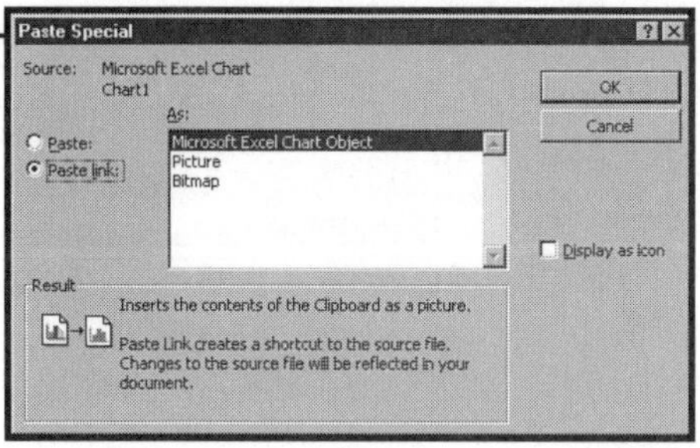

FIGURE 29.24

Pasting a link inside Word, using **Paste Special**.

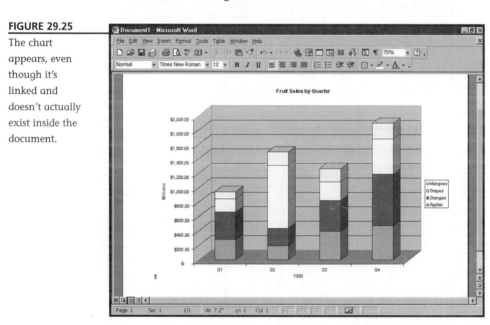

4. You'll see the chart inside your Word document (see Figure 29.25). Even though you can see and print the picture, Word only stores a little pointer to the picture. It takes up almost no space. Even better, if the picture changes in test.xls, it'll change in the Word document also.

FIGURE 29.25

The chart appears, even though it's linked and doesn't actually exist inside the document.

5. Let me show you how that works. Close this document and give it a name like, oh, `temp.doc`. Flip back to Excel and change the number in **cell B3** to zero (see Figure 29.26).

6. Click the **Chart1** tab to see how the new data changes the chart (see Figure 29.27). The first column looks short, right?

7. Now go back to Word and open temp.doc. Voilà! The first column gets chopped off here too (see Figure 29.28).

I THOUGHT YOU SAID THE PICTURE WASN'T PUT IN THE DOCUMENT

Look at the bottom of Figure 29.24, where it says this action **Inserts the content of the Clipboard as a picture**. That isn't really true. When you run a **Paste link**, Word puts a link to the picture inside your document—a pointer that tells Word where to find the picture when Word needs to retrieve it. The picture isn't there at all.

FIGURE 29.26

Change the data in test.xls.

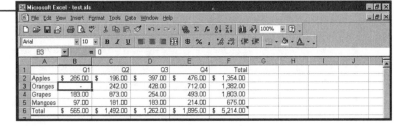

FIGURE 29.27

The new data takes effect in Chart1.

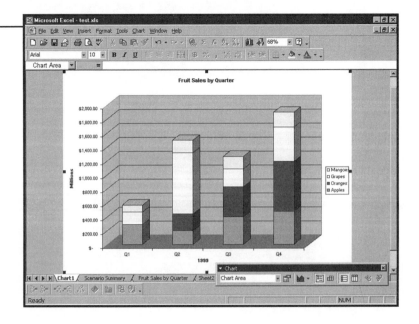

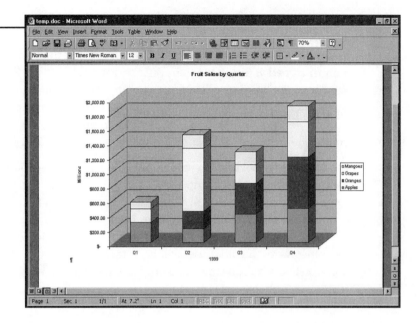

Open the document in Word and the link gets updated, bringing in the latest version of the chart.

8. There's another big difference in the way Word behaves when it has linked—as opposed to embedded—data. Try double-clicking the chart in Figure 29.28. You might expect Word to pull a werewolf and bring in the Excel menus and toolbars. It doesn't. Instead, Word actually shifts over to Excel and presents you with the chart, as it did in Figure 29.23.

And that pretty well shows you the relative benefits of copying, embedding, and linking.

Which Is Best?

Ah, you ask such tough questions…

The best way to bring Excel data into Word documents is the way that creates the fewest headaches for you! Here are the salient points:

- When you copy data, there's no memory of where it came from, so it's hard to change any calculated numbers. If you keep a copy of the original spreadsheet around, though, making changes isn't too hard, and copying isn't difficult at all. Copied data doesn't take up much room at all, and it always travels with the document, so any program that can read Word documents will be capable of seeing the copied data.

- Embedding spreadsheets adds the convenience of having Excel a double-click away for modifying data. Other people will be able to read the data with any program that can view Word documents, but if they want to change the data in any way, they have to have Excel running on their PC. The data is in the document, so the .doc file can get quite big, particularly if you use **Paste Special** to do the embedding. But because the data is in the file, you don't have to worry about sending multiple files to anybody who wants to read your document.

- Linking is very cool but has several drawbacks. You have to send the linked file along with the document. Worse, the linked file has to be in precisely the same location on the disk, or Word won't be capable of finding it. (For example, if you originally linked data from the workbook c:\someplace\ mysheet.xls, that workbook has to be in the same location on another machine before the other user will be able to see the data.) Most of all, Word and Excel have to run simultaneously to make linking work—and that requires a fairly powerful machine.

Ya pays yer money and ya takes yer chances...

Sharing Data Between Word and PowerPoint

There's a special tunnel between Word and PowerPoint, which, at least in theory, allows you to create presentations directly from Word documents.

The trick lies in formatting your Word document so PowerPoint can figure out what in the world to do with the text in the document. PowerPoint looks for paragraphs formatted with these specific styles:

- Heading 1 paragraphs in Word, when transferred to PowerPoint, start new slides. PowerPoint puts the contents of Heading 1 paragraphs in the Title box, up at the top of the slide. So when you want to start a new slide, format your Word paragraph with the Heading 1 style.

- Heading 2 paragraphs become the highest-level bulleted text in the Text box at the bottom of the slide. (PowerPoint calls these second-level bullet points, but they're actually the highest level text on the slide, aside from the slide title.)

- Similarly, Heading 3 paragraphs become third-level bullet points, Heading 4 paragraphs become Fourth level, and so on.

If you already have a Word document formatted with those specific styles, you're way ahead of the game. If you don't, you'll have to create a document and apply those styles. (In fact, if you're starting from scratch, you may well find it easier to use PowerPoint directly—forget about Word—and work in PowerPoint's Outline view.)

Here's an interesting way to use the tunnel to quickly generate a Q&A slide show, based on a great idea I pilfered from Paul Somerson at *PC Computing*.

EXERCISE

Turn a Document into a Presentation

1. Start Word.

2. Create a document with the appropriate styles. In Figure 29.29, I've written a document with three Heading 1 paragraphs and three Heading 2 paragraphs interlaced. Alternatively, if you have a nicely formatted Word document with those styles already applied, open it.

FIGURE 29.29

The Word document must have Heading x styles applied in the appropriate places.

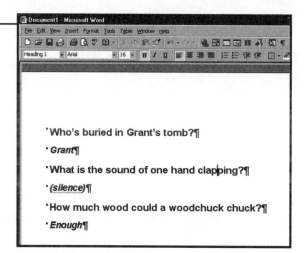

3. When the document looks right, click **File**, **Send To**, **Microsoft PowerPoint** (see Figure 29.30).

4. PowerPoint comes up in Normal view, with each of the Heading 1 paragraphs identified as titles of their own slides. Note that PowerPoint hasn't created a title slide for the beginning of the presentation. Nor has it applied any sort of formatting. This (see Figure 29.31) is one bare-bones presentation.

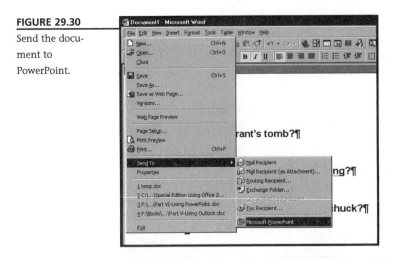

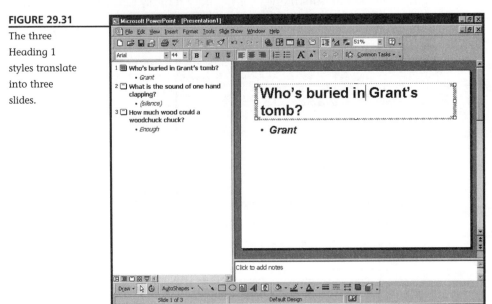

5. These slides really need a lot of cosmetic surgery, but I'll only work on the
basics. Click **View**, **Master**, **Slide Master** to bring up the one slide that
controls how all the slides in this presentation will appear. I want the title
(the Heading 1 questions in the original Word document) to appear centered
from left to right, near the middle of the slides; and I want the body (the
Heading 2 answers in the .doc) to appear at the bottom. So I clicked and
dragged a bit, and came up with what you see in Figure 29.32.

FIGURE 29.32

The Slide
Master for this
presentation.

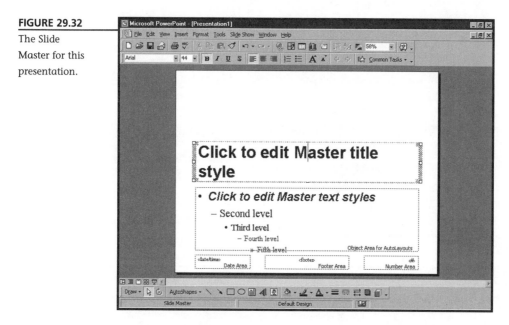

FIGURE 29.32

The Slide
Master for this
presentation.

6. I want some text to appear at the beginning of each slide. (I'd call this a
title, but that name's already been taken, and I'd only confuse you!) I clicked
on the **Text Box** 📦 icon on the Drawing toolbar, clicked and dragged to
create a location for this text, and then typed CRRRRAZY QUESTIONS in the
new text box, as shown in Figure 29.33. Because that text box appears on
the Slide Master, it will also appear on all the slides.

FIGURE 29.33

Use a text box
in the Slide
Master to put
text on all
slides.

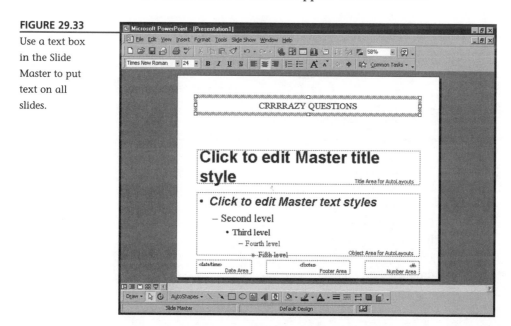

7. Next, I clicked the **Slide Sorter View** 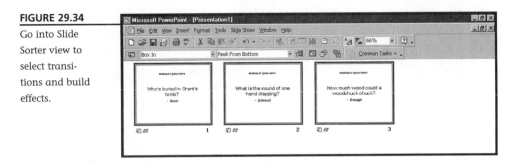 icon on the View bar to flip PowerPoint over to Slide Sorter view. I then selected all three slides (**Edit**, **Select All**) and chose **Box In** for a Slide Transition Effect (the left drop-down box on the toolbar), and **Peek From Bottom** for a Text Preset Animation (the right drop-down box), as shown in Figure 29.34.

FIGURE 29.34

Go into Slide Sorter view to select transitions and build effects.

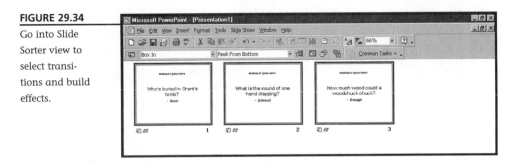

8. Click **Slide Show**, **View Slide Show**, and PowerPoint runs through the presentation. Each slide with a question appears, in turn. Then, when you click the slide, the answer to the question slides into view (see Figure 29.35).

FIGURE 29.35

The presentation, including a boxy transition between slides and answers, appears with the click of a mouse.

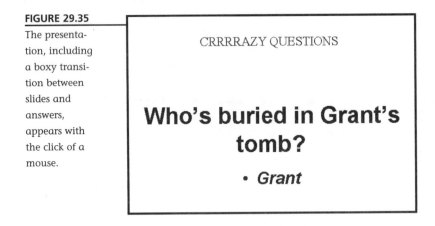

CRRRRAZY QUESTIONS

Who's buried in Grant's tomb?

- *Grant*

Conversely, there's another tunnel from PowerPoint back into Word that will dump a presentation out in a Word-friendly format. To use it, bring up the presentation you want to move in PowerPoint, and then click **File**, **Send To**, **Microsoft Word**. You'll have a few options—you can even run a **Paste link** to link the Word document back to the presentation—but they're pretty self-explanatory.

Sharing Data Between PowerPoint and Excel

I covered this link in Chapter 28, "Making Presentations Look Better," simply because I couldn't bear to tell you how to use a cheap Excel substitute with PowerPoint when the real thing works much better.

Woody Leonhard

TEACHES

OFFICE ON THE WEB

WHAT A DIFFERENCE A VERSION NUMBER MAKES! Microsoft was caught a bit flat-footed when the Web burst forth on the mainstream computing scene. Office 97 contained Microsoft's quick and dirty response to the Web challenge. The Web components available in Office 97 weren't so much integrated features as they were slapped-on last-minute modifications.

Office 2000, on the other hand, has the Web in its veins. If you can create a Word document, Excel spreadsheet, or PowerPoint presentation, and you have a Web (or intranet) site set up, making a simple Web page takes minutes, at most.

Choose the Right Tools

If you're going to do any serious Web work, you're much better off with Web-specific packages such as FrontPage or any of its many competitors. (FrontPage, of course, is part of the Premium Edition of Office 2000.) The other Office applications don't even come close to FrontPage's creation, modification, and management capabilities.

However, if you already know Word, Excel, or PowerPoint, or have an existing document, spreadsheet, or presentation that you'd like to publish on the Web, Office's tools make it easy. I'll show you how.

Open and Save Files on the Net

Brace yourself for some weird new terminology.

There are, quite literally, millions of files available on the Internet. When I speak of "files" here, I'm not talking about Web pages—what I mean is good old-fashioned computer files, free for the plucking.

The most common way to pull files off the Internet, or to put them on the Internet, is via something called FTP (File Transfer Protocol). You don't need to understand what FTP actually entails. All you need to know is that when you see FTP, you're looking at something that lets you read and write files on the Internet.

WHAT'S THE DIFFERENCE BETWEEN THE INTERNET, WEB, AND INTRANET?

The Internet (commonly called *the Net*), as you probably know, is a massive collection of computers and the phone lines that connect them. Yes, this is the information superhighway you've read about, but it doesn't really work like a superhighway.

The World Wide Web (also known as *the Web*) sits on top of the Net. It consists of another massive collection of computers, called Web servers, interconnected via the Net, which contain Web pages. The Web pages, as you've probably discovered, refer to each other via links; click a link and you move to a different Web page, whether it sits on the same Web server or halfway around the world.

Intranets act much like the Web, except they're usually designed so access is limited to people inside one company. The details can get a bit hairy, but if your company has a network, chances are good it already has an intranet—whether it uses that intranet or not.

For more information about the Net, the Web, intranets, and how Office fits into all of them, check out:

- *Special Edition Using Microsoft Office 2000*, by Ed Bott and Woody Leonhard, Que, ISBN 0-7897-1842-1

- *Platinum Edition Using Microsoft Office 2000*, by Laura Stewart, Que, ISBN 0-7897-1841-3

Word, Excel, and PowerPoint all have the capability to open and save files on the Internet, using FTP. Here's how.

EXERCISE

Open a File on the Net

1. Start Word. Click **File**, **Open**.

2. In the Open dialog box, click the down arrow to the right of **My Documents**. As you can see in Figure 30.1, the entries at the bottom of that list refer to Internet Locations (FTP) and FTP Locations. An Internet Location or FTP Location (which is the same thing, in this case) is just a place on the Internet where you can pick up or drop off files.

> **WHAT'S LOG ON AS ANONYMOUS?**
> Some places on the Net require you to have a user ID and password before you can retrieve files or store files in that location. Other sites, called *Anonymous FTP sites*, don't care if you have an ID or password. Most software company support sites, such as `ftp.microsoft.com`, are anonymous because they want to allow anybody to come in and download files.

FIGURE 30.1

The Open dialog box directly supports retrieving files from the Net.

3. Choose **Add/Modify FTP Locations**. Word responds immediately with the Add/Modify FTP Locations dialog box, as shown in Figure 30.2.

4. If you have a favorite site on the Net for storing files, enter it here. If you're just learning, try using Microsoft's main file storage site, known as `ftp.microsoft.com`.

> **WHAT ABOUT INTERACTIVE WEB COMPONENTS?**
> Microsoft's marketing machine churns out some great concepts, doesn't it? In this case, the implementation of the marketing concept is pretty spectacular—and may even be useful from time to time.
>
> Here's the idea: You can publish an Excel spreadsheet, PivotTable, or PivotChart on the Web.
>
> *continues*

5. Click **OK** and you're back in the Open dialog box, as shown in Figure 30.3. Now this is the most important part of this exercise: *Back up everything before you proceed!*

6. At the risk of repeating myself, make sure you back up everything before you try to connect to the FTP site. There's at least a very small chance Word will lock up your machine when you try to connect. Don't say I didn't warn you!

7. Double-click **ftp://ftp.microsoft.com**. If you're lucky, Office will connect to the FTP site and show you a list of folders and files available on the site.

8. You're pretty much on your own at this point. Just navigate the site as if it were your hard drive.

The Word, Excel, and PowerPoint **File**, **Save As** dialog boxes contain similar facilities for letting you save files on the Net. They, too, can occasionally lock up your machine, so be careful to save everything (on your hard drive or on your local network) before trying to connect.

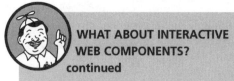

WHAT ABOUT INTERACTIVE WEB COMPONENTS? continued

People viewing the Web page can interact with the spreadsheet or PivotCritter exactly the same way they would interact with it in Excel—and they can do it in their Web browser even if they don't have Excel installed on their machine.

This makes for great theater: seeing a good demo of the "Interactive Web Component" feature will leave you speechless. (Microsoft also hopes it'll leave you with your wallet wide open.)

While it's certainly okay to "oooh" and "aaah" at the demo—the technology involved is quite impressive—realize that there are significant limitations. The Web server you use must be running Windows NT, with the Office Server Extensions (only a small percentage of all public Web servers run OSE). The Web surfer must be using Internet Explorer 4.01 or later, and they must download and install the Office Web Components (which they can get by installing Office 2000, or—if their company has a site license for Office 2000—by downloading and installing the components from their corporate server). In short, TANSTAAFL.

(SciFi acronym for the day: TANSTAAFL, pronounced "tahn-stahful," is short for "There Ain't No Such Thing As A Free Lunch." Another wonderful addition to the English language from Robert Heinlein.)

If your Web server and Web page viewers can meet all those stringent requirements, you can get at Excel's Interactive Web components by checking the box marked **Add Interactivity** in the Save As Web Page dialog box.

FIGURE 30.2

You must tell Office, in advance, which Net locations you want to use to retrieve or store data, and how to log on to the location.

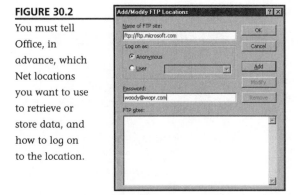

FIGURE 30.3

The Microsoft FTP site has been added to the Open folder list.

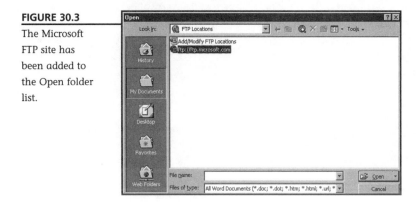

Browse

Just as Word, Excel, and PowerPoint have access to files on the Net, they can also flip over to your Web browser.

 EXERCISE

Search the Web from Word

1. Start Word.

2. Bring up the Web toolbar by right-clicking on a blank area in any handy toolbar and choosing **Web**. Word responds by placing the Web toolbar below the Formatting toolbar, as shown in Figure 30.4.

3. While you would think, just looking at the toolbar in Figure 30.4, that Word would be capable of leaping out to the Web, reality isn't quite so wonderful. Yes, you can use the Web-style navigation buttons to move forward or backward among open documents or to jump to a document. But if you try to do anything that requires the Web, such as clicking the **Search the Web** 🔍 icon, Word brings up your Web browser, as you can see in Figure 30.5.

4. If you poke around a bit, the rest of Office's Web browsing support proves equally underwhelming. For example, although all the Office applications have Microsoft on the Web entries on their Help menus (see Figure 30.6), clicking any of them merely launches your Web browser. There's no connection between the application and the Help topics, so you'll find yourself frequently flipping back and forth between Web page and application.

WHAT ABOUT WEB DISCUSSIONS?

Well, yes, Web discussions for Word documents are pretty cool if your company has everything set up to support them. Basically, you publish your document as a Web page, and then invite collaborators to come in and make comments. The comments appear as fully threaded remarks, so replies to remarks are kept together. In some cases that can be helpful, as long as the collaborators remember to refresh their view of the Web page frequently (to ensure they can see all the most current remarks). When all the comments are in, you can open the document in Word and incorporate the remarks into the document.

The restrictions, though, are anything but simple. It's a lot like using Interactive Web Components, which I mentioned earlier in this chapter. You have to have a server running Windows NT and the Office Server Extensions. The people participating in the discussion must be running Internet Explorer 4.01 or later, and must have Office 2000 installed. (While it's theoretically possible to participate in a discussion without having Office 2000 installed, you have to jump through several bothersome hoops.)

If your company has Web discussions enabled, by all means check with your network administrator and get the name of your company's Discussion Server. Then go into Word and click **Tools**, **Online Collaboration**, **Web Discussions**.

FIGURE 30.4

The Web toolbar makes an appearance.

FIGURE 30.5

Click **Search the Web** from inside Word and you're propelled to your Web browser, which goes to a predefined Microsoft Web site.

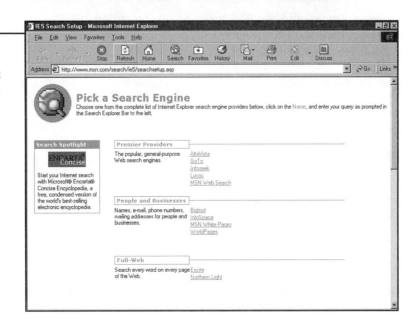

FIGURE 30.6

Microsoft on the Web entries all lead to your Web browser, with an appropriate page loaded.

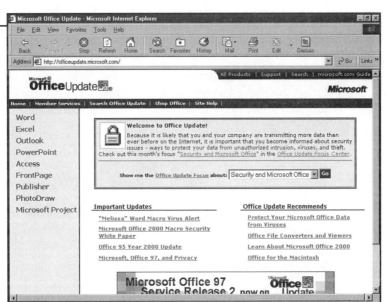

Hyperlinks

Word, Excel, and PowerPoint all support hyperlinking. In particular, it's very easy to create a hot hyperlink from your document to a Web page—and if you then post your document on the Web, the hyperlink continues to work.

☞ *I discuss some forms of Word hyperlinks in the section on "Hyperlinks" in Chapter 13, on **page 248**. You might want to look over that section again to refresh your memory on hyperlinking and hot spots.*

Let's put a hyperlink on a PowerPoint presentation slide. The link will be hot, so if you click it while giving a presentation, and the presentation PC is connected correctly to the Net, the Web page you specify will appear on the screen during the presentation. Cool, no?

EXERCISE

Hyperlinking a PowerPoint Slide to the Web

1. Start PowerPoint, and open Generic Presentation.ppt. If you aren't in Slide Sorter View, click the **Slide Sorter View** 🔳 icon on the View bar.

2. Let's put the hot link on slide 8, the one marked **Next Steps**. Click that slide, and then click the **Normal View** icon on the View bar.

3. In Figure 30.7, I've used **Insert**, **Picture** to put a picture from the Clip Gallery in the lower-right corner. Then I used the **Text Box** 🔳 tool on the Drawing toolbar to stick the text **Check Que's Web page** on the slide, and the **Arrow** 🔳 icon to draw an arrow from the text to the picture.

4. Click once on the picture. We're going to set up the picture so it's hot.

5. Click the **Insert Hyperlink** 🔳 icon on the Standard toolbar. PowerPoint knows that what you've selected—in this case, the picture—is supposed to be hot, and it presents you with the Insert Hyperlink dialog box, as shown in Figure 30.8.

6. Type a favorite URL (that is, a Web address) in the box marked **Type the file or Web page**. In Figure 30.8, I've set the picture up to link to the Macmillan Computer Publishing Web page, www.mcp.com.

7. Now run the slide show by clicking **Slide Show**, **View Show**. When you get to slide 8, let your cursor hover over the picture. You'll see a ScreenTip advising you of where the hot link leads—in this case, to http://www.mcp.com (see Figure 30.9).

FIGURE 30.7
A clip art picture, a text box, and an arrow placed on the slide.

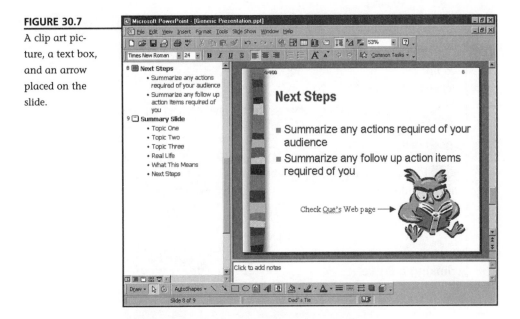

FIGURE 30.8
Type the URL (Web address) to which you want to link.

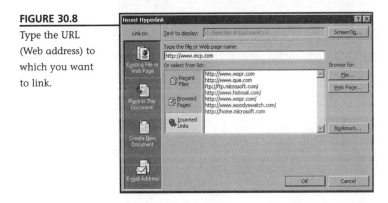

8. Click the hot picture. Your Web browser should come up with the indicated page loaded, as shown in Figure 30.10.

FIGURE 30.9

The picture is hot; clicking it will lead to www.mcp.com.

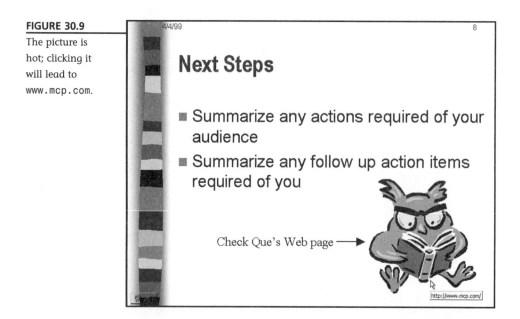

FIGURE 30.10

Clicking the hot picture brings up your Web browser with the indicated page loaded.

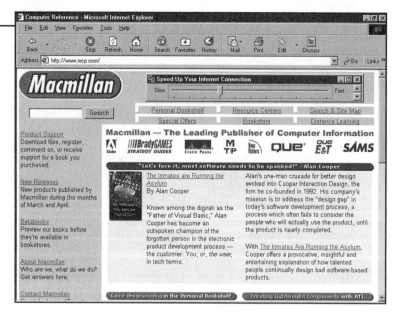

Anything you can select in any Word document, Excel workbook, or PowerPoint slide can become a hot hyperlink. That includes text, pictures, ranges, charts—just about anything you can imagine. Simply select whatever you want to turn into a link, click the **Insert Hyperlink** 🔗 icon, and type the Web address.

Open and Save Web Pages

Office does an excellent job of converting Word documents, Excel spreadsheets, and PowerPoint presentations to HTML—the format needed to post a document on the Web.

While I won't go so far as to claim that HTML is a "native file format" for Office—that is, you can save any Office document in HTML format, and then open it up and get back precisely the same document you started with—I will have to admit Office is pretty darn close to perfect. It's very rare that a round-trip to HTML and back will have any noticeable effect on any Office document.

That's a wonderful development for anybody who wants to put Office documents on the Web; it means you can publish Web pages almost as easily as saving the document in the first place.

WHAT'S HTML?

HTML (Hypertext Markup Language) is the language used on the Web, the language understood by Web browsers such as Internet Explorer and Netscape. When Excel saves a spreadsheet as HTML, that means it converts the spreadsheet to HTML code and saves the HTML code. The process is amazingly similar to printing a spreadsheet: When you have Excel print a spreadsheet, it converts the spreadsheet into a code that can be understood by your printer, and then ships that code to the printer.

After Excel has saved a spreadsheet as HTML, you can take the resulting HTML code and put it on a Web page. When a Web browser sees that HTML code, it should interpret the HTML so the stuff that shows up on the screen looks just like your original spreadsheet. Again, it's quite similar to a printer, where the intelligence inside the printer interprets the code sent to it by Excel.

The terms *Web page* and *HTML file* can be used interchangeably: Any HTML file can be used as a Web page, and every Web page is an HTML file.

EXERCISE

Publish a Document to the Intranet

1. I'm going to assume that you have access to your company's intranet. In most cases, you'll have to get the intranet's URL (such as `http://ourserver/public`) from your company's system administrator, and you'll have to arrange in advance for permission to post pages on that URL. (If you have a Web page already, with write access, you have everything you need.)

2. Start Word, and create a document you'd like to publish as a Web page. In Figure 30.11, I've created a biography page, complete with background color and photograph.

FIGURE 30.11

My bio. Yeah.
Really.

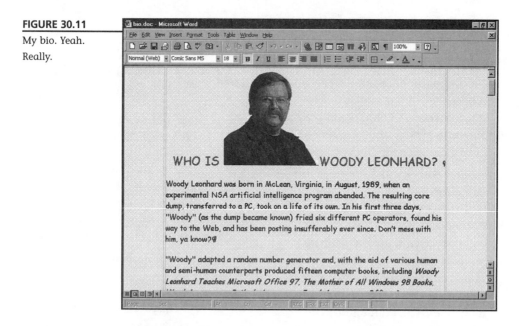

3. Click **File**, **Save As Web Page**. Word responds with the Save As dialog in Figure 30.12. Click the **Web Folders** icon in the lower-left corner. We're going to set up a folder for your company's intranet.

FIGURE 30.12

When you save
a Word docu-
ment as a Web
page, you work
with the same
Save As dialog
box you've
come to know
and ignore.

4. Click the **Create New Folder** icon. Word responds with its Add Web Folder Wizard, shown in Figure 30.13.

5. Follow the steps in the wizard to establish a Web folder. Once it's available, saving the Web page to the folder is as simple as saving a file to any other folder. Similarly, you can open Web pages contained in the folder as readily as you would open documents in any other location.

FIGURE 30.13

Word has a wizard to make it easy to add Web folders to the Save As (and Open) dialog.

If you aren't too picky about how your Web pages look, Word, Excel, and PowerPoint will create and maintain entire Web sites, using the hyperlinking techniques discussed in the preceding section.

To end the book on an upbeat note: PowerPoint 97 was notorious for generating "Web" files that just wouldn't work on many Web sites. PowerPoint 2000, by contrast, seems to have solved all the old problems. You should feel reasonably confident that, if you save a PowerPoint presentation as a Web page, the Web site generated (see Figure 30.14) will likely work on almost any server.

FIGURE 30.14

The Generic Presentation, saved as a Web page, and viewed with Internet Explorer 5. Note all the navigation aids that make it easy to change slides.

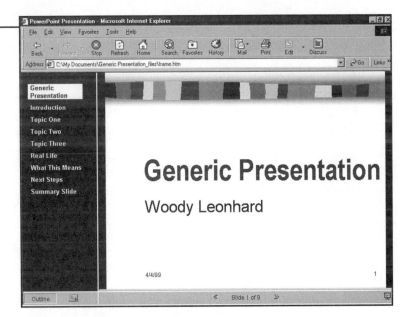

Anyway, there you have it: what I figure every beginning Office user should know. You're ready for the big time now. Pick up a copy of *Special Edition Using Microsoft Office 2000*, and use it as a reference when you get stuck. Give Office a little push every now and then, and see what new things you can learn.

Most of all, remember to keep watching WOW (www.woodyswatch.com) for the very latest developments in the land of Office.

Good luck!

Index

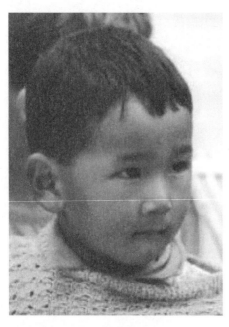

In 1959 the Communist Chinese invaded Tibet, driving its 24-year-old leader, the Dalai Lama, into exile. The Chinese unleashed a pogrom of ethnic and cultural genocide. Tibetans were imprisoned, tortured, murdered; their artistic, religious, and cultural heritage reduced to rubble. Reliable estimates place the number of Tibetans slaughtered since the Chinese invasion at 3 million. According to Amnesty International and other leading human rights organizations, arbitrary arrest, torture, and Chinese government-sanctioned killings in Tibet continue to this day.

The Dalai Lama settled in northern India. Millions of Tibetans followed him into exile. Most moved into refugee camps scattered throughout Nepal and India. Life in the camps is hard. Few families have more than one room to call their own. Many eke out a hand-to-mouth existence as subsistence farmers, manual laborers, handicraft workers, traders—often with "shops" consisting of no more than a couple of pieces of bamboo and a plastic tarp.

The Tibetan Children's Fund was founded in 1993 to provide food, shelter, and education for Tibetan refugee children living in northern India. TCF's center of operation is in Darjeeling—renowned to Westerners as a source of tea, but better known to Tibetans and many other Asians as a respected center of education. For more than a hundred years, English-language boarding schools in and around Darjeeling have prepared leaders of government, education, and commerce.

As of this writing, TCF sponsors 150 Tibetan children around Darjeeling. The children are chosen for their scholastic ability and financial need. TCF volunteers (who pay for their own trips to India) interview the children and their parents, select the children, and monitor their progress in school each semester. Scholastic evaluation emphasizes proficiency in English, math, the sciences, and humanities.

A little hard currency goes a long way in India. U.S. $60 will sponsor a refugee child for a full year in one of the government-run schools. U.S. $250 covers a full year—including tuition, room, and board—in one of the top English-language schools.

TCF is an all-volunteer organization. Overhead expenses are paid by TCF's corporate sponsors. Every penny donated by individuals goes straight to the children. If you would like to help a deserving Tibetan refugee child, please contact:

Tibetan Children's Fund
P. O. Box 473, Pinecliffe, CO USA 80471
Voice: 303-642-0492, Fax: 303-642-0491
Part of the profits from the sale of this book are donated to the TCF.